OXFORD STUDIES IN EUROPEAN LAW

General Editors: PAUL CRAIG AND GRÁINNE DE BÚRCA

European Law and New Health Technologies

European Law and
New Health
Technologies

Edited by
MARK L FLEAR
ANNE-MAREE FARRELL
TAMARA K HERVEY
and
THÉRÈSE MURPHY

OXFORD
UNIVERSITY PRESS

OXFORD

UNIVERSITY PRESS

Great Clarendon Street, Oxford, OX2 6DP,
United Kingdom

Oxford University Press is a department of the University of Oxford.
It furthers the University's objective of excellence in research, scholarship,
and education by publishing worldwide. Oxford is a registered trade mark of
Oxford University Press in the UK and in certain other countries

Published in the United States of America by Oxford University Press
198 Madison Avenue, New York, NY 10016, United States of America

British Library Cataloguing in Publication Data
Data available

Library of Congress Cataloguing in Publication Data
Data Available

ISBN 978-0-19-965921-0

General Editors' Preface

Health is central to all our lives, so too is technology. This collected set of essays brings both together, and analyses them from the perspective of European law. It is however in accord with the very nature of the subject matter that European law in this context connotes not just EU law, but also the Council of Europe, the OECD, the World Health Organization, and the European Patent Office.

The cross-jurisdictional focus thus befits the nature of the subject matter, which defies pigeon holing into 'the national' or 'the European', where the latter is composed solely of EU law. Regulations emanating from the EU thus provide part of the story, but only part, and the overall picture is complemented by initiatives from the other European and international organizations that impact on this important area.

This collection is moreover of interest and value because it demonstrates multi-level governance in action within a particular sectoral area, shaped by a plethora of inter-institutional relationships, and reveals also the interplay of different cultural values within the overarching frame of constitutional pluralism.

The edited collection has four parts, the first of which sets the scene through three chapters, which deal respectively with the defining features of the EU's approach to regulation of new health technologies; the Council of Europe, human rights, and regulation of new technologies; and a chapter that maps the science and technology that underpins subsequent discussion.

Part two addresses European legal approaches to new health technologies, through the medium of case studies on particular issues that have more general relevance for the overall project. To this end there are chapters on innovative tissue engineering, 'orphan' medicines, patent law, and product liability law, with the aim of highlighting problems, deficiencies, and challenges within the existing system.

The focus in the third part of the book turns to regulatory theory and regulatory innovation, with chapters on risk and legitimacy; the continuing role of existing regulations for emerging health technologies; the medical-industrial complex in EU pharmaceutical regulation; and the governance of nanoproducts in the EU.

This is followed in part four by a series of chapters that address new techniques for researching European law and health technology, which draw on a range of disciplines and methodologies, including science and technology studies, discourse analysis, qualitative interviews and empirical analysis. The different parts of the overall analysis are brought together in the editors' conclusion, which revisits issues posed at the outset of the study.

The collection will be of interest to scholars of EU law, regulation, governance, and human rights, as well as those with a more direct concern for health regulation.

Paul Craig and Gráinne de Búrca

Acknowledgements

The editors would like to thank the Economic and Social Research Council for its funding (award number RES-451-26-0764) of the two-year research seminar series in *European Law and New Health Technologies* that gives this volume its name. We also want to acknowledge support, both financial and administrative, that was provided by the following: the School of Law and Institute of Governance at Queen's University Belfast; the Sheffield Health Law and Policy research group, the Sheffield Centre for International and European Law, the Sheffield Institute for Biotechnology, Law and Ethics, and the School of Law at the University of Sheffield; the Centre for Social Ethics and Policy and the Institute for Science Ethics and Innovation at the University of Manchester; and the School of Law and the Human Rights Law Centre at the University of Nottingham.

With this support, we were able to organize seminars on *Core Research Questions and Developing Research Capacities* (Sheffield, November 2009); *Legitimating Techniques* (Nottingham, March 2010); *European Law and New Health Technologies* (Belfast, November 2010); and *Challenges and Opportunities* (Manchester, March 2011). We would like to express our thanks to all those who attended, chaired, acted as discussant, or gave papers at those four seminars in the ESRC seminar series, and at the companion events: the student human rights conference on the theme of new technologies and human rights, run by the Human Rights Law Centre at the University of Nottingham in March 2010; and the University Association for Contemporary European Studies funded 'Author meets Reader' event in Sheffield in November 2009.

Without the time and efforts of our contributors this collection would not have been possible—so our thanks to them. We particularly appreciate their efforts to work across the disciplinary boundaries that so often divide scholarship—their openness to doing so contributed greatly to our enjoyment of this project and, as we hope others will agree, to the quality of this publication. In terms of developing the ideas in the papers given at the seminars into chapters appropriate for publication, we are also grateful to the many colleagues who were generous enough to provide independent and rigorous peer reviews of the chapters that comprise this collection: Amel Alghrani, Margaret Brazier, Roger Brownsword, Helen Busby, Emilie Cloatre, John Coggon, Sarah Devaney, Marie Fox, David Fraser, Emily Jackson, Kirsty Keywood, Bettina Lange, Bob Lee, Sheelagh McGuinness, John Morison, Aoife Nolan, Barbara Prainsack, Malcolm Ross, Colin Scott, Sally Sheldon, Paul Torremans, Andrew Webster, and Noel Whitty.

Our thanks must also go to Paul Craig and Gráinne de Búrca, the editors for the series in which this collection appears, as well as the whole Oxford University Press editorial team. In preparing the manuscript for submission, we were able to rely on student research assistance from Luke Mooney, Abi Stark, and Neel Thomas, and we are grateful for their help.

Mark Flear, the principal investigator for this project, and principal editor of this collection, would like to convey his personal thanks to everyone involved. In particular he warmly acknowledges his fellow editors for their unstinting hard work, insight, and all round support.

Foreword

Roger Brownsword

While working as one of the specialist advisers to the House of Lords Select Committee on Stem Cell Research—a committee that was set up in order to consider the implications of approving the Human Fertilisation and Embryology (Research Purposes) Regulations 2001—I heard many views about the necessity and legitimacy of conducting human embryonic stem cell research. Not surprisingly, a range of opinions (both prudential and ethical) was expressed by scientists and researchers, by religious groups, by patients' groups, by bioethicists, and so on. However, one of the most striking statements made to the Committee, and a part of the evidence that has remained with me, came from a witness who was wheelchair-bound. Her central point was very simple: according to this witness, even if human embryonic stem cell research fulfilled its promise, leading to therapies that would enable her to dispense with the use of her wheelchair, she still rejected such research as fundamentally immoral. In the event, this view has not prevailed in the United Kingdom where the regulatory framework allows for the licensing of such research; but, elsewhere in continental Europe, it is widely accepted that it is indeed immoral to use human embryos for research purposes and, in these places, the regulatory environment is more restrictive.

There are two points that we might take from this. One point is that there can be a tension between, on the one hand, projects and practices (research and clinical) that deliver effective and reliable health care benefits and, on the other, what we regard as 'acceptable' health care techniques and technologies. For each society, there will be limits to the licence that health care practitioners are granted; researchers, health care technologists, and clinicians do not operate with a carte blanche. The other point is that, in Europe, there seem to be many different views about what those limits are, as well as why the limits are where they are—the objection, for example, that using human embryos for research purposes compromises human dignity has much less resonance in the United Kingdom than in, say, France, Germany, or Italy. What is more, it is evident that new health technologies (whether involving reproductive techniques, the sequencing or manipulation of the human genome, nano-medical diagnostics and (possibly) therapeutics, or fMRI imaging, and so on) are particularly prominent in agitating public opinion and in provoking the articulation of these deep value differences.

Against this backcloth, it is a pleasure to introduce this exciting collection of essays gathered under the banner of 'European Law and New Health Technologies', in which the editors and contributors seek to establish whether there is a distinctively European way of regulating new health technologies. Or, to put this in slightly different terms, the focal question in the collection is whether the regulatory space populated by health technologies in Europe, together with the operative regulatory environment, is distinctive. In response to that question, the editors highlight the ways in which so much of European regulatory thinking (within both the EU and the Council of Europe) is orientated towards the regional market (for health care technologies) qualified by considerations of risk (where both prospective costs and benefits attract attention), human rights, and ethics. But, of course, there are difficult balances to be made in relation to this quartet of leading considerations, not least finding the right balance between regulatory restriction for the sake of, say, safety or respect for human rights and regulatory support (or relaxation) for the sake of innovation (and the market). So, for example, where it is judged that health care technologies might be dangerous or harmful relative to humans and the environment, the risks need to be regulated at an acceptable level; and, even if these risks are effectively managed, regulators will be pressed to ensure that the development and application of these technologies are compatible with respect for human rights as well as ethically acceptable. At the same time, however, regulators will be criticized if the limiting measures of precaution or restriction are seen as stifling innovation or unnecessarily delaying life-saving technologies in reaching the market.

In their closing remarks, the editors sketch some of the further lines of inquiry that are invited by their research focus. These include: first, the way that the ideas of market, risk, human rights, and ethics play in legitimating regulatory purposes and practices (leading to questions about the distinction between legitimacy and legitimation). For example, following the ECJ's well-known decision in the DocMorris case (Case C-322/01), regulators might have sought to *legitimate* the opening up of the German market for non-prescription drugs to a Dutch internet pharmacy by referring to the fundamental freedoms within the single market; but it does not follow that we should accept the *legitimacy* of the ECJ's decision or of the background regulatory scheme. Similarly, it does not follow that the wheelchair-reliant witness to whom I have referred should accept the *legitimacy* of the 2001 Regulations even though their sponsors sought to *legitimate* them by reference to the therapeutic promise of human embryonic stem cell research. Secondly, there is the important question of whether the law (in a fairly broad, but specifically European, sense) has the capacity to respond to the multi-faceted demands that we make of regulators and of the regulatory environment. Quite apart from the questions of risk and legitimacy, is the law able to craft and to maintain an adequate connection with health care technologies, and how effectively are regulators able to ensure that there is compliance? For example, European data protection law and modern information technologies, having rapidly parted company, now urgently need reconnection; and the proliferation of biobanks and databases raises questions about the practicalities of securing the confidentiality of health care data. Thirdly, the relationships between law, new health technologies, and identity invite further examination. Up to a point, new health technologies (and their underlying scientific bases) shed new light on what kind of beings we are and this can shape our sense of who we are. However, there is also the possibility that Europeans might participate in communitarian and democratic projects in such a way that they express themselves through the resulting regulatory regime, thereby announcing the relationship that they see themselves as having with new technologies in the health field—for example, some might make a strong statement about their sense of identity by eschewing any application of 'enhancing' technologies. Finally, there are distributive and redistributive issues to address. For instance, one reason for eschewing technologies that enhance human performance might be because there is a worry about this leading to a widening of the gap between the privileged and the rest. However, this line of reasoning might be coupled with thoughts about solidarity which also apply in relation to insurance and genetic profiles—at once, for Europeans, questions of markets, risks, human rights, and ethics compete for consideration.

The landscape of legal scholarship is now thoroughly European; but it is only recently that lawyers have thought more systematically about the regulatory environment (of which traditional law is a material, if not always the decisive, part) and the impingement of 'new' technologies. By putting the spotlight on European law and new health technologies, this collection helps readers to gain a sense of the way in which the landscape is changing as well as to home in on health care technologies as an important sub-field within the larger regulatory enterprise.

Contents

PART V. BRINGING IT ALL TOGETHER

Table of Cases

EUROPEAN PATENT OFFICE

ITALY

UNITED KINGDOM

UNITED STATES

Table of Instruments and Legislation

Directives

List of Abbreviations

AG	Advocate-General
APA	American Psychiatric Association
ART	assisted reproductive technology
ASPD	antisocial personality disorder
ATMP	Advanced Therapy Medicinal Products
ATMP	advanced therapy medicinal product
BPAI	[US] Board of Patent Appeals and Interferences
CAT	Committee for Advanced Therapies
CBRC	Cross-border reproductive care
CEDAW	Convention on the Elimination of All Forms of Discrimination against Women
CESCR	Committee on Economic, Social and Cultural Rights
CFI	Court of First Instance
CHMP	Committee for Medicinal Products for Human Use
CII	computer-implemented invention
CJEU	Court of Justice of the European Union
CoE	Council of Europe
COMP	Committee for Orphan Medicinal Products
CPMP	Committee for Proprietory Medicinal Products
DHV	decellularized homograft valve
DSM	Diagnostic and Statistical Manual of Mental Disorders
EC	European Community
ECD	expanded criteria donation
ECHR	European Convention on Human Rights
ECJ	European Court of Justice
ECLA	European Classification system
ECRI	European Commission against Racism and Intolerance
ECtHR	European Court of Human Rights
EEA	European Economic Area
EEC	European Economic Community
EGE	European Group on Ethics in Science and New Technologies
ELSI	ethical, legal, and social implications
EMA	European Medicines Agency
EMEA	European Medicines Evaluation Agency
EPC	European Patent Convention
EPO	European Patent Office/European Patent Organization
ERA	European Research Area
ESBAC	Emerging Science and Bioethics Advisory Committee
ETEPSnet	European Techno-Economic Policies Support Network
EU	European Union
EUCFR	European Charter of Fundamental Rights
EUTCD	EU Tissues and Cells Directive
FDA	Federal Drug Administration
FP	Framework Programme
GCP	good clinical practice
GLP	good laboratory practice
GMMO	genetically modified micro-organism
GMO	genetically modified organism

hESC	human embryonic stem cell
HFEA	Human Fertilisation and Embryology Authority
HGC	Human Genetics Commission
HSC	Hospital for Sick Children [Canada]
HTA	Health Technology Assessment
ICCPR	International Covenant on Civil and Political Rights
ICD	International Classification of Disease
ICESCR	International Covenant on Economic, Social and Cultural Rights
IP	intellectual property
IPC	International Patent Classification
iPS	induced pluripotent stem cells
ISO	International Organization for Standardization
IVF	*in vitro* fertilization
MDG	Millennium Development Goals
MHRA	Medicines and Healthcare product Regulatory Agency
MS	Member State
NHBD	non-heart-beating donation
NHS	National Health Service
NHSC	National Horizon Scanning Centre
NHT	new health technology
NICE	National Institute for Health and Clinical Excellence
NIHR	National Institute for Health Research
nyr	not yet reported
OECD	Organisation for Economic Co-operation and Development
OMC	Open Method of Coordination
OMP	orphan medicinal product
PACE	Parliamentary Assembly of the Council of Europe
PHI	public health interventions
QALY	quality adjusted life year
REACH	Registration, Evaluation, Authorisation and Restriction of Chemicals
STS	science and technology studies
TE	tissue engineering
TFEU	Treaty on the Functioning of the European Union
TIC	technologies of health information and communications
TRIPs	World Trade Organization Agreement on Trade-Related Aspects of Intellectual Property Rights
UDBHR	Universal Declaration on Bioethics and Human Rights
UDHR	Universal Declaration of Human Rights
UN	United Nations
UNMD	UN Millennium Declaration
USAID	US Agency for International Development
WHO	World Health Organization
WMA	World Medical Association
WTO	World Trade Organization

List of Contributors

John Abraham is Professor of Sociology and Director of the Centre for Research in Health and Medicine (CRHaM) at University of Sussex. As Specialist Expert Adviser to the UK House of Commons Parliamentary Health Select Committee, he was centrally involved in its 8-month 'Inquiry into the Influence of the Pharmaceutical Industry' (2005). His main research interests are in pharmaceutical regulation worldwide. He is author of three books on the politics and sociology of pharmaceuticals in UK, US and EU, namely, *Science, Politics and the Pharmaceutical Industry* (Routledge 1995), *The Therapeutic Nightmare: The Battle over the World's most Controversial Sleeping Pill* (Earthscan 1999), and *Regulating Medicines in Europe: Competition Expertise and Public Health* (Routledge 2000), and is editor of *Regulation of the Pharmaceutical Industry* (Palgrave 2003).

Richard Ashcroft is Professor of Bioethics at the School of Law, Queen Mary, University of London. He is co-Director of the Centre for the Study of Incentives in Health, and co-editor of *Principles of Health Care Ethics* (2nd edn, Wiley-Blackwell 2007).

Gordon Bache completed his PhD at the School of Law, University of Sheffield in 2011, which was based on his thesis entitled *Beyond Bias and Burden: A multi-causal account of compromise in medicines regulation in England and the EU.* He has written on the reimbursement of medicinal products in the EU, and it is this subject matter that forms the basis of his current work.

Siân M Beynon-Jones is a Wellcome Trust Research Fellow in Biomedical Ethics, University of York. She works on the co-construction of gender and expert knowledge in the context of contemporary reproductive medicine, with a particular focus upon temporal ordering practices. She has also co-authored articles that engage with these themes in the related field of bioscience policy-making.

Nik Brown is Reader in Sociology at the University of York. He has published widely on the politics and regulation of the biological sciences and co-authored *New Medical Technologies and Society* (Polity Press 2004, with Andrew Webster). He is interested in biopolitical theory and has researched and written on a range of empirical cases including blood, stem cells, biobanking, reproductive biology and transplantation.

Courtney Davis is Lecturer in Sociology at University of Sussex. She has published numerous articles on sociology and politics of pharmaceuticals in journals, such as *Social Science & Medicine*, *Social History of Medicine*, *Science, Technology & Human Values*, and *Social Studies of Science*. As Director of the Centre for Corporate Accountability she has also given expert testimony to Parliamentary Inquiries in the UK.

Bärbel Dorbeck-Jung is Professor of Regulation and Technologies at the University of Twente, Netherlands. She has published widely on topics related to governance, legislation and self-regulation, good governance and the rule of law, computer law, health care law and technological regulation. She also leads projects of the Dutch NanoNext Programme Risk and Technology Assessment.

Anne-Maree Farrell is Associate Professor, Faculty of Law, Monash University, Australia. She researches in health law and policy, with specific interests in the regulatory governance of human biological materials (blood, organs and stem cells) and health technologies, as well as medical malpractice and patient safety. She has published widely in a range of internationally recognised journals and edited collections. Her books include *The Politics of Blood: Ethics Innovation and the Regulation of Risk* (CUP 2012) and she is a co-editor of *Organ Shortage: Ethics Law and Pragmatism* (CUP 2011).

Mark L Flear is a Lecturer in Law at Queen's University Belfast and a Member of the Northern Ireland DNA Database Governance Board. His main field of interest lies in the governance of life itself, and attempts to query legal and regulatory decision-making in that area, so-called biopolitics. Within this broad field he focuses on the European and global dimensions of two substantive areas: public health and new health technologies. A key focus of this research is public or citizen participation. Work on these areas has appeared in several leading journals, including *Common Market Law Review, European Integration online Papers, Human Rights Law Review, Maastricht Journal of European and Comparative Law* and *Medical Law Review*. He is currently completing (under the working title) *The Biopolitics of EU Public Health Governance: HIV/AIDS, Cancer and Pandemic Influenza* (Hart forthcoming). Mark's research has been funded by the AHRC, the British Academy, ESRC, School of Law of Queen's University Belfast, and UACES.

Sjef Gevers is Emeritus Professor of Health Law at the University of Amsterdam, Netherlands. He has published widely in national and international journals on the legal aspects of health care. For almost 20 years, he was one of the editors-in-chief of the *European Journal of Health Law*. His present activities include membership of the Central Disciplinary Court of the Netherlands.

Tamara K Hervey is Jean Monnet Professor of European Union Law at the School of Law, University of Sheffield. She is author of eight books/edited collections and over 60 articles and book chapters on European social and constitutional law, in particular its application in practice in health fields; on the regulation of tobacco in the EU context; on European public health law and policy; on the governance of stem cell research in the EU; on the European Group on Ethics in Science and New Technologies; on social security and welfare; and on equality law; as well as on the phenomenon of 'new governance' in the EU, in particular as an alternative or supplement to 'command and control' means of regulation in social fields. Her publications include E Mossialos, G Permanand, R Baeten and TK Hervey (eds), *Health Systems Governance in Europe: The Role of European Union Law and Policy* (CUP 2010); TK Hervey and JV McHale, *Health Law and the European Union* (CUP 2004); and TK Hervey and J Kenner (eds), *Economic and Social Rights under the EU Charter of Fundamental Rights* (Hart 2003). She is also interested in research methodologies, particularly in the context of EU law, as seen in R Cryer, TK Hervey, B Sokhi-Bulley and A Bohm, *Research Methodologies in EU and International Law* (Hart 2011).

Nils Hoppe is Full Professor for Regulation in the Life Sciences at Leibniz Universitaet, Hannover, Germany. He has published widely on ethical and legal issues in relation to regenerative medicine, tissue engineering and biobanking. He is the director of the Centre for Ethics and Law in the Life Sciences (CELLS) in Hannover, a fellow and Open Section council member of the Royal Society of Medicine, visiting fellow at the University of Oxford and a visiting professor at the European School of Molecular Medicine at the University of Milan, Italy.

Thérèse Murphy is Professor of Law and Critical Theory at the University of Nottingham. Her most recent book is *Health and Human Rights* (Hart 2013).

Mónica Navarro-Michel is Reader of Civil Law, University of Barcelona, Spain. She writes in the area of medical and health technologies. Her most recent book is *Tort Law. Cases and Materials* (coauthor with Encarna Roca), in Spanish.

Rory O'Connell is Professor of Human Rights and Constitutional Law at the Transitional Justice Institute/School of Law, University of Ulster. He is the author of *Legal Theory in the Crucible of Constitutional Justice* (Ashgate 2000) and has published articles in several journals, including the *International Journal of Constitutional Law, Legal Studies*, and the *European Human Rights Law Review*. He is a former member of the Budget Analysis Project Team at the Queen's University of Belfast.

Gearóid Ó Cuinn is an Academic Fellow at Lancaster University Law School. His recent doctoral research was funded by the Wellcome Trust and focused on the public health governance of pandemic influenza. He also has a strong interest in the sociology of human rights law and practice. He is co-director of Ceartas, Irish Lawyers for Human Rights, a non-profit organisation that develops innovative legal actions to protect and promote human rights internationally.

Amanda Odell-West is a Lecturer at the School of Law, University of Manchester. Her research focuses around the role of exclusions from and exceptions to patentability in driving or constraining innovation, translational health care research, and the impact on medical practice and health care provision from a comparative perspective. She is currently working on *Patent Law: Creating Wealth from Health?* (Edward Elgar forthcoming).

Martyn Pickersgill is Wellcome Trust Senior Research Fellow in Biomedical Ethics, University of Edinburgh. He has held grants and fellowships from the AHRC, ESRC, Newby Trust and Wellcome Trust on the social and ethical dimensions of neuroscience, neurology and psychology. He has published in journals including *BioSocieties*, *Sociology of Health and Illness*, *Social Studies of Science*, and *Science, Technology and Human Values*. Martyn's co-edited collection (with Ira van Keulen), *Sociological Reflections on the Neurosciences* (Emerald 2011), was shortlisted for the 2012 British Sociological Association Medical Sociology Book Prize. He is currently working with Emilie Cloatre on the edited collection, *Knowledge, Technology and Law: Interrogating the Nexus* (Routledge forthcoming). Martyn is also on the Editorial Board of the journal *Sociology of Health and Illness*. He has been a visiting scholar at Harvard University, the London School of Economics, the University of Manchester, the University of Groningan, and the US National Institutes of Health, as well as a Wellcome Trust Public Engagement Ambassador. In 2011 Martyn was elected as an inaugural member of the Young Academy of the Royal Society of Edinburgh.

Elen Stokes is a Lecturer at Cardiff Law School, and a Research Associate of the Sustainable Places Research Institute, Cardiff University. Her work explores the ways in which the law mediates and manages risks and scientific uncertainties, particularly those associated with new technologies. She is especially interested in the consequences of applying traditional forms of regulation to rapidly evolving fields, such as nanotechnology and synthetic biology. Elen is a Research Affiliate to the Dutch NanoNext Programme Risk and Technology Assessment.

Keith Syrett is Professor of Public Health Law at Cardiff Law School. He is the author of *Law, Legitimacy and Rationing: a Contextual and Comparative Perspective* (CUP 2007) and *The Foundations of Public Law: Principles and Problems of Power in the British Constitution* (Palgrave Macmillan 2011). He has written extensively on the relationship between law and the rationing of healthcare with a particular interest in techniques and institutions of health technology assessment, especially NICE in the UK. He also has an interest in the role for legal intervention in population health, especially in the context of climate change, and was the founder of the Worldwide Universities Network 'Global Health Justice Network' research grouping. He is a Solicitor of the Supreme Court of England and Wales, Secretary of the British Association for Canadian Studies, a Fellow of the Royal Society of Medicine, and a member of the editorial board of *Medical Law International*.

Ilke Turkmendag is Mildred Blaxter Post Doctoral Fellow at PEALS (Policy, Ethics and Life Sciences Research Centre), Newcastle University. She is primarily interested in interdisciplinary research on socio-ethical and legal aspects of the life sciences with particular reference to human reproductive technologies and stem cell research. Her recent work involves regulation of gamete donation in the UK, and the ethical, legal and social aspects of the uses of reproductive tissue, cells and embryos in stem cell science. She has published widely, including in *International Journal of Law, Policy and the Family*, *Journal of Law and Society*, and *Sociology of Health & Illness*.

Amanda Warren-Jones is a Senior Lecturer at the School of Law, University of Sheffield. She is currently researching the factors that affect the development of medical innovation. Her research interests have evolved from patenting medical innovation, to consider the wider regulation and decision-making which affects medical technology. Her first book, *Patenting rDNA: Human and Animal Biotechnology in the United Kingdom and Europe* (Lawtext Publishing 2001) was favourably reviewed in the IIC, cited in Cornish's Intellectual Property Textbook and referenced as core reading by the New Zealand Patent Office. More recent work has been cited by the President of the European Patent Office in the WARF decision (G2/06, 2006), as well as in international research publications and teaching materials.

Regulators

Belen Crespo Sanchez-Eznarriaga is Director of the Agencia Española de Medicamentos y Productos Sanitarios (the Spanish Medicines Agency).

Emily Jackson is a Professor of Law at the London School of Economics. She was a Member of the Human Fertilisation and Embryology Authority from 2003–2012, and its Deputy Chair from 2008. Recent publications include *Medical Law* (2nd edn, OUP 2010), *Debating Euthanasia* (Hart 2011) and *Law and the Regulation of Medicines* (Hart 2012).

Mihalis Kritikos is a Senior Associate in White and Case, a law firm specialising in the environment and risk regulation. He is also Assistant Professor in Vesalius College-VUB. Previously he worked as a Research Programme Manager for the Research and Innovation Directorate General of the European Commission dealing with legal, ethical and governance issues arising at the design and development of a wide range of new and emerging technological applications.

Previously he won the 2008 UACES Prize for the Best Thesis in European Studies in Europe. He has published widely in the in the fields of climate change, risk regulation, technology assessment, sustainable management strategies, access to genetic resources, licensing requirements, regulatory compliance and regulatory control of new and emerging risks. He is currently completing a monograph on GMO regulation in Europe.

Graeme Laurie is Professor of Medical Jurisprudence in the School of Law at the University of Edinburgh. Form 2007–2011 he was Director of the AHRC Research Centre for Studies in Intellectual Property and Technology Law (aka SCRIPT) and he is also Founding Director of the JK Mason Institute for Life Sciences, Medicine and the Law. His policy work has included Chairmanship of the UK Biobank Ethics and Governance Council and the Privacy Advisory Committee in Scotland.

Jonathan Montgomery is Professor of Health Care Law at the University of Southampton, where he has worked since 1984. He is Chair of the Health Research Authority, The Nuffield Council of Bioethics and the Advisory Committee on Clinical Excellence Awards. He has over twenty years of NHS board experience and has chaired provider trusts, a strategic health authority, and primary care trusts. From 2009–2012 he was chair of the Human Genetics Commission. He has served on a number of working parties looking into bioethical issues, including the Organ Donation Taskforce's work on presumed consent, the Committee on the Ethical Aspects of Pandemic Influenza, the Nuffield Council of Bioethics Working Party on Public Health Ethics, and the Medical Ethics Committee of the BMA. He chaired a Strategy Committee on Brain Banking for the UK Clinical Research Collaboration and was the founding chair of the Scientific Steering Committe of the UK Brain Banks Network.

His research emphasises the need to understand the institutional context in which the law regulates health care practice and has been described in Journal of Medical Ethics as 'some of the most important and interesting legal analysis of medical law as a discipline'. In 2005 he was elected to honorary fellowship of the Royal College of Paediatrics and Child Health.

1

European Law and New Health Technologies: The Research Agenda

Mark L Flear, Anne-Maree Farrell, Tamara K Hervey,
and Thérèse Murphy

What do the following people have in common: Elizabeth Adeney, Cameron Brown, Daniel and Danielle Stanley, Tony Nicklinson, Gemma Pepper, Rob Summers, Sam Yates and Philippa Bradbury, Patrick Kane, Matthew Green, Corporal Andrew Garthwaite? The answer is that their health has been the subject of recent media attention from the BBC—either because of cutting-edge technology or because of the implications of its use, from the point of view of European law, or because of both. We could, of course, produce dozens of similar lists using different media sources, from across Europe. And this would be to exclude the countless others who do not make the news. Developments in health care and medical treatments, and their relationships with law, are it seems exciting topics, replete with practical, ethical, constitutional, economic, sociological, and myriad other (including mundane) dimensions.

Health is, of course, a matter of fundamental importance, both as a human right in itself, and as a factor in a productive workforce and therefore a healthy economy. New health technologies promise improved quality of life, and the potential for the prevention of disease and management or alleviation of disability in the future. New health technologies are also a key area of 21st-century knowledge societies and economies, offering potential for growth and economic development. At the same time, new health technologies present significant challenges, perhaps most notably concerning questions of their safety, efficacy, desirability, and value for (public) money. New health technologies, actual and potential, consequently evoke diverse responses, ranging from hope to fear and from hype to the ennui of quotidian familiarity. Managing these responses, in complex democratic societies, is in part conditioned by how well we feel that the law is fitted to the challenge of providing appropriate constraints, incentives, and protections to those operating in, and affected by, the field of new health technologies.

All that said, we hardly need further justify our research agenda in this book. The relationships between new health technologies and law *matter*—that is why we have chosen to investigate them. But why *European* law? Of course, to guard against the possible dangers arising from new health technologies, and to maximize the benefits, all European governments regulate their development, marketing, and public financing. These regulatory arrangements are not drafted from a clean sheet: they are conditioned by what has gone before, in terms of institutional path dependencies, and in terms of a quite specific European history of relationships between health, experimentation, innovation, economic models, human dignity, and human rights. At a level of generality, given shared histories, institutions, and cultural framings, there may be something distinctive about the 'European' way of regulating new health technologies. Part of our research agenda is to consider that question.

More crucially, because of the ways in which those European countries are embedded in multiple, overlapping legal orders and institutional forms at European level, European governments regulate new health technologies within the contexts of those European legal systems. Put simply, especially when viewed as a multilevel pluralist legal system, the law of new health technologies within Europe *is* European law. For sure, the detailed instrumental embedding of those bodies of law varies between national settings, as some of the chapters of this book show. National and European legal and regulatory institutions are in non-hierarchical relationships, so that we could not talk simply of national 'implementation' of 'top-down' European law of new health technologies. Rather, we conceptualize our research agenda through a set of more complex, and hence interesting, institutional interrelationships, which are increasingly understood through a lens of constitutional pluralism. A range of European institutions are relevant to and brought into view by this lens, including the OECD, WHO (Europe), and the European Patent Office. The most prominent are the European Union (EU), and the Council of Europe (CoE): those are our main focus in this book. Let us be clear—by 'European law' we do *not* mean only the law of the EU; law emanating from other European institutions, in particular the CoE, is also an important and necessary part of our agenda.

In this realization, our research agenda at once occupies a new place within legal scholarship. Scholarly treatment of health law normally operates within the context of a particular national jurisdiction, even if it reflects increasing awareness of extra-jurisdictional influences, in particular from international human rights law. Yet, especially (though not only) in the context of new health technologies, such scholarship can offer only a partial picture. We cannot understand the national legal terrain without developing a clear understanding of the *European* legal contexts within which those laws are proposed, promulgated, implemented, applied, revised, adjudicated upon, and otherwise contested. Equally, while legal scholars have considered relationships between European law and new technologies more generally, our focus on *health* technologies allows for a more specific basis for analysis and critique.

Hence, this book offers the first systematic attempt at scholarship on European law and new health technologies. In so doing, it asks whether there is—or might yet be—a European law *of* new health technologies. If there is, its significance will resonate not just within Europe but across transnational and global contexts, as those in other parts of the world faced with similar challenges respond, either by varying degrees or types of take-up or by aversion.

The purpose of the book is to analyse European law (in the broad sense outlined earlier) and its relationships with new health technologies. We have not defined 'new health technologies' prescriptively, but rather have allowed the contributors to the book, all of whom are experts, to determine which technologies are of most interest and salience. As such, we have conceptualized both 'European law' and 'new health technologies' in broad, inclusive, and dynamic ways. Our collective research agenda focuses around the following interrelated questions: What—if any—are the defining features of European law approaches to new health technologies? What is the significance of European law to such technologies? To what extent, and if so, how is European law on new health technologies legitimated? In particular, what are—and what should be—the roles of markets, risk, human rights, and ethics in European law approaches to new health technologies?

Thus the agenda which we set ourselves requires both the central disciplinary modes and methods of legal scholarship and those of other cognate disciplines. Legal scholarship grapples with questions such as: What is the relevant law applicable to a particular set of facts in a range of health (or health technology) settings? How is the relevant law created, interpreted, applied, adjudicated, modified, contested? Who are the key actors involved in these processes? What are the expectations and relative successes of different types of actor (individual patients, health care professionals, industry actors, patient groups . . .) in utilizing the law? To what extent does law achieve its intended effects, and what unintended consequences ensue from particular legal strategies? How do different bodies of law (for instance, human rights law, intellectual property law, trade law) interact where they meet over a new health technology? The answers to these types of question get us quite a long way in unravelling our research agenda. But to gain a more holistic understanding, other disciplinary methods are also needed.

Our approach is therefore to combine more 'traditional' legal scholarship with regulatory theory, bioethics, and approaches inspired by sociology, social theory, and science and technology studies (STS). The contributors to this book are substantive experts, but also represent a reasonably diverse group in terms of disciplinary and methodological backgrounds. More importantly, all who participated in the research demonstrated a willingness to be open to (and in some cases to experiment with) unfamiliar approaches. For sure, the legal occupies centre stage in the book. Given our topic, the centrality of law to that topic, and the need to understand that centrality (how it is produced or not produced, disrupted or displaced, and its advantages and disadvantages alike), it could not be otherwise. But it is our firm view that the investigation of 'European law and new health technologies' cannot but be such a cross-disciplinary activity. It would not be possible to pursue our research agenda without the sorts of methodological innovation of which this book is an example.

To this end, the book is structured into five distinct parts. The first, scene-setting, part, considers the definitional challenges implicit in our research agenda (what is 'new', what is 'health', what is 'technology', what is 'European', and what is 'law'?). These are questions to which we return in the conclusion. In Part I, readers will also find detailed discussion of the two principal legal orders at issue here: those of the EU and the CoE. Part II is focused around legal approaches. Adopting many of the standard tools of legal scholarship, Part II uses selected case studies on topics of salience (innovative tissue engineering, 'orphan' medicines, patent law, and product liability law) to interrogate the contributions of European law in its various forms to the regulation of new health technologies, highlighting problems, deficiencies, and challenges. In Part III, we turn to regulatory theory and regulatory innovation. Drawing on the insights of regulatory theory, and on the relevance to law of institutional regulatory arrangements, and the interactions between institutions at national, sub-national, and supranational levels, Part III considers questions of legitimacy and effectiveness of regulatory structures and mixes, in the context of the risks (as well as market opportunities) inherent in new health technologies. Part IV brings to bear new techniques for researching European law and new health technologies. Drawing on a range of approaches and methods from sociology, in particular, science and technology studies, content and discourse analysis, and qualitative interviews, this part considers the interfaces between European law, politics, society, and new health technologies.

Interwoven between the parts are several 'regulators' perspectives'—shorter, largely unreferenced pieces written in a personal capacity by those who are able to reflect on our research agenda from the point of view of the regulatory processes with which the authors are most familiar. The threads of the analysis are brought together in the editors' conclusion (Part V), in which we return explicitly to the research agenda described earlier, highlighting the book's core research findings and setting the forthcoming agenda. In that discussion, we explicitly defend our central claim—concerning the extent to which, through our investigation into the relationships between European law and new health technologies, we have defined a new field of scholarship: European law of new health technologies.

PART I

SETTING THE SCENE

2

The Defining Features of the European Union's Approach to Regulating New Health Technologies

*Gordon Bache, Mark L Flear, and Tamara K Hervey**

A. Introduction, Scope, and Approach

The brief for this chapter is to determine the defining features of the relationships between European Union (EU) law and new health technologies, by reference to risk, ethics, rights, and markets. The chapter contributes towards the book's broad research agenda, which asks:

What are the defining features of the European law approach to new health technologies and what is the significance of European law to such technologies? How is European law or governance to be legitimated? In particular, what are the roles of risk, ethics, rights, and markets in the European law approach?

A more complete understanding of the *European* law approach to regulating new health technologies involves consideration of other European institutions, in particular the Council of Europe[1] and the European Patent Office.[2] This chapter considers only *European Union* law.

In our research, we mapped the EU's regulatory environment for a hypothetical new health technology, through the 'cycle of innovation', from idea to initial research, through pre-clinical, clinical research, and marketing, to post-market regulation (see Figure 2.1). Drawing from our analysis of the detailed contents of this map, the chapter considers the ways in which EU regulation of new health technologies is 'framed'. By 'frames', we mean discursive devices, that organize experience and knowledge,[3] and both constitute[4]

* This chapter was written with the support of ESRC Seminar Series RES-451-26-0764 (Principal Investigator: Mark L Flear, Co-Investigators: Anne-Maree Farrell, Tamara K Hervey, Thérèse Murphy) and a version was presented at the first seminar in the series, Sheffield, 13 November 2009. The chapter was also presented at the conference on *Regulation in the Age of Crisis*, Dublin, 17–19 June 2010 and at the Wellcome Trust workshop on *Regulating Health Technologies*, London, 12–13 May 2011. We are grateful to the participants at those events for their useful comments and suggestions and to Roger Brownsword and Thérèse Murphy for their thought-provoking peer reviews.

[1] See Chapters 3 and 13 in this collection.
[2] See Chapter 7 in this collection.
[3] E Goffman, *Frame Analysis: An Essay on the Organisation of Experience* (Harvard University Press 1974); M Rein and D Schön, 'Problem Setting in Policy Research' in C Weiss (ed), *Using Social Research in Public Policy Making* (Lexington Book 1977) 235–51; DA Snow and others, 'Frame Alignment Processes, Micromobilization and Movement Participation' (1986) 51 *American Sociological Review* 464; M Hajer and D Laws, 'Ordering through Discourse' in M Moran, M Rein, and R E Goodin (eds), *The Oxford Handbook of Public Policy* (OUP 2006).
[4] S Jasanoff, 'The Idiom of Co-production' in S Jasanoff (ed), *States of Knowledge* (Routledge 2004) 2–3.

and contribute to the process of conveying ideas and values.[5] We are interested in four frames: markets, risk, rights, and ethics.[6] Our approach is to examine the functions and aims of the regulation and its rationales, as expressed in the (significant) legal and policy documentation itself. We recognize that this approach is limited in that it does not seek external verification of conclusions, for instance through social science methods of 'triangulation'. However, it is appropriate for our research task here, in that the very notion of 'framing' implies that discourse—including legal discourse—has power and significance and that its study is important and valuable in itself.

Our original intuitions with respect to the research questions were as follows: the 'internal market' and markets in general are the dominant frame for EU regulation of new health technologies; risk is also an important framing device, particularly because of its link to the internal market; rights and ethics appear to be an important part of the regulatory environment, but their role is essentially that of legitimating devices. Our analysis tested these hypotheses, finding that some were more accurate than others, and that all needed to be adjusted in view of different new health technologies, and the different regulatory strategies that the EU deploys. Analyses such as that on which we report in this chapter help to illuminate the ways in which different frames relate and perhaps compete within the EU's law and policy on new health technologies, and how some frames endure with greater stability than others.[7]

A range of measures of EU (hard) law, soft law, and opportunities for funding (all command, control, or steering instruments), along with judicial decisions interpreting these provisions, comprise the EU's regulatory environment for new health technologies. (We have not included discussion of new health technologies *as* regulation.[8]) For the purposes of this chapter, our focus is the EU-level of the multilevel governance order[9] that comprises the EU. We recognize that a more complete picture of framing of regulation[10] of new health technologies would involve consideration also of regulatory instruments at national level and regional level where power is devolved,[11] as place and scale of regulation makes important differences to frames.[12] Developing such a multilevel analysis proved unfeasible within the confines of this chapter.

[5] VA Schmidt, 'Discursive Institutionalism: The Explanatory Power of Ideas and Discourse' (2008) 11 *American Review of Political Science* 303.

[6] The focus on those four frames is determined by the book's research agenda. Of course, other frames could also have been drawn out, for instance, the idea that innovation itself is a major frame in EU regulatory thinking on new health technologies, in that the EU might be seen to be concerned to create the 'right' regulatory environment to encourage innovation in health technologies. Where we discuss this idea, we note its relationship to our four frames, in particular the market frame.

[7] M Hajer and D Laws, 'Ordering through Discourse' in M Moran, M Rein, and RE Goodin (eds), *The Oxford Handbook of Public Policy* (OUP 2006) 263–4.

[8] See K Yeung and M Dixon-Woods, 'Design-Based Regulation and Patient Safety: A Regulatory Studies Perspective' (2010) 71 *Social Science & Medicine* 502.

[9] Multilevel governance approaches to the study of the EU conceptualize the EU as a regulatory order, nested in and interacting with, a range of other regulatory orders. See, seminally, L Hooghe and G Marks, *Multilevel Governance and European Integration* (Rowman & Littlefield 2001).

[10] The term 'regulation' has a wide range of meanings, depending on audience, context, and disciplinary focus, see R Baldwin, M Cave, and M Lodge, 'Regulation, the Field and the Developing Agenda' in R Baldwin, M Cave, and M Lodge (eds), *The Oxford Handbook on Regulation* (OUP 2011). Black's popular definition of regulation is 'the intentional use of authority to affect behaviour of a different party according to set standards, involving instruments of information-gathering and behaviour modification', see J Black, 'Critical Reflections on Regulation' (2002) 27 *Australian Journal of Legal Philosophy* 1. This understanding of regulation places hard law with other ways of shaping behaviour and social outcomes, such as 'soft law', social norms, the market—and technologies themselves.

[11] See Chapter 5 in this collection.

[12] eg EU law on genetically modified crops at EU level is about markets and risk, whereas at the level of a regional authority, eg Wales, the framing devices in the relevant discourse are more

'Health technologies' per se are not defined as a single regulatory category by the EU. For instance, the Patients' Rights Directive defines 'health technologies' as medicinal products, medical devices, or medical and surgical procedures as well as measures for disease prevention, diagnosis, or treatment used in health care.[13] EU marketing legislation distinguishes 'medicinal products'[14] from 'medical devices',[15] and several subcategories are also found in EU law and regulation, including 'biotechnology medicine' or 'biotechnology-derived pharmaceutical';[16] 'advanced therapy medicinal products' (ATMPs);[17] and 'nanomedicine'.[18] Our analysis draws on regulation of all these categories of new health technologies and more. Much of the EU's regulation of *new* health

about sovereignty, see eg RG Lee and E Stokes (eds), *Economic Globalisation and Ecological Localisation: Socio-Legal Perspectives* (Wiley-Blackwell 2009).

[13] Parliament and Council Directive 2011/24/EU of 9 March 2011 on the application of patients' rights in cross-border healthcare [2011] OJ L88/45, Art 3(l).

[14] Parliament and Council Directive 2001/83/EC of 6 November 2001 on the Community code relating to medicinal products for human use [2001] OJ L311/67 (Community Code (as amended)), has two limbs to its definition of 'medicinal product'. These are medicinal product by 'presentation' ('[a]ny substance or combination of substances presented for treating or preventing disease in human beings'—Community Code, art 1(2)) and by 'function' ('any substance or combination of substances which may be used in or administered to human beings either with a view to restoring, correcting or modifying physiological functions by exerting a pharmacological, immunological or metabolic action, or to making a medical diagnosis').

[15] Defined by Council Directive 93/42/EEC of 14 June 1993 concerning medical devices [1993] OJ L169/1 to include 'any instrument, apparatus, appliance, software, material or other article, whether used alone or in combination, including the software intended by its manufacturer to be used specifically for diagnostic and/or therapeutic purposes and necessary for its proper application, intended by the manufacturer to be used for human beings' for one or more of several purposes. These purposes are: 'diagnosis, prevention, monitoring, treatment or alleviation of disease; diagnosis, monitoring, treatment, alleviation of or compensation for an injury or handicap; investigation, replacement or modification of the anatomy or of a physiological process; [or] control of conception', see Art 1(2). To fall within this definition, the device must 'not achieve its principal intended action in or on the human body by pharmacological, immunological or metabolic means', but it 'may be assisted in its function by such means', Art 1(2).

[16] The terms 'biotechnology medicine' or 'biotechnology-derived pharmaceutical' are generally used (EMA, 'S6 Preclinical Safety Evaluation of Biotechnology-Derived Pharmaceuticals' CHMP/ICH/302/95) to cover the medicines derived from the processes listed in sec 1 of the Annex (recombinant DNA technology, controlled expression of genes coding for biologically active proteins in prokaryotes and eukaryotes including transformed mammalian cells, hybridoma and monoclonal antibody methods) to Parliament and Council Regulation (EC) 726/2004 of 31 March 2004 laying down Community procedures for the authorisation and supervision of medicinal products for human and veterinary use and establishing a European Medicines Agency [2004] OJ L311/67.

[17] Advanced therapy medicinal products (ATMPs) are still classed as medicinal products and are included in sec 1a of the Annex to Parliament and Council Regulation (EC) 726/2004 of 31 March 2004 laying down Community procedures for the authorisation and supervision of medicinal products for human and veterinary use and establishing a European Medicines Agency [2004] OJ L311/67. Under the definition of ATMPs, Parliament and Council Regulation (EC) 1394/2007 of 13 November 2007 on advanced therapy medicinal products and amending Directive 2001/83/EC and Regulation (EC) No 726/2004 [2007] OJ L324/121, includes gene therapy medicinal products, somatic cell therapy medicinal products, tissue engineered products and combined ATMPs. So far as we are aware, only one ATMP has been authorized by the EMA, ChondroCelect—a tissue-engineered product for which TiGenex gained EU marketing authorization on 5 October 2009; see A Mahalatchimy, 'Access to Advanced Therapy Medicinal Products in the EU: Where do we stand?' (2011) 18 *European Journal of Health Law* 305.

[18] The European Medicine's Agency's, *Reflection Paper on Nanotechnology-Based Medicinal Products for Human Use* EMEA/CHMP/79769/2006, London, 20 June 2006, uses the term 'nanomedicinal product'; Amended proposal for a Council Decision concerning the 7th framework programme of the European Atomic Energy Community (Euratom) for nuclear research and training activities (2007–2011) (presented by the Commission pursuant to art 250(2) of the EC Treaty) COM/2006/0364 final highlights the importance of 'nano-medicine' under the theme of 'Nanosciences, Nanotechnologies, Materials and new Production Technologies'. Moreover see: B Dorbeck-Jung,

technologies is through its regulation of *all* health technologies, and thus, in drawing the map on which the analysis in this chapter relies, we did not focus only on the novel. Moreover, some apparently 'new' health technologies are not particularly new in time. For example, recombinant insulin and growth hormone (defined as 'biotechnology medicines') have been on the market in the EU since the 1980s.

The opening section of the chapter reports on our map of the key elements of EU regulation of new health technologies.[19] We drew our map by considering the regulatory environment relevant to new health technologies at different stages in the cycle of innovation (see Figure 2.1). This approach is justified by the need to contain a wide-ranging analysis, in terms of substantive coverage, in a chapter-length piece, and by the research agenda, which is to produce a map, from which to discuss the 'frames' of EU regulation of new health technologies in general, not a detailed substantive analysis of the application of EU law to specific new health technologies.[20] Our map covers the regulatory environment from the initial basic research up until the point at which a new health technology reaches the market and/or a patient receives treatment under a health care system. The approach of 'mapping' may appear simple, descriptive, technical, and theoretically or analytically innocuous. However, presenting our map involved not only methodologically-based decisions such as determining what constitutes 'EU law'[21] and 'regulation',[22] but also determining which elements of the regulatory environment belong on the map at all (for instance, does the REACH legislation[23] belong there?,[24] does data protection legislation?[25]). With some reluctance, especially given the significant EU legal intervention in the pharmaceutical market after the

DM Bowman, and G Van Calster (eds), *Governing Nanomedicine: Lessons from Within, and for, the EU Medical Technology Regulatory Framework* Special Issue (2011) 33 *Law and Policy* 215.

[19] There is no single piece of existing literature that sets out and describes all the legislation and other regulatory tools which we include in our map—there is no book on 'EU New Health Technology Law'. Emily Jackson's *Law and the Regulation of Medicines* (Hart 2012) covers some of the same ground, but does not include medical devices.

[20] See, for examples of this, Chapters 5 and 12 in this collection.

[21] As well as what counts as 'EU regulation', within a multilevel governance system (n 9).

[22] See Yeung and Dixon-Woods (n 8).

[23] Parliament and Council Regulation (EC) 1907/2006 of 18 December 2006 concerning the Registration, Evaluation, Authorisation and Restriction of Chemicals (REACH), establishing a European Chemicals Agency, amending Directive 1999/45/EC and repealing Council Regulation (EEC) No 793/93 and Commission Regulation (EC) No 1488/94 as well as Council Directive 76/769/EEC and Commission Directives 91/155/EEC, 93/67/EEC, 93/105/EC and 2000/21/EC [2006] OJ L136/3; Parliament and Council Directive 2006/121/EC of 18 December 2006 amending Council Directive 67/548/EEC on the approximation of laws, regulations and administrative provisions relating to the classification, packaging and labelling of dangerous substances in order to adapt it to Regulation (EC) No 1907/2006 concerning the Registration, Evaluation, Authorisation and Restriction of Chemicals (REACH) and establishing a European Chemicals Agency [2006] OJ L136/281.

[24] It does not, see Parliament and Council Regulation (EC) No 1907/2006 of 18 December 2006 concerning the Registration, Evaluation, Authorisation and Restriction of Chemicals (REACH), establishing a European Chemicals Agency, amending Directive 1999/45/EC and repealing Council Regulation (EEC) No 793/93 and Commission Regulation (EC) No 1488/94 as well as Council Directive 76/769/EEC and Commission Directives 91/155/EEC, 93/67/EEC, 93/105/EC and 2000/21/EC [2006] OJ L396/1, Art 2(5)(a), which states that the REACH legislation does not apply to the extent that a substance is used in medicinal products; and Art 2(6) which states that it does not apply to medical devices, covered by the *leges speciales* discussed in this chapter.

[25] It does, see Parliament and Council Directive 95/46/EC of 24 October 1995 on the protection of individuals with regard to the processing of personal data and on the free movement of such data [1995] OJ L281/31, which includes data in health care settings, including research and development of new health technologies. See also Proposal for a Regulation of the European Parliament and of the Council on the protection of individuals with regard to the processing of personal data and on the free movement of such data (General Data Protection Regulation) COM(2012) 11 final.

AstraZeneca case,[26] we decided, for instance, to exclude consideration of EU competition law, which at least arguably has an important indirect effect on the regulation of new health technologies because of its constraining and enabling effects on the global pharmaceutical industry,[27] on the basis that its effects on new health technologies were too remote. We also had to determine which EU regulatory instruments belong at which point(s) on the map. Particular measures of EU law, or other regulatory instruments, do not necessarily apply at only one stage in the 'life span' of a new health technology (see Figure 2.3). The drawing of the map—which we regarded as merely a preliminary stage in our overall research agenda—in fact represents a significant piece of original research. Moreover, we are aware that the very way in which we drew our map—which essentially involves a cycle from idea to market and/or health care system—*in itself* may have coloured our analysis of the framing of regulation of new health technologies in the EU.

The remainder of the chapter presents the results of our analysis of the contents of the map, with respect to our central research questions—what are the roles of risk, ethics, rights, and markets as framing devices for the EU's regulation of new health technologies? Our conclusions were reached through a close reading of the relevant legal and policy documentation, with a view to determining the dominant 'frames', in the sense of discourse analysis, and to unpicking the ways in which different frames interact, co-produce, and constitute EU regulation of new health technologies. Of course, within the confines of a chapter-length work, it is not possible to report the detail of our evidence, but we have sought to illustrate our general points with pertinent examples in each case.

B. The Map

As noted earlier, we began our task of mapping the EU's regulation of new health technologies by considering the different stages in the 'cycle of innovation' (see Figure 2.1). We have conceptualized this as a circular process, beginning with an idea,[28] which drives basic research, leading (where successful) to non-clinical, pre-clinical, and clinical research, and from there (where successful) to marketing of new health technologies, then the monitoring of those technologies within the market, leading to development of consumer/professional/patient demand and hence ideas that lead to improved new health technologies, with the cycle beginning again. What is already in the market, and consumer demand, itself also drives the innovation

---

[26] EU competition law has been used by national authorities to challenge the use by pharmaceutical and other companies of regulatory structures, in particular intellectual property bodies, to delay entry into the market of generic competitors. The European Commission fined AstraZeneca €60 million in 2005 for such behaviour, on the basis that it was an 'abuse of a dominant position', unlawful under Art 102 TFEU. In 2008, the Commission began a sector-wide inquiry into the practice of making 'allegedly misleading representations' to patent authorities as part of a strategy on AstraZeneca's part to protect its leading product, Losec, from generic competition, even after the patent on its active ingredient had expired. The CFI upheld the Commission in all important respects in the judicial review of its decision, see Case T-321/05 *AstraZeneca v Commission* [2010] ECR I-2805 and the CJEU has since upheld the CFI, Case C-457/10-P 6 December 2012.

[27] EU competition law applies to situations where smaller enterprises license larger enterprises to undertake clinical development, and the need to comply with EU anti-monopoly laws can affect what research into NHTs is feasible in practice. See, eg L Hancher, 'The EU Pharmaceuticals Market: Parameters and Pathways' in E Mossialos, G Permanand, R Baeten, and T Hervey (eds), *Health Systems Governance in Europe: The Role of EU Law and Policy* (CUP 2010) 635.

[28] This could be an 'idea in the mind of a scientist', or, equally, an 'idea in the mind of a venture capitalist'.

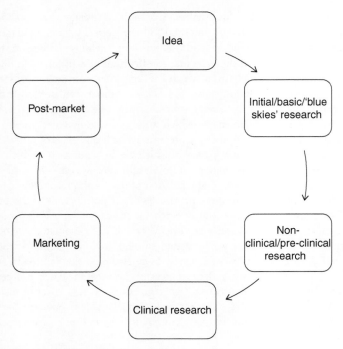

Figure 2.1 The cycle of innovation

processes, as well as the development of scientific knowledge and understanding, or the desire to benefit from intellectual property rights, which can lead to only small innovations, designed to enable renewed patents. Within our map, we have mainly conceptualized new health technologies as products, but they could equally be new processes or procedures,[29] or even texts.[30]

From this cycle of innovation, we drew up a list (a long list!) of all the different EU regulatory measures that affect the different stages in the map.[31] Our central focus is legislation, but we also included soft law, such as guidance and elements of regulation through 'steering', such as the availability of EU funding and the ability to rely on intellectual property rights in the development of new health technologies. Our initial analysis involved categorizing these measures into a typology of relevant EU regulation, a heuristic device that takes account of the different regulatory types that we came

[29] eg the use of ICT in health care settings, such as new technologies that allow remote management of chronic conditions, such as blood pressure or glucose monitoring, movement sensors, bed/chair occupancy sensors. See, eg J Hendy, J Barlow, and T Chrysanthaki, 'Implementing Remote Care in the UK: An Update of Progress' (2011) 17 *Eurohealth* 21; E Hanson and L Magnusson, 'The role of ICT Services to Promote Ageing in Place: A Swedish Case Study' (2011) 17 *Eurohealth* 24.

[30] See Chapter 15 in this collection.

[31] Similar approaches have been used by regulatory authorities in the Member States. See, in the UK context, the 'UK Stem Cell Tool Kit' <www.sc-toolkit.ac.uk/home.cfm> accessed 7 May 2012; the 'Clinical Trials Tool Kit' <www.ct-toolkit.ac.uk/> accessed 7 May 2012; the 'Experimental Medicine Tool Kit' <www.em-toolkit.ac.uk/home.cfm> accessed 7 May 2012; and the 'Data and Tissues Tool Kit' <www.dt-toolkit.ac.uk/home.cfm> accessed 7 May 2012.

Funding

FP funding - Decision 1982/2006/EC OJ 2006 L 412/1
Public health programme funding -Decision 1350/2007/EC OJ 2007 L 301/3
EGE Opinions on funding

 Protection of intellectual property

Directive 98/44/EC on the legal protection of biotechnological inventions OJ 1998 L 213/13 - Case C-377/98 *Biotechnology*
[2001] ECR I-7079; Case C-34/10 *Brüstle* [2011] ECR I-
Supplementary Protection Certificate Regulation 1768/92 OJ 1992 L 182/1
Special protection for orphan and paediatric new health technologies - Regulation 1901/2006/EC OJ 2006 L 378/1;
Regulation 141/2000/EC OJ 2000 L 18/1

 Regulation of research processes

Good Laboratory Practice Directives 2004/9/EC and 2004/10/EC OJ 2004 L 50/28&44; Good Clinical Practice Directive
2005/28/EC OJ 2005 L 91/13; Clinical Trials Directive 2001/20/EC OJ 2001 L 121/34, as amended
Special Legislation on paediatric and orphan trials - Regulation 1901/2006/EC OJ 2006 L 378/1; Regulation 141/2000/EC OJ
2000 L 18/1
Medical Devices legislation (see below)
EMA Guidance - principles of Good Laboratory Practice; Guidance on ATMPs; Good Clinical Practice Guidance
Animal Protection Directive - Directive 2010/63/EU -OJ 2010 L 276/33
Directives on GMOS and GMM-Os -Council Directive 90/219/EC OJ 1990 L 117/1, Directive 2001/18/EC OJ L 106/1

 Data protection

Data Protection Directive 95/46/EC OJ 1995 L 281/31

 Marketing and product safety legislation

Market authorisation for medicinal products legislation - Directive 2001/83/EC OJ 2001 L 311/67; Regulation 726/2004/EC
OJ 2004 L 136/1; Regulation 1901/2006/EC OJ 2006 L 378/1; Regulation 1394/2007 on advanced therapy medicinal
products OJ 2007 L 324/121; Regulation 1901/2006/EC on medicinal products for paediatric use OJ 2006 L 378/1;
Regulation 141/2000/EC on orphan medicinal products OJ 2000 L 18/1; Directive 2011/62/EU on falsified medicines OJ 2011
L 174/74; Legislation on manufacture and import of products used in clinical trials
Medical Devices legislation – Directive 90/385/EEC on active implantable medical devices OJ 1990 L 189/17 as amended;
Directive 98/79/EC on in vitro diagnostic medical devices OJ 1998 L 331/1 as amended
CE certification; General Product Safety Directive 2001/95/EC OJ 2002 L 11/4
Advertising and patient information – Directive 2001/83/EC, Articles 86-100
Guidance and soft law eg MEA Guidelines; MEDDEVs standards
Blood Safety Directive 2002/98/EC OJ 2002 L 33/30; Human Tissue Directive 2004/23/EC OJ 2004 L 102/48; Human Organs
Directive 2010/53/EU OJ 2010 L 207/14

 Monitoring and surveillance

Directive 2010/84/EU on pharmacovigilance OJ 2010 348/74; Directive 2001/83/EC, Articles 101-108b, as amended, most
recently by Regulation 1235/2010/EU on pharmacovigilanceand ATMPs OJ 2010 L 348/1 and Directive 2010/84/EU OJ 2010
L 348/74
Product Liability Directive 85/374/EEC OJ 1985 L 210/29

 Pricing, reimbursement, coverage in health care systems

Transparency Directive 89/105/EEC OJ 1989 L 40/8
Patients' Rights Directive 2011/24/EU OJ 2011 L 88/45

Figure 2.2 Typology of relevant EU regulation

across in drawing up our list. We found seven broad types of EU regulation of new
health technologies: funding; protection of intellectual property; regulation of research
processes; data protection; marketing and product safety legislation; post-market monitoring and surveillance, and product liability; and pricing, reimbursement, and coverage in national health care systems (see Figure 2.2). The process of drawing up the list
also revealed gaps or areas where there is little or no EU regulation of new health
technologies, for instance in the area of novel surgical techniques.

Funding includes the EU's 'Framework Programmes', administered by DG Research
and the public health programmes, administered by DG SANCO. The work of the
European Group on Ethics in Science and New Technologies (EGE), such as its

Opinion No 22,[32] feeds into the interpretation and development of these programmes. The EU's regulatory mode here is 'steering' rather than 'command and control'[33]—the availability of funding streams to support development of certain types of new health technologies (and not other types) is intended to encourage particular types of behaviour. Similarly, the EU's intellectual property law has the effect, through the incentive of exclusive intellectual property rights, such as patent protection, of steering behaviour in particular ways.[34] The decision of the Court of Justice of the European Union (CJEU) in the *Brüstle* case[35] has been widely interpreted as encouraging certain types of research, in particular that using adult stem cells,[36] or certain types of industry behaviour, for instance keeping manufacturing processes for new technologies a trade secret,[37] or investing in non-European companies.[38]

In terms of regulating research processes, EU legislation covers 'good laboratory practice'[39] (GLP), and 'good clinical practice' (GCP),[40] requiring Member States to set standards for the planning, performance, reporting, and archiving of research, and in particular to establish systems of monitoring and inspection. This EU legislation draws from the OECD's work on good laboratory/clinical practice since the 1990s[41] and on

---

[32] On the ethics review of human embryonic stem cell Framework Programme 7 research projects 20 June 2007 <http://ec.europa.eu/bepa/european-group-ethics/docs/publications/opinion_22_final_follow_up_en.pdf> accessed 7 May 2012.

[33] This 'steering' is what Daintith calls 'government by dominium'. See T Daintith, 'The Techniques of Government' in J Jowell and D Oliver (eds), *The Changing Constitution* (OUP 1994) 209.

[34] T Hervey and H Black, 'The European Union and the governance of stem cell research' (2005) 12 *Maastricht Journal of European and Comparative Law* 3; Chapter 7 in this collection.

[35] Case C-34/10 *Oliver Brüstle v Greenpeace* [2011] ECR I-nyr.

[36] A Abbott, 'Stem Cells: The Cell Division' (2011) 480(7377) *Nature* <www.nature.com/news/stem-cells-the-cell-division-1.9634> accessed 7 May 2012; see, eg G Puppinck, '*Brüstle* Case: The Court of Justice of the European Union Reaffirms that a Process Involving the Destruction of an Embryo Cannot be Patented (*Turtle and Beyond*, 18 October 2011) <www.turtlebayandbeyond.org/2011/eu/brustle-case-the-court-of-justice-of-the-european-union-reaffirms-that-a-process-involving-the-destruction-of-an-embryo-cannot-be-patented/> accessed 7 May 2012; S Ertelt, 'European Union Court Bans Stem Cell Patents if Embryo Destroyed' (*Life News*, 10 August 2011) <www.lifenews.com/2011/10/18/european-union-court-bans-stem-cell-patents-if-embryo-destroyed/> accessed 7 May 2012.

[37] S Jenei, 'EU's Court of Justice: Stem Cells Unpatentable if an Embryo is Destroyed' (*Patent Baristas*, 24 October 2011) <www.patentbaristas.com/archives/2011/10/24/eus-court-of-justice-stem-cells-unpatentable-if-an-embryo-is-destroyed/> accessed 7 May 2012; Though see C Langer, 'The European Court of Justice Bars Stem Cell Patents in Land mark Decision' (2012) The Bolt; *Berkley Technology Law Journal* <http://btlj.org/2012/01/05/the-european-court-of-justice-bars-stem-cell-patents-in-landmark-decision/> accessed 7 May 2012—who argues that the ruling may not have much effect at all.

[38] *EuroStemCell*, 'European Court Bans Stem Cell Patents' (*EuroStemCell*, 18 October 2011) <www.eurostemcell.org/story/european-court-bans-stem-cell-patents> accessed 8 May 2012; A Blackburn-Starza, 'Ban on Embryonic Stem Cell Patents by European Court of Justice' (*BioNews*, 24 October 2011) <www.bionews.org.uk/page_109818.asp> accessed 8 May 2012; C Drew, 'Human Embryonic Stem Cells in the EU' (*Winston & Strawn LLP*, Patent News, November 2011) <www.winston.com/siteFiles/Publications/HumanEmbryonicStemCells.pdf> accessed 8 May 2012.

[39] Parliament and Council Directive 2004/10/EC of 11 February 2004 on the harmonisation of laws, regulations and administrative provisions relating to the application of the principles of good laboratory practice and the verification of their applications for tests on chemical substances [2004] OJ L50/44; Parliament and Council Directive 2004/9/EC of 11 February 2004 on the inspection and verification of good laboratory practice (GLP) [2004] OJ L50/28.

[40] Parliament and Council Directive 2001/20/EC of 4 April 2001 on the approximation of the laws, regulations and administrative provisions of the Member States relating to the implementation of good clinical practice in the conduct of clinical trials on medicinal products for human use [2001] OJ L121/34, which requires the Commission to establish principles relating to good clinical practice and detailed rules in line with those principles, see Commission Directive 2005/28/EC of 8 April 2005 laying down principles and detailed guidelines for good clinical practice as regards investigational medicinal products for human use, as well as the requirements for authorisation of the manufacturing or importation of such products [2005] OJ L91/13.

[41] See *OECD*, 'Good Laboratory Practice (GLP)' (*OECD*) <www.oecd.org/document/1/0,3746, en_2649_37465_48477249_1_1_1_37465,00.html> accessed 8 May 2012.

International Standards for audit, accreditation, and technical competence.[42] In practice, the detailed regulation for many new health technologies here is found in soft law 'guidance notes', issued by the European Medicines Agency (EMA).[43] Given that many new health technologies are derived from biotechnological processes, for our purposes, key guidance documents[44] include pre-clinical safety evaluation of biotechnology-derived pharmaceuticals (ICH S6).[45] Again, the regulatory mode is steering, rather than command and control, because compliance with the guidance is not mandatory. However, compliance is normally required for studies used to support applications for clinical trial authorization or market authorization for products, giving the 'soft law' a 'hard' effect in practice.

Concern with animal welfare across the internal market motivates the EU's regulation of the use of animals in the context of scientific research,[46] which includes research into new health technologies. EU regulation of genetically modified micro-organisms (GMMOs)[47] and release into the environment of genetically modified organisms (GMOs)[48] is intended to prevent harmful release of such organisms, and particularly applies in the food sector. However, it also applies to medicines that use GMMOs and GMOs, that are developed and marketed within the EU, and for that reason we have placed it in this part of our typology. As far as we are aware, there have not as yet been any new health technology products that are, or consist of, GMMOs or GMOs as defined in these Directives. There are hopes that food could be engineered to contain vaccines, which could then be easily transported to developing states.[49] Such products would be covered by medicinal products legislation rather than GMO legislation, subject to the requirement for an equivalent environmental risk assessment.[50]

However, GMOs such as plants, animals, and microbes have been used as expression systems for medicinal products. An example of early stage research involving GMOs, and related to new health technologies, is the EU-funded project TERPMED. This project hopes to derive new bioactive molecules from genetically modified plants, a

[42] Eg, *ISO*, 'ISO/IEC 17000:2004, Conformity Assessment-Vocabulary and General Principles' (*ISO*) <www.iso.org/iso/catalogue_detail?csnumber=9316> accessed 8 May 2012; *ISO*, 'ISO 9000:2005 Quality Management Systems-Fundamentals and Vocabulary' (*ISO*) <www.iso.org/iso/iso_catalogue/catalogue_ics/catalogue_detail_ics.htm?csnumber42180> accessed 8 May 2012; *ISO*, 'ISO 15189: 2007, Medical Laboratories-Particular Requirements for Quality and Competence' (*ISO*) <www.iso.org/iso/iso_catalogue/catalogue_ics/catalogue_detail_ics.htm?csnumber=42641> accessed 8 May 2012.

[43] *European Medicines Agency*, 'Non-Clinical Guidelines' (*European Medicines Agency*) <www.ema.europa.eu/htms/human/humanguidelines/nonclinical.htm> accessed 8 May 2012.

[44] Such as, Non-Clinical Safety Studies For The Conduct Of Human Clinical Trials For Pharmaceuticals (ICH M3[R2]) CPMP/ICH/286/95; Non-Clinical Safety Studies For The Conduct Of Human Clinical Trials For Pharmaceuticals (ICH M3[R2]) CPMP/ICH/286/95; Safety pharmacology studies for human pharmaceuticals (ICH S7A) CPMP/ICH/539/00; Duration of chronic toxicity testing in animals (rodent and non-rodent toxicity testing) (ICHS4A) CPMP/ICH/300/95; Carcinogenicity: testing for carcinogenicity of pharmaceuticals (ICH SIB) CPMP/ICH/299/95.

[45] CPMP/ICH/302/95.

[46] Directive 2010/63/EU on the protection of animals used for scientific purposes [2010] OJ L276/33, which repeals Directive 86/609/EEC from 2013 (Art 62) and replaces point (a)(iv) of Art 8 of Regulation 1069/2009, with reference to the new Directive (Art 63). Hervey is grateful to the organizers of the Wellcome Trust and AHRC Workshop *Research With Living Beings*, University of Keele, 30 June–1 July 2011 for the invitation to participate in a discussion of this relatively new Directive.

[47] Council Directive 90/219/EC of 23 April 1990 on the contained use of genetically modified micro-organisms [1990] OJ L117/1.

[48] Parliament and Council Directive 2001/18/EC of 12 March 2001 on the deliberate release into the environment of genetically modified organisms and repealing Council Directive 90/220/EEC [2001] OJ L106/1.

[49] M Paul and JK-C Ma, 'Plant-made Pharmaceuticals: Leading Products and Production Platforms' (2011) 58 *Biotechnology and Applied Biochemistry* 58; KM Everett and others, 'Development of a Plant-Made Pharmaceutical Production Platform' (2012) 10(1) *BioProcess International* 16.

[50] Directive 2001/18/EC, Art 5; also see EMA, Guideline on Environmental Risk Assessments for Medical Products Consisting of, or Containing, Genetically Modified Organisms (GMOs), Doc. Ref. EMEA/CHMP/BWP/473191/2006—Corr.

process often referred to as 'pharming'. Another example is ATryn, which was approved via the centralized procedure in 2007, and which is expressed in the milk of transgenic goats. Moreover, as the EGE confirms, transgenic animals are used and have the potential to be used '[i]n fundamental bio-medical research to improve our genetic and physiological knowledge; [t]o make models of human diseases; [and] [a]s an alternative source of tissues and organs for "xenotransplantation".'[51]

The EU's data protection legislation, said to be the most stringent in the world,[52] covers trials involving human data. In the nanotechnology field, new health technologies such as subcutaneous radio-frequency identification microchips, used to monitor the health of individuals, send human data to an external device, and thus themselves must comply with EU data protection law. Many of the pieces of EU legislation in our categories of regulation of research processes,[53] protection of intellectual property,[54] product safety legislation,[55] monitoring and surveillance,[56] and pricing, reimbursement, and coverage in health care systems[57] refer explicitly to the EU's Data Protection Directive 95/46/EC.[58] This Directive, which itself refers directly to Council of Europe human rights law,[59] and also draws on the work of the OECD,[60] requires that 'personal data', that is, information relating to an indentified or identifiable natural person, be processed according to principles set out in national law concerning matters such as fairness, legitimacy of purpose, and accuracy. In principle, data concerning

[51] Group of Advisors on the Ethical Implications of Biotechnology (now the European Group on Ethics in Science and New Technologies), Opinion No 7 on the ethical aspects of genetic modification of animals, 21 May 1996 <http://ec.europa.eu/bepa/european-group-ethics/docs/opinion7_en.pdf> accessed 8 May 2012. See Chapter 16 in this collection.

[52] E Kosta and D M Bowman, 'Treating or Tracking? 'Regulatory Challenges of Nano-Enabled ICT Implants' (2011) 33 *Law and Policy* 256, 260.

[53] Parliament and Council Directive 2001/20/EC of 4 April 2001 on the approximation of the laws, regulations and administrative provisions of the Member States relating to the implementation of good clinical practice in the conduct of clinical trials on medicinal products for human use [2001] OJ L121/34, Recital 17, Art 3.

[54] Parliament and Council Directive 98/44/EC of 6 July 1998 on the legal protection of biotechnological inventions [1998] OJ L213/13; Council Regulation (EEC) No 1768/92 of 18 June 1992 concerning the creation of a supplementary protection certificate for medicinal products [1992] OJ L182/1; Parliament and Council Regulation (EC) No 1901/2006 of 12 December 2006 on medicinal products for paediatric use and amending Regulation (EEC) No 1768/92, Directive 2001/20/EC, Directive 2001/83/EC and Regulation (EC) No 726/2004 [2006] OJ L378/1; Parliament and Council Regulation (EC) No 141/2000 of 16 December 1999 on orphan medicinal products [2000] OJ L18/1.

[55] Directive 2001/83/EC on the Community code relating to medicinal products for human use, as amended, Art 54a; Parliament and Council Directive 2010/45/EU of 7 July 2010 on standards of quality and safety of human organs intended for transplantation [2010] OJ L207/14, Recital 22, Arts 16 and 17; Parliament and Council Regulation (EC) No 1394/2007 of 13 November 2007 on advanced therapy medicinal products and amending Directive 2001/83/EC and Regulation (EC) No 726/2004 [2007] OJ L324/121, Recital 22; Parliament and Council Directive 2004/23/EC of 31 March 2004 on setting standards of quality and safety for the donation, procurement, testing, processing, preservation, storage and distribution of human tissues and cells [2004] OJ L102/48, Recital 24; Parliament and Council Directive 2002/98/EC of 27 January 2003 setting standards of quality and safety for the collection, testing, processing, storage and distribution of human blood and blood components and amending Directive 2001/83/EC [2003] OJ L33/30, Recital 25, Art 2.

[56] Parliament and Council Regulation (EU) No 1235/2010 of 15 December 2010 amending, as regards pharmacovigilance of medicinal products for human use, Regulation (EC) No 726/2004 laying down Community procedures for the authorisation and supervision of medicinal products for human and veterinary use and establishing a European Medicines Agency, and Regulation (EC) No 1394/2007 on advanced therapy medicinal products [2010] OJ L348/1, Recital 23.

[57] Parliament and Council Directive 2011/24/EU of 9 March 2011 on the application of patients' rights in cross-border healthcare [2011] OJ L88/45, Recital 25, Arts 2, 4, 5, 10, 14.

[58] [1995] OJ L281/31 (n 25).

[59] European Convention on Human Rights and Fundamental Freedoms, Art 8.

[60] *OECD*, 'OECD Guidelines on the Protection of Privacy and Transborder Flows of Personal Data' (*OECD*, 23 September 1980) <www.oecd.org/document/18/0,2340,en_2649_34255_1815186_1_1_1_1,00.html> accessed 8 May 2012.

health may not be processed, but this rule is subject to exceptions, such as where explicit consent is given[61] (relevant in research settings involving new health technologies), or 'where processing of the data is required for the purposes of preventive medicine, medical diagnosis, the provision of care or treatment or the management of health care services, and where those data are processed by a health professional subject under national law or rules established by national competent bodies to the obligation of professional secrecy or by another person also subject to an equivalent obligation of secrecy'[62] (relevant in treatment settings involving new health technologies).

A significant amount of EU legislation on new health technologies, and supporting guidance, is aimed at product safety of medicines and medical devices. Dating back to the 1960s, this legislation is concerned to prevent medicines or medical devices reaching the EU market unless they are safe, efficacious, and of appropriate quality. The legislation sets detailed rules with respect to the requirements for granting marketing authorizations, either by national authorities, or, more likely in the case of new health technologies, by the 'centralized' procedure involving the EMA. The rules with respect to medicines (defined by 'presentation'[63] and by 'function'[64]) are consolidated in the 2001 'Community Code relating to medicinal products for human use', itself amended regularly since then.[65] Medical devices legislation covers 'active implantable medical devices' used for diagnosis, prevention, monitoring, treatment, or alleviation of disease,[66] which do not achieve their intended purpose by pharmacological, immunological, or metabolic means. *In vitro* diagnostic medical devices are covered by a separate Directive 98/79/EC.[67] The medical devices legislation creates a special, sector specific, version of the general system of 'CE' product safety certification, a process governed in general in the EU by the 'General Product Safety Directive'.[68] As such, it is more of an industry-based regulatory system than that pertaining to medicines.[69] As noted earlier, these marketing rules interact with EU law on the research process, for marketing authorizations cannot be given without compliance with principles of good laboratory/clinical practice.[70] Moreover, the relevant legislation also covers the research process. For this reason, the legislation appears twice in our typology.

Perhaps more controversially in a European context, we have included, in the category of 'product safety legislation' in our typology, legislation concerned with safety with respect to human tissue, blood, and organs. In terms of its own categories of

[61] Directive 95/46/EC, Art 8(2)(a).
[62] Directive 95/46/EC, Art 8(3).
[63] 'Any substance or combination of substances presented for treating or preventing disease in human beings'—Community Code, art 1(2).
[64] 'Any substance or combination of substances which may be used in or administered to human beings either with a view to restoring, correcting or modifying physiological functions by exerting a pharmacological, immunological or metabolic action, or to making a medical diagnosis.'
[65] Most recently in 2011, see Parliament and Council Directive 2011/62/EU of 8 June 2011 amending Directive 2001/83/EC on the Community code relating to medicinal products for human use, as regards the prevention of the entry into the legal supply chain of falsified medicinal products [2011] OJ L174/74.
[66] Directive 90/385/EEC, as amended, Art 1(2)(a). The Directive also covers devices used in 'diagnosis, monitoring, treatment, alleviation of or compensation for an injury or handicap, investigation, replacement or modification of the anatomy or of a physiological process and to control conception.'
[67] [1998] OJ L331/1, as amended.
[68] Directive 2001/95/EC [2002] OJ L11/4.
[69] B Dorbeck-Jung and N Chowdhury, 'Is the European Medical Products Authorisation Regulation Equipped to Cope with the Challenges of Nanomedicines?' (2011) 33 *Law and Policy* 276, 282.
[70] eg Recital 4 of Directive 2004/10/EC provides that the EU's marketing legislation lays down 'that non-clinical tests on pharmaceutical products are to be carried out in accordance with the principles of... [GLP] in force in the Community for chemical substances, compliance with which is also required by other Community legislation'; see also Directive 2005/28/EC, Recital 3.

competence, the EU certainly does not do so: these pieces of legislation are based on what is now Article 168 TFEU, not on the internal market legal basis of (now) Article 114 TFEU, which is the basis of the EU's competence to adopt product safety legislation in general. Adopting measures such as the Blood Safety Directive,[71] the Human Tissue Directive,[72] and the Human Organs Directive[73] on the basis of internal market competence, and product safety in the internal market, was not politically feasible as human tissue, blood, or organs are not regarded as 'products' in European cultures.[74] However, functionally speaking, this legislation performs essentially the same role in the regulation of new health technologies as other EU product safety legislation, so for that reason it is included in this part of our typology.

EU legislation concerning post-market monitoring and surveillance[75] requires Member States to operate a pharmacovigilance system, which imposes reporting obligations on health care professionals of suspected adverse reactions, and requires those who hold marketing authorizations to undertake pharmacovigilance. For ATMPs, there is an additional requirement for a plan to ensure the follow-up *efficacy* of the product[76] and a traceability requirement.[77] Member States share pharmacovigilance information through the EMA and its Pharmacovigilance Risk Assessment Committee, using the 'Eudravigilance' database.[78]

Post-market liabilities for harm are covered by the Product Liability Directive,[79] which provides that producers are liable for damage caused by a defect in products. However, a key point that has generally excluded producers of new health technologies

---

[71] Parliament and Council Directive 2002/98/EC of 27 January 2003 setting standards of quality and safety for the collection, testing, processing, storage and distribution of human blood and blood components and amending Directive 2001/83/EC [2003] OJ L33/30.

[72] Parliament and Council Directive 2004/23/EC of 31 March 2004 on setting standards of quality and safety for the donation, procurement, testing, processing, preservation, storage and distribution of human tissues and cells [2004] OJ L102/48.

[73] Parliament and Council Directive 2010/53/EU of 7 July 2010 on standards of quality and safety of human organs intended for transplantation [2010] OJ L207/14; see Corrigendum to Parliament and Council Directive 2010/45/EU of 7 July 2010 on standards of quality and safety of human organs intended for transplantation [2010] OJ L243/68, which makes it clear that the correct number is Directive 2010/53/EU.

[74] T Hervey and J McHale, *Health Law and the European Union* (CUP 2004) 343–8; A-M Farrell, 'Is the gift still good? The politics and regulation of blood safety in the European Union' (2006) 14 *Medical Law Review* 155; A-M Farrell, 'The Politics of Risk and EU Governance of Human Material' (2009) 16 *Maastricht Journal of European and Comparative Law* 41; A-M Farrell, 'Adding Value? EU Governance of Organ Donation and Transplantation' (2010) 17 *European Journal of Health Law* 51; A-M Farrell, *The Politics of Blood: Ethics Innovation and the Regulation of Risk* (CUP 2012).

[75] Parliament and Council Regulation (EU) No 1235/2010 of 15 December 2010 amending, as regards pharmacovigilance of medicinal products for human use, Regulation (EC) No 726/2004 laying down Community procedures for the authorisation and supervision of medicinal products for human and veterinary use and establishing a European Medicines Agency, and Regulation (EC) No 1394/2007 on advanced therapy medicinal products [2010] OJ L348/1; Parliament and Council Directive 2010/84/EU of 15 December 2010 amending, as regards pharmacovigilance, Directive 2001/83/EC on the Community code relating to medicinal products for human use [2010] OJ L348/74; Directive 2001/83/EC, Arts 101–8b, as amended.

[76] Parliament and Council Regulation (EC) No 1394/2007 of 13 November 2007 on advanced therapy medicinal products and amending Directive 2001/83/EC and Regulation (EC) No 726/2004 [2007] OJ L324/121, Art 14(1). For other medicinal products, generally only safety studies are requested.

[77] Regulation (EU) No 1394/2007, Art 15.

[78] Regulation 1235/2010/EU on pharmacovigilance and advanced therapy medicinal products [2010] OJ L348/1.

[79] Council Directive 85/374/EEC of 25 July 1985 on the approximation of the laws, regulations and administrative provisions of the Member States concerning liability for defective products [1985] OJ L210/29.

from liability is the so-called 'development risks defence' which states that it is a defence to show 'that the state of scientific and technical knowledge at the time when he put the product into circulation was not such as to enable the existence of the defect to be discovered.' The most notable successful product liability claim relevant to new health technologies is the English case of *A v National Blood Authority*[80] relating to hepatitis C infected blood. The application of the development risk defence was excluded in this case due to the fact that the national blood authority knew that the product could be contaminated, even if there was no mechanism for preventing this fact. During our research, we did not find any other successful litigation under the Product Liability Directive relating to new health technologies.[81] However, this is most likely due to the preference for settling claims out of court.[82]

Finally in our typology is the very small selection of EU regulation that covers the pricing of pharmaceuticals, medical devices, and other new health technologies, and inclusion within the 'basket of care' in a particular national health system. In principle, such matters are a question of national competence, even though that means significant discrepancies in pricing and thus in practice no single European market in the relevant products.[83] Member States are obliged only to disclose information on national pricing arrangements for pharmaceuticals[84] (not other new health technologies) and to authorize access to health care in other Member States, paid for by the home Member State, under the (restricted) conditions of the Directive on patients' rights in cross-border health care.[85]

---

[80] *A v National Blood Authority*, The Times, 4 April 2001 (QB).

[81] Another example, relating to medical devices, is *Foster v Biosil* (2000) 59 BMLR 178 which related to a ruptured breast implant. In this case, it was made clear that the claimant had to establish that a specific design or manufacturing defect caused the rupture and it was not enough simply to point to the rupture. Presumably the PIP breast implant scandal of late 2011/2012 will lead to litigation, and in that instance it seems that substandard materials were used, which would constitute a design or manufacturing defect. See, eg BBC News, 'PIP Breast Implant Boss Jean-Claude Mas Faces Charges' (*BBC News*, 27 January 2012) <www.bbc.co.uk/news/world-europe-16736385> accessed 8 May 2012.

[82] eg see Opren case which was settled with no admission of fault—see *Davies v Eli Lilly & Co* [1987] NLJ Rep 1183; *Davies v Eli Lilly & Co* [1987] 3 All ER 94, [1987] 1 WLR 1136 and the Myodil case see Ernest Jellinek, 'Myodil arachnoiditis iatrongenic and forensic illness' (2002) 2 *Practical Neurology* 237. This is the likely outcome of litigation arising from the PIP breast implant scandal.

[83] L Hancher, 'Creating the Internal Market for Pharmaceutical Medicines: An Echternach Jumping Process?' (1991) 28 *Common Market Law Review* 821; L Hancher, 'The EU Pharmaceuticals Market: Parameters and Pathways' in E Mossialos and others (eds), *Health Systems Governance in Europe: The Role of EU Law and Policy* (CUP 2010).

[84] Directive 89/105/EEC on the transparency of measures regulating the pricing of medicinal products for human use and their inclusion in the scope of national health insurance schemes [1989] OJ L40/8; for discussion, see T Hervey and J McHale, *Health Law and the European Union* (CUP 2004) 323–7; the Commission has proposed an amendment to this Directive, responding to changes in the pharmaceuticals market and pressures on national health systems leading to more complex pricing arrangements, in particular concerning generics, see Proposal for a Directive of the European Parliament and the Council relating to the transparency of measures regulating the prices of medicinal products for human use and their inclusion in the scope of public health insurance systems COM (2012) 84 final.

[85] Directive 2011/24/EU [2011] OJ L88/45. These are essentially, without prior authorization from the home Member State, non-hospital care, where no specialized cost-intensive medical infrastructure or medical equipment is involved, and no particular risk to the patient, or concern about the quality of the care, is involved, Art 8(2); it is also possible for Member States to justify refusal to authorize access to cross-border health care on the grounds of 'overriding reasons in the public interest', such as planning requirements ('planification'); avoiding waste of financial, technical or human resources; preservation of treatment capacity or medical competence in the state concerned, Art 4 (3); See Van de Gronden and others (eds), *Health Care and EU Law* (Springer 2011); S de la Rosa, 'The Directive on Crossborder Healthcare or the Art of Codifying Complex Caselaw' (2012) 49 *Common Market Law Review* 15.

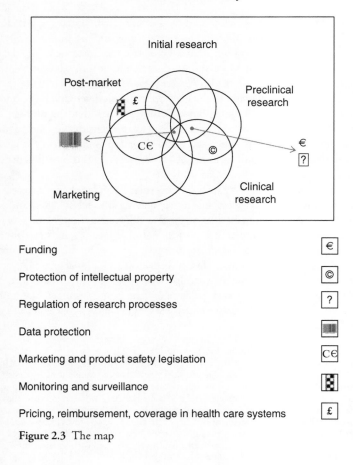

Funding   €

Protection of intellectual property   ©

Regulation of research processes   ?

Data protection   ▓

Marketing and product safety legislation   CE

Monitoring and surveillance   ▦

Pricing, reimbursement, coverage in health care systems   £

Figure 2.3 The map

Putting our cycle of innovation and our typology of EU regulation of new health technologies together, we are able to draw the following map (Figure 2.3) which illustrates what types of EU regulation are involved at each stage of the cycle.

To summarize our conclusions so far, there is a great deal of overlap in the categories, because the structure of EU regulation (and in particular legislation) does not follow the cycle of innovation. Rather, almost everything refers to the market, either regulation of access to the market for new health technologies (the most densely 'populated' area on our map), or regulation of research into new health technologies with a view to eventual marketing, or regulation of consumer safety once a new health technology is on the market. Our first conclusion, therefore, consistent with our original hypotheses, is that the market is a (perhaps the) dominant frame in EU regulation of new health technologies. But what of the other frames? We turn now to explore each of our four frames in turn.

C. Frames

What are the roles of risk, ethics, rights, and markets as framing devices for the EU's regulation of new health technologies? To what extent does analysis of the map support our intuitions that the 'internal market' and markets in general are the dominant frame for EU regulation of new health technologies; risk is also an important framing device, particularly because of its link to the internal market; rights and ethics appear to be an important part of the regulatory environment, but their role is essentially that of legitimating devices?

1. Markets

Overall, the dominant focus, orientation, rationale, and justification for EU law on new health technologies is the market, in particular the internal market (that is, the market across the EU), but also the global market. The legal basis (the part of the EU Treaties giving formal power to the EU to adopt law) for the vast majority of relevant EU law is Article 114 TFEU, which concerns the EU's competence to create and sustain the internal market. A typical expression of the underpinning rationale for EU law regulating new health technologies is

Trade in medicinal products within the [EU] is hindered by disparities between certain national provisions, in particular between provisions relating to medicinal products..., and such disparities directly affect the functioning of the internal market.[86]

The oldest EU legislation in this field concerns marketing authorization for medicinal products.[87] The EU regulatory agencies, especially the EMA, but also those that support the CE product safety certification system, operate within a market frame. Their existence is justified by the need for a favourable regulatory environment for European industry, with harmonized arrangements for placing new health technologies on the market, and optimal regulatory conditions to encourage innovative technology that will compete in the global market. For instance,

... high-technology medicinal products requiring lengthy periods of costly research will continue to be developed in Europe only if they benefit from a favourable regulatory environment, particularly identical conditions governing their placing on the market throughout the [EU].[88]

The largest density of EU regulatory activity falls within our 'marketing' category. But more importantly, most of the legislation that falls into our other categories also points to or cross-refers to marketing as its justification or at least part of its rationale. For example, in the context of EU research funding, new health technologies are highlighted in the FP7 objectives.[89] Much of the focus of FP7 is on 'translational research', which attempts to translate basic research into usable (hence marketable) technologies. However, basic research such as '[r]esearch on the brain and related diseases', or basic research in the nanotechnology field, such as research into the genes behind kidney

---

[86] Directive 2001/83/EC, as amended, Recital 4.

[87] Directive 65/65/EEC on the approximation of provisions laid down by law, regulation or administrative action relating to proprietary medicinal products [1965] OJ L22/369, OJ Spec Ed 1965–6 I p 24.

[88] Council Directive 87/22/EEC of 22 December 1986 on the approximation of national measures relating to the placing on the market of high-technology medicinal products, particularly those derived from biotechnology [1987] OJ L15/38, Recital 2.

[89] In references to, say, 'the development and validation of new therapies... diagnostic tools and medical technologies'. The activities to be funded include '[i]nnovative therapeutic approaches and intervention' ie '[t]o research, consolidate and ensure further developments in advanced therapies and technologies with potential application in many diseases and disorders such as new therapeutic tools for regenerative medicine'. See FP7 Work-programme (2011) <http://ec.europa.eu/research/health/pdf/fp7-health-2012-orientation-paper_en.pdf> accessed 8 May 2012).

disease risk,[90] is also listed as a relevant activity.[91] But in FP7 even basic research is framed as a driver of growth, rather than, for instance, of increased knowledge and understanding, or an ethic of increased welfare in a broader sense. Optimal regulation for innovation is framed as centrally concerned with the market.

The EU's FP funding is part of a move towards creating a European Research Area (ERA), which is deemed necessary in order to 'reinvigorate research in Europe'.[92] Crucially, although funding under FP6 and FP7[93] is limited by the principle of 'European added value', it must enable discourse between researchers in different Member States so that the competitiveness of the industry is improved.[94] Research is explicitly linked to and framed by the Lisbon Strategy as part of the so-called 'knowledge triangle' of research, education, and innovation. Indeed, research is

the driver for the production and exploitation of knowledge . . . [making it] above all a linchpin in the implementation of the Lisbon strategy to make Europe the most dynamic and competitive, knowledge-based economy in the world, capable of sustaining economic growth, employment and social cohesion.[95]

Another example is the EU's Directive 98/44/EC on the legal protection of biotechnological inventions, which is justified by the idea that differences in legal protection for such inventions between Member States create barriers to trade in the internal market.[96] This was challenged in Case C-377/98 *Netherlands v Parliament and Council (Biotechnology)*[97] but the CJEU rejected the argument, finding that the Directive 'in fact aims to prevent damage to the unity of the internal market'.[98] The market frame is

---

[90] Projects that contributed towards this research were EURODIA (Functional genomics of pancreatic beta cells and of tissues involved in control of the endocrine pancreas for prevention and treatment of type 2 diabetes), ANEUPLOIDY (Understanding the importance of gene dosage imbalance in human health using genetics, functional genomics and systems biology), EUROSPAN (European special populations research network: quantifying and harnessing genetic variation for gene discovery), GENECURE (Applied genomic strategies for treatment and prevention of cardiovascular death in uraemia and end stage renal disease), EPIC (European prospective investigation into cancer, chronic diseases, nutrition and lifestyle), HYPERGENES (European network for genetic-epidemiological studies: building a method to dissect complex genetic traits, using essential hypertension as a disease model), and EUNEFRON (European network for the study of orphan nephropathies). The website for the FP offers many other examples of funded research that is of relevance to new health technologies.

[91] Amended proposal for a Council Decision concerning the 7th framework programme of the European Atomic Energy Community (Euratom) for nuclear research and training activities (2007–2011) (presented by the Commission pursuant to Art 250(2) of the EC Treaty) COM/2006/0364 final.

[92] European Commission, 'Communication from the Commission to the Council, The European Parliament, the Economic and Social Committee and the Committee of the Regions: Towards a European Research Area' COM(2000) 6 final, 5.

[93] Parliament and Council Decision No 1982/2006/EC of 18 December 2006 concerning the Seventh Framework Programme of the European Community for research, technological development and demonstration activities (2007–2013) [2006] OJ L412/1.

[94] See T Hervey and J McHale, *Health Law and the European Union* (CUP 2004) 243–4. The focus of the 6th FP is on the new instruments of integrated projects and networks of excellence. Studies on the 4th FP have shown that on average research teams originate from four to six countries; see R Gusmão, 'Research Networks as a Means of European Integration' (2003) 23 *Technology in Science* 386, 388.

[95] European Commission, Communication on 'Building the ERA of Knowledge for Growth', COM(2005) 118 final, 2.

[96] Parliament and Council Directive 98/44/EC of 6 July 1998 on the legal protection of biotechnological inventions [1998] OJ L213/13, Recitals 5, 6, and 7.

[97] Case C-377/98 *Netherlands v Parliament and Council (Biotechnology)* [2001] ECR I-7079.

[98] Case C-377/98, para 18.

strong here, and has been judicially confirmed. Specifically, harmonization is justified by the need to foster the internal market:

uncoordinated development of national laws on the legal protection of biotechnological inventions in the [EU] could lead to further disincentives to trade, to the detriment of the industrial development of such inventions and of the smooth operation of the internal market.[99]

EU law on pre-clinical and clinical research also links directly to marketing authorization, as does EU law on pharmacovigilance. The latter, with respect to medicinal products, also refers to the Community Code for marketing such products,[100] and with respect to medical devices, refers to the need to harmonize safety levels to guarantee free movement within the internal market.[101]

However, we also found three important counter-examples to the overall dominant frame of markets, each of which is discussed in more detail in the relevant section, and which reveal more nuanced relationships between the different frames. The most important of these is the risk frame. However, risk, in particular patient or rather 'consumer' safety, is a framing device that appears, in general, only *alongside* the market frame, in a supporting capacity. So in virtually all the previous examples we cite, the relevant market frame is closely related to risk as a framing device.[102] For instance, the preambles of the EU legislation on marketing of medicinal products, such as those cited earlier,[103] begin with the need to 'safeguard public health', conceptualized as a patient or consumer safety matter, but move quickly to the reason for needing to do so as protecting and promoting the market in those products. A typical example is

While the fundamental objective of the regulation of medicinal products is to safeguard public health, this aim should nevertheless be achieved by means that do not impede the free movement of safe medicinal products within the Union.[104]

Another example of the risk-market connection is the Product Liability Directive, where the frame is basically risk focused, but the internal market frame underpins safety concerns. The same can be said for some post-market regulation, such as the prohibition on advertising for prescription-only medicines,[105] which has recently been under pressure through litigation.[106] The EU legislation on regulation of human materials is similar: the central concern of this legislation is fostering confidence in different national risk regulation systems, and so encouraging innovation. However, the rationale for this is again the building of the internal market, and its 'fit' with other areas of EU new health technology regulation, such as marketing authorization,[107] also suggests a close relationship between risk and the market.

---

[99] Directive 98/44/EC, Recital 7.

[100] Parliament and Council Directive 2010/84/EU of 15 December 2010 amending, as regards pharmacovigilance, Directive 2001/83/EC on the Community code relating to medicinal products for human use [2010] OJ L348/74, Recitals 1 and 4.

[101] Directive 90/385/EEC, Recital 3.

[102] Incidentally, this appears to be the case for other regulatory systems applicable to new health technologies, for instance that of the WHO, see R C Eccleston *A Model Regulatory Program for Medical Devices: An International Guide* (PAHO, WHO, US FDA 2001) 3–4.

[103] See nn 86–8.

[104] Directive 2010/84/EU, Recital 4.

[105] Directive 2001/83/EC Art 88.

[106] Case C-316/09 *MSD Sharp & Dohme GmbH v Merckle GmbH* [2011] ECR I-nyr.

[107] An example of a recently marketed NHT that contains a product derived from plasma is M-M-RVAXPRO (<www.ema.europa.eu/ema/index.jsp?curl=pages/medicines/human/medicines/000604/human_med_000907.jsp&murl=menus/medicines/medicines.jsp&jsenabled=true> accessed 8 June

A second very important counter-example to the overall focus on markets as the dominant frame is found with respect to paediatric clinical research and regulation of medicinal products for paediatric use;[108] and the regulation of 'orphan' medicines (those indicated for a rare disease or if the product's development would not be commercially viable without incentives[109]). In all of these instances, we found a different configuration of the place of the market as a framing device—EU regulation is said to create incentives for the development of new health technologies that would not be developed (or would not be developed so quickly) under normal market conditions. We might call this an ethics or rights-based approach to markets. In this context, ethics and rights (in particular the concept of non-discrimination) interact differently with the dominant frame than markets in the standard case discussed earlier. Ethics and rights justify interference in and departure from a market frame.

The third counter-example to the overall dominance of the market frame is where EU law affects pricing of new health technologies and their coverage under national health systems. In spite of the implications of failure to adopt a market frame here, that is, the economies of scale and efficiencies implied in a larger single European market, there is virtually no EU-level legislation or other regulatory instrument on pricing of pharmaceuticals, and there is none at all on medical devices. Some recent developments, such as the move towards (eventual) common EU-level health technology methodologies for assessing new health technologies,[110] through sharing national health technology assessments, found in the Directive on Patients' Rights to Cross-Border Healthcare,[111] are based in rights, not markets, and also to some extent on promoting efficiency in the public sector. However, it should be noted here also that other recent developments, in particular the Commission's proposal on transparency,[112] where the rationale for creating a tighter timeline[113] for pricing and reimbursement decision-making and fostering more effective enforcement,[114] are very much based on a market rationale.

With respect to the market frame, then, our original intuitions are broadly accurate, but our research revealed several important exceptions. We turn now to the second of the 'frames' that define the features of the EU law approach to new health technologies, that of risk.

2. Risk

We have already noted (looking at medicinal products, product liability, and post-market regulation) that risk, in the sense of patient safety or more accurately

---

2012), which was authorized via the centralized procedure in 2006 and contains recombinant albumin (recombumin).

[108] Regulation 1901/2006/EC.

[109] Regulation 1901/2006/EC, Art 3.

[110] That is, the 'toolkit' used to inform or support a specific technology appraisal decision (such as made by NICE in the English context).

[111] Art 15(2)(b) provides that one of the objectives of the health technology assessment network shall be to support Member States in the provision of objective, reliable, timely, transparent, comparable Regulation 1901/2006/EC, and transferable information on the relative efficacy as well as on the short- and long-term effectiveness, when applicable, of health technologies and to enable an effective exchange of this information between the national authorities or bodies.

[112] Proposal for a Directive of the European Parliament and the Council relating to the transparency of measures regulating the prices of medicinal products for human use and their inclusion in the scope of public health insurance systems COM(2012) 84 final.

[113] The proposal is for 30 days (rather than 180) for generics; and for 120 days (rather than 180) for innovative products.

[114] Which to date has been woefully inadequate.

consumer safety,[115] is a significant frame in EU regulation of new health technologies, and that the dominant place of risk frames is alongside those of markets, in a supporting role, or embedded within a market frame or vice versa. Three further examples where risk can be seen to support markets are research funding, protection of intellectual property, and product safety. In research funding and knowledge creation leading to the ERA, funding is partly about reducing the risks to commerce by supporting research[116]—a different type of risk to consumer safety. Protection of intellectual property is also linked to those risks, but again as being ultimately oriented towards markets.[117] In product safety,[118] for instance, risk-related concerns are implicated in the standards of 'quality and safety of tissues and cells intended for human applications' which aim at ensuring a high standard of protection for human health.[119] The language of quality and safety permeates EU product safety legislation.[120] The constant reference point is the aim of getting new products to market, in such a way that consumers will have confidence in their quality and safety (risk supporting the market).

Probably the best example of where a concern with risk is found alongside and supporting a market frame in EU regulation of new health technologies is the EU's regulation of research processes. We consider three examples here: GMO/GMMO and animal research regulation; the regulation of pre-clinical research through GLP; and regulation of clinical research through GCP.

EU legislation concerned with GMO/GMMO and animal research is based on Article 114 TFEU, that is, the internal market legal basis. The centrality of risk is necessitated in internal market legislation by Article 114(3) TFEU, which provides that the Commission,

in its proposals . . . concerning health, safety, environmental protection and consumer protection, will take as a base a high level of protection, taking account in particular of any new development based on scientific facts.

This provision therefore installs important countervailing concerns in the internal market's regulatory environment, but such that these concerns (all of which are risk-based) aid and abet the establishment and functioning of the internal market. So, for instance, the EU's GMO legislation is based on the idea that it is 'necessary to approximate the laws of the [Member States] . . . concerning the deliberate release

[115] In this chapter, we are concerned with risk in the sense of patient/consumer safety. This is not to say that other forms of risk are irrelevant—eg risk to traditional technologies; the risk of not innovating; the risk of damage to trust in governments/regulators/the EU.

[116] Parliament and Council Decision No 1982/2006/EC of 18 December 2006 concerning the Seventh Framework Programme of the European Community for research, technological development and demonstration activities (2007–2013) [2006] OJ L412/1.

[117] eg it is noted that 'in the field of genetic engineering, research and development require a considerable amount of high-risk investment and therefore only adequate legal protection can make them profitable'; Directive 98/44/EC, Recital 2.

[118] See, eg Directive 2004/23/EC [2004] OJ L102/48.

[119] Directive 2004/23/EC, Art 1.

[120] See, eg Directive 2004/23/EC, Recitals 1–5, 8, 11, 13, 15, 19, 28, 31, 32; Arts 1, 8, 9, 11, 16–24, and of course the title of the Directive; Parliament and Council Directive 2011/62/EU of 8 June 2011 amending Directive 2001/83/EC on the Community code relating to medicinal products for human use, as regards the prevention of the entry into the legal supply chain of falsified medicinal products [2011] OJ L174/74, Recitals 3, 4, 7, 11. This Directive aims to prevent falsified medicines, which can include new health technologies, such as the monoclonal antibody, Avastin, see the report to the effect that some samples of Avastin had salt, starch, and various chemicals, but none of the life-saving active ingredients, see B Berkrot, 'Fake Avastin Had Salt, Starch, Chemicals: Roche' (*Reuters*, 27 February 2012) <www.reuters.com/article/2012/02/27/us-avastin-idUSTRE81Q29X20120227> accessed 8 May 2012.

into the environment of GMOs and to ensure the safe development of industrial products utilizing GMOs.'[121] The link between managing risks to human health and the environment and the bringing of new products to market is made even more explicit in Directive 2010/63/EU on animal protection, which explains that safety and efficacy of such new products must be demonstrated by testing, which involves research on animals.[122] Member States must therefore recognize test data which complies with EU legislation on test methods.[123] Here risk is deployed to support a discourse of widening/deepening markets by adding new products.

Risk assessment and risk monitoring, licensing, and inspection, by EU-mandated national competent authorities, are the primary modes of regulation deployed by the EU in the area of regulation of research processes. So, for instance, Directive 90/219/EC provides that Member States must ensure that a risk assessment is carried out by anyone using GMMOs.[124] National competent authorities are required by the Directive to monitor matters such as the suitability of containment and other protective measures, waste management, and emergency response measures. Detailed guidance on risk has been developed by EU agencies, such as the EMA. Directive 2010/63/EU on animal research also concerns risk management through licensing, inspection, and the institution of a 'competent authority'.[125] Member States must ensure that all breeders, suppliers, and users of animals in scientific research are authorized by and registered with the 'competent authority', and that they comply with the Directive.[126] Regular inspections must take place to ensure compliance.[127] In these examples, the 'right' regulatory approach, to support innovation, is conceptualized as containing and managing the risks inherent in innovation. A strong discourse of risk provides the rationale for this legislation and regulatory activity, even if the key focus of the primary legislation is the EU's internal market.

The same is true for our second example: pre-clinical research. Medicinal new health technologies that are eventually manufactured must satisfy health and safety concerns and be based on clear scientific and technical justification. For novel agents, recent disasters such as the TGN1412 incident, where the first-in-human (Phase I) trials resulted in the need for intensive care following multiple organ failure in six trial participants,[128] mean that there is likely to be a great deal of precaution before allowing

---

[121] Directive 2001/18/EC, Recital 7.   [122] Directive 2010/63/EU, Recital 42.

[123] Recital 42, Art 2(2); Art 46 (with an exception for data that needs further testing for the protection of public health, safety, or the environment).

[124] Directive 90/219/EC, defined in Art 2(b)(i) as 'a microorganism in which the genetic material has been altered in a way that does not occur naturally by mating and/or natural recombination.' According to Annex I: 'Techniques of genetic modification referred to in Article 2(b)(i) are, *inter alia*: 1. Recombinant nucleic acid techniques involving the formation of new combinations of genetic material by the insertion of nucleic acid molecules produced by whatever means outside an organism, into any virus, bacterial plasmid or other vector system and their incorporation into a host organism in which they do not naturally occur but in which they are capable of continued propagation. 2. Techniques involving the direct introduction into a micro-organism of heritable material prepared outside the micro-organism including microinjection, macro-injection and micro-encapsulation. 3. Cell fusion or hybridisation techniques where live cells with new combinations of heritable genetic material are formed through the fusion of two or more cells by means of methods that do not occur naturally.' They do not include, eg, *in vitro* fertilization.

[125] Directive 2010/63/EU (n 122) Art 59.

[126] Directive 2010/63/EU, Art 20 (1).

[127] Directive 2010/63/EU, Art 34 (1).

[128] Zosia Kmietowicz, 'Rules for Drug Trials should be Tightened, say experts' (2006) 333 *British Medical Journal* 276.

first-in-human trials.[129] EU law[130] requires that all laboratories carrying out tests on chemical products must comply with the OECD's principles of GLP.[131] The importance of risk is apparent in, for instance, allowing Member States to 'provisionally prohibit or make subject to special conditions the marketing of that substance on its territory' where application of the GLP principles demonstrates that a chemical substance examined under the Directive nevertheless 'presents a danger to man and the environment'.[132] Echoing the OECD's definition of GLP,[133] the EMA's principles of GLP operate and reinforce a mutually supportive interaction between markets and risk.[134] The EMA has adopted a long list of 'Scientific Guidelines for Human Medicinal Products'.[135] Conducting a GLP-compliant study—which is normally required for studies used to support applications for clinical trial authorization or market authorization for products (noted earlier)—costs significantly more than a non-GLP-compliant study, because of the documentation and data management requirements. The costs of generating such pre-clinical data can be particularly significant for smaller enterprises developing new health technologies. This higher cost is justified by the need to ensure safety and quality in products (a risk discourse) that eventually reach the market (a market discourse embedded within and supported by a risk discourse).

Furthermore, the EU has also adopted soft law guidance on non-clinical studies that enhances risk regulation by providing guidance on how to 'fulfil a legal obligation'.[136] Enterprises may take alternative approaches to that suggested in guidance, but these must be 'appropriately justified'.[137] The key principle is that '[t]he nonclinical safety studies, . . . should be adequate to characterize potential adverse effects that might occur under the conditions of the clinical trial to be supported.'[138] Risk is also central to the key guidance documents noted earlier, such as ICH S6. Risk analysis, management, avoidance, and reduction are central in the discourse, as seen in safety concerns with respect to 'biotechnology-derived pharmaceuticals' (such as cytokines, plasminogen activators, recombinant plasma factors, growth factors, fusion proteins, enzymes, receptors, hormones, and monoclonal antibodies). Although partial exceptions from GLP

---

[129] eg Geron has taken a long time to progress to clinical development, even though it has substantial pre-clinical data for its human embryonic stem cell derived products; see <www.geron.com/products/> accessed 2 June 2011. Geron has now ceased recruiting new patients to its trial of GRNOPC1, its first product from human embryonic stem cells to enter clinical testing, though it is following up the patients from its Phase I trial for 15 years, see <http://cell-therapies.geron.com/grnopc1> accessed 8 June 2012.

[130] Art 1(1), Directive 2004/10/EC provides that Member States 'shall take all measures necessary to ensure that laboratories carrying out tests on chemical products . . . comply with the principles of [GLP] . . . as laid down in Annex I to this Directive.' See also Recital 8 of Directive 2004/10/EC.

[131] These are appended to Directive 2004/10/EC in Annex 1.

[132] Directive 2004/10/EC, Art 5(2).

[133] Directive 2004/10/EC, in 2.1 of Annex 1.

[134] They do so by 'defining a set of rules and criteria for a quality system concerned with the organisational process and the conditions under which non-clinical health and environmental safety studies are planned, performed, monitored, recorded, reported and archived', 'Good Laboratory Practice Compliance' (*European Medicines Agency*) <www.ema.europa.eu/Inspections/GLP.html> accessed 8 May 2012.

[135] 'Non-Clinical Guidelines' (European Medicines Agency) <www.ema.europa.eu/htms/human/humanguidelines/nonclinical.htm> accessed 8 May 2012.

[136] EMA, 'Procedure for European Union Guidelines and Related Documents within the Pharmaceutical Legislative Framework' London, 18 March 2009, Doc. Ref. EMEA/P/24143/2004 Rev. 1 corr. P4.

[137] EMA (n 136) 5.

[138] EMA, 'ICH Topic M 3 (R2) Non-Clinical Safety Studies for the Conduct of Human Clinical Trials and Marketing Authorization for Pharmaceuticals', CPMP/ICH/286/95, June 2009.

are permitted for studies employing specialized test systems, which are often needed for biopharmaceuticals, and need not necessarily impede progress to marketing authorization, the overall basis of the trials must be informed by safety concerns. There is additional specific guidance for ATMPs.[139] For gene therapy medicinal products, there is guidance on quality, pre-clinical and clinical aspects of gene transfer medicinal products,[140] and non-clinical studies required before first clinical use of gene therapy medicinal products.[141] There is also guidance on biological active substances produced by stable transgene expression in higher plants.[142] For cell and tissue engineered products, there is the guidance on human cell-based medicinal products,[143] xenogenic cell-based medicinal products,[144] and reflection papers on particular types of product, for example stem cell-based medicinal products[145] and cartilage replacement products.[146] Some of this guidance covers the clinical research stages too, and it is framed in terms of its relationship with EU legislation on marketing authorizations. In these instances, therefore, the risk discourse, which remains central, is directly related to the discourse of the market, and in particular the desirability of safe and efficacious novel products reaching the market.

Moving from our second example (pre-clinical research) to our final example of risk discourse (clinical research), the Clinical Trials Directive makes reference to 'the protection of clinical trial subjects—and in particular the weighing of risks and inconveniences with benefits . . . ':[147]

The clinical trial subject's protection is safeguarded through risk assessment based on the results of toxicological experiments prior to any clinical trial, screening by ethics committees and Member States' competent authorities, and rules on the protection of personal data.[148]

Risks to people who cannot consent are given special consideration.[149] Further protections are provided in the prohibition on the carrying out of obsolete or repetitive tests within the EU or in third countries.[150] Risk is also important in relation to specific requirements on the manufacture and import of investigational medicinal products,[151] labelling,[152] the verification of compliance of investigational medicinal products with good clinical and manufacturing practice through inspections,[153] and notification of adverse reactions.[154] Suspected serious unexpected adverse reactions that are fatal or life-threatening must be notified to the competent authorities in the Member States. Risk here appears to be a strong and stand-alone framing device.

---

[139] A number of draft guidelines are also currently in the adoption process, eg Draft ICH Topic S6 (R1) Preclinical Safety Evaluation of Biotechnology-Derived Pharmaceuticals CHMP/ICH/302/95, November 2009.

[140] CHMP/GTWP/234523/09.

[141] EMEA/CHMP/GTWP/125459/2006.

[142] EMEA/CHMP/BWP/48316/2006.

[143] EMEA/CHMP/410869/2006.

[144] EMEA/CHMP/CPWP/83508/2009.

[145] EMA, Reflection paper on stem cell-based medicinal products, CAT/571134/09.

[146] EMA, Reflection paper on *in-vitro* cultured chondrocyte containing products for cartilage repair of the knee, CAT/CPWP/568181/2009.

[147] Directive 2001/20/EC, Art 3.   [148] Directive 2001/20/EC, Recital 2.

[149] They should be included in clinical trials only 'when there are grounds for expecting that the administering of the medicinal product would be of direct benefit to the patient, thereby outweighing the risks', see Directive 2001/20/EC, Recital 3. See later, concerning the frames and particularly vulnerable individuals.

[150] Directive 2001/20/EC, Recital 6.   [151] Directive 2001/20/EC, Art 13.

[152] Directive 2001/20/EC, Art 14.   [153] Directive 2001/20/EC, Art 15.

[154] Directive 2001/20/EC, Art 16.

But the Clinical Trials Directive goes further than these general legislative obligations, in that it requires the Commission to establish principles of good clinical practice (GCP) and detailed rules in line with those principles. These rules are established by the EMA, in accordance with International Conference on Harmonisation of Technical Requirements for Registration of Pharmaceuticals for Human Use (ICH) harmonized standards.[155] All clinical trials falling within the scope of the Directive must be designed, conducted, and reported in accordance with GCP, and this again is framed in terms of risk. Directive 2005/28/EC,[156] which lays down guidelines of GCP, contains additional requirements relating to the investigational medicinal product used in the clinical trial, detailed requirements of data collection and handling, and provisions on inspections mechanisms. And it is here that the relationship between risk and markets as frames reappears: this Directive (and thus the detailed guidance based thereon) refers to the marketing of medicinal products as its underlying basis (risk embedded within markets).[157]

Overall, then, our discussion here on framing supports other commentaries that have (implicitly) argued that EU regulation of new health technologies is essentially focused on risk-benefit balance.[158] We would agree that that balance is crucial to EU regulation of new health technologies, but would go further, and claim that the balance should be read in the context of an overarching market frame. That is to say, a risk-benefit balance is constructed in EU law as crucial to ensure consumer confidence in novel products within the market place, and thus to optimize their production.[159] It is also constructed to support industry bringing novel products to market. While others have argued that risk (often instantiated as 'patient safety') and 'access to new markets, trade and profits' are in an oppositional relationship in the global context,[160] our research on the EU context suggests the two frames are constructed as mutually supportive, not oppositional. The EU's approach to risk in new health technologies produces a particular construction of the EU market in new health technologies: as a safe market for consumers/patients. Moreover, in general, we discern marginally stronger discourses of market than of risk in primary legislation, and strong discourses of risk in soft law, such as detailed guidance documents. Thus risk discourse is embedded within and justified by market discourse.

However they relate, markets and risk are crucially important frames for EU regulation of new health technologies. What, then, of the other frames—of rights and ethics—under consideration in this book?

---

[155] EMA, CHMP 'E6: Guideline for Good Clinical Practice' (CPMP/ICH/135/95).

[156] Commission Directive 2005/28/EC of 8 April 2005 laying down principles and detailed guidelines for good clinical practice as regards investigational medicinal products for human use, as well as the requirements for authorisation of the manufacturing or importation of such products [2005] OJ L91/13.

[157] Directive 2005/28/EC, Recital 3.

[158] In the context of new health technologies using nanotechnology, see B Dorbeck-Jung and N Chowdhury, 'Is the European Medical Products Authorisation Regulation Equipped to Cope with the Challenges of Nanomedicines?' (2011) 33 *Law and Policy* 276; in the context of new health technologies using biotechnology and also GMO regulation, see A Spina, 'European Networks in the Regulation of Biotechnologies' (2010) 35 *European Law Review* 197.

[159] Dorbeck-Jung and Chowdhury (n 158).

[160] C Altenstetter, 'Medical Device Regulation and Nanotechnologies: Determining the Role of Patient Safety Concerns in Policymaking' (2011) 33 *Law and Policy* 227.

3. (Human) Rights and Ethics

A strong concern with (human) rights[161] and ethics[162] can be seen in three key examples drawn from our map: research funding and intellectual property rights promoting research; safety in research processes and products; and consent in research processes. But in each of these, rights and ethics seem to operate less as a stand-alone frame, and more as a link, inflection and support, or even as a 'false front', for the other frames—especially markets, but also risk. There are, nevertheless, important counter-examples to this overall conclusion about the place of (human) rights and ethics in EU regulation of new health technologies, particularly concerning certain types of new health technologies. These might be characterized as embodying an ethics or (human) rights-based approach to markets. In some areas of our map, all the frames at issue in this chapter disappear almost entirely. Even so, those counter-examples still reference markets. In general, we suggest, in EU regulation of new health technologies, (human) rights and ethics are used more as a means of legitimating other framing choices than as a frame in themselves.

Our first example of a strong ethics and human rights discourse concerns research funding. The former chair of the EGE has said that several of the EGE's opinions (presumably including those concerning funding under the FPs) are based on a 'human rights oriented approach'.[163] Rights are also implicated in, for instance, references to the importance of knowledge in the ERA for the well-being of citizens,[164] and the idea that those participating in research should respect and observe the fundamental rights and principles recognized 'in particular by the Charter of Fundamental Rights of the European Union'.[165] Most pertinent is Article 3(2) EUCFR on the right to integrity of the person, which states in 'the fields of medicine and biology' there shall be respect of 'the free and informed consent of the person concerned, according to the procedures laid down by law', 'the prohibition of eugenic practices, in particular those aiming at the selection of persons', 'the prohibition on making the human body and its parts as such a source of financial gain', and 'the prohibition of the reproductive cloning of human beings'.

Ethics figure in EU research funding decisions, for instance, in relation to FP7, a 'proposal which contravenes fundamental ethical principles ... shall not be selected'.[166] The legitimating function of ethics can be made out more clearly by reference to the advisory opinions[167] submitted to the European Commission by the

---

[161] For the purposes of this chapter, we do not distinguish between human rights as law and human rights as discourse, although of course the two are very different in many important practical respects.

[162] We are acutely aware that human rights and ethics are seen as separate and very different frames by others in this collection and elsewhere in the literature, not least because ethics, unlike human rights, do not attach to a discernible discrete body of law. We originally intended to discuss each separately. However, we found while writing this chapter, which is concerned with painting a fairly 'broad-brush' picture, that it was not satisfactory to separate out these two frames, as to do so would involve a great deal of unnecessary repetition, given that they are intertwined, and that their roles in the EU regulation of new health technologies are, in our view, similar.

[163] G Hermerén, 'Accountability, Democracy, and Ethics Committees' (2009) 2 *Law, Innovation and Technology* 153.

[164] European Commission, Communication on 'Building the ERA of Knowledge for Growth', COM(2005) 118 final, 2.

[165] Regulation 1906/2006, Recital 27.

[166] Regulation 1906/2006/EC, Art 15(2).

[167] See: European Commission—Bureau of European Policy Advisers <http://ec.europa.eu/european_group_ethics/avis/index_en.htm> accessed 8 May 2012.

body[168] which became the EGE in 1997.[169] Relevant opinions range from synthetic biology,[170] prenatal diagnosis,[171] and products derived from human blood or human plasma,[172] and have been used to support EU funding of controversial research on new health technologies.[173] Here, the introduction of ethics is linked to the avoidance of regulatory uncertainty and potentially harmful confused public debate: see, for example, 'hESC research needs appropriate measures to be put in place to promote the public governance and science–society dialogue with regard to its aims, achievements and failures',[174] implicitly to ensure that confusion does not adversely influence the climate for industrial development of biotechnology. Moreover, while (bio)ethics[175] is deemed to express and foster EU citizenship, and provide a democratic basis for governance through the representation of the values of EU citizens,[176] such that 'European integration must mean more than establishing a single market; progress in science and technology must be given a human, social and ethical dimension, otherwise European citizenship cannot be established',[177] ethics is figured as an expert-generated discourse and as such is dissociated from the EU's citizenry.[178] This is an example of ethics as a frame that appears to play one role (democratic legitimation of EU regulation), whereas in practice it (also) plays another (production of an expert-led EU regulatory environment that supports innovation in new health technologies).

There is a strong ethical and human rights discourse surrounding the patenting of biotechnological products in the EU. Directive 98/44/EC on the legal protection of biotechnological inventions, Recital 16, notes the importance of dignity and integrity of the person and asserts that 'the human body . . . cannot be patented'. Under Article 7, the EGE 'evaluates all ethical aspects of biotechnology'.[179] The Directive also seeks to support the development of new products or processes to promote public health, to

---

[168] Group of Advisers on the Ethical Implications of Biotechnology, appointed in 1991.

[169] The EGE's mandate was renewed in 2001 and 2005, and on the last occasion 'to cover all areas of the application of science and technology'; Commission Decision 2005/754/EC of 11 May 2005 on the renewal of the mandate of the European Group on Ethics in Science and New Technologies [2005] OJ L127/17.

[170] EGE Opinion 25–17/11/2009—Ethics of Synthetic Biology.

[171] EGE Opinion 23–16/01/2008—Ethical Aspects of Animal Cloning for Food Supply.

[172] EGE Opinion 2–12/03/1993—Products Derived from Human Blood or Human Plasma.

[173] EGE Opinion 10–11/12/1997—Ethical aspects of the 5th Research Framework Programme; and EGE Opinion 22–13/07/2007—The Ethics Review of hESC FP7 Research Projects.

[174] EGE Opinion 22 at 43.

[175] More generally, see N S Jecker and others, *Bioethics. An Introduction to the History, Methods, and Practice* (Jones and Bartlett Publishers 1997); MLT Stevens, *Bioethics in America. Origins and Cultural Politics* (Johns Hopkins University Press 2000).

[176] Through the EGE the 'Commission aims to promote responsible research in Europe and to keep the rapidly advancing progress in science in harmony with the *ethical values of all Europeans*' (n 49). Emphasis added.

[177] Original mandate of the GAEIB, the predecessor to the EGE, see: <http://ec.europa.eu/european_group_ethics/archive/1991_1997/bilan_en.htm> accessed 13 April 2011; cited Report of the Expert Group on Science and Governance, to DG Research, *Taking European Knowledge Society Seriously* (European Commission 2007) 48 <http://ec.europa.eu/research/science-society/document_library/pdf_06/european-knowledge-society_en.pdf> accessed 8 June 2012.

[178] See further M Flear and A Vakulenko, 'A Human Rights Perspective on Citizen Participation in the EU's Governance of New Technologies' (2010) 10 *Human Rights Law Review* 661, 684–7.

[179] The EGE's predecessor, the GAEIB, gave various opinions, including on Directive 98/44/EC Opinion 3—30/09/1993—Opinion on Ethical Questions Arising from the Commission Proposal for a Council Directive for Legal Protection of Biotechnological Inventions; Opinion 8—25/09/1996—Ethical Aspects of Patenting Inventions Involving Elements of Human Origin (taken 'in account' in the drafting of the Directive, recital 19 Directive 98/44/EC); Opinion 16—07/05/2002—Ethical Aspects of Patenting Inventions Involving Human Stem Cells.

tackle world hunger,[180] and to treat rare diseases.[181] The references to global development and to particularly needy groups suggest an element of a different kind of ethical rationale behind the Directive, that of global justice,[182] and may link to human rights in the sense of a growing emphasis of the human rights obligations of the global North and West, including the EU, concerning international assistance and cooperation.[183]

Strong discourses drawing on individual human rights and ethics (and in particular human dignity and a particularly Judeo-Christian notion of integrity of the human body) are found in some interpretations of the Directive. The *Brüstle* case[184] is a prominent recent site for these discourses, especially Advocate-General Bot's Opinion. The Opinion begins by opposing 'different philosophies and religions' and 'the continual questioning of science'[185] and by opposing 'the economic functioning of the market' and 'competition'[186] on the one hand, and 'the fundamental values of the Union' on the other.[187] The EU, according to Advocate-General Bot, 'is not only a market to be regulated', but it 'also has values to be expressed', in particular the value of human dignity.[188] This oppositional duality is unusual in official EU discourse. The EGE, for instance, is at pains to avoid placing 'science' in opposition to 'ethics', but prefers to reconstruct that relationship as mutually supportive.[189] In its decision in *Brüstle*, the Court avoids the question by characterizing its decision as concerning only 'legal' interpretation, and not broaching 'questions of a medical or ethical nature'.[190] Having set up the opposition, Advocate-General Bot then moves to defend the position that a single EU definition of embryo, in the context of Directive 98/44/EC, is necessary, as the Directive is a harmonization measure, and thus separate nationally-based definitions would run counter to its underlying objective.[191] Referring explicitly and regularly to the ethical discourse mainly within, but also surrounding, the Directive, Advocate-General Bot takes the view that all totipotent cells, whatever the means by which they are obtained, are 'embryos' in the sense of the Directive.[192] Likewise, the blastocyst is an 'embryo'.[193] Pluripotent cells (embryonic stem cells) are *not* embryos.[194] They are

---

[180] Directive 98/44/EC, Rectial 11.

[181] Directive 98/44/EC, Recital 18.

[182] N Daniels, *Just Health Care* (CUP 1985); N Daniels, *Just Health: Meeting Health Needs Fairly* (CUP 2008).

[183] See M Nowak, 'Human Rights Conditionality in the EU' and B Simma, J Aschenbrenner, and C Schulte, 'Human Rights Considerations in Development Cooperation Activities of the EC' in P Alston (ed), *The EU and Human Rights* (OUP 1999); B Toebes and others (eds), *Health and Human Rights in Europe* (Intersentia 2012). For discussion of the right to health in this context, see B Toebes, 'The Right to Health' in A Eide, C Krause, and A Rosas (eds), *Economic, Cultural and Social Rights* (Kluwer 2001) and T Hervey, 'We Don't See a Connection: The "Right to Health" in the EU Charter and European Social Charter' in de Búrca and de Witte (eds), *Social Rights in Europe* (OUP 2005).

[184] *Oliver Brüstle* (n 35); Opinion of AG 10 March 2011.

[185] *Oliver Brüstle* (n 35) para 39.

[186] We would suggest he means 'competitiveness', taking the statements in context.

[187] *Oliver Brüstle* (n 35) para 44. The language used in this para is particularly striking—it talks of 'the cost of sacrificing' the Union's fundamental values.

[188] *Oliver Brüstle* (n 35) para 46.

[189] H Busby, T Hervey, and A Mohr, 'Ethical EU Law: The Influence of the European Group on Ethics in Science and New Technologies' (2008) 33 *European Law Review* 803.

[190] *Oliver Brüstle* (n 35) para 30.

[191] *Oliver Brüstle* (n 35) paras 50–61; confirmed by the Court in paras 25–9.

[192] *Oliver Brüstle* (n 35) paras 85, 91.

[193] *Oliver Brüstle* (n 35) para 95.

[194] *Oliver Brüstle* (n 35) paras 98, 100. The Court took a slightly different approach, finding that any human ovum after fertilization; any non-fertilized human ovum into which the cell nucleus from a mature human cell has been transplanted; and any non-fertilized human ovum whose division and further development have been stimulated by parthenogenesis are 'human embryos' in the sense of Art 6(2)(c) of

elements of the human body.[195] However, because these embryonic stem cells have been removed from the blastocyst (which is an embryo) and the process of so doing by definition destroys the blastocyst ('embryo'), products or processes based on those embryonic stem cells are not patentable.[196] A strong narrative of ethics, and in particular the dignity of the human body, runs through all of Advocate-General Bot's Opinion, especially this part. For instance, he states that 'to make an industrial application of an invention using embryonic stem cells would amount to using human embryos as simple base material. Such an invention would exploit the human body.'[197] He likens such a process to the taking of human organs for trafficking.[198] In this context, then, although the analysis nods to (as it must, given the legal basis of the Directive) the creation of the internal market, it begins somewhere very different (philosophies, religions, beliefs[199]) and very swiftly and definitely departs from any questions of markets, competitiveness, or even trade.[200]

Nevertheless, usually (Advocate-General Bot excepted) the discourse of ethics around Directive 98/44/EC operates essentially as a legitimating device for the central aim of the legislation, which is about strengthening the competitiveness of the European market for biotechnological products. The work of the EGE serves to educate European publics, thereby enhancing the ethical acceptability of biotechnological inventions, and hence allowing their contribution to European competitiveness to be more effectively harnessed.[201] The general principle behind Directive 98/44/EC on the legal protection of biotechnological inventions is that inventions which meet the general requirements of patenting cannot be exempted from patent protection merely because

the Directive, see paras 30–8. The Directive excludes from patentability where the technical teaching which is the subject of the patent application requires the prior destruction of human embryos, or their use as base material. The Court left it to the national court to decide whether a stem cell obtained from a human embryo at the blastocyst stage is such a 'human embryo'; see paras 30–8.

[195] Here the AG refers to Directive 2004/23/EC the tissue safety directive, which applies to adult and embryonic stem cells.

[196] Directive 2004/23/EC, paras 103–5; 109–10.

[197] Directive 2004/23/EC, para 110.

[198] Directive 2004/23/EC, para 106.

[199] Directive 2004/23/EC, paras 39–40.

[200] The 'economic and financial issues' (para 41) concerned are swept away cursorily with a reference to research deriving pluripotent stem cells from mature human cells, even though the process (carried out in Kyoto University, Japan) there is subject to patent which presumably excludes European companies from entering into that particular market until the patent expires. See Takahashi and others, 'Induction of Pluripotent Stem Cells from Adult Human Fibroblasts by Defined Factors' (2007) *Cell*, doi:10.1016/j.cell.2007.11.019; more seriously, Yamanaka's research group's work was subsequently shown to be highly problematic, as the first attempts produced a cancer-producing protein. See, G Tiu, 'Stem Cell Pioneer Yamanaka Discovers New Factor, Glis1, For iPS Cell Production' (*Asian Scientist*, 9 June 2011) <www.asianscientist.com/in-the-lab/yamanaka-transcription-factor-glis1-program-ips-cells/> accessed 8 May 2012; Maekawa et al, 'Direct reprogramming of somatic cells is promoted by maternal transcription factor Glis1' (2011) 474 *Nature* 225, DOI: doi:10.1038/nature10106. It is interesting to note that the European competitiveness discourse (with a nod to ethics in the sense of patient well-being) was the way in which Professor Brüstle framed his disappointed response to the AG's Opinion: 'One wonders why the EU spends millions of euros supporting the development of therapies based on embryonic stem cells, if practical progress towards the clinic is blocked by patenting restrictions. While stem cell technologies are already beginning to reach patients in the US and Asia, we are still discussing policy issues and wasting Europe's valuable competitive edge.' See *NeuroStemCell*, 'Stem cell patents and the European Court of Justice' (*NeuroStemCell*, 28 April 2011) <www.neurostemcell.org/stem-cell-patents -and-the-european-court-of-justice/> accessed 8 May 2012; *EuroStemCell*, 'Stem cell patents and the European Court of Justice' (*EuroStemCell*) <www.eurostemcell.org/stem-cell-patents> accessed 8 May 2012.

[201] H Busby, T Hervey, and A Mohr, 'Ethical EU Law: The Influence of the European Group on Ethics in Science and New Technologies' (2008) 33 *European Law Review* 803.

they concern biological material which may also have occurred in nature.[202] This general position is qualified so that certain products and processes,[203] including where commercial exploitation would be contrary to *ordre public* or morality,[204] cannot be the subject of a patent. Examples of such products or processes include 'the use of human embryos for industrial or commercial purposes'.[205] This provision does bring an element of ethical discourse within the terms of the Directive. The Court's approach in *Brüstle* reflects a framing of ethics as supporting competitiveness within the internal market.[206] However, the framing of the ethics also refers back to the market—the question of *ordre public* or morality is structured by the legislation as an *exception* to the general rules of the Directive. Again, then, the market frame is the dominant one, and ethics again works to support and legitimate EU involvement and the market-oriented approach.

EU regulation of research through intellectual property[207] concerns rights to the 'foreground'[208] or results, 'including those related to copyright, design rights, patent rights, plant variety rights or similar forms of protection' and information, 'whether or not they can be protected'.[209] There are detailed provisions on ownership,[210] dissemination and use,[211] and access rights.[212] These are important to human rights, especially in relation to vulnerabilities, exclusions, and protections for research subjects. In addition, inconsistency with ethical principles can constitute grounds for the Commission's objection to the transfer of ownership or grant of exclusive licence of 'foreground' to 'third parties established in a third country not associated' to FP7.[213] In general, however, rights and ethics are little mentioned in discussions of the ERA.

Turning to our second example, the regulation of research processes and product safety, the references to safety and the protection of human health and the environment, such as those found in legislation on GMOs/GMMOs, product safety legislation such as on blood safety, safety of products involving human tissue and cells, as well as articulating a risk frame, also highlight the importance of rights—particularly vulnerabilities and the need for protections—as a supporting rationale and frame for internal market legislation that again flows from Article 114(3) TFEU. Competitiveness also features in the preparatory documents for Directive 2010/63/EU on animal research, which refer explicitly to the Lisbon Agenda on EU competitiveness, and the 'highly diversified, unequal competitive environment for industry and the research

---

[202] Directive 98/44/EC, Art 3.

[203] Plant and animal varieties, essentially biological processes (Directive 98/44/EC, Art 4), simple discovery of genes (Directive 98/44/EC, Art 5(1)).

[204] Directive 98/44/EC, Art 6. The morality clause in Art 53(a) European Patent Convention been revised so that it corresponds to the Directive; see Rules 23b–e of the Implementing Regulations. For critical comment on this change see D Beyleveld and R Brownsword, *Human Dignity in Bioethics and Biolaw* (OUP 2001) 197–9.

[205] Directive 98/44/EC, Art 6(2)(c).

[206] See, eg *Oliver Brüstle* (n 35) para 34 'The context and aim of the Directive [to remove obstacles to trade and to the smooth functioning of the internal market . . . and thus to encourage industrial research and development in the field of genetic engineering, para 27] show that the EU legislature intended to exclude any possibility of patentability where respect for human dignity could thereby be affected.'

[207] For a discussion of intellectual property as an indirect mode of regulation in this area see: T Hervey and H Black, 'The European Union and the Governance of Stem Cell Research' (2005) 12 *Maastricht Journal of European and Comparative Law* 3.

[208] Generally 'foreground' is the 'property of the participant carrying out the work generating that foreground', see Regulation 1906/2006, Art 39(1).

[209] Regulation 1906/2006, Art 2(4).   [210] Regulation 1906/2006, Arts 39–43.

[211] Regulation 1906/2006, Arts 44–6.   [212] Regulation 1906/2006, Arts 47–51.

[213] Regulation 1906/2006, Art 43.

community' across the EU. They go on to claim that the 'proposal strikes a balance in promoting European research and competitiveness while at the same time being at the forefront in ensuring that full regard is paid to animal welfare.'[214] Thus, the discourse of market is placed in opposition to that of ethics. Even the European Parliament's proposals, which are almost entirely concerned with just two issues—animal welfare and transparency—begin with the need to eliminate regulatory disparities in the internal market.[215] So even where the policy discourse adopts a different focus (in this case ethics), that discourse is ultimately framed by a market discourse, to which the ethics discourse is in some sense subsidiary.

In product safety, the EU's blood,[216] human tissue and cells,[217] and human organs[218] safety legislation implicates ethics. One way it does this is by reference to the EGE,[219] which has provided guidance.[220] An ethic of altruism is also reflected in the hortative provision that Member States shall endeavour to ensure voluntary and unpaid donation of blood,[221] tissues and cells,[222] and organs.[223] This principle of altruism is a strong articulation of an ethical discourse placed in opposition to that of the market[224]—yet the fact that this is not a binding legal obligation reflects the reality of markets in human materials within the EU.[225] Again, voluntary blood and tissue donation is to be encouraged so as to ensure consumer confidence in the quality and safety of the relevant products and the ethical and human rights elements of their production, showing that the market is the constant reference point.

Our third and final example is the notion of consent, critically important to human rights and ethical decision-making, given its focus on autonomy.[226] Consent is embedded across the Clinical Trials Directive,[227] and is connected with the 'protection of human rights and the dignity of the human being with regard to the application

[214] COM(2008) 543; Council position 26 May 2010—Position of the Council at first reading with a view to the adoption of a directive of the European Parliament and of the Council on the protection of animals used for scientific purposes 6106/10.

[215] European Parliament legislative resolution of 5 May 2009 on the proposal for a directive of the European Parliament and of the Council on the protection of animals used for scientific purposes (COM(2008)0543—C6-0391/2008–2008/0211(COD)).

[216] See Directive 2001/83/EC, Art 1(10) on medicinal products deriving from human blood or plasma; the Blood Safety Directive 2002/98/EC [2002] OJ L33/30.

[217] Directive 2004/23/EC on Tissue and Cells [2004] OJ L102/48.

[218] Parliament and Council Directive 2010/45/EU of 7 July 2010 on standards of quality and safety of human organs intended for transplantation [2010] OJ L207/14.

[219] Directive 2004/23/EC, Recital 33.

[220] eg EGE Opinion 2—12/03/1993—Products Derived from Human Blood or Human Plasma; EGE Opinion 11—21/07/1998—Ethical Aspects of Human Tissue Banking. For a full list, see <http://ec.europa.eu/bepa/european-group-ethics/publications/opinions/index_en.htm> accessed 8 June 2012.

[221] Directive 2002/98/EC, Art 20.

[222] Directive 2004/23, Art 12 (1).

[223] Directive 2010/45/EU, Recital 19, Art 13.

[224] See, seminally, R Titmuss, *The Gift Relationship*, edited by A Oakley and J Ashton (LSE Books 1997).

[225] Farrell, *The Politics of Blood: Ethics, Innovation and the Regulation of Risk* (n 74).

[226] There are different figurations of consent and other so-called 'bioethical floaters'; see further: R Brownsword, 'Human Dignity, Ethical Pluralism, and the Regulation of Modern Biotechnologies' in T Murphy (ed), *New Technologies and Human Rights* (OUP 2009); R Brownsword and D Beyleveld, *Human Dignity in Bioethics and Biolaw* (OUP 2001); R Brownsword and D Beyleveld, *Consent in the Law* (Hart 2007).

[227] Parliament and Council Directive 2001/20/EC of 4 April 2001 on the approximation of the laws, regulations and administrative provisions of the Member States relation to the implementation of good clinical practice in the conduct of clinical trials on medicinal products for human use [2001] OJ L121/34, Recitals 3, 4, 16, Arts 2, 3, 4, 5.

of biology and medicine, as for instance reflected in the 1996 version of the Helsinki Declaration.'[228] Moreover, special protection is envisaged for those 'who are incapable of giving legal consent to clinical trials'.[229] A strong human rights and ethics frame expresses the EU regulation of new health technologies approach with respect to a particularly vulnerable subset of Europeans. A European database bringing together information on the content, commencement, and termination of clinical trials is subject to protections for confidentiality,[230] invoking a discourse of rights to privacy. Cross-references to the Data Protection Directive are embedded throughout EU clinical trials regulation. But we have already noted that protection of the individual in the context of the Clinical Trials Directive occurs principally through a risk frame. Similarly, Directive 2005/28/EC[231] on GCP frames the rights of individual trial subjects as concerning their protection from risk. For instance, the first principle of GCP is that 'The rights, safety and well being of the trial subjects shall prevail over the interests of science and society.'[232] Likewise, in the Blood Safety Directive and in Directive 2004/23/EC on tissue and cells[233] the notion of consent[234] and of data protection and confidentiality[235] brings in a rights-based discourse. Nevertheless, the constant reference point is the aim of getting new products to market, in such a way that consumers will have confidence in their quality and safety, and in the human rights and ethical elements of their production (ethics and rights supporting the market). Equally, although in the context of medical devices regulation, the EU's data protection and privacy laws, which are framed on the basis of rights to 'privacy by design',[236] require ICT-enabled devices/implants to have 'built-in privacy . . . features', the basis of the Data Protection Directive is that of the internal market.

In other words, in general, in the EU regulation of new health technologies, rights/ethics and markets/risk are linked,[237] with the former supporting, justifying, and complementing the latter, rather than as a free-standing frame of its own.

---

[228] Directive 2001/20/EC, Recital 2.   [229] Directive 2001/20/EC, Recitals 3, 4.

[230] Directive 2001/20/EC, Recital 9 and Art 11(3).

[231] Commission Directive 2005/28/EC of 8 April 2005 laying down principles and detailed guidelines for good clinical practice as regards investigational medicinal products for human use, as well as the requirements for authorisation of the manufacturing or importation of such products [2005] OJ L91/13.

[232] Directive 2005/28/EC, Art 2 (1).

[233] Directive 2004/23/EC [2004] OJ L102/48.

[234] Directive 2004/23/EC, Art 13.

[235] Directive 2004/23/EC, Art 14.

[236] Kosta and Bowman (n 52) 260. On the specific rights of the relevant patient ('data subject'), see 268–9.

[237] A closer analysis could be carried out to explore the nuances of this relationship, in particular whether it might manifest as zero-sum, in which rights might be 'turned off' where risk suggests it is necessary. Or are rights and ethics in the frame of 'risk', in the sense that they are important concerns that the market ignores at its peril? For discussion of this in relation to new technologies see, eg S Franklin, 'Embryonic Economies: The Double Reproductive Value of Stem Cells' (2006) 1 *BioSocieties* 71 <http://eprints.lse.ac.uk/943/1/Franklin_Embryonic_economies_2006.pdf> accessed 8 May 2012; T Murphy, 'Taking Revolutions Seriously: Rights, Risk and New Technologies' (2009) 16 *Maastricht Journal of European and Comparative Law* 15. More generally see: S Franklin, 'The Reproductive Revolution: How Far Have We Come?', *BIOS Working Papers No. 2* (BIOS, London School of Economics and Political Science, 2008) <www.lse.ac.uk/collections/BIOS/workingpapers/002.pdf> accessed 18 April 2012; or as inaugural lecture <www2.lse.ac.uk/PublicEvents/pdf/20051124 -Franklin_TheReproductiveRevolution.pdf> accessed 8 June 2012; L Lazarus and BJ Goold, 'Security and Human Rights: The Search for a Language of Reconciliation' in BJ Goold and L Lazarus (eds), *Security and Human Rights* (Hart 2007) 4. Also see: GJ Annas, *American Bioethics: Crossing Human Rights and Health Law Boundaries* (OUP 2005); LO Gostin, 'When Terrorism Threatens Health: How Far are Limitations on Personal and Economic Liberties Justified?' (2003) 55 *Florida Law Review* 1105; I Loader and N Walker, *Civilising Security* (CUP 2007); B Von Tigerstrom, *Human Security and International Law: Prospects and Problems* (Hart 2007).

However, there are at least two important counter-examples to this general position. Principal among these are paediatric clinical research and medicinal products; and the regulation of 'orphan' medicines. Here, rights and ethics are a much more dominant frame than in general EU regulation of new health technologies. Although the regulatory environment is shaped through the creation of incentives for research, trials, and getting safe products to market, the relevant discourse is framed in terms of providing benefits for (deserving) vulnerable groups, so through an ethic of collective responsibility for the less-well-off, through promoting their rights.

Turning first to new health technologies for children, a special set of provisions of EU law applies to medicinal products for paediatric use.[238] Many medicinal products currently used to treat children have not been subject to clinical trials involving the paediatric population. Although Regulation 1901/2006/EC is based on Article 114 TFEU, and is therefore framed by markets, it is noted that 'market forces alone have proven insufficient to stimulate adequate research into, and the development and authorisation of, medicinal products for the paediatric population.'[239] As such, the specifics of the paediatric population are not necessarily catered to, and this engenders risk, rights, and ethics concerns. Some of these are noted: 'inadequate dosage information which leads to increased risks of adverse reactions including death, ineffective treatment through under-dosage, non-availability to the paediatric population of therapeutic advances...'[240] The Regulation seeks to shape 'obligations and rewards and incentives in order to foster'[241] the development of safe medicinal products for children.[242] However, a balance must be struck between public health and the internal market such that the former 'must be achieved by means that do not impede the free movement of safe medicinal products within the [EU]'.[243]

Special provisions for EU-wide data collection of paediatric studies,[244] a special regulatory committee (the Paediatric Committee) and an EU 'network of excellence'[245] operate within the general EU and ICH framework.[246] The network, as well as other incentives, such as assessment by the EMA of paediatric investigation plans, fee waivers for scientific advice, information and transparency measures, and research funding under the FP[247] are supported by EU funds.[248] A special paediatric use marketing authorization is available through the general EU marketing authorization system.[249] An applicant for such a marketing authorization is able to refer to data contained in the

---

[238] The main legislation being Regulation 1901/2006/EC on medicinal products for paediatric use.

[239] Regulation 1901/2006/EC, Recital 2.

[240] Regulation 1901/2006/EC, Recital 3.

[241] Regulation 1901/2006/EC, Recital 6.

[242] Regulation 1901/2006/EC, Recital 4.

[243] Regulation 1901/2006/EC, Recital 5.

[244] The database on clinical trials established by Directive 2001/20/EC 'should include a European register of clinical trials of medicinal products for paediatric use comprising all ongoing, prematurely terminated, and completed paediatric studies conducted both in the Community and in third countries' Recital 31 and Art 41.

[245] How it 'should contribute to the work of strengthening the foundations of the European Research Area in the context of Community Framework Programmes for Research, Technological Development and Demonstration Activities, benefit the paediatric population and provide a source of information and expertise for industry, see Recital 31 and Art 44.

[246] Directive 2001/20/EC, and ICH guideline E11 on the development of medicinal products for the paediatric population, are noted as important reference points for the Committee's work; see Recital 8.

[247] Regulation 1901/2006/EC, Recital 30 and Art 40.

[248] Regulation 1901/2006/EC, Recital 35.

[249] Regulation 1901/2006/EC, Recital 19.

dossier of a medicinal product which is or has been authorized in the EU, in order to provide an 'incentive to encourage small and medium-sized enterprises to develop off-patent medicinal products for the paediatric population'.[250] Again, this is an example of the regulatory environment being focused towards eventual marketing of new health technologies. The legislation cross-refers to marketing authorizations as its underlying justification. Nevertheless, a strong rights-based and ethical frame runs through the EU's special regulatory environment for paediatric new health technologies.

Secondly, we see a similar ethical and rights-based frame for the EU's law on 'orphan drugs'. A series of special arrangements, designed to incentivize innovation in this area by disrupting normal market processes, apply to such new health technologies. Before an enterprise begins the process of applying for a market authorization for a new health technology, they may apply for their medicine to be designated as an orphan drug.[251] A drug may be classified as being an orphan medicinal product if it is indicated for a rare disease or if its development would not be commercially viable without incentives.[252] Obtaining orphan drug status means that the enterprise may obtain early assistance from the EMA in designing the study protocols for clinical research. A further incentive is the waiving of fees paid to the EMA.[253] Orphan medicinal products also gain ten years of market exclusivity on the granting of a marketing authorization. Since such products are often not protected by a patent, rather than having the benefit of a supplementary protection certificate as with patent-protected products, market exclusivity is extended to twelve years when the requirement for data on use in the paediatric population is fully met.[254] This arrangement is noted as providing the 'strongest incentive for industry to invest in the development and marketing of orphan medicinal products'.[255] Orphan drug designation means that the enterprise may also have access to incentive schemes made available by individual Member States. For example, until recently France had put in place tax breaks for enterprises developing orphan medicinal products.[256] Many companies developing new health technologies seek orphan drug status for their products, like Genzyme, which markets recombinant enzymes. Products such as Cerezyme have reached blockbuster status, that is, sales of more than $1 billion or more in a year. The significant cost and regularity of treatment has meant that relatively few patients are needed to generate significant turnover. In spite of the apparent ethical discourse about what sufferers of orphan diseases deserve, and the consequent need to distort market processes, orphan drug development is not a charitable activity—it can be a highly profitable business![257] An ethics or rights-based approach to markets can be commercially beneficial.

---

[250] Regulation 1901/2006/EC, Recital 20.

[251] By the Committee on Orphan Medicinal Products. See Parliament and Council Regulation (EC) No 141/2000 of 16 December 1999 on orphan medicinal products [2000] OJ L18/1.

[252] Regulation 141/2000, Art 3.

[253] Regulation 141/2000, Recital 7.

[254] Regulation 1901/2006/EC, Recital 29.

[255] Regulation 141/2000, Recital 8.

[256] See RR Shah, 'Regulatory Framework for the Treatment of Orphan Diseases' in A Mehta, M Beck, and G Sunder-Plassmann (eds), *Fabry Disease: Perspectives from 5 Years of FOS* (Oxford PharmaGenesis 2006) available at <www.ncbi.nlm.nih.gov/books/NBK11567/> accessed 8 May 2012.

[257] Andrea Faeh is highly critical of the discourse of ethic and concern for those with rare diseases found in the EU legislation, arguing that national reimbursement conditions and discretion of pharmaceutical companies concerning the markets into which they release novel orphan medicines mean that, in practice, EU law and policy does little or nothing towards a just distribution of health care, see A Faeh, 'A Just Distribution of Health Care in the Case of Orphan Medicinal Products: Aligning the Interests of European Economic Integration and National Welfare Policy' (2012) 14 *European Journal of Social Security* 21.

Regulation 141/2000/EC on orphan drugs is based on Article 114 TFEU, and the need for a harmonized approach is justified by the avoidance of distortions of competition and barriers to cross-border trade within the EU.[258] Moreover, action to stimulate the development of orphan medicinal products 'is best taken at ... [EU] level in order to take advantage of the widest possible market and to avoid the dispersion of limited resources.'[259] The Regulation is also framed in terms of the imperative of the EU to provide a regulatory environment that gives EU-based companies the chance to compete with companies based in the USA and Japan, that already had systems of incentivizing the development of orphan drugs in place.[260] Notwithstanding this 'classical' internal market frame, a strong discourse of non-discrimination (which can be seen as rights-based or ethical) surrounds the Regulation: sufferers of orphan diseases are framed as entitled to 'the same quality of treatment as other patients';[261] and 'the same quality, safety and efficacy' of medicinal products.[262]

Some have suggested that at least some EU regulation of new health technologies does not address ethical or human rights questions at all.[263] Undergirding such views is the distribution of competence between the EU and its Member States, in which ethics are configured in accordance with the principle of subsidiarity in Article 5 TEU. The latter operates to determine when the EU can act on competences it shares with the Member States, such as in the area of the internal market, which includes the vast majority of EU regulation of new health technologies. While operating to limit occasions when the EU legislates in place of its Member States, where the EU does legislate, ethical content is determined by committees and national governments.[264] That said, while the EU tends to avoid the harmonization of ethics across the Member States, it does seek to create a framework—a frame—in which national ethical differences are squared with the imperative of creating and optimizing the internal market. Nevertheless, in the context of our two counter-examples, the regulatory environment works to legitimate the internal market through concrete outputs to deserving groups, who would not otherwise be well served through 'normal' market processes. Moreover, this building of incentives into the regulatory environment also references the market in terms of justifications for interference with normal market processes as a way of creating certain types of new health technologies.[265]

In our final example, we consider an area of the map where we would expect a strong market frame, but where actually all four of our frames almost disappear: the regulation of pricing of new health technologies and their coverage under national health

---

[258] Regulation 141/2000, Recital 3.   [259] Regulation 141/2000, Recital 3; also Recital 4.
[260] Regulation 141/2000, Recitals 2 and 8.   [261] Regulation 141/2000, Recital 2.
[262] Regulation 141/2000, Recital 7.
[263] eg the ATMP Regulation does not interfere with national decisions on whether to allow the use of any specific type of human cells, such as embryonic stem cells, see A Mahalatchimy, 'Access to Advanced Therapy Medicinal Products in the EU: Where do We Stand?' (2001) 18 *European Journal of Health Law* 305; see also M Lee, 'Risk and Beyond: EU Regulation of Nanotechnology' (2010) 35 *European Law Review* 799, who argues that for all its apparent concern with ethics, EU regulation is essentially only concerned with risk (safety); and HDC Roscam Abbing 'Patients' Rights in a Technology and Market Driven-Europe' (2010) 17 *European Journal of Health Law* 11, who argues that the 'common European human rights framework' (ie that of the Council of Europe) ought to be embedded into EU law where patients cross borders to receive health care, where health care crosses borders (eg direct-to-consumer screening technology), or in the context of cross-border medical research.
[264] M Tallacchini, 'Governing by Values. EU Ethics: Soft Tool, Hard Effects' (2009) 47 *Minerva* 281, 293–5.
[265] eg Regulation 1901/2006/EC, Recital 5 notes that a balance must be struck between public health and the internal market such that the former 'must be achieved by means that do not impede the free movement of safe medicinal products within the Community'.

(insurance) systems. The reason for this is again the allocation of competences between the EU and its Member States.

A true single market for new health technologies across the EU would involve harmonized rules on the pricing for new health technologies. Of course, such a single market would imply profound effects on the administration and financing of national health (insurance) systems, as the principal purchasers of new health technologies within the EU. Because of that political reality, the EU has adopted only minimal rules towards such a single market, applicable only to pharmaceuticals. The Transparency of Pharmaceuticals Pricing Directive[266] is aimed only towards ensuring sufficient openness to ensure that EU law on free movement of goods is being respected, requiring no more than judicially reviewable national decisions as to inclusion or exclusion of (novel) pharmaceuticals within national health (insurance) systems.[267]

Equally, a single market in health services involving new health technologies would imply EU-level decisions about which new health technologies would be covered in the 'basket of care' provided by national health (insurance) systems. In both case law where mobile patients have sought to rely on a discourse of EU internal market law (in particular, that of free movement of services[268]) and in legislation,[269] the EU has eschewed the regulation of pricing and coverage of new health technologies within national health (insurance) systems. The Patients' Rights Directive, while invoking the discourse of rights in general, reinforces the rule (already present in the jurisprudence of the CJEU[270]) that there is no 'right' in EU law to cross-border health care if the treatment sought is not covered in the 'basket of care' within the home Member State. One reason for such disparities of coverage is that new health technologies are recognized and covered within different Member States at different times, because health technology assessment is a national affair.[271] Such decisions are for Member States to take, based on whatever combination of discourses in rights (to health care), ethics (in terms of social welfare, equality, equity), risk (for instance, through involving expert-led technocratic decision-making procedures), or markets they wish. The only caveat is that the arrangements for inclusion and pricing of new health technologies within national health (insurance) systems must not breach internal market law[272]—

---

[266] Council Directive 89/105/EEC of 21 December 1988 relating to the transparency of measures regulating the prices of medicinal products for human use and their inclusion in the scope of national health insurance systems [1989] OJ L40/8.

[267] The European Commission has proposed an amendment to the Directive: European Commission, Proposal for a Directive relating to the transparency of measures regulating the prices of medicinal products for human use and their inclusion in the scope of public health insurance systems COM (2012) 84 final. See further: T Hervey and J McHale, *Health Law and the European Union* (CUP 2004) 323–7.

[268] See, eg, Case C-157/99 Geraets-Smits *and Peerbooms* [2001] ECR I-5473, involving novel multidisciplinary treatment of Parkinson's disease, and innovative neurostimulation therapy respectively; and Case C-173/09 *Elchinov* [2010] ECR I-8889, involving attachment of radioactive plates or proton therapy to treat eye cancer.

[269] Directive 2011/24/EU, Recitals 7, 33; Art 7(3).

[270] See most recently Case C-173/09 *Elchinov* [2010] ECR I-8889; see also the EFTA Court in Cases E-11/07 and 1/08 *Rindal* (2008).

[271] For discussion of judicial oversight of health technology assessment in three jurisdictions, see K Syrett, 'Health technology appraisal and the courts: accountability for reasonableness and the judicial model of procedural justice' (2011) 6 *Health Economics, Policy and Law* 469.

[272] As found in Parliament and Council Directive 2011/24/EU (n 13), and the case law leading to it, such as C-158/96 *Kohll v Union des Caisses de Maladie* [1998] ECR I-1931; Case C-368/98 *Vanbraekel* [2001] ECR I-5363; Case C-157/99 *Geraets-Smits* [2001] ECR I-5473; Case C-385/99 *Müller-Fauré/Van Riet* [2003] ECR I-4509; Case C-56/01 *Inizan* [2003] ECR I-12403; Case C-8/02

so here the market frames again, albeit in a relatively weak and indirect form. The (highly remote) prospect of an EU-level process of health technology assessment[273] is covered in EU legislation for the first time in the 2011 Patients' Rights Directive. Recital 58 reads:

The constant progress of medical science and health technologies presents both opportunities and challenges to the health systems of the Member States. Cooperation in the evaluation of new health technologies can support Member States through economies of scale and avoid duplication of effort, and provide a better evidence base for optimal use of new technologies to ensure safe, high-quality and efficient healthcare. Such cooperation requires sustained structures involving all the relevant authorities of the Member States, building on existing pilot projects and consultation of a wide range of stakeholders. This Directive should therefore provide a basis for continued Union support for such cooperation.[274]

The discourse here is of competitiveness through economies of scale in the internal market, and also that of risk (patient safety). But even the frames of markets and risk are weak: the dominant discourse is about respect for national autonomy. Ethics and rights disappear almost entirely where EU regulation interfaces with systemic decisions involving redistributive consequences for national health (insurance) systems. The reason for this disappearance is the allocation of competences within the EU.

D. Conclusions

We were right: markets are key to the EU approach to regulation of new health technologies. The structure of EU regulation of new health technologies flows through to the market—the entire discourse and the way that the regulatory measures fit together, cross-refer each other, and are justified, essentially refers to the marketing of new health technologies. Risk—in the sense of patient or consumer safety—is also a very strong element of the frame, but in general risk per se is not a 'stand-alone' element of the frame—virtually all the elements of EU regulation of new health technologies that frame through risk do so with the importance of markets underlying that frame, and risk as a frame supports the market. Still, risk is a stronger element of the frame than we originally thought, at least in certain areas of the map, such as pre-clinical and clinical research, and certain innovative new health technologies, such as nanotechnologies.

Rights and ethics map back to markets in much the same way that risk does, and they do operate more as legitimating devices or even as 'false fronts'—but their role is greater than we originally envisaged. This is more the case in certain modes of EU regulation, such as 'steering' through funding, in certain areas in the 'map' such as regulation of research, in relation to certain new health technologies such as paediatrics and orphan medicines, and in relation to certain 'vulnerable' people, such as those who cannot consent, children, and sufferers of rare diseases. All the frames almost disappear where EU regulation interfaces with systemic decisions with redistributive consequences, leaving

---

Leichtle [2004] ECR I-2641; Case C-372/04, *Watts* [2006] ECR I-4325; Case C-444/05 *Stamatelaki* [2007] ECR I-3185; Case C-208/07 *von Chamier-Glisczinski* [2009] ECR I-6095, para's 64, 66 and 85; Case C-211/08 *Commission v Spain* [2010] ECR I-5267; Case C-173/09 *Elchinov v Natsionalsa zdravnoosiguritelna kasa* [2010] ECR I-8889.

[273] For further discussion, see T Hervey, 'Co-operation between health care authorities in the Proposed Directive on patients' rights in cross-border health' in J van de Gronden and others (eds), *Health Care and EU Law* (Asser Press 2011).

[274] Directive 2011/24/EU, Recital 58.

only a weak market frame. Hence our overall intuition, that markets are the dominant frame in the EU approach to regulating new health technologies, is sustainable.

The frames, although seemingly conceptually distinct, are constructed in EU regulation of new health technologies to overlap significantly. An attempt to unravel the separate frames more precisely was not possible in this chapter, which is concerned with a broad research question about the EU approach to regulating new health technologies, across a wide range of different types of regulation (Figure 2.2), although it would be feasible in the context of a 'micro' study, focused on one aspect of the regulatory landscape. What we have been able to show here, however, suggests that the EU's approach to risk, (human) rights, and ethics is, in general, all about the need to 'protect' the EU market. It embodies a form of 'race to the top' in terms of regulation, in that it articulates the idea that the EU's market is safer, more respectful of human rights, and more ethical than other markets. This way of framing the market departs from the traditional idea that markets as a rationale for regulation are all about free trade, whereas risk, (human) rights, and ethics imply barriers to free trade. The way that each other frame maps back to markets, and the inter-connected nature of the frames, therefore suggest another important feature of the EU approach to the regulation of new health technologies—the EU's approach is to 'bootstrap' all the other frames onto the market frame, as if there were no such inherent tension between them.

In these final paragraphs of our chapter, we turn to some more general conclusions from our research, with respect not only to EU regulation of new *health* technologies, but also new technologies more generally. We reflect on what legal analyses like that in this chapter can bring to the study of science and technology and consider some potential future research agendas.

The dominance of markets throughout EU regulation of new health technologies implies one important dimension of co-production. The internal market as the dominant frame for EU engagement not only shapes the regulatory environment encountered by new health technologies, as we have shown. The frame also helps to constitute new health technologies, in particular by subtly shaping what is researched and developed such that new health technologies help to optimize economic growth. Like other technologies, new health technologies thus have norms and values built into them by the very framing privileged in their regulation,[275] and moreover, reflect and reproduce those norms and values.[276] Thus our analysis of frames by implication frustrates the distinction often made in legal scholarship between the law and science.[277] This insight also helps to counter the potentially dangerous idea that law is unable to 'keep up' with technology—the so-called problem of 'pace' highlighted by Brownsword[278]—which links to the potential for the 'rule of technology' (and the implied irrelevance or uselessness of law) as a means of regulating behaviour and social outcomes.[279] As such, our analysis reinforces a wider constructive response by legal scholarship that emphasizes the continued efficacy and relevance of law as a way of

---

[275] S Jasanoff (ed), *Reframing Rights* (MIT Press 2011) 13.
[276] S Jasanoff, 'The Idiom of Co-production' in Jasanoff (n 4) 2–3. Original emphasis.
[277] For further discussion see: T Murphy and N Whitty, 'Risk and Human Rights in UK Prison Governance' (2007) 47 *British Journal of Criminology* 798.
[278] See further: R Brownsword, 'So What Does the World Need Now? Reflections on Regulating Technologies', in R Brownsword and K Yeung (eds), *Regulating Technologies: Legal Futures, Regulatory Frames and Technological Fixes* (Hart Publishing 2008).
[279] R Brownsword, 'Code, Control and Choice: Why East is East and West is West' (2005) 25 *Legal Studies* 1; L Lessig, *Code: And Other Laws of Cyberspace* (Basic Books 1999).

shaping new (health) technologies. This type of legal scholarship conceives law as reaching well beyond the few formal articulations of (enforceable) rights throughout (EU) law[280] on new (health) technologies, and engages with the panoply of regulation. Legal entitlements and responsibilities are revealed as more than formal articulations in legal instruments (constructed 'above', by the state or 'supra-state' (here, the EU)), but have social meaning when they are worked out in practice, through the products and processes of science and technology (constructed 'below' by active citizens).[281] There is scope for repetition of the type of analysis we carried out here in the context of different technologies and different regulatory orders.

Our analysis implicitly highlights EU regulation of novel (health) technologies as an important site for engagement over questions such as what and whom is worthy of protection, the matter of who and what interests might be privileged, and the various and disparate ways in which this manifests. Incidentally, we also reveal some of the roles of various public and private actors in EU regulation. As such, our analysis also exemplifies within one case study the growing ties between EU regulation, its citizens, and wider publics. In this respect, our analysis fits with Jasanoff's idea of EU regulation as expressing 'bioconstitutionalism'.[282] This term decentres law and judicially enforceable rights and obligations on public and private legal persons within the EU[283] to emphasize the many different relations constituted by EU regulation of its subjects,[284] whether they be EU citizens or those without EU citizenship but who are nevertheless affected by EU regulation.[285] Of course, the multilevel nature of this regulation needs to be more fully explored, but our analysis of frames highlights some important features of EU bioconstitutionalism and why it is worthwhile exploring further.

[280] 'Inquiry has to focus as well on what we view as the *basic building blocks of rights*: that is, on social commitments concerning what is worth protecting and why, for and against whom, through which kinds of social and institutional agency, by what means, to what extent, and through what processes. It is at this deeper level, that one may *elucidate the impacts of science and technology on the very notion of rights*—not only as they are formally construed by courts, but also as they are tacitly understood and worked out by scientists, lawyers, and policymakers; articulated in research practices; hardened into material technologies, or built into professional discourses and political practices.' Jasanoff (n 275) 16. Emphasis added.

[281] See Jasanoff (n 275) 15; T Murphy, 'Repetition, Revolution, and Resonance' in T Murphy (ed), *New Technologies and Human Rights* (OUP 2009). The idea that citizens are 'active' not passive is a core idea of Science and Technology Studies.

[282] Jasanoff (n 275).

[283] The traditional view of EU constitutionalism: P Craig, 'Constitutions, Constitutionalism, and the European Union' (2001) 7 *European Law Journal* 125; K Lenaerts, 'Constitutionalism and the Many Faces of Federalism' (1990) 38 *American Journal of Comparative Law* 205; MP Maduro, *We the Court: the European Court of Justice and the European Economic Constitution* (Hart 1998); E Stein, 'Lawyers, Judges and the Making of a Transnational Constitution' (1981) 75 *American Journal of International Law* 1; JHH Weiler, *The Constitution of Europe* (CUP 1999), in particular 'The Transformation of Europe' and 'The Reformation of European Constitutionalism'. See also: P Craig and G de Búrca (eds), *The Evolution of EU Law* (OUP 1999); A-M Slaughter, A Stone Sweet, and JHH Weiler (eds), *The European Courts and National Courts—Doctrine and Jurisprudence: Legal Change in Social Context* (Hart 1998); A Stone Sweet, *Governing With Judges: Constitutional Politics in Europe* (OUP 2000).

[284] For definition and discussion see: Baldwin, Cave, and Lodge (n 10); J Black, 'Critical Reflections on Regulation' (2002) 27 *Australian Journal of Legal Philosophy* 1.

[285] In the context of new health technologies, see ML Flear, 'The EU's Biopolitical Governance of Advanced Therapy Medicinal Products' (2009) 16(1) *Maastricht Journal of European and Comparative Law* 113; see further: ML Flear and S Ramshaw (eds), 'Symposium: New Technologies, European Law and Citizens' (2009) 16(1) *Maastricht Journal of European and Comparative Law*.

EU regulation, especially its production and deployment of knowledge through to material embodiments (Figure 2.1), as in our example of new health technologies, also involves practices of 'state' (or 'supra-state')-making, and of governance.[286] EU engagement with new (health) technologies is central to the European project of rule, as it provides legitimating support for the wider project of European integration itself, and other, usually national, actors who require EU action in order to support their own legitimacy.[287] Our analysis here supports the idea that EU regulation of new technologies, as part of a response to perceived regulatory failures in the use and institutionalization of scientific knowledge in national and EU structures, such as GMOs in food, or the BSE crisis of the 1990s,[288] is framed by markets. Risk—often instantiated as consumer safety and communicated through assurances that EU standards for new (health) technologies have been met—has been grafted on to that core market concern, as for instance in the EU's *European Governance* White Paper.[289] EU risk-based regulation thus renders the EU auditable and inspectable as it relates to consumers,[290] and builds and maintains their confidence so that they consume new (health) technologies, which demonstrates in turn the EU's general tendency to govern through market freedom.[291] We have also shown how rights and ethics are used to aid and abet—and essentially legitimate—that ordering of frames. Overall, the production of new (health) technologies as concrete 'outputs'[292] that deliver innovation and prosperity can be seen to build the EU's identity and relationships with its citizens and others, and legitimate its activity.

This analysis affirms long-standing theorizations of the EU integration process, including Monnet's vision of a united Europe, neofunctionalism,[293] and a vision of the EU as a 'regulatory state'.[294] The overarching steer for EU law and regulation as being about economic optimization was subsequently reinforced by the Lisbon Strategy

---

[286] S Jasanoff, 'The Idiom of Co-production' in Jasanoff (n 4) 3; G Majone, 'The Rise of the Regulatory State in Europe' (1994) 17 *West European Politics* 77.

[287] C Lord, 'Legitimacy, Democracy and the EU: When Abstract Questions Become Practical Problems', *Policy Paper 03/00*, available at <www.mcrit.com/scenarios/visionsofeurope/documents/one%20Europe%20or%20Several/C%20Lord.pdf> accessed 8 May 2012.

[288] M Everson and E Vos, 'The Scientification of Politics and the Politicisation of Science' in M Everson and E Vos (eds), *Uncertain Risks Regulated* (Routledge-Cavendish 2009).

[289] European Commission, 'European Governance: A White Paper', COM(2001) 428 final.

[290] Power describes these sorts of techniques as '*increasingly framed* as an organizational *strategy to manage public expectations*' (M Power, *Organized Uncertainty* (OUP 2007) 20–1. Emphasis added). On risk as a legitimating device, also see: J Black, 'The Emergence of Risk-Based Regulation and the New Public Risk Management in the United Kingdom' [2005] *Public Law* 512.

[291] See further: M Foucault, *The Birth of Biopolitics: Lectures at the Collège de France, 1978–1979* (Palgrave Macmillan 2008); cf T Lemke, '"The Birth of Biopolitics": Michel Foucault's Lecture at the Collège de France on Neo-liberal Governmentality' (2001) 30(2) *Economy and Society* 190; W Brown, *Edgework* (Princeton UP, 2005) 39–44.

[292] F Scharpf, 'Economic Integration, Democracy and the Welfare State' (1997) 4(1) *European Public Policy* 18; on performance: D Beetham, *The Legitimation of Power* (Macmillan 1991); D Beetham and C Lord, *Legitimacy and the EU* (Longman 1998); F Scharpf, 'Problem-solving Effectiveness and Democratic Accountability in the EU' (2003) *MPIfG Working Paper 03/1* <www.mpifg.de/pu/workpap/wp03-1/wp03-1.html>; cf R Brownsword and H Somsen, 'Law, Innovation and Technology: Before We Fast Forward—A Forum for Debate' (2009) 1 *Law, Innovation and Technology* 1.

[293] eg E Haas, *The Uniting of Europe: Political, Social and Economic Forces 1950–1957* (Stanford UP 1968). See further: P Craig, 'The Nature of the Community: Integration, Democracy and Legitimacy' in Craig and de Búrca (n 283) 6.

[294] G Majone, 'Europe's "Democratic Deficit": The Question for Standards' (1998) 4(1) *European Law Journal* 5; G Majone, 'The Politics of Regulation and European Regulatory Institutions' in J Hayward and A Menon (eds), *Governing Europe* (OUP 2003).

and now in Europe 2020. In the health sphere, this focus was given specific form[295] in the European Commission's *Together for Health*.[296] It can also be suggested that the wider use of the specific ordering of the frames for EU engagement with new (health) technologies for legitimacy actually gains in importance in light of de-legitimating events, such as the 'No' votes in national referenda on EU Treaty amendments, and the recent economic and financial crises.[297]

Overall, EU engagement with new (health) technologies imagines and projects a vision of the EU and its institutions, such as the European Commission, the EMA, and EGE. Underpinning that engagement,[298] we can discern a presumption of a European identity that serves to legitimate EU activities; a process of knowledge production—an epistemology—that constitutes an ontological enactment of the EU; and a choice made about how to rule, which is implicit in the relative importance of each of the frames.

[295] ML Flear, 'The Open Method of Coordination on Health Care After the Lisbon Strategy II: Towards a Neoliberal Framing?' (2009)13(1) *European Integration online Papers* (Art 12).

[296] European Commission, 'White Paper, Together for Health: A Strategic Approach for the EU 2008–2013', COM(2007) 630 final; European Commission, 'Commission Staff Working Document Accompanying White Paper, Together for Health: A Strategic Approach for the EU 2008–2013', SEC (2007) 1376. For an overview of initiatives, see European Commission, 'Commission Staff Working Document, Report on European Governance (2003–2004)', SEC(2004) 1153.

[297] For a good summary see: CJ Bickerton, 'Legitimacy through Action', available at <www.nottingham.ac.uk/shared/shared_icmcr/Docs/bickerton.pdf> accessed 8 May 2012.

[298] S Jasanoff, 'The Idiom of Co-production' in Jasanoff (n 4) 8.

3

Fixed Points in a Changing Age? The Council of Europe, Human Rights, and the Regulation of New Health Technologies

*Rory O'Connell and Sjef Gevers**

A. Introduction

The Council of Europe is an intergovernmental organization set up after the Second World War by ten countries; it now has forty-seven Member States. Its aims include protecting human rights, democracy, and the rule of law; encouraging the development of Europe's cultural identity and diversity; and helping consolidate democratic stability in Europe by backing political, legislative, and constitutional reform.[1] The Council, with its headquarters in Strasbourg, covers many of the major issues facing European societies, such as human rights, the media, legal cooperation, social cohesion, education, culture, local democracy, and regional planning.[2] There is some overlap between the remit of the Council of Europe and the European Union (EU), though legally and institutionally these are distinct organizations as discussed in Section B.[3]

The key questions in this chapter are first, to what extent has the Council been involved with regulation of new health technologies (NHTs) and secondly, what is the nature of its interventions? In considering this, the chapter will focus on the theme of (human) rights, although it also address ethical issues when we come to discuss dignity. Technological change may seem to threaten the status of human rights as fundamental standards—much less fixed points[4]—in political democracies, with authors wondering how human rights can survive the challenge of rapidly evolving technology,[5] or even how human rights might be meaningful in a 'posthuman' age.[6]

In addressing these questions, the chapter is structured as follows. Section B describes the system of multilevel regulation within the Council of Europe, identifying the relevant Council of Europe institutions and texts. Section C considers the importance of flexibility and variability in the Council's interventions relating to NHTs; a particular focus is the European Court of Human Rights (ECtHR) and the margin of appreciation doctrine. The theme of rights and especially autonomy-related

---

* We would like to thank the anonymous reviewers and Thérèse Murphy for their detailed constructive advice on this chapter.

[1] Council of Europe in Brief, 'Objectives' <www.coe.int/aboutCoe/index.asp?page=nosObjectifs &l=en> accessed 15 May 2012.

[2] See Council of Europe website <www.coe.int> accessed 16 May 2012.

[3] The EU is the focus of Chapter 2 in this collection.

[4] 'Good old Watson! You are the one fixed point in a changing age': Arthur Conan Doyle, 'His Last Bow' in *Sherlock Holmes: The Complete Illustrated Short Stories* (Chancellor Press 1994) 808.

[5] C Gearty, *Can Human Rights Survive?* (CUP 2006) 148–9.

[6] U Baxi, *Human Rights in a Posthuman World: Critical Essays* (OUP 2007).

rights (non-interference, privacy, etc) is the subject of Section D; equality rights and the right to health are also considered. Section E examines how the Council treats dignity. Section F revisits some of the governance-related discussion of the earlier sections, highlighting the Council's standards that encourage public discussion of these sensitive questions.

B. A Multi-Layered System

First, let us consider the multi-layered framework that is the Council of Europe. Section 1 presents the general structure of the Council. Section 2 discusses the general human rights framework with a special focus on the European Convention on Human Rights (ECHR). Section 3 covers the Council of Europe's work more specifically in relation to biomedicine; including the Biomedicine (or Oviedo) Convention and related protocols. Section 4 discusses the relationship between the Council of Europe and the EU.

1. The Council of Europe System

The Council of Europe was established by the Statute of the Council of Europe in 1949.[7] It is an international organization which uses intergovernmental working methods. These are very different from the working methods of the supranational EU; in particular, the legal instruments of the Council of Europe are not directly effective in national law and they are not supreme over conflicting national law.

The Council's seat is in Strasbourg; and its principal institutions are the Committee of Ministers and the Parliamentary Assembly of the Council of Europe (PACE). The Committee of Ministers consists of the Foreign Minister from each Member State,[8] while the PACE includes representatives from the legislatures of the Member States.[9] These institutions are served by a Secretariat.[10] The work of the Council typically leads to treaties that are open for adoption by the Member States (and sometimes non-Member States). As of 2012, there are more than 200 such treaties, the most relevant of which will be presented in the next two sections.[11]

Apart from elaborating treaties, the Council has other mechanisms that may be relevant. The Committee of Ministers established a Committee of Experts on Bioethics (CAHBI) in 1982, which was subsequently renamed the Steering Committee on Bioethics (CDBI) and is now the Committee on Bioethics (DH-BIO).[12] The Council of Europe has a long-standing involvement in technical cooperation and standard setting in the fields of blood transfusion and transplantation medicine.[13] Harmonization of laws and policies may also result from the recommendations issued by the

---

[7] European Social Charter (ETS) 1.

[8] Statute of the Council of Europe, 1949, Art 14.

[9] Statute of the Council of Europe, 1949, Art 25.

[10] Statute of the Council of Europe, 1949, Art 10.

[11] See the Treaty Office of the Council for the full list: <www.conventions.coe.int> accessed 16 May 2012.

[12] <www.coe.int/t/dg3/healthbioethic/cdbi/default_en.asp> accessed 6 June 2012.

[13] For more on this, see P van Aken, 'The Contributions of the Council of Europe to Blood Transfusion and Transplantation' in H Roscam Abbing and others (eds), *Health, Ethics and Human Rights; The Council of Europe Meeting the Challenge* (Council of Europe 2004) 59 ff; European Directorate for the Quality of Medicine and Health Care <www.edqm.eu/en/Background_Mission-65.html> accessed 17 May 2012.

Committee of Ministers[14] or by PACE;[15] although these recommendations are not binding, they could influence national developments. There are now about fifty such recommendations on bioethics,[16] including several on NHTs (for example, xenotransplantation[17] and stem cell research[18]).

2. Council of Europe Human Rights Framework

Human rights are of considerable importance to new technologies,[19] biomedicine, and bioethics.[20] Questions raised by NHTs are often framed in terms of human rights issues.[21] The Council of Europe has adopted treaties that set out human rights standards and create institutions to monitor the observance of those standards. There is now an extensive Council of Europe archipelago of such instruments; we will first introduce the ECHR before mentioning some of the other treaties.

The European Convention for the Protection of Human Rights and Fundamental Freedoms, 1950 (European Convention on Human Rights or ECHR) was innovative in establishing an international court—ECtHR—to hear complaints that a state had breached an individual's rights. Every member of the Council of Europe is a party to the ECHR and accepts the jurisdiction of the ECtHR to hear individual applications. The decisions of the Court are directly binding (as a matter of international law) on the Member States. The ECtHR sits in different formations—single judge, Committees, Chambers, and the Grand Chamber.[22] The single judge formation and committees decide admissibility issues; the seven-judge Chambers are the primary forum for deciding the merits of cases, while the 17-judge Grand Chamber hears cases involving 'serious' questions of the interpretation of the ECHR, cases where there may be differing Chamber judgments, and referrals (appeals) from parties to a Chamber judgment.[23]

The ECHR rights are primarily though not exclusively civil and political in character. Surprisingly, given the context of the ECHR's birth, there is no explicit reference to the uses and misuses of technology such as the Nazis' experimentation on human beings,[24]

---

[14] Statute of the Council of Europe, 1949, Art 15.

[15] Statute of the Council of Europe, 1949, Art 23.

[16] Collected at <www.coe.int/t/dg3/healthbioethic/Texts_and_documents/default_en.asp> accessed 17 May 2012.

[17] Among others there are PACE Recommendation 1399 (1999) on xenotransplantation and Committee of Ministers Recommendation Rec(2003)10 on xenotransplantation 2003. On these, see Chapter 16 in this collection.

[18] PACE Resolution 1352 (2003) on human stem cell research.

[19] T Murphy and G Ó Cuinn, 'Works in Progress: New Technologies and the European Court of Human Rights' (2010) 10 *Human Rights Law Review* 601.

[20] F Francioni, 'Genetic Resources, Biotechnology and Human Rights: the International Legal Framework' in F Francioni (ed), *Biotechnologies and International Human Rights* (Hart 2007); J Sándor, 'Human Rights and Bioethics: Competitors or Allies? The Role of International Law in Shaping the Contours of a New Discipline' (2008) 27 *Medicine & Law* 15.

[21] See UNESCO declarations such as the Universal Declaration on the Human Genome and Human Rights 1997; Universal Declaration on Bioethics and Human Rights 2005. For a defence of the latter document's reliance on human rights see R Andorno, 'Global Bioethics at UNESCO: in Defence of the Universal Declaration on Bioethics and Human Rights' (2007) 33 *Journal of Medical Ethics* 150.

[22] Art 26 ECHR as amended by Protocol 14.

[23] Arts 30 and 43 ECHR as amended by Protocol 14.

[24] R Ashcroft, 'Could Human Rights Supersede Bioethics?' (2010) 10 *Human Rights Law Review* 639, 641.

eugenic,[25] or nuclear technology. There is no reference to the benefits of technology akin to the Universal Declaration of Human Rights (UDHR) provisions on rights to 'share in scientific advancement and its benefits' or to the 'protection of the moral and material interests resulting from any scientific' production.[26] Nor is there a provision equivalent to article 7 of the International Covenant on Civil and Political Rights, 1966 (ICCPR) prohibiting medical experimentation without consent. Furthermore, there is no reference to dignity in the ECHR, even though dignity features as a value in the UDHR[27] and as a right in the German Constitution of 1949.[28]

That said, the rights in the ECHR are very general in nature and have a wide scope; thus, several may affect NHTs. These include the right to life (Article 2), the right to be free from torture, inhuman or degrading treatment (Article 3), the right to respect for private and family life (Article 8), the right to marry and to found a family (Article 12), the principle of non-discrimination (Article 14), and the right to property (Article 1 of the First Protocol to the ECHR[29]). Some of these rights—notably Article 8—are 'qualified' rights, that is, they might be limited where necessary in a democratic society to protect a legitimate public interest (this is the famous proportionality doctrine). Other rights, such as Articles 2 and 3 are more 'absolute' in character; in principle for instance, no legitimate interest can justify the infliction of torture. In respect of many rights, 'positive obligations' exist. These are obligations on the state to take steps to protect rights rather than merely refraining from interfering with them.[30]

While much of the discussion in this chapter will be on the ECHR, the other human rights treaties and institutions within the Council of Europe may also affect the regulation of NHTs. The ECHR is complemented in the field of social and economic rights by the European Social Charter system, notably the original 1961 Charter and the Revised Charter of 1996.[31] Article 11 of both treaties requires states to respect the right to protection of health; this includes removing the causes of ill-health; promotion of health and individual responsibility; and preventing diseases and accidents. Article 13 of both treaties includes the right to social and medical assistance. The 1996 Charter adds several rights, of which the most relevant is the right to non-discrimination in the enjoyment of Charter rights (Article E).

Other human rights institutions may have some relevance to the regulation of NHTs. For instance, the Committee for the Prevention of Torture, which has the power to visit any place of detention.[32] Or the two Council of Europe institutions that are concerned with minority rights and the fight against racism: the Advisory Committee of the Framework Convention on National Minorities and the European

---

[25] IV Motoc, 'The International Law of Genetic Discrimination: The Power of "Never Again"' in T Murphy (ed), *New Technologies and Human Rights* (OUP 2009) 225.

[26] UDHR 1948, Art 27.

[27] Mentioned in the Preamble, Arts 1, 22, and 23.

[28] Art 1.

[29] Intellectual property (IP) rights are potentially relevant here; for more on the intersection of IP and human rights see LR Helfer and G Austin, *Human Rights and Intellectual Property: Mapping the Global Interface* (CUP 2011).

[30] A Mowbray, *The Development of Positive Obligations under the European Convention on Human Rights by the European Court of Human Rights* (Hart 2004); B Dickson, 'Special Issue on Positive Obligations and the European Court of Human Rights' (2010) 61 *Northern Ireland Legal Quarterly*.

[31] European Social Charter 1961, ETS 35; the Revised European Social Charter 1996, ETS 163.

[32] Established by the European Convention for the Prevention of Torture and Inhuman or Degrading Treatment or Punishment, 1987, ETS 126. Every Council of Europe state has ratified this.

Commission against Racism and Intolerance (ECRI).[33] These bodies might be relevant if there were problems with failures to develop health resources particularly relevant to ethnic minorities or with discriminatory impacts of NHTs. The example of ECRI also indicates that the Council of Europe is active in human rights promotion in many fields even where there is no formal treaty. These fields include the rights of women and children, and people with disabilities. Finally, a Commissioner for Human Rights has a general mandate to promote human rights.[34]

3. The Biomedicine Convention and its Protocols

Alongside the general human rights framework, the Council of Europe has adopted several texts on human rights and biomedicine.[35] The most prominent is the Convention on Human Rights and Biomedicine 1997 (the Oviedo Convention or Biomedicine Convention), which came into force in 2000.[36] By May 2012, twenty-nine Council of Europe states had ratified this Convention.

This human rights instrument sought to address developments in modern biology and medicine. Whereas protecting human rights in the context of scientific research and advanced medicine lies at the heart of the Biomedicine Convention, its scope is not restricted thereto. In fact, its provisions are as relevant for everyday health care provision as for highly technical medical procedures and medical research.[37] As to more specific health technologies, reference can be made to several provisions in the Biomedicine Convention. The most important ones are those that more or less limit genetic testing, interventions on the human genome, and sex-selection to medical purposes (Articles 12–14), protect living donors in case of organ or tissue removal (Articles 19–20), and prohibit making a profit from the human body and its parts (Article 21). The Biomedicine Convention has been supplemented with four additional protocols which, among other matters, prohibit reproductive cloning and regulate organ transplantation.[38]

4. Relationship with Other Organizations

Of course, other international organizations are also contributing to the development of basic principles relating to NHTs. At the European level, the most direct regulatory companion of the Council of Europe is the EU.[39] Substantial differences exist between

[33] The former is established by the Framework Convention for the Protection of National Minorities, 1995, ETS 157.

[34] Resolution (99)50 of the Committee of Ministers, 7 May 1999.

[35] Much of this material is available at <www.coe.int/t/dg3/healthbioethic/> accessed 17 May 2012.

[36] Convention for the Protection of Human Rights and Dignity of the Human Being with Regard to the Application of Biology and Biomedicine, 1997, ETS 164.

[37] J Dute 'The Leading Principles of the Convention on Human Rights and Biomedicine' in J Gevers, E Hondius, and JH Hubben (eds), *Health Law, Human Rights and the Biomedicine Convention* (Martinus Nijhoff 2005) 4 and 11.

[38] Additional Protocol to the Convention for the Protection of Human Rights and Dignity of the Human Being with regard to the Application of Biology and Medicine, on the Prohibition of Cloning Human Beings, 1998, ETS 168; Additional Protocol to the Convention on Human Rights and Biomedicine concerning Transplantation of Organs and Tissues of Human Origin, 2002, ETS 186; Additional Protocol to the Convention on Human Rights and Biomedicine, concerning Biomedical Research, 2005, ETS 195; Additional Protocol to the Convention on Human Rights and Biomedicine concerning Genetic Testing for Health Purposes, 2008, ETS 203.

[39] See Chapter 2 in this collection.

the two organizations, in history, membership, mission, and objectives, as well as in institutional order and legal instruments. As to the last point: the EU Member States are subject to a common legal order with much more regulatory potential than exists in the intergovernmental Council of Europe.

Nevertheless, although their perspectives and roles are different, there is some overlap between their activities with regard to health technologies, and that overlap seems to be increasing. One aspect of this is that the EU has been concerning itself more with human rights. In 2000 it adopted a (then non-binding) Charter of Fundamental Rights which includes several rights directly relevant to health technology such as the right to dignity,[40] a detailed right to physical integrity that explicitly lays down standards in the field of medicine,[41] a prohibition on genetic discrimination,[42] and a right to health care.[43] Since the Treaty of Lisbon (2009) the EU has further strengthened its commitment to human rights by conferring on this Charter the same legal force as the EU Treaties,[44] and paving the way for the EU to accede to the ECHR.[45] Perhaps most significantly the EU is now venturing into technical domains such as blood transfusion and organ donation that were previously the almost exclusive area of intergovernmental coordination via the Council of Europe. It is not surprising, therefore, that in drawing-up Directives and undertaking other initiatives in these areas, the EU has been called upon not to duplicate the work of the Council, to coordinate its activities with 'Strasbourg', and to make use of the pan-European expertise in these fields.[46] This is not only a matter of economical use of resources, but also of avoiding the adoption of inconsistent or even conflicting standards.[47]

5. Conclusion on a Multi-Layered Framework

The role of the Council of Europe in regulating NHTs consists of different parts, situated at different levels. Its first contribution is that the human rights framework provides a general normative context for the development, introduction, and use of NHTs. Secondly, the Council has developed rules and recommendations specifically in relation to biomedicine, including NHTs. These sources, notably the Biomedicine Convention, form a potentially important common framework for biomedical research in general and provide basic principles with regard to some NHTs in particular.

Having set out the institutions and texts which form the basis of the Council's engagement in this field, the next sections address some of the characteristics of that engagement. The first point emphasized will be the variable and flexible nature of that engagement.

C. A Variable and Flexible System

The Council of Europe's approach to regulation in this field is subject to important qualifications. The intergovernmental nature of the Council, considered in section 1,

---

[40] Art 1.   [41] Art 3.   [42] Art 21.   [43] Art 35.

[44] See Arts 2 and 6 of the Treaty on the European Union; see ML Flear and A Vakulenko, 'A Human Rights Perspective on Citizen Participation in the EU's Governance of New Technologies' (2010) 10 *Human Rights Law Review* 661, 667–8.

[45] Art 6(2) of the Treaty on European Union; Art 17 of Protocol 14 to the ECHR.

[46] See A-M Farrell, 'Adding Value? EU Governance of Organ Donation and Transplantation' (2010) 17 *European Journal of Health Law* 51, 65, and 77.

[47] JKM Gevers, 'Medical Research Involving Children' (2008) 15 *European Journal of Health Law* 103, 106.

lends itself to a variable approach to regulation, in particular because not all states have ratified the Biomedicine Convention. Moreover as explained in section 2, even in relation to the most impressive achievement of the Council—the ECHR—the doctrine of the margin of appreciation affords considerable flexibility to Member State activity in this field.

1. Variability in an Intergovernmental System: Soft Law, Treaties, and Not So Hard Law

The Council of Europe's intergovernmental nature renders it radically different from the supranational, even proto-federal, EU. In the EU, states have pooled their sovereignty and created a new legal order; many of the legal instruments of the EU benefit from the doctrines of direct effect and supremacy; the EU Commission can take action against Member States, and so on. None of this exists in the Council of Europe which remains in many ways a traditional international organization.

For example, the Council makes use of 'soft law' instruments—these are the Recommendations of the Committee of Ministers or PACE, as well as guidance issued by other committees within the Council of Europe architecture. As their name indicates these are not formally legally binding even as a matter of international law.

Of course, the conventions or treaties developed by the Council of Europe can be examples of hard law, that is, legally binding as a matter of international law for those states that have ratified the treaties. The ECHR, ratified by all Council of Europe states, is the leading example of this. Nevertheless, even in relation to the development of treaties, the intergovernmental approach leads to a variable form of regulation. Most notably, states are not required to ratify all Council of Europe conventions. Of the forty-seven Council of Europe states,[48] only twenty-nine have ratified the Biomedicine Convention.[49] Among the states that have not ratified the Biomedicine Convention, are Germany, Russia, Poland, and most of the founders of the Council (Belgium, Ireland, Italy, Luxembourg, the Netherlands, Sweden, and the United Kingdom).[50]

Furthermore, even though a treaty is not 'soft law', some of the Council of Europe treaties are not such hard law either. In the first place, some are 'framework' treaties, that is, they establish general principles which have to be completed by national measures, rather than detailing rights or rules which could be relied on in court. The intention of the Committee of Ministers and of PACE was that the Biomedicine Convention would be such a framework convention.[51] While it provides fundamental principles relating to a number of fields (for example, consent, private life, and right to information), other issues are to be further elaborated in additional protocols.

Many of the Biomedicine Convention provisions are very abstract. This holds in particular for the general provisions in the first chapter of the Convention, such as Article 1 on the protection of the dignity and identity of all human beings including respect, without discrimination, for their integrity, and Article 2 according to which the interests and welfare of the human being shall prevail over the sole interest of science

---

[48] The Biomedicine Convention is open to ratification by some non-Council of Europe states.

[49] As of 16 May 2012. See <http://conventions.coe.int/Treaty/Commun/ListeTraites.asp?CM=8&CL=ENG> for details of ratifications and reservations to all Council of Europe treaties.

[50] Furthermore, Millard suggests that the many East European states which ratified the Convention did so more out of a desire to show their human rights credentials than on the basis of any thorough examination of the issues: F Millard, 'Rights Transmission by Mimesis: the Biomedicine Convention in Central Europe' (2010) 9 *Journal of Human Rights* 427.

[51] Council of Europe, *Explanatory Report to the Biomedicine Convention 1997*, para 4.

and society. The principle of 'equitable access to health care' (Article 3) is heavily caveated with references to 'available resources', 'appropriate' measures, and 'appropriate' quality. Furthermore, the Convention does not address some controversial issues: these include decisions about when life begins and ends, and the right to dispose of the dead body.[52] The Additional Protocol on Genetic Testing for Health Purposes also exemplifies that, in the process of standard setting, areas of disagreement tend to be avoided, since it does not deal with the controversial issues of pre-implantation and prenatal screening or with using the information resulting from genetic testing for non-health care purposes such as access to private insurance cover.

There is, however, ambiguity in the Biomedicine Convention: the term 'framework' is not used, while many of the provisions are sufficiently specific to be 'self-executing' (that is, so specific that courts could rely on them to decide cases without the need for further national implementation measures), as acknowledged in the Council of Europe's own Explanatory Report on the Convention.[53] For example, Chapter II provides detailed rules on consent, while Chapter V specifies protections for research subjects. Article 11 contains a clear rule prohibiting discrimination on grounds of genetic heritage; Article 14 prohibits sex selection except for serious medical reasons. These and other provisions of the Convention belie its 'framework' character.

However, it is not just the 'framework' nature of some treaties that makes them akin to soft law guidelines. Some conventions lack a rigorous or indeed any enforcement mechanism. The Biomedicine Convention, for instance, provides for no monitoring or enforcement mechanism other than the possibility for the Secretary General of the Council of Europe to request a state to report on how it implements the Convention.[54] There is the possibility for a state party or the Steering Committee on Bioethics (now the Committee on Bioethics) to ask the ECtHR to give an advisory opinion on the Biomedicine Convention's interpretation.[55] While the Biomedicine Convention lacks any enforcement mechanism, at least one possibility exists for its indirect judicial protection. The ECtHR sometimes relies on other international treaties to interpret the ECHR[56] and it may so rely on the Biomedicine Convention. The ECtHR has referred occasionally to the Biomedicine Convention,[57] but these references do not seem to have significantly influenced the Court's reasoning.[58]

Having highlighted the problematic legal nature of some of the relevant Council conventions, we now turn to the ECHR.

2. Flexibility: The ECHR and the Margin of Appreciation

At first glance, the ECHR does not seem to suffer from the problems affecting the other Council of Europe treaties. Every Council of Europe state has ratified it, and there is a well-established (albeit overloaded) individual complaints mechanism. Despite these

---

[52] HDC Abbing, 'The Convention on Human Rights and Biomedicine—An Appraisal of the Council of Europe Convention' (1998) 5 *European Journal of Health Law* 377, 378.

[53] Council of Europe (n 51) para 20.

[54] Art 30.

[55] Art 29.

[56] The ECtHR invoked the Aarhus Convention 1998 and the Rio Declaration on the Environment and Development 1992 in *Tătar and Tătar v Romania* App no 67021/01 (27 January 2009, ECtHR).

[57] Eg *Glass v United Kingdom* (2004) 39 EHRR 15; *MAK and RK v United Kingdom* (2010) 51 EHRR 14.

[58] Murphy and Ó Cuinn (n 19) 610–11. In a case on the sterilization of a Roma woman without her informed consent, there are several references to the Biomedicine Convention. Nevertheless, a violation could have been found on the basis of Art 3 ECHR even without relying on the Biomedicine Convention: *VC v Slovakia* App no 18968/07 (8 November 2011, ECtHR).

important advantages, one should not expect too much from the ECtHR in the field of NHTs. Partly this is because the ECHR contains few technology-specific references; and partly because the ECHR was originally perceived as a set of minimum standards. Neither of these factors fully explains why we do not find detailed guidance from the ECtHR however: the ECtHR is adept at interpreting the Convention to meet the evolving needs of European society, and even speaks of the ever-increasing standards required by human rights law.[59] Instead, the key reason why detailed guidance is lacking is the ECtHR's margin of appreciation doctrine.

The ECtHR speaks of a margin of appreciation, that is, a degree of deference that is due to the states in their implementation of the ECHR. This margin is required because the responsibility to ensure the observance of rights falls primarily on the states (Article 1); the ECtHR's role is merely supervisory. Sometimes the ECtHR recognizes a wide margin of appreciation in cases where a supranational court is ill placed to second guess the decisions of the national authorities (for example, cases involving national security, planning decisions, economic policy). Most pertinently for our purposes, a wide margin of appreciation often applies where there are no common European standards (no 'European consensus', in the language of the Court); this might be because sensitive moral or ethical issues are involved, or because states are grappling with the challenges posed by rapidly evolving technology. Both these points are very relevant to NHTs.

The margin of appreciation does not amount to a 'trump' card for the state however. Even where a wide margin of appreciation is justified, the ECtHR may find that other factors require a more intensive scrutiny. Furthermore, the margin of appreciation may vary over time. The clearest example of both these possibilities is the ECtHR's approach to gender reassignment surgery. In gender reassignment cases in the 1980s, the ECtHR allowed the states considerable freedom of manoeuvre though also indicating that the issues had serious implications for the persons affected and that regulations in this area should be kept under review in light of 'scientific and societal developments'.[60] By the 1990s,[61] and even more so in the 21st century, as demonstrated by *Goodwin v United Kingdom*, this margin of appreciation had narrowed dramatically. In *Goodwin*, the ECtHR noted there was an 'international trend' favouring recognition of the new sexual identity of someone who had undergone gender reassignment surgery.[62] It criticized the United Kingdom for effectively ignoring the repeated admonitions of the ECtHR that this was an area of law that needed to be kept under review; after about fifteen years[63] of such warnings, the matter was no longer within the national margin of appreciation, irrespective of the fact that there was no *European* consensus on the issue.[64]

It is not easy to predict how the ECtHR will evaluate the margin of appreciation and this makes the task of predicting the ECtHR's approach in this area 'difficult and dangerous'.[65] Certainly, the margin of appreciation has been prominent in cases involving new technologies including NHTs.

---

[59] *Siliadin v France* (2006) 43 EHRR 16, para 149.
[60] *Rees v United Kingdom* (1987) 9 EHRR 56, para 47.
[61] *B v France* (1992) 16 EHRR 1.
[62] *Goodwin v United Kingdom* (2002) 35 EHRR 18, para 85.
[63] Sometimes the erosion of the margin of appreciation happens even more quickly as seen in the cases concerning the right of a gay single person to adopt: compare *Fretté v France* (2004) 38 EHRR 21 to *EB v France* (2008) 47 EHRR 21 [GC].
[64] *Goodwin v United Kingdom* (n 62) paras 85, 92–3.
[65] Murphy and Ó Cuinn (n 19) 620.

In *Evans v United Kingdom*,[66] one of the issues was whether under Article 8 there exists a positive obligation on the state to ensure that a woman who has embarked on treatment for the purpose of giving birth to a genetically related child, should be permitted to proceed to implantation of the embryo notwithstanding the withdrawal of consent by her former partner (the male gamete provider). National legislation gave both parties a right to withdraw their consent to the use of the gametes. The ECtHR held that Article 8 covered the right to respect for the decision to become a parent and, in particular, that it covered the right to respect for the decision to become a parent in the genetic sense.[67] The Court noticed that there was no European consensus, either as to the relative importance of the interest at stake or as to the best means of protecting it. Since several aspects of IVF treatment give rise to 'sensitive moral and ethical issues against a background of fast moving medical and scientific developments, and since the questions raised by the case touch on areas where there is no clear common ground among the member states', the margin of appreciation must be a wide one.[68] Against this background, the Court concluded that there had been no violation of Article 8. Four judges dissented, seeing the UK legislation as a disproportionate restriction on the applicant's rights given her particular circumstances. They criticized the majority's use of 'the margin of appreciation principle as a merely pragmatic substitute for a thought-out approach to the problem of the proper scope of review.'[69]

Disagreement over the margin of appreciation also figured in *SH and others v Austria*, another assisted reproduction case, albeit one where the Grand Chamber reversed a Chamber judgment.[70] The complaints were brought by two couples, both depending (for medical reasons) on IVF combined with gamete (ova or sperm) donation in order to have a child genetically related to themselves. Austrian law did not allow this combination as it prohibited the use of donated ova, and prohibited the use of donated sperm for IVF; the legislation 'permitted only homologous methods—such as using ova and sperm from the spouses or from the cohabiting couple itself—and methods which did not involve a particularly sophisticated technique and were not too far removed from natural means of conception.'[71] The Austrian legislature had adopted such rules to balance the right to procreate, the rights of children, and the value of human dignity.[72]

The Chamber considered that moral considerations or social acceptability might be relevant when deciding whether to permit assisted reproduction, but could not justify a complete ban on a specific assisted reproductive technique. Once a state has decided to allow assisted procreation, it must adopt a coherent legal framework. The Chamber found that there was not sufficient justification for the difference in treatment between couples who, for medical reasons, need to resort to gamete donation in combination with IVF and couples who can have a child making use of assisted procreation procedures that do not include that particular technique.[73]

The Grand Chamber, however, reversed this decision, reaffirming that there was a wide margin of appreciation in situations where there was no European consensus,[74]

[66] *Evans v United Kingdom* (2008) 46 EHRR 34 [GC].
[67] *Evans v United Kingdom* (n 66) paras 71–2.
[68] *Evans v United Kingdom* (n 66) para 81.   [69] Joint dissenting opinion at para 12.
[70] *SH v Austria* (2010) 52 EHRR 6 (Chamber); *SH v Austria* App no 57813/00 (3 November 2011, GC).
[71] *SH* [GC] para 19.
[72] *SH* [GC] para 19.
[73] *SH* (Chamber) (n 70).
[74] The German and Italian Governments intervened in the case; the German Government argued that restrictions on certain IVF techniques were justified to protect the interests of the child and to prevent the possibility of 'split motherhood'; Italy argued that there should be a wide margin of appreciation given the lack of a European consensus in this area. There were also four NGO

especially where the case raised 'sensitive moral or ethical issues' and the states were balancing the legitimate interests of different parties.[75] This wide margin of appreciation did not just benefit the decision whether to permit the use of assisted reproduction technologies but also extended to the detailed rules adopted in any legislation.[76] The Grand Chamber found that the Austrian legislation was within the margin of appreciation. However, the judgment does include language indicating that the ECtHR might decide differently in a few years. The Grand Chamber noted there was an 'emerging consensus' permitting gamete donation for IVF, albeit that this was not yet based on settled principles.[77] The judgment concluded with a word of caution for the Austrian Government, highlighting that this was an area where there were 'particularly dynamic developments in science and law' and that the states needed to keep their legislation under review; the Grand Chamber mentioned the *Goodwin* case in this context presumably as an example that the ECtHR may decide to narrow the margin of appreciation if states do not act themselves.[78] As in *Evans*, four judges issued a strongly argued dissent, criticizing the majority's use of the margin of appreciation and the idea of a European consensus.[79]

The ECtHR regards one particular decision as being firmly within the national margin of appreciation: this is the decision on the status of the embryo.[80] In its early abortion decisions, the ECtHR was reluctant to enter this moral and ethical thicket:[81] Judge De Gaetano, in dissent, has described the ECtHR case law as 'exceptionally pusillanimous'.[82] During the 21st century, the modern Court has had the opportunity to revisit this question in cases from France, Poland, and Ireland.[83] In 2011, in *A B and C v Ireland*, the Grand Chamber reaffirmed that the decision as to when life begins falls within the national margin of appreciation. This is not because of a lack of European consensus on when abortion should be permitted; on the contrary, the Grand Chamber thought there was evidence of a European consensus permitting abortion in circumstances prohibited by Ireland.[84] Nevertheless, the Grand Chamber concluded that there was 'no European consensus on the scientific and legal definition of the beginning of life' and the issues concerned 'rights claimed on behalf of the foetus and those of the mother [that] are inextricably interconnected'; in those circumstances, at least where— as in Ireland—there had been extensive public debate on this question, the state was entitled to a wide margin of appreciation.[85] A significant number of judges issued separate and dissenting opinions in this case.[86]

---

interveners, two of which argued for upholding the Austrian regulation, while the other two argued there was no justification for the Austrian ban.

[75] *SH* [GC] (n 70) para 94.

[76] *SH* [GC] (n 70) para 97.

[77] *SH* [GC] (n 70) para 96.

[78] *SH* [GC] (n 70) para 118.

[79] Joint dissenting opinion of Judges Tulkens, Hirvelä, Lazarova Trajkovska, and Tsotsoria. On *Evans* and *SH*, see also Chapter 13 in this collection.

[80] Baxi (n 6) 236 indicates that courts may need to grapple with questions about the status of artificial intelligence or artificial life forms in the future.

[81] *Bruggeman and Scheuten v Germany* (1981) 3 EHRR 244.

[82] *RR v Poland* (2011) 53 EHRR 31, dissenting opinion at para 5.

[83] *Vo v France* App no 53924/00 (8 July 2004, ECtHR); *Tysiac v Poland* App no 5410/03 (20 March 2007, ECtHR); *RR* (n 82) *A B and C v Ireland* (2011) 53 EHRR 13 [GC].

[84] *A B and C* (n 83) para 235. On this case, see also Chapter 17 in this collection.

[85] *A B and C* (n 83) para 237.

[86] See notably the joint partly dissenting opinion of Judges Rozakis, Tulkens, Fura, Hirvelä, Malinverni, and Poalelungi, as well as concurring opinions by Judge López Guerra (joined by Judge Casadevall), and Judge Geoghegan.

The margin of appreciation figures prominently in any ECtHR consideration of NHTs. Its use has frequently been decisive, though it has also been controversial as is evident from the significant number of dissenting judges in these major cases. The cases demonstrate that the doctrine affords states considerable flexibility in the regulation of NHTs. Indeed, at one point during discussions about xenotransplantation, a representative of the ECtHR suggested that the ECHR 'should be understood as a legal instrument aimed at securing individual rights and as such it may be of limited relevance to policy issues in the field of bioethics.'[87]

Notwithstanding these comments and the pervasiveness of the margin of appreciation doctrine, we are not devoid of any guidance from the ECtHR. The margin of appreciation does not inevitably function as a trump card for national governments: there may be countervailing factors that narrow the margin of appreciation and—as *Goodwin* indicates—the doctrine may even evaporate. In short, as the next part demonstrates, the Council of Europe provides important minimum standards—even in this sensitive and rapidly evolving area—for the protection of rights.

D. Rights

As we have highlighted, a key feature of the Council of Europe's approach to the regulation of NHTs is that it allows a considerable degree of flexibility to the states. This does not mean that the Council of Europe provides infinitely malleable standards. The Council exists to protect and promote human rights, democracy, and the rule of law. However much flexibility may be required, the approach is still a rights-based one, and this comes across both in the Biomedicine Convention and in the case law of the ECtHR. To illustrate this important point, the next three sections examine how Council instruments protect autonomy type rights (for example, non-interference, privacy, but also personal development), and to some extent equality rights and the right to health.

1. Autonomy

Key to the ideal of autonomy is the right to not to be subject to physical (including medical) intervention without one's consent. The importance of autonomy in the Biomedicine Convention is emphasized by the early and detailed chapter on 'Consent'; this comes as the first chapter after the one laying out general principles. It establishes the general principle that any medical intervention requires 'free and informed consent' that may be withdrawn at any time.[88] There are specific safeguards for persons who are not able to give their consent,[89] while there is also a requirement to consider the previously expressed wishes of a person who is no longer able to give consent.[90]

Chapter V, on biomedical research, is also relevant. After stating that 'research in the field of biology and medicine shall be carried out freely, subject to the provisions of this Convention and other legal provisions ensuring the protection of the human being', this chapter contains basic principles on the protection of persons undergoing research (including persons not able to consent to research) and on research with embryos *in vitro*. Whereas the drawing-up of an intended additional protocol on embryo protection has as

---

[87] *Explanatory Report on Draft Recommendation Rec (2003) on Xenotransplantation* 19 June 2003 <https://wcd.coe.int/ViewDoc.jsp?id=39603&Site=CM> accessed 11 June 2012.

[88] Art 5.

[89] Arts 6–8.

[90] Art 9. This is the closest the Biomedicine Convention comes to considering living wills.

yet been unsuccessful,[91] the principles on the protection of persons undergoing research have been further elaborated in the Additional Protocol on Biomedical Research. This provides more detailed rules on ethical review, information and consent, research with persons not able to consent, some specific forms of research, safety and supervision, confidentiality, and the right to information.

A further aspect associated with autonomy is the right to respect for private life and in particular personal information. The Biomedicine Convention accords this protection in Chapter III, immediately following the chapter on consent. Article 10 specifically covers the right to know any information collected about one's health and the right not to be informed of such information.

Consent has also been covered in a number of rulings by the ECtHR. One of the more interesting is *Glass v United Kingdom*.[92] Doctors had administered diamorphine to a severely disabled minor and had put a 'do not resuscitate' (DNR) notice in his notes, without the agreement of the child's family. The ECtHR observed that any consent should be 'free, express and informed'; in the absence of such consent, the doctors could only treat the child on the basis of a court order.[93] The ECtHR also observed that the UK *general* approach—that parental consent is required and outside emergency circumstances can only be overridden by a court order—was compatible with the Biomedicine Convention (the United Kingdom has not signed, much less ratified this Convention).[94] Although this general approach was compatible with the ECHR and Biomedicine Convention, the specific actions under review in the instant case breached Article 8. Moreover, as found in *VC v Slovakia*, a case involving sterilization of a Roma woman, medical intervention without free and informed consent may violate not just Article 8 but also Article 3's prohibition on inhuman or degrading treatment.[95]

Autonomy also implies the right to keep some information private and to control the use of personal data, including biological data. This, in turn, implies that states must have regulations in place to protect the confidentiality of medical records.[96] An interesting example is the Article 8 case of *S and Marper v United Kingdom* on the retention of tissues, DNA profiles, and fingerprints for forensic purposes.[97] In this case, the ECtHR held that in addition to their highly personal nature, cellular samples contain much sensitive information about an individual, including information about his or her health. Moreover, samples contain a unique genetic code of great relevance to both the individual and his or her relatives. Given the nature and the amount of personal information contained in cellular samples, the ECtHR concluded that their retention per se was an interference with the right to respect for the private lives of the applicants.[98] In reaching this conclusion, the Court relied on the concern that the rapid evolution in both information technology and genetics might give rise to 'novel', possibly unforeseeable threats to the right to private life.[99] The Court reached the same

---

[91] Te Braake, 'Research on Human Embryos' in Gevers, Hondius, and Hubben (n 37).

[92] *Glass v United Kingdom* (n 57).

[93] *Glass v United Kingdom* (n 57) paras 82, 83.

[94] *Glass v United Kingdom* (n 57) para 75.

[95] *I v Finland* (2009) 48 EHRR 31.

[96] *I v Finland* (2009) 48 EHRR 31.

[97] *S and Marper v United Kingdom* (2009) 48 EHRR 50 [GC]. For further discussion, see R Brownsword and M Goodwin, *Law and the Technologies of the Twenty-First Century* (CUP 2012).

[98] *S and Marper* (n 97) para 73.

[99] *S and Marper* (n 97) para 71. Along these lines see also the partial dissent of Judge Zupančič in *Tătar and Tătar v Romania* App no 67021/01 (27 January 2009, ECtHR) where he says that Art 8 has a 'primordial value' and cannot be limited because of a lack of 'absolute certainty' especially in the context of modern illnesses.

view about the DNA profiles though with slightly more hesitation.[100] The Court held that the permanent storage of samples after the end of a criminal investigation, irrespective of the gravity of the offence, the age of the suspect, or whether there was a conviction, was disproportionate.[101] Although this case was about forensic use, it has direct implications in the health field, for instance with regard to the safeguards in case of storage and use of DNA samples for diagnostic and research purposes. Furthermore, the ECtHR was careful to indicate that the use of technology to achieve a desirable social good did not in any sense render human rights outmoded: 'modern scientific techniques' could not be 'allowed at any cost and without carefully balancing the potential benefits of the extensive use of such techniques against important private-life interests.'[102]

Autonomy-type rights do not merely protect rights of non-interference or privacy, however. Autonomy may extend to a right to personal development, to discover more about one's own origins, or to self-realization. The ECtHR has long held that Article 8 provides that people have a right to know about their origins, upbringing,[103] and parents;[104] though this right can de defeated by other legitimate interests.[105] In *Evans* the Grand Chamber of the ECtHR confirmed that Article 8 includes 'the right to personal autonomy, personal development and to establish and develop relationships with other human beings and the outside world', including the right to decide whether to become parents.[106] The Grand Chamber also recognized that *Evans* concerned a clash between these Article 8 rights of two private persons as well as wider concerns.[107] As we have already seen, however, the Member States have a wide margin of appreciation when discharging their positive obligations in respect of this right.

Although the margin of appreciation in these cases is wide, its invocation does not necessarily mean the state wins. *Dickson v United Kingdom* is a striking example of how the state may sometimes be found to have exceeded its margin of appreciation.[108] The two applicants were married; they had met while in prison. The husband had been jailed for murder and would not be released before 2009. The Home Secretary (an executive minister) refused them permission to use artificial insemination facilities to have a child, deeming the situation was not sufficiently exceptional to justify this. The Grand Chamber reaffirmed the earlier finding in *Evans* that Article 8 covered the right to respect for the wish to become genetic parents.[109] In *Dickson*, there were competing legitimate interests,[110] but the Grand Chamber concluded that the decision-making framework in the United Kingdom did not allow these interests to be balanced appropriately; the framework was heavily weighted against the interests of applicants and did not allow for a proper proportionality assessment of the decision to

---

[100] *S and Marper* (n 97) paras 74–7. The ECtHR also held that the retention of fingerprints constituted such an interference: para 86.

[101] *S and Marper* (n 97) paras 119–26.

[102] *S and Marper* (n 97) para 112.

[103] In the case of a child brought up in care: *Gaskin v United Kingdom* (1990) 12 EHRR 36.

[104] Everyone 'should be able to establish details of their identity....' *Mikulic v Croatia* App no 53176/99 (7 February 2002, ECtHR) para 54.

[105] *Odievre v France* (2003) 38 EHRR 43.

[106] *Evans v United Kingdom* (n 66) para 71, citing *Pretty v United Kingdom* (2002) 35 EHRR 1.

[107] *Evans v United Kingdom* (n 66) paras 73–4.

[108] *Dickson v United Kingdom* (2008) 46 EHRR 41 [GC].

[109] *Dickson v United Kingdom* (n 108) para 66.

[110] In *Dickson*, the ECtHR identifies a number of possibly conflicting interests and the need to balance them in paras 75, 76, 78, 81.

allow or deny permission to use such techniques.[111] That said, the deep diversity of views that marks this area of law is indicated by yet another joint dissenting opinion (by five judges), while the British judge changed his views as to the existence of a violation when sitting on the Grand Chamber, as compared to his views on the Chamber.[112]

2. Equality

Equality (along with autonomy and dignity) is one of the key principles underpinning human rights law and figures in every major human rights instrument. Article 1 of the Biomedicine Convention speaks of guaranteeing everyone 'without discrimination, respect for their integrity and other rights'. There is also a specific prohibition of discrimination based on 'genetic heritage' in Article 11. The principle of equality is also reflected in the provisions to protect persons who are not able to give consent themselves whether due to age or lack of capacity; special requirements are in place to safeguard these vulnerable groups.[113] Article 4 of the Biomedicine Convention requires states to provide 'equitable' access to health care. The Explanatory Report to the Biomedicine Convention explains that equitable access requires the 'absence of unjustified discrimination', though it does not require 'absolute equality'.[114]

Within the ECHR, non-discrimination figures as an accessory or parasitic right in Article 14; this guarantees non-discrimination in the enjoyment of other ECHR rights. The Council has adopted Protocol 12 that provides for a free-standing right to non-discrimination, though only eighteen states have ratified it.[115] Moreover, historically, the ECtHR has made limited use of the Article 14 clause and, though this has started to change in the last ten years,[116] any such evolution seems to have bypassed the area of NHTs, at least for now.

In *Evans*, the applicant sought to invoke Article 14 in conjunction with Article 8, arguing that she, being unable to conceive without the use of IVF, was subjected to the will of the sperm donor, while a woman not in her position was not so subject. The majority judgment, however, did not grapple with the possible issue of sex discrimination under Article 14, reasoning that the Article 8 discussion had addressed the issues.[117] The dissenters conceptualized the equality issue somewhat differently from the manner presented by the applicant. The dissenters argued that this situation called for different treatment of differently situated persons. In effect, the national legislation treated men and women in a symmetrical manner but this did not take account of the different situation of men and women concerning reproduction. The dissenters thought that the national authorities should have taken account of the 'excessive physical and emotional burden and effects' on the applicant in this case.[118]

The non-impact of Article 14 is also evident in *SH v Austria*. The Chamber found a breach of Article 14, but the Grand Chamber declined to consider the Article, relying

---

[111] *Dickson v United Kingdom* (n 108), paras 82–4.

[112] Joint dissenting opinion of Judges Wildhaber, Zupančič, Jungwiert, Gyulumyan, and Myjer; separate opinion of Judge Bratza.

[113] Arts 6, 7, 17, 20.

[114] Explanatory Report available at <http://conventions.coe.int/Treaty/en/Reports/Html/164.htm> accessed 29 May 2012.

[115] Protocol No 12 to the Convention for the Protection of Human Rights and Fundamental Freedoms, 2000, ETS 177. Ratification figures accurate as of 29 May 2012.

[116] R O'Connell, 'Cinderella Comes to the Ball: Article 14 and the Right to Non-Discrimination in the ECHR' (2009) 29 *Legal Studies* 211.

[117] *Evans v United Kingdom* (n 66) paras 93–5.

[118] *Evans v United Kingdom* (n 66), dissenting opinion at para 15, referring to *Thlimmenos v Greece* (2001) 31 EHRR 15.

on its assessment that Article 8 had not been breached. Moreover, even where the ECtHR has found a violation of the ECHR it has frequently declined to consider a discrimination argument. The ECtHR adopted this approach in *VC v Slovakia* even though, as noted by Judge Mijović in dissent, discrimination was the 'very essence' of the case.[119] In addition, in *Dickson*, where the issue was one of discriminatory access to artificial insemination facilities, the ECtHR did not mention discrimination or equality.

Despite this, the ECtHR has protected equality rights in its jurisprudence, even if it has preferred to rely on other provisions to do so. So, for example, the *Dickson* case clearly redressed some of the inequality inherent in requiring prisoners to show exceptional reasons before being granted access to artificial insemination techniques. In *VC,* the rights of Roma women were upheld, and the ECtHR spoke of the need under Article 8 for 'safeguards giving special consideration to the reproductive health of the applicant as a Roma woman'.[120] Finally, in *S and Marper*, the ECtHR noted concern about the disproportionate presence of young persons and ethnic minorities on the national database.[121]

The attitude of the ECtHR to equality rights in this field is therefore a mixed one. While it has upheld equality interests, it has frequently done so using a substantive provision of the ECHR rather than the non-discrimination provision. In this field at least, the ECtHR remains unwilling to use the non-discrimination clause to examine claims that involve *systematic* disadvantage imposed on women (*Evans*) or ethnic minorities (*VC*).

3. Right to Health

Neither the Biomedicine Convention nor the ECHR mention the right to health. As is notorious, the drafters of the ECHR left most socio-economic rights out of the ECHR.[122] Still, this has not stopped the ECtHR offering some indirect protection to these rights by expansively interpreting the mainly civil and political rights in the ECHR.[123] The ECtHR has sometimes relied on Articles 2, 3, and 8 to protect aspects of the right to health in specific contexts. It has laid down the principles that states have a positive obligation to secure to 'citizens their right to effective respect for the physical and psychological integrity', which requires 'the provision of a regulatory framework of adjudicatory and enforcement machinery protecting individuals' rights and the implementation, where appropriate, of specific measures . . .'.[124] The ECtHR has developed these principles in cases involving blood transfusion, environmental threats, right to information about health, and the provision of health care. These cases include suggestions as to how the ECtHR might approach questions of the management of risk to health.

---

[119] She also criticized the majority for failing to take account of the indirect discrimination case law as developed in *DH v Czech Republic* (2008) 47 EHRR 3, dissenting opinion of Judge Mijović.

[120] *VC v Slovakia* (n 58) para 154.

[121] *S and Marper* (n 97) para 124.

[122] *Collected Edition of the Travaux Preparatoires, Volume 1* (Martinus Nijhoff 1975) 194.

[123] I Koch, *Human Rights as Indivisible Rights: The Protection of Socio-economic Demands under the European Convention on Human Rights* (Martinus Nijhoff 2009); E Palmer, 'Protecting Socio-Economic Rights Through the European Convention on Human Rights: Trends and Developments in the European Court of Human Rights' (2009) 2 *Erasmus Law Review* 397.

[124] *A B and C v Ireland* (n 83) para 245.

The ECtHR has considered several cases involving blood transfusion services;[125] some of the principles adopted in those cases may also apply to the use of newer health technologies (for example, xenotransplantation, modifications of the human genome). In *Oyal v Turkey*, a child was infected with HIV after he received a contaminated blood transfusion.[126] The child and his family received some compensation but this was sufficient only to cover one year's medical expenses.[127] The ECtHR reiterated that the ECHR 'lays down a positive obligation on States to take appropriate steps to safeguard the lives of those within its jurisdiction'.[128] These obligations included adopting regulations for public and private hospitals to ensure they took steps to protect the right to life; the state must also provide for adequate judicial accountability.[129] In this case, the redress offered to the family was insufficient; the ECtHR indicated the courts should have ordered such compensation as would provide for life-time treatment and medication.[130]

The right to health has figured in the environmental rights case law of the ECtHR.[131] The ECtHR has found that threats to health originating from environmental problems can violate Articles 2 and 8, and has imposed positive obligations on the states in this area. Notably these obligations include the duty to carry out studies[132] and to provide information to those affected,[133] the duty to have in place legislative and administrative structures to prevent harm,[134] and the duty to provide for remedies.[135] In addition, in at least one case, the ECtHR has invoked the 'principle of precaution' to stress that the absence of scientific certainty should not be a reason to delay the adoption of effective and proportionate protective measures.[136]

The ECtHR has, in turn, relied on these environmental rights cases to develop the right to information in particular health-related contexts.[137] It has affirmed that there may be a positive obligation to adopt 'regulations concerning access to information about an individual's health'[138] including, in appropriate cases, access to the results of genetic testing where these are available.[139] In addition, in a special context where the applicant (a former soldier) had participated in chemical warfare tests during the 1960s, the ECtHR insisted that the state provide an 'effective and accessible procedure' to enable the applicant to access information that would permit him to assess any health risk.[140]

---

[125] See eg *GN v Italy* App no 431 34/05 (1 December 2009; and 15 March 2011).

[126] *Oyal v Turkey* (2010) 51 EHRR 30.

[127] *Oyal v Turkey* (n 126) para 37.

[128] *Oyal v Turkey* (n 126) para 53.

[129] *Oyal v Turkey* (n 126) para 54.

[130] *Oyal v Turkey* (n 126) para 72.

[131] *Hatton v United Kingdom* (2003) 37 EHRR 28 [GC]; *Taşkın v Turkey* (2004) 42 EHRR 50; *Giacomelli v Italy* (2007) 45 EHRR 38.

[132] *Tătar and Tătar v Romania* App no 67021/01 (27 January 2009, ECtHR) para 88.

[133] *Guerra v Italy* (1998) 26 EHRR 357.

[134] *Öneryildiz v Turkey* (2005) 41 EHRR 20 [GC]; *Di Sarno v Italy* App no 30765/08 (10 January 2012, ECtHR).

[135] *Taşkın v Turkey* (2004) 42 EHRR 50, paras 122–125.

[136] *Tătar and Tătar v Romania* (n 132) paras 109, 120. See also the concurring opinion of Judge Zupančič in *Băcilă v Romania* App no 19234/04 (30 March 2010, ECtHR).

[137] *Roche v United Kingdom* (2006) 42 EHRR 30 [GC]; *KH v Slovakia* (2009) 49 EHRR 34; *I v Finland* (2009) 48 EHRR 31.

[138] *RR v Poland* (n 82) para 188.

[139] *RR v Poland* (n 82) para 197.

[140] *Roche v United Kingdom* (n 137) para 162, 167.

The ECtHR is, however, reluctant to require states to provide medical care;[141] this comes across in extradition or deportation cases where an individual is being sent to a home country which offers markedly inferior health facilities.[142] That said, in one special context, the provision of health care is required: this is where an individual is detained and so cannot look after his or her own health. For example, the ECtHR has required states to take steps to provide proper treatment for prisoners with hepatitis C,[143] HIV Aids,[144] anorexia,[145] and other problems; to protect a prisoner with lung disease from passive smoking;[146] and to provide the same health care as is available to the general public, including a dental prosthesis.[147]

Recently, though, the ECtHR has identified one situation where the ECHR requires medical treatment for someone not in detention; this is where national law provides a right to specific medical treatment. In *Panaitescu v Romania*, the applicant (who died before the Court judgment), had been entitled under national law to receive free cancer medication. This entitlement was confirmed by a national court, but the court's judgment was not fully implemented. In these circumstances, the ECtHR found a violation of Article 2, the right to life.[148]

This last case demonstrates how the ECtHR can uphold the right to health even though the right is not specified in the text of the ECHR. While the absence of the right to health from the ECHR is relatively unsurprising (given the text's orientation towards civil and political rights), the absence of a right to health from the Biomedicine Convention is more surprising. Article 1 of the Biomedicine Convention refers to 'equitable access to health care' which is a narrower notion than the right to health.[149] An obligation to provide 'equitable access to health care' is nevertheless important, even if qualified (states must take into account 'health needs and available resources'; states must take 'appropriate' measures to provide care of 'appropriate' quality).[150] The Explanatory Report on the Convention specifies, however, that this does not create an individual right.[151] The Biomedicine Convention therefore does not go as far as Article 12 of the International Covenant on Economic, Social and Cultural Rights 1966 or Article 11 of the European Social Charter 1961.

On a more critical interpretation, the situation regarding the right to health in the Biomedicine Convention may be worse. Critics of the dignity-orientation in this text might object that the Convention discourages or even prohibits certain interventions that might promote the right to health in the longer term. On this critical view, the Biomedicine Convention paradoxically impedes the realization of the right to health. It is time to turn to the most controversial aspect of the Biomedicine Convention, its invocation of human dignity.

---

[141] *Nitecki v Poland* App no 65653/01 (21 March 2002, ECtHR); *Pentiacova v Moldova* (2005) 40 EHRR SE23 63.

[142] *N v United Kingdom* (2008) 47 EHRR 39, para 44 [GC]. This limits the earlier judgment in *D v United Kingdom* (1997) 24 EHRR 423 to relatively extreme situations.

[143] Violation of Art 3: *Poghosyan v Georgia* App no 9870/07 (24 February 2009, ECtHR).

[144] Violation of Art 3: *AB v Russia* App no 1439/06 (14 October 2010, ECtHR).

[145] Violation of Art 3: *Raffray Taddei v France* App no 36435/07 (21 December 2010, ECtHR).

[146] Violation of Art 3: *Elefteriadis v Romania* App no 38427/05 (25 January 2011, ECtHR).

[147] Violation of Art 3: *VD v Romania* App no 7078/02 (16 February 2010, ECtHR).

[148] *Panaitescu v Romania* App no 30909/06 (10 April 2012, ECtHR), para 37.

[149] F Callard, 'Between Legislation and Bioethics: The European Convention on Human Rights and Biomedicine' (2010) 45 *Ethics in Psychiatry* 73, 79.

[150] Art 1.

[151] Council of Europe (n 51) para 26.

E. Dignity

The concept of dignity is often central in any discussion of human rights, bioethics, and NHTs.[152] Being unavoidable does not, however, make it straightforward, for at least three reasons.

First, the relationship between dignity and human rights is both unclear and contested.[153] Thus, dignity might provide the foundation for human rights; this appears to be the role assigned to dignity in the UDHR 1948. Or dignity might be a right itself, as in the German Constitution of 1949 or the Hungarian or South African Constitutions.[154] Equally, dignity might function as an interpretative value in a human rights scheme, that is, it may be a value that influences the interpretation of rights.[155]

This last aspect suggests that dignity may be best conceived as an ethical value; in this role, dignity might serve as a legitimate reason to restrict the development of NHTs or even to restrict the exercise of rights. This is perhaps the tension highlighted by Roger Brownsword who identifies two versions of dignity: one (dignity as empowerment) is associated with human rights while the other (dignity as constraint) is more concerned with restricting certain applications of biomedical technology.[156] In the latter version, dignity sometimes appears as a sophisticated version of the 'yuck factor' and acts as a 'non-negotiable, one line, reason' to reject certain policies.[157]

Disagreement about dignity is not, however, limited to questions of its relationship with human rights. A second reason for complexity is that authors disagree on what dignity means; whilst we might agree with Kant that dignity attaches to that which is 'exalted above all price', we may not agree with him that it is rooted in autonomy.[158] Furthermore, a third problematic aspect of dignity is that there is no agreement on the subject who is entitled to dignity: this might be the human individual or the human species; dignity might attach to entities that are not autonomous human persons;[159] depending on our conception of dignity we could meaningfully talk of the dignity of the severely incapacitated, embryos, dead bodies, or even non-human animals.[160] The Preamble to the Biomedicine Convention itself draws attention to some of these tensions when it speaks about the need to respect the human being 'both as an

---

[152] D Beyleveld and R Brownsword, *Human Dignity in Bioethics and Biolaw* (OUP 2001).

[153] On the different uses of human dignity in human rights see C McCrudden, 'Human Dignity and Judicial Interpretation of Human Rights' (2008) 19 *European Journal of International Law* 655; T Khaitan, 'Dignity as an Expressive Norm: Neither Vacuous Nor a Panacea' (2012) 32 *Oxford Journal of Legal Studies* 1.

[154] Art 54 of the Hungarian Constitution; section 10 of the South African Constitution 1996.

[155] Section 39 of the South African Constitution.

[156] R Brownsword, 'Human Dignity, Ethical Pluralism, and the Regulation of Modern Biotechnologies' in Murphy (n 25) 26.

[157] T Caulfield and R Brownsword, 'Human Dignity: A Guide to Policy Making in the Biotechnology Era?' (2005) 7(1) *Nature Reviews Genetics* 72, 72 and 74.

[158] I Kant, *The Moral Law (Groundwork of the Metaphysic of Morals)* (Hutchinson 1948) 77, 79.

[159] Dwyer discusses how Beyleveld and Brownsword (n 153) differ from Gewirth in analysing the question of how to treat creatures that are not clearly agents even though all rely on an agency-oriented conception: D Dwyer, 'Beyond Autonomy: The Role of Dignity in "Biolaw"' (2003) 23 *Oxford Journal of Legal Studies* 319, 325.

[160] JR Herrmann, 'Use of the Dead Body in Healthcare and Medical Training: Mapping and Balancing the Legal Rights and Values' (2011) 18 *European Journal of Health Law* 277. In one case the ECtHR has referred to the 'right to respect for the dead' as a factor to consider when deciding whether a DNA test can be carried out on a deceased person in order to determine paternity: *Jaggi v Switzerland* (2008) 47 EHRR 30, para 39. The ECtHR held (5–2) that Art 8 required the test in that case, noting that the deceased's Art 8 rights would not be affected by the test: see para 42. The ECtHR has declared admissible a case about the treatment of dead bodies: *Sabanchiyeva v Russia* App no 38450/05 (6 November 2008, ECtHR).

individual and as a member of the human species', thereby highlighting the collective as well as the individual notion of dignity.

These differences over the relationship between dignity and rights, the meaning of dignity, and the subject of dignity, make universal agreement on dignity unlikely. We may well find that there are distinct national differences in how dignity should be understood. Susan Millns, for instance, highlights that there is a difference between the treatment of dignity in the decisions of the constitutional tribunals of France and Germany (specifically in relation to abortion).[161] One might also speculate whether there is a distinctively European conception of dignity as distinct from an Asian, African, or American (US) notion. One might even point to the Biomedicine Convention as an explicit step in articulating a European conception of dignity, but the very patchy ratification of this Convention makes it difficult to confirm that it expresses a pan-European consensus on dignity.

Even if it does not represent a pan-European consensus, the human dignity orientation is strong in the Biomedicine Convention, as evidenced, for instance, by the restrictions on genetic testing and interventions on the human genome, and the prohibition of sex selection and creating embryos for research purposes. This is not surprising, because issues of life, health, and death raise ethical concerns. The Preamble to the Biomedicine Convention speaks of the importance of ensuring the 'dignity of the human being'—and this is both as an individual and as a species. The Preamble also warns of the dangers to human dignity posed by the misuses of biology and medicine. If one looks at the substance of all the rules in the Biomedicine Convention, their focus is on protection of human dignity as well as the protection of rights (discussed earlier). The idea of dignity (and specifically dignity as a constraint) is exemplified in the limitations or prohibitions placed on interventions on the human genome,[162] sex selection,[163] creation of embryos for research,[164] and reproductive cloning.[165] Dignity is also embedded in the prohibition on making a financial gain out of the human body.[166] Apart from the Biomedicine Convention and its protocols,[167] the Council of Europe has adopted a number of recommendations that also touch on dignity and ethics.[168] As a result of these provisions the Biomedicine Convention may not only facilitate technological developments, but also slow them down or bring them to a halt where they are incompatible with human dignity.

The invocation of dignity (especially dignity as constraint) in the Biomedicine Convention has provoked considerable criticism. Millns sees the reliance on dignity as both 'remarkable' but also 'fuzzy'.[169] Cutas has argued that the Convention's notion

---

[161] S Millns, 'Consolidating Bio-rights in Europe' in F Francioni (ed), *Biotechnologies and International Human Rights* (Hart 2007).

[162] Art 13.

[163] Art 14.

[164] Art 18(2).

[165] Art 1(1) of the Additional Protocol on the Prohibition of Cloning Human Beings.

[166] Art 21. See also Chapter VI of the Additional Protocol on Transplantation of Organs and Tissue of Human Origin.

[167] The Additional Protocol on Transplantation of Organs and Tissue of Human Origin prescribes that the dead body must be treated with respect (Art 18); the requirement of ethical approval for research on human subjects is imposed by the Additional Protocol on Biomedical Research: Chapter III.

[168] Examples include R (2001) 5 on organ transplantation waiting lists and waiting times, R (2003) 10 on xenotransplantation, R (2003) 12 on organ donor registries, R (2005) 11 on the role and training of professionals responsible for organ transplantation, and R (2006) 16 on the quality improvement programmes for organ donation.

[169] Millns (n 161) 76.

of dignity is not coherent with some of the classic expositions of the concept; indeed according to Cutas, the Convention's position is impious in seeking to deny the freedom to choose that God bestowed on man.[170] Hottois is similarly sceptical, arguing that the Biomedicine Convention contains 'techno-scientophobic accents'[171] and enshrines value judgements that are not universally shared.[172]

The text of the ECHR—unlike the Biomedicine Convention—does not explicitly mention the term 'dignity'. It is only in the 13th Protocol that one finds a preambular reference to this value. Despite this, in the last decade or so, ECtHR judges have increasingly woven the value into their judgments and individual opinions.[173] In *Goodwin*, the ECtHR indicated that society could be expected to suffer some inconveniences if this was necessary to enable post-operative transsexuals to 'live in dignity and worth in accordance with the sexual identity chosen by them at great personal cost'.[174] In the recent case of *MS v United Kingdom*, the ECtHR said that the detention of the mentally ill applicant for three days in police custody without access to psychiatric treatment 'diminished excessively his fundamental human dignity'.[175]

Dignity has also appeared in ECtHR cases as a factor in the justification of limits on rights, particularly in relation to the qualified Article 8 right. States can regulate or limit this right to protect a wide range of legitimate public interests; thus, dignity might figure as a legitimate reason to regulate or limit rights claims, especially bearing in mind the margin of appreciation. This is all the more true as national legislation in this field will be concerned about regulating and balancing the rights of different individuals. The ECtHR mentions this explicitly in *Evans*, when it explains that the UK's regulations on IVF were adopted with a view to show '[r]espect for human dignity and free will' by assuring each donor of the right to withdraw consent.[176] In *SH v Austria*, the Grand Chamber accepted that Austrian legislation, intended to respect (one conception of) human dignity, was compatible with the Convention.[177] These cases suggest that where states regulate (or restrict) access to NHTs in the interests of protecting a particular conception of dignity, then the ECtHR may well find the regulation to be compatible with the ECHR.

Despite this emergence of dignity as a value in the ECtHR case law, a clash between dignity (as understood in the Biomedicine Convention) and the ECHR is conceivable. A state might for instance *permit* a practice proscribed by the dignity-oriented clauses of the Biomedicine Convention. In the *SH* case, the separate opinion of Judge De Gaetano draws attention to this problem; in this opinion the judge criticizes the *Dickson* case for making dignity play 'second fiddle to advances in medical science'.[178]

---

[170] D-E Cutas, 'Looking for the Meaning of Dignity in the Bioethics Convention and the Cloning Protocol' (2005) 13 *Health Care Analysis* 303, 307.

[171] G Hottois, 'A Philosophical and Critical Analysis of the European Convention of Bioethics' (2000) 25 *Journal of Medicine and Philosophy* 133, 137.

[172] Hottois (n 171) 141.

[173] As well as the cases discussed in the text, there are references to dignity in *Odievre v France* (2003) 38 EHRR 43, *VC v Slovakia* (n 58); and the concurring opinion of Judge Zupančič in *Băcilă v Romania* (n 136).

[174] *Goodwin v United Kingdom* (n 62) para 91.

[175] *MS v United Kingdom* App no 24527/08 (3 May 2012, ECtHR) para 44.

[176] *Evans v United Kingdom* (n 66) para 89.

[177] *SH v Austria* (n 71) para 113.

[178] *SH v Austria* (n 71) para 3 of Judge De Gaetano's opinion. Judge Marcus-Helmons alludes to this possibility in one of the Cypriot cases; his partly dissenting opinion also suggests that Art 2 should be interpreted to include the 'freedom to seek to enjoy the best physically available treatment'. *Cyprus v Turkey* (2001) 35 EHRR 30 [GC], paras O-V16–17.

Judge De Gaetano asserts that dignity may require the prohibition of 'certain acts in order to bear witness to the inalienable value and intrinsic dignity of every human being'.[179] Despite Judge De Gaetano's opinion, it is not obvious that the ECHR would allow a successful challenge to a state measure on the ground that it violated human dignity (as opposed to an identifiable person's rights). The margin of appreciation doctrine and the possibility to offer justifications for the restriction of qualified rights might impede such arguments; furthermore, the ECHR's standing requirement may be a problem. If, for instance, a state permitted the sale of organs (with the consent of the donor), it would require some expansive interpretation of the ECHR to find such a policy violated a right (perhaps the Article 3 right not to be subject to degrading treatment) but even if this could be done the standing requirement would have to be addressed even before this could be considered. The ECHR has a relatively strict standing requirement in that only a victim (or a dead victim's family) can bring an application to the ECtHR. It is not clear that anyone is a victim in the case of the voluntary sale of organs, and this is even more problematic when one considers who might be a victim in a case about alterations to the human genome.[180] While these factors make it difficult to use the ECHR to challenge policies incompatible with the dignity-oriented provisions of the Biomedicine Convention, the possibility is not excluded. For instance, a person who agreed to sell organs might change their mind, and argue that no one could legitimately consent to such a sale (as degrading treatment) any more than one could consent to being sold as a slave.

F. Governance

We have drawn attention, throughout the chapter, to the variable and flexible nature of the Council of Europe approach in relation to NHTs. This possibility for flexibility is important because states may adopt very different approaches to regulation in this field. These might range from market-based approaches to systems that rely heavily on regulation and proscription; they might include approaches that involve a mix of different forms of regulation (markets as well as statutory regulation, voluntary regulation as well as formal law, indirect as well as direct regulation, procedural as well as substantive law, general principles as well as technology-specific legislation). All these approaches are possible within the Council of Europe framework thanks to the variable and flexible nature of the standards involved. It would, however, be unsatisfactory if that were all we could say about the Council of Europe framework in this field.

Fortunately, we can say rather more. We have already noted that the Council of Europe instruments—including the ECHR which has been ratified by all Council Member States—requires respect for a minimum core of rights. These include autonomy-type rights (the consent principle, respect for private life), but also to some extent equality and the right to health. These rights set a minimum standard for regulation. Their implications could, however, be pushed further. For instance, important possible implications may be to: ensure adequate information on the benefits and risks of the use of the technology in question; help and protect persons who cannot make decisions of their own; ensure the quality and safety of new technological applications

---

[179] *SH v Austria* (n 71) para 6.
[180] In its environmental case law the ECtHR has said that there is no Convention right to 'nature preservation' though the Art 8 right might be affected by environmental pollution: *Fadeyeva v Russia* App no 55723/00 (9 June 2005, ECtHR) para 68.

for the public; and see to it that the use of NHTs does not increase existing social inequalities.[181]

Moreover, beyond the protections of these rights, both the Biomedicine Convention and the ECHR encourage certain principles for governance in this area. The Biomedicine Convention does this explicitly in Article 28 which concerns public debate:

Parties to this Convention shall see to it that the fundamental questions raised by the developments of biology and medicine are the subject of appropriate public discussion in the light, in particular, of relevant medical, social, economic, ethical and legal implications, and that their possible application is made the subject of appropriate consultation.

Given the importance of the issues raised by NHTs, it is desirable that their regulation be publicly debated in a democratic society. This Article in the Biomedicine Convention is, of course, mainly hortatory; however, the ECtHR jurisprudence includes comments which, at the very least, nudge states in the direction of having public, informed debates on these matters. For example, the conclusion in *Evans* that the United Kingdom had not breached its positive obligations under Article 8 rested in part on the fact the United Kingdom had undertaken 'an exceptionally detailed examination of the social, ethical and legal implications of developments in the field of human fertilisation and embryology'; the resulting legislative framework was 'the fruit of much reflection, consultation and debate'.[182] Similarly, in *A B and C*, the case on Ireland's abortion laws, the ECtHR was influenced by the extent of public deliberation on the topic.[183]

The Chamber judgment in *SH* initially went further, in requiring legislative distinctions within an assisted reproduction regime to be shown to be justified. As explained earlier, the Grand Chamber reversed this decision: however, despite this reversal, the non-discrimination clause—Article 14 ECHR—may still have a role to play in ensuring the rationality of legislative distinctions in this field. If a state failed to offer *any* rational justification for a distinction, then this might breach Article 14. Furthermore, even though the Austrian legislation survived the Grand Chamber's scrutiny, the Court laid down a marker for the Austrian Government, noting that the Austrian Parliament had 'not, until now, undertaken a thorough assessment of the rules governing artificial procreation, taking into account the dynamic developments in science and society.'[184] This was potent advice that the Austrian authorities should remember that the ECtHR's use of the margin of appreciation could evolve.[185] While the ECtHR did not find a violation in either *Evans* or *SH*, it did find a violation in *Dickson*. One of the reasons for finding a violation was that the UK Parliament had never considered how to balance the competing interests in that case on access to artificial insemination facilities for prisoners; indeed, the policy had been adopted prior to the incorporation of the ECHR into domestic law.[186]

These cases have important implications for the quality of democratic governance when it comes to the regulation of NHTs. They imply that there must be actual public deliberation on the balancing of interests that is required in such regulation. In one sense, this is a typical judicial 'procedural' response to avoid deciding difficult substantive questions. On the other hand, however, it can be seen as encouraging the democratic debate which is essential for any responsible decision-making in this field.

---

181 Baxi (n 6) 216 warns of this last danger.   182 *Evans v United Kingdom* (n 66) para 86.
183 *A B and C v Ireland* (n 83) para 237.   184 *SH v Austria* (n 70) para 117.
185 *SH v Austria* (n 70) para 118.   186 *Dickson v United Kingdom* (n 108) para 83.

G. Conclusion

Having examined in detail the approach of the Council of Europe to the regulation of NHTs, we suggest that there are five key facets of the Council's engagement in this area.

First, the approach of the Council of Europe is a multi-layered one, ranging from the very general basic principles incorporated in the ECHR to the detailed technical rules laid down in the technical guidance documents elaborated in the fields of blood transfusion and organ donation. The more general rules do not only have a wider scope, they also have a stronger legal status ('hard law', instead of the 'soft law' of recommendations and guidelines). On the other hand, the fundamental rights embodied in the ECHR regulate NHTs only in an indirect way. The guidance provided by recommendations and comparable documents relates much more directly to their development and use. The Biomedicine Convention and its Additional Protocols are somewhere in the middle between fundamental rights and technology-specific standards.

Secondly, the Council of Europe framework for regulation in this area is flexible and variable. This stems partly from the intergovernmental nature of instruments like the Biomedicine Convention, and partly from the ECtHR's margin of appreciation doctrine. Flexibility, as we have seen, is qualified: the margin of appreciation may change over time (*Goodwin*) and is subject to the possibility that the ECtHR may find factors that justify more intense scrutiny (*Dickson*). While this flexibility, in the guise of the margin of appreciation, has been criticized as 'pusillanimous' and merely a 'pragmatic substitute for a thought-out approach', this feature of the Council of Europe's system is eminently understandable given that NHTs raise issues of deep and reasonable disagreement.[187]

Thirdly, despite this flexibility, the human rights framework is not infinitely malleable but serves at least two vital functions. The first function is to secure a minimum level of respect for human rights, especially autonomy-type rights such as the requirement of free and informed consent (*Glass*, *VC*), and the right to respect for private life (*S and Marper*), but also the right to health (*Oyal*) and, to at least some extent, the right to equality and non-discrimination. The second function is that it indicates which interests need to be considered, promoted, and balanced in whatever national regulatory framework is adopted.

Fourthly, there is a difference in approach between the Biomedicine Convention and the ECHR; while both arguably rely on notions of dignity, in the former case this is explicit and, more importantly, is linked to the ethical idea of dignity as constraint. Despite this difference, the potential for any actual clash is largely, though not entirely, avoided by the intergovernmental character of the former and the margin of appreciation doctrine and victim standing requirement in the latter.

Finally, while the Council of Europe permits states considerable flexibility in how they regulate NHTs (subject to respect for human rights), the Biomedicine Convention and the ECtHR jurisprudence encourage the need for informed public debate on these questions in a democratic society.

In conclusion, the Council of Europe approach to the regulation of NHTs is a multi-layered, variable, and flexible one. All, however, is not variability and vicissitude; the human rights framework provides, if not fixed points, certainly fixed reference points in our ever-changing age.

---

[187] T Murphy, 'Repetition, Revolution and Resonance: An Introduction to New Technologies and Human Rights' in Murphy (n 25) 10.

4

Mapping Science and New Health Technologies: In Search of a Definition

*Amanda Warren-Jones**

Technological development is a key human endeavour, but part of mankind's social responsibility is ensuring that advancement is not sought at any cost. In consequence, new technology is regulated by different mechanisms at critical developmental stages. The gravity of the regulatory task becomes most obvious in the context of health care. In this context, products and processes are rigorously regulated at a level commensurate to the risk inherent in applying new technology to those in need of medical intervention. The complexity of regulation is apparent in just a few examples of developmental stages: research funding is subject to ethical, scientific, and political considerations; and clinical trials are subject to scientific analysis through a market authorization system, as well as the analysis of ethical review bodies, and principles of good clinical practice while trials are on-going. This complexity is compounded by the form of regulation changing according to the nature of the health technology: specifically, medicines are subject to different forms of oversight in comparison to devices, both of which are different to the regulation of treatment protocols. In addition, regulation precedes the creation of technology (for example, research funding regulates the general focus of scientific research even before medical innovation occurs) and continues for as long as the product/process is used (for example, pharmacovigilance,[1] risk management plans,[2] and product liability[3] regulate market safety).

The current regulatory framework for health technology innovation has arisen from the need to secure a safe and effective system of health care: providing new forms of medical treatments; prophylactics;[4] diagnostics and monitoring mechanisms; as well as increasing mankind's knowledge of the human body. With the prospect of reducing deaths and enhancing the quality of life, it cannot be doubted that everyone has a stake in ensuring that health technology regulation (whether aimed at isolated aspects of

---

* This chapter is based on a paper entitled 'Mapping Science and New Health Technologies: an overview of current debates in Europe' presented at the ESRC Research Seminar Series 'European Law and New Health Technologies', Seminar 1: Introducing the Core Research Questions and Developing Research Capacity (Mapping the Research Agenda) (ERSC Research Seminar Series 2009).

[1] This is a system for ensuring the safety of medicines while they are marketed and includes activities such as adverse drug reaction reportage which enables a doctor (or patient in some instances) to identify side effects of pharmaceuticals.

[2] These are often required by pharmaceutical companies as part of the process of market authorization and relate to plans for ensuring safety in the event that clinical trials data has not identified risks that actually arise once the product is put on the market.

[3] This refers to a system of legal protection against manufacturers/suppliers of products which are dangerous, defectively manufactured, or do not provide sufficient warnings at the point of sale.

[4] Preventative treatments such as vaccinations.

regulation,[5] or not,[6] or at discrete technological applications within medicine,[7] or at technology collectively[8]) is effective and that it is fully negotiated by all affected parties: policymakers, regulators, scientists (including engineers, computer programmers, doctors, etc.), academics, and the public. This fully inclusive approach may not require a shared system of values,[9] but it does require at least a shared understanding of terms[10] in order to appreciate what is being regulated. This is a crucial first step which must be achieved before it becomes possible to consider how to regulate.

New or emerging technologies have become a particular focus of diverse multi-disciplinary debates[11] because of the increasingly complex nature of recent scientific advances (such as biotechnology[12], nanotechnology,[13] tissue engineering,[14] and mono-clonal antibody technology).[15] In consequence, discourse on these new technologies

---

[5] eg T Murphy (ed.), *New Technologies and Human Rights* (OUP 2009); H Busby, T Hervey, and A Mohr, 'Ethical EU Law? The Influence of the European Group on Ethics in Science and New Technologies' (2008) 33(6) *European Law Review* 803; A Cygan, 'Public Healthcare in the European Union: Still a Service of General Interest?' (2008) 57(3) *International & Comparative Law Quarterly* 529; M Steffen (ed.), *Health Governance in Europe: issues, challenges and theories* (ECPR Studies in European Political Science, Routledge 2005); A Arundel, 'Biotechnology Indicators and Public Policy' *OECD Science, Technology and Industry Working Papers 2003/5* (OECD 2003); SJR Bostyn, 'The Prodigal Son: the Relationship Between Patent Law and Health Care' (2003) 11(1) *Medical Law Review* 67; PA Kaufert, 'Health Policy and the New Genetics' (2000) 51 *Social Science and Medicine* 821; JE Paul and P Trueman, '"Fourth Hurdle Reviews", NICE, and Database Applications' (2001) 10 *Pharmacoepidemiology and Drug Safety* 429.

[6] eg TK Hervey and JV McHale, *Health Law and the European Union* (CUP 2004).

[7] eg SR Donnelly, 'Patentability of Human Embryonic Stem Cells' (2011) 20 *Dalhousie Journal of Legal Studies* 151; JB Krauss and T Takenaka, 'A Special Rule for Compound Protection for DNA Sequences—Impact of the ECJ "Monsanto" Decision on Patent Practice' (2011) 93(2) *Journal of the Patent and Trademark Office Society* 189; LJ Valverde and I Linkov, 'Nanotechnology: Risk Assessment and Risk Management Perspective' (2011) 8(1) *Nanotechnology Law and Business* 25.

[8] Special Issue, 'Material Worlds: Intersections of Law, Science, Technology, and Society' (2012) 39(1) *Journal of Law & Society*, in particular: A Faulkner, B Lange, and C Lawless, 'Introduction', 1; J Lezaun, 'The Pragmatic Sanction of Materials: Notes for an ethnography of legal substances', 20; C Rooke, E Cloatre, and R Dingwall, 'The Regulation of Nicotine in the United Kingdom: How Nicotine Gum Came to be a Medicine, But Not a Drug', 39; and A Mahalatchimy, E Rial-Sebbag, V Tournay, and A Faulkner, 'The Legal Landscape of Advanced Therapies: Material and institutional implementation of European Union rules in France and the United Kingdom', 131; and from other sources: MC Roco, 'Possibilities for Global Governance of Converging Technologies' (2008) 10 *Journal of Nanopart Research* 11–29; Symposium, 'Toward a General Theory of Law and Technology' (2007) 8(2) *Minnesota Journal of Law, Science & Technology*.

[9] R Brownsword, 'Regulating Human Genetics: New Dilemmas for a New Millennium' (2004) 12(1) *Medical Law Review* 14.

[10] Roco (n 8) particularly 24–5.

[11] Exemplified in nn 5–9, and at nn 17, 27, 28, 30, 32, 37, 38, and 40.

[12] This broadly refers to a raft of procedures known as 'recombination', which alter genomic DNA (in the nucleus of cells), such as splicing (a form of 'cut and paste' of small parts of the genomic DNA), and extends to more dramatic genomic interventions, such as cloning (which involve the whole of the genomic DNA).

[13] This broadly relates to similar interventions as recombination on an atomic/molecular scale (as opposed to the micro-organism scale of biotechnology), but is not confined to biological matter (this enables miniscule machines to be made, which can be utilized to perform repairing functions, for example).

[14] Also known as regenerative medicine, tissue engineering enables new human tissue to be grown for transplantation either with or without the use of scaffolds to create structural elements. Eg, the artificial growth of skins cells for the treatment of burn victims, the creation of a human nervous system, and the use of a scaffold to create a human ear (which although lacking aural capacity, provides a cosmetic benefit).

[15] Also known as 'hybridoma technology', this involves the creation of immortal cell production systems which manufacture antibodies designed to fight a specific disease.

inevitably encounters difficulties in successfully exchanging information (both among specialists and with the public) because terminology and concepts are not standard. This is only made worse by the technology not being established or easily comprehensible. The absence of shared understanding results in failure to reach a consensus (or form opinions). Therefore, deciding how to regulate new health technologies (for example, through the creation and evolution of relevant regulatory bodies; the development of institutional aims; the formation and implementation of policies and regulatory principles; and the ensuing debates which facilitate regulatory improvement and adaptation) can only be undertaken once the concept of what is being regulated ('new health technology' (NHT)) has become a broadly shared frame of reference.

This chapter argues that the concept of NHT is not presently clearly defined and that the absence of a common vocabulary prevents a shared dialogue and hampers effective regulation. After exploring the scope for using interpretive tools, this chapter proposes a common vocabulary, in the form of a definition which is predominantly derived by 'mapping' existing terms (see Figure 4.1), to overcome difficulties with communication and enabling regulation to become more easily accessible.

Section A reviews current approaches to defining NHT within policy, academic, and scientific discourses.[16] Examining disparate fields of expertise identifies a fundamental mismatch in terminology between individual disciplines, as well as problems associated with rationalizing language for technology which is so rapidly evolving. An analysis of a sample of relevant regulation (governing tissue engineering) demonstrates that this disjointed terminology has impaired the effectiveness of regulation.

The analysis in Section A is evidenced predominantly in the context of Europe for three reasons. The first reason is to align this chapter with the content of other contributions to this book. Secondly, technology in Europe is subject to a mix of EU-wide, national and Europe-wide regulatory measures and bodies, which creates a particularly pressing need to have a reasonably common frame of reference which represents the broadest of these geographical options. Having common terminology is especially pertinent given current difficulties with achieving EU-wide policies which are inclusive of all Member States.[17] Thirdly, although technology is global, the jurisdictional nature of regulation means that a supranational focus enables detailed exemplification to be provided in support of the proposed definition of NHT, while retaining global relevance through recourse to international standards and a brief assessment of a comparator region (the USA).

Section B discusses the scope of possible meanings[18] which can be accorded to NHT using literal and non-literal interpretation. This section of the chapter uniquely argues that an appreciation of the full scope of meaning can be identified by supplementing accepted interpretive tools with patent law principles for interpreting claims. Patent law

---

[16] These sources reflect the affected parties identified earlier for which there is sufficient evidence from which to draw conclusions.

[17] eg S Peers, 'The Constitutional Implications of the EU Patent' (2011) 7(2) *ECL Review* 229; N Fenanda and M Fabio, 'Constitutionalizing Tobacco: The Ambivalence of European Federalism' (Summer 2005) 46(2) *Harvard International Law Journal* 507; TK Hervey, 'Buy Baby: The European Union and Regulation of Human Reproduction' (1998) 18(2) *Oxford Journal of Legal Studies* 207.

[18] The relationship between definitions, meanings, and understanding as distinct terms is subject to dispute (eg U Wybraniec-Skardowska, 'Meaning and Interpretation I' (2007) 85 *Studia Logica* 105), but outside these specialist fields these are generally considered on their ordinary meaning, as aspects of conveying information or concepts in a comprehensible form (eg RC Anderson and RW Kulhavy, 'Learning Concepts from Definitions' (1972) 9(3) *American Educational Research Journal* 385).

may seem a surprising source of inspiration on which to base such an analysis but, as an established system for regulating new technology which has not yet been conceived of (or labelled), it is highly relevant to interpreting NHT. Consequently, the principle of purposive construction (as understood in patent law) is utilized as a logical basis for determining the scope of meaning of NHT, guiding the subsequent mapping.

The core value of this chapter is represented by sections C and D, together with Figure 4.1, because collectively they represent and explain the definition of NHT. Adopting the principle of purposive construction, section C describes how the map definition of NHT captures and interfaces ('mapping') the terminology and understanding of relevant disciplines involved in health technology (namely science, regulation, policy, and academia). It identifies that this process yields an organizing three-level nomenclature, facilitating the use of the map definition to users. It then discusses how purposive construction operates by construing the three key terms ('health', 'technology', and 'new') relative to each other. This section concludes by discussing the limiting parameters which are necessarily imposed in order to rationalize the content and location of terms within the map definition.

Section D discusses the value of the map definition to different interest groups involved in developing health technology and demonstrates the map's utility, exemplifying its flexibility and ability to remain relevant even where the map definition relates to technology as fast changing as advancements in health care.

A. Current Approaches to Defining New Health Technology

1. A Composite Phrase

It is expected that, if a generally accepted meaning of the phrase NHT exists, it would be apparent from policy, academic, and scientific literature. For policymakers in the EU, one of the most authoritative sources is the European Medicines Agency's (EMA) current policy document entitled *Road map to 2015*.[19] This identifies 'new and emerging science' as comprising 'personalised medicine, nanotechnologies, novel-novel drug development, regenerative medicine, synthetic biology, as well as advances to streamline non-clinical and clinical development.'[20] In focusing on 'science' rather than 'technology', the EMA's description provides a partial definition of NHT: any technology arising from these 'sciences' is regarded as 'new and emerging'. New technologies which arise from established sciences remain outside the scope of the EMA's terminology, unless they are focused on efficiency. A more encompassing definition would be expected from Europe's New and Emerging Science & Technology (NEST)[21] initiative, but this provides only a non-exhaustive list of examples of innovation[22] supported by the EU, and more broadly states that it is focused on 'unconventional and visionary research with the potential to open new fields for European science and technology, as well as research on potential problems uncovered by science.'[23]

---

[19] *Road Map to 2015: The European Medicines Agency's Contribution to Science, Medicines and Health* (2011) <www.ema.europa.eu/ema/index.jsp?curl=pages/about_us/general/general_content_000292.jsp&mid=WC0b01ac05800293a4> accessed January 2012.

[20] *Road Map* (n 19), 9.

[21] <http://cordis.europa.eu/nest/> accessed January 2012.

[22] Innovation refers to the product/process which implicitly encapsulates the technology, but can be used interchangeably with the scientific advancement, or its application.

[23] <http://cordis.europa.eu/nest/whatis.htm> accessed January 2012.

A more exhaustive account is provided in the 2006 report *Consequences, opportunities and challenges of modern biotechnology for Europe* (*Bio4EU*) produced by the European Techno-Economic Policies Support Network (ETEPSnet).[24] While this account is also more widely cast than health technology, it is notable that it adopts a similar, list-based approach to defining new technology.

A contemporary approach, used by both policymakers and regulators in identifying suitable technologies for Health Technology Assessment (HTAs),[25] is horizon scanning. Scanning is conducted through organizations such as the European Information Network on New and Changing Health Technologies (EuroScan),[26] which operate a database comprising examples of recent innovations. In addition, horizon scanning is also conducted using the internet to identify relevant technology, as well as incoming regulatory requirements.[27] In reviewing the use of the Euroscan database, Ibargoyen-Roteta and others describe 'emerging health technologies' as 'those techniques or procedures used in clinical practice that are just before being accepted or adopted into the healthcare system. . . . those that have passed the clinical trials phase but whose use is not yet widespread.'[28]

Obviously this is a definition which is confined to the context of HTAs. It could not form the basis of a multi-disciplinary debate, because this definition necessarily excludes technology as understood by medical researchers and most of the technology regulated by the patenting system (which relates to technology not publicly disclosed, and this generally means that patenting precedes the human phase of clinical trials).[29] In the United Kingdom, the National Horizon Scanning Centre (NHSC) (which is part of the National Institute for Health Research (NIHR)) assesses individual technology in discrete subject areas, which mirror medical specialities (for example, musculoskeletal, ENT, paediatrics, and neonatology). The NHSC provides an early warning service to the National Institute for Health and Clinical Excellence (NICE) of NHTs that are three years ahead of gaining market entry.[30] The NHSC does not claim to offer a complete review of all NHTs,[31] which limits its value in identifying NHT comprehensively, but it is notable that it recognizes sub-categories: medical devices; pharmaceuticals; and diagnostic and screening tests. Consequently, none of the existing systems of horizon scanning offer an accepted definition of NHT, because such databases

---

[24] Rolled into the JFC Reference Report of the same name, Joint Research Centre of the European Commission, 2007.

[25] HTAs are a tool for post-market authorization regulation which focuses upon a comparison of new/ emerging technologies with existing technologies. For more see: MV Garrido, FB Kristensen, CP Nielsen, and R Busse, *Health Technology Assessment and Health Policy-Making in Europe* (World Health Organization 2008) <www.euro.who.int/_data/assets/pdf_file/0003/90426/E91922.pdf> accessed January 2012.

[26] European Information Network on New and Changing Health Technologies, *EuroScan: Status Report* (2005) <http://euroscan.org.uk/mmlib/includes/sendfile.php?id=44> accessed January 2012.

[27] K Douw, H Vondeline, D Eskildsen, and S Simpson, 'Use of the Internet in Scanning the Horizon for New and Emerging Health Technologies: A Survey of Agencies Involved in Horizon Scanning' (2003) 5(1) *Journal of Medical Internet Research* e6 <www.jmir.org/issue/year/2003> accessed January 2012.

[28] N Ibargoyen-Roteta and others, 'Differences in the Identification Process for New and Emerging Health Technologies: Analysis of the EuroScan Database' (2009) 25(3) *International Journal of Technology Assessment in Health Care* 367.

[29] European Patent Convention (EPC) 2010, Art 54; *Fomento v Mentmore* [1956] RPC 87.

[30] M Fung, S Simpson, and C Packer, 'Identification of Innovation in Public Health' (2010) 33(1) *Journal of Public Health* 123. Notably NICE's role is changing with the implementation of the UK Health and Social Care Act 2012.

[31] The NHSC invites submission of new technology that it should review: see <www.nhsc -healthhorizons.org.uk/suggest-a-topic/> accessed January 2012.

comprise non-exhaustive examples of technologies which are designed to be searchable, rather than having a unifying concept(s) which distinguishes definitions.

Academic articles on policy, within which NHT is a key focus of analysis, routinely do not define the phrase.[32] This could indicate that NHT is an implicitly understood concept which does not need a detailed definition. In light of policy documents and relevant organizations attempting to indicate examples of NHTs, it is more likely that omitting a definition is a response to the pace with which health technology progresses: a precise enumeration of specific technology, innovation, or scientific advances gives commentary based upon it a limited 'shelf-life' of relevance. Specificity is traded in for longevity.

Within a broader tranche of academic debate, NHT as a composite phrase tends not to be found in relevant literature. Technology transfer articles define 'technology'.[33] Patent law commentary discusses new technologies, but either as specific technology[34] or broader technological categories such as biotechnology.[35] Patent law commentary contributes to debates on NHTs by considering examples of it, but does not use the phrase itself. NHTs are listed in the patent register (describing technology which is far from clinical trial completion), or recognized in the classification system (which comprises all existing technological categories).[36] However, this is entirely incidental, because the aim is not to provide information about NHTs or to define it as a composite phrase, but to identify inventions and track the state of existing knowledge as a basis for judging patentability.

Within scientific discourse, there is also no apparent discussion on the definition of NHT. Fustero and Arredondo briefly discussed 'health technology innovation', which incorporated a definition of 'health technology' as being a 'well accepted ... [concept that] covers, not only the equipment and devices, but also the organization systems, their processes, the Information Systems and the different services that support the provision of Health services.'[37] This is a reasonably comprehensive definition in extending a core understanding of 'health technology' as meaning any technology utilized in the context of health, which would include eHealth and Health 2.0/ Medicine 2.0[38] (albeit that it omits overt reference to products such as pharmaceuticals and it is far from clear what else is covered by being 'well accepted'). However, this still raises problems with understanding this concept when qualified by 'new': with an established definition of 'public health interventions' (PHI) Fung, Simpson, and Packer

[32] eg O Golan, P Hansen, G Kaplan, and O Tal, 'Health Technology Prioritization: Which Criteria for Prioritizing New Technologies and What are Their Relative Weights?' (2011) 102 *Health Policy* 126; K Murphy, C Packer, A Stevens, and S Simpson, 'Effective Early Warning Systems for New and Emerging Health Technologies: Developing an Evaluation Framework and an Assessment of Current systems' (2007) 23(3) *International Journal of Technology Assessment in Health Care* 324.

[33] eg B Bozeman, 'Technology Transfer and Public Policy: A Review of Research and Theory' (2000) 29 *Research Policy* 627.

[34] eg G Bernstein, 'In the Shadow of Innovation' (2010) 31(6) *Cardozo Law Review* 2257; Donnelly (n 7); Krauss and Takenaka (n 7).

[35] eg Bostyn (n 8); W Helwegen, 'The Research Exemption from a Nanotechnology Perspective' (2010) 32(7) *EIPR* 341.

[36] eg the International Patent Classification (IPC) or the European Classification system (ECLA) organize information within families according to priorities, within categories of increasing specificity.

[37] SC Fustero and AG Arredondo, '"The Biomedical Engineer as a Driver for Health Technology Innovation' (2010) 32nd Annual International Conference of the IEEE EMBS, 6844 <www.ncbi.nlm. nih.gov/pubmed/21096299> accessed January 2012.

[38] For more see: H Oh, B Hughes, R Mayoral, and E Randeree, 'Definition of Health 2.0 and Medicine 2.0: A Systematic Review' (2010) 12(2) *Journal of Medical Internet Research* e18 <www.jmir. org/2010/2/e18/> accessed January 2012.

encountered problems in defining 'innovation in PHI' by empirical analysis.[39] So, a partial definition cannot substitute for an understanding of the composite phrase NHT, and extrapolation may not be easily derived from 'health technology'.

The International Organization for Standardization (ISO) lays down technical and definitional norms for 'health and medicine' as a separate category, but does not comprehensively define either term, let alone defining them within the context of new technology. Instead, articles on medical science revolve around specific technological progress, such as how the body's internal 'clock' regulates cellular regeneration,[40] or the progress of late-stage clinical trials on a new malaria vaccine.[41]

This analysis indicates that the use of the phrase NHT is confined to policy sources and commentary on health regulation. Patent law commentary and scientific articles contribute to these debates only by using technology-specific analyses or technological categories. In addition, the only apparent regulatory commentary which provides a definition of NHT actively excludes patent law commentators/practitioners/policymakers and the scientific/medical research communities by utilizing a description hinged on post-clinical trials technology. This indicates that there is a clear mismatch in the terminology used by the fields of expertise which are involved in the development of health technology. If there is no generally accepted meaning of NHT as a composite phrase, is there an accepted meaning for each of the individual terms?

2. Individual Terms

Standard definitions of 'new', 'health', or 'technology' as individual terms can be assessed utilizing the same sources of evidence as noted earlier. In the context of patent law, 'new' refers to what is unknown,[42] but in the context of medicine, 'new' has a range of meanings depending upon the precise context. To a medical researcher, it refers to something which is untested, but to a medical practitioner it is something which is untried. Consequently, 'new' has a broad range of possible definitions, none of which are generally accepted.

The widest conception of 'health' can be found in the Constitution of the World Health Organization (WHO), which states that:

Health is a state of complete physical, mental and social well-being and not merely the absence of disease or infirmity. The enjoyment of the highest attainable standard of health is one of the fundamental rights of every human being without distinction of race, religion, political belief, economic or social condition.[43]

This definition of health encapsulates technology aimed at alleviating disease, enhancing normal human biological functions (for example, creating 'supermen'), and technology which ameliorates a wide array of social factors which negatively affect the quality of life. For example, bioremediation[44] would be caught by this definition of health because (in

---

[39] (n 31).

[40] P Janich and others, 'The Circadian Molecular Clock Creates Epidermal Stem Cell Heterogeneity' (2011) 480 *Nature* 209.

[41] The RTS,S Clinical Trials Partnership, 'First Results of Phase 3 Trial of RTS,S/AS01 Malaria Vaccine in African Children' (2011) 365 *New England Journal of Medicine* 1863.

[42] Art 54, EPC 2010.

[43] WHO, *Basic Documents*, amending the Forty-fifth edition, Supplement, October 2006 <www.who.int/governance/eb/who_constitution_en.pdf> accessed January 2012.

[44] This refers to using micro-organisms to remove environmental pollutants.

incorporating 'oil molecule consuming micro-organisms'[45] which ensure that the oceans remain unpolluted) it enhances human health by facilitating swimming. The introduction of a system of debt relief would be included, because being free of financial concerns has a positive mental impact on people. In fact, it is difficult to imagine any technology that would not be caught by such a broad definition of health.[46]

In comparison with the normal meaning of terms such as 'health care', which is focused on the provision of resources designed to address disease/injury/malfunction, the WHO definition of 'health' more broadly includes social goals aimed at equitable access to care, enhancements, and arguably extends to causative factors of disease/malfunction. Notably, the WHO definition was adopted from the wording of the Declaration of Alma-Ata, which emerged from the International Conference on Primary Health Care held in Russia in 1978. Even if this source is regarded as limiting the definition of 'health' to primary health care (meaning health within the community), the difficulty is that any services/products/information which are provided by consultants (secondary health care), hospital specialists (tertiary health care), and diagnosticians or researchers (quaternary health care) are removed from the definition. This creates a definition which excludes a commonsense meaning of 'health', because it includes the services of a water provider, but excludes anything done by a cardiologist.

The International Covenant on Economic, Social and Cultural Rights 1966 (ICESCR), in creating a right to 'the highest attainable standard of physical and mental health',[47] adopts a similar approach to 'health' as the WHO. The ICESCR describes the right not just as a matter of tackling disease and ill-health,[48] but as addressing environmental factors[49] which trigger sickness. This is an understanding of 'health' which is about requiring minimum standards of sanitation and prophylactic treatments to minimize the incidence of epidemics or pandemics (which is indicative of public health), and a preventative and causative approach to care (indicative of private health). In adopting this standard, the UN General Assembly were clear in their rejection of the WHO conception of 'health', in preference to 'health' emanating from:

a wide range of socio-economic factors that promote conditions in which people can lead a healthy life, and extends to the underlying determinants of health, such as food and nutrition, housing, access to safe and potable water and adequate sanitation, safe and healthy working conditions, and a healthy environment.[50]

Consequently, the ICESCR provides a narrower understanding of 'health' that does not permit for enhancements, is not confined to primary health care (inherently being focused to health care generally) and is arguably not focused on equitable access

---

[45] See *Diamond v Chakrabarty* [1980] 447 US 303.

[46] The scope of the definition is not captured by the World Health Survey questionnaires (<www.who.int/healthinfo/survey/instruments/en/index.html> accessed January 2012), and is not fully represented in the WHO Quality of Life reports, which focus on discrete areas such as mental health and substance abuse (eg <www.who.int/mental_health/media/en/76.pdf> accessed January 2012).

[47] Art 12. This is a United Nations (UN) Treaty which has been almost globally adopted: for more see <http://treaties.un.org/Pages/ViewDetails.aspx?src=TREATY&mtdsg_no=IV-3-a&chapter=4lang=en> accessed June 2012.

[48] Art 12(2)(c).

[49] Art 12(2)(b) and (c).

[50] Committee on Economic, Social and Cultural Rights, 'Substantive Issues Arising in the Implementation of the International Convention on Economic, Social and Cultural Rights' (2000) 22nd Session, General Comment 14 (E/C.12/2000/4) <www2.ohchr.org/english/bodies/cescr/comments.htm> accessed June 2012, p 2, point 4.

(as is the WHO definition), but instead targets resources to aspects of direct need in securing wellness. However, the understanding conveyed by this definition of 'health' is far broader than simply addressing health care, because the Committee on Economic, Social and Cultural Rights[51] considers 'health' (in the sense of providing the means to achieve wellness)[52] to be the responsibility not just of individual nations, but of corporations and individuals within those countries.[53]

This understanding of health as a nexus for various states of wellness dependent on multiple factors is further expanded by international instruments, identifying the right to health as extending to the right to access[54] health care for a specified range of social groups. For example, ensuring: access to health care irrespective of the 'race, colour, or national or ethnic origin' of the patient;[55] equal access to health care for women,[56] specifically recognizing the need to ensure access in rural areas,[57] and in securing working conditions for women which comply with health and safety standards;[58] access to health care for migrants which is equivalent to nationals in accessing emergency medical care (limited to protecting life and not causing irreparable damage),[59] and permits migrant workers,[60] and their families,[61] to access health care provided they have met relevant requirements (for example, in the United Kingdom this could mean payment of National Insurance in order to gain access to health care under the NHS); access to the best achievable health care for children, including all forms of childcare which affect the child's well-being (such as the quality of parenting);[62] and that disability does not prevent access to health care or diminish its quality.[63]

These international measures are supported by the EU[64] and the provisions are recreated through a range of European instruments (which facilitate more detail in the provisions without representing a broader commitment to a right to health where secondary sources are taken into account). For example, European instruments overtly: include the provision of occupational health and health and safety in the workplace;[65] identifying the right to health (as in the ICESCR), but more overtly addressing the

---

[51] Created to monitor the implementation of the ICESCR.

[52] A 'right to the enjoyment of a variety of facilities, goods, services and conditions necessary for the realization of the highest attainable standard of health' (n 51) p 3, point 9.

[53] Committee on Economic, Social and Cultural Rights, 'Statement on the Obligations of States Parties Regarding the Corporate Sector and Economic, Social and Cultural Rights' (2011) 46th Session (E/C.12/2011/1) <www2.ohchr.org/english/bodies/cescr/> accessed June 2012.

[54] 'Access' is used in its ordinary English sense, and does not necessarily reflect the Committee on Economic, Social and Cultural Rights' approach, which includes: availability (existing in sufficient quantity); accessibility (without discrimination, physically and economically obtainable, and known about); acceptability (provided ethically); and quality(scientifically and medically): (n 53) pp 4–5.

[55] International Convention on the Elimination of All Forms of Racial Discrimination 1965, Art 5 (e)(iv).

[56] Convention on the Elimination of All Forms of Discrimination against Women 1979 (CEDAW), Art 12.

[57] CEDAW, Art 14(2)(b).

[58] CEDAW, Art 11(1)(f).

[59] International Convention on the Protection of the Rights of All Migrant Workers and Members of their Families 1990, Art 28.

[60] (n 59) Art 43(e).

[61] (n 59) Art 45(c).

[62] Convention on the Rights of the Child 1989, Art 24.

[63] Convention and Optional Protocol on the Rights of Persons with Disabilities 2006, Art 25.

[64] eg the ICESCR is adhered to by the EU <http://eeas.europa.eu/human_rights/esc/index_en.htm> accessed June 2012.

[65] European Social Charter 1961, Art 3.

causative agents of ill-health,[66] and the right to access 'advisory and educational facilities';[67] as well as ensuring the provision of 'care necessitated by . . . [the] condition' of all EU nationals where they do not have sufficient resources to provide for their own care.[68]

A much narrower approach to 'health' is that represented by the United Nations (UN) Millenium Declaration 2000,[69] which initially represented a commitment to promote health only in respect of ameliorating mortality during childbirth and in children until the age of five, the spread of HIV/AIDS,[70] and promoting access to essential medicines in developing countries.[71] The current Millenium Development Goals (MDG)[72] aim at maternal health, beyond merely preventing death, to include reproductive health[73] and aim to reduce the incidence of malaria and other serious diseases.[74] This is an approach which, in common with the ICESCR, directs resources to areas of greatest need. The current MDG are set to expire in 2015 and it is predicted that the goals will be unmet,[75] which is not totally surprising given that the MDG Gap Task Force Report 2012 identifies only 50 per cent of public sector health care facilities and 69 per cent of private facilities currently provide essential medicines.[76] This represents only a minimal improvement over the 2011 report.[77]

Notably, the definition of 'essential medicines' is provided by the WHO and relates to: 'medicines that satisfy the priority health care needs of a population'. They are selected with regard to disease prevalence, safety, efficacy, and comparative cost-effectiveness.[78] This is akin to a 'public health emergency medicine' definition, but interestingly includes the idea that an understanding of 'health' can be limited on the basis of effectiveness and cost. As such, it refocuses 'health' as a matter of resource management, rather than as a human condition.

In addition, the MDG to provide essential medicines is being pursued whilst developing countries are implementing the Agreement on Trade-Related Aspects of Intellectual Property Rights 1994 (TRIPs). TRIPs promotes access to essential medicines by specifically providing that individual nations can permit innovations to be freely used where there is a 'national emergency or other circumstances of extreme urgency',[79] which would enable essential medicines to be provided without liability for licensing fees.[80] However, the overall effect of the implementation of TRIPs-based

---

[66] European Social Charter, Art 11(1).   [67] European Social Charter, Art 11(2).

[68] European Social Charter, Art 13, importing the European Convention on Social and Medical Assistance 1953.

[69] <www.un.org/millennium/declaration/ares552e.htm#> accessed June 2012.

[70] Millennium Declaration, Development Goal III, Resolution 19.

[71] Millennium Declaration, Development Goal III, Resolution 20.

[72] Available at <www.un.org/millenniumgoals/> accessed June 2012.

[73] MDG 5B.

[74] MDG 6C.

[75] UN Committee for Development Policy, 'Report on the Fourteenth Session' (12–16 March 2012), Supplement No 13 (E/2012/33), pp 9–13 <www.un.org/en/development/desa/policy/cdp/cdp_ecosoc/e_2012_33_en.pdf> accessed June 2012.

[76] Available at <www.undp.org/content/undp/en/home/librarypage/mdg/mdg-gap-task-force-report -2012/>, p61 accessed October 2012.

[77] MDG Gap Task Force Report 2011 <www.un.org/en/development/desa/policy/mdg_gap/mdg_gap2011/mdg8report2011_engw.pdf> accessed June 2012.

[78] WHO, 'Essential Medicines' (June 2010) Factsheet No 325 <www.who.int/mdiacentre/factsheets/fs325/en/index.html> accessed June 2012.

[79] Art 31(b).

[80] An interpretation supported by the World Trade Organization (WTO), 'Declaration on the TRIPs Agreement and Public Health' (9–14 November 2001), Ministerial Conference Fourth Session (WT/MIN(01)/DEC/W/2) ('Doha Declaration'), para 5(c).

patent rights on pharmaceuticals globally is to shift pharmaceutical industry markets: newly TRIPs-compliant countries (for example, India) are constrained to produce generics which must wait for branded drugs to come off patent, spreading the generics market out from developed countries with robust pre-TRIPs patent protection; while the market demand for copycat drugs (globally subject to patent rights, but unprotected nationally) left by newly generic-producing countries is likely to be met by countries with little existing manufacturing capacity, creating new centres of copycat drug production globally. Crucially, while this shift is occurring, access to cheaper copycat drugs in the most impoverished countries is severely restricted. This shift has been exacerbated by pharmaceutical sector trade practices (for example, bi-lateral agreements), in concert with international trade law and policy which is operated in favour of industry because of shared economic interests,[81] forcing harsher conditions to be introduced in developing countries than those laid down in TRIPs and making it even more difficult for those countries to gain access to innovative medicines.

To counter this, instruments such as the Doha Declaration[82] and the Paragraph 6 Decision[83] have permitted developing countries which lack the capacity to manufacture medicines to gain access to crucial medicines (enabling them to be compulsorily licensed nationally) by manufacture occurring in other countries. While this does not directly identify any definitions of 'health' that would be relevant in this analysis, it does demonstrate that innovation of new technologies is of critical importance in framing an understanding of NHT. In addition, it highlights the importance for any definition of NHT to be valuable in a practical sense. For example, it must be able to accommodate a cohesive understanding of 'health' as both public and private, as well as enable 'health' to be understood either as public or private in order to permit for regulatory exceptions to be created.

In addition, national constitutions may be explored in search of a definition of 'health' which could be universally applied. For example, the Socialist Constitution of the Democratic People's Republic of Korea (North Korea's constitution) states in Article 72 that:

Citizens are entitled to free medical care, and all persons who are no longer able to work because of old age, illness or a physical disability, the old and children who have no means of support are all entitled to material assistance. This right is ensured by free medical care, an expanding network of hospitals, sanatoria and other medical institutions, State social insurance and other social security systems.

It is to be doubted that such an understanding of 'health', which is implicitly focused on the state's duty to preserve the life of its citizens beyond a context purely of health care, could be globally utilized where compliance demands a financial commitment and social restructuring that could not be implemented in most countries. In addition, this creates difficulties with establishing the extent to which the wording and meaning is driven by national considerations (for example, in North Korea the expectations of citizens that 'health' means 'life preserving only', without addressing 'quality of life' issues which may be implicitly expected by citizens in other countries). The

---

[81] eg imposing requirements for specific forms of protection to be provided (such as data exclusivity) through measures such as trade sanctions or free trade agreements (eg the Chile–USA Free Trade Agreement), often referred to as 'TRIPs plus provisions'.

[82] (n 80).

[83] General Council WTO, 'Implementation of Paragraph 6 of the Doha Declaration on the TRIPS Agreement and Public Health' (1 September 2003) WT/L/540 and Corr.1 <www.wto.org/english/tratop_e/trips_e/implem_para6_e.htm> accessed June 2012.

acceptability of such definitions is also problematic where its source becomes known and inevitably raises political objections (demonstrated here by the definition emanating from a communist regime, which would be likely to be objected to by capitalist countries).

A shared definition of NHT must rely upon a narrower interpretation of 'health' than those examined so far (with the exception of construing it as 'essential medicines', which is far too narrow for practicality). This analysis identifies that what is required is a definition which is far less idealistic,[84] can be considered separately from its causative factors, and is more closely related to the contexts of its use.

For instance, the WHO definition could be limited to only one aspect of well-being (for example, physical health), but physical, social, and mental states are inextricably linked and this is precisely the rationale for their incorporation within the WHO Constitution. Beyond this, the WHO adopts a three-step approach to epidemiology: the first step focuses on behavioural factors (for example, smoking, diet, and exercise); the second step relates to physical measurements (for example, height, weight, and blood pressure); and the third step assesses biochemical factors (for example, serotonin, dopamine, or cholesterol levels).[85] This three-step approach provides a basis for a narrower definition of health, which centres upon the relationship between the factors of health and their impacts. A definition which rests upon this relationship enables distinctions to be drawn between factors with direct/indirect impacts, which could further narrow the scope of technologies captured by 'health'. For example, 'health' could be limited to describing only a direct relationship between well-being and physical, social, and mental factors. Therefore, stress would be a direct factor contributing to conditions such as coronary heart disease (bringing it within 'health'), but the reduction of debt would be only an indirect factor, because it causes the stress which results in heart disease but cannot directly cause a heart attack (taking it outside 'health'). The difficulty is that this distinction shifts the debate from the scope 'health' to what is meant by 'direct'.

Alternatively, the WHO's International Classification of Disease (ICD)[86] could be used to refine the meaning of health as being no wider than disease, defined as a 'medically recognised malfunction'. This approach has the benefit of coming from an internationally accepted standard. It also circumvents ethical issues created by an interpretation of health which incorporates expanding human physiology beyond 'normal' parameters: equating health with 'ameliorating disease' removes enhancement of human physiology (for example, creating supermen), and the imposition of impairments (for example, intentionally causing deafness).

The term 'technology' faces similar difficulties because, in the absence of an accepted meaning, arbitrary distinctions must be made. Ambiguity centres upon the degree to which 'technology' can be understood independently of pure science on the one hand,

---

[84] JS Larson, 'The World Health Organization's Definition of Health: social versus spiritual health' (1996) 38 *Social Indicators Research* 181.

[85] WHO, 'WHO STEPwise Instrument: Core and Expanded—The WHO STEPwise Approach to Chronic Disease Risk Factor Surveillance' (2009) <www.who.int/chp/steps/STEPS_Instrument_v2.1.pdf> accessed September 2011; beyond the medical context, other disciplines have assessed the social and public policy implications arising from such health factors: eg DA Kindig, 'Population Health Terminology' (2007) 85(1) *The Milbank Quarterly* 139; A Steptoe and M Marmot, 'Socioeconomic Status and Coronary Heart Disease: A Psychobiological Perspective' (2004) 30 *Population and Development Review* 133; JS House, 'Understanding Social Factors and Inequalities in Health: 20th Century Progress and 21st Century Prospects' (2001) 43 *Journal of Health and Social Behaviour* 125.

[86] ICD-10 came into force in 1994 and is an internationally applied benchmark for medical practice: <http://apps.who.int/classifications/apps/icd/icd10online/> accessed January 2012.

and specific individual applications on the other. This is a more difficult distinction to achieve in the context of a contemporary technological developmental sphere such as biomedicine, which is universally recognized as having blurred former distinctions between pure and applied science.[87] Indeed, an analysis of the scientific literature identifies that new technology is progressing so quickly that terminology has not been clearly delineated.[88] This can be exemplified by 'bioengineering'. The Merriam-Webster Online Dictionary[89] defines 'bioengineering' as 'the application of biological techniques (as genetic recombination) to create modified versions of organisms (as crops)' and links the term with 'genetic engineering'.

The same definition also applies to 'biotechnology', and this is variously referred to as 'biological engineering', 'biological systems engineering', and 'biomedical engineering' depending upon the context of the application (for example, medicine, agriculture) and on the context of the use (for example, science makes distinctions based on 'systems' as a discrete discipline, but it is grouped with 'biotech' in non-science commentary). Confusion also arises where the same term is used to describe widely divergent forms of technology. For example, 'synthetic biology' refers to the chemical reproduction of biological materials such as plants, but also refers to the creation of artificial life forms (for example, through the use of Biobricks),[90] which are entirely divergent disciplines.

This analysis suggests that there is no accepted definition of NHT either as a complete phrase or as individual terms identified from European sources. The situation is no different in the USA. For example, the Centre for Strategic & International Studies Global Health Policy Centre report, *Policies and Practices to Advance Global Health Technologies*[91] does not define 'new technology' even though it is the focus of the report. Similarly, the US Agency for International Development (USAID), which is charged with funding and managing new health technology, does not define NHT.[92]

Irrespective of the geographical source of the evidence, it is apparent that NHT is not universally used as a composite phrase. It is an undefined expression adopted by policymakers/academics on regulation, and often not used by academics in other fields or by scientists. Neither is there an accepted meaning of the terms in isolation. This is an issue of communication which impairs the ability to resolve dilemmas identified in separate debates. For example, without standardized terms empirical analyses of health technology per se or discrete applications cannot be correlated to legal, regulatory, or scientific analyses. Arguably the absence of accepted terminology has already proved a problem in framing regulation effectively. This point can be exemplified through an assessment of regulating tissue engineering in the EU.

---

[87] eg S Thambisetty and K Kumaramangalam, 'Peer Review and Patents: Why the Goose that Lays the Golden Egg is a Red Herring' (2008) 30(5) *EIPR* 171; P Mirowski and R Van Horn, 'The Contract Research Organization and the Commercialization of Scientific Research' (2005) 35(4) *Social Studies of Science* 503; D Chalmers and D Nicol, 'Commercialisation of Biotechnology: Public Trust and Research' (2004) 6(2–3) *International Journal of Biotechnology* 116; TF Gieryn, 'Boundary-work and the Demarcation Between Science from Non-science: Strains and Interests in Professional Ideologies of Scientists' (1983) 48(6) *American Sociological Review* 781.

[88] Oh and others (n 38); W Hersh, 'A Stimulus to Define Informatics and Health Information Technology' (2009) 9 *BMC Medical Informatics and Decision Making* 24.

[89] Recognized as being authoritative in legal jurisprudence: eg *T315/03 HARVARD Oncomouse* [2005] EPOR 31.

[90] For more on this see: <http://biobricks.org/http://biobricks.org/> accessed January 2012.

[91] (2009) <www.ghtcoalition.org/files/CSIS_Paper_elias_policiespractices.pdf> accessed January 2012.

[92] eg USAID, *USAID Research: Policy Framework, Principles and Operational Guidance* 2011–15 <www.usaid.gov/policy/ads/200/polframe.pdf> accessed January 2012.

3. Effect on Regulation

This section of the chapter focuses on the regulation of tissue engineering in the context of the EU to demonstrate that the absence of agreed terminology may well have resulted in regulation which is less effective than is ideal. It is not possible to undertake an exhaustive analysis of tissue engineering,[93] so three negative impacts will be focused upon. The first is the fragmented development of regulation on tissue engineering, which has resulted in regulation being inaccessibly spread across too many instruments. The second impact is the need to engage with impenetrable definitions identifying the scope of specific regulatory instruments. The third and final impact is the lack of fit with existing scientific terminology. In order to understand how the problems with regulation relate to the science, a general understanding of the science is required.

Tissue engineering broadly concerns the use of cells/tissue to repair/replace existing malfunctions in components of the human body. Although tissue engineering is often used interchangeably with 'regenerative medicine', the latter term has become synonymous with stem cells,[94] leaving the former to describe the creation of parts of the human body (and this can extend to whole organs). Consequently, tissue engineering (using cells/tissue to create tissue/body parts/whole organs for transplantation) is a term which intersects with three related forms of technology: antisense technology (using RNA to interrupt a cell's normal function);[95] somatic gene therapy (using DNA to genetically change an adult cell's function); and stem cell technology (using a master cell which divides at an accelerated rate and can be reprogrammed to a specific cellular function). In terms of applications of these three forms of technology, tissue engineering intersects with transplantation and therapy. Antisense technology is confined to a form of therapy for its application. Somatic gene therapy is obviously therapeutic, but the products used in the therapy (DNA encased in a delivery vehicle and usually placed in a host cell) can be harnessed to produce bio-pharmaceuticals/biologics (for example, Erythropoietin or tissue-Plasminogen Activator produced naturally by human cells which are engineered to a manufacturing-scale), or utilized as toxicology models. Finally, stem cell technology can be utilized in any of the applications identified.

This demonstrates that technologies are often referred to by different terms, are closely related scientifically, and interlinked within contexts of application. This makes regulating these technologies much more difficult to achieve. The first problem which

---

[93] For additional critique see: Mahalatchimy and others (n 9); M Favale and A Plomer, 'Fundamental Disjunctions in the EU Legal Order on Human Tissue, Cells & Advanced Regenerative Therapies' (2009) 16 *Maastricht Journal of European and Comparative Law* 89; ML Flear, 'The EU's Biopolitical Governance of Advanced Therapy Medicinal Products' (2009) 16 *Maastricht Journal of European and Comparative Law* 113. For a comparative analysis see: B von Tigerstrom and E Schroh, 'Regulation of Stem-Cell Based Products' (2007) 15 *Health Law Journal* 175.

[94] This refers to a form of 'master' cell which has the capacity to develop into different cells either within a limited range, the same biological 'family', or almost any cell, depending on the type of stem cell. Cells which can develop into any cell (including a whole human) are excluded legally in Europe and the USA: Case C-34/10 *Brüstle v Greenpeace* (2011) <http://eur-lex.europa.eu/LexUriServ/Lex-UriServ.do?uri=CELEX:62010CJ0034:EN:HTML> accessed December 2011, German Patent (DE 19756864, EP1040185); Comments of the President of the EPO on WARF (President Pompidou), G2/06, 28 September 2006; *Stem Cells/Wisconsin Alumni Research Foundation (WARF)* [2006] EPOR 31; [2009] EPOR 15. (USA) WARF (US No 7,029,913 was rejected by the BPAI (USPTO Appeal Boards, *Foundation for Taxpayer and Consumer Rights v WARF* [2010] BPAI No 001854) and is currently subject to *inter partes* re-examination pending before the USPTO (Control No 95/000,154).

[95] This disrupts the production of proteins, but cannot result in the production of a different protein, for example.

demonstrates this difficulty arises from the fast pace with which NHTs develop, which can result in fragmented regulatory instruments.

a. Fragmented regulation

The general market authorization procedure which permits new medicinal products to be introduced into use by the public as a whole is laid down in Directive 2001/83/EC (Medicinal Products Directive), which defines its remit as extending to:

any substance or combination of substances which may be administered to human beings with a view to making a medical diagnosis or to restoring, correcting or modifying physiological functions in human beings is likewise considered a medicinal product.[96]

This provision is drafted with sufficient ambiguity that it easily accommodates the cells and tissue used in tissue engineering. However, the scope of the Medicinal Products Directive was subsequently amended by Directive 2003/63/EC (amending Directive),[97] and the distinction in Recital 9 between products used in genomic intervention ('gene therapy medicinal products') and those used in cellular intervention ('cell therapy medicinal products') was carried into the new Annex I to the Medicinal Products Directive.

Despite this amendment, which accommodates both gene therapy and stem cell technology, Regulation 1394/2007/EC on Advanced Therapy Medicinal Products (ATMP Regulation)[98] was introduced to govern the market authorization (and other relevant procedures) of tissue engineered products. According to Recital 5 of the ATMP Regulation, products based on gene therapy and stem cell technology were incorporated into the ATMP Regulation because they are as technologically complex and novel as tissue engineering, providing a reason for them to be considered alongside tissue products. Notably, in Recital 3 the ATMP Regulation accepted the Annex I meanings of both the gene and cell therapy medicinal products, and added a definition of 'tissue engineered products' as resting upon viability: viable cells/tissues (are tissue engineered products) and non-viable biological materials (do not fall within the remit of the ATMP Regulation).

The sample discussed here represents a limited range of regulatory measures relevant to tissue engineering and yet it requires three separate legal instruments (the ATMP Regulation, the Medicinal Products Directive, and the amending Directive) in order to identify the scope of the ATMP Regulation's applicability. Outside market authorization procedures, the EU Tissues and Cells Directives (EUTCD)[99] which once governed 'donation, procurement and testing, processing, preservation, storage and distribution' for tissue engineered products are now reduced to covering only donation, procurement,

---

[96] Directive 2001/83/EC Community Code relating to medicinal products for human use (28.11.2001) OJ L311/67, Art 1(2)(b).

[97] (27.6.2003) OJ L159/46.

[98] Regulation 1394/2007/EC on Advanced Therapy Medicinal Products (10.12.2007) OJ L324/121.

[99] Comprising: Directive 2004/23/EC setting standards of quality and safety for the donation, procurement, testing, processing, preservation, storage and distribution of human tissues and cells (7.4.2004) OJ L102/48; Directive 2006/17/EC as regards certain technical requirements for the donation, procurement and testing of human tissues and cells (9.2.2006) OJ L38/40; Directive 2006/86/EC as regards traceability requirements, notification of serious adverse reactions and events and certain technical requirements for the coding, processing, preservation, storage and distribution of human tissues and cells (25.10.2006) OJ L294/32.

and testing.[100] This means that how these products are handled is determined by four separate legal instruments, depending on the nature of the 'handling'. In comparison with effective regulation (for example, a single instrument with accessible definitions), this is a confusing array of regulatory instruments for a legal specialist and is obviously a greater problem to navigate for those actually handling these cells/tissues.

The ATMP Regulation compounds this complexity in dealing with the applications of tissue engineered products. This can be demonstrated through the ATMP's departure from accepted mechanisms for resolving overlaps and in its scope of application, which has been defined around existing regulatory provisions for related applications. It is to this the chapter now turns.

b. Impenetrable descriptions defining scope

It is impossible to read the ATMP Regulation without realizing that its remit is defined by a complex series of conditions which distinguish overlapping applications. For example, Recital 4 recognizes that many of the products falling within the ATMP Regulation will also be contained within medical devices, which are separately regulated by Directive 93/42/EEC (as amended) (Devices Directive).[101] The usual approach to resolving overlaps in the Devices Directive and the Medicinal Products Directive is dictated by the 'principal mode of action', but Recital 4 of the ATMP Regulation stipulates that products take priority irrespective of the 'mode of action'. Similarly, adult stem cells which are used for regenerating spinal cord, for example, would be categorized as both a 'somatic cell therapy medicinal product' and a 'tissue engineered product', so Article 2(4) stipulates that such overlaps are classified as the latter.

Transplantation is implicitly excluded,[102] as is gene therapy conducted on individual patients[103] and clinical trials are directed to align with the principles for commercial-scale use which is covered in the ATMP Regulation.[104] Given the definition of what is included is principally in Article 2, the ATMP Regulation utilizes more provisions to define what is excluded than included. This is indicative of regulation that relies upon artificial divisions and these are generally more difficult to enforce. The confusion caused by the ATMP Regulation is further evidenced in the failure to employ existing interpretations of scientific terminology, discussed in the next subsection.

c. Lack of fit with existing terminology

The overall lack of clarity in the ATMP Regulation is exacerbated when its scope is explored.[105] The Regulation creates a new collective term of 'advanced therapies', but (as identified in subsection A above) the utilization of many of the cells within its remit are also utilized for non-therapeutic purposes (for example, as toxicology models). Annex I defines advanced therapy medicinal products as those 'based on manufacturing processes focussed on various gene transfer produced bio-molecules, and/or biologically advanced

---

[100] (n 99) Art 3, limiting the applicability of Directive 2004/23/EC (part of the EUTCD).

[101] Concerning medical devices (12.7.1993) OJ L169/1.

[102] (n 99) Recital 2.

[103] (n 99) Recital 6, Art 28.

[104] (n 99) Recital 16, Art 4.

[105] Although additional clarity is provided in the EMA's *Guideline on Human Cell-Based Medicinal Products* (2008) EMEA/CHMP/410869/2006 <www.emea.europa.eu/docs/en_GB/document_library/Scientific_guideline/2009/09/WC500003894.pdf> accessed January 2012.

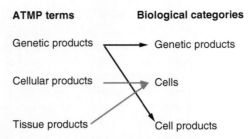

Figure 4.1 Mapping the ATMP to accepted scientific technology

therapeutic modified cells as active substances or part of active substances.'[106] This definition arguably includes the genetically-altered cell nucleus, its delivery vector, and even the cell *ex vivo* (outside a living person) into which it is placed provided it is in the context of therapy, but excludes 'factory cells' (which comprise exactly the same elements, but are not produced for therapeutic use), as well as the products subsequently harvested.[107] Regulatory divisions based on context of use are extremely difficult to navigate, let alone to enforce and are highly unlikely to withstand continued technological progress. It is in recognition of this that the ATMP Regulation set up the Committee for Advanced Therapies (CAT), but it is inescapable that some degree of simplification of the existing regulations is going to be required in future.

The division between products under the ATMP Regulation also shifts established scientific distinctions (see Figure 4.1). Under the ATMP Regulation there are three discrete product categories: genetic products (DNA/RNA and cells comprising them); cellular products (somatic stem cells); and tissue products (manufactured cells or tissue with/without scaffolds). These categories do not align with biological categories comprising: genetic products (DNA/RNA), cells (somatic, germ-line), and cell products (proteins, enzymes).

In addition, the use of the term 'somatic' is usually used to distinguish different forms of gene therapy (for example, germ-line gene therapy, meaning an inheritable intervention,[108] as distinct from somatic gene therapy which affects a change on adult cells only), but under the ATMP Regulation 'somatic' is used to limit the scope of stem cells (including adult stem cells, but only ambiguously extending to cells biologically regressed).

It can be concluded that the existing ATMP Regulation fails to be clearly accessible, because of the absence of standard terms and ignoring standard scientific terms where they do exist. Precisely why the ATMP Regulation was necessary when all of the technologies fit within the existing definition in the Medicinal Products Directive is beyond the scope of this chapter. What is pertinent here is that the use of language in existing regulatory measures (exemplified by the ATMP Regulation) results in a system which is difficult to navigate, understand, and implement. This cannot result in effective regulation.

---

[106] (n 97) Part IV.

[107] Regulation 726/2004/EC for the authorization and supervision of medicinal products for human and veterinary use and establishing the EMA (30.4.2004) OJ L136/1 applies.

[108] This is generally regarded as impermissible, eg Convention for the Protection of Human Rights and Dignity of the Human Being with regard to the Application of Biology and Medicine: Convention on Human Rights and Biomedicine (EST 164 (1997) <http://conventions.coe.int/Treaty/en/Treaties/html/164.htm> accessed January 2012), Art 13.

Key terms, such as NHT, are fundamentally important to multi-disciplinary discourse and to working towards more effective regulation. One means of creating a common meaning of NHT is to explore the scope of possible interpretations that could be attributed to it. It is to this that this chapter now turns.

B. Scope of Possible Meanings of New Health Technology

1. Principles of Interpretation

Definitions and interpretation are an important aspect of any academic discipline.[109] In legal discourse, the standard approach to understanding terms is to adopt a literal interpretation[110] and to resolve ambiguity by utilizing a context-based, non-literal interpretation.[111] A literal interpretation rests upon a reasonably narrow understanding of the core meaning of words and generally derives from a dictionary definition. Conversely, a non-literal interpretation enables a broader approach to be taken to the scope of meaning that particular words convey. In order for any non-literal interpretation to be authoritative, it must be appropriately evidenced. There are broadly three approaches to adopting a non-literal interpretation: intent-based;[112] identified context-based;[113] or purposive.[114]

In addition, understanding phrases requires interpretation of more than simply the sum of the individual words: it requires an appreciation of the phrase as having a 'composite' meaning.[115] This is the scope of meaning derived from the literal interpretation attributed to the individual words, in addition to an appreciation of what the words mean collectively. For example, NHT yields a composite meaning comprising the meaning of 'new', 'health', and 'technologies', *and* an understanding of NHT as a combined phrase.

Importantly, patent law[116] pays close attention to the meaning of words in patent claims, because it is this that defines the scope of the legal right granted.[117] The effect of

---

[109] eg as a tool to understand the social significance of institutions and cultural artefacts (JW Mohr, 'Measuring Meaning Structures' (1998) 24 *Annual Review of Sociology* 345); in understanding the practical role that definitions play in the successful marketing of new products (S Bhattacharya, V Krishnan, and V Mahajan, 'Managing New Product Definition in Highly Dynamic Environments' (1998) 44(11) *Management Science* S50); or using philosophical and epistemological theories in order to analyse the formation of mathematical definitions (C Ouvrier-Buffet, 'Exploring Mathematical Definition Construction Processes' (2006) 63(3) *Educational Studies in Mathematics* 259).

[110] *Exxon Corp v Exxon Insurance* [1982] RPC 69 (Justice Graham) at 77.

[111] Vienna Convention on the Law of Treaties 1969, Art 31; (UK): *Investors Compensation Scheme Ltd v West Bromwich Building Society* [1998] 1 WLR 896 (Lord Hoffmann) at 913; *Antaios Cia Naviera SA v Salen Rederierna* [1984] 3 All ER 229 (Lord Diplock) at 233; (USA): *Markman v Westview Instruments* [1996] 517 US 370; *Texas Digital Systems v Telegenix* (Fed Cir 2002) 308 F3d 1193; *Phillips v AWH Petroleum* (Fed Cir 2005) 415 F3d 1303.

[112] This gains legitimacy as the intention of the legislator, evidenced by preparatory legislative materials or from collateral records. It is inapplicable to defining NHT, which is not a legislative term.

[113] This gains legitimacy from a wide range of evidence (eg existing theories; standard practice; or social need), but is inapplicable to NHT because there is no accepted meaning, no pressing social need, and no rationale for elevating any specific theory.

[114] This gains legitimacy from the rationality inherent in ensuring that the law is performing the job that it currently has: eg what the claim writer intended, tempered by how the reasonable recipient would understand the claim (explored later).

[115] eg (n 111) 89 (Lord Justice Oliver).

[116] In common with other areas of law, eg in banking law, *Re Sigma Finance Corp* [2010] 1 All ER 571 (Lord Mance) at point 12.

[117] s 72(1)(c), UK Patents Act 1977 (as amended), requires an invention be disclosed 'sufficiently' to enable an ordinarily skilled person in the field to recreate it. In combination with s 72(1)(d), claims

this legal approach is that claims are framed on an understanding of the meanings of individual words, together with their meanings relative to each other.[118] To take this to its logical conclusion would be to suggest that a full scope of literal meaning for NHT should be supplemented by understanding 'health technologies', 'new technologies', and 'new health', an approach which becomes obviously unworkable when it is explored in the context of NHT, to which the discussion now turns.

2. Literal Interpretation: Exploring Possible Scope

In order for a literal interpretation of NHT to be established, there must be a valid means of determining the scope of the individual words, together with their composite meaning. Assessing the terms individually, the term 'new' can be interpreted as being 'novel' or 'innovative', but 'new' is inherently a relative term, because it can be distinguished from concepts such as being old or mainstream. So the first ambiguity is what is 'new' relative to? It cannot be relative to what is known, because (other than in patent law) it is a practical impossibility to discuss 'new' in the sense of the unknown. Indeed, 'new' might be relative to clinical trials, first commercial use, or rely on predating a mainstream usage. 'New' might be oriented to the time when the technology was developed (but even if this can be agreed, is this triggered by a post-scientific publication or post-patent publication?). The choice of limit on 'new' has the effect of drastically changing the amount of technology that is captured by the phrase NHT, so it cannot be arbitrary. The same is equally true of 'health', which at its narrowest means ill-health or the amelioration of medically recognized malfunctions,[119] but at its widest can address well-being from public as well as personal perspectives. In terms of 'technology', there is a similar definitional breadth of scope: 'technology' can be narrowly construed as 'only that part of innovation which relates to the science which underpins it'; or at its broadest can mean 'knowledge' or 'skill'.

Exploring the composite relationships between the terms hinges just as much on the scope of the terms individually. On a literal construction, NHT describes the scope of all technology as restricted to the context of health-related advancements ('health technology'). This may reduce the scope of technology, but it does not result in a useful definition because this still comprises a range: at its broadest being understood as including all well-being-related knowledge, and at its narrowest only including those techniques which are used in treating medically recognized conditions. Similarly, 'new' distinguishes technologies temporally ('new technology'), but again only provides a range of broad to narrow meanings. Finally, 'health' evolves over time, so 'new health' limits the meaning of health to a contemporary interpretation. For example, health in

---

are limited if they are not justified by the applicant's contribution to the field, or in a reproducible form: *Biogen v Medeva* [1997] RPC 1; *Generics (UK) Ltd v Lundbeck* [2007] EWHC 1040; [2008] EWCA Civ 311.

[118] Most jurisdictions expect applicants to seek skilled advice from Patent Agents (eg in the United Kingdom: *Kirin-Amgen v Transkaryotic Therapies (No 2)* [2005] RPC 9, at 187), but irrespective of who wrote the claim, courts construe it as being a mix of patent law terminology (eg 'comprising' and 'consisting of' defining entirely distinct relationships between two objects); technical terminology (eg agreed or independently corroborated by dictionary or expert evidence); and the applicant's specific meaning (tempered by how it is received by the 'ordinarily skilled person in the field'). For more on claim constructions and purposive construction: (UK) *Improver Corp v Remington* [1990] FSR 181 (Lord Hoffmann) at 189; *Catnic Components Ltd v Hill & Smith Ltd* [1982] RPC 183 (Lord Diplock) at 243; (USA) eg Orsenga K, 'Linguistics and Patent Claim Construction' (2006) 38 *Rutgers Law Journal* 61.

[119] *MEDI-PHYSICS/Treatment by Surgery* [2010] EPOR 25.

the 21st century diverges significantly in comparison to the Middle Ages, where expectations about longevity and quality of life vastly differ.

This discussion demonstrates that not only do the individual terms identify a range of meanings, but so do their interrelationships. The problem created is that, overall, a literal interpretation does not identify a meaning of NHT, it only describes an array of options leading to the capture of so many interpretations that they cannot be utilized in practice in any context. Fundamentally, a literal interpretation is ambiguous, because it provides no mechanism for reducing the scope from an array of equally possible meanings.

3. New Health Technology Purposively Construed

Purposive construction represents a possible solution, because it combines literal and non-literal interpretations. Where a literal interpretation does not resolve ambiguity, a non-literal interpretation is adopted by combining the meaning intended by the provider of the terminology with the understanding of its recipient.[120] The fundamental purpose of a definition of NHT is to facilitate multi-disciplinary discourse and the formulation of effective regulation based on a common understanding, which is capable of evolving over time. Consequently, in this context, a non-literal interpretation accommodates a narrower meaning of NHT than a literal interpretation, because a non-literal interpretation must rationalize existing language used in policy/regulatory academic discourse mapped to that used in other academic/scientific discourses. A commonly agreed meaning, here represented by the map definition, must provide the broadest meaning that will be accessible to disparate parties involved in the advancement of health technology, tempered by the need to be useful in those contexts. Inherently, individual users of the map definition should be able to adopt narrower interpretations within the map's broader scope, but it must be possible to locate every debate or regulatory instrument within the map definition (providing the common reference).

This establishes a theoretical basis for interpreting NHT purposively (combining literal and non-literal interpretation) as a phrase comprising pre-existing discrete descriptive terms (information capture from a range of disciplines) interrelated in an organizing scheme (mapped) to identify the composite relationships between the terms. Fundamentally, a purposive construction of NHT must address the needs of users and receivers of the mapped terms in order to provide an accessible and shared definition. Precisely how this is achieved in the context of discrete terms from disparate disciplines, how it relates to the individual and composite meanings of NHT, and the limiting factors which can ensure that the map definition retains its applicability are what this chapter now focuses upon.

C. Explaining the Map Definition of New Health Technology

1. Mapping and a Three-Level Nomenclature

The construction of a purposive definition of NHT necessitates the creation of three organizing levels (see Figure 4.1). First, 'categories of general health technologies'

---

[120] EPC 2010, Art 69 and the Protocol to Art 69; discussed in more detail in C Wadlow, 'Requiem for a noun: the "terms of the claim" (1953–2007)' (2011) 33(3) *EIPR* 146; (UK): *Catnic* (n 118) (Lord Diplock) at 241–3; *Kirin-Amgen* (n 118), at 185; and explored in some detail in *Deutsche Trustee Co Ltd v Fleet Street Finance Three plc, Party A* [2011] EWHC 2117 (Ch), points 42–50.

Table 4.1 Mapping Group A categories

Patent Terminology	Regulatory Bodies Terminology	Group A
Products	Pharmaceuticals & Herbals	Materials used in treatments
	Devices	General Medical Equipment/Devices
Methods of Using Products in Treatments by: Surgery	Processes (eg therapies)	Medical Procedures
Methods of Using Products in Treatments by Therapy		Treatments
Methods of Using Products in Treatments by Diagnosis	Surveillance	Information-Gathering/ Diagnostics
Process		Testing

(Group A), which represents the broadest category, providing a macro perspective. Secondly, 'technological groups' (Group B) representing the median perspective. Thirdly, 'specific applications of technology' (Groups C1&2), comprising the narrowest/micro perspective.

Group A draws upon established categories within patent legislation and medical practice (Table 4.1), representing the most generic and most specific existing groupings of health technology (respectively). The patent system draws distinctions between products, processes, and methods of using products which in a medical context, results in distinctions being made between medical procedures such as surgery, treatments such as therapies, and diagnosis.[121] Regulatory bodies (for example, EMA, the UK Medicine and Healthcare product Regulatory Agency (MHRA)) utilize distinctions between: products (pharmaceuticals or herbals); devices; processes such as therapies; and surveillance such as pharmacovigilance. Between these are commonalities, which can be rationalized into a generally accepted list of health technologies, represented by Group A (Table 4.1 and Figure 4.1).

Group B is reached through analysis of the interface between science and academic literature on patenting/regulation and regulatory instruments/policy documents. Group C (1&2) is derived from scientific journals.

The creation of these different categories enables links to be made between the general category (Group A), the technological groups (Group B), and individual examples of technological applications which evidence them (Group C (1&2)). For example, 'gene therapy' refers to treatments which target genomic DNA for the purpose of treating/curing a malfunction/disease. This is done by excising or splicing existing genomic instructions, which are causal factors in malfunctions/diseases, whilst the genomic DNA is still in the nucleus of somatic (adult) cells. This definition includes these genomic processes conducted *in vivo* (within the patient), but also include *in vitro* (within a lab) processes, which additionally refers to the need to harvest the somatic cells before they are genetically manipulated and the protein product/genomic materials (for example, DNA, amino acids, or polypeptide chains) administered to a patient

[121] EPC 2010, Art 53(c).

(providing the capacity for administration to a third party). Clearly, 'targeting genomic DNA for the purpose of treating/curing' as a definition fails to distinguish the context in which the intervention occurs and this could mean that regulation aimed at specific interventions would not easily identify the technological applications which fall within its remit.

Utilizing the sample of the map definition above (Table 4.2, text in bold), it becomes clear that the definition of 'gene therapy' permits a distinction to be made between *in vivo* interventions, excluding *in vitro* processes (identified in C2) which harvest protein products/genomic material for use as treatments (because this comes within the meaning of 'biologics', which are a discrete technological group). The ordinary meaning of 'gene therapy' also includes processes performed on cells outside the human body for the purposes of testing drugs, but these cannot be regarded as a form of 'treatment'. The map definition distinguishes all of these applications. Comparatively, a descriptive definition such as 'targeting genomic DNA for the purpose of treating/curing' cannot convey this degree of detail or easily draw distinctions without confusing the definition user.

In addition, genomic material is a biomaterial when administered within gene therapy (Group A, 'materials used in treatments'), distinguishing it from the factory cells (a biotool: Group A 'general medical equipment/devices'), the cellular/genomic materials they produce (biologics: Group A 'general medical equipment/devices'), and their use specifically for cellular toxicology models (Group A 'testing'). This demonstrates that the map definition overcomes many of the problems with delineating different applications/aspects of the same basic technology faced by the ATMP Regulation (discussed in subsection A3). This illustrates how the map definition can support sophisticated distinctions between applications of technology and specific contexts, but still create a cohesive understanding of 'gene therapy'.

The map definition also enables 'gene therapy' to be understood as both a form of technology (Group B) and an application context for the technology entitled 'therapeutic cloning' (Group C2) (Table 4.2, italic text), which is important because there is a clear scientific distinction between the methods used to create cloned/stem cells and those used to effect gene therapy. Consequently, cloning and gene therapy must be regarded as separate forms of technology, but this example highlights that some forms of technology inherently convey their application while others do not. It also demonstrates the blurring that already occurs in distinguishing 'technology' and 'application', justifying the amalgamation of 'technology', 'innovation', and 'application' within a purposive construction (discussed at subsection C2).

It is entirely possible to undertake all of the same processes described with somatic cell gene therapy with germ-line cells (for example, sperm or ova). Germ-line gene therapy is not patentable[122] and would be unlikely to be granted market authorization through organizations such as the EMA/UK MHRA.[123] Consequently, it is a form of technology which is not applied in practice, which removes it from the map definition.

This exemplification demonstrates that, even with the benefit of established scientific and legal terminology, the definitions of particular technological groups must be

---

[122] The Biotech Directive (Directive 98/44/EEC on the Legal Protection of Biotechnological Inventions, 6 July 1998: [1998] OJ L213 EC 30 July 1998) excludes this through Recital 40, which states that it is 'important to exclude unequivocally from patentability processes for modifying the germ line genetic identity of human beings' and this is given legal force in Art 6(2)(b) on the grounds of immorality/being contrary to '*ordre public*'.
[123] (n 108).

Table 4.2 Mapping overlaps between technology and applications

A: General Category	B: Technological Groups	C1: Sample of Specific Example(s) of Technology	C2: Applications of Sampled Technology
TREATMENTS	*Gene Therapy* (somatic cell)	HACs(HumanArtificial Chromosomes)	Recombination requiring physical delivery/splicing, which cannot be achieved by simple drug delivery methods (eg injection in fluid)
	Biologics	Direct Therapeutics'anti-cancer agent—DT1-015 (carmustine, intratumoral)	Drug treatment for cancer
	Therapeutic Cloning	Non-embryonic Stem Cells (eg piPSCs/iPSCs)	Harvested and used in: *gene therapy*; drug treatment; organ, tissue or bone replacement; drug testing
TESTING	Toxicology Modelling	Chemical toxicity testing utilizing cells genetically engineered to express reliable levels of CYP enzymes	Used to determine substrate specificities and specific species differences
MATERIALS USED IN TREATMENTS	Bionanotechnology	DNA nanotubes, liposomes	*Delivery vehicles for Gene Therapy*; enhance drug absorbsion
GENERAL MEDICAL EQUIPMENT/ DEVICES	Bio-/other materials	Polymers or Silicons	Treatment of Acquired Brain Injury, etc.
	Biotools	DNA printers, probes, knockout mice, oncomouse, bio-engineered factor cells	Use in HGP, stages I–III; used as test models

narrowed in order to prevent overlaps that would have the effect of incorporating specific applications in more than one sub-category. It also identifies a need for filters that remove technologies which are not capable of progressing beyond a research phase. These limitations are discussed in more detail in subsection C3.

The map definition enables conclusions to be reached about the scope of the categories used. Group A must be comprehensive if the map definition is to be regarded as 'finished' (in as much as any capture of changing information can be regarded as completed). Group B must be as comprehensive as possible, but additionally includes advances in existing fields of expertise which are not separately listed (for example, chemical drugs, etc.), because they are not in themselves innovative fields of technology, even though discrete innovations will arise within them. Groups C1&2 provide only a single example of each technological group. This is because the groups are relative to the scope for change and the uses that the map definition will be put to. Group A are highly unlikely to change unless there is a new context in which a product/process is used. Group B will change only if a new scientific/technical sphere is developed. Group C will change all the time, so it exemplifies the other groups as technology is captured in 2012, but will need sporadic updating. This identifies that Figure 4.1 is incomplete: Groups B and C are limited, because it is not possible to list every existing field of expertise or every form of innovation. However, from these examples it should be obvious where new additions should be placed. Before exploring the principles and restrictions imposed on the map definition to prevent overlaps and rationalize duplicates, it is necessary to identify the overarching limits imposed upon NHT in order to arrive at this map definition.

2. Purposively Construing New Health Technology Relative to its Components

To obtain a useful and inclusive meaning of NHT, the relativity of the terms ('new', 'health', and 'technology') is paramount: if a broad interpretation is taken in construing one term, the interpretation of other terms must compensate in order to ensure that the capture of information is manageable, while still being as encompassing as possible. The relationship between the terms identifies that 'health' determines the broader context, 'technology' determines the narrower aspect, and 'new' determines the temporal quantity of information.

This means it is critical that 'health' is stringently limited in order to capture a manageable quantity which still encompasses divergent specialist fields. Making 'health' too broad would result in an unworkably vast map, because it forces the capture of information across every context. Consequently, 'health' is construed as meaning ill-health or the amelioration of a medically recognized disease or malfunction, rather than extending to interpretations incorporating well-being. This interpretation permits a commonality to be achieved in grouping widely divergent contexts to contentious issues, without having to qualify individual aspects of the contexts. For example, using Pre-implantation Genetic Diagnosis to ensure that a child is deaf, using technologies to artificially prolong life (without curative purposes), or using mind-enhancing drugs to increase normal mental abilities raise completely different contentions in comparison to using drugs/equipment/fertility treatments to cure/prevent diseases. This approach also justifies an otherwise arbitrary distinction between pharmfoods (which are included) and nutriceuticals (which are not).[124] Prophylactic treatments (such as vaccines) are included because, although preventative, they are primarily aimed at disease.

With a narrow definition of 'health', broader constructions of 'technology' and 'new' are possible. 'Technology' can be broadly construed as including technology, innovation, application, and knowledge. It could extend to systems, but this recasts 'health' as an incidental aspect of a much broader cache of systems management, incorporating mechanisms for organizing health care systems (as well as other fields). Consequently, systems are excluded from the definition of 'technology'. More specifically, technological fields such as toxicogenomics,[125] bioremedial technology, and bioweaponry[126] are all excluded, because they are insufficiently focused on ameliorating ill-health.

---

[124] Pharmfoods refer to the genetic manipulation of food in order to effect a pharmaceutical benefit and can be distinguished from nutriceuticals, which merely enhance well-being by increasing the vitamin/mineral value of specific food.

[125] This is an area which explores the toxicological effects on cells on a molecular level, which promises (amongst others) to enhance risk assessment of environmental influences on cellular activity and identify new targets for pharmaceutical development, as such it is about causative factors of disease/malfunctions.

[126] This refers to advancements in using micro-organisms (eg infectious agents such as vectors) to target specific genetic or geographical enemies and cause cellular damage which will either incapacitate the targeted population or cause death.

'New' could be construed narrowly (for example, meaning technology post-clinical trials, or arbitrarily picking the last three years to align with horizon scanning parameters), but this excludes academic disciplines at the beginning of the innovation chain (for example, scientists, patent commentators), as well as limiting the visibility of potential technological developments for policymakers and regulators. To include all groups, 'new' commences from first publication (whether in a scientific journal or the patent register)[127] and includes technologies at any stage before becoming mainstream/ routine. This approach includes developments in the medical research phase, because (in common with those going through clinical trials or market authorization procedures) they are not marketed even though they are administered. It also includes early market entry technology (for example, it has not yet been accepted or become sufficiently prevalent, but excluding mere lack of take-up).

The non-literal interpretation of NHT proposed in this chapter leads to a narrow construction of 'health', which facilitates a reasonably broad interpretation of 'technology' and a broad understanding of 'new'. This approach to defining NHT captures a scope of meaning which is applicable to policymakers, regulators, medical and scientific researchers, as well as academic commentators. Consequently, it complies with purposive construction. The ability to update the map definition, providing it with an enduring relevance, relies upon understanding the limitations which must be imposed in order to create a cohesive reference point and it is to these limitations that the assessment now turns.

3. Explaining Specific Limits Imposed on the Map Definition

As a general rule, terminology conveys its core, literal interpretation. For example, 'treatments' are products physically applied to patients to ameliorate medically recognized conditions and 'testing' is technology which assesses the effectiveness of those treatment products. Some exploration of overlaps and exceptions is necessary to enable future updating of the map definition, which of necessity represents current technology, but which needs to be flexible for future use.

Overlaps are resolved by the dominant use/technique categorizing the technology but, where this is not clear, a hybrid approach is adopted.[128] For example, bioinformatics[129] (Table 4.3, Group B) is a form of 'general medical equipment' (Group A), because it creates functioning disease models for testing treatments, making bioinformatics comparable to 'laseroptics' (a medical tool that enables diagnostic analysis). However, bioinformatics also relates to data-mining, which is a purely 'information-gathering/diagnostic' activity, so the duality is represented in aligning with one category and adopting the shading of another.

Where the core meaning of categories cannot be determined, this resulted in artificial categories being created. For example (Table 4.4), 'materials used in treatments'

---

[127] Equal in being measures of 'first known'.

[128] This is particularly relevant in adopting the map for regulatory purposes and it is notable that this is in line with the customary approach diverged from by the ATMP Regulation, discussed earlier.

[129] This refers to the use of computing techniques (such as data-mining and imaging) to biology in order to facilitate the identification of new information about the way in which, eg, biological systems operate and diseases progress, as well as giving researchers new mechanisms for interfacing and dealing with vast amounts of information.

Table 4.3 Mapping overlaps to dominant use

A: General Category	B: Technological Groups	C1: Sample of Specific Example(s) of Technology
GENERAL MEDICAL EQUIPMENT/ DEVICES	Medical Professionals' Tools	Optics (eg lasers, fibre optics), Portable Imaging (eg Magnetic Resonance Imaging, MRI; Radiographic Imaging; microscopes)
	Bioengineering	Prosthetics that interface with muscular signals; bionic eyes
	Bioinformatics	Data-Mining
INFORMATION-GATHERING/ DIAGNOSTICS	BioBanks/ CellBanks/…	Repositories for DNA/cells/tissue

Table 4.4 Creating artificial subdivisions where dominant use is not clear

A: General Category	B: Technological Groups	C1: Sample of Specific Example(s) of Technology
TREATMENTS	Gene Therapy (somatic cell)	HACs (Human Artificial Chromosomes)
	Therapeutic Cloning	Non-embryonic Stem Cells (eg piPSCs/iPSCs)
	Monoclonal Antibodies	Trastuzumab
TESTING		
MATERIALS USED IN TREATMENTS	Bio-/other materials	**Polymers or Silicons**
	Bionanotechnology	DNA nanotubes, liposomes
	Nanotechnology	Buckytubes/Buckyballs,nanoparticles such as copolymers/polymers/polysaccharides
GENERAL MEDICAL EQUIPMENT/ DEVICES	Biotools	DNA printers, probes, knockout mice, oncomouse, bioengineered factory cells
	Medical Professionals' Tools	Optics (eg lasers, fibre optics), Portable Imaging (eg Magnetic Resonance Imaging, MRI Radiographic Imaging; microscopes)
	Patient-Based Tools	Wheelchairs; mechanical prosthetics; sensory responsive equipment
	Biomechanics	Physiometric analysis: measures movement relative to level of injury/risk
	Bioengineering	Prosthetics that interface with muscular signals; bionic eyes

accommodates the use of products not traditionally associated with 'treatments', such as polymers[130] developed for use in Acquired Brain Injuries (ABI).[131] Polymers are administered in an emergency medical context, making them 'treatments', but they do not cure/improve primary ABI damage, taking them outside a core definition of 'treatment'. Similarly, polymers are administered invasively, directly to the patient, preventing their categorization as medical equipment (which is generally reserved for medical devices, scanning, or imaging equipment). As a result, they are classed as 'materials used in treatments'.

The introduction of biobanks, cell and/or tissue banks,[132] which utilize information as a diagnostic tool and as a key source of future medical technology, expands the 'diagnostic' category to a wider interpretation than traditionally accepted (Table 4.5). Consequently, 'information-gathering/diagnostics' represents the distinction between the tests which enhance medical understanding of ill-health (which fall within it), and tests which precede this phase and are generally not directly related to reaching a medical prognosis, such as testing treatments during research procedures, and which are categorized as 'testing'.

Table 4.5 Accommodating technology which challenges general categorization

A: General Category	B: Technological Groups	C1: Sample of Specific Example(s) of Technology
TREATMENTS		
TESTING	Toxicology Modelling	Chemical toxicity testing utilizing cells geneticall engineered to express reliable levels of CYP enzymes
	Synthetic Biology	BioBricks
MATERIALS USED IN TREATMENTS		
GENERAL MEDICAL EQUIPMENT/ DEVICES	Bioinformatics	Data-Mining
INFORMATION-GATHERING/ DIAGNOSTICS	BioBanks/CellBanks/ Tissue Banks	Repositories for DNA/cells/ tissue
	Genetic Screening: *in vitro* Diagnostic Tests	TREK's Yeast On susceptibility plate
	Genetic Screening: *in vivo* Diagnostic Tests	'Xenomics' molecular diagnostic test kit detects *in vivo* cell death from urine/other body fluids
	Human Genome Project	eg Work by NIH and MRC

[130] Polymer is a term for molecules which are comprised of a chain of smaller atomic units (known as monomers). While they can be made of anything, DNA would be one example of a polymer, because it is comprised of smaller base pairs (called nucleotides), which are vertically bound together by sugar and phosphate bonds.

[131] AO Koob, JM Colby, and RB Borgens, 'Behavioural Recovery from Traumatic Brain Injury After Membrane Reconstruction Using Polyethylene Glycol' (2008) 2(1) *Journal of Biological Engineering* 9.

[132] Biobanks, cell/tissue banks refer to research organizations/repositories which store genetic material.

This analysis demonstrates two main points. First, it identifies the organizing principles of the map definition, making it easy to revise in accordance with technological developments in the future. Secondly, it demonstrates the benefits of constructing a definition as a map. This latter aspect requires further analysis, to which the final subsection of this chapter turns.

D. Utility to Users

As discussed in subsection C1, regulation of NHT may need to develop incrementally as technology emerges, but to be effective it must be underpinned by a shared interpretation of the technological scope to which it applies. The same is equally true of regulatory bodies: with so many organizations responsible for the oversight of health technology, it is crucial that the policies of regulatory bodies and the guidance they issue are easily accessible to everyone. Within academic discourse there is a need for a common understanding of NHT, to facilitate multi-disciplinary debate. Adopting too broad a definition of NHT makes meaningful analysis unachievable, because it creates too many provisos which must be qualified. This can be demonstrated by the safety of artificially enhanced food requiring an accepted and shared understanding of pharmfoods, which does not rely on first being distinguished from nutriceuticals.

Adopting too narrow a definition of NHT means academic, policy, or public debates are fragmented and do not penetrate every field of significance. For example, ethical issues raised by scientific methods to create pluripotent stem cells are likely to be relevant in therapeutic cloning,[133] and collaterally relevant in cell banking and gene therapy, which may not be appreciated in regulating any of these areas. Adopting a definition of NHT which lacks detail dilutes the value of social understanding generally, as well as attenuating regulation and policy. Adopting a definition that is not inclusive of all the specialist fields affected by it misses opportunities for rationalizing regulation across diverse fields. Clearly, this is not the case with the map definition, which encourages links to be spotted between vastly different areas of expertise (Table 4.6).

The map definition developed in this chapter provides a multilevel nomenclature, comprised of a common framework derived from all relevant specialist fields and presented in a readily accessible form. Further, it accommodates the need for both broad generalizations and for specific examples, enabling the user to decide which is required. This means that use of a broad generalization can be traced to its specific details (for example, making it easier to frame regulation without the need for an awkward preamble) and use of a specific example can be tracked to other instances in which contentious issues are the unifying factor.

The utility of the map definition in regulatory and academic debates can be exemplified for clarity. In the absence of the map, a social scientist exploring specific issues raised by NHT in risk analysis may explore their specialist area in the context of a discrete technological application (for example, analysing the risk management of biomaterials) or may discuss risk analysis across an undefined/social science-based tacit understanding of NHT.

---

[133] Therapeutic cloning refers to the process of generating cells/tissue through copying and this can include the generation of stem cells.

Table 4.6 Using the map definition to understand the broader relevance of a narrow analysis: facilitating multidisciplinary exchange

A: General Category	B: Technological Groups	C1: Sample of Specific Example(s) of Technology
TREATMENTS	Gene Therapy (somatic cell)	HACs (Human Artificial Chromosomes)
	Therapeutic Cloning	Non-embryonic Stem Cells (eg piPSCs/iPSCs)
TESTING		
MATERIALS USED IN TREATMENTS		
GENERAL MEDICAL EQUIPMENT/DEVICES		
INFORMATION-GATHERING/ DIAGNOSTICS		
PROCEDURES	Scientific Technique	Protein-Induced Pluripotent Stem Cells (PiPSCs)

Table 4.7 Using the map definition to identify the field of inquiry (more broadly and more narrowly) and as a short cut for readers

A: General Category	B: Technological Groups	C1: Sample of Specific Example(s) of Technology	C2: Applications of Sampled Technology
TREATMENTS			
TESTING	Toxicology Modelling	Chemical toxicity testing utilizing cells genetically engineered to express reliable levels of CYP enzymes	Used to determine substrate specificities and specific species differences
	Synthetic Biology	BioBricks	Drug Testing
MATERIALS USED IN TREATMENTS	Bio-/other materials	Polymers or Silicons	Treatment of Acquired Brain Injury, etc.
	Bio-nanotechnology	DNA nanotubes, liposomes	Delivery vehicles for Gene Therapy; enhance drug absorbsion
	Nanotechnology	Buckytubes/Buckyballs, nanoparticles such as copolymers/ polymers/polysaccharides	
GENERAL MEDICAL EQUIPMENT/ DEVICES	Biotools	DNA printers, probes, knockout mice, oncomouse, bioengineered factory cells	Used in HGP, stages I–III; used as test models

The map definition (Table 4.7) identifies that these issues have a broader technological application. This enables the researcher to develop analyses of discrete technologies (for example, biomaterials), individual examples of technology (for example, polymers), or of broader categories (eg, 'treatments', which are inherently implicated by 'materials used in treatments'). In addition, it enables the researcher to see potential links to other forms of products used in health care. For example, one option would be to make connections to polymers/copolymers used within nanotechnology (changing the scale of the product). Another option is to consider the risks inherent in other forms of health care products, such as biotools (changing the context of use from a 'material used in treatment' to 'general medical equipment/devices' where use occurs in a research context). The researcher could use the map definition to identify links with BioBricks (identifying a new form of technology such as synthetic biology[134] with which to compare/contrast issues of risk), or identify other examples of biomaterials (for example, changing from polymers to silicons, or exploring other materials not specifically exemplified on the map definition). Irrespective of which option the researcher decides upon, the readers of the analysis will easily be able to understand it in all of those contexts, because the map enables both the user and receiver to explore the links between discrete technological areas, examples, and categories.

E. Conclusion

Health technologies are highly regulated, and new developments are the most contentious and arguably the most in need of effective management if the social benefits they promise are to be realized. At present, the use of the phrase NHT is confined to policy documents, regulatory organizations, and commentary, but there is no implicitly understood or generally accepted meaning of the phrase. The absence of a common understanding of NHT inhibits multi-disciplinary debate and consequently impairs regulation. A useful and workable interpretation of NHT must rationalize fragmented scientific terminology, aligning it with existing categories utilized in policy, regulatory, academic, and scientific contexts.

In order to achieve such an understanding of NHT, the full scope of meaning must be explored. Standard principles of legal interpretation identify that a literal meaning of 'new', 'health', and 'technology' are supplemented by NHT as a composite phrase. Principles of patent claim construction suggest the additional incorporation of the relationship between the words. The impracticality of adopting a literal interpretation is abundantly clear when this construction is applied to NHT: it yields only a range of possible meanings, with no clear mechanism to guide a specific choice between options. This chapter argued that purposive construction, which centres interpretation upon its fundamental purpose as a context-based mechanism of communication, is an appropriate method for limiting the scope of meaning. This approach mediates the meaning of phrases between the intentions of the framer and the understanding of the recipient. The analysis in this chapter demonstrates how purposive construction can be used to construct a map definition of NHT as a three-level nomenclature underpinned by: 'health' understood narrowly as ill-health; 'technology' understood reasonably broadly as synonymous with innovation, application, and knowledge, but excluding

---

[134] In this context, this refers to the creation of entirely new organisms or the basic genetic building blocks from which to develop new organisms.

systems; and 'new' understood inclusively as spanning first publication right up until mainstream use. The resultant map definition presents three levels (broad generalization, technological group, and individual exemplification), which are drawn from relevant sources concerned with health technology. This approach has the effect of identifying NHT as a composite phrase (collectively described by the mechanisms used to resolve the inherent lack of interface between specialist areas, guided by the need for utility, inclusiveness, and longevity, and represented by the map as a whole), as well as rationalizing and categorizing scientific terminology to furnish detail in relation to specific technological applications.

Progress in health technology has become increasingly specialist and, as it spans diverse scientific disciplines (such as biology, mathematics, chemistry, and computers), there is increasing pressure for policymakers, regulators, academic commentators, and practitioners in law/medicine to consider the implications of NHTs from an equally informed mix of interfacing specialist fields. This chapter provides a new starting point from which policymaking, regulation, and academic discourse can determine how to regulate, using this map definition of NHT as the foundation of a shared understanding of what is being regulated.

Map definition: New Health Technologies

A: General Category	B: Technological Groups	C1: Sample of Specific Example(s) of Technology	C2: Applications of Sampled Technology
TREATMENTS	Gene Therapy (somatic cell)	HACs (Human Artificial Chromosomes)	Recombination requiring physical delivery/splicing, which cannot be achieved by simple drug delivery methods (eg injection in fluid)
	Biologics	Direct Therapeutics' anti-cancer agent -DJT1-015 (carmustine, intratumoral)	Drug treatment for cancer
	Therapeutic Cloning	Non-embryonic Stem Cells (eg piPSCs/iPSCs)	Harvested and used in: gene therapy; drug treatment; organ, tissue or bone replacement; drug testing
	Monoclonal Antibodies	Trastuzumab	Drug Treatment for metastatic breast cancer
	Antisense Technology	OGX-011 (secondary form of treatment): Inhibits clusterin, with effect of making resistant tumours susceptible to normal cancer treatments	Drug treatment (Antisense Treatments are limited to removing/reducing protein activity, but cannot correct cellular effects)
	Tissue Engineering	Artificial Skin; nervous systems; ears	Burns victims / Nerve network, human ear, human heart, etc.
	Xenotransplantation	'humanisation' on a genetic level of pig hearts	Transplantation (Immutran licensed to do trials currently)
	Pharmfoods	Lettuce containing insulin	Treatment of diabetes
TESTING	Toxicology Modelling	Chemical toxicity testing utilising cells genetically engineered to express reliable levels of CYP enzymes	Used to determine substrate specificities and specific species differences
	Synthetic Biology	BioBricks	Drug Testing
MATERIALS USED IN TREATMENTS	Bio-/other-materials	Polymers or Silicons	Treatment of Acquired Brain Injury, etc.
	Bionanotechnology	DNA nanotubes, liposomes	Delivery vehicles for Gene Therapy; enhance drug absorbsion
	Nanotechnology	Buckytubes/Buckyballs, nanoparticles such as copolymers/polymers/ polysaccharides	
GENERAL MEDICAL EQUIPMENT/ DEVICES	Biotools	DNA printers, probes, knockout mice, oncomouse, bio-engineered factory cells	Used in HGP, stages I-III; used as test models
	Medical Professionals' Tools	Optics (eg lasers, fibre optics); Portable Imaging (eg Magnetic Resonance Imaging, MRI; Radiographic Imaging; microscopes)	Used in treatments and diagnosis
	Patient-Based Tools	Wheelchairs; mechanical prosthetics; sensory responsive equipment	Rehab & Life enhancement

(continued)

A: General Category	B: Technological Groups	C1: Sample of Specific Example(s) of Technology	C2: Applications of Sampled Technology
	Biomechanics	Physiometric analysis: measures movement relative to level of injury/risk	Used to prevent lifting-related injuries in the workplace; used to identify level of injury to facilitate return-to-work
	Bioengineering	Prosthetics that interface with muscular signals; bionic eyes	Limb/organ replacement
	Bioinformatics	Data Mining	Creates/organises Information; creates functioning disease models
INFORMATION GATHERING/ DIAGNOSTICS	BioBanks/CellBanks/ Tissue Banks	Repositories for DNA/cells/tissue	Information; Starting Materials
	Genetic Screening: In Vitro Diagnostic Tests	TREK's YeastOne susceptibility plate	Used to identify and develop drugs for 'Super Bugs', created by increased antibiotic resistance
	Genetic Screening; In Vivo Diagnostic Tests	Xenomics' molecular diagnostic test kit detects in vivo cell death from urine/other body fluids	Use in detecting neuro-degenerative diseases, eg. Alzheimers, strokes, etc.
	Human Genome Project	eg Work by NIH & MRC	Sequenced the human genome; identifying links with diseases, identifying links with proteins and other microbiological products
PROCEDURES	Surgical Techniques	Irreversible Electroporation (IRE) Technique	Microsecond electrical pulses punch nanoscale holes in the membranes of target (tumour) cells, without harming the integrity of the surrounding cellular structure
	Medical Technique	Motor Cortex Stimulation	Alleviates severe chronic facial pain
	Scientific Technique	Protein Induced Pluripotent Stem Cells (PiPSCs)	Uses four proteins to regress pluripotent stem cells into embryo-like stem cells, notably with no requirement for genetic alterations/additions
	Diagnostic Technique	Breath analysis for volatile organic compounds (under investigation)	Breast Cancer Detection

Strategies of Regulation: Illustrations from the Work of the Human Genetics Commission

*Jonathan Montgomery**

Not all regulators are alike. Nor do all regulatory issues require the same approach. This piece reflects on factors that affect the selection of regulatory options in the context of the work of a UK body that was not a 'regulator' in the sense of formally overseeing the activity of others. The Human Genetics Commission (HGC) did not directly wield legal power, but it had a recognized place in UK bioethical governance. It was established in 2000 to provide the UK Governments with advice on the ethical, legal, and social issues arising from Human Genetics and it adopted different approaches in various pieces of its work. It was disbanded in 2012 as part of the reconfiguration of non-governmental bodies, colloquially known as the 'bonfire of the quangos' (an acronym for quasi-autonomous non-governmental organizations), and partly replaced by an internal expert committee of the Department of Health in England to be known as the Emerging Science and Bioethics Advisory Committee (ESBAC).

The Commission can point to a number of regulatory successes in the instigation of legal interventions, such as the crime of DNA theft under the Human Tissue Act 2004. However, in other pieces of work different modes of regulation have emerged. Its interim recommendation in 2001 that there should be a moratorium on the use of predictive genetic testing in insurance led to such a moratorium being announced by the Association of British Insurers later that year, which has been periodically renewed by agreement with the governments of the day. In other areas the Commission was not able to convince its audiences of the wisdom of its views, as in the need for legal protection against genetic discrimination. Here, the Commission recommended in 2002 that consideration needed to be given to specific legislation protecting people against discrimination on the basis of genetics. It considered that existing discrimination provisions (specifically the protections against unequal treatment on the basis of disability or the perception of disability) were inadequate to achieve this (a view that persisted even after the amendment of the Disability Discrimination Act 1995 following the EU Employment Directive 2000). The Disability Rights Task Force (1999) was not convinced. The HGC's suggestion that the UK's Equality Act 2010 should include specific genetic discrimination provisions was also rejected. Nevertheless, the Commission sought to keep the issue alive by convening a high-level seminar with the Arts and Humanities Research Council and recommending in its

---

* The views expressed here are personal and do not represent the formal views of the Human Genetics Commission.

consideration of the report of that seminar that the Equality and Human Rights Commission should continue to monitor evidence of genetic discrimination and keep the need for legislative change under review (*The Concept of Genetic Discrimination: A Seminar Report and Reflections and Recommendations* 2011).

These examples illustrate how the Commission needed to consider the opportunities for both short and longer term intervention and also a range of regulatory options. In some cases a specific and immediate legal intervention can be promoted. Where that failed it was necessary to consider how influence might be brought to bear over a longer time frame or through less direct regulatory approaches. Thus, it is necessary to consider the type of normative intervention that is ultimately most likely to promote the activities and behaviours that have been identified as desirable. Such regulatory strategies are sometimes obscured by the more explicit consideration of substantive issues in the final published reports, which are the activities that generally receive the most attention. It may, however, be equally important to consider how decisions were taken on how best to frame inquiries when they are established and also how recommendations are championed once the conclusions of the deliberations have been reached. These can be messy and difficult to disentangle; the context in which a report is published may be different from that in which it was initiated, the degree to which the 'regulator' can control the reception of its reports is limited, and the conclusions that are reached may be unanticipated. Nevertheless, some scoping of how choices of regulatory strategy may be made is possible.

It will be grouped here under two headings. The first concerns issues relating to the art of the possible that result in the investigations being framed on the basis that some possibilities that are theoretically open are to be regarded as fixed for the purpose of the inquiry. This would include an assessment of the constraints put in place by aspects of the regulatory framework that are regarded as given (at least at the point of time in question), the realities of technological possibilities in the proximate future (distinguishing hyperbolic speculation from plausible developments within the regulatory time horizon), and socio-political and economic contexts that are not expected to be amenable to influence within the time frame of the inquiry.

The second concerns which actors' behaviour the regulator should set out to influence. This might cover both providers and consumers of services. It could address governmental, professional, and trade bodies. It might be concerned to shape the terms of public debate, either directly or through opinion formers such as various media. Each of these aspects of consideration is likely to colour the prudent selection of regulatory measures that are likely to be effective. The regulator's task in this is neatly captured by Reinhold Niebuhr's prayer to be granted the serenity to accept the things that cannot be changed, the courage to change the things that should be changed, and the wisdom to tell the difference.

These points can be elaborated in relation to the issue of genetic tests directly available to consumers without the intermediary of health service provision. The HGC had explored issues arising from the possibilities of widely available genetic testing in *Genes Direct* (2003) and *More Genes Direct* (2007) before it embarked on a specific piece of work on direct-to-consumer tests that led to the publication of *A Common Framework of Principles for Direct-to-Consumer Genetic Testing* (2010). Rather than proposing the extension of formal regulation beyond that already in place under the EU *In Vitro* Diagnostic Devices Directive, this framework sought to establish a consensus on high-level principles through a collaborative process involving stakeholders from mainland Europe and the USA as well as the United Kingdom who represented public, professional, regulatory bodies, governments, and charities, as well as companies providing direct testing services. The principles included standards of scientific quality, marketing, the categorization of tests including those where results should only be communicated by an appropriate health professional, and issues relating to the genetic testing of children.

The proposal of a code of good practice were criticized by some for lack of courage, shying away from recommending a ban of a practice in which it saw many pitfalls. However, a number of features of the context were significant in explaining why this approach made sense to the Commission. First, the market about which concerns had been raised was a transnational one. Test kits might be bought and marketed in the United Kingdom but it was highly likely that the actual testing would be carried out abroad, especially in the USA. Given the nature of internet marketing it was also possible that the marketing and purchase would also occur in the USA, swabs of samples being taken by the consumers in the United Kingdom when kits were sent to them, and then sent abroad for analysis. In this context, development of agreed principles for a code of practice had a better chance of securing acceptance from US providers of services than proposing regulatory restrictions at either UK or European level (even without taking into account the time that it might take to implement such restrictions). Once standards were in existence, they would also enable responsible testing companies to differentiate themselves from less reputable providers by using their compliance as a selling point and thereby giving a market advantage to good practice. Indirect force might be given to the standards where health professionals were involved via the requirements of professional ethics. In a world where there was clear demand for the services, the framework of principles might also serve to educate consumers to make better informed choices so that they were less likely to over-estimate the reliability, accuracy, or significance of results.

This could be achieved more quickly than a more formal regulatory approach would have permitted. This approach did not preclude the adoption of further regulatory options in the future. The intention of the Commission had been to return to the regulatory questions, but its abolition ended its work in the area. However, even in the absence of such interventions, the principles have already had an impact in international discussions and can therefore be seen as providing the foundation for further regulatory action but nevertheless as powerful in their own right. Further, they created an environment where interventions by regulators in different countries were more likely to adopt a common approach and consequently more likely to establish a consistent regulatory framework that had a chance to work robustly in a global cross-border market. Thus, in both the case of genetic discrimination and the direct-to-consumer testing, it could be said that the HGC was playing a long game—seeking to frame and influence the policy debates of the future even where it thought that early progress was unlikely. In part, this was a reaction to limitations placed on the authority and shelf life of the Commission following the announcement that it was to be wound down after the General Election of May 2010. However, this is not the whole picture. All regulators need to consider influencing strategies as part of their work and to shape the environment in which they work in order to achieve their long-term goals.

PART II

LEGAL APPROACHES TO EUROPEAN LAW AND NEW HEALTH TECHNOLOGIES

5

Innovative Tissue Engineering and Its Regulation—The Search for Flexible Rules for Emerging Health Technologies

*Nils Hoppe**

A. Introduction

Advances in tissue engineering techniques have resulted in the potential for ground-breaking new health technologies for human use. In some instances, the innovative leap represented by these products is significant and the potential benefit for patients, and in some cases for particularly vulnerable patient groups, is substantial. At the same time, recent regulatory initiatives at European level have made an attempt at determining European Union (EU)-wide minimum standards in relation to some aspects of working with human tissues and cells for use in humans. The implementation of these standards in the EU's Member States (MSs)—from procurement over manufacture to marketing authorization—seems at first glance not to have led to the desired level of regulatory harmony and the categorization of such products in individual MSs may well represent an obstacle for market entry in the case of particularly innovative products.

This can arguably be traced back to at least two reasons. First, the complex character of these products: whilst in some instances, tissue engineered products fall squarely under the definitions envisaged in the appropriate EU instruments, some innovations do not and slight deviations in domestic implementation of the Directives lead to a heterogeneous regulatory landscape and the potential for a regulatory corset unable to facilitate the bedside deployment of very innovative research results.[1] Secondly,

* This chapter's descriptive parts rely heavily on work undertaken by a number of colleagues in relation to an overview study of the legal situation in a number of MSs (unpublished) and information gathered during the course of an FP7 project (Tiss.EU, 2007–2011). I am grateful for the work of Anna Ocka Böhnke (EU and German law), Shawn Harmon (UK), Aurelie Mahalatchimy and Emmanuelle Rial-Sebag (France). I am also extremely grateful to Samir Sarikouch (MHH) for advice on the technical aspects of DHV development and to Samantha Pegg for discussions and advice in relation to poisoning offences. Any errors and inaccuracies are, of course, my own.

[1] I acknowledge that there is an ongoing discussion on how the law might deal with fast-moving regulatory targets (see eg R Brownsword and K Yeung (eds), *Regulating Technologies—Legal Futures, Regulatory Frames and Technological Fixes* (Hart 2008) and R Brownsword, *Rights, Regulation, and the Technological Revolution* (OUP 2008)). Whilst I would suggest that it is clear that health innovations never occur in a legal vacuum (the law's most abstract norms will usually always encompass the status quo), it is evident that where we choose to regulate specifically, the quality and efficacy of such regulation is a paramount concern. It is the aim of this chapter to investigate whether specific regulation in the area of regenerative medicine comes up to the standard we are entitled to expect.

regulatory activity in relation to material derived from the human body is traditionally generally very prohibitive and legislators are reluctant to make such cells and tissues available in an unrestricted fashion.[2] This raises issues of regulatory quality and serious ethical concerns in relation to ensuring that innovative health technologies are made available swiftly and safely. In order to illustrate the functioning of EU regulatory initiatives and their interplay with disparate MS implementations in the context of new health technologies, I will use a therapeutic intervention currently being developed in the context of a large-scale translational regenerative medicine cluster in Hannover as an example.

A particularly promising field of tissue engineering is that of substantially altering human donor heart valves to increase the transplant's lifetime and recipient tolerance. Classically available therapeutic interventions for replacing dysfunctional pulmonary heart valves include xenografts (usually bovine or porcine), allografts (from post-mortem donors), or artificial valves. Innovative tissue engineering processes permit the decellularization of certain grafts, essentially a washing process which removes vital cells and leaves only a collagen scaffold behind. This scaffold has mechanical properties comparable to native valves and there is an expectation that this innovation will lead to an 'alternative source to create viable, nonimmunogenic, and biologically active grafts'.[3] Early reports indicate that the decellularized homograft valve (DHV) manifests a number of advantages over the outlined conventional treatments.[4] First, the quick manufacturing process and short time from manufacture to deployment in a patient mean that potentially deleterious cryogenic preservation processes[5] can generally be avoided. Secondly, the lack of vital donor cells after decellularization increases recipient tolerance of the graft by dramatically reducing immunogenicity which may result in increased preservation of good valve function. Thirdly, there is some evidence to suggest that the scaffold is homogeneously populated by autologous cells, leading to excellent organismic integration. Finally, there is preliminary evidence to suggest that classic problems of heart valve transplantation, such as infections and calcification of the transplant, may occur in fewer cases with DHV.

These last three observations contribute to the DHV increasingly looking like the gold standard for the treatment of children and young adults: this patient group has a much higher immunological competence (less immunogenicity of the valve is therefore a distinct advantage) and an excellent physical integration means a reduced necessity to subsequently reoperate to refit appropriately sized valves. The expected longer lifetime of the DHV contributes to longer time spans between reoperations, significantly

---

[2] See N Hoppe, *Bioequity—Property and the Human Body* (Ashgate 2009).

[3] S Cebotari, I Tudorache, A Ciubotaru, D Boethig, S Sarikouch, A Goerler, A Lichtenberg, E Cheptanaru, S Barnaciuc, A Cazacu, O Maliga, O Repin, L Maniuc, T Breymann, and A Haverich, 'Use of Fresh Decellularized Allografts for Pulmonary Valve Replacement May Reduce the Reopera-tion Rate in Children and Young Adults—Early Report' (2011) 124 *Circulation* S115, S115.

[4] Cebotari and others (n 3).

[5] There is evidence, the statistical significance of which is not undisputed, that cryogenic preserva-tion leads to a reduced elasticity of the valve. Other reported effects include deterioration of some structures following possible ice formation. See K Schenke-Layland, N Madershahian, I Riemann, B Starcher, KJ Halbhuber, K König, and UA Stock, 'Impact of Cryopreservation on Extracellular Matrix Structures of Heart Valve Leaflets' (2006) 81 *Ann Thorac Surg* 918; cf CJ Gerson, RC Elkins, S Goldstein, and AE Heacox, 'Structural Integrity of Collagen and Elastin in SynerGraft Decellular-ized-Cryopreserved Human Heart Valves' (2012) 64 *Cryobiology* 33 and GL Converse, M Armstrong, RW Quinn, EE Buse, ML Cromwell, SJ Moriarty, GK Lofland, SL Hilbert, and RA Hopkins, 'Effects of Cryopreservation, Decellularization and Novel Extracellular Matrix Conditioning on the Quasi-static and Time-dependent Properties of the Pulmonary Heart Valve Leaflet' (2012) 8 *Acta Biomater-ialia* 2722.

reducing the risk associated with transplant degeneration and the general risk associated with cardithoracic surgery. Early reports therefore provide initial evidence that the DHV is, or at least will be, significantly superior to other treatment options, reduces the risk and burden to the patient, and is particularly relevant to vulnerable patient groups (children and young adults). From this premise there is ample ground to assume not only an ethical justification for advancing the development of this type of treatment but beyond that also an ethical duty to make it available. I will briefly address these ethical aspects at a later stage but first I will turn to the regulatory problems the DHV encounters in the current setting.

Developing, and ultimately routinely deploying, a new health technology such as the DHV clearly requires a close adherence to the appropriate regulatory framework for the type of health product it is. The regulatory landscape in relation to health products covers a number of different types of products[6] (outlined in more detail later), displaying different characteristics and attracting different kinds of these complex regulatory frameworks. It seems clear that a medicinal product (such as a headache tablet) and a medical device (such as a pacemaker) ought not be regulated in exactly the same kind of way—the former having to be metabolized by the organism for its chemical effect, the latter usually only exhibiting a mechanical or electrical effect.[7] It also seems plainly obvious that the first concern in relation to regulating health products must be the safety of the product[8]—the great rigidity of the rules relevant when bringing a new health technology from the lab bench to the patient's bedside is therefore eminently plausible. At the same time, this unyielding framework with its rigid product classes seems to have two significant effects. On the one hand, it may well cause less legal certainty and more confusion and thereby shackle the development of highly innovative tissue engineered products and significantly delay their bedside availability. On the other hand, much of the regulation, which hinges on the exact type of innovative product in question, has a direct impact on the research and development process for that innovation, for example in terms of testing, improving, and clinical trials. Certainty of downstream regulatory frameworks is therefore paramount, even when still at the earliest research and developmental stage. Weber and others write in this context that '[t]he local classification of boundary cases according to different categories provided by European regulations has implications for the harmonization of tissue practices in terms of requirements for cell processing and clinical practice across Europe, and the developmental pathway of cell-based therapies.'[9]

---

[6] Even the use of the term 'product' in this context holds potential for terminological confusion as the law crucially distinguishes between *devices* and *products*, whilst intuitively, all of the objects under discussion here could be described as products. I have tried to prevent any inadvertent pre-emptive normative categorization in this chapter by using the term 'artefact' where there was potential for confusion.

[7] The distinction between a mechanical interference and a, potentially self-induced but other-designed, chemical intervention in the human body can plausibly be argued to be a reason the law also makes an explicit distinction between offences against the person that involve direct force and those that do now, in particular poisoning and related offences (such as Offences Against the Person Act 1861, ss 22, 23, 24).

[8] Indeed, where the relevant instruments outlined in this chapter do not specifically regulate product or device safety aspects, the EU's general product safety rules come into play. Art 1(2) Directive 2001/95/EC on general product safety [2001] OJ L11/4.

[9] S Weber, D Wilson-Kovacs, and C Hauskeller, 'The Regulation of Autologous Stem Cells in Heart Repair: Comparing the UK and Germany' in C Lenk, N Hoppe, K Beier, and C Wiesemann (eds), *Human Tissue Research—A European Perspective on the Ethical and Legal Challenges* (OUP 2011) 166.

The current regime (flowing from the EU's, for the most part relatively recent, regulatory activity) in relation to tissue engineered products addresses issues of safety and quality in the context of transferring tissues and cells from one human (donor) to another (recipient). The relevant Directive[10] expressly relies on definitions of cells and tissue which seem to neglect the role played by connective tissue, in particular the extracellular matrix component, which is the part that provides structure (made up largely of collagen, which is a protein). Even within the area of tissue engineering an exact definition of what is meant has so far not been achieved and, unsurprisingly, the DHV seems not to sit comfortably with those definitions that have been offered so far.[11] Whilst it is derived from the human body, the decellularization process entails the complete removal of all vital donor cells from the collagen matrix (and provides potentially for the subsequent repopulation with recipient cells in situ). Technically, it is therefore probably much closer to an autograft than an allograft. The stipulations of the Human Tissue Directive, whilst relevant in relation to procurement and transfer of the original homograft, seem to come to the end of their usefulness after the decellularization process has finished.

An additional layer of regulatory complexity is invoked by the forced analogy to medicinal products inspired by the EU templates and fleshed out by some MSs' implementation of the EU Directives (see later). A heart valve functions solely on mechanical principles and exhibits no pharmacological, immunological, or metabolic function. The classification as a medicinal product seems to be aimed at establishing the highest possible level of safety and protection for a process which is so far seen as being unpredictably novel. Additionally, the current regulatory regime in relation to human tissue-derived products seems to be based on a prohibitive stance which leads to overregulation.[12] The overregulation, in turn, leads to an inability to categorize innovative tissue-derived products appropriately and swiftly, representing a significant obstacle in relation to product testing, authorization, and market entry, manifestly to the detriment of society and individual patients. The criticism developed in this chapter is not aimed at advocating a regulatory 'race to the bottom' on the basis of managed competition by means of privatization and deregulation to achieve an economic advantage for a particular industry. Rather, the idea is to foster an appropriate regulatory framework to ensure that life-saving and -improving medical innovations reach the

---

[10] Directive 2004/23/EC on setting standards of quality and safety for the donation, procurement, testing, processing, preservation, storage and distribution of human tissues and cells [2004] OJ L102/48 (the Human Tissue Directive).

[11] Trommelmans, Selling, and Dierickx, for example, define 'Tissue Engineering' as '"the creation of new tissue for the therapeutic reconstruction of the human body, by the deliberate and controlled stimulation of selected target cells, through a systematic combination of molecular and mechanical signals"... The in vitro combination of donated, cultured, and substantially altered human cells with supporting structures (scaffolds) and biomolecules such as growth factors yields metabolically active constructs, known as human tissue engineered products (HTEPs)' (L Trommelmans, J Selling, and K Dierickx, 'Informed Consent When Donating Cells for the Production of Human Tissue Engineered Products' in C Lenk, N Hoppe, K Beier, and C Wiesemann (eds), *Human Tissue Research—A European Perspective on the Ethical and Legal Challenges* (OUP 2011) 149). A decellularized homograft valve, devoid of vital cells and metabolically inactive, does not answer this description either. This certainly makes the DHV an interesting case study to test the robustness and versatility of the relevant regulation.

[12] Based on the problematic notion of making the human body available as a resource—mostly motivated by an apprehension of creating fertile ground for exploitation of vulnerable individuals or merely making the human body a means to an end. See N Hoppe, 'A Sense of Entitlement: Individual vs. Public Interest in Human Tissue' in C Lenk, J Sandor, and B Gordijn (eds), *Biobanks and Tissue Research: The Public, The Patient and the Regulation* (Springer 2011) for a criticism of these positions.

patient as soon as reasonably possible. Regulation has to be either appropriate or absent—inappropriate regulation is a manifestation of injustice.

In the following sections, I am going to outline the EU's initial regulatory impetus in the context of the DHV (as an example of a contemporary innovative health technology). As the relevant EU instruments (bar the regulations in relation to advanced therapy medicinal products (ATMP, see Section 2)) must be implemented into domestic law to deliver their regulatory payload, I will briefly discuss their implementation in German, UK, and French law before contrasting these implementations in order to illustrate the degree of current disparity. The selection of three Member States for this illustration is based on the density of information available after completion of a relevant EU project[13] and the interesting jurisdictional differences raised by these Member States' legal systems. I will conclude with a discussion of the actual effect achieved and whether any meaningful convergence or harmonization has occurred before, finally, addressing a number of paramount ethical concerns resulting from this regulatory process.

B. EU Legal Framework

When looking at the EU's regulatory activity in the field of health, it is worth remembering the very limited Treaty competence the EU technically has in this area, with a clear assumption in favour of MSs' capacity to better regulate health systems at domestic level.[14] This certainly has not stopped the EU from steering developments in health policy and, far from this being some kind of competence creep worthy of criticism,[15] it is a process owed to the desirable meta-policy quality of the area of health[16]—aspects such as the freedoms of movement, consumer protection, and public health are clearly part of the overall construct that is health and in this way the MSs have simply bought into collateral influences of health policy directly or indirectly from other policy areas. In the interests of ensuring a common standard of quality and safety of health products across all MSs, the EU has developed a number of regulatory devices setting these standards. Depending on the exact type of artefact under consideration, these artefacts can be subject to, inter alia, the Medical Devices Directive,[17] the Medicinal Products Directive,[18] the Human Tissue Directive, or the Advanced Therapy Medicinal Products Regulations.[19] In order to identify the governance framework for an artefact, and thus appreciate how a certain new health technology ought to be developed, tested, and brought to the bedside, it is necessary to be clear what type of technology it is in regulatory terms (not least in order to ensure that clinical trial design will satisfy the regulatory requirements). I will look at the definitions of artefacts

---

[13] Tiss.EU—Evaluation of Legislation and Related Guidelines on the Procurement, Storage and Transfer of Human Tissues and Cells in the European Union an Evidence-Based Impact Analysis. FP7 Grant No. 202204.

[14] For a great overview, which by now is sadly out date, see M McKee, 'The Influence of European Law on National Health Policy' (1996) 6 *Journal of European Social Policy* 263.

[15] S Greer, 'Uninvited Europeanization: Neofunctionalism and the EU in Health Policy' (2006) 13 *Journal of European Public Policy* 134.

[16] N Hoppe, 'On the Europeanization of Health Law' (2010) 17 *EJHL* 323.

[17] Directive 93/42/EEC concerning medical devices [1993] OJ L169/1.

[18] Directive 2001/83/EC on the Community code relating to medicinal products for human use [2001] OJ L311/67.

[19] Regulation (EC) No 1394/2007 of the European Parliament and the Council on advanced therapy medicinal products and amending Directive 2001/83/EC and Regulation (EC) No 726/2004 [2007] OJ L324/121 (ATMP Regulations).

in these instruments in turn and apply them to the example of the decellularized homograft valve.

1. Medical Devices

A medical device classically ranges in complexity from a thermometer used to measure a patient's temperature to an implanted defibrillator. In order to delimit its scope, the Medical Devices Directive uses a negative definition of characteristics to differentiate between a medical device and a medicinal product. Article 1(2)(a) of the Medical Devices Directive states that a medical device is defined as any instrument, apparatus, appliance, software, material, or other article '. . . which does not achieve its principal intended action in or on the human body by pharmacological, immunological or metabolic means, but which may be assisted in its function by such means.'

The Medical Devices Directive goes on, in Article 1(5)(f), to state that certain artefacts derived from a human donor do not fall under its regulation '. . . transplants or tissues or cells of human origin nor to products incorporating or derived from tissues or cells of human origin, with the exception of devices referred to in paragraph 4a.'[20]

A DHV is technically quite close to a transplant in that the transplantable pulmonary donor valve is simply improved between explantation and implantation by the removal of immunogenic material. It clearly also, however, falls squarely into the exception 'products incorporating *or derived from* tissues or cells of human origin'[21] in that whilst no vital cells remain, the collagen matrix is derived from a human donor valve. Far from unintentionally neglecting to address this type of tissue engineered health technology, the Medical Devices Directive proceeds explicitly to exclude animal-derived avital cell structures from its application. Article 1(5)(g) reads '. . . transplants or tissues or cells of animal origin, unless a device is manufactured utilizing *animal tissue which is rendered non-viable or non-viable products derived from animal tissue.*'[22]

This to some extent suggests that the legislator was aware of the possibility of avital (or non-viable) cell structures. The failure to include such artefacts in the context of human cells is unlikely to be an oversight and begs the question whether the legislator has deliberately left a built-in ambiguity to cater for subsequent interpretational scope at domestic level. I will return to this question. The consequence of the Medical Devices Directive's negative definition of its remit is that a decellularized tissue engineered artefact, derived from human donor tissue, cannot be a medical device. As the Medical Devices Directive has actively differentiated between medical devices and medicinal products, I will turn to the regulatory classification of medicinal products.

2. Medicinal Products

A medicinal product is what is commonly referred to as a pharmaceutical product. Intuitively, these products are thought to include some sort of chemical compound which causes some kind of biochemical reaction in the patient or assist in diagnostic processes, that is, either a medicine or maybe a contrast medium. Medicinal products are therefore defined in Article 1(2) of the Medicinal Products Directive in very similar terms:

  (a) Any substance or combination of substances presented as having properties for treating or preventing disease in human beings; or

---

[20] Para 4a of Art 1 referred to here concerns blood and plasma products.
[21] Art 1(5)(f) Emphasis added.   [22] Emphasis added.

(b) Any substance or combination of substances which may be used in or administered to human beings either with a view to restoring, correcting or modifying physiological functions by exerting *a pharmacological, immunological or metabolic action, or to making a medical diagnosis.*[23]

It seems immediately striking that the term substance does not comfortably describe the nature of tissue engineered constructs, though the common language definition ('a particular kind of matter with uniform properties', as per the *Oxford English Dictionary*) could, at a stretch, be applied to the collagen making up the DHV scaffold. It seems doubtful that this type of health technology is what the legislator had in mind when defining the rules surrounding medicinal products.

In the case of any such doubt about the categorization of a certain artefact, the Medicinal Products Directive claims general priority (Article 2(2)), a claim which has judicially been hesitantly applied[24] and seems to be rooted solely in the assertions contained in recital 7 of the preamble to a directive[25] amending the Medicinal Products Directive:

In order to take account both of the emergence of new therapies and of the growing number of so-called 'borderline' products between the medicinal product sector and other sectors, the definition of 'medicinal product' should be modified so as to avoid any doubt as to the applicable legislation when a product, whilst fully falling within the definition of a medicinal product, may also fall within the definition of other regulated products. This definition should specify the type of action that the medicinal product may exert on physiological functions. This enumeration of actions will also make it possible to cover medicinal products such as gene therapy, radio-pharmaceutical products as well as certain medicinal products for topical use. Also, in view of the characteristics of pharmaceutical legislation, provision should be made for such legislation to apply. With the same objective of clarifying situations, where a given product comes under the definition of a medicinal product but could also fall within the definition of other regulated products, it is necessary, in case of doubt and in order to ensure legal certainty, to state explicitly which provisions have to be complied with.

The stated aim is to create legal certainty whilst also ensuring the highest possible level of quality, safety, and efficacy—which, following this reasoning for decellularized artefacts, is assumed to lie in medicinal products rather than medical devices regulation. This is, presumably, because the array of pre-clinical and clinical trials required for such products leads to a more robust evidence base in relation to the technology's safety. In the case of purely mechanical technologies, closer to an implant in character, it seems unclear whether this stipulation is merely overly onerous or simply nonsensical. What also remains is the question of how the requirement of 'a pharmacological, immunological or metabolic action' can be reconciled with the purely mechanic function of tissue engineered vessels. Some helpful details can be gleaned from the European Commission's (non-binding) guidelines on the demarcation of Product Directives.[26] Here, the three terms are defined briefly. Pharmacological is held to be an interaction between molecules (not applicable), immunological means the

---

[23] Emphasis added.
[24] See Case C-140/07 *Hecht-Pharma v. Staatliches Gewerbeaufsichtsamt Lübeck* [2009] ECR I-41.
[25] Directive 2004/27/EC amending Directive 2001/83/EC on the Community code relating to medicinal products for human use [2004] OJ L136/34.
[26] European Commission, 'Borderline Products, Drug-delivery Products and Medical Devices Incorporating, as an Integral Part, an Ancillary Medicinal Substance or an Ancillary Human Blook Derivative' (Guidance Document, 2-1/3 rev 3, undated) <http://ec.europa.eu/health/medical-devices/files/meddev/2_1_3_rev_3-12_2009_en.pdf> accessed 11 May 2012.

mobilization of a specific immune reaction (again, not applicable, quite the opposite), and metabolic is held to mean an alteration of the normal chemical processes (debatable, though it seems fairly clear that without a pulmonary valve, a patient's metabolism would be affected).

A valid argument against this criticism may be that, when it is to be applied to technology such as a DHV, this part of the definition of medicinal product simply becomes a legal fiction which ought not to be read literally. This may fit in well with the possibility that some interpretational scope was left for medical devices legislation at MS level. The upshot here certainly is that whilst neither the Definition of medicinal product nor the actual content of the instrument seem to work well with getting decellularized heart valves from bench to bedside, the Directive claims jurisdiction unless other explicit rules are in existence. Regardless of whether one subscribes to a literal reading or not, the legal framework here simply does not seem to work well for the technology in question.

3. Advanced Therapy Medicinal Products

ATMP are products for human use which are based on the very latest advances in tissue engineering, gene therapy, and somatic-cell therapy.[27] The ATMP Regulations were also designed to encompass the latest developments in these emerging fields. Recital 1 of the preamble states:

New scientific progress in cellular and molecular biotechnology has led to the development of advanced therapies, such as gene therapy, somatic cell therapy, and tissue engineering. This nascent field of biomedicine offers new opportunities for the treatment of diseases and dysfunctions of the human body.

The Preamble acknowledges that, so far, a reasonable definition of tissue engineering has been difficult but continues to address the issue at stake here:

a legal definition of tissue engineered products remains to be laid down. *When products are based on viable cells or tissues, the pharmacological, immunological or metabolic action should be considered as the principal mode of action.* It should also be clarified that *products which do not meet the definition of a medicinal product, such as products made exclusively of non-viable materials which act primarily by physical means, cannot by definition be advanced therapy medicinal products.*[28]

This, at first glance, seems to be very helpful. Artefacts consisting of viable cells which deploy some kind of pharmacological, immunological, or metabolic effect ought to be subsumed under medicinal products. Those which do not contain viable material and act primarily by physical means (such as the DHV) cannot be ATMP—but are suggested also not to be meeting the requirements of a medicinal product. The actual unhelpfulness of the recital becomes evident when we look at the consequence of this triumvirate of instruments (the Medical Devices Directive, Medicinal Products Directive, and the ATMP Regulations). Whilst the interpretative scope provided by the wording of the Directives is amplified by the freedom accorded to MSs in relation to achieving a Directive's aim in the domestic setting, the regulation is hard, direct, and uncompromising in its effect. The outcome seems to be this: the

---

[27] European Medicines Agency, 'Advanced Therapies' (2011) <www.ema.europa.eu/ema/index.jsp?curl=pages/regulation/general/general_content_000294.jsp&jsenabled=true> accessed 11 May 2012.
[28] Recital 3. Emphasis added.

DHV is not a medical device, it is not by definition a medicinal product, and it is not an advanced therapy medicinal product. Read together with the catch-all jurisdiction claimed in the Medicinal Products Directive, the DHV looks set to be nothing tangible in terms of categorization but subject to regulation designed for controlling pharmaceutical products. In other words, this is the worst of all worlds in that it imposes pharmaceutical industry standards on a research, trial, and manufacturing process which can only be adapted to these regulations with the greatest difficulty.[29] The regulatory effect on the ground is determined by how individual MSs have implemented the two Directives and—after a brief look at the role played by the Human Tissue Directive— I will turn to a quick comparison of a small group of MSs' implementations.

4. Human Tissue Directive

The Human Tissue Directive deals only with human applications (that is, therapeutic use but also including cells and tissue applied in clinical trials in humans) and claims regulatory competence over any products derived from human tissues or cells. Article 2(1) outlines:

This Directive shall apply to the donation, procurement, testing, processing, preservation, storage and distribution of human tissues and cells intended for human applications and of manufactured products derived from human tissues and cells intended for human applications.

The Directive then qualifies its application and, where manufactured artefacts are covered by other Directives, limits itself to regulating merely the donation, procurement, and testing of such artefacts (Article 2(1)). This is especially the case where the artefact in question is manufactured industrially. At the same time, the Human Tissue Directive lays down important rules in relation to the licensing and documentation obligations for establishments working with human tissues and cells. It therefore creates a detailed normative backdrop for the steps taken in relation to procuring human tissues and cells before any product categorization is taking place and should be read together with the other Directives.

In the context of a decellularized, tissue engineered artefact, this combination of definitions and instruments seems to lead to a very heterogeneous mixture of a number of different norms, originally designed to address fundamentally different products: despite the lack of metabolic, immunological, or pharmacological activity, the Medicinal Products Directive claims dominion (save for questions of donation procurement and testing where the Tissue Directive comes into play). The ATMP Regulations suggest that, for very sensible reasons, decellularized tissue artefacts are not medicinal products, but nor are they advanced therapy medicinal products. Whilst this suggests that decellularized products are simply not categorized, they are clearly by no means unregulated: they seem to be firmly subject to the rules developed for pharmaceutical products.

C. Member State Implementation

The discussion of the EU regulatory framework in the context of a new health technology such as the DHV leads to the question how individual MSs have implemented these

---

[29] A detailed discussion would exceed the remit of this chapter, though it seems evident that a clinical trial design with double-blind or placebo controlled set-ups seem difficult to perform here. Any objection to this point on the basis that medical devices are also subject to performing appropriately in clinical trials essentially underpins this chapter's main argument.

instruments into domestic law, and whether this implementation has led to any meaningful convergence or harmonization. I will look, very briefly, at how Germany, the United Kingdom, and France have implemented these Directives and which effect, if any, this has had on the regulatory categorization of a DHV.

1. Germany

The Directives outlined earlier were eventually all implemented in German law (with some reluctance in implementing the requirements of the Human Tissue Directive). In particular, the definitions relevant to the DHV context were taken directly from the Directives. This leads to the same categorization of transplants, medicinal products, and medical devices. The one significant deviation from the Directives is that the German legislator has declined to create a separate class for such tissue-based artefacts and has instead subsumed them largely under the category of medicinal products. Whilst human tissue-derived technologies do fall under different marketing authorization rules to other medicinal products, there is substantial criticism of the style of implementation.[30] First, the systematic inclusion of all tissue-derived artefacts under medicinal products seems to lack any meaningful basis in European legislation. Secondly, the legislative mechanism for the implementation of the Human Tissue Directive[31] leads to unfortunate domestic legal fragmentation: it amends existing primary and secondary law but does not constitute a coherent single text. This process may well have been more enjoyable for lawyers but is unfortunately a lot less useful to practitioners. Another dimension adding complexity in this context is that whilst there is an oversight body dealing with technical categorizations at a federal level (the Paul-Ehrlich-Institut in Langen), approval also needs to be sought at the level of each federal state.[32]

The wholesale adoption of established medical devices terminology leads to an exclusion of tissue engineered artefacts, even if they only have mechanical functions and not any of the typical medicinal products characteristics outlined earlier. Additionally, any artefacts which do not contain vital tissues or cells cannot be categorized as an ATMP under the relevant German legislation.[33] Therefore, tissue engineered technologies of this type are medicinal products, or 'tissue preparations' (*Gewebezubereitungen*), under the current German legal regime, a category introduced to distinguish between advanced therapies and less risky therapies.[34] In other words, the path taken by the German legislator may deviate from the impetus given by the Directive, but the result is essentially the same.

2. United Kingdom

One preliminary issue to bear in mind in relation to the regulatory situation in the United Kingdom is that the bulk of existing tissue governance frameworks was only

---

[30] Bundesärztekammer (Federal Medical Chamber), 'Stellungnahme *zum Entwurf eines Gewebegesetzes* (*Consultation Paper in Response to the Draft of a Human Tissue Act*)' (2006) <www. bundesaerztekammer.de/downloads/ZStell.pdf> accessed 11 May 2012.

[31] Gesetz über Qualität und Sicherheit von menschlichen Geweben und Zellen (Gewebegesetz) 20 July 2007 (BGBl. I S. 1574) [Act on Quality and Safety of Human Tissues and Cells (BGBl (Federal Law Gazette) I p. 1574)].

[32] Weber and others (n 9) 164.

[33] Para 4(9) Gesetz über den Verkehr mit Arzneimitteln (Arzneimittelgesetz—AMG) (BGBl. I S. 3394), amended on 22 December 2011 (BGBl. I S. 2983) [Act on Trade in Medicinal Products (BGBl. (Federal Law Gazette) I p. 3394) as amended (Federal Law Gazette I p 2983)].

[34] Weber and others (n 9).

partly triggered by EU-level activity. Following the revelations of the Royal Liverpool Children's Inquiry, which investigated the removal, retention, and disposal of children's organs and tissues at Alder Hey Children's Hospital in Liverpool, a new regulatory framework was implemented.[35] This framework significantly exceeded the EU parameters in scope (for example, by also addressing research and not merely therapy). At the same time, the subsequent implementation of the Human Tissue Directive entailed rather less controversy in the United Kingdom than elsewhere as the subject matter had already been extensively publicly discussed. The implementation through a statutory instrument[36] was therefore closely aligned with the original EU legislation.

Weber and others, in the context of clinical trials of stem cell therapies but writing on the issue of cell-based therapies as a whole, point out that the EU-derived regulatory categorization results in a graded approach in the United Kingdom, based on risk:

Thus the conduct of clinical trials employing stem cells in the UK has become set within two variable processes that are centred on a graded approach to overseeing the risks posed by cells in medical applications. This approach involves an assemblage of authorities and mechanisms which take over from each other in setting technical conditions for cell processing and carrying out trials according to GCP principles. The ensuing interfaces between authorities and processes of oversight require negotiations between different actors regarding the classificatory status of tissues and cells and the appropriate regulatory mechanisms.[37]

The EU-level medicinal products legislation is implemented through both the Medicines Act 1968 as well as the Medicines for Human Use (Marketing Authorizations Etc) Regulations 1994.[38] The latter define 'relevant medicinal product' as a 'medicinal product for human use to which Chapters II to V of Council Directive 65/65/EEC apply' (reg 1(2)). The equivalent definition of medicinal products with its exclusion of tissue-derived products is again included in the appropriate regulations (Medical Devices Regulations 2002,[39] reg 3(d)) '[t]hese regulations shall not apply to ... transplants or tissues or cells of human origin incorporating or derived from tissues or cells of human origin.'

On the basis of this set of definitions and exclusions, the same types of product categories are established as elsewhere: medical device, transplant, and medicinal product (including ATMP). Where there is doubt about the appropriate classification of an artefact, the Medicines and Healthcare products Regulatory Authority (MHRA) is consulted. The MHRA's guidelines, issued from time to time, give an indication of how an innovative tissue engineered technology might be classified. In relation to collagen-based scaffolds, the MHRA has indicated that the exclusion derived from the Medical Devices Directive results in such artefacts certainly not being classified as a medical device,[40] despite the intuitive clarity of the product's main characteristics resembling a medical device, and despite similar technologies being classified as such in the USA.[41] At the same time, neither the definitions for medicinal product nor ATMP fit in relation to decellularized tissue engineered technologies. This leaves the

---

[35] House of Commons, 'The Royal Liverpool Children's Inquiry Report' (TSO 2001).

[36] Human Tissue (Quality and Safety for Human Application) Regulations 2007, SI 2007/1523.

[37] Weber and others (n 9).

[38] Medicines for Human Use (Marketing, Authorisations etc.) Regulations 1994, SI 1994/3144.

[39] Medical Devices Regulations 2002, SI 2002/618.

[40] Medicines and Healthcare products Regulatory Agency, *Bulletin No. 17, Medical Devices and Medicinal Products Annex 1*, N. 7/8 (MHRA 2009).

[41] US Food and Drug Administration, 'FDA Clears for Market First Decellularized Heart Valve' (FDA 2008) <www.fda.gov/NewsEvents/Newsroom/PressAnnouncements/2008/ucm116855.htm> accessed 11 May 2012.

dilemma that there appears to be no suitable regulatory category. The rather unhelpful guidance provided by the MHRA does not shed light on this problem either:

Tissue scaffolds containing bioactive materials are likely to be medicinal products.... Human tissue derived fillers may be regulated as medicinal products, or may come within the Code of Practice for human derived therapeutic products—verify with the Medicines Borderline Section at MHRA. Note that the legislation covering human tissues and cells and regulations on advanced therapy products may also apply to such products.[42]

It is not immediately clear how much guidance is provided by text which revolves around terms such as 'likely' and 'may'. In any case, the outcome seems to be that a DHV may be likely to be, in the fullness of time and all things being equal, possibly regulated as a medicinal product.

3. France

Again, the domestic implementation of all relevant Directives (apart from some aspects in relation to assisted reproduction) was done on the basis of very much the same wording as was foreseen in the European instruments. The Human Tissue Directive was implemented into French law by means of an array of individual norms, much like the German system. In terms of the types of product categories, French law does have a surprise in store. Products are classified as either transplants, medical devices, medicinal products (including ATMP), or non-industrial human cell therapies. The differentiation between industrial and non-industrial manufacture is also made in relation to medicinal products: non-industrially manufactured artefacts are exclusively subject to French law. The separate category of non-industrial human cell therapies is also subject to exclusive French jurisdiction.[43] The eligibility for marketing authorization for these types of technologies is, other than for medicinal products, undertaken by the Agence française de sécurité sanitaire des produits de santé in consultation with the Agence de la Biomédicine. Again, it is clear that a classification as a medical device, on the basis of the DHV's predominantly mechanic properties, would be the intuitive first choice. On the basis of the fairly direct transposition of the Directives, French law also introduces a distinction for technologies generated from human tissue, which excludes the DHV from a medical devices classification.

The additional dimension in French law is that, depending on whether the artefact in question is being manufactured industrially or not, French law may provide an additional classification as a *'preparation de thérapie cellulaire'*. The absence of vital cells does not exclude such a classification. Individual rules for the manufacture, storage, and distribution of such an artefact are contained in Decret no 2008-968.[44] Where the artefact is manufactured industrially, it is likely to be regulated as a borderline product. In this case, as in the other discussed jurisdictions, the aim is to achieve the highest possible level of protection for the receiving patients. In the case of innovative tissue engineered technologies, this may well lead to a categorization as a medicinal product,

---

[42] Text at n 37.

[43] Though EU medicinal products legislation makes a point of treating products that are the result of an 'industrial process' or a 'substantial manipulation' as resulting in riskier therapies: Weber and others (n 9) 163.

[44] Décret no 2008-968, 16 September 2008, relatif aux conditions d'autorisation des activités portant sur les tissus et leurs dérivés, les préparations de thérapie cellulaire, de thérapie génique et de thérapie cellulaire xénogénique, et aux conditions d'autorisation de ces produits [concerning the conditions of authorisation of activities relating to the tissues and their derivatives, the preparations for cell therapy, gene therapy and xenogeneic cell therapy, and the conditions of authorization of those products], NOR: SJSP0813071D.

as the rules concerning marketing authorization, clinical trials, and patient safety processes are likely to lead to a higher degree of patient protection. Where the manufacture of the artefact in question is non-industrial, exclusive French jurisdiction applies. This is likely to be the case were the DHV generally produced in hospitals on a per-patient basis. Additionally, the fact that the production of a decellularized homograft valve is always dependent on a donor valve being available and thus subject to the same issues of scarcity as other allografts seems to speak against an industrially viable process.

D. Discussion

1. General

Before launching into a comprehensive criticism on the unsuitability of the regulatory framework outlined in this chapter, it is worth bearing in mind that it is simply the nature of law to create abstract rules for highly individualized cases. It follows from this fact that in the occasional individual case, this may lead to inappropriate or unfair results. This is, of course, one of the reasons why there is often ample flexibility in interpreting these abstract rules. In the context of regulating medical products, there is a reasonable amount of plausibility in suggesting that the cascade of categorization norms—negative definitions, finite lists of product characteristics, and a final catch-all provision for borderline or doubtful products—is intended to give the regulatory framework the maximum possibly flexibility in order to encompass innovative health technologies, regardless of whether they were visible on the horizon at the time of legislating or not. In terms of regulating risky activities, the firewall approach (prohibit everything and then open up windows of permission one at a time) seems to be the method of choice to avoid inadvertent under-regulation. In the instant case, the result is a rather disparate regulatory landscape where an entity wishing to produce a DHV in Germany would be subject to different rules to one producing a DHV in the United Kingdom or in France. Weber and others consider this to be an expression of different attitudes towards managing risks and uncertainty:

Our analysis suggests that Germany and the UK have taken different routes in regulating biomedical developments in novel cell therapies. Germany has adopted a streamlined approach in which a single regulatory body oversees the integrity of research as well as tissue practices. Its legislative framework aims to be comprehensive by classifying all tissues and cells in human application as medicinal products. In contrast, the UK's regulatory structure separates tissues and cells on the basis of their assumed biological 'riskiness'. This is complemented by an assemblage of institutional mechanisms set up to ensure the ethical and risk-controlled conduct of research—as evidenced by the MHRA, the HTA, the GTAC, the Department of Health Research Governance Framework, and non-statutory good practice guidance.[45]

Whilst the primary tenor of the EU instruments briefly discussed earlier is ensuring safety and quality, regulating for these common standards across the Union is also a facet of facilitating the common market. A side effect in this case seems to be a high level of health protection (potentially by removing the DHV from the market altogether) but a low degree of congruence in marketing authorization terms, which opens up the possibility of actors gravitating towards the jurisdiction with the most permissive regulatory set in the EU. This counteracts any attempts at establishing a level playing field within the Union and impacts negatively on the mobility of the services

---

[45] Weber and others (n 9) 165.

or the products (simply put, just because a DHV might be available in one MS does not mean that it can simply also be made available in another without restriction). Additional to these issues, which are more or less policy issues, there is also a question of whether the legislative impetus given by the EU was, in terms of securing legal certainty, helpful in bringing MS jurisdictions closer together or not. Legal certainty, in this context, would mean that compliance requirements during the course of developing, testing, and marketing an innovative health technology are much more clearly defined, thus easier to adhere to and therefore have a beneficial effect on availability (as well as also being the declared aim of the regulatory activity, as we have seen in the Preamble to Directive 2004/27/EC[46]). Quite the opposite seems to be the case here— at the time of drafting some of these Directives and Regulations, the likely innovations of tissue engineering were clearly visible and, as outlined earlier, were in some cases also identified in the detailed Preambles of the Directives. The question boils down to a balancing act between legal certainty for producers (ability to translate innovation to the market) and legal certainty for patients (certainty of quality and safety across the EU). Actively failing to legislate for these new health technologies and instead implementing a general jurisdiction for non-categorized health technologies within the remit of medicinal products, suggests that there is a certain degree of acquiescence in relation to decelerating these products' translational progress towards the clinic.

2. Ethics

I have suggested earlier that, over and beyond what may be criticized so far as being merely a complaint about the regulatory aesthetics of EU product legislation in the context of tissue engineering, there are also significant ethical issues at work here. The main lines of argument that present themselves here are that an emerging superior treatment standard might be unavailable because of bureaucratic obstacles, the treatment's particular relevance to vulnerable patient groups, risk benefit assessments, and allocation of scarce resources. In the context of health regulation, the reflection of these issues often takes place in an interdependent system of, oftentimes conflicting, perspectives of utilitarianism, human rights, and notions of human dignity.[47] As briefly outlined earlier, this chapter does not advocate an economics-based regulatory race to the bottom; rather, the appropriateness of the regulation should underpin a speedy availability of promising interventions, to the benefit of health systems, purchasers, and patients.

Any new health technology which yields a manifest advantage over conventional treatments ought to be made available as soon as responsibly possible, lest we systematically treat individuals with the second-best option longer than absolutely necessary. The rationale behind this argument is also visible when, for example, stopping rules are defined in the design of most clinical trials:[48] where the experimental intervention within a cohort proves so significantly superior to other treatment arms in the trial, there is a fundamental ethical basis for aborting the trial to avoid patently disadvantaging a group of patients or research participants. The ethical argument can be

---

[46] Text at n 23.

[47] Roger Brownsword calls this the 'bioethical triangle' and points out that regulation is made difficult by the competing interests generated by these three angles: R Brownsword, *Rights, Regulation, and the Technological Revolution* (OUP 2008) 36.

[48] For a detailed discussion, see NMP King and LR Churchill, 'Assessing and Comparing Potential Benefits and Risks of Harm' in EJ Emanuel, C Grady, RA Crouch, RK Lie, FG Miller, and D Wendler (eds), *The Oxford Textbook of Clinical Research Ethics* (OUP 2008).

expanded to a pragmatic legal one where best practice and state-of-the-art standards are drawn upon to establish whether a medical professional has been negligent in the care she provides to an individual.

In the context of the decellularized homograft valve, a major patient group for this type of technology is that of children and young adults which adds a dimension of the treatment being particularly addressed to a vulnerable patient group and one for which treatments are very often not specifically available because of the difficulties encountered in terms of proofing safety in reasonably sized trials with child cohorts. Additionally, the current conventional approach of implanting homografts or artificial valves in young patients entails an acquiescence to onerous and risky subsequent reoperations to fit appropriately sized valves after the patient has grown. Any appropriate risk-benefit assessment would therefore have to take into account future risk associated with cardiothoracic surgery to balance against the risk of a potentially unproven treatment.

An additional ethical point that can convincingly be made here is that decellularizing homograft valves (rather than using them as conventional allografts) increases the likelihood of longer term and successful implantation. This addresses issues of maximizing the use made of a scarce and valuable health resource. A more economical allocation system would simply be the one where each patient required only one valve in her lifetime, rather than five or more. This would also entail minimizing the risk and harm caused to patients (by providing a more suitable and less immunogenic graft) and making the most of the 'gift of life' given by the donor, whether cadaveric or not.[49] It is clear that more reflection is required in relation to the range of risks and benefits that highly innovative health technologies entail and the question of regulation is not a trivial one: governance and regulation in the area of emerging health technologies is increasingly turning into an area that carries as much ethical significance as the deployment of a potentially risky intervention—where legislators regulate faultily or hastily they are just as blameworthy as where they fail to regulate a risk appropriately.

The criticisms I have levelled at the current regulatory regime do not aim at this regime being merely restrictive for research and development of innovative health technologies. Restrictive regulations have an appropriate place in biomedical governance frameworks when they serve the purpose of encouraging a measured and controlled development of new health technologies at a time when the potential risks are difficult to gauge. Indeed, others have hailed the inclusion of tissue- and cell-based preparations under medicinal products law as creating a future-proof regulatory structure. Weber and others write:

The second regulatory route centres on the expansion of innovations in the production of cellular therapies and tissue engineering...These may entail a combination of live tissue currently classified as 'biological', synthetic structures classified as 'medical devices', and drugs classified as 'pharmaceuticals', and expand beyond the scope of existing regulatory frameworks for medicinal products, medical devices, or biologicals. Here, efforts have focused on resolving regulatory inconsistencies in the definition of such products and establishing appropriate controls for product safety to facilitate uniform marketization across Europe.[50]

The tendency seems, therefore, to be to err on the side of caution and categorize highly innovative technologies in a more stringent way as a means of regulating risk. Weber and others go on to write:

---

[49] Valves can technically also be harvested from explanted recipient hearts during the course of a heart transplantation.
[50] Weber and others (n 9) 162.

Rather than implementing a separate framework for tissue-engineered products, provisions for all cell-based therapies were integrated into existing EU medicinal products regulation. Consequently, cellbased therapies have been aligned more closely with pharmaceutical products under the auspices of the European Medicines Agency (EMEA) as the established European agency of oversight. This change has been interpreted as ensuring rigorous regulation of future cell therapeutics . . . [51]

This seems to be a very optimistic assessment and, ironically, one which fails to foresee tissue engineered innovations or cell-based therapies which are simply not biologically active (whilst there is evidence, as we have seen, that the legislators, at least at EU level, had knowledge of the technology when drafting the rules). The fault seems generally to lie in the fact that there is a complete lack of clarity of how a technology such as a decellularized homograft valve is to be categorized and therefore regulated. This lack of legal certainty seriously impedes the next developmental steps to be taken as the actors developing these technologies are not in a position to decide what type of pre-clinical and clinical trials will be necessary to satisfy the regulatory demand.

In the case of technologies such as the DHV, the legislator has opted not to create a regulatory framework which is able to address non-vital tissue engineered structures and has instead opted to subject these types of artefact to onerous and ill-fitting medicinal products regulation. Whilst this may have been a wait-and-see attitude towards the novelty of the innovation with the highest level of possible protection for subsequent patients in mind, it very much seems to fail to recognize the reality in the wards where a clearly safe and superior treatment option will be significantly delayed. One of the reasons behind this attitude may well be an apprehension of undefined biological risks.[52] Another reason may be a diffuse inability easily to accept that tissue engineered technologies derived from donors can simply be the best therapeutic option and do not necessarily open up the human body to undesirable exploitation as a mere means to an end. Whilst it is clear that there cannot be a discrete regulatory category for each emerging technology, regulation needs to be flexible enough to encompass the unexpected but desirable in an appropriate fashion. To paraphrase Aristotle, biotechnology regulation ought to be a leaden rule.

---

[51] Weber and others (n 9) 162.   [52] Weber and others (n 9) 162.

6

Looking After the Orphans? Treatments for Rare Diseases, EU Law, and the Ethics of Costly Health Care

Keith Syrett

A. The Nature of the Problem

An 'orphan drug' technology may be defined as one which is developed for the treatment of a rare medical condition, that is, a condition which has a low prevalence across the population.[1] There is no universally agreed definition of what constitutes low prevalence in this context. In the USA, where the pressure to incentivize research and development of such drugs first arose, the Orphan Drug Act 1983 merely defines 'rare disease or condition' as 'any disease or condition which occurs so infrequently in the United States that there is no reasonable expectation that the cost of developing and making available in the United States a drug for such disease or condition will be recovered from sales in the United States of such drug.'[2] The subsequent Rare Diseases Act 2002 specifies a prevalence of less than 200,000 persons in the USA[3] (representing a prevalence ratio of approximately 1 affected individual per 1,560 persons on 2011 population figures).[4] Other jurisdictions which have adopted similar legislation employ differing definitions of prevalence, ranging from a total patient population of 2,000 in Australia (a ratio of approximately 1 affected individual per 11,350 people) to 50,000 in Japan (a prevalence ratio of approximately 1 affected individual per 2,540 people).[5]

---

[1] It should be noted that 'rare diseases' are sometimes seen as a subset of a broader category of 'orphan diseases'. Eg Eurordis, a Europe-wide non-governmental patient alliance, regards orphan diseases as comprising both rare and neglected diseases, the latter being defined as common, communicable diseases that primarily affect patients in developing countries and into which minimal research and drug development takes place because the market is regarded as unprofitable: Eurordis, 'Rare Diseases: Understanding this Public Health Priority' (2005) 6 <www.eurordis.org/IMG/pdf/princeps_document-EN.pdf> accessed 30 September 2011.

[2] Pub. L. No.97–414, section 2, amending Chapter V of the Federal Food, Drug and Cosmetic Act 1938.

[3] Pub. L. No.107–280, section 2(a)(1). This figure had first been inserted by the Health Promotion and Disease Prevention Amendments of 1984, Pub. L. No.98–551. The subsection proceeds to give examples of such diseases: 'Huntington's disease, amyotrophic lateral sclerosis (Lou Gehrig's disease), Tourette syndrome, Crohn's disease, cystic fibrosis, cystinosis, and Duchenne muscular dystrophy.'

[4] Source: Population Reference Bureau, 'The World at 7 Billion: 2011 World Population Data Sheet' <www.prb.org/Publications/Datasheets/2011/world-population-data-sheet/data-sheet.aspx> accessed 30 September 2011.

[5] See Canadian Organization for Rare Disorders, 'Challenges in Preventing and Managing Rare Conditions in a Publicly-Funded Healthcare System' <www.raredisorders.ca/library.html> accessed 30 September 2011 (population figures updated to 2011).

Within the European Union (EU), rare diseases have been defined as those with a prevalence of 'less than 5 per 10,000 in the Community',[6] and this is taken as the threshold for the applicable provision of EU law which will be discussed subsequently in this chapter. The statistical prevalence criterion is supplemented by two other factors. First, the conditions (which are specified to include those of genetic origin)[7] should be life-threatening or chronically debilitating, and secondly, their prevalence is such that 'concerted efforts are needed to address them [the diseases]'.[8] The latter criterion points towards the need for action in respect of rare diseases to be taken at Union level, notwithstanding the principle of subsidiarity set out in Article 5(3) TEU. This rationale is spelled out in more detail in the applicable Regulation (to be discussed later), which refers to the need to 'take advantage of the widest possible market', to 'avoid the dispersion of limited resources', and to prevent uncoordinated action being taken by Member States (MS) with deleterious consequences for competition and intra-Community trade;[9] as well as in Council Recommendation 2009/C 151/02, which states that:

The specificities of rare diseases—a limited number of patients and a scarcity of relevant knowledge and expertise—single them out as a unique domain of very high added value of action at Community level. This added value can especially be achieved through gathering national expertise on rare diseases which is scattered throughout the Member States.[10]

If numbers of patients are, indeed, limited in the manner suggested in the Council Recommendation, it might be queried why conditions of this type warrant the attention of policymakers and legislators. The answer lies in the 'paradox of rarity'.[11] Although patient numbers for individual diseases may be small, the total number of affected persons across the Union is far from insignificant: Council Recommendation 2009/C 151/02 states that between 6 per cent and 8 per cent of the Union suffer from a rare disease, equivalent to 27–36 million people,[12] or more than the combined population of the Benelux countries. As Eurordis argues, 'even though the "diseases are rare, rare diseases patients are many". It is therefore "not unusual to have a rare disease".'[13] Furthermore, rare diseases are characterized by considerable heterogeneity and diversity: the Council cites an estimation that 5,000–8,000 such diseases exist,[14] and notes that many of these are of even lower prevalence than the legally defined threshold, alluding to a further (informal) categorization of 'ultra-orphan' diseases which has sometimes been adopted.[15] Nonetheless, certain common features of such

---

[6] European Commission, Health and Consumer Protection Directorate-General, 'Useful Information on Rare Diseases from an EU Perspective' (European Commission 2004) 1.

[7] In fact, the majority of rare diseases have identified genetic origins: Eurordis estimates the figure to be 80 per cent: Eurordis (n 1) 4.

[8] European Commission, Health and Consumer Protection Directorate-General (n 6).

[9] Regulation (EC) No 141/2000 of the European Parliament and of the Council of 16 December 1999 on orphan medicinal products [2000] OJ L18/1 (OMP Regulation).

[10] Council Recommendation 2009/C 151/02 of 8 June 2009 on an action in the field of rare medical diseases (Council Recommendation on action in the field of rare diseases) [2009] OJ C151/8, para 18.

[11] Eurordis (n 1) 4.

[12] Council Recommendation on action in the field of rare diseases, para 5.

[13] Eurordis (n 1) 4.

[14] Council Recommendation on action in the field of rare diseases, para 5. Orphanet, a reference portal for information on rare diseases and orphan drugs which is partly funded by the European Commission, lists 5,954 diseases in its inventory: see <www.orpha.net/consor/cgi-bin/index.php?lng=EN> accessed 30 September 2011.

[15] See eg National Institute for Health and Clinical Excellence (NICE), 'Appraising Orphan Drugs' (2006) <www.nice.org.uk/niceMedia/pdf/smt/120705item4.pdf> accessed 30 September 2011, para 2.5.

conditions have been identified: a level of severity ranging from severe to very severe; chronic, degenerative, and frequently life-threatening character; incurability; generally early onset; association with a lack or loss of autonomy; significant psychosocial burden; and difficulty in management of the disease.[16]

Although cumulatively the total number of patients suffering from such conditions may be greater than is generally assumed, those patients tend to be geographically dispersed. As a consequence, diagnostic information on the nature and management of the disease, clinical expertise in addressing it, and availability of and access to treatments (always assuming that treatments have been developed) tend to be unevenly distributed. This increases the sense of isolation felt by those who suffer from rare diseases,[17] and is necessarily troubling for those MS governments which wish to uphold foundational values of solidarity and equity within their health systems.

However, the problem is not a straightforward one to resolve at national level. Profit-seeking manufacturers of pharmaceuticals and medical devices are unlikely to prioritize research and development of new health technologies to treat conditions in situations where the costs of such activities may not be recouped given relatively small patient populations in a particular country, especially in view of the difficulty of conducting clinical trials in the absence of reliable patient databases. The problem can be self-perpetuating: inadequate research and development leads to a lack of professional and public awareness and low status as a public health objective; in turn, the lack of prominence accorded to such conditions translates back into limited attention on the part of the manufacturers. Although this pattern has, to some degree, begun to alter as a consequence of pressure imposed by patient organizations in recent years, rare diseases continue to present an awkward policy challenge.

This chapter will analyse the manner in which the policy problem presented by rare diseases has been addressed through the mechanisms of EU law. An account of the legal framework will highlight that action at EU level is designed to ensure that new health technologies to treat such diseases are made more widely *available*—that is, that they can, in principle, be acquired and provided—than might otherwise be the case. However, while this may alleviate certain of the difficulties noted earlier, a crucial obstacle remains for those who wish to obtain these technologies. EU law does not guarantee that a particular individual or physician will be able to *access* such a treatment, because a MS may choose to deny or restrict provision within the national health system over which it has responsibility. The high cost of such technologies (or at least, a *perception* of their high cost) is the most important, albeit not the sole, factor explaining the existence of such limitations. This in turn raises difficult questions as to the extent to which obligations of a normative type might compel a MS to permit access, given that only finite resources are available to fund a health system. It will be argued that certain steps might be taken, both at EU and MS level, to minimize the 'blockages' to access, but that ultimately elicitation of citizen preferences is likely to be crucial to legitimation of the highly challenging ethical choices which inevitably shape policy on provision of treatment for rare diseases.

The Institute recommends classification of 'ultra-orphan' conditions as those with a prevalence of less than 1 in 50,000 people in the United Kingdom: para 4.2.

[16] Eurordis (n 1) 5.
[17] Eurordis (n 1) 13.

B. EU Law: The Regulation on Orphan Medicinal Products

Legislative action at EU level was triggered by a European Commission proposal of July 1998.[18] Prior to this, rare diseases had been identified as a priority area in the field of public health,[19] and the Commission had also proposed a programme of action including provision of information on rare diseases and support for patient organizations.[20]

Noting that research and development of products to treat such conditions was prohibitively expensive, but that an ethical obligation existed to provide patients with the benefits of medical progress notwithstanding that patient populations for particular diseases might be small, the Commission expressed the view that 'it is ... up to the public authorities to provide the necessary incentives and to adapt their administrative procedures so as to make it as easy as possible to provide these patients [ie those with rare diseases] with medicinal products which are just as safe and effective as any other medicinal product and meet the same quality standards.'[21] To this end, and by reference to the regimes established in the USA in 1983 and Japan in 1995, the Commission identified 'the key element in an effective policy of support for orphan medicinal products research and development ... [as being] the creation of an official system for recognizing orphan medicinal products and granting exclusive marketing rights for a sufficient period of time from the date when the medicinal product is actually placed on the market.'[22] Its proposed Regulation, as amended, was accepted by the Council and approved by the European Parliament, entering into force on 22 January 2000.

As proposed by the Commission, the stated objectives of Regulation (EC) No 141/ 2000 are twofold. First, it establishes a procedure by which orphan medicinal products may be designated and approved for marketing in the EU. Secondly, it provides incentives for their research, development, and marketing.

Article 3 of the Regulation sets out the definition of an orphan medicinal product (OMP). For designation to take place, the sponsor (that is, manufacturer) of such a product must demonstrate first, that it is intended for the diagnosis, prevention, or treatment of a condition of a certain degree of severity, ranging from 'life-threatening' to 'serious and chronic'. Secondly, it must be shown that the product either fulfils a prevalence stipulation—defined as a disease which affects no more than 5 in 10,000 persons across the EU at the time when the application for OMP status is made; or an insufficient return condition, that is, 'that without incentives it is unlikely that the marketing of the medicinal product in the Community would generate sufficient return to justify the necessary investment.' Additionally, the sponsor must demonstrate an absence of an alternative, authorized, satisfactory method for diagnosis, prevention, or treatment of the condition or that, if such a method does exist, that the new product will 'be of significant benefit to those affected by that condition'.

---

[18] Commission, 'Proposal for a European Parliament and Council Regulation (EC) on orphan medicinal products' COM (98) 450 final.

[19] Commission 'Communication on the Framework for Action in the Field of Public Health' COM (93) 559 final.

[20] Commission, 'Communication concerning a programme for Community action concerning rare diseases within the framework for action in the field of public health; Proposal for a European Parliament and Council decision adopting a programme of Community action 1999–2003 on rare diseases in the context of the framework for action in the field of public health' COM (97) 225 final.

[21] Commission Proposal (n 18) 2.

[22] Commission Proposal (n 18) 3.

Designation of OMPs is carried out by a Committee for Orphan Medicinal Products (COMP), established within the European Medicines Agency (EMA).[23] COMP has both scientific evaluation and public health functions. In addition to examination of applications for designation, it advises the Commission on the establishment and development of a policy on OMP products in the Union and assists the Commission in liaison on an international level, and with patient organizations. Assessment of OMPs for marketing authorization purposes, as with all medicines for human use, is conducted by the Agency's Committee for Medicinal Products for Human Use (CHMP).[24]

Various incentives for manufacturers of OMPs are set out in Articles 6–9 of the Regulation. Protocol assistance may be provided at any point prior to the submission of an application for marketing authorization: in such an instance, the manufacturer may request the Agency's advice on the conduct of tests and trials necessary to establish the product's quality, safety, and efficacy for the purposes of grant of marketing authorization. OMPs also have direct access to the centralized procedure for application for marketing authorization, meaning that a single Union-wide authorization will be granted if application is successful (as distinct from the need to seek authorization simultaneously in various EU states, or through a process of mutual recognition, which arises from use of the national authorization process).[25] Manufacturers of OMPs also benefit from a reduction or waiving of fees payable in connection with an application for marketing authorization, and are eligible for research and development grants made available by the Union or MS.

However, the incentive which is likely to be most decisive in stimulating the development of new OMPs is market exclusivity, which is governed by Article 8. This provides that, subsequent to the grant of marketing authorization for an OMP, 'the Community and the Member States shall not, for a period of ten years, accept another application for a marketing authorization, or grant a marketing authorization or accept an application to extend an existing marketing authorization, for the same therapeutic indication, in respect of a similar medicinal product.'

This provision, which compares with a period of seven years under the Orphan Drug Act 1983 in the USA,[26] precludes marketing of cheaper generic products within the Union during that time. An additional application for marketing authorization for a similar medicinal product for the same therapeutic indication may nonetheless be granted if the holder of the authorization for the original product gives consent, or if the latter is unable to supply sufficient quantities of the product, or if the applicant for marketing authorization of the second product can demonstrate that it is safer, more effective, or otherwise clinically superior to the original OMP.[27]

Furthermore, under Article 8(2), the period of market exclusivity may be reduced to six years if, after the end of the fifth year, the conditions for designation as an OMP

---

[23] OMP Regulation, Art 4.
[24] See Regulation (EC) No 726/2004 of the European Parliament and of the Council of 31 March 2004 laying down Community procedures for the authorization and supervision of medicinal products for human and veterinary use and establishing a European Medicines Agency [2004] OJ L136/1, Art 5.
[25] OMP access to the centralized procedure was optional until 2005 but is now mandatory: see Directive 2004/27/EC of the European Parliament and of the Council of 31 March 2004 amending Directive 2001/83/EC on the Community code relating to medicinal products for human use [2004] OJ L136/34.
[26] Section 2(a), amending s 527(a) of the Federal Food, Drug and Cosmetic Act 1938.
[27] OMP Regulation, Art 8(3).

are no longer met. Significantly, it is provided that this shall include a situation 'where it is shown on the basis of available evidence that the product is sufficiently profitable not to justify maintenance of market exclusivity.' The review procedure under Article 8(2) is triggered by an indication from a MS to EMA that at least one of the criteria for designation are no longer being met, following which COMP will conduct an assessment and produce an opinion, which forms the basis of the Commission's ultimate decision as to whether or not market exclusivity should be maintained.[28] This review procedure is 'expected to be the exception'.[29]

The Regulation is deemed by many to have been a success. Indeed, organizations representing the biopharmaceutical industry have proclaimed it as 'one of the most successful EU healthcare policies overall'.[30] The basis for such an evaluation is the increased availability of OMPs across the Union subsequent to enactment of the Regulation. Prior to 2000, only eight products fitting the definition of an OMP had been granted marketing authorization in the EU.[31] By the end of 2010, a further sixty-three products had been authorized,[32] while 877 designations had been granted by the Commission as at July 2011.[33] Such increased availability of new health technologies carries the potential to benefit large numbers of patients: Eurordis estimates that 2.5–2.6 million EU citizens may potentially make use of these newly authorized products.[34] Resources spent upon research and development of OMPs have also significantly increased, from approximately €150 million in 2000, to more than €490 million in 2009.[35]

The positive stakeholder evaluation of the Regulation is shared by the Commission. A 2006 general report on the experience acquired as a result of the Regulation and of the public health benefits which it has yielded,[36] concluded that 'the response to the orphan legislation in the EU has far exceeded initial expectations',[37] although it noted that it was too early to assess the full impact upon public health. Similarly, a Communication of 2008 proclaimed that 'the EU policy for orphan drugs is a success'.[38] However, both documents sounded a similar note of caution:

---

[28] Commission, 'Guideline on aspects of the application of Article 8(2) of Regulation (EC) No 141/2000 of the European Parliament and of the Council: Review of the period of market exclusivity of orphan medicinal products' 2008/C 242/07 [2008] OJ C242/8, section 3.

[29] Commission Guideline (n 28).

[30] European Biopharmaceutical Enterprises/European Association for Bioindustries, 'Assessment of the Impact of Orphan Medicinal Products (OMPs) on the European Economy and Society' (2010) 3 <www.europabio.org/positions/OHE_Consulting_Impact_of_OMPs_November2010%20FINAL. pdf> accessed 30 September 2011.

[31] European Biopharmaceutical Enterprises/European Association for Bioindustries (n 30) 1.

[32] S Aymé and C Rodwell (eds), '2011 Report on the State of the Art of Rare Disease Activities in Europe of the European Union Committee of Experts on Rare Diseases—Part I: Overview of Rare Disease Activities in Europe and Key Developments in 2010' (European Union 2011) 38.

[33] COMP, 'Monthly Report' (July 2010) EMA/COMP/399953/2011 Corr., 4 <www.ema.europa. eu/ema/index.jsp?curl=pages/news_and_events/document_listing/document_listing_000201.jsp &murl=menus/about_us/about_us.jsp&mid=WC0b01ac0580028e78> accessed 30 September 2011.

[34] <www.eurordis.org/content/celebrating-10-years-orphan-drug-regulation-europe> accessed 30 September 2011.

[35] European Biopharmaceutical Enterprises/European Association for Bioindustries (n 30) 2.

[36] OMP Regulation, Art 10 requires the Commission to publish such a report.

[37] Commission, 'Staff Working Document on the experience acquired as a result of the application of Regulation (EC) No 141/2000 on orphan medicinal products and account of the public health benefits obtained' SEC(2006) 832 13.

[38] Commission, 'Communication to the European Parliament, the Council, the European Economic and Social Committee and the Committee of the Regions on Rare Diseases: Europe's Challenges' COM (2008) 679 final, 3.

The full benefits of the EU orphan regulations require optimal synergies between action on Community and on Member State level. Incentives at the European Union level need to be translated into rapid access of patients to the new products throughout the entire Community and they need to be supplemented by incentives at Member State level. In this regard, the past experience was not entirely satisfactory.[39]

Member States do not yet ensure full access to each authorised orphan drug approved.[40]

In order to understand the problems to which OMPs, once designated and authorized, may give rise, it is therefore necessary to address the issue of access to such products.

C. Availability and Accessibility of Orphan Medicinal Products

In the context of the discussion in this chapter, it is especially important to distinguish the *availability* of a medical treatment or service, including an OMP, from *access* to it. Availability refers to the fact that the product has received marketing authorization, and that it can therefore, in principle, be purchased or prescribed. The Regulation on Orphan Medicinal Products is designed to incentivize availability throughout the EU, although it does not follow that launch of a new product in a given country will follow immediately upon the granting of marketing authorization through the centralized EMA procedure.

By contrast, accessibility refers to the capacity of a patient to obtain the treatment or service, on the recommendation of a treating physician, within a given health system. As the European Committee of Experts on Rare Diseases observes, this is contingent upon overcoming certain 'administrative hurdles' erected within a given health system.[41] Pricing, reimbursement, and distribution of medical treatments and services are matters for a MS, in accordance with the strong expression of the principle of subsidiarity in Article 168(7) TFEU, which states that:

Union action shall respect the *responsibilities of the Member States* for the definition of their health policy and for the organisation and delivery of health services and medical care. The responsibilities of the Member States shall include the management of health services and medical care and the allocation of the resources assigned to them.[42]

Accordingly, it is quite possible that a new OMP may be *available* as a consequence of having been granted marketing authorization at EU level, but not *accessible* within a given MS health system because a choice has been made not to reimburse it or include it in a national or local formulary. This does, indeed, appear to be the case in practice. A survey of pricing and access to OMPs in ten EU countries indicates that, of those products which have been granted EU marketing authorization, access ranges from 93 per cent of products in France to 25 per cent in Greece, translating into 98 per cent of patients with access in the former country to 34 per cent in the latter.[43] Unsurprisingly,

---

[39] Commission Staff Working Document (n 37) 13.
[40] Commission Communication (n 38) 3.
[41] Aymé and Rendall (n 32) 39.
[42] Emphasis added. See also Directive 2011/24/EU of the European Parliament and of the Council of 9 March 2011 on the application of patients' rights in cross-border health care (Patients' Rights Directive) [2011] OJ L88/46, para 7: 'this Directive respects and is without prejudice to the freedom of each Member State to decide what type of healthcare it considers appropriate. No provision of this Directive should be interpreted in such a way as to undermine the fundamental ethical choices of Member States.'
[43] Y Le Cam, 'Inventory of Access and Prices of Orphan Drugs across Europe: a collaborative work between National Alliances on Rare Diseases and Eurordis' (2011) <http://img.eurordis.org/newsletter/pdf/mar-2011/ERTC_13122010_YLeCam_Final.pdf> accessed 30 September 2011.

this is regarded as a problem not only by the Commission, as outlined in the preceding section, but also by patient organizations such as Eurordis[44] and representatives of the biopharmaceutical industry.[45]

D. Why Limit Access to Orphan Medicinal Products?

There are three main reasons why a MS might choose to restrict access to OMPs in the national health system for which it is responsible.

The first of these turns upon the argument that evidence of the clinical effectiveness of such products is sometimes weak. Since it is mandatory for OMPs to proceed through the centralized marketing authorization process in the EMA, it is the responsibility of the CHMP to evaluate the efficacy (as well as the safety and quality) of the product,[46] the manufacturer having, upon request, been provided with protocol assistance by the Scientific Advice Working Party within the Committee as to the evidence which must be established. The Committee has acknowledged that 'conduct, analysis, and interpretation of studies in rare conditions at times may be constrained to varying degrees by the prevalence of the disease',[47] given that small patient populations may render randomized controlled trials, the so-called 'gold standard' of clinical evidence,[48] problematic or impossible. Accordingly, it permits the adoption of different and less common methodological approaches to obtaining controlled evidence, provided that patient interests remain protected.[49] Nonetheless, the Committee also notes that most OMPs submitted for authorization are based upon evidence obtained from randomized controlled trials, concluding that 'deviation from such standards is, therefore, uncommon and should only be considered when completely unavoidable and would need to be justified.'[50]

However, acceptance by EMA of the clinical efficacy of a new product for the purposes of marketing authorization in the EU is an entirely distinct process from evaluation of clinical effectiveness for the purposes of pricing, reimbursement, or inclusion in a national formulary. As discussed in the preceding section, this is the responsibility of MS governments, and both the criteria which are applied and the evidence which is required may differ from, and be more restrictive than, that employed by CHMP. For example, reimbursement in France is conditional not on clinical effectiveness per se, but upon proof of 'clinical added value', which measures the relative effectiveness of the product in relation to existing therapies: while it is more

---

[44] See Eurordis (n 34): 'Another significant challenge remains to translate market authorisations into real availability for patients in every Member State.'

[45] European Biopharmaceutical Enterprises/European Association for Bioindustries (n 30) 3: 'the biggest challenge faced currently in respect of orphan drugs is the unequal access to them across Member States following centralised marketing approval. There are large differences in the number of available OMPs across the EU.'

[46] In accordance with Directive 2001/83/EC of the European Parliament and of the Council of 6 November 2001 on the Community code relating to medicinal products for human use [2001] OJ L311/67.

[47] CHMP, 'Guideline on Clinical Trials in Small Populations', CHMP/EWP/83561/2005 (2006) 3 <www.ema.europa.eu/docs/en_GB/document_library/Scientific_guideline/2009/09/WC500003615.pdf> accessed 30 September 2011.

[48] See eg M Meldrum, 'A Brief History of the Randomised Controlled Trial: From Oranges and Lemons to the Gold Standard' (2000) 14 *Hematology/Oncology Clinics of North America* 745. For criticism, see eg J Grossman and F Mackenzie, 'The Randomised Controlled Trial: Gold Standard or Merely Standard?' (2005) 48 *Perspectives in Biology and Medicine* 516.

[49] CHMP (n 47) 10.

[50] CHMP (n 47) 3.

likely that products which have been designated OMP status will fulfil this criterion than those which have not, this will not always be the case.[51]

The distinction between the two levels of evaluation can therefore be explained as follows.[52] For marketing authorization (EMA) purposes, the decision is an all-or-nothing one (the product is authorized or not) and is based upon the benefit of the doubt; while for pricing/reimbursement/formulary (national agency) purposes, the decision is a relative one (in view of alternatives, the product merits reimbursement or inclusion in the national formulary) and the evidence of effectiveness is more critically scrutinized, even though a 'lower' standard of evidence may still be acceptable than is the case for other medical treatments and services.[53]

The second justification for restricting access to OMPs within a health system is to respond to 'gaming' by manufacturers. It is possible for sponsors of an OMP to manipulate the incentives established by the Orphan Medicinal Product Regulation in a number of ways. One scenario is where a manufacturer obtains marketing authorization for a slightly modified variant of a product which is already available on an unlicensed basis, thus largely bypassing the research and development stage but still taking advantage of the incentives—especially market exclusivity—which the Regulation confers.[54] A further strategy is to obtain marketing authorization for a disease which meets the prevalence criterion established in the Regulation, but then to broaden its application so that it treats more common conditions, some of a non-orphan character, while still maintaining the benefit of the incentives provided by the Regulation.[55] Other questionable practices include 'sub-setting' (splitting a disease into sub-categories, each of which has orphan status) and 'salami-slicing' (creating artificial orphan subsets of a non-orphan condition).[56]

In reality, although such activities may generate a degree of outrage and form a basis for critique of the legislation,[57] they are unlikely in themselves to afford a rationale for restricting access. Rather, they connect to the third—and, undoubtedly, the most

---

[51] See A Denis, S Simoens, C Fostier and others, *Policies for Rare Diseases and Orphan Drugs* (Belgian Health Care Knowledge Centre (KCE) 2009) 47.

[52] See A Denis, L Mergaert, C Fostier and others, 'Issues Surrounding Orphan Disease and Orphan Drug Policies in Europe' (2010) 8 *Applied Economics and Health Policy* 343, 345–6.

[53] eg betaine anhydrous for the treatment of homocystinuria was approved by EMA on the basis of a literature review. It was not recommended for use by the Scottish Medicines Consortium because the evidence of clinical efficacy was regarded as insufficient, even though the Consortium recognized the difficulties involved in assessing effectiveness in this disease area: see M Garau and J Mestre-Ferrandiz, 'Access Mechanisms for Orphan Drugs: a Comparative Study of Selected European Countries' (2009) 52 *OHE Briefing* 13.

[54] For an illustration, see D Nicholl, D Hilton-Jones, J Palace and others, 'Open Letter to Prime Minister David Cameron and Health Secretary Andrew Lansley' (2010) 341 *British Medical Journal* 1079. In Case T-264/07 *CSL Behring GmbH v European Commission and another* [2010] All ER (D) 76, the manufacturer argued that an application for designation of human fibrinogen as an OMP should be granted by EMA, notwithstanding that the product had received marketing authorization in a number of European countries from 1966 onward, because the therapeutic indication ('treatment of congenital deficit in fibrinogen') differed from that specified in the marketing authorization ('treatment of specific haemorrhaging'). This argument was rejected by the General Court. For discussion, see G Bache and T Hervey, 'Incentivising Innovation or Supporting Other Interests? European Regulation of Orphan Medicinal Products' (2011) 19 *Medical Law Review* 123.

[55] See N Hawkes and D Cohen, 'What Makes an Orphan Drug?' (2010) 341 *British Medical Journal* 1076, 1078. An example is imatinib, which has now been approved for use for six indications by the EMA and ten by the Federal Drug Administration in the USA.

[56] See Denis, Mergaert, Fostier and others (n 52) 344. For discussion of the latter strategy in the context of orphan drug legislation in the USA, see W Yin, 'R&D policy, agency costs and innovation in personalised medicine' (2009) 28 *Journal of Health Economics* 950.

[57] See especially Nicholl, Hilton-Jones, Palace and others (n 54).

significant—justification, which is the price of OMPs. Orphan drugs tend to be expensive: a study of ten OMPs commissioned by the Commission found that the average cost per patient was about ten times higher than that of other non-orphan products which were themselves considered expensive because they were innovative and/or treated severe conditions.[58] This may be explained in part by the need to recoup expenditure on research and from small patient populations, and in part by the fact that Article 8 of Regulation 141/2000 precludes competition from cheaper generic products during the period of market exclusivity. But can the cost of provision of such products be met, and sustained, by a health system?

This issue is highly contentious. Perhaps unsurprisingly, stakeholders who have an interest in increasing access to OMPs seek to demonstrate that cost should not present a problem to health systems. Eurordis argues that increased costs to health systems since the adoption of the Regulation on Orphan Medicinal Products in 2000 are primarily attributable to two new product families: imatinib for various forms of cancer, and enzyme replacement therapies, and that 'the remainder of orphan drugs represent less than 1 per cent of national healthcare costs'.[59] While acknowledging that 'at an individual level, treatment of a rare disease is more costly than treating the majority of common illnesses',[60] the organization emphasizes that the *absolute* or *overall* cost to a health system (or, more broadly, to society) is not as great as is commonly supposed. It reaches this conclusion on the basis of a number of factors.

First, low prevalence of rare diseases means that the number of patients seeking access to a particular costly treatment will be low. Secondly, not all of those who seek access will actually receive a product, given that drugs are not always effective in every patient affected by a given pathology and that specialist centres and facilities remain relatively inaccessible. Thirdly, the cost of treatment does not increase proportionally with the rarity of the disease. Fourthly, in the absence of treatment, there would be costs to be borne in the form of frequent hospitalizations and reduced capacity for work.

By contrast, those who are charged with making choices upon the allocation of health care resources for particular populations tend to emphasize the *individual* costs of particular products, and the *opportunity costs* of treatments which must be foregone if the OMP is provided. For example, those responsible for the commissioning of health services in the West Midlands area of England have noted that the decision of the National Specialized Commissioning Advisory Group to place no restrictions upon the use of enzyme replacement therapy to treat lysosomal storage diseases, which more than doubled the expenditure of Primary Care Trusts upon such treatment in 2005–6, had significant consequences for access to other treatments:

The increase levied on West Midlands Primary Care Trusts for this single service was greater than the entire increase in all acute regionally commissioned services, including several high cost and growing specialty areas such as blood and marrow transplantation, blood products for haemophiliacs, neonatal intensive care and special care services for babies, paediatric intensive care, adult and paediatric burns services, and laboratory and clinical genetics services.[61]

---

[58] Alcimed, 'Study on Orphan Drugs, Phase I: Overview of the Conditions for Marketing Orphan Drugs in Europe' (2005) 37 <http://ec.europa.eu/health/files/orphanmp/doc/pricestudy/final_final_report_part_1_web_en.pdf> accessed 30 September 2011.

[59] Eurordis Statement, 'Orphan Drugs: Rising to the Challenge to Ensure a Better Future for 30 Million Patients in Europe' (2009) 2 <www.eurordis.org/publication/orphan-drugs-rising-challenge-ensure-better-future-30-million-patients-europe> accessed 30 September 2011.

[60] Eurordis Statement (n 59) 7.

[61] A Burls, D Austin, and D Moore, 'Commissioning for Rare Diseases: View from the Frontline' (2005) 331 *British Medical Journal* 1019, 1020–1. At the date in question, the National Specialized

Further research undertaken on behalf of the Department of Health and the National Health Service (NHS) for England has concluded that the total cost to the NHS in England and Wales of providing this type of treatment to all patients with lysosomal storage disorders could amount to £32 million per year, while the cost of treating 'ultra-orphan' cancer conditions could total between £21.7 million and £139.2 million annually.[62]

The differing approaches to the assessment of the cost of OMPs suggest that it is rather simplistic to draw the conclusion that 'the potentially high cost of new drugs for rare conditions could result in a disproportionately large impact of these conditions on health service budgets.'[63] A plausible case can be made that the present (or recent) amount expended by European health systems on OMPs stands at acceptable levels,[64] but that—especially given the time-lag between designation as an OMP and marketing authorization—levels of expenditure are likely to increase significantly in the near future.[65] However, it might also be argued that the *perception* of the expense entailed in provision of OMPs is as important in shaping decisions and policies to limit access to such treatments as is their actual cost. Such a view is held, for example, by Eurordis which has commented upon 'the *fear*... that their cost is so exorbitant that they represent a considerable expense to the community'.[66]

The question of whether the cost of OMPs can be borne by a health system—and, moreover, by society—is, of course, not simply a matter of finance. It also hinges upon social value judgements as to the just distribution of health care in circumstances in which resources are finite. That is, we need to ask not only whether we *can afford* to provide access to OMPs, but also whether we *should* provide access to OMPs, especially given other calls upon scarce health care resources. It is this ethical dimension which, arguably, is the most contentious and intractable aspect of orphan drug policy, and it will now be considered.

E. The Ethics of Access to Orphan Medicinal Products

It is well known that there are a number of principles of justice which might offer an ethical basis upon which the distribution of finite health care resources may be carried out.[67] Those principles are as pertinent to the OMP context as they are elsewhere in health care; indeed, the high cost of such products and the severely debilitating and/or

---

Commissioning Advisory Group had oversight of the commissioning of all specialized NHS services for children and adults with rare conditions.

[62] K Miles, C Packer, and A Stevens, 'Quantifying Emerging Drugs for Very Rare Conditions' (2007) 100 *Quarterly Journal of Medicine* 291, 294–5.

[63] Miles, Packer, and Stevens (n 62) 295.

[64] An analysis of expenditure in five European countries concludes that the average expenditure on OMPs as a percentage of overall drug expenditure was 1.7 per cent in 2007: J Orofino, J Soto, M Casado and others, 'Global Spending on Orphan Drugs in France, Germany, the UK, Italy and Spain during 2007' (2010) 8 *Applied Health Economics and Health Policy* 301.

[65] Denis, Simoens, Fostier, and others forecast an increase of 145 per cent in expenditure upon orphan drugs in Belgium in the period 2008–13: this would represent approximately 4 per cent of the total expenditure on pharmaceuticals and over 10 per cent of all hospital expenditure on pharmaceuticals: (n 51) 84.

[66] Eurordis Statement (n 59) 6. Emphasis added.

[67] For discussion, see eg R Cookson and P Dolan, 'Principles of Justice in Healthcare Rationing' (2000) 26 *Journal of Medical Ethics* 323; J Butler, *The Ethics of Health Care Rationing: Principles and Practices* (Cassell 1999).

life-threatening nature of the conditions for which they are developed tend to raise the ethical questions which are generated by scarcity in an especially acute form. More generally, Brownsword's model of the 'bioethical triangle' alerts us to the existence of a 'background ethical plurality': distinct ethical perspectives which frame the debate as to the legitimacy of regulatory activities in a biotechnological context.[68] The three leading positions which Brownsword identifies can be applied to OMPs—utilitarianism underpins principle (1) in the following section (and may play a part in principle (2)(a) if scientific advancement serves to maximize future health gain at a level greater than the costs incurred in achieving it); human rights, principle (2)(d); and dignity, principles (2)(b), (d), and (less overtly) (a).

This plurality is, as Brownsword notes, contested.[69] Thus, it will be seen that adoption of a utilitarian perspective suggests restriction or denial of access to OMPs, while human rights and dignity arguments operate in favour. This is problematic for those who seek to obtain OMPs because a utilitarian approach to the issue of access to new health technologies has recently become widely embedded in policymaking at MS level. Weighty countervailing ethical arguments will thus be needed if adverse national policy preferences are to be displaced. It will, however, be argued that both the human rights and dignitarian approaches possess weaknesses which mean that they are unlikely to 'trump' utilitarianism in this context. It is also unclear that there is public support for such an outcome.

1. Health Maximization and Health Technology Assessment

The ethical principle which is least favourable to OMPs is that which pursues the objective of the maximization of aggregate population health. This approach is problematic for those who seek to argue for access to OMPs because it entails a comparison of the health benefits gained to the population through provision of the treatment or service with the costs to the health system of making such provision (both in monetary terms and, more broadly, in respect of health which is foregone). The number of patients who will benefit from access to OMPs within any given MS health system is small (albeit that, cumulatively, the patient population across the Union runs into several millions), but the price of such products tends to be high. Hence—given the finite resources available for health care—if sufficient funds are to be set aside to provide an OMP, significant numbers of patients with other (perhaps more common) conditions will be unable to receive treatments which can no longer be afforded. Consequently, there may well be a net *decrease* in aggregate population health if OMPs are routinely offered.

Another way of expressing this is to consider the impact on a health system of permitting access to OMPs in terms of the cost per quality adjusted life year (QALY) of particular products of such type. In their discussion of the issues raised by the commissioning of enzyme replacement therapies on the NHS, Burls, Austin, and Moore report that the four licensed treatments have costs per QALY of between £252,000 and more than £450,000.[70] Similarly, the National Institute for Health and Clinical Excellence (NICE) in the United Kingdom has noted that one group of OMPs, the beta-interferons and glatiramir acetate for multiple sclerosis, have a cost per QALY in

---

[68] See R Brownsword, *Rights, Regulation and the Technological Revolution* (OUP 2008) 32.
[69] Brownsword (n 68) 69.
[70] Burls and others (n 61) 1020.

excess of £700,000.[71] It estimates that, in general, 'ultra-orphan' products can be expected to cost between £200,000 and £300,000 per QALY.[72]

This is substantially higher than the usual threshold of £20,000 to £30,000 which the Institute applies to determine whether a health care intervention can be considered to be cost-effective for the purposes of its technology appraisal guidance to the NHS in England and Wales.[73] While this is a 'soft' decisional threshold insofar as interventions with a cost per QALY above the higher of these two figures may still be evaluated as cost-effective by NICE if adequate reasons and evidence exist in support of such a conclusion,[74] it nonetheless points to a significant obstacle to access to OMPs, both in the NHS and in other health systems across the EU.[75]

In light of continued and increasing pressures on already overstretched budgets for health care, a number of countries worldwide—including several in Europe[76]—have recently sought to employ methods of health technology assessment (HTA) to assess the clinical and cost-effectiveness of (mainly) new health care interventions, with a view to minimizing or eliminating expenditure upon treatments or services which offer little clinical benefit and/or which represent poor 'value for money'. Although processes and methodologies vary, HTA is likely to have the effect of limiting access to OMPs, as representatives of the biopharmaceutical industry have observed:

There are large differences in the number of available OMPs across the EU. This can be linked to demographic and economic factors but also to the application of HTA methodologies to appraise orphan drugs that can lead to high rates of rejection and significant delay to access to new OMPs. The increasing demand for HTA to inform healthcare decisions will therefore represent a major challenge in terms of access to OMPs, which are unlikely to meet standard HTA requirements.[77]

The difficulty which HTA presents for those who argue for the expansion of access to OMPs is that this form of activity, when feeding into policy decisions on reimbursement, pricing, or coverage of new health technologies,[78] is necessarily focused upon maximization of health at a population level. As the preceding discussion indicates, this is especially problematic where the institution undertaking HTA employs QALY methodology in order to make recommendations on the cost-effectiveness of an

---

[71] NICE (n 15) para 4.1.2.   [72] NICE (n 15) para 4.9.

[73] NICE, *Guide to the Methods of Technology Appraisal* (NICE, 2008) paras 6.2.22–6.2.24.

[74] NICE (n 73) para 6.2.25. Note that a higher threshold applies in the case of certain life-extending treatments for patients with short life expectancy: see NICE, 'Supplementary Advice to the Appraisal Committees: Appraising life-extending, end of life treatments' (2009) <www.nice.org.uk/media/E4A/79/SupplementaryAdviceTACEoL.pdf> accessed 30 September 2011.

[75] Although it should be noted that drugs for 'ultra-orphan' diseases are likely to be even less cost-effective than OMPs simply because the lower rates of prevalence make it more difficult for manufacturers to recoup research and development costs through sales, with the consequence that prices will tend to be higher still.

[76] See C Sorenson, M Drummond, and P Kavanos, *Ensuring Value for Money in Healthcare: the role of health technology assessment in the European Union* (World Health Organization on behalf of the European Observatory on Health Systems and Policies 2008).

[77] European Biopharmaceutical Enterprises/European Association for Bioindustries (n 30) 3.

[78] A distinction is sometimes drawn between *assessment*, which is defined as the scientific/technical process of gathering and analysing information on a health technology; and *appraisal*, which refers to decision-making or policy advice on that technology, on the basis of a synthesis of the scientific evidence combined with other factors such as social values. See eg A Stevens and R Milne, 'Health Technology Assessment in England and Wales' (2004) 20 *International Journal of Technology Assessment in Health Care* 11. However, HTA is commonly used to refer to both forms of activity, and it is accordingly used here.

intervention, but even where QALYs are not generally used,[79] the goal of standard methods of HTA may still be viewed as increasing the efficiency of the provision of health care.[80] Given high prices, small target populations, and limited evidence as to clinical effectiveness, OMPs do not readily fulfil this objective. Accordingly, modification of the applicable ethical principles, as well as the clinical and health economic methodologies and rules employed by agencies conducting HTA, is likely to prove necessary if OMPs are to overcome this 'fourth hurdle' to access.[81]

In this respect, the recent EU-level commitment to supporting and facilitating cooperation and exchange of scientific information within a voluntary network connecting national HTA agencies,[82] may prove to be a significant development. While it is, as yet, too early to judge whether a harmonized European approach to the ethical values which inform national HTA decisions might be adopted—and, if so, whether any such approach will signal a departure from the goal of health maximization which operates unfavourably to OMP provision—the interest shown by the existing collaborative network, EUnetHTA, in assuring 'ethical . . . healthcare for citizens across Europe',[83] suggests at least that the issue will feature prominently on the agenda of the network when it is formally established as a permanent entity in 2014–15.

2. Other Ethical Bases: Do OMPs Warrant Special Treatment?

There are a number of countervailing ethical arguments for granting OMPs special status for funding and inclusion within the coverage offered by a health system notwithstanding that they do not satisfy the criteria normally applied within an HTA process. However, each of these suffers from certain weaknesses, as will be seen.

a. *Scientific advancement*

First, it might be contended that encouragement of research and development of new OMPs will stimulate further scientific and medical advances, and that there is therefore a moral obligation of beneficence towards existing patients and a commitment to future generations, in addition to a more generalized duty to develop scientific knowledge.[84] This rationale is well captured in an observation made by William Harvey in 1657, which is frequently cited in modern-day accounts of orphan drugs and their regulation:

Nature is nowhere accustomed more openly to display her secret mysteries than in cases where she shows traces of her workings apart from the beaten path; nor is there any better way to

---

[79] eg in Germany. See Institute for Quality and Efficiency in Healthcare (IQWiG), *General Methods for the Assessment of the Relation of Benefits to Costs* (IQWiG 2009) 4.

[80] See Sorenson and others (n 74). Eg NICE is statutorily obliged to have regard to 'the broad balance between the benefits and costs of the provision of health services . . . in England': Health and Social Care Act 2012, s 233(1)(a).

[81] See M Drummond, D Willson, P Kavanos and others, 'Assessing the economic challenges posed by orphan drugs' (2007) 23 *International Journal of Technology Assessment in Health Care* 36, 38. The 'fourth hurdle' of cost-effectiveness supplements the other three: safety, efficacy, and quality. For discussion, see R Taylor, M Drummond, G Salkeld and others, 'Inclusion of cost-effectiveness in licensing of new drugs: the fourth hurdle' (2004) 329 *British Medical Journal* 972.

[82] Patients' Rights Directive, Art 15(1).

[83] <www.eunethta.eu/Public/About_EUnetHTA/EUnetHTA-Vision/> accessed 30 September 2011.

[84] See C Gericke, A Riesberg, and R Busse, 'Ethical Issues in Funding Orphan Drug Research and Development' (2005) *Journal of Medical Ethics* 164, 166.

advance the proper practice of medicine than to give our minds to the discovery of the usual law of Nature than by careful investigation of cases of rarer forms of disease.[85]

This justification appears especially potent in cases where development of the OMP yields insights into treatment of more common conditions. In such situations, the claim (outlined previously and considered in further detail later) that it is inequitable to allocate resources to treat those with rare diseases if as a consequence those with more common illnesses lose out, is weakened, at least in the longer term. It is therefore unsurprising that members of COMP have pointed to the Committee's willingness to grant OMP designation to products classified as 'innovative' (including stem cell therapies, nanotechnology, and monoclonal antibodies),[86] and have claimed that 'the challenges that have been encountered in the research and development of drugs for rare conditions have fostered creative approaches that could also be applied to drug development for common diseases.'[87] However, it is notable that neither the Regulation nor any of the associated documents make specific reference to the scientific advancement rationale per se as a justification for incentivizing development of OMPs within the EU. Instead research and development are linked to other ethical claims, as will next be discussed. This suggests that the argument is unlikely to prove sufficiently strong on its own to displace the maximization of population health objective which underpins HTA, especially as scientific advances are inherently unpredictable in nature.[88]

b. Equity

The second, and predominant, ethical claim which underpins EU action in the field of rare diseases is expressed in the second recital to Regulation 141/2000: 'patients suffering from rare conditions should be entitled to the *same quality of treatment as other patients*'.[89] The argument, therefore, is one of equity, supplemented by related claims of universality and solidarity. This is underlined by Council Recommendation 2009/C 151/02, which describes such principles (as well as that of 'access to good quality care') as being 'of paramount importance to patients with rare diseases'.[90] In so doing, it makes reference to the earlier Council 'Conclusions on common values and principles in European Union Health Systems', a statement which 'sets out the common values and principles that are shared across the European Union about how health systems respond to the needs of the populations and patients that they serve',[91] and which explains the principles as follows:

---

[85] Letter from William Harvey to John Vlackveld (24 April 1657): see eg M Field and T Boat (eds), *Rare Diseases and Orphan Products: Accelerating Research and Development* (National Academies Press 2010) 15; K Westermark and others, 'European Regulation on Orphan Medicinal Products: 10 Years of Experience and Future Prospects' (2011) 10 *Nature Reviews Drug Discovery* 341, 341; Gericke, Riesberg, and Busse (n 84).

[86] Westermark and others (n 85) 343.

[87] Westermark and others (n 85) 349. See also Commission Communication (n 38) 2: 'Research on rare diseases has proved to be very useful to better understand the mechanism of common conditions such as obesity and diabetes, as they often represent a model of dysfunction of a single biological pathway.'

[88] See C McCabe, A Tsuchiya, K Claxton and others, 'Orphan Drugs Revisited' (2006) 99 *Quarterly Journal of Medicine* 341, 343–4.

[89] OMP Regulation. Emphasis added.

[90] Council Recommendation on action in the field of rare diseases, para 2.

[91] [2006] OJ C146/1, Annex.

Universality means that no-one is barred access to healthcare; solidarity is closely linked to the financial arrangement of our national health systems and the need to ensure accessibility to all; equity relates to equal access according to need, regardless of ethnicity, gender, age, social status or ability to pay.[92]

The equity argument is widely invoked as a principle of justice which might determine how health care resources should be allocated. It finds expression in theoretical work which argues that the basis for distribution should be securing 'fair equality of opportunity',[93] or a 'fair innings' for all.[94] Ostensibly, it appears just that a patient suffering from a rare disease who has the same personal characteristics (insofar as these are considered relevant to distribution of health care), prognosis, and capacity to benefit as a patient suffering from a more common condition should have the same capacity to access treatment as the latter; after all, clinical need is generally considered to be the primary determinant of access.[95]

However, the picture changes once the fact of resource scarcity is recognized. If we assume that the cost of the OMP is higher than the cost of a drug to treat a common condition (and, as discussed previously, there is reason to believe that this is the case at least at the level of *individual treatments* if not necessarily as an *overall burden upon the system*), then—given a finite budget for health care—treating patients with relatively expensive OMPs is likely to carry the opportunity cost that insufficient resources remain to treat some patients with more common conditions. As well as being problematic from the perspective of maximization of population health, such a situation is also inequitable, for it implies that the health of those with prevalent diseases is valued less than those with rare diseases. Accordingly, as McCabe, Claxton, and Tsuchiya argue, 'the idea that decisions should be made based on valuing health outcome more highly for no other reason than rarity of the condition seems unsustainable and incompatible with other equity principles and theories of justice.'[96]

c. Non-abandonment

A third justification for according OMPs special status when decisions are being taken as to which treatments and services should be provided within a health system derives from the principle of non-abandonment. The very word 'orphan' conveys a sense that patients with rare diseases have been discarded by society. Many would regard such a situation as morally unacceptable from a perspective rooted in equity or rights;[97] moreover, it may be argued that utility may be derived from the hope that treatment will be offered for a rare and serious condition,[98] and from an 'enhanced feeling of

---

[92] [2006] OJ C146/1, Annex.

[93] See especially N Daniels, *Just Health Care* (CUP 1985) and *Just Health: Meeting Health Needs Fairly* (CUP 2008).

[94] See A Williams, 'Intergenerational Equity: An Exploration of the "Fair Innings" Argument' (1997) 6 *Health Economics* 117.

[95] See R Klein, P Day, and S Redmayne, *Managing Scarcity* (Open University Press 2006) 25: 'justice requires that people with equal needs should receive equal treatment'; further, Cookson and Dolan (n 67) 324.

[96] C McCabe, K Claxton, and A Tsuchiya, 'Orphan Drugs and the NHS: Should we Value Rarity?' (2005) 331 *British Medical Journal* 1016, 1018. See also D Hughes, B Tunnage, and S Yeo, 'Drugs for Exceptionally Rare Diseases: Do they Deserve Special Status for Funding?' (2005) 98 *Quarterly Journal of Medicine* 829, 832.

[97] See Gericke and others (n 84) 166.

[98] E Nord, J Richardson, A Street and others, 'Who Cares About Cost? Does Economic Analysis Impose or Reflect Social Values?' (1995) 34 *Health Policy* 90.

security derived from knowing that one lives in a compassionate society, where those in desperate need are not ignored.'[99]

A particular species of this ethical argument is the 'rule of rescue'. According to this principle, a moral obligation exists to save individuals who are in immediate peril, notwithstanding that considerable resources may be expended upon doing so:

Our moral response to the imminence of death demands that we rescue the doomed. We throw a rope to the drowning, rush into burning buildings to snatch the entrapped, dispatch teams to search for the snowbound. This rescue morality spills over into medical care, where our ropes are artificial hearts, our rush is the mobile critical care unit, our teams the transplant services. The imperative to rescue is, undoubtedly, of great moral significance.[100]

It is argued that an ethical obligation of this type exists to treat those suffering from rare diseases and that this justifies departure from the maximizing principle inherent in HTA.[101] Indeed, Australia's HTA agency, the Pharmaceutical Benefits Advisory Committee, explicitly draws a connection between the 'rule of rescue' and the rarity of a condition as a rationale for reversing a recommendation to deny state subsidy for a medicine on the ground that the product is not cost-effective.[102]

However, both the weight and applicability of the 'rule of rescue' in this context may be queried. First, it might plausibly be argued that what is described is a psychological phenomenon, 'a concept that explains the observed instinctive reactions of individuals to tragic events in urgent circumstances',[103] which carries potent symbolic value.[104] But if it is to function as a 'rule' which can guide decision-making in particular circumstances, it requires further normative justification, and the precise nature of this justification is ambiguous given the 'head-on clash of values' which is inherent in the concept.[105]

Secondly, we might question whether those who suffer from rare diseases fit the criteria of the 'rule of rescue': to what extent do they resemble the paradigm cases of the trapped miner or the shipwrecked mariner? Schöne-Seifert has enumerated five 'uncontested imperatives' of the concept,[106] the absence of any one of which, she claims, weakens any inherent moral obligation deriving from the 'rule' and its consequent suspension of the calculus of costs and benefits normally associated with priority-setting in health care. Of the five features—visibility or identifiability of the victims; acutely impending death of the victims; a reasonable chance of effective rescue; acceptable risks of costs to the rescuers; and exceptionality of occurrence—it may be argued that only the last is always characteristic of rare diseases, although each of

---

[99] J McKie and J Richardson, 'The Rule of Rescue' (2003) 56 *Social Science and Medicine* 2407, 2411.

[100] A Jonsen, 'Bentham in a Box: Technology Assessment and Healthcare Allocation' (1986) 14 *Law Medicine and Healthcare* 172, 174.

[101] Hughes and others (n 96) 833.

[102] Pharmaceutical Benefits Advisory Committee, *Guidelines for preparing submissions to the Pharmaceutical Benefits Advisory Committee (Version 4.3)* (Commonwealth of Australia 2008) 168.

[103] McCabe and others (n 96) 343.

[104] See McKie and Richardson (n 99) 2414.

[105] McKie and Richardson (n 99) 2417. One significant point of ethical contention, which for reasons of space cannot be explored in detail here, is whether it is justifiable, as the 'rule' apparently requires, to accord priority to identified individuals over 'statistical lives', given that this conflicts with the principle of equity. For further discussion, see B Schöne-Seifert, 'The "Rule of Rescue" in Medical Priority-Setting: Ethical Plausibilities and Implausibilities' (2009) 0 *Rationality, Markets and Morals* 421, 424–5 <www.rmm-journal.de/downloads/030_schoene_seifert.pdf> accessed 30 September 2011; McCabe and others (n 96) 343.

[106] Schöne-Seifert (n 105) 423.

the others *may* be present in a given case. This suggests, furthermore, that the ethical rationales underpinning the 'rule of rescue' and non-abandonment of those suffering from rare diseases can be distinguished, notwithstanding their apparent elision by Australia's HTA agency. As Cookson, McCabe, and Tsuchiya remark, 'the moral imperative behind Rule of Rescue relates to the fact of imminent peril. It is not clear why it should make any difference from an ethical point of view whether the cause of imminent peril is rare or common.'[107]

d. Rights

A final ethico-legal argument may be constructed on the basis of rights. Regulation 141/2000 does not explicitly invoke the discourse of rights, but it does refer to *entitlement*. Such entitlement could be of a moral character, grounded in the dignity owed to all human beings as autonomous individuals. Alternatively (or additionally), it could take a legal form and be rooted in a right to health as a matter of human rights law. In this regard, it might be noted that Directive 2011/24/EU on the application of patients' rights in cross-border health care, which *is* expressed in the language of 'rights', contains a provision relating to patients suffering from rare diseases.[108] The Charter of Fundamental Rights of the European Union, which now has binding legal status equal to the Treaties,[109] also contains a 'right to benefit from medical treatment',[110] which could extend to those suffering from rare diseases. In principle, various articles of the European Convention on Human Rights might also be applicable to this context,[111] although the margin of appreciation afforded on ethically controversial questions by the Strasbourg Court, coupled with a reluctance to impose disproportionate allocative burdens on state authorities, appears likely to render this avenue relatively unproductive for patients.

There is no doubt that a claim grounded in rights possesses significant 'normative cachet',[112] either on its own or as a supplement to the other ethical arguments identified here, particularly that based upon equity and universality. As such, it is a highly potent discursive tool for those who seek to argue for special status for OMPs, functioning to 'raise awareness and . . . [to] provide a means of framing debate'.[113] However, the extent to which it can be regarded as sufficiently decisive to justify varying the standard principles and practices of HTA depends upon the reading of rights which is adopted in a situation in which health care resources are scarce, or perceived to be so. Drawing upon the work of TH Marshall, Newdick has distinguished between rights of a civil and political variant, which are individualist in orientation, and rights which arise from social citizenship—including the right to

---

[107] R Cookson, C McCabe, and A Tsuchiya, 'Public Healthcare Resource Allocation and the Rule of Rescue' (2008) 34 *Journal of Medical Ethics* 540, 541.

[108] Art 13.

[109] Art 6(1) TEU.

[110] Art 35. For discussion, see T Hervey, 'The "Right to Health" in EU Law' in T Hervey and J Kenner (eds), *Economic and Social Rights under the EU Charter of Fundamental Rights—a Legal Perspective* (Hart 2003) 202–6.

[111] Notably Art 2 (right to life), Art 3 (prohibition of inhuman or degrading treatment or punishment), Art 8 (right to respect for private and family life), and Art 14 (prohibition of discrimination in respect of enjoyment of other rights).

[112] Hervey (n 110) 197.

[113] J McHale, 'Fundamental Rights and Health Care' in E Mossialos, G Permanand, R Baerten, and others, *Health Systems Governance in Europe: the Role of European Union Law and Policy* (CUP 2010) 314.

health—which serve 'not simply to promote liberty, but to [promote] reciprocity, mutuality and community'.[114] The essential function of such rights is to reduce inequality, with the consequence that:

they are often *relative* rights in the sense that they are subject to regulations intended to promote the public objectives of the fund whilst retaining financial balance in the interests of the needs of other people. Rather than being enforceable in the abstract, they can only be measured against the needs of others and the resources available to the resource-allocator.[115]

On this approach, a rights-based claim to access an OMP would not suffice to accord special status to the latter, since the right does not necessarily trump the community interest in equitable allocation of scarce resources.

As a matter of EU law, however, the argument from rights cannot wholly be dismissed as insufficiently strong to warrant special treatment for OMPs. Ostensibly, the stated basis for EU action on this issue is economic—harmonization in order to achieve completion of an internal market under what is now Article 114 TFEU— rather than grounded in human rights. Yet, as McHale has noted, jurisprudence of the Court of Justice of the European Union has been significant 'in arguably constructing a "right to healthcare" through the application of "economic" free movement principles rather than human rights principles . . . [and this] has led to concerns at the national level as to their impact on resource allocation.'[116] If this jurisprudence were to be applied to the OMP context, access to such products could be regarded as a component of a species of EU citizenship in which rights, founded upon an individualistic understanding, are decoupled from national territories. Arguably, this would have 'corrosive' consequences for social solidarity at MS level as resources are diverted from 'poorly represented, less visible, less articulate groups'.[117]

The prospects of the case law evolving in this direction in respect of OMPs as well as other medical treatments and services must now be assessed in light of Directive 2011/24/EU on the application of patients' rights in cross-border health care. Veitch argues that 'the objective of the Directive is to set out rules by which to improve the functioning of the internal market and the free movement of goods, persons, and services, rather than to create mechanisms by which Member States can circumvent these';[118] it thus functions as a codification of the preceding jurisprudence through which a 'right to healthcare' has been constructed. He therefore regards the Directive as retaining a strong individualist flavour. However, it should be noted that the specific provision of the Directive which relates to rare diseases is oriented merely towards supporting MSs 'in co-operating in the development of diagnosis and treatment capacity', and that the Directive also preserves the freedom of a MS to make ethical choices and to determine the type of health care which it considers appropriate.[119] There is little

[114] C Newdick, 'Citizenship, Free Movement and Health Care: Cementing Individual Rights by Corroding Social Solidarity' (2006) 43 *Common Market Law Review* 1645, 1647.

[115] Newdick (n 114) 1648. Emphasis in original.

[116] McHale (n 113) 303. The principal basis of these 'patient mobility' cases is what is now Art 56 TFEU (freedom to provide services). See eg Case C-158/96 *Kohll* [1998] ECR I-1931; Case C-157/99 *Geraets-Smits and Peerbooms* [2001] ECR 5473; Case C-385/88 *Muller-Fauré* [2003] ECR 4509; Case C-372/04 *Watts* [2006] ECR I-4325.

[117] Newdick (n 114) 1646.

[118] K Veitch, 'Juridification, Medicalisation and the Impact of EU Law: Patient Mobility and the Allocation of Scarce Resources' (2012) 20 *Medical Law Review* 362, 384.

[119] Patients' Rights Directive, Art 13. Note, however, provision for establishment of a permanent voluntary HTA network by Art 15, which (as discussed previously) may in due course impact upon ethical choices made at MS level: n 82 and accompanying text.

here to suggest that the issue of access to OMPs is now to be understood predominantly in terms of individualistic rights, as Newdick had feared.[120] Nonetheless, it is certainly plausible that an 'increased reference to the rhetoric of rights'[121] will characterize future demands for access to OMPs in both the judicial and political arenas.

3. Conclusion

In sum, the preceding dignitarian and rights-based ethical rationales cannot be said unequivocally to point towards granting special status to OMPs and consequent suspension of the standard utilitarian principles and methodologies of HTA, although the claim founded on 'rights' appears to provide the most persuasive mode of discourse and likely means of challenging denial of access in the future.

Neither is it wholly clear whether public opinion would support special treatment of OMPs. In this regard, a NICE Citizen's Council Report on ultra-orphan drugs of 2004 reported that twenty (of twenty-seven) of the membership considered that the Institute should sometimes or always vary its normal assessment of cost-effectiveness to permit NHS expenditure on ultra-orphan drugs where necessary, but that seven members were of the opinion that the standard methodologies and principles of HTA should be applied to such products.[122] More recently, a survey conducted in Norway found 'little compelling evidence... to support the existence of a societal preference for rarity in itself, a finding that supports the view that treatments for rare disease should not be exempt from standard considerations of cost effectiveness.'[123] In light of such public ambivalence and ethical ambiguity, one might conclude that limiting access to OMPs within a health system on the ground of cost-(in)effectiveness is unlikely to generate significant levels of public opposition, with the obvious exception of those who suffer from the disease in question and organizations which represent the interests of such patients.

F. Unblocking the Bottleneck of Access?

The Commission has described MS decision-making on pricing, reimbursement, and health system coverage as a 'bottleneck in access to orphan drugs'.[124] Strategies which have been proposed to alleviate this problem include enhanced collaboration at EU level on scientific assessment of the added therapeutic value of OMPs;[125] and establishment and implementation of plans, strategies, or other public health measures for rare diseases at MS level.[126]

---

[120] Newdick (n 114) 1660.

[121] T Hervey and J McHale, *Health Law and the European Union* (CUP 2004) 410.

[122] NICE Citizen's Council Report, *Ultra Orphan Drugs* (2004) 4 <www.nice.org.uk/niceMedia/pdf/Citizens_Council_Ultraorphan.pdf> accessed 30 September 2011. The Council is a deliberative body, with membership selected to be broadly representative of the population of England, which provides advice on the social values which the Institute should consider when producing its guidance.

[123] A Desser, D Gyrd-Hansen, J Olsen and others, 'Societal Views on Orphan Drugs: Cross-sectional Survey of Norwegians aged 40 to 67' (2010) 341 *British Medical Journal* c4715, 6.

[124] Commission Communication (n 38) 6.

[125] Commission Communication (n 38) 6. The establishment of the voluntary HTA network by Art 15 of Directive 2011/24/EU is likely to be of particular value in this context: n 82 and accompanying text.

[126] Council Recommendation on action in the field of rare diseases, Recommendation I.

As previously noted, the Directive on the application of patients' rights in cross-border health care makes specific mention of continued problems for rare disease sufferers, stating that, notwithstanding previous EU action in the field, 'some patients affected by rare diseases face difficulties in their quest for a diagnosis and treatment to improve their quality of life and to increase their life expectancy.'[127] The inclusion of rare diseases within the wide-ranging provisions of the Directive suggests a continued foregrounding of the issue at EU level, with particular emphasis being placed upon the development of European reference networks in the rare disease context.[128] These are voluntary arrangements between health care providers and centres of expertise in the MSs, and are intended to 'serve as research and knowledge centres, updating and contributing to the latest scientific findings, treating patients from other Member States and ensuring the availability of subsequent treatment facilities where necessary.'[129] As noted previously, the Directive also seeks to enhance access to treatment for rare diseases by seeking to make patients, health professionals, and those commissioning health care aware of the possibility of referral for treatment in another MS even where treatment is unavailable 'at home',[130] for example because an OMP has not successfully navigated the national HTA process.

It is, of course, premature to judge what effect the Directive will have, especially given the multiplicity of factors which may have a bearing upon its transposition.[131] However, one might legitimately harbour doubts as to its likely impact in this particular context. Although measures designed to pool expertise may assist, the primary stumbling-block to access to OMPs remains their cost (or perceived cost), especially in times of financial stringency when access even to treatments for more common conditions may be restricted within a health system.[132] This renders them highly likely not to satisfy the criteria applied by institutions operating standard HTA criteria. Yet, as discussed in the preceding section, the ethical case for varying those criteria in favour of OMPs is far from incontrovertible.

Given that it lacks competence over matters relating to the organization, management, and financing of health care services, the scope for the EU to address the central issue of access is limited. However, two possible courses of action might be pursued if widening access is considered to be an important policy goal. First, more extensive information on the overall cost of an OMP to a health system (that is, the price of the product multiplied by its frequency of utilization) could be derived through data derived from standardized patient registries, coordinated through the European reference network system.[133] This would permit a more accurate assessment of how much may need to be spent *in total* within a health system if access to an OMP is

---

[127] Patients' Rights Directive, para 55.
[128] Patients' Rights Directive, Art 12.
[129] See <http://ec.europa.eu/health/rare_diseases/european_reference_networks/erf/index_en.htm> accessed 30 September 2011.
[130] Patients' Rights Directive Art, 13(b).
[131] For concerns expressed by Eurordis in this regard, see <www.rarediseaseblogs.net/2011/03/04/the-new-eu-directive-on-cross-border-health-care-introduce-a-new-paradigm-for-the-provision-of-healthcare-services-to-rare-diseases-patients-in-europe/> accessed 30 September 2011. D Dimitrakopoulos, 'The Transposition of EU Law: "Post-Decisional" Politics and Institutional Autonomy' (2001) 7 *European Law Journal* 442 provides a general discussion of the factors which may affect transposition.
[132] See eg 'Patients Denied Key Treatments Due to NHS Cost-Cutting, Surgeons Warn', *The Guardian* (18 April 2011).
[133] See Commission, Pharmaceutical Forum, Pricing and Reimbursement Working Group, *Improving access to orphan medicines for all affected EU citizens* (2008) 4–5.

permitted, rather than focusing upon the cost of treating a single patient, or delivering a single QALY. If it does, indeed, prove to be the case that the total budgetary impact is minimal given small patient populations, many of the misgivings as to the affordability of OMPs would seem to be misplaced.

Secondly, should cost continue to prove an obstacle to access, there may be a case for critically scrutinizing the market exclusivity period of ten years. Such a strategy need not entail wholesale reform: robust application of the profitability criterion for reduction of the period of marketing exclusivity contained in Article 8(2) at all stages (initiation by the MS, assessment by COMP, and final decision by the Commission) might serve to reduce price levels of OMPs. It should, however, be noted that the assumption that exclusivity is a driver of the high price of OMPs is far from proven.[134] Furthermore, an approach of this type would inevitably generate considerable opposition from pharmaceutical companies, potentially negating the incentivizing effect of the Regulation.[135]

There are also steps which might be taken by MS governments, even if they remain attached to the existing principles and methodologies of HTA. First, greater flexibility in the regime for pricing and reimbursement of medicines may widen access while maintaining a degree of control of costs. Conditional pricing schemes, which allow rapid access to OMPs subject to later price adjustment on the basis of further evidence provided by post-launch studies, have been recommended for use in this context,[136] and are employed in a number of EU states.[137] Related pricing practices,[138] such as risk-sharing (where the manufacturer bears a proportion of the cost of the product to the health system) and value-based pricing (where the price of the product is determined by its value to patients and a health system, based upon criteria such as innovation or capacity to respond to unmet need) may also assist in restraining expenditure on OMPs.

A second option would be to focus attention not upon the cost of an OMP, but upon the ethical principles which militate against their inclusion within the basket of health services, especially those maximizing principles which generally underpin HTA. From this perspective, the task for those seeking a means to unblock the 'bottleneck' of access would be to demonstrate that society *does* accord value to provision of treatments for uncommon conditions, even if this means that those with more frequently occurring diseases may lose out as a consequence.

---

[134] See Alcimed, 'Study on Orphan Drugs, Phase II: Considerations on the application of article 8.2 of EC regulation No.141/2000 concerning orphan drugs' 8 <www.maladiesrares.be/documents/Alcimed2.pdf> accessed 30 September 2011.

[135] Alcimed (n 134) 7.

[136] Pharmaceutical Forum (n 133) 4.

[137] eg France operates an 'Authorization for Temporary Use' system which applies inter alia to orphan drugs, while the Netherlands has a regulation which conditionally reimburses orphan drugs used in teaching hospitals for a period of three years, during which period the manufacturer is required to conduct cost-effectiveness research in order to secure full listing. For further discussion, see Commission, Pharmaceutical Forum, Pricing and Reimbursement Working Group, *Risk-sharing practices and conditional pricing of pharmaceuticals* (2008).

[138] These approaches are normally separated in the literature, but have also been viewed as mere variants on 'agreements concluded by payers and pharmaceutical companies to diminish the impact on the payer's budget of new and existing medicines brought about by either the uncertainty of the value of the medicine and/or the need to work within finite budgets': J Adamski, B Godman, G Ofierska-Sujkowska, and others, 'Risk-sharing Arrangements for Pharmaceuticals: Potential Considerations and Recommendations for European payers' (2010) 10 *BMC Health Services Research* 153, 3 <www.biomedcentral.com/1472-6963/10/153> accessed 30 September 2011.

As previously discussed, there is some uncertainty as to the position of the public on this question and the evidence to date is somewhat limited. However, an opportunity to ascertain the views of the public in a more comprehensive manner may present itself through the development of plans or strategies for rare diseases by MSs, which the Council has recommended should take place as soon as possible and ideally by the end of 2013 at the latest.[139] Since these plans are 'aimed at guiding and structuring relevant [MS] actions in the field of rare diseases within the framework of . . . health and social systems',[140] it would seem imperative to gather information on the importance that the public assigns to making treatments available for rare conditions. If this were to be done in such a way as to foster a broad public debate upon the appropriateness and feasibility of a health system making provision for orphan drugs,[141] an additional purpose would be served in facilitating social learning on the need for trade-offs in this context. Building public understanding of the difficult choices which must necessarily be made may contribute to securing the legitimacy and, thus, the long-term stability, of the framework through which access to OMPs is determined.

Of course, it may be the case that elicitation of social values in this way will demonstrate that the public *does not* favour modification of maximizing principles in order to accommodate wider access to OMPs. Provided that such an outcome is premised upon broadly accurate information as to the likely overall cost of such products to a health system, it should be respected. This is so notwithstanding the powerful pull of principles of scientific advancement, equity, universality, non-aban-donment, and entitlement which justify the action which has been taken at the EU level to make OMPs available. Ultimately, a health system is 'part of the social fabric of every country',[142] both reflective of and constitutive of shared social values and norms; moreover, it is the citizens of that country who fund it, whether through taxation or forms of social insurance. While many of those values may be common across the EU,[143] choices as to the scope of a health system—including those as to the accessibility or otherwise of OMPs—must therefore remain at MS level, as EU law has recently reiterated.[144]

---

[139] Council Recommendation on action in the field of rare diseases, Recommendation I.

[140] Council Recommendation on action in the field of rare diseases, para 1(a).

[141] This could be done be way of deliberative mechanisms, such as citizen juries or deliberative polling. For a discussion of the use of such processes in the health context, see J Abelson, PG Forest, J Eyles and others, 'Deliberations about Deliberative Methods: Issues in the Design and Evaluation of Public Participation Processes' (2003) 57 *Social Science and Medicine* 239. One problem with such an approach is that it tends to be expensive. Eg a series of deliberative events and mechanisms linked to the UK Government's White Paper *Our health, our care, our say* (2005) cost £1.05 million, while nine citizen juries held on 18 September 2007 in connection with 'The NHS Next Stage Review' cost £868,930.02: *House of Commons Debates* vol. 451, cols.1219–20W (30 October 2007).

[142] L Gilson, 'Trust and the development of health care as a social institution' (2003) 56 *Social Science and Medicine* 1453, 1461.

[143] See especially Council Conclusions (n 91).

[144] Patients' Rights Directive, para 5: 'decisions about the basket of healthcare to which citizens are entitled . . . must be taken in the national context'.

7

Exclusions in Patent Law as an Indirect Form of Regulation for New Health Technologies in Europe

Amanda Odell-West

A. Introduction: Patent Law as Indirect Regulation

This chapter considers the effects of the 'medical' and 'morality' exclusions in patent law on several important new health technologies, including biotechnologies and nano-therapeutics. The patent system, grounded on incentive theory, is justified on the basis of its role in promoting innovative activity and economic performance,[1] and provides a means of capturing and commodifying the otherwise intangible capital of new knowledge. These benefits are achieved in part by providing a tranche of time during which an investor may secure a return on its investment, taking into account market, financial, management, and technological risks associated with a particular invention. Exclusions in law tend to be justified on the basis that patent protection is not an end in itself, but serves public policy objectives. The exclusions which are the focus of this chapter were not intended as part of any formal governing arrangements outside the sphere of patents, but nevertheless indirectly regulate aspects of the European health care market.

A patent is a twenty-year state-granted monopoly awarded to the patentee for a new technical invention, in exchange for full disclosure about how to work the invention (where this might otherwise be kept a trade secret), thereby encouraging others to make improvements and further advance the state of the art. This type of intellectual property right is negative—it prevents others from encroaching upon the technical territory defined by the 'claims' in the specification which the patentee makes about the invention. A patent can be enforced to prevent others from copying (or dealing with the invention in any manner prohibited under national laws) without permission, during the period the patent is in force.

Patent rights are personal (intangible) property rights[2] that allow the right holder to control the knowledge required to perform the invention. In the context of market economies, knowledge is considered a 'free good', because public use does not exhaust it. Neither is its social value diminished by widespread use. A 'public good' which is also a 'free good' has no market, not only because it is inexhaustible but also because it is non-excludable (one cannot stop others copying the fruit of that knowledge).[3] A patent creates property in an invention by imposing an artificial scarcity on the knowledge resource required for its operation.[4]

---

[1] Organisation for Economic Co-operation and Development, 'Patents and Innovation: Trends and Policy Challengers' (OECD 2004).

[2] Art 64 European Patent Convention (EPC) 2000 (The Convention on the Grant of European Patents, as revised by the Act revising Art 63 EPC of 17 December 1991 and the Act revising the EPC of 29 November 2000 EPC, contained in the 14th edition of the European Patent Convention (2010)).

[3] M Fisher, *Fundamentals of Patent Law* (Hart 2007).

[4] Fisher (n 3), 135.

Thus, the principal economic justification for patent rights is the public interest in competition, innovation, and creativity. As technological change and wider creativity are key drivers of innovation, the return on investment embodied in a patent right serves the public interest responsively, promoting economic growth. Where competition, innovation, and creativity may be restricted in consequence of the abuse of an intellectual property right, state or supranational intervention to control anti-competitive activity becomes legitimate.[5] This justification for patent law is reflected in the 'incentive to invent' theory[6]—the idea that, but for the patent system, the invention would not exist and/or secrets would not be disclosed.[7] However, the effects of the patent system on innovation and economic growth are, at best, ambiguous.[8] In terms of innovation, it is probably the return to *investor* which is more crucial[9] than the return to the patentee. What matters is not whether people would cease to be creative or inventive without the patent system. Rather, patent law seeks to promote the type of incentive that is required to prompt investment in the inventive process.

In itself, a patent gives no positive right commercially to exploit an invention. Therefore, patent law does not directly regulate the development and marketing of new technologies in any field, including that of health. However, faced with research and development costs involved in bringing an invention up to market, absence of patent protection may amount to a disincentive to enterprises operating in the new health technology sector. One of the major problems faced by new health technology seed and start-up enterprises (particularly in biotechnology and nanotechnology) is access to the first round of funding, either through debt or venture capital investment.[10] The protection available for new health technologies through the patent system is thus a key driver in determining which new health technologies are in fact developed. In this sense, patent law is a means of indirect regulation of new health technologies.[11]

---

[5] HL McQueen, 'Towards Utopia or Irreconcilable Tensions? Thoughts on IP, Human Rights and Competition Law' (2005) 2(4) *SCRIPTed* 452. A recent example is afforded in Case-A431 *Ratiopharm v Pfizer*, Italian Competition Authority, Decision No 23194, 11 January 2012, in which Pfizer was found to have abused its dominant position with the intention to hinder the entry of generic firms, thereby infringing Art 102 TFEU.

[6] PJ Heald, 'A Transaction Cost Theory of Patent Law' (2005) (66) *Ohio State Law Journal* 473 <http://dx.doi.org/10.2139/ssrn.385841> accessed May 2012. For analysis of post-classical economic theories of patent protection, see Fisher (n 3), Ch 5.

[7] Other justifications for patent law include the 'natural right' theory (the natural property right in ideas) (see P Laslett (ed), *Locke's Two Treatises of Government* (CUP 1960). 'Of Property' is one of the most famous, influential and important chapters in the Second Treatise of Government); 'just reward' theory (where fair reward is commensurate to the usefulness of the invention to society) and 'exchange' theory (based on a contract or 'bargain' metaphor between the state and the inventor) (see F Malchup and E Penrose, 'The Patent Controversy in the Nineteenth Century' (1950) 10(1) *Journal of Economic History* 1). In respect to the requirement of sufficiency of disclosure in a patent specification, it is argued exchange theory engenders potential confusion and error: S Thambisetty, 'Sufficiency of Disclosure in the Common Law' in Ng, Bently, and D'Agostino (eds), *The Common Law of Intellectual Property* (Hart 2010).

[8] UK Intellectual Property Office and Strategic Advisory Board for Intellectual Property Policy, 'The Economic Value of Intellectual Property: Research Agenda and Plan of Action' (2009) 5.

[9] M Fisher (n 3).

[10] M Cardullo, 'Intellectual Property—The Basis for Venture Capitalist Investments' <www.wipo.int/sme/en/documents/venture_capital_investments.htm> accessed September 2011.

[11] Noting that EU patent law is used to 'steer' behaviour in the field of stem cell research and innovation, see T Hervey and H Black, 'The European Union and the Governance of Stem Cell Research' (2005) 12 *Maastricht Journal of European and Comparative Law* 3.

'Regulation', broadly understood, is an umbrella term encompassing standard setting, directing conduct, monitoring compliance, detecting non-compliance, and enforcement.[12] The concept of regulation can be said to concern the 'channeling' of behaviour. It is not, however, co-extensive with the concept of law[13]—the relationship between law and regulation is better described as intersectional.[14] Patent law's indirectly regulatory effects arise from various mechanisms, in particular exclusions from patentability for subject matter that falls within certain categories;[15] exceptions to the monopolistic rights conferred by a patent;[16] and exceptions to permit certain acts without the authorization of the patent holder but with the authorization of a judicial or government body.[17] The way in which patent law indirectly regulates new health technologies is further supported by the requirements for patentability,[18] and through any later validity proceedings which could limit or extinguish patent rights. This may occur, for example, as a counter to infringement proceedings if the patent was invalidly granted. Through the incentives and disincentives it offers, patent law encourages commercial behaviour deemed to be desirable, and discourages commercial behaviour that is not desirable, for instance because it might breach fundamental principles safeguarding the dignity and integrity of human beings.[19]

To understand the effects of patent law, it is important to appreciate that patent law is unapologetically semantic, in that the specific, and highly technical, language of a patent is what determines the legal position. The law does not require that patents be understood by a member of the general public, but rather by a skilled worker in the technical field of the invention. The precise wording deployed thus determines whether the intended monopoly return on the patent can be achieved. In considering whether an exclusion should apply, it is often necessary to first establish what the 'invention' actually *is*. Where this is not obvious from the patent specification, it must be construed. This involves a question of law determined solely by reference to the patent, rather than what the invention might seem, in terms of function or anything else, to an onlooker. So, in the context of this chapter, whether a particular new health technology falls within, for instance, the medical exclusion, depends on *how* and what *exactly* is being claimed and, in turn, whether this offends the medical exclusion.

The chapter proceeds as follows. First, the legal framework for patents in Europe is outlined, with a brief description of the main relevant instruments and institutions (the TRIPs Agreement; the European Patent Organization and European Patent

---

[12] eg see R Baldwin and J Black, 'Really Responsive Regulation' (2008) 71(1) *Modern Law Review* 59; L Lessig, *Code: Version 2.0* (Basic Books 2006).

[13] See Llewellyn's description of 'law-jobs'—conflict resolution mechanisms, conflict avoidance measures ('preventive channelling'), recognized power structures, and ensuring shared goals ('net drive'): KN Llewellyn, 'The Normative, The Legal and the Law-Jobs: The Problem of Juristic Method' (1940) 49 *Yale Law Journal* 1355.

[14] For full treatment, see R Brownsword, *Rights, Regulation and the Technological Revolution* (OUP 2008) 7 ff.

[15] Art 52(2) EPC.

[16] Including non-commercial use, experimental use, and the 'Bolar' exemption, subject to TRIPs, Art 30.

[17] eg TRIPs Art 31 providing for compulsory licences; government/Crown use.

[18] A patentable invention must be novel, inventive (non-obvious), capable of industrial application and must not fall within the prohibited class deemed not to be regarded as inventions (Art 52(2) EPC 2000).

[19] Art 6(2) of the Treaty on European Union, concerning respect for fundamental rights as guaranteed by the European Convention for the Protection of Human Rights and Fundamental Freedoms.

Convention; and European Union (EU) law). Secondly, the chapter explains the rules concerning the two important exclusions in European patent law with respect to new health technologies: the morality and medical exclusions. Finally, the chapter considers the implications of these rules for the development of new health technologies in four fields.

B. The Legal Framework for Patents in Europe

In Europe, the interpretation and application of patent law falls to the relevant appellate authorities in European states, the European Patent Organization,[20] and the Court of Justice of the European Union (CJEU). All of this decision-making takes place within the overall framework of World Trade Organization's Agreement on Trade-Related Aspects of Intellectual Property Rights 1994 (the TRIPs Agreement).[21] The TRIPs Agreement binds the EU (as a WTO member) and all members of the WTO, which includes the twenty-seven EU Member States and most other European states[22] individually. It is a multilateral treaty which does not define substantive law, but instead mandates WTO members to align domestic laws to provide the minimum level of protection and enforcement required by the Agreement.[23] TRIPs is not 'directly effective', that is, it does not provide rights upon which individuals may rely.[24] However, the interpretation of legislation (including EU legislation) must be effected in a manner that conforms with the TRIPs Agreement where possible.[25]

The patent system in Europe is the remit of the European Patent Organization (EPO), based in Munich. Its legal instrument is the European Convention on the Grant of European Patents 2000 (EPC).[26] In spite of the name of this instrument, there is, at the time of writing, no unitary European patent. Patents are granted centrally at the EPO, but must be validated in the Member States requested by the patentee.[27] Membership of the European patent system extends beyond the boundaries of the EU—there are thirty-eight Member States of the European Patent Organization[28] and two 'extension states'.[29]

---

[20] Comprising the Opposition Division, Technical Board of Appeal, and Enlarged Board of Appeal (rising in priority sequentially).

[21] Annex 1C of the Agreement establishing the World Trade Organization, (the TRIPs Agreement 1994), approved by Council Decision 94/800/EC of 22 December 1994 concerning the conclusion on behalf of the European Community as regards matters within its competence [1994] OJ L336/1.

[22] Depending upon how one defines 'European states', of course. Azerbaijan, Belarus, Bosnia and Herzogovina, Kazahkstan, Russian Federation, Serbia, Tajikistan, Uzbekistan are 'observer governments', see <www.wto.org/english/thewto_e/whatis_e/tif_e/org6_e.htm> accessed September 2011.

[23] The TRIPs Agreement is justiciable under the WTO dispute settlement procedure. Patents are provided for in section 5, TRIPs.

[24] *Monsanto v Cefetra* [2011] All ER (EC) 209.

[25] *Monsanto* (n 24).

[26] Convention on the Grant of European Patents (EPC 2000) (n 2).

[27] This involves significant translation costs and delay. For further information, see: European Commission (SEC 2010/797) Summary of Impact Assessment <http://documents.epo.org/projects/babylon/eponet.nsf/0/2031D832895C4AB6C12577750049A8BF/$File/ia_sec_2010_0797_en.pdf> accessed May 2012.

[28] The twenty-seven EU Member States, and Albania, Switzerland, Croatia, Iceland, Liechtenstein, Monaco, FYROM, Norway, Serbia, San Marino, Turkey, see <www.epo.org/about-us/organisation/member-states.html> accessed May 2012.

[29] Bosnia and Herzogovina, and Montenegro, see <www.epo.org/about-us/organisation/member-states.html> accessed May 2012.

As part of its internal market law, the EU legislature has adopted laws on supplementary protection certificates for medicinal products,[30] special compulsory licensing provisions for pharmaceuticals to be exported to developing countries,[31] and its best known piece of legislation concerned with patenting: Directive 98/44/EC on the Legal Protection of Biotechnological Inventions (the Biotech Directive).[32]

The EPO is institutionally and legally separate from the EU. That said, synchronization between the EU and the EPO on matters concerning patent law and policy is desirable on a strategic level. Cooperation avoids obstacles to obtaining patent protection or seeking enforcement in EU Member States, which operating different rules or policies would otherwise cause. The EPO elected to implement the provisions of the Biotech Directive into the EPC.[33] Had it not done so, obtaining and enforcing biotechnology patents in the EU would have been a very confusing affair, fragmenting the system for patent protection in the EU and engendering a situation contrary to the principles of a single market. Fragmentation of the system causes negative effects on the functioning of the EU's internal market as evidenced by the current process required for patent validation, in the absence of a pan-European patent. As a result of fragmentation, data exists to suggest that patent 'borders' are being erected around individual Member States, 'reducing the commercial value of patented inventions, impeding cross-border activities and leaving business opportunities unexploited.'[34] The European Commission has actively involved itself in patent matters from time to time; at present this is focused on efforts towards the creation of a unitary European patent and court.[35]

To summarize, the framework for patents in Europe involves a fragmented, but cooperative, relationship between multiple institutions, expressed in a plethora of regulatory instruments and practices. In order to appreciate more precisely how patent law indirectly acts as a form of regulation on innovation in health technologies, the chapter now turns to examine the main legal provisions which determine patentability in European contexts.

---

[30] Regulation (EC) 469/2009, establishes a supplementary protection certificate for a maximum period of five years for medicinal products at the EU level. This measure aims to compensate for the period that elapses between the filing of a patent application for a new medicinal product and the authorization to place the product on the market: Regulation (EC) 469/2009 [2009] OJ L152/1, Art 13(1).

[31] Regulation (EC) 816/2006, on compulsory licensing of patents relating to the manufacture of pharmaceutical products for export to countries with public health problems [2006] OJ L157/1.

[32] [1999] 2 OJ EPO 101–19.

[33] Implementing Regulations to the Convention on the Grant of European Patents, Part II, Chapter V, Rules 26–30.

[34] European Commission, (SEC 2010/797) Summary of Impact Assessment 2/3.

[35] Proposal for a Regulation of the European Parliament and of the Council implementing enhanced cooperation in the area of the creation of a unitary patent protection, COM (2011) 215; Proposal for a Council Regulation on the Community patent—COM (2000) 412; Opinion 1/09 of the Court (Full Court) of 8 March 2011 on the compatibility of the draft agreement for a unified patent litigation system and Court, with the Treaties. The EU has also recently considered patentability of computer implemented inventions, see Proposal for a Directive of the European Parliament and of the Council on the patentability of computer-implemented inventions, COM/2002/0092 final—COD 2002/0047, rejected: see also Comments of the President on Programs for Computers OJ EPO 1/2011, 10 [G3/08].

1. Main Legal Provisions

Article 27(1) TRIPs states that patents shall be available for any inventions in all fields of technology provided that they are novel, inventive, and industrially applicable, although WTO Members may exclude patentability in the two cases discussed in this chapter (the morality and medical exclusions) and in the case of a third exclusion concerning plants, animals and micro-organisms.[36] Otherwise ' . . . patents are available and patent rights enjoyable without discrimination as to the place of invention, the field of technology and whether products are imported or locally produced.'

Likewise, the European Patent Convention, Article 52(1) provides that European patents shall be granted for any inventions in all fields of technology, provided they are novel, involve an inventive step (are non-obvious), and are susceptible of industrial application. In addition, the subject of the patent must not fall within the prohibited class deemed not to be regarded as inventions.[37] For instance, 'discoveries' are not patentable, as they do not constitute inventions. New health technology inventions, such as those using nanotechnology or biotechnology, must meet the same criteria as those in any other technical field, hence the usual substantive criteria are applied and interpreted in accordance with Rules 26–29 of the Implementing Regulations to the Convention on the Grant of European Patents ('Implementing Regulations') (the wording of which is identical to Articles 5 and 6 of the Biotech Directive, see later); and the Biotech Directive is a supplementary means of interpretation. In particular, the recitals preceding the provisions of the Biotech Directive are to be taken into account (although they do not have legal force).

Pursuant to international obligations incumbent on the EU and Member States that have signed the TRIPs Agreement, patent protection must be guaranteed in EU law for products and processes in all areas of technology.[38] Accordingly, the Biotech Directive requires Member States to protect biotechnological inventions under national patent law.[39] Although there is no definition of a biotechnological invention, the Directive provides for the patentability of inventions that are novel, inventive, and industrially applicable, 'even if they contain a product consisting of or containing biological material or a process by means of which biological material is produced, processed or used.'[40] Article 5 of the Directive provides that 'the human body, at the various stages of its formation and development' cannot constitute a patentable invention;[41] 'whereas an element that is isolated from the human body or otherwise produced by means of a technical process, including the sequence or partial sequence of a gene, may constitute a patentable invention.'[42] Article 9 of the Biotech Directive covers the scope of protection, and confirms that, on a product containing or consisting of genetic information, that protection extends to 'all material, save as

---

[36] Art 27(3)(b) TRIPs: Members may also exclude from patentability: '(b) plants and animals and other micro-organisms, and essentially biological processes for the production of plants or animals other than non-biological and microbiological processes.'

[37] Art 52(2) EPC.

[38] Art 27(1) TRIPs.

[39] Directive 98/44/EC on the legal protection of biotechnological interventions [1998] OJ L213/13, Art 1(1) (see also Recital 12).

[40] Biotech Directive (n 39) Art 3. Also, inventions concerning a microbiological or other technical process or a product obtained by means of such a process: Art 4(3).

[41] Biotech Directive (n 39) Art 5(1).

[42] For analysis of Art 5, see A Odell-West, 'Gene-uinely Patentable? The Distinction in Biotechnology Between Discovery and Invention in US and EU Patent Law' (2011) 3 *IPQ* 304.

provided in Article 5(1), in which the product is incorporated and in which the genetic information is contained and performs its function.'

2. Exclusions

a. *The morality exclusion*

The 'morality exclusion' is found in Article 27(2) TRIPs:

Members may exclude from patentability inventions, the prevention within their territory of the commercial exploitation of which is necessary to protect *ordre public* or morality, including to protect human, animal or plant life or health or to avoid serious prejudice to the environment, provided that such exclusion is not made merely because the exploitation is prohibited by their law.

This provision is facilitative, not mandatory. However, its presence in the TRIPs Agreement allows a WTO Member to enact a morality exclusion without fear of WTO dispute proceedings being mounted for having implemented an inconsistent measure under TRIPs. The thrust of the morality exclusion (in this context the protection of human life and health) is bolstered by Article 8(1) TRIPs which allows WTO Members to adopt measures necessary to protect human health and nutrition, and to promote the public interest in sectors of vital importance to their socio-economic and technologic development.

Accordingly, the European Patent Convention, Article 53(a), provides that

European patents shall not be granted in respect of: inventions the commercial exploitation of which would be contrary to 'ordre public' or morality; such exploitation shall not be deemed to be so contrary merely because it is prohibited by law or regulation in some or all of the Contracting States. . . .

The Biotech Directive stipulates that patent law must be applied so as to respect the fundamental principles safeguarding the dignity and integrity of the person.[43] More detail is provided in Article 6, which repeats the wording of the EPC, but augments it with examples:

1. Inventions shall be considered unpatentable where their commercial exploitation would be contrary to *ordre public* or morality . . .
2. On the basis of paragraph 1, the following in particular, shall be considered unpatentable:
   (a) processes for cloning human beings
   (b) processes for modifying the germ line genetic identity of human beings
   (c) uses of human embryos for industrial or commercial purposes
   (d) processes for modifying the genetic identity of animals which are likely to cause them suffering without any substantial medical benefit to man or animal, and also animals resulting from such processes.

The EU is founded (in part) on the value of human dignity.[44] Accordingly, a patent must not be granted (or maintained) that offends the morality exclusion provisions of the Biotech Directive, which were enacted to require, '. . . ethical considerations so as to prevent the economic functioning of the market giving rise to

---

[43] See Recital 16 in the Preamble.
[44] The Charter of Fundamental Rights of the European Union [2000] OJ C364/1, Preamble.

competition at the cost of sacrificing the fundamental values of the Union.'[45] The interpretation of Article 6 is also to correspond with 'ethical or moral principles recognized in a Member State', which supplement standard legal examination under patent law.[46] However, Member States do not have unlimited discretion to determine its scope, and any application of the exclusion can be subject to review by the CJEU.[47] The purpose of the non-exhaustive list is to provide national courts and patent offices with a general guide in interpreting the meaning of morality and *ordre public*. '[P]rocesses which offend against human dignity such as the production of chimeras from germ cells or totipotent human or animal cells are obviously also excluded.'[48]

b. The medical exclusion

Article 27(3)(a) TRIPs provides for a medical exclusion. It allows WTO Members to exclude from patentability 'diagnostic, therapeutic and surgical methods for the treatment of humans or animals.' Like the morality exclusion, it is not mandatory, but permissive.

The exclusion from patentability of methods to treat the human body is the same as that enacted in the EPC, at Article 53 which provides:

European patents shall not be granted in respect of: . . . c) methods for treatment of the human or animal body by surgery or therapy and diagnostic methods practised on the human or animal body; this provision shall not apply to products, in particular substances or compositions, for use in any of these methods.

The exclusion of such methods of treatment from patentability was not a new provision. Prior to the coming into force of the EPC 1973, these methods were excluded from patentability under the national laws of many European countries.[49]

The medical exclusion in the EPC has three separate limbs (surgery, therapy, and diagnostic methods)[50] and is a complex area of law that has required two referrals to the EPO's Enlarged Board of Appeal in recent years to interpret the scope and meaning of the latter two limbs. The policy behind the medical exclusion is to 'ensure that those who carry out innovative methods of medical treatment of humans (or the veterinary treatment of animals) should not be restricted by patents':[51] it is based on socio-ethical and public health considerations.[52] The Board in *Wellcome/PIGS I* considered the relevant preparatory documents which led to the EPC 1973 and concluded that the object of the provision (Article 53(c)) is to exclude from patentability 'treatment intended to cure or alleviate . . . suffering.'[53] The Enlarged Board of Appeal has expressly stated that

---

[45] According to AG Bot, Opinion of 10 March 2011, in Case C-34/10 *Brüstle v Greenpeace* [2011] ECR I-nyr, at para 44.
[46] Biotech Directive (n 39) Recital 39.
[47] Case C-377/98 *Netherlands v Parliament and Council (Biotechnology)* [2001] ECR I-7079.
[48] Biotech Directive (n 39) Recital 38.
[49] See in particular Conference document BR/219/72, para 27.
[50] Notably both products (such as pharmaceuticals) used in these methods (as discussed earlier) and known products which have new therapeutic effects can be patented (Arts 53(c) and 54(5) EPC 2000).
[51] Wellcome/PIGS I [1988] EPOR 1, point 3.7.
[52] Cornea/THOMPSON OJ EPO 8/1995, 512, point 2.4.
[53] Wellcome/PIGS I (n 51), point 3.7.

the intention of Article 53(c) EPC is only to free from restraint *non-commercial* and *non-industrial* medical and veterinary activities.[54]

C. Patents and the Regulation of New Health Technologies

How do the requirements of the morality and medical exclusions in European patent law indirectly regulate new health technologies? In what ways do these rules of patent law affect the development or invention of new health technologies in European contexts? The following section explores these questions, focusing on particular health care fields where new technologies are being developed: stem cell therapy; gene-based diagnostics and therapy; nanomedicine; and human performance enhancement.

1. Stem Cell Therapy and the Status of the Human Embryo

Embryonic stem cells hold great promise for tissue engineering and regenerative medicine,[55] because of their capacity for indefinite renewal and ability to form all differentiated cell types, except placental cells. Though instinctively, most right-minded people might baulk at the notion of using human embryos for patented, industrial purposes, it is worth considering whether it would make any difference to that assessment if those uses were to attempt quantum leaps in the treatment of major, intractable diseases where any embryos 'used' were left-over from IVF cycles otherwise bound for incineration, rather than specifically created for an industrial purpose. Awareness of these issues is presently raised in the United Kingdom with the recent announcement that Moorfields Eye Hospital (London) is authorized to carry out the first clinical trial in Europe using human embryonic stem cells.[56] Scientific regulation of human embryonic stem cell research has been embroiled in legal and ethical controversies over the destruction of human embryos and their production through nuclear cell transfer ('therapeutic cloning') for years.[57] European patent law forms part of that regulation.

The Biotech Directive provides that the human body[58] (at whatever stage of its formation) is excluded from patentability, as are processes for cloning human beings.[59] Accordingly, stem cell therapies broadly fall into one of two groups; those that involve human embryonic stem cells (hESCs) and those that do not. The latter (such as adult stem cells, or iPS cells)[60] are generally patentable subject matter, as long as EPC criteria are otherwise met, but inventions concerning stem cells derived through use of human embryos for industrial or commercial purposes are specifically excluded pursuant to the morality exclusion. EPO jurisprudence concerning this provision has developed in a way that Article 53(a) in conjunction with Rule 28(c) EPC[61] forbids the patenting

---

[54] Second Medical Indication/EISAI OJ EPO 3/1985, 64, point 22.

[55] L O'Leary, J Fallas, E Bakota, and others, 'Multi-Hierarchical Self Assembly of a Collagen Mimetic Peptide From Triple Helix to Nanofibre and Hydrogel' (2011) 10 *Nature Chemistry* 1038. New method for making synthetic collagen useful as scaffold for regenerating new tissues and organs from stem cells.

[56] F Walsh, 'Europe's First Embryonic Stem Cell Trial at Moorfields' *BBC News* (22 September 2011) <www.bbc.co.uk/news/health-15028881> accessed September 2011.

[57] J Savulescu and R Saunders, 'The Hinxton Group Considers Transnational Stem Cell Research' (2006) 36(3) Hastings Centre Report. See also <www.aaas.org/news/releases/2011/media/0208 hinxton_consensus_document.pdf> accessed August 2011.

[58] Biotech Directive (n 39) Art 5(1).

[59] Biotech Directive (n 39) Art 6(2)(a), supported by Recitals 40 and 41.

[60] 'Induced pluripotent cells', made by reversing adult cells taken from tissues such as skin.

[61] Rule 28(c) EPC transposes Biotech Directive (n 39) Art 6(2)(c).

of claims directed to products which can be prepared exclusively by a method that necessarily involves the destruction of human embryos, based on respect for the principle of human dignity.[62] This is so even where the claims defining the invention[63] in the patent do not include a step or feature reciting use of an embryo or even removal of cells from an embryo. The claim need not be directed to cells from an embryo, or even to a method of proliferating cells taken from an embryo as such, to fall foul of the exclusion.[64]

The question at what point in human development an entity becomes a 'human embryo' for the purposes of the Directive has only recently been clarified, by the CJEU following a reference for a preliminary ruling concerning the exclusion of inventions that use embryos for commercial and industrial purposes.[65] In particular, the CJEU was required to adjudicate upon whether, for the purpose of Article 6(2)(c) of the Directive, a human embryo is legally categorized as such from the moment of gamete fusion or at some later developmental stage. The point was in issue because the invention under patent derived from the destruction of a blastocyst (the entity which has developed five to six days after fertilization). If the blastocyst was to be classed as a human embryo, the invention in suit may be construed as falling foul of the 'industrial use' morality exclusion. The case from which these questions arose concerned a German patent for neural crest cells which are pluripotent stem cells derived from a blastocyst, for the treatment of neural defects such as Parkinson's disease. The referral also encompassed inter alia the question whether an entity created by nuclear transfer,[66] or stimulated by parthenogenesis,[67] are included within the definition of 'human embryo.'

The CJEU[68] emphasized that the text of the Directive must be regarded as 'designating an autonomous concept of EU law which must be interpreted in a uniform manner throughout the territory of the Union.'[69] Following the Advocate-General's view that the CJEU was not being called upon to determine questions of a medical or ethical nature, the CJEU restricted itself to a purely legal interpretation.[70]

Use of human biological material under EU patent law must be consistent with regard for fundamental rights, especially the dignity of the person.[71] The CJEU determined that the legislature intended to exclude any possibility of patentability where respect for human dignity could be compromised and that a wide meaning of the concept 'human embryo' was appropriate.[72] Therefore, any ovum rendered capable of commencing the process of development is within the concept of 'human embryo.' The CJEU clarified that this encompasses any human ovum: (a) upon being fertilized; (b) into which a mature cell nucleus has been transferred; or (c) which has been stimulated to develop by parthenogenesis, thereby precluding the invention concerned from patentability under EU law.

---

[62] *Comments of the President of the EPO on WARF (President Pompidou)* [G2/06], 28 September 2006.

[63] Art 69(1) EPC; *Conor Medsystems Inc v. Angiotech Pharmaceuticals Inc* [2008] UKHL 49 (Lord Hoffmann) para 17.

[64] *Comments of the President of the EPO on WARF (President Pompidou)* (n 62); *California Institute of Technology* [2003] ED EP 93921175.1 (unreported); *Edinburgh Patent* [2003] EP 94913174.2 (unreported).

[65] Case C-34/10 *Brüstle v Greenpeace e V* (n 45).

[66] By transplanting a nucleus from a mature human cell into an unfertilized ovum (a type of cloning).

[67] Stimulation of an unfertilized ovum to duplicate its genetic material and further cell division (another type of cloning).

[68] Case C-34/10 *Brüstle v Greenpeace e V* (n 45).

[69] At para 26.

[70] At para 30.

[71] Reflected by Recital 16, noted at para 32.

[72] At para 34.

Notably, the Court departed from the reasoning of Advocate-General Bot on whether a pluripotent cell falls within the meaning of 'human embryo.' The Advocate-General distinguished totipotent and pluripotent cells. Totipotent cells, in his Opinion, represent the 'first stage of the human body which they will become.'[73] Totipotent cells, howsoever produced,[74] are therefore 'embryos' because they possess full capacity for subsequent division and specialization, ultimately leading to a human being.[75] He reasoned that 'embryo' must include the blastocyst, because this constitutes one of the stages of the development of the human body.[76] On the other hand, according to the Advocate-General, pluripotent cells lack capacity to develop into a human[77] and in isolation cannot be classed as an embryo.[78] Inventions relating to pluripotent cells are thus patentable subject matter, subject to the caveat that the cells must not be obtained to the detriment of an embryo, 'whether its destruction or modification.'[79] Embryonic pluripotent stem cells are elements isolated from the human body within meaning of Article 5(2) of the Directive.[80] In evidence to the CJEU, Mr Brüstle (the inventor) said that embryonic stem cells are obtained from the 'internal cellular mass of the blastocyst.' The Advocate-General reasoned that an element (internal cellular mass) of the human body in the course of its development (the blastocyst) is therefore isolated in order to proliferate the cells contained in that cellular mass.[81] This reinforces the reasoning that pluripotent cells are not within the concept of human embryo and therefore cannot be conceived as 'a stage in the formation and development of the human body', which pursuant to Article 5(1) of the Directive cannot constitute a patentable invention. So, the pluripotent cell was brought within the meaning of Article 5(2) of the Directive, elevating its status in patent terms to that of a patentable invention, provided it was not obtained by destroying an embryo. In less detailed reasoning, the CJEU held that, if obtained from a blastocyst, such pluripotent cells are *not* necessarily outside of the exclusion, if capable of commencing the process of developing into a human being. The matter, in future, will turn upon whether scientific evidence exists to demonstrate this capability.[82]

Prior to this case being brought, there had been some debate in the literature that the meaning of the words concerning the morality exclusion provision: 'uses . . . for industrial or commercial purposes' in Article 6(2)(c) of the Directive might necessitate the excluded 'uses' to be repetitive, mechanical, or chemical and related to the technical processing (of raw materials).[83] Such a meaning, so the argument ran, could not apply to a product derived from a human embryo, it could only apply to processes that directly claim (and require) repetitive use of the human embryo. The meaning of these words was adjudicated upon by the EPO's Enlarged Board of Appeal in 2009 in the *WARF* (stem cell culture) case.[84]

In considering the meaning of 'uses . . . for industrial or commercial purposes', the Enlarged Board of Appeal in the *WARF* case rejected outright the appellant's assertion

---

[73] At para 85.   [74] At para 91.   [75] At para 84.
[76] At para 94.   [77] At paras 93 and 119.
[78] At para 98.   [79] At para 109, basing this on reasons of *ordre public* and morality.
[80] At para 101.   [81] At para 101.   [82] At para 37.
[83] See eg M Rowlandson, '*WARF/Stem Cells* (G2/06): The Ordre Public and Morality Exception and Its Impact on the Patentability of Human Embryonic Stem Cells' (2010) 32(2) *EIPR* 67, 70; P Torremans, 'The Construction of the Directive's Moral Exclusions Under the EPC' in A Plomer and P Torremans (eds), *Embryonic Stem Cell Patents: European Law and Ethics* (OUP 2009). This argument is rejected by S Sterckx and J Cockbain, 'Assessing the Morality of the Commercial Exploitation of Inventions Concerning Uses of Human Embryos and the Relevance of Moral Complicity' (2010) 7(1) *SCRIPTed* 83.
[84] *Comments of the President of the EPO on WARF (President Pompidou)* (n 62).

that the prohibited 'use for industrial and commercial purposes' must be explicitly claimed. It did so by applying a literal construction to that Article which refers to the invention in the context of its exploitation and not in the context of claims. Therefore the teaching contained in the patent as a whole, having regard to the entire specification, became relevant. This allowed the Enlarged Board of Appeal to take into account (unclaimed) embryonic destruction because WARF's human stem cell cultures had to be made before their use could be employed. As such the Enlarged Board of Appeal held that WARF's invention fell into the exclusion. It asserted the broad interpretation of the relevant implementing rule was properly supported by its legislative history. The finding was further reinforced by the fact that WARF's invention did not concern 'a therapeutic or diagnostic purpose to be applied to the embryo which was useful to it',[85] an exception to the prohibition of industrial and commercial uses.

In *Brüstle*, the reasoning of the CJEU concerning the meaning of 'uses ... for industrial or commercial purposes' was premised on a statement that the purpose of the Directive is limited to the patentability of biotechnological inventions and does not extend to regulate the use of embryos in research. The CJEU held that the words 'uses ... for industrial or commercial purposes' in Article 6(2)(c) of the Directive include 'use' in scientific research, if the end result of that 'use' becomes the subject matter of a patent application.[86] Such use, the CJEU reasoned, cannot be separated from the monopoly or attendant patent rights unless that use is for therapeutic or diagnostic purposes, to be applied to the embryo and 'useful to it.' If this is the case, the subject matter falls outside the exclusion, and the invention is patentable. The CJEU explicitly observed that this interpretation was identical to that adopted by the Enlarged Board of Appeal in *WARF* concerning the equivalently worded exclusion in the European Patent Convention.[87]

Explicitly agreeing for a second time with the Enlarged Board's interpretation in *WARF* as regards inventions that 'require destruction of a human embryo' in order to be developed or worked, the CJEU observed that the effect of skilful claim drafting could be exercised to render the exclusion redundant. Even where human embryonic destruction occurs long before implementation of the later invention subject to a patent application, such subject matter falls foul of the exclusion.

At present, although large numbers of patents over stem cell-related inventions exist, these are fragmented between public and private institutions. Considerable difficulty exists in convincing the pharmaceutical industry and private investors to finance clinical development of stem cell products and therapies.[88] This reluctance is allegedly based on uncertainty surrounding the patentability of human embryonic stem cells,[89] complicated by freedom to operates reservations. This latter concern comes from the sheer volume of existing stem cell patents which already exist and would create 'thickets' (meaning vast numbers of legal rights, which are close/overlapping in scope, making them impenetrable to navigate either to obtain licences in order to innovate onwards, or around which to invent). The consequence is that the prospect of bringing stem

[85] Recital 42, Biotech Directive (n 39).

[86] At para 43.

[87] At paras 45 and 51.

[88] J Lebkowski, 'Discussions on the Development of Human Embryonic Stem Cell Based Therapies' (2009) 4 *Regenerative Medicine* 569.

[89] T Caulfield and others, 'The Stem Cell Research Environment: A Patchwork of Patchworks' (2009) 5 *Stem Cell Reviews and Reports* 82 at 84–5, cited by Y Joly, 'Clinical Translation of Stem Cell Therapies—Intellectual Property and Anticipatory Governance' (2010) 7(2) *SCRIPTed* 265.

cell-related products onto the health care market is greatly reduced and it is this which may deter the investor.

In *Brüstle*, the CJEU has gone some way in reducing that uncertainty, by reaching an identical conclusion on what amounts to the same point of law as the Enlarged Board of Appeal in *WARF*. However, the tangible effects of the decision on the advancement of stem cell science and investment in Europe remain to be seen. On one view, patenting in the hESC field within Europe is now constrained, which may drive researchers (and cash) out of Europe. If it is accepted that the patent system provides an important, if not key, incentive to invest in costly, cutting edge but high-risk research, then non-patentability removes that incentive and research and development expenditure which cannot be recouped will not be undertaken. Funding for hESC research in Europe may eventually dry up because products or processes that involve human embryonic destruction, including stem cells howsoever produced if otherwise capable of commencing the process of development into a human being, cannot be patented.[90]

Some may take comfort in the view that the ruling seems to focus on inventions that rely on traditional (destructive) methods for generating embryonic stem cells, but provides a continuing basis for patentability of processes for generating human embryonic stem cells and products derived from those cells where non-destructive techniques can be used, such as single blastomere technology. However, the fact that the CJEU was unable to differentiate a pluripotent stem cell from 'a human embryo' in the same way as Advocate-General Bot means that patentability will turn upon evidence as to the capability of the cell, 'to commence the process of development as a human being' irrespective of whether it is produced by a newer, non-destructive method. This position does little to promote the legal changes sought after by the industry.

2. Gene-Based Diagnostics and Therapy

Research into uses of genes for both diagnostic and therapeutic procedures continues to be dynamic. Although predisposition testing is now common place, personalized medicine (for example, pharmacogenomics) and gene therapy are at more of an experimental stage. Somatic gene therapy involves manipulation of gene expression to an individual's cells. Research is currently focused on creating non-toxic gene therapy delivery vectors, with some recent success.[91]

In terms of indirect regulation by the medical exclusion, in common with 'therapy', 'diagnostic methods' in Article 53(c) EPC does not preclude from patentability all methods related to diagnosis. In order to fall within the exclusion, a claim directed to a diagnostic method must include all the following phases:[92] (a) the examination phase, involving the collection of data; (b) the comparison of this data with standard values; (c) assessment, finding of any significant deviation (for example, a symptom) during the comparison; and (d) the attribution of the deviation from the standard to a particular clinical picture, for example, the deductive medical 'decision phase' (diagnosis for

---

[90] For more see, eg M Grund and SJ Farmer, '*Brüstle v Greenpeace*: The End of the Road for Human Embryonic Stem Cells Patents' (2012) 12(2) *Bio-Science Law Review* 39; E Bonadio, 'Stem Cell Industry and Beyond: What Is the Aftermath of *Brüstle*?' (2012) 3(1) *European Journal of Risk Regulation* 93.

[91] E Teixeira da Silva, E Andreoli de Oliveria, A Février and others, 'Supramolecular Polymorphism of DNA in Non-cationic Lα Lipid Phaser' (2011) 34(8) *The European Physical Journal* 112.

[92] *Treatment by surgery/MEDI-PHYSICS* OJ EPO 3/2011, 134; *CYGNUS/Diagnostic Methods* [2006] EPOR 15.

curative purposes). A diagnostic method must be 'practised on the human...body.' Hence, each of the preceding technical method steps relating to phases (a) to (c) must be performed on a human. The type or intensity of the interaction is not decisive: this criterion is fulfilled if the performance of the technical method step in question necessitates the presence of the body. Direct physical contact with the body is not required. In the context of quasi-medical conditions or perceived deficiencies (see later), a medical practitioner does not have to be involved, either by being present or by bearing the overall responsibility in the procedure. Methods for merely obtaining information (data, physical quantities) from the living human body (for example, X-ray investigations, medical imaging techniques such as magnetic resonance imaging, and blood pressure measurements) fall outside the exemption (patentable).[93] This demonstrates that, although medical products/devices/methods of diagnosis are clearly patentable, a line is drawn between those which will inhibit the role of medical professionals in being able to make clinical decisions (unpatentable), and those which will not (patentable). There is no equivalent provision relating to the exclusion of methods of treatment of the human body by therapy, surgery, or diagnostic methods practised on the body, in the Biotech Directive. But although a diagnostic method does not offend the medical exclusion, it might nevertheless be assessed for compliance with the morality exclusion.

There is no objection, in principle, to inventions relating to somatic gene therapy, including claims for first and subsequent medical use of gene sequences in vectors for use in gene therapy.[94] Recital 40 of the Biotech Directive[95] refers to consensus within the EU, that interventions in the human germ-line offend against *ordre public* and morality. Therefore, gene therapy that results in modification of human germ-line genetic identity is 'unequivocally excluded'[96] from patentability.

Although discussion of the basic substantive criteria is outside the central focus of this chapter, it is worth briefly noting the requirement of industrial application in respect to gene-based inventions, which has been the subject of litigation in the United Kingdom and the EPO.[97] In order for a gene-based invention to be patentable, it must first be a type that is not excluded subject matter.[98] The link between the requirement for an invention with that of industrial application (utility) has become paramount for this assessment. The new gene product or process cannot be considered an invention, where the morality exclusion provisions would be offended. In *Monsanto v Cefetra*,[99] the CJEU interpreted Article 9 of the Biotech Directive to the effect that the scope of any European patent based on an isolated gene sequence is contingent on there being a credible function cited in the patent and that the gene is actually capable of performing the function for which it was patented. Thus, in terms of gene-based diagnostics, a step involving a comparison with a reference molecule or allelic variant thereof will continue to be (otherwise) patentable, although the public interest in having access to gene-based diagnostics which are exclusively licensed remains potentially problematic and may

---

[93] C:IV: para 4.8.1.

[94] See eg EP-A-0 773 785 with the title 'Treatment of cancer using HSV mutant', concerning Swiss claims to a viral vector using mutant herpes simplex virus.

[95] Implemented by Art 6(2)(b) providing that processes for modifying the germ line genetic identity of human beings are unpatentable.

[96] Some evidence suggests that gene therapy may interfere with the Weissman Barrier thought to prevent inheritance of manipulated gene expression in the parent to a subsequent generation: PY Reaves and others, 'Permanent Cardiovascular Protection From Hypertension by the AT1 Receptor Antisense Gene Therapy in Hypertensive Rat Offspring' (1999) 85 *Circulation Research* 44.

[97] *Human Genome Sciences Inc v Eli Lilly* [2011] UKSC 51 and *Neutrokine/HUMAN GENOME SCIENCES* [2009] EP 96939612.6 (unreported).

[98] Biotech Directive (n 39) Art 5(1).   [99] *Monsanto* (n 24).

mean that alternative legal mechanisms for redress should be explored.[100] However, researchers are no longer restricted by (absolute) product patents over gene sequences, which required licences to be obtained in order to develop new diagnostic indications, methods, or treatments.[101]

Now surrounded by much less hype than when the human genome was first sequenced, a pharmacogenetic test seeks to detect the presence or absence of, or change in, a particular gene or chromosome in order to predict response to a medicine.[102] In this way, drug therapy can be tailored to the patient's genetic profile, hence the term 'personalized medicine.' The aim of pharmacogenomics is to identify a correlation between a genetic anomaly and the efficacy or safety of drug therapy.[103] This type of research is developing in two main directions: (a) to identify specific genes and gene products associated with various diseases, and (b) to identify genes and allelic variants that affect response to drugs. This is one reason why some patients experience adverse drug reactions[104] due to genetic variation. So, a pharmacogenetic test might be indicated where a drug has a narrow therapeutic index and is efficacious in only 25 per cent in the population, rather than a wide therapeutic index, efficacious in 90 per cent of the population.

There are a number of concerns about pharmacogenetic tests, which include privacy and data protection (for example, in regard to health insurance discrimination, or right of insurers to access genetic data), as well as ethical issues (such as incidental disclosure of non-paternity, or other family members' right to know, or not know, about a genetic risk).[105] In terms of patentability,[106] the fact that, in developing predictive genetic tests of drug response, the major gene candidate should be 'well documented as being functionally relevant'[107] will defeat novelty as regards patenting use of the gene, and may also be sufficient to render the resultant genetic test unpatentable on the ground of obviousness. 'Inventive step' is an elusive legal concept and cannot be predicted with any degree of reliability in any technical field, but a drug delivery vector is otherwise patentable. It is possible that claims based on novel dosage regimes depending on genetic variation will also be claimed, following the decision of the Enlarged Board of Appeal in *ABBOTT RESPIRA-TORY/Dosage Regime*, which will have the effect of lengthening the period of exclusivity granted to any specific medical product.[108] Patent law prohibits legal protection for

---

[100] A Odell-West, 'The Legacy of Myriad for Gene-Based Diagnostics' (2009) 4 *Journal of Intellectual Property Law & Practice* 267.

[101] Monsanto (n 24). See also Odell-West (n 42).

[102] Nuffield Council on Bioethics, *Pharmacogenetics: Ethical Issues* (Nuffield Council 2003) 94.

[103] A gene variant connected to response to common asthma drugs has been recently reported: K Tantisira, J Lasky-Su, M Harada and others, 'Genomewide Association Between GLCCI1 and Response to Glucocorticoid Therapy in Asthma' (2011) 10 *NEJM* 1056.

[104] It has been suggested that 1 in 15 hospital admissions in the United Kingdom are due to adverse drug reactions, 'The Cost of Adverse Drug Reactions' (Editorial) (1997) 16 *Adverse Drug React Toxicol Review* 75.

[105] See: M Pirmohamed and G Lewis, 'The Implications of Pharmacogenetics and Pharmacogenomics for Drug Development and Health Care' in E Mossialos, M Mrazek, and T Walley (eds), *Regulating Pharmaceuticals in Europe* (Open UP 2004) available at <www.openup.co.uk> accessed September 2011; R Wilkinson, 'When is My Genetic Information Your Business?' Biological, Emotional and Financial Claims to Knowledge' (2010) 19 *Cambridge Quarterly of Healthcare Ethics* 110.

[106] It is noteworthy that a recent (unanimous) decision of the US Supreme Court has held that a diagnostic test to determine drug efficacy (non-genetic, personalized medicine) merely recites a 'law of nature' and is not patentable subject matter under Federal patent law: *Mayo v Prometheus Labs* 566 US (2012). This decision may carry implications for contested claims to similar inventions in the EU as being mere 'discoveries' and therefore excluded subject matter.

[107] G Tucker, 'Pharmacogenetics—Expectations and Reality' (2004) 329 *British Medical Journal* 4.

[108] *ABBOTT RESPIRATORY/Dosage Regime* [2010] EPOR 26.

genetic applications (for example, germ-line gene therapy) which could have a long-term effect on future generations, ensuring that the survival of mankind is not at risk by ill-advised interference with the inheritable 'gene pool.'

3. Nanomedicine

Nanotechnology and nanomedicine[109] involve entities with a controlled geometrical size of at least one functional component below 100 nanometres (one billionth of a metre) in one or more dimensions susceptible of making physical, chemical, or biological effects.[110] The EU is the largest public investor in nanotechnology research, and the field of nanomedicine is growing exponentially across all areas of medical technology and most clinical disciplines.[111] Increasing ability to engineer and manufacture at the nanoscale heralds the possibility of a multitude of novel applications for medical imaging, mini-aturized diagnostics (that can be implanted for early diagnosis of illness),[112] drug delivery, regenerative medicine, and biomaterials, such as self-organizing scaffolds to foster a new generation of tissue engineering and bio-mimetic materials, with the long-term potential of synthesizing organ replacement.[113] These developments are fully expected to change health care 'in a fundamental way.'[114]

Nanotechnology has considerable potential in the field of therapeutic medicine and surgery.[115] However, new nano-treatments that involve even one surgical step (element) may also be regulated by operation of the 'surgery' limb of the medical exclusion,[116] now expanded to cover most types of surgery.[117] A 'once and for all' redefinition of the meaning of 'treatment by surgery' to delimit the exact boundaries was deemed not to be possible given the myriad technical situations to which it might apply.[118] However, the Enlarged Board of Appeal, after reviewing the legal history and the *ratio legis* of the exclusions from patentability in Article 53(c), found nothing to justify limiting the term to curative surgery, that is, surgical methods pursuing a *therapeutic* purpose.[119] The Enlarged Board of Appeal ruled that if (a) maintaining the life and health of the patient is important, (b) the method comprises an invasive or 'substantial physical intervention', (c) requiring medical expertise to execute, and (d) involves a significant health risk even when carried out in a non-tortious manner, then the method is excluded from patentability by Article 53(c) EPC. Thus, in addition to

---

[109] Nanoscience is the study of phenomena and material properties at nanoscale, while nano-medicine is defined by the European Science Foundation as, 'the science and technology of diagnosing, treating and preventing disease and traumatic injury, of relieving pain, and of preserving and improving human health, using molecular tools and molecular knowledge of the human body'.

[110] Definition used at the EPO.

[111] The Institute of Nanotechnology at <www.nano.org.uk> accessed August 2011.

[112] The 'Cardiovascular Innovation Award' (Medical Futures) was recently awarded to the 'Nano-technology for Implanted Devices Team', headed by Professor Sir Magdi Yacoub, Cardiothoracic Surgeon, National Heart & Lung Institute, Imperial College London.

[113] The NanoMedicine Network <www.nano.org.uk/nanomednet/index.php?option=comcontent&task=section&id=10&Itemid=79> accessed August 2011.

[114] B Roszek, WH de Jong, and RE Geertsma, 'Nanotechnology in Medical Applications: State-of-the-Art in Materials and Devices' (RIVM report 265001001/2005).

[115] As surgical procedures become less invasive, nanotechnology is expected to play a significant role, eg through non-invasive procedures performed outside the body, or the development of nanoscale tools for surgery.

[116] See A Odell-West, 'Protecting Surgeons and Their Art? Methods for Treatment of the Human Body by Surgery under Article 52(4) EPC' (2008) 30(3) *EIPR* 102–8.

[117] *Treatment by surgery/MEDI-PHYSICS* (n 92).

[118] Treatment by surgery/MEDI-PHYSICS (n 92).

[119] Treatment by surgery/MEDI-PHYSICS (n 92).

'therapeutic' surgery, cosmetic (non-therapeutic) surgical methods now fall within the ambit of the exclusion, which also carries implications for new enhancement technologies, discussed later.

Although some products are already commercially available,[120] a good deal of research remains to be done,[121] including risk assessment studies on long-term safety, especially concerning toxicological aspects of nanoparticles entering the human body.[122] All inventions (including those involving nanotechnology) must meet basic patent criteria under the EPC 2000; and only man-made inventions may be patented and not mere 'discoveries.'[123] Where inventions concern natural substances, the discovery-invention dichotomy that continues to plague gene patenting may arise.[124] So, where a claimed nano-invention concerns a pre-existing natural substance[125] (such as a complex protein), it may be considered a discovery rather than an invention, and therefore will not attract patent protection. This, in turn, could negatively affect incentives for commercial development of the technology, or drive researchers out of Europe to jurisdictions which take a less restrictive view of what constitutes a discovery.

A detailed discussion of novelty and inventive step is outside the scope of this chapter. But they are worth briefly mentioning here in that these requirements may be particularly difficult to meet in nanomedicine. For example, where the invention is a miniature version of something that already exists, such as a cardiac pacemaker, miniaturization per se does not necessarily infer either novelty or inventiveness. Yet a miniature version of a known device may be considered 'new' if its technical effect attributable to its size is enhanced, such that it is reasonable to assume the size was purposefully selected to achieve this new effect.[126] Miniaturization may also be considered inventive if it was not obvious to the skilled addressee that miniaturization would achieve the new technical effect (for example, enhanced power). As the technological field is so new, some of the methods when applied to a highly specific problem may exceed even expert knowledge, and the EPO is emphasizing the heightened requirements for disclosure (particularly clarity) in this field.[127]

---

[120] Such as surgical blades and suture needles, contrast-enhancing agents for magnetic resonance imaging, bone replacement materials, wound dressings.

[121] For an overview, see: ETC Group, 'Nanotech Rx/Medical applications of nano-scale technologies: what impact on marginalised communities?' (2006) <www.etcgroup.org/upload/publication/593/01/etc06nanotechrx.pdf> accessed June 2011.

[122] OECD, 'Current Developments/Activities on the Safety of Manufactured Nanomaterials' (No. 29) (March 2011) <www.oecd.org/officialdocuments/displaydocumentpdf?cote=env/jm/mono(2011)12&doclanguage=en> accessed August 2011; also, 'Characterising the Potential Risks Posed by Engineered Nanoparticles: A Second Government UK Research Report' (Department for Environment, Food and Rural Affairs 2007), available at <www.defra.gov.uk/publications/files/pb12901-nanoparticles-riskreport-071218.pdf> accessed September 2012.

[123] Art 52(1) EPC.

[124] The USA and Australia are presently grappling with this dichotomy. The Biotech Directive provides for the patenting of isolated DNA, but for criticism of the provisions see Odell-West (n 42).

[125] Assessment of exposure of humans (and the environment) to engineered nanoparticles has been hampered because of difficulties in distinguishing between engineered and naturally occurring nanoparticles: 'Characterising the potential risks posed by engineered nanoparticles: A second Government UK Research Report' (2007).

[126] European Patent Office, 'Nanotechnology and Patents' <http://documents.epo.org/projects/babylon/eponet.nsf/0/623ECBB1A0FC13E1C12575AD0035EFE6/$File/nanotech_brochure_en.pdf> accessed August 2011.

[127] EPO (n 126).

In 2008, the EU issued a Recommendation on a code of conduct for 'responsible nanosciences and nanotechnologies research',[128] which has since become the remit of the 'NanoCode project' funded under the 7th Framework Programme (FP7). This includes the stipulation that '[nanosciences and nanotechnologies] research organizations should not undertake research aiming for non-therapeutic enhancement of human beings... solely for the illicit enhancement of the performance of the human body.'[129] The European Group on Ethics in Science and New Technologies (EGE)[130] observed there is a 'fine line' between medical and non-medical uses of nanomedical methods for diagnostic, therapeutic and preventive purposes.[131] Others are more forthright, contending that nanotechnologies intended for use in the body will erase the distinction between 'therapy' and 'enhancement.'[132] Blurring the line between what is generally considered to be therapeutic as opposed to cosmetic will make claiming non-medical methods more difficult. Moreover, the blurring between products and methods implicit in nanotechnologies adds to the more general problem of illogicality in patent law that patents for products to treat the human body are allowed, but patents for methods to treat the human body are not.[133]

Although the purpose of patent law is to support high risk, cutting edge innovation, where non-contentious (patentable) claims to a method of treatment cannot be extricated from therapy or surgery and are therefore unpatentable, this might constitute a disincentive to future investors and/or lay the patent open to attack by competitors. A new technology enterprise needs to devote its money, time and resources to technology development and commercialization, and cannot usually afford litigation.[134] However, it might be argued that discouraging cosmetic/non-therapeutic inventions is a beneficial indirect effect of patent law.

4. Human Performance Enhancement Technologies

Technologies considered under the umbrella of 'human enhancement' range from the relatively mundane (drugs already long on the market) to interventions arising from combination high-end technological fields. They encompass oral medications for various enhancement purposes, reconstructive and cosmetic surgery, tissue engineering, genetic modification, bioengineering (bionic prosthetic limbs that may be operated by the patient following nerve transplantation and artificial intelligence),[135] and various other processes using ICT neuroimplants, such as deep brain stimulation. These applications may be prescribed as therapeutic treatments to restore function in the case of disease or injury, but controversially may also be used to 'enhance' normal

---

[128] Commission Recommendation (2008/345/EC) of 7 February 2008 on a code of conduct for responsible nanosciences and nanotechnologies research (notified under document number C(2008) 424) [2008] OJ L116/46.

[129] Commission Recommendation (2008/345/EC) of 7 February 2008 on a code of conduct for responsible nanosciences and nanotechnologies research (notified under document number C(2008) 424) [2008] OJ L 116/46, at 4.1.16.

[130] EGE, *Opinion on the Ethical Aspects of Nanomedicine* (Opinion No 21), 17 January 2007.

[131] EGE (n 130) 41–2.

[132] ETC Group (n 121).

[133] Odell-West (n 116).

[134] '... the risk of expensive litigation may be sufficient to reduce the probability of venture capital financing', M Cardullo (n 10).

[135] N Bowdler, 'Bionic Hand for Elective Amputation Patient' *BBC News* (18 May 2011) <www.bbc.co.uk/1/hi/health/8677/32.stm> accessed September 2011.

functioning. The latter raises issues in respect to the therapy/non-therapy distinction in patent law.

Consider the case of oral medications that may be used as enhancers in some capacity. Most drugs are developed to treat disorders. The discovery of a non-therapeutic indication, though fortuitous, is usually incidental.[136] Yet some drugs are being developed *primarily* to enhance normal functioning,[137] though clearly there are degrees of cognition or performance 'enhancement.' An example frequently referred to in the literature is propanolol, belonging to a common group of drugs called beta-blockers. This is a beta-adrenoceptor blocking drug, and core staple in the treatment of irregular heart rhythm, hypertension, and heart attack. Propanolol may also be used to alleviate some symptoms of anxiety; the pharmacological guidance is that patients with palpitation (irregular heart beat), tremor, and tachycardia (fast heart rate) probably respond best.[138] The point being, that a clinical picture to indicate treatment of anxiety should pre-exist; it is not an effective treatment for anxiety across the board. Beta-blockers do not affect psychological symptoms of anxiety such as worry, tension, and fear; but they do reduce autonomic symptoms such as palpitation and tremor. In terms of anxiety, 'beta-blockers are indicated for patients with predominantly somatic symptoms; this, in turn, may prevent the onset of worry and fear.'[139] Taking propanolol before one's grade 6 piano examination will not enhance musical ability beyond that which pre-exists, but it can reduce the onset of fear and trembling, which of course affects ability to perform.[140] Thus, beta-blockade does not equate to 'performance (ability) enhancement' in the same way that say, 'EPO'[141] or gene doping[142] does in sport. Yet treatment of anxiety with a beta-blocker does not lack therapeutic effect, so it is difficult to see how it could be patented purely as a non-therapeutic 'enhancer.' Where the technical effects of a new invention (such as a new drug) lie at the fringes of the therapeutic/non-therapeutic boundary, these can be difficult to distinguish for the purposes of patent law. Where the effects are inextricable, no patent protection over the medical method can be given, because of the effect of the medical exclusion.

However, where a method claim includes dual therapeutic (unpatentable) and non-therapeutic (patentable) effects, if clearly and solely directed to the latter, the non-therapeutic method will not fall under Article 53(c) EPC.[143] This can be exemplified by considering a claim to the use of deep brain stimulation[144] for both enhancement and

---

[136] Such as rogaine (active ingredient minoxidil) to treat high blood pressure; can be used to promote hair growth; or viagra (active ingredient sildenafil) to treat impotence; can be used to enhance sexual performance. Both marketed by Pfizer.

[137] A Chatterjee, 'The Promise and Predicament of Cosmetic Neurology' (2006) 32 *Journal of Medical Ethics* 110–13, commenting that ampakines and CREB modulators are being developed to augment normal encoding mechanisms with the purpose of acquisition of long-term memory, citing T Tully, R Bourtchouladze, R Scott, and others, 'Targeting the CREB Pathway for Memory Enhancers' (2003) 2 *Nature Reviews Drug Discovery* 267.

[138] British National Formulary No 62 (September 2011) at 4.2 <www.icmje.org> accessed September 2012.

[139] British National Formulary No 62 (n 138).

[140] Beta-blockers are prohibited (in competition only) in certain sports such as golf, darts, bridge, and skiing: World Anti-Doping Code; 2012 Prohibited List, at section P2.

[141] Erythropoietin, a banned substance in and out of competition (n 140) at section S2.

[142] Gene doping (transfer of nucleic acid sequences or the use of normal or genetically modified cells) with the potential to increase sport performance, is entirely prohibited (n 140) at section M3.

[143] *DU/PONT/Appetite Suppressant* OJ EPO 9/1986, 301. The language of the claims clearly covered a method of cosmetic use unrelated to the therapy of a human or animal body.

[144] Discussed in section 4.

therapy. A claim for a method directed to use of deep brain stimulation for 'non-therapeutic memory enhancement', where the surgical step is successfully omitted[145] or disclaimed,[146] may not be objectionable under Article 53(c);[147] whereas a similar claim to treat Parkinson's disease would prima facie offend the medical exclusion. In this example, the two claimed technical effects are at least divisible, creating the possibility of the non-therapeutic element to be patented.

The law on implanted devices more generally has hinged on whether the claimed method has a therapeutic purpose or effect. For example, in a case concerning a heart pacemaker, the Board clarified that a claim could contain;

nothing but technical features directed to a technical operation performed on a technical object and a subsequent technical operation performed on a human or animal body, but such a claim would be unallowable under Article 52(4) [now Article 53(c)] EPC if it *defines* a method for treatment of such a body by therapy or surgery.[148]

In that case, the claimed features of sensing ventricular pressure and using this and/or its time derivative to control the pacer in accordance with the required cardiac output, *defined* the use of the pacer to carry out physical actions, amounting to a method for treatment of a human body by therapy. In *Blood Separation Systems/FENWAL*[149] the invention concerned a blood separation system and included claims for operating the device, whereupon Article 53(c) was invoked. The Board noted that, if a method solely related to operating a device with no functional link between it and the effects produced on the body, the method will not constitute an Article 53(c) 'method of treatment.' But where a functional link exists, the method is excluded from patentability.[150]

The difficulty of distinguishing therapeutic and non-therapeutic effects is part of a broader problem in health care, concerning the point at which a risk factor, or non-medical 'issue' (such as a sedentary lifestyle, erectile dysfunction, or male pattern baldness[151]) becomes a disorder, necessitating medical attention. Historically, this has been a decision for the medical profession alone, though Walley argues this is no longer the case as other stakeholders including the general public, third party payers of health services, and the pharmaceutical industry also have a legitimate role to play in making these decisions.[152] A lifestyle 'wish' may become 'medicalized' by doctors themselves where a biomedical cause (such as a genetic trait) or treatment is found; or where lifestyle choices (such as obesity or cigarette smoking) associated with long-term public health concerns, are depicted as amenable to medical intervention.[153]

---

[145] Omission to be decided on a case-by-case basis, and use must comply with Art 123(2) and (3), 83, and 56 EPC: Treatment by surgery/MEDI-PHYSICS (n 92); *Cardiac pacing/TELECTRONICS OJ EPO 5/1996, 274.*

[146] Articles 84, 56, and 83 EPC must be fulfilled/compatible with any disclaimer and conditions in *Disclaimer/PPG* OJ EPO 8-9/2004, 413 and *Disclaimer/GENETIC SYSTEMS* OJ EPO 8-9/2004, 448.

[147] Although objection to this invention on the ground of morality and *ordre public* is very likely to succeed.

[148] *Cardiac Pacing/TELECTRONICS* (n 145), at 1.1 reasons for the decision. Emphasis added.

[149] *Blood Separation Systems/FENWAL* [2011] EP 961403.3 (unreported).

[150] *ABBOTT RESPIRATORY/Dosage Regime* (n 108).

[151] E Festa, J Fretz, R Berry, and others, 'Adipocyte Lineage Cells Contribute to the Skin Stem Cell Niche to Drive Hair Cycling' (2011) 146(5) *Cell* 761. Source of signals that trigger hair growth discovered—may lead to new treatments for baldness.

[152] T Walley, 'Should We Pay for Lifestyle Drugs?' in Mossialos and others (n 105).

[153] Walley (n 152) 300.

Closely linked to this debate is 'disease-mongering',[154] a phrase coined to mean the practice of promoting illness in order to create markets for treatment. Parens argues that markets for cosmetic surgery have been created, '... by convincing people that they possess defects that only surgery can repair', citing the example of women with small breasts being labelled 'micromastic' or thigh dimples as 'cellulite', conditions requiring treatment.[155] It is postulated that disease-mongering will result in enhancements becoming naturalized until viewed as necessary corrections.[156] Areas ripe for disease-mongering are the markets for memory enhancement and memory attenuation. In respect of the latter, research is being conducted on prophylactic use of propanolol to prevent post-traumatic stress disorder.[157] It is argued that the process of disease-mongering through 'over-medicalization' of bad memories, and its subsequent exploitation by the pharmaceutical industry, is the most immediate social concern in respect to memory-attenuating drug usage.[158]

If painful memories, or being of average-range strength, or intelligence[159] come to be considered impediments as a result of companies being able to target patients indirectly through disease awareness campaigns,[160] sponsorship of materials, and press releases,[161] the difficulty of distinguishing healing from enhancement will be increased. This blurring of the line has repercussions for indirect regulation of enhancements by patent law to the extent that claims to a process or method must be sufficiently delimited from therapy and surgery to be patentable. Where this is not possible, no patent protection can be given, thereby exerting a constraining regulatory effect which might not necessarily be in the public interest. So, for example, the patentee in *Antimicrobial agent/ FUJISAWA PHARMACEUTICAL CO* sought to claim both medical and non-medical uses for a new antimicrobial agent. The claim to the non-medical use was as follows, '[u] se of an effective amount of FR109615 or salts thereof as an antimicrobial agent.' This was held by the Technical Board of Appeal to cover non-medical use, but the wording also directly covered a method for the treatment of the human or animal body by (antimicrobial) therapy. Hence, following Article 53(c) EPC, this was not patentable.[162]

Deep brain stimulation (DBS) is a method that employs a deep brain stimulation electrode connected to an implantable pulse generator in the chest through which brain activity is modulated, and is used mainly in the treatment of advanced Parkinsonian symptoms.[163] DBS is thought to have some effect on memory and the possibility of using it to enhance normal memory in otherwise

---

[154] H Wolinsky, 'Disease Mongering and Drug Marketing' (2005) 6 *European Molecular Biology Organisation Report* 7.

[155] E Parens (ed), *Enhancing Human Traits: Ethical and Social Implications* (Georgetown University Press 1998).

[156] Parens (n 155).

[157] RK Pitman, KM Sanders, RM Zusman, and others, 'Pilot Study of Secondary Prevention of Posttraumatic Stress Disorder With Propranolol' (2002) 51(2) *Biological Psychiatry* 189.

[158] M Henry, JR Fisherman, and SJ Youngner, 'Propranolol and the Prevention of Post-Traumatic Stress Disorder: Is it Wrong to Erase the "Sting" of Bad Memories?' (2007) 7(9) *The American Journal of Bioethics* 12.

[159] J Harris and A Chatterjee, 'Is it Acceptable for People to Take Methylphenidate to Enhance Performance?' (2009) 338 *British Medical Journal* 1532, for countering views on use of chemical cognitive enhancers. See also G Hagger-Johnson and L Hagger, '"Super kids": Regulating the Use of Cognitive and Psychological Enhancements in Children' (2011) 3(1) *Law, Innovation and Technology* 137.

[160] Harris and Chatterjee (n 159).

[161] Walley (n 152).

[162] *Antimicrobial agent/FUJISAWA PHARMACEUTICAL CO* [1999] EP 88305828.1 (unreported).

[163] But also epilepsy, psychiatric illnesses, and intractable pain: see patent no. EP1062973, 'A multifunction electrode for neural stimulation'.

healthy individuals has been raised.[164] Although the use of DBS for non-therapeutic enhancement is unlikely to become a reality in the near future (if at all), the very significant risks associated with it are not limited to brain surgery. Invoking potential infringement of Articles 1 (human dignity), 3 (right to the integrity of the person), and 8 (protection of personal data) of the Charter of Fundamental Rights of the European Union (2000),[165] the EGE has advised the Commission that the use of ICT implants (such as DBS) to change memory[166] should be banned.[167] As a medical method for memory enhancement, indirect regulation of DBS through the patent system would (subject to novelty and inventive step) be partly contingent on method claims being sufficiently directed to uses for non-therapeutic (enhancement) purposes. As already indicated, objections based on morality would present a major hurdle to such an invention. Given the robust views of the EGE on the ethical position of using DBS for enhancement purposes, these are likely to succeed before any tribunal in Europe.

In respect to oral medications used for memory enhancement/attenuation, a second medical use patent may be sought for a new and inventive indication[168] thereby effectively prolonging the monopoly over the known drug.[169] Although not a new phenomenon in patent law, following amendment of the second medical use provision (Article 54(5)) in EPC 2000, a potential problem may arise where a drug (for instance, a beta blocker) is re-patented following the discovery of a new indication but where the former use (for example, in cardiology) has come off-patent. Under these circumstances, the medical practitioner who prescribes the generic version for enhancement purposes (for example, prior to a patient retaking their driving test for the fifth time), simply because it is cheaper than the patented version, infringes the second medical use patent in force; a situation contrary to the policy of the medical exclusion—and one yet to be legally clarified.[170] This is because, prior to amendment, second medical use interpreted in *Second Medical Indication/EISAI* allowed purpose-limited claims to the process for making a drug ('Swiss type' claims); whereas Article 54(5) EPC seemingly provides for purpose-limited claims to the substance or composition (the drug). The other point to note is that second medical use is only available for use in Article 53(c) EPC methods of treatment. Thus where the proposed second use falls outside this provision, which may be the case where the enhancement is non-therapeutic, there can be no second medical use patent.[171]

The exclusionary provisions for 'methods of treatment' have already resulted in convoluted distinctions between discrete treatments, which do not totally correlate to divisions between solely therapeutic methods, and those excluded irrespective of purpose. New innovations (such as bioengineering and DBS) promise to blur these distinctions more broadly, requiring new distinctions to be made between medically necessary treatments and enhancements. This represents a moral 'slippery slope',

---

[164] J Ong, 'Deep Brain Stimulation: The Quest for Cognitive Enhancement' (2008) 5 *The Science in Society Review* 4 <http://triplehelixnus.files.wordpress.com/2011/01/nus-fall08.pdf> accessed September 2011.

[165] [2000] OJ C364/1 Preamble: '. . . Conscious of its spiritual and moral heritage, the Union is founded on the indivisible, universal values of human dignity, freedom, equality and solidarity; it is based on the principles of democracy and the rule of law.'

[166] Or to change identity, self perception and perception of others; or as a basis for cyber-racism; or to enhance capabilities in order to dominate others (at 33).

[167] EGE, *Opinion on Ethical aspects of ICT Implants in the Human Body* (Opinion No 20), 16 March 2005, 33.

[168] *ABBOTT RESPIRATORY/Dosage Regime* (n 108).

[169] Pursuant to Art 54(5) EPC.

[170] For further comment see: Julian Cockbain's amicus brief, relating to *ABBOTT RESPIRATORY/Dosage Regime*, dated 21 May 2009.

[171] *Second Medical Indication/EISAI* (n 54).

in which society risks an exponential increase in the expectations of wellness and the insistence that novel medicines and treatments be available. Indirect regulation by the patent system is effected where claims are directed to a method of treatment that improves the normal performance of the human body for a therapeutic purpose, as these would be excluded from patent protection. However, unlike methods of treatment by surgery, *non-therapeutic* methods of treatment by therapy (for example, methods for cosmetic, enhancement, life-style,[172] or hygiene purposes) are otherwise patentable. For example, in *Increasing energy in vivo/BIOENERGY INC*, the invention concerned the administration of ribose to normal healthy subjects engaged in physical activity to enhance skeletal muscle performance.[173] The following claim, '[u]se of ribose for enhancing skeletal muscle performance of normal healthy subjects', did not offend the medical exclusion because the use of ribose was limited to normal healthy subjects and was not a method of treatment of the human body by therapy,[174] and was patentable.

Therefore, methods for human 'enhancement' that have therapeutic and non-therapeutic indications fall under Article 53(c) EPC, if the claimed method is not limited to non-therapeutic applications.[175] but if the two claimed technical effects are at least divisible, the non-therapeutic element may be otherwise patentable. Where patent protection is either unavailable or a patent is highly vulnerable to challenge, this is likely to deter investors and restrict development of the technology. Uncertainty about the availability of patent protection due to operation of the exclusions may negatively influence private (and to some extent public[176]) sector investment.

D. Conclusion

In the context of new health technologies, the patent system exerts an indirect regulatory effect, in part through the basic requirements for patentability of inventions, but through the operation of the moral and medical exclusions to patentability. As a strong patent position is usually a prerequisite for investment, be it through bank credit or venture capital, patent law de facto indirectly regulates the types of treatments for which capital may be attracted in order to fund the very significant developmental costs associated with the stem cell, gene therapy, and nanomedical fields in order to bring new therapies, devices, or products up to market. The various institutions regulating patents in Europe prohibit both the patenting of medical methods of treatment of the human (or animal) body and the patentability of inventions the commercial exploitation of which offends morality and/or *ordre public*.

The medical exclusion means that methods of treatment of the human body (the art of 'being a doctor') cannot be patented. Some of the new health technologies arising in nanomedicine and biotechnology engender a fine line between medical and non-medical uses of methods for diagnostic, preventative or therapeutic purposes. Where potentially patentable claims over a novel method of treatment simply cannot be extricated from what is otherwise a treatment of the human body by 'therapy' or 'surgery', this might constitute a disincentive to future investors and/or lay the patent

---

172 May be defined as a method that is used either for non health problems or for problems that lie at the margins of health and well-being.

173 *Increasing energy in vivo/BIOENERGY INC* [2010] EP 99928759.2 (unreported).

174 *Increasing energy in vivo/BIOENERGY INC* (n 173) 4 (reasons for the decision).

175 *Blood Separation System/FENWAL* [2011] EP 961403.3 (unreported).

176 Given that the public sector is increasingly subject to pressure to capture intellectual property and commercialize innovation.

open to attack by competitors. A new technology enterprise, which needs to devote its money, time, and resources to technology development and commercialization, cannot normally afford litigation.[177]

The fine line complexity adds to an illogicality within patent law that patents for *products* to treat the human body (pharmaceuticals) are allowed, whereas patents for *methods* to treat the human body are not. This is so notwithstanding that both products and methods used to treat the human body (within the meaning of the law) fall exclusively within the domain of the medical practitioner. Moreover, at what point a risk factor or non-medical personal health care 'issue' becomes a disorder (something necessitating medical therapeutic intervention) is highly contentious. The distinction between medical and non-medical is particularly relevant to emerging health treatments that are aimed exclusively at the cosmetic or enhancement market.

It is, therefore, important that the meanings of methods of treatment by 'therapy' or 'surgery', barred by the medical exclusion, are legally precise and certain. As the case law demonstrates, appellate tribunals have been required to grapple with the precise boundaries of the therapy/non-therapy distinction. This distinction, already blurry,[178] is likely to become more so if 'enhancements' are normalized as therapy. This may restrict 'method of treatment' claims, affecting development of cosmetic, non-therapeutics, and treatments with dual market potential, where the effects are inextricably linked, contrary to the public interest in some instances.

The argument here should not be over-stated. Of course, patent law is just one strand of the regulatory environment for new health technologies—others, such as marketing permission, may be much more important in terms of development of new health technologies in Europe. And patent law's role of indirect regulation is secondary to the primary purpose of patent law—the legal protection of technical innovation. But to return to the point that patent law is unapologetically semantic, if regulatees (patent attorneys and patent holders) are able to navigate around the medical and morality exclusions by employing highly technical, formulaic language with careful deployment of disclaimers and the like, exclusions may in some cases be avoided. Biotechnology cases involving potential breaches of human dignity are becoming an exception to this generalization, serving to remind us that the primary purpose of patent law is the legal protection of technical innovation only where this conforms to acceptable ethical and moral standards (and does not unduly fetter basic medical practice). As the chapter has shown, the law must be precise and certain to support the regulators (patent examiners and judges) satisfactorily in their deliberations about the application of the morality exclusion to the subject matter before them.

The uncertainties (such as what counts as 'cosmetic' or 'therapeutic'), perceived illogicality (allowing patents for products to treat the human body, but not for methods), and potentially undesirable consequences of patent law for the development of new health technologies (such as patent thickets or reduction in venture capitalist investment), suggest that the time is ripe for a re-assessment of patent law's indirect regulatory roles in this context. Such a re-assessment should include greater public input into patent law policy[179] to inform questions about morality and human dignity, alongside creativity, Europe's competitive edge and economic growth.

---

[177] Cardullo (n 10).   [178] Odell-West (n 116).

[179] In agreement with the Beyleveld and Brownsword thesis (D Beyleveld and R Brownsword, 'Mice, Morality and Patents' (Common Law Institute of Intellectual Property 1993)), Drahos also urges the establishment of an independent multi-disciplinary Ethics Board assigned to the EPO to hear contested Art 53 cases; P Drahos, 'Biotechnology Patents, Markets and Morality' (1999) 21(9) *EIPR* 441.

8

New Health Technologies and Their Impact on EU Product Liability Regulations

Monica Navarro-Michel

A. Introduction

Product liability is a concern of the industrial age. The growth of mass production and changes in distribution chains, have had an enormous impact on the law, particularly with regards to liability. As we move into (or continue to be in) a technological age, we need to identify whether or not laws which have traditionally applied to 'products' also apply to new health technologies,[1] as well as to identify the legal problems that may emerge as we try to fit the new reality into the old legal mould.[2] The European Union (EU) has taken significant strides in relation to ensuring product safety,[3] particularly in the case of medicinal products since the first Directive was adopted back in 1965.[4] The legal debate on new health technologies is focused mainly on risk prevention and safety, which are mechanisms of *ex ante* protection.[5] In contrast, this chapter seeks to explore the challenges that arise between new health technologies and one aspect of risk governance, namely *ex post* compensatory mechanisms, which arise once damage has in fact occurred.

The purpose of this chapter revolves around three ideas: risk, market, and rights. First, I explore whether EU product liability legislation has had an impact on the market and on rights. The European Council approved Directive 85/374/EEC of 25 July 1985 on the approximation of laws, regulations and administrative provisions of the Member States (MSs) concerning liability for defective products,[6] (hereinafter

---

[1] New health technologies include a wide array of products and even procedures, some of which may not even be technically new, although a novel application may be given to an existing and well-known technology such as assisted reproductive technoloiges (ART), for example. It includes a wide variety of concepts: medicinal products, medical devices, products derived from the human body (eg organs, blood, tissue) applied as treatment, medical and surgical procedures, any measures taken in relation to disease prvention, diagnosis of treatment used in health care.

[2] For reference on the mismatch or disconnection between regulatory framework and new technologies see, among others, R Brownsword, *Rights, Regulation, and the Technological Revolution* (OUP 2008) and R Brownsword and K Yeung (eds), *Regulating Technologies. Legal Futures, Regulatory Frames and Technological Fixes* (Hart 2008).

[3] Commission 'European Governance: A White Paper' COM (2001) 428 final, recognizes that the EU needs to respond to the expectations of its citizens, including taking the lead in seizing opportunities to further the globalization of economic and human development, as well as in responding to concerns over safety.

[4] Council Directive 65/65/EEC of 26 January 1965 on the approximation of provisions laid down by law, regulation or administrative action relating to proprietary medicinal products [1965] OJ L229/369.

[5] Even the Universal Declaration on Bioethics and Human Rights adopted by UNESCO's General Conference on 19 October 2005 in Art 20 includes a reference to risk assessment and management: 'appropriate assessment and adequate management of risk related to medicine, life sciences and associated technologies should be promoted'.

[6] At European level, attention was first given by the Council of Europe's European Convention on Products Liability in regard to Personal Injury and Death, 27 January 1977.

referred to as the Product Liability Directive or, simply, the Directive), with the main aim of minimizing the 'existing divergences [which] may distort competition and affect the movement of goods within the common market'. Implementation of the Directive led to a curtailment of patients' rights in some MS, where national legislation had previously been more favourable to victims.

The first section of this chapter highlights inconsistencies at EU level in relation to product liability. There is currently no uniformity within MS product liability legislation which, of itself, is not necessarily negative, except for the fact that the European Commission (Commission) and the Court of Justice of the European Union (CJEU) insist on total harmonization. However, the main problem lies not so much in a lack of uniformity, as in uncertainty and curtailment of patients' rights. This is particularly relevant for new health technologies, since lack of harmonization affects some technologies in particular, such as pharmaceuticals and human tissue products. The second section of this chapter explores in further detail those differences and it highlights how new health technologies present new legal problems or, more often than not, aggravates or accentuates legal problems which are already in existence. Focus will be placed on two specific issues which affect new health technologies in particular. On the one hand, there is the development risk defence which offers manufacturers the opportunity of avoiding liability if the state-of-the-art scientific and technical knowledge at the time the product was put into circulation meant that they were unable to discover the existence of the defect. On the other hand, there is the interplay between product safety and liability regulation: this will be analysed in the third section of the chapter.

B. EU Legislation and Its Impact on Member State Legislation

Implementation of Directives into the national law of MSs creates a conflict when the level of protection given by national or internal laws is higher that the one provided by EU legislation. Victims' pre-existing legal entitlements may be curtailed if the expected level of harmonization is absolute. This is particularly relevant for new health technologies, as in some MSs medicines have been singled out and those who have suffered harm as a result of defective medicinal products have been given a higher level of protection than those who suffered harm through the use of other defective products.

1. Conflict With Existing National Laws

Traditionally, the buyer of a defective product could make a claim against the manufacturer under the rules of contract and the latent defects guarantee; when the victim had not bought the product, s/he had to rely on tort law. In most MS, tort law is based on a general principle of liability for fault,[7] and negligence is a difficult requirement to establish. The Product Liability Directive intended to bring about a solution to some of the legal obstacles found in relation to bringing product liability claims. Strict liability was introduced which made negligence irrelevant.[8] In addition, privity of contract was held not to bar the non-buyer from making a claim against the manufacturer, thus allowing users and third parties alike to obtain compensation from the producer.

These legal advantages were outweighed by two different issues. In some MSs, the obstacles the Directive sought to overcome in relation to the making of product liability

---

[7] See eg Art 1382 French Code civil; Art 1902 Spanish Civil Code; § 823 I German Civil Code (BGB).
[8] It turns out that it is not as strict as the Preamble intended as the Directive reintroduces negligence in its provisions.

claims had already been surmounted through victim-friendly interpretation of traditional rules by national courts (allowing a direct claim against the manufacturer (either
applying contract rules or tort law); the introduction of a rebuttable presumption of
fault);[9] or by specific rules for consumer protection. The Directive came with a set
of rules that were unfavourable to victims, and which had previously been unknown in
relation to product liability claims: it introduced an additional requirement of proof of
defect, new defences available to the defendant (most notably, the development risk
defence), a threshold, damage caps, and an expiry date. This meant that the manufacturer would not be liable according to the liability system established in the Directive
once ten years had passed since the date that the product had been put into circulation.

The Directive was not well received by MSs, such as Germany, that offered a higher
level of protection to victims, either in general terms or in relation to specific products.
When harmonization is exhaustive or maximum, it does not provide a basis on which
MSs are able to adopt more stringent regulation in line with national prerogatives. One
of the reasons given to account for the delay in implementation in some MSs, such as
Spain (1994) and France (1998), was that they were reluctant to implement a Directive
that appeared to offer less protection to victims than their own national law or case law
respectively. I will now focus on the German, Spanish, and French legislation prior to
the implementation of the Product Liability Directive.[10]

a. Germany

Claims made by victims of defective products were initially based on contract law, which
offered some advantages when compared to tort law.[11] The seminal judgment of the
German Supreme Court in November 1968,[12] known as the *Newcastle disease case* which
involved contaminated vaccines for animals, proposed a tort-based approach to product
liability that has not been challenged since such time.[13] In 1989, Germany transposed the
Directive into national law through the adoption of the Product Liability Act.[14] Originally, this was not an attractive basis for liability, since German law did not award damages
for non-pecuniary loss on the basis of strict liability. Therefore, victims preferred to make
claims based on negligence, which had become victim-friendly due to the reversal of
proof introduced by the Bundesgerichtshof. Since the 2002 BGB (the German Civil
Code) reform, damages for pain and suffering can now also be awarded on the basis of a
strict liability claim, which subsequently widened the remit of the Product Liability Act.

There is a special category of products regulated outside the German Product
Liability Act. The Federal Pharmaceutical Act of 1961 (AMG)[15] was amended in

---

[9] In Spain, the reversal of proof was first introduced by case law and applied generally to 'difficult
cases'. Currently, the rules of evidence make it mandatory to take into account the availability of
evidence to each party (see Art 217.6 of the Spanish Law of Civil Procedure, Ley 1/2000, 7 January, de
Enjuiciamiento Civil).

[10] It is important to note that prior to the Product Liability Directive, national product liability laws
in these MSs had been adopted as a direct consequence of specific health scandals involving either
pharmaceutical products or food.

[11] See BS Markesinis and H Unberath, *The German Law of Torts* (4 edn, Hart 2002) 94.

[12] *Bundesgerichtshof* 51, 91.

[13] G Wagner, 'Development of Product Liability in Germany' in S Whittaker (ed), *The Development of Product Liability* (CUP 2010) 122.

[14] *Produkthaftungsgesetz*, 15 December 1989 (BGB I.I.2198) [German Product Liability Act].

[15] *Arzneimittelgesetz*, AMG, 1961. The law is referred to as Medicinal Products Act as a result of the
translation of the Law provided by the Federal Ministry of Justice <www.juris.de>. It is also referred to
as the Pharmaceutical Act by leading scholars, such as Markesinis and Unberath (n 11).

1976[16] to include provisions on civil liability for damage caused by defective drugs. This legislation was introduced as a consequence of the *Thalidomide* scandal of the late 1960s.[17] Under § 84 AMG, the manufacturer is held to be strictly liable and may not use the development risk defence, as it is considered responsible even when the adverse effects of the drug only become discernable following marketing. The proviso is that the side effects must have been known at the time of treatment and the application of the drug in such circumstances would have been unreasonable. In contrast, there is no liability for the consequences of a drug that adversely affects the health of patients, but which is without a reasonable alternative at the time of treatment, and the benefits of which outweigh the side effects at such point in time.[18]

b. Spain

Product liability is set out in the General Law 26/1984, 19 July, for the Protection of Consumers and Users[19] (hereinafter referred to as LGDCU, following the Spanish acronym). This legislation was passed after the *colza* or rape-seed oil affair. Given its social and economic impact, this 'affair' proved to be the biggest consumer scandal that Spain had ever seen. The case involved a mass poisoning which resulted in more than 30,000 victims, who died or suffered a variety of personal injuries after consumption of denatured rape-seed oil.[20] The LGDCU provided for two liability regimes: a general one based on the principle of liability for negligence, with a rebuttable presumption of fault,[21] as well as a strict liability regime.[22] The latter applied to products and services that are required to meet certain levels of purity, efficiency, or security (undergoing technical, professional, or systematic controls);[23] and to specific products and services including medicines, food, and food products.[24] These provisions removed the distinction between liability in contract and liability in tort, since it applied to both without distinction, and all subjects in the distribution chain were to be held jointly and severally liable.[25]

The Product Liability Directive was implemented in 1994, with the adoption of the Product Liability Act[26] (hereinafter referred to as LRPD, following the Spanish acronym). Since such time, Articles 25 to 28 LGDCU have been held to be inapplicable to liability for damages caused by defective products included in the LRPD. Both laws are now included in unamended form in Legislative Decree 1/2007, 16 November, on the General Law for the Protection of Consumers and Users and other laws (LGDCU 2007). Current reference should be made to this law.[27]

---

[16] Such amendments have been in force since 1 July 1978.

[17] Thousands of children were born with severe physical disabilities (including absence of limbs and incomplete development of organs) after their mothers had taken *Thalidomide* during pregnancy for morning sickness.

[18] Wagner (n 13) 140.

[19] Ley 26/1984, de 19 de Julio, General para la Defensa de los Consumidores y Usuarios (LGDCU) [Spanish Law for the Protection of Consumers and Users].

[20] For details, see M Martín-Casals and JS Feliu, 'The Development of Product Liability in Spain' in S Whittaker (ed), *The Development of Product Liability* (CUP 2010) 251–6.

[21] Art 26 LGDCU.

[22] Art 28 LGDCU.   [23] Section 1 LGDCU.

[24] Art 28(2) LGDCU. Specific products include: food products, cleaning products, cosmetics, medicines and pharmaceutical products, health care services, gas and electricity services, electrical appliances, means of transportation, motor vehicles, toys and other products targeted at children.

[25] Art 27.2, LGDCU.

[26] Ley 22/1994, de 6 de Julio, de Responsabilidad Civil por los Daños Causados por Productos Defectuosos (LRPD) [Spanish Product Liability Act].

[27] It is important to note that EU Directives set out aims and objectives which are to be met by MSs, but that MSs are then free to choose the form and methods of implementation. See Art 288 of

c. France

Before 1985, French product liability law rested heavily on contract law. The buyer of a defective product was able to make a claim against the manufacturer based on the rules of contract. This was attributable to the interpretation given to both the latent defects guarantee and *action directe*.[28] When the victim had not bought the product, s/he had to rely on tort law and, in the 1960s, the Cour de cassation held that putting a defective product into circulation constituted an act of negligence. Given the precedent of no-fault liability for things (*responsabilité du fait des choses*), applied to the keeper of things,[29] it seemed unfair that the professional manufacturer or seller only be held liable for negligence. Even though the divide between liability in contract and liability in tort remained essential, the situation of victims was scarcely affected by their contractual status:[30] the difficulty in either case lay in proving that the damage had been caused by a defect in the product and that this defect existed at the time the product left the defendant's hands. Nonetheless, it was held that both the manufacturer and the seller would be held liable on a no-fault basis.

When the Product Liability Directive was implemented into national law in France, it was considered to be too restrictive. When the contaminated blood scandal (*affaire du sang contaminé*) emerged in the mid to late 1980s, the Cour de cassation decided that the undiscoverable nature of the virus constituted no defence for the blood supplier.[31] The biggest point of contention between consumer-friendly and industry-friendly Members of Parliament was the development risk defence.[32] Notwithstanding criticism from the then European Court of Justice, it took France thirteen years to implement the Directive, which it finally did through Law no 98-389 of 19 May 1998 on liability for defective products, which inserted the provisions into the French Civil Code as set out in Articles 1386-1 to 1386-13.

Before formal implementation of the Product Liability Directive under French law in 1998, the Cour de cassation had developed a new product liability regime along similar lines to that proposed in the Directive. The court decided that manufacturers and sellers must supply products without any 'safety defect' (*défaut de sécurité*), as

the Consolidated Version of the Treaty on the Functioning of the European Union (TFEU) (ex Art 249 Treaty of the European Community (EC)).

[28] The latent defects guarantee establishes that the buyer can obtain damages, but only if the seller knew of the defect (Art 1645 *Code civil*). The Cour de cassation established that when the seller is a professional dealer, there is an irrebuttable presumption of knowledge of the existence of the defect. This finding, coupled with *action directe*, allowed victims to sue the manufacturers of defective products. French law has a very liberal conception of privity of contract. There are various cases in which a person who has not entered a contract can nevertheless raise a claim in contract, notably when there is a chain of contract alongside which there had been a transfer of property of a thing (*chaine contractuelle translative de propriété*). The claimant may make a claim against a party with whom he has not entered into a contract (*action directe*).

[29] See Art 1384 *Code civil*. French courts have long recognized the concept of no-fault liability. At the end of the 19th century, the courts developed the concept of no-fault liability for things (*responsabilité du fait des choses*) based on a liberal interpretation of Art 1384 *Code civil*. Given the claimant's difficulty in obtaining compensation for damages from the manufacturer (eg manufacturer not easily identifiable; difficulty in proving fault; problems of remoteness), the attention of the French courts turned from the manufacturer to the owner of the thing.

[30] JS Borghetti, 'The Development of Product Liability in France' in S Whittaker (ed), *The Development of Product Liability* (CUP 2010) 97.

[31] Cassation 1er, 12 April 1995, *Juris- Classeur Periodique* 1995.II.22467; see also P Jourdain, *Juris-Classeur Periodique* 1995.I.3893, no 20.

[32] Borghetti (n 30) 106.

defined in the Directive.[33] The liability for non compliance of the *obligation de sécurité* raised a number of troubling questions for the courts and Parliament: it was the first time that French judges had implemented an EU Directive on their own initiative. This was considered to be contrary to the way things had previously been done within the French politico-legal system, as judges were meant to apply the law, not to create it.

2. The CJEU's Trilogy of Cases

Regardless of what it claims to be, an EU Directive that gives options to MS or that defers to national law is a Directive which aims at minimum harmonization. What is puzzling is that the CJEU has stressed repeatedly that the Product Liability Directive establishes a conclusive scheme that must not be amended by MSs. The CJEU has insisted on maximum harmonization for product liability and if consumers' rights are to be curtailed, then so be it. In judgments given on 25 April 2002 in the three cases of *Commission v France*,[34] *Commission v Greece*,[35] and *González Sánchez v Medicina Asturiana SA*,[36] the CJEU stated that 'the margin of discretion available to the MSs in order to make provision for product liability is entirely determined by the Directive itself.'[37] Discrepancies in the French[38] and Greek[39] implementation laws were not within the terms of the Directive and should therefore not be allowed. The CJEU stated that the Directive did not allow MSs to maintain a general system of product liability different from that provided for in the Directive; however, this did not preclude the application of approaches to contractual or non-contractual liability based on other grounds, such as fault or a warranty for latent defects.[40]

The Product Liability Directive states that 'this Directive shall not affect any rights which an injured person may have according to the rules of the law of contract or non-contractual liability or a special liability system existing at the moment when this Directive is notified.'[41] Taken literally, this would appear to respect the higher levels of protection afforded under MS legislation if and/or when they existed prior to the adoption of the Directive. However, that was not the interpretation given by the CJEU which held that such provision 'must be interpreted as meaning that the rights conferred under the legislation of a MS on the victims of damage caused by a defective product under a general system of liability as having the same basis as that put in place by the Directive may be limited or restricted as a result of the Directive's transposition into the domestic law of that State.'[42] The CJEU concluded that the Directive 'contains

---

[33] P Le Tourneau, *Droit de la responsabilité et des contrats* (Dalloz 2004) nr 6075, notes that the Cour de cassation developed this case law in order to compensate for the fact that French legislators had not transposed the Product Liability Directive into French law.

[34] C-52/00 *Commission v France* [2002] ECR I-3827.

[35] C-154/00 *Commission v Greece* [2002] ECR I-3879.

[36] C-183/00 *Maria Victoria González v Medicina Asturiana SA* [2002] ECR I-3901.

[37] *Commission v France*, para 16; *Commission v Greece*, para 12; *Maria Victoria González Sánchez v Medicina Asturiana SA*, para 25.

[38] The Commission held that there had been a failure correctly to transpose the Product Liability Directive under French law, in particular there had been a failure to include a threshold of € 500 for damage to property; it extended liability to the supplier; and it increased the producer's burden of proof in the context of reliance being placed on the development risk defence.

[39] The Commission held that Greek transposition laws had been contrary to the Product Liability Directive because it omitted the threshold of € 500.

[40] *Commission v France*, para 22; *Commission v Greece*, paras 17–19; *Maria Victoria González Sánchez v Medicina Asturiana SA*, para 27.

[41] Art 13 Council Directive 85/374/EEC.

[42] See *Maria Victoria González Sánchez v Medicina Asturiana SA*.

no provision expressly authorizing the MS to adopt or maintain more stringent provisions ... to secure a higher level of consumer protection',[43] and the Directive may require restriction of consumer rights within its specific domain. The basis for this is market-related: since different degrees of consumer protection for defective products entail a negative effect on the functioning of the internal market, then they should be eliminated. Therefore, the CJEU insisted on maximum harmonization to achieve a single market at the expense of consumer's rights. France and Greece sought to argue on the basis of an evolutionary interpretation[44] of the EC Treaty, given the growing importance of consumer protection within the EU.[45] However, the CJEU dismissed such arguments, as this Treaty competence had been inserted into the EC Treaty following the adoption of the Product Liability Directive.[46]

Consequently, EU product liability legislation remains frozen in 1985, the year the Directive was adopted, regardless of either subsequent Treaty reforms at EU level or the higher level of consumer protection demanded by society.[47] In general, legal scholars have been uncomfortable with this curtailment of consumer protection.[48] The CJEU's insistence on maximum harmonization does not sit comfortably with the likelihood of different approaches adopted by Member States in relation to the implementation of Directives. This has long been a feature of the implementation process involving EU Directives, provided that a certain level of minimum harmonization is met. It is important to note that there are a number of optional provisions in the Directive, such as the state-of-the-art defence, and financial limits.[49] Such provisions were adopted by Germany, Spain, and Portugal.[50] However, there are a number of issues where deference is shown to national law, including in relation to damages covering both the categories of damages to be compensated and the quantum of loss. The Directive also provides for compensation for damage caused by death or personal injury and for damages to property intended for private use, however, the amount of compensation to be awarded is to be determined in line with national law.[51] Important differences also remain as between MSs with respect to compensation for non-pecuniary loss and third party rights to compensation.[52] As long as MSs provide an effective remedy, however, then the CJEU does not appear to be concerned about differences in approach in these areas.[53] In

---

[43] *Commission v France*, para 18; *Commission v Greece*, para 14; *Maria Victoria González Sánchez v Medicina Asturiana SA*, para 27.

[44] Evolutionary or dynamic interpretation is used by the European Court of Human Rights (ECtHR) to introduce the necessary degree of flexibility with respect to the application of the European Convention of Human Rights (ECHR). In *Tyrer v United Kingdom*, App no 5856/72 ECHR, 25 April 1978, the ECtHR stated that the ECHR is a 'living instrument' and it should be interpreted in light of 'present day conditions'.

[45] At the time, Art 153 EC contained a reference to the need to ensure 'a high level of consumer protection'. Currently, Art 12 TFEU refers to 'consumer protection requirements shall be taken into account in defining and implementing other Union policies and activities'.

[46] *Commission v France*, para 15; *Commission v Greece*, para 11.

[47] See J Joussen, 'L'Interpretazione (teleologica) del Diritto Comunitario' (2001) 4 *Rivista Critica di Diritto Privatto* 491.

[48] P Le Tourneau, *Responsabilité des vendeurs et des fabricants* (Dalloz 2002) 76: 'punishing France for giving greater protection to victims seems unfortunate and may reinforce resentment towards European institutions.'

[49] It cannot be less than €70 million, see Art 16 Council Directive 85/374/EEC.

[50] Originally, a cap on damages was also established in Greece, although it was removed when the law was re-enacted in 1994.

[51] Art 9 Council Directive 85/374/EEC.

[52] As loss of maintenance, non-pecuniary loss for death of a loved one, or psychiatric harm.

[53] Case C-203/99 *Veedfalds v Arhus Amtskommune* [2001] ECR I-3569, para 27: 'although it is left to national legislatures to determine the precise content of those two heads of damage, nevertheless,

conclusion, the fact that the Directive provides for certain derogations or defers to national law in certain respects 'does not mean that in regard to the matters which it regulates harmonization is not complete'.[54]

At a theoretical level, there is no tension between harmonization and the existence of so many differences at MS level, where there is minimum harmonization which does, in fact, permit such differences. The conflict appears when emphasis is placed on complete or maximum harmonization which does not allow for differences. This tension could be reduced if both the Commission and the CJEU stopped insisting on the latter approach. By 2006, the Commission appeared finally to acknowledge that the approach taken by MSs in relation to the transposition of the Product Liability Directive had in fact been based on minimum harmonization,[55] and since such time has omitted any reference to the level of harmonization achieved as between MSs.[56] The question was whether the CJEU would follow suit.

3. The Right to Compensation versus The Internal Market

EU regulation on product liability has proved ineffective in terms of harmonization of laws and, what is worse, in some MSs it has had a negative impact on patients' rights. There are a number of arguments as regards product liability that have been repeated by the Commission and the CJEU: it is important to create a level playing field; disparities between MSs undermine competition; and in relation to the tension between the interests of victims and those of the internal market, the latter always wins. This approach is echoed in the first Recital in the Preamble to the Product Liability Directive, which states that discrepancies between MS regulations 'may distort competition and affect the movement of goods within the common market and entail a differing degree of protection of the consumer against damage caused by a defective product to his health or property.' The European Economic Community (EEC as it then was) was first and foremost concerned with the 'common market' since at the time there was no EU legislative competence in relation to consumer protection. Therefore, the Product Liability Directive *had* to be justified on economic grounds. Given that the Directive was originally adopted pursuant to Article 100 EEC,[57] this legal basis provided no scope for MSs to maintain or establish provisions which departed from Community harmonizing measures.[58] But what if the effective functioning of the internal market was not under threat and harmonization measures proved to be unnecessary?

First of all, there is a general assumption that there is (or can be) a single market in all products, although that is not entirely true, particularly with respect to new health technologies. For example, let us consider the pharmaceutical industry which is unlike any other industry.[59] It deals with essential products where the interests of the industry converge with that of health policy. It is an industry of innovation heavily dependent

---

save for non-material damage whose reparation is governed solely by national law, full and proper compensation for persons injured by a defective product must be available in the case of those two heads of damage.'

[54] *Commission v France*, para 19; *Commission v Greece*, para 15; *Maria Victoria González Sánchez v Medicina Asturiana SA*, para 28.

[55] Commission's *Third Report* (2006).

[56] Commission's *Fourth Report* (2011).

[57] Art 115 TFEU (ex Art 94 EC).

[58] *Commission v France*, para 14; *Commission v Greece*, para 10; *Maria Victoria González Sánchez v Medicina Asturiana SA*, para 23.

[59] See TK Hervey and JV McHale, *Health Law and the European Union* (CUP 2004) 328.

upon investment in research and development and its profitability relies to a large extent on patent protection. Demand also works differently, since it is not based on choice between competing products with respect to quality and price. National governments and health professionals maintain special positions as main purchasers or prescribers of pharmaceuticals, and the patient-consumer does not usually pay the full price of the product.[60] We nevertheless need to proceed on the assumption that there is in fact a single market for pharmaceuticals in line with the approach taken at EU level.

Secondly, although the Directive was heralded as a piece of legislation that benefits victims of defective products, it has not significantly affected the nature and number of product liability claims.[61] There is a perceived increase in the number of cases that have been brought in recent years but it is thought to be mainly due to external factors, such as greater consumer awareness and better organization of consumer groups or improved means of accessing information.[62] Thirdly, the perception of the pharmaceutical industry is that alleged disparities have not played an important role in the conduct of their businesses or altered competition in any significant way.

It is worth considering the Lovells Report on the application of the Directive published in 2003. The Report set out the findings from a study carried out on behalf of the Commission which sought to analyse and compare the extent to which the Directive was being used, as well as its impact on consumer protection across the EU.[63] It involved surveying hundreds of participants, including producers, consumer representatives, lawyers, and academics on the practical effects of the Directive. One of the questions posed to producers, insurers, and legal participants was the following: Does any disparity in product risks between Member States discourage the marketing in one Member State of products from another? Only 12 per cent answered yes, but if we look at the answers given by producers (who are the ones making decisions about marketing products), then only 6 per cent answered yes.[64]

Finally, the Commission has adopted a position which seems inconsistent with its previously held views: namely, disparities between MS legislation 'do not create significant trade barriers or distort competition in the EU'.[65] So, why was such insistence placed on complete harmonization? If rights have been curtailed and consumer protection diminished in the interests of the market and this has turned out to be an unnecessary or unrealized fear, then has the time come to introduce or reinstate the

---

[60] Hervey and McHale (n 59), 286 ff.

[61] This leads to a debate on the gap between the law in theory and the law in practice. Reimann has argued that the Directive has influenced the law on the books rather than the law in action. He states that this illustrates how deceptive and ineffective mere black-letter law harmonization can be (see M Reimann, 'Product Liability in a Global Context: the Hollow Victory of the European Model' (2003) 2 *European Review of Private Law* 128). Cavaliere has argued that the minimal impact of product liability law may be due to compensation provided by the welfare state, as well as the significant costs associated with access to justice in Europe (see A Cavaliere, 'Product Liability in the European Union: Compensation and Deterrence Issues' 18 (2004) *European Journal of Law and Economics* 299).

[62] Commission's *Fourth Report* (2011) 4.

[63] The full title is 'Product Liability in the European Union. A Report for the European Commission' (February 2003).

[64] Lovells Report (n 63) 27.

[65] This is mentioned for the first time in the Commission's *Third Report* (2006) 9, and confirmed in the *Fourth Report* (2011) 11. The *Third Report* also stated that 'total harmonization ... is not only unrealistic, but also unnecessary in view of the limited impact (if any) that its absence would have on the internal market.' This was a surprising admission from the Commission. See D Fairgrieve and G Howells, 'Rethinking Product Liability: A Missing Element in the European Commission's Third Review of the European Product Liability Directive' (2007) 70 *Modern Law Review* 962, 966.

higher level of protection which is already provided by some MSs? When the measures taken by the EU to protect the single market prove to be unnecessary, then is it time to throw them in the proverbial legal wastebasket? Is there a real need for reform or is the negative impact on victims' rights based primarily on ideological grounds? Some may argue that it is not necessary to amend legislation when, in practice, the protection of victims is otherwise assured (except perhaps in Austria where the Product Liability Directive has had a positive impact in the way in which claims are made).[66] With respect to rights, however, language is important and the striking feature of the Directive is that the market is (still) the primary concern of the EU.[67]

Developments at EU level in other areas do assist with claims for compensation, such as a broadening of access to justice, as well as consumer protection more generally. In addition, the issue of prevention is now of increasing concern for the EU. In the area of product liability, however, the market still prevails. It is also interesting to note that one of the mantras used to justify the Product Liability Directive is that it strikes 'an appropriate balance on the whole between producers/suppliers interests and those of consumers'.[68] However, if the Commission seeks to rely on the Lovells Report to justify such a conclusion, then the argument is not convincing as consumer interest groups were under-represented in the survey.[69]

C. New Health Technologies and the Development Risk Defence

Even though conceptualization and characterization of health technologies per se may not appear to be very important, it is relevant not only to ascertain whether they fit within the mould of 'product' (as defined by the Product Liability Directive), but also more importantly to see if they fit within the exception provided by national legislation with regards to the availability of the development risk defence. 'Product' is defined in very broad terms by the Directive as 'all movables'.[70] New health technologies, as far as they involve a 'thing' rather than a procedure, would be included within the scope of the Directive.

Some MSs make a distinction between products in general, which include medical devices and medicines, with respect to the so-called development risk defence. It is a defence that is available to the producer of medical devices, but not to the producer of pharmaceuticals. The distinction between a medical device and a medicine, which may generally be considered irrelevant, becomes a matter of great importance in some MSs. However, this distinction is not always an easy one to make, as will become

---

[66] Lovells Report (n 63) 19.

[67] The Commission has not adopted an approach which is consistent with its own conclusions, as it insists on the need to curtail further differences between MSs. It concludes that the supplier's no-fault liability may not be left to the MSs, as the Council suggested in 2002 (see Council Resolution of 19 December 2002 on the amendment of the liability for defective products Directive [2002] C26/02).

[68] Commission's *Third* (2006) and *Fourth* (2011) Reports.

[69] Respondents to the survey set out in the Lovells Report were mainly producers (48 per cent), followed by members of the legal profession (24 per cent), insurers (19 per cent), and lastly, consumer representatives (8 per cent). Lovells Report (n 63) 6. This may explain the degree of satisfaction registered with the Product Liability Directive. See S Whittaker, *Liability for Products. English Law, French Law, and European Harmonization* (OUP 2005) 665. The Commission's own investigations and reports reflect 'more a practical sense of the difficulty in piecing together a fresh compromise rather than a general agreement on the fairness of its provisions'.

[70] Directive 99/34/EC of 10 May 1999 amending Directive 85/374 on the approximation of the laws, regulations and administrative provisions of the Member States concerning liability for defective products [1999] OJ L141/20, Art 2, extended the scope of product liability to include raw agricultural products and game, after the BSE crises, also known as 'mad cow disease'.

apparent in the following section. This section will focus on pharmaceuticals and human tissue products as examples of health technologies, as legislation in some MSs provides different approaches to liability in each case.

1. The Availability of the Development Risk Defence for Medicines

The Product Liability Directive states that the producer shall not be liable if it shows 'that the state of scientific and technical knowledge at the time when he put the product into circulation was not such as to enable the existence of the defect to be discovered.'[71] In short, the producer shall not be liable for an undiscoverable defect. This is a substantial departure from the law of negligence where, in principle, the claimant has to prove that the defendant knew or ought to have known about the risk. The CJEU has stated that it is up to the producer to prove that it was impossible to discover the defect on the basis of an objective assessment of the available level of scientific and technical knowledge, including the most advanced level.[72] This knowledge must have been accessible at the time the product was put into circulation, that is, published in international scientific journals. The defence is about knowledge or foreseeability of the risk of harm, not about avoidability.

The adoption of the development risk defence was optional, as the Directive allowed MSs to exclude it.[73] Most MSs have implemented it, except Finland and Luxembourg. Other MSs have implemented it, except for specific categories of product. For example, Germany excludes drugs from the operation of the development risk defence;[74] Spain excludes medicines, foods, and food products used for human consumption;[75] and France excludes human body parts or products derived from the human body.[76] Such exceptions under national law are justified (or at least explained) by the fact that these countries have suffered health scandals involving medicines or food products (for example, Thalidomide, colza oil, contaminated blood as previously mentioned).

This defence is said to be a significant factor in achieving a satisfactory compromise between the need to stimulate innovation and consumers' legitimate expectations of safer products.[77] Removing it would stifle innovation, lead to higher insurance costs, and, in some cases, such risks would not be insurable at all. This would potentially have an impact on market structure and competition.[78] Reality proves otherwise: the German pharmaceutical industry is subject to strict liability and unable to use the development risk defence, and yet two German companies are among the leading pharmaceutical industries in the world.[79] It is important to remember that the defence

---

[71] Art 7(e).

[72] Case C-300/95 *Commission v United Kingdom* [1997] ECR I-2649. The Commission challenged the United Kingdom's implementing legislation, arguing that it had failed to adopt the precise terms of the development risk defence. This was because it called for a subjective assessment, with emphasis being placed on the conduct of a reasonable producer. The CJEU decided that it should not be assumed that the United Kingdom's product liability legislation would be interpreted in a way that was inconsistent with the Product Liability Directive. In the case *A & Others v National Blood Authority* [2001] 3 All ER 289, the High Court followed the lead from the CJEU and looked directly at the language of the Directive rather that at the implementing legislation on the issue.

[73] Art 15.

[74] § 84 AMG.

[75] Art 140.3 LGDCU 2007, which is identical to the previous Art 6.3 LRPD.

[76] Art 1386-12 *Code civil*.

[77] As stated in F Rosselli (on behalf of the Commission), 'Analysis of the economic impact of the development risk clause' (2004) 135.

[78] Rosselli (n 77) paras 3–4. If it did, however, there are options to consider such as increasing patent protection or marketing exclusivity, see R Goldberg, *Causation and Risk in the Law of Tort. Scientific Evidence and Medicinal Product Liability* (Hart 1999) 249.

[79] See Top 50 pharmaceutical companies at <www.pharmexec.findpharma.com>.

was included in the Directive after pressure was exerted by the United Kingdom for its inclusion in order to safeguard producers' interests. It was only when the defence was included that the United Kingdom agreed to be bound by the Directive.[80]

In Spain, the position is that the development risk defence is generally available, except in the case of manufacture of pharmaceuticals. This exception has, in turn, another exception. When the medicine in question has been manufactured by a hospital or service within the public health care system, then the defence becomes available. Public authorities' liability is established pursuant to Law 30/1992[81] which states that 'there is no liability for damages caused by acts or circumstances which were unforeseeable or unavoidable according to the scientific or technical knowledge available at the time such damages occurred, notwithstanding the health care or economic benefits that the law may provide for such cases.' This was introduced by way of an amendment in 1999 in response to the contaminated blood scandal.[82] It introduces a distinction between private and public hospitals in that the former would be liable in particular situations where the latter would not. This has been criticized on the grounds that it is both unfair and unjustifiable, as well as the fact that the development risk defence has been re-introduced in a piece of legislation that deals not with product liability law, but public authorities' liability.[83] One may question whether the types of distinction that have been made in Spain and France with respect to specific kinds of products or in the context of public or private health care (Spain), is in accordance with EU law. Leaving the German case aside which is specifically mentioned in the Directive,[84] the CJEU has stated that the Directive[85] enables MSs to remove the exemption from liability for development risks, but 'it does not authorize them to alter the conditions under which the exception is applied'.[86]

2. Medical Devices and Medicines

Medical devices and medicinal products, both of which are considered to be 'products' within the remit of the product liability regime, are also regulated in two different EU Directives for evaluation and authorization purposes. Council Directive 93/42/EEC, of 14 June 1993, concerning medical devices,[87] states that *medical device* 'means any instrument, apparatus, appliance, software, material or other article, whether used alone or in combination, including the software intended by its manufacturer to be used specifically for diagnostic and/or therapeutic purposes and necessary for its proper

[80] R Goldberg, 'The Development Risk Defence and the CJEU' in R Goldberg and J Lonbay, *Pharmaceutical Medicine, Biotechnology and European Law* (CUP 2000) 185, 186.

[81] Art 141 Law 30/1992, 26 November, on the legel regime of public administrations and common administrative procedure.

[82] Law 4/1999, 13 January.

[83] For further discussion on this point, see M Martin-Casals, 'Spanish Product Liability Today—Adapting to the "New" Rules' in D Fairgrieve (ed), *Product Liability in Comparative Perspective* (CUP 2005) 56 ff.

[84] Recital 13 of the Directive refers implicitly to the Germany's AMG.

[85] Art 15.

[86] Case C-52/00 (n 34) para 47. The French Civil Code initially required the producer to take appropriate steps to avoid the consequences of a defective product in order to be able to invoke the development risk defence.

[87] As amended by Directive 2007/47/EC of the European Parliament and the Council of 5 September 2007 amending Council Directive 90/385/EEC on the approximation of the laws of the Member States relating to active implantable medical devices, Council Directive 93/42/EEC concerning medical devices and Directive 98/8/EC concerning the placing of biocidal products on the market [2007] OJ L247/21.

application, intended by the manufacturer to be used for human beings',[88] for the purposes mentioned in the provision.[89] According to Directive 2001/83/EC of the European Parliament and of the Council of 6 November 2001 on the Community code relating to medicinal products for human use, *medicinal product* mean 'any substance or combination of substances presented for treating or preventing disease in human beings. Any substance or combination of substances which may be administered to human beings with a view to making a medical diagnosis or to restoring, correcting or modifying physiological functions in human beings is likewise considered a medicinal product.'[90] Spain and Germany have similar definitions.[91]

In terms of interpreting these definitions, let us consider by way of example, drug delivery through nanotechnology. Is it a device or a product? The development of pharmacogenetics and nanotechnology-based medicinal products presents challenges with respect to the way in which drugs are prescribed and delivered to patients. These developments also pose legal challenges in relation to how the final product should be characterized. A solution to these problems can be found by looking at more traditional ways to deliver medicines. This issue is addressed in the Directives referred to previously which deal with evaluation and authorization but they may also be useful for compensation purposes. Certain medical devices are intended to administer medicinal products (syringes, droppers). Where a medical device is intended to administer a medicinal product that device shall be covered under both Directive 93/42 with regard to the device and Directive 2001/83 with regard to the medicinal product. If, however, the device and the medicinal product form a *single integral unit*, which is intended exclusively for use in a *given combination* and which is *not reusable* (for example, a syringe marketed pre-filled), then that single product will be covered under Directive 2001/83.[92] In such circumstances, it would be considered exclusively as a medicinal product for compensation purposes. The key issue then becomes how to determine when a product should be considered as a single integral unit and when the components should be considered distinguishable, as well as re-usable. If a medical device is labelled as intended for single use only, and a decision to re-use it is made (either by a physician or the health care service), then this may have consequences in terms of product liability. This is because the re-processor or re-user will be deemed the manufacturer of the new device.[93]

Let us take the further example of a substance being incorporated into an active implantable medical device. In this case, 'particular account shall be taken of the principal mode of action of the product'[94] in order to ascertain when Directive 2001/83 (medicinal products) applies as opposed to Council Directive 90/385/EEC of 20 June 1990 on the approximation of the laws of the Member States relating to active implantable medical devices. Where an active implantable medical device is intended to administer a medicinal product, then both Directives will be applicable.[95]

---

[88] Art 1(2)(a).

[89] Which are 'diagnosis, prevention, monitoring, treatment or alleviation of disease; diagnosis, monitoring, treatment, alleviation of or compensation for an injury or handicap; investigation, replacement or modification of the anatomy or of a physiological process, control of conception, and which does not achieve its principal intended action in or on the human body by pharmacological, immunological or metabolic means, but which may be assisted in its function by such means.'

[90] Art 1(2).

[91] Art 8, Ley 29/2006, de 26 de Julio, de garantías y uso racional de los medicamentos y productos sanitarios [Law 29/2006, 26 of July, on the Guarantees and Rational Use of Medicines and other Medical Devices]; Section 2(1) AMG.

[92] Art 1(3), Council Directive 93/42/EEC, as amended in 2007 (see n 87).

[93] As suggested by C Hodges, 'The Reuse of Medical Devices' (2000) 8 *Medical Law Review* 157, 166.

[94] Art 1(6) as amended by Directive 2007/47.

[95] Art 1(3) Council Directive 90/385/EEC on the approximation of the laws of the Member States relating to active implantable medical devices.

Where an active implantable medical device incorporates, as an *integral part*, a medicinal product, and it acts upon the body with action that is ancillary to that of the device, then it is an active implantable medical device,[96] even if the medicinal product is derived from human blood or human plasma (a human blood derivative).[97] An example of this product is a heparin-coated catheter. In the UK Medicines and Healthcare products Regulatory Agency's (MHRA) opinion,[98] 'integral' means a single component product (for example, coated or incorporated within) rather than a pack containing the two components (that is, a drug or a device).

The Commission has published a manual which examines products which are on the borderline between medical devices and medicinal products.[99] However, the manual is not legally binding and therefore national authorities may reach completely different conclusions in relation to a given product. It nevertheless offers useful guidance on this issue as it provides an explanation as to how to deal with a borderline product and provides examples. For instance, eye drops will be considered medicinal products if they are used or administered with a view to making a medical diagnosis, or to restore, correct, or modify physiological functions, and have a pharmacological, immunological, or metabolic principal mode of action. However, they will be medical devices when used for disinfecting, cleaning, rinsing, or hydrating contact lenses. When intended to alleviate soreness, discomfort, or irritation caused by environmental factors (dust, heat, smoke, etc.) eye drops will be medical devices or medicinal products depending on their mode of action. Another example mentioned in the manual is plasters with capsaicin. They are intended to be used as local analgesia in order to treat muscular, rheumatic, or neuralgic pains. Given that the plaster is acting as a carrier for the substance, the product achieves its principal intended action by pharmacological means and should therefore be considered a medicinal product.

3. Organs and Other Products Derived from the Human Body

According to Directive 2001/83/EC, the substance which comprises a medicinal product may include 'any matter irrespective of origin which may be human' (for example, human blood and human blood products).[100] Prior to this Directive, the CJEU had stated that an organ for transplantation was a medicinal product for all legal effects and purposes in the well-known case of *Veedfalds v Arhus Amtskommune*.[101] There have been different approaches taken by MSs, however, in relation to whether the development risk defence applies in relation to such 'products'. In Spain, the term 'medicine' includes 'blood, plasma and any substance with human origin (fluids, glands, excretions, secretions, tissue and any other substances) as well as its derivatives, when used for therapeutic purposes.'[102] In Germany, the term 'medicinal product' does not apply to organs intended for transplantation.[103] The rules applicable to manufacturers lack uniformity, given such differing legal definitions. The Spanish categorization of

---

[96] Art 1(4) Council Directive 90/385/EEC.

[97] Art 1(4)(a) Council Directive 90/385/EEC.

[98] MHRA 'Medical Devices and Medicinal Products' Bulletin no 17, last amended in February 2011.

[99] 'Manual on borderline and classification in the Community regulatory framework for medical devices' (released on 23 August 2011). This manual has been issued by the Working Party on borderline and classification comprised of Commission services, experts of MSs and other stakeholders.

[100] Art 1(3).

[101] Case C-203/99 of 10 May 2001 (n 53).

[102] Art 46 of the Spanish Law 29/2006, 26 of July, on the Guarantees and Rational Use of Medicines and other Medical Devices.

[103] § 2(3) 8 AMG.

medicines encompasses human organs, whereas the German one does not; therefore the defendant would not be able to benefit from the development risk defence in Spain (unless a publicly funded hospital were involved), but would be able to do so in Germany. In France, the defence would not be available as organs are human body parts and no distinction is made between public or private hospitals.

The potential also exists for product liability claims when the use of assisted reproductive technologies (ART) involving donor-assisted conception produces children with genetic defects. Sperm could then be subject to product liability, with the producer being the ART clinic.[104] Blood supplied by a blood service may also be considered a product in line with the Directive. Given the difficulties victims have experienced in making successful claims arising out of the receipt of contaminated blood, however, special compensation funds have been created in MSs, such as France and Spain.[105]

Are hospital-prepared products put into circulation if they never leave the sphere of control of the producer? The answer is yes, according to the aforementioned case of *Veedfalds*. One of the main issues here was whether the hospital in question had actually put the product (perfusion fluid used to prepare the kidney for transplantation) into circulation. The CJEU decided that the provision of a specific medical service, which consisted of preparing an organ for transplantation, meant that it had been put into circulation. Whenever the producer puts the product at the disposal of a third party, whether it is the consumer or the conveyor, then this requirement is met. It is put into circulation 'when it is used during the provision of a specific medical service', regardless of the payment (or lack thereof) made by the user.

The producer is excluded from liability if the product was neither manufactured by it for sale or any form of distribution for economic purposes, nor manufactured or distributed by it in the course of its business.[106] In the *Veedfalds* case, the hospital invoked this defence but the CJEU held that a defective product which had been manufactured and used in the course of a specific medical service did not fall within the scope of this provision, even if it was financed entirely from public funds and provided without the patient having to pay for the product as such.

D. The Relationship Between Safety and Defectiveness

The EU is particularly interested in promoting a high level of product safety,[107] establishing requirements governing the testing of new medicines; criteria for quality safety and efficacy; and rules relating to marketing authorization, labelling, and advertising. This part of the chapter explores the relationship between product safety

---

[104] Even in the USA, where laws usually exempt blood, blood products, and human tissues and organs from product liability suits, there are some exceptions. In the state of New York, where no such 'blood shield laws' exist, sperm is considered a commercial product and has given rise to a successful product liability claim (see N MacReady, 'Sperm is Subject to Product Liability Laws in the US (2009) 10 *The Lancet Oncology* 451).

[105] In France, it was established pursuant to Law 91-1406, 31 December, and in Spain, by Law 14/2002, 5 June, on social benefits for persons with hemophilia or other congential coagulopathies who have developed hepatits C as a result of having received treatment with coagulation concentrates in the public health care system, and other tax rules, and Royal Decree 377/2003, 28 March, which establishes the procedure to obtain social benefits for persons with hemophilia or other congenital coagulopathies who have developed hepatitis C as a result of having received treatment with coagulation concentrates in the public health care syste, amended by Royal Decree 477/2006, 21 March.

[106] See Art 7(c) Council Directive 85/374/EEC.

[107] Directive 2001/95/EC of the European Parliament and of the Council of 3 December 2001 on general product safety [2001] OJ L11/4 and Regulation (EC) No 765/2008 setting out the requirements for accreditation and market surveillance relating to the marketing of products and repealing Regulation (EEC) No 339/93 [2008] OJ L218/30.

and product liability regulation. It analyses two issues: first, the role safety plays in the definition of a defective product; and secondly, whether compliance with safety regulations may be used by manufacturers as a defence. The challenge of disconnection between regulation and technological development comes to the fore once again.

1. When is a Product Defective?

According to the Product Liability Directive, a product becomes defective 'when it does not provide the safety which a person is entitled to expect'.[108] Although reference is made under English law to the 'consumer expectation test', the defectiveness of the product should be determined by reference 'to the lack of the safety which the *public at large* is entitled to expect', as stated in the Preamble to the Directive. It is the general public's expectations that are assessed and not those of regulatory authorities, judges, victims, or producers. The 'public at large' is not a knowledgeable purchaser making informed choices, but the ignorant general public.

There is some debate as to whether we should take into account the social perception of risk,[109] or the scientific perception of risk.[110] The latter is based on probabilities, and therefore would seem to be always reasonable, whereas the former includes other variables, and may be unreasonable. Given the text of the Product Liability Directive, social perception will be relevant.[111] The expectation of the general public as regards product safety is not factual but normative. It has been argued that 'the general public is not entitled to expect the safety the product *actually has*, which can be 99.9 per cent, but it is entitled to expect the safety the product *ought to have*.'[112] So even if the general public were informed about manufacturing defects, and the fact that products would not always be 100 per cent free of manufacturing defects, this does not shift the burden of risk to the victim.

To a large extent, the concept of a safe product (Product Safety Directive)[113] runs parallel to the concept of a non-defective product (Product Liability Directive). There is perhaps surprisingly, however, no correlation between the two concepts. An unsafe product is not necessarily defective if there is sufficient information about the adverse effects, for example,[114] and a safe product may be defective because of a manufacturing defect, which only affects some products during the manufacturing process, that are otherwise well designed. The reason for this is that the Product Liability Directive aims to provide a mechanism for financial compensation and balances the risks between the interests of the individual manufacturer and the individual victim. In contrast, the

---

[108] Art 6.

[109] DA Kysar, 'The Expectations of Consumers' (2003) 103 *Columbia Law Review* 1700, 1768.

[110] MA Geistfeld, *Principles of Products Liability* (Foundation Press 2006) 44–5.

[111] Contrast this with the USA, where the *Restatement (Third) of Torts: Product Liability* has introduced the professional judgement test. Since expectations of safety will be influenced by what physicians say, the learned intermediary rule for drugs and medical devices applies. Section 6(c) states: 'A prescription drug or medical device is not reasonably safe due to defective design if the foreseeable risks of harm posed by the drug or medical device are sufficiently great in relation to its foreseeable therapeutic benefits that a reasonable health-care provider, knowing of such foreseeable risks and therapeutic benefits, would not prescribe the drug or medical device for any class of patient.'

[112] C van Dam, *European Tort Law* (OUP 2006) 380, having analysed contaminated blood cases in several European jurisdictions. Emphasis added.

[113] Directive 2001/95/EC of the European Parliament and of the Council of 3 December 2001 on general product safety [2001] OJ L11/4, revised in 2004.

[114] Information plays a key role in determining whether a product is defective. When Art 6(1)(a) of the Directive refers to 'the presentation of the product' as a circumstance to be taken into account, it includes information and directions for use. However, information per se is not enough to exonerate producers from liability if it is possible to produce a safer product with no extra financial burden, and this higher safety level does not affect the benefit of the product.

Product Safety Directive is focused on prevention and thus seeks to balance the risks between the individual manufacturer and the public at large.[115]

The defectiveness of the product must be determined on the basis of safety regulation that was in force when the product was put into circulation.[116] This deviates from the general rules of negligence that take into account the state of the art at the time immediately before the realization of the risk.[117] Again, we face the problem of determining when a product is put into circulation. The Explanatory Memorandum to the first Draft Product Liability Directive referred to the fact that 'normally, an article has been put into circulation when it has been started off on the chain of distribution.'[118] National law in the area in some MSs does provide definitions, such as the Belgian law,[119] the Italian law,[120] and the Irish law—'products put into circulation *in any* Member State'—which must be compared to the broad definition of 'supplied' as understood under English law.[121]

In the case of *Declan O'Byrne v Sanofi Pasteur MSD Ltd and Sanofi Pasteur SA,* the CJEU found that the relevant time is when it leaves the producer's sphere of control: when the product 'is taken out of the manufacturing process and enters a marketing process in the form in which it is offered to the public in order to be used or consumed'.[122] It also stated that complex manufacturing and distribution arrangements within international groups of companies is a reality, so ascertaining industry's interests in the context of new health technologies can be quite difficult.

A number of important issues need to be addressed, given the global reach of the pharmaceutical industry. If a product is marketed for the first time in the USA, the dates to take into account are potentially the date when it was imported into the European Economic Area (EEA),[123] or the date it was distributed in each specific MS. According to the Directive, a person who imports into the EEA a product for sale, hire, leasing, or any form of distribution in the course of its business shall be deemed to be a producer within the meaning of the Directive.[124] This means that if a product is manufactured in China, then the victim can file a claim against the company that imported the product into the EEA. But if the importer has the product in storage for a couple of years before finally distributing it, would the product be put into circulation at the time the product was introduced in the EEA, or at the time it was supplied to the distributor? In a different scenario, if there is no novelty in the product, would a change of producer affect when it is put into circulation? What about generic medicines? All these issues require careful examination. They have not been fully addressed to date by the CJEU.

In 2000, the Commission published a *Guide to the implementation of directives based on the new approach and the global approach* ('Blue Guide'), which states that the placing on the market happens when the product is transferred from the stage of manufacture with the intention of distribution or use on the Community market.[125] According to

---

[115] Van Dam (n 112) 372. Compare with G Howells, 'The Relationship between Product Liability and Product Safety—Understanding a Necessary Element in European Product Liability through a Comparison with the U.S. Position' (2002) 39 *Washburn Law Journal* 305, 307: product liability litigation as a means of regulatory control may not be as necessary in Europe, given the nature and scope of product safety regulatory regimes.

[116] Art 6(1)(c) Council Directives 85/374/EEC.

[117] Van Dam (n 112) 378.   [118] Recital 11.

[119] Art 6, Loi relative à la responsabilité des produits défectueux 1991 [Liability for Defective Products]: a product is put into circulation when the producer intends to indicate its use by transferring it to other people or using it for the advantage of third parties.

[120] Italian Presidential Decree 224 of 24 May 1988 (art 6(1)(c)) is now contained in arts 114 to 127 of the Legislative Decree 6 September 2005 no 206 approving the *Codice del Consumo.*

[121] Consumer Protection Act 1987.

[122] C-127/04 *O'Byrne v Sanofi Pasteur MSD Ltd and Sanofi Pasteur SA* [2006] ECR I-1313.

[123] Includes the MSs of the EU, as well as Norway, Iceland, and Liechtenstein.

[124] Art 3(2) Council Directive 85/374/EEC.   [125] Blue Guide, 18.

the guide, placing on the market is considered not to have happened where a product is held in inventory by the manufacturer. To state otherwise would incentivize manufacturers to produce large quantities of products in accordance with 'old' legal requirements, stockpile them in their warehouses, and then sell them over an extended period of time. Such criteria would appear to be applicable to new health technologies.[126]

2. The Defence of Regulatory Compliance

EU regulation of medicinal products is the oldest, most extensive, and most complex of any product regulatory system.[127] In areas where regulatory standards exist, should compliance with regulatory standards for products provide a defence against a finding of liability? The pharmaceutical industry has argued strongly in support of the introduction of a defence of regulatory compliance.[128] It has been argued that the defence should be applicable in circumstances where the product is fully compliant with the existing regulatory regime. It has been suggested that it is not for the courts to second-guess or undermine regulations that deal comprehensively with the safety of particular products.

There are two strong arguments that can be made in opposition to introducing such a defence. First, the differing pace at which technological developments take place and the necessary amendments to regulatory frameworks that follow is inevitable. Technology tends to advance faster than the law. This regulatory disconnection is not necessarily a bad thing;[129] however, liability should not be put on hold while regulatory consensus is reached. Secondly, product liability is (theoretically) based on strict liability, where the 'reasonable manufacturer' standard, which includes compliance with regulatory norms, is not a shield against liability. Courts in France and Spain are very clear on this issue and do not allow the defence of regulatory compliance in tort-based cases. An approach to fault that is dependent upon economic analysis may tend to support a deferential approach to regulators,[130] but it is contrary to the strict liability principle enshrined in the Directive. The Commission has not submitted any proposal for the introduction of such a defence,[131] although we may assume that the industry will continue to lobby for its introduction.

This defence of regulatory compliance must be distinguished from the defence which is already available in the Product Liability Directive: the producer shall not be liable if it shows 'that the defect is due to compliance of the product with mandatory regulations issued by the public authorities.'[132] The manufacturer may not use as a defence the fact that the product has complied with mandatory legislation issued by public authorities; however, it could be used as a defence if it was obliged to manufacture the product in a specific way which subsequently turned out to be defective.

It is interesting to draw a comparison with Directive 2001/95, which establishes a presumption of safety when a product conforms to national or EU regulation.[133] In the absence of such regulation, the circumstances to be taken into account are, among others, the state of the art of the technology, as well as reasonable consumer

---

[126] Interpretative Document of the Commission's services placing on the market of Medical Devices (16 November 2010).

[127] C Hodges, *European Regulation of Consumer Product Safety* (OUP 2005) 38.

[128] As explained in the Commission's *Third Report* (2006) 11.

[129] As Brownsword (n 2) 288, has observed, 'in the interest of regulatory legitimacy and democracy, it is important to take time out to debate the developments that have taken place and to determine how the regulatory framework should be adjusted.'

[130] M Lee, 'Safety, Regulation and Tort: Fault in Context' (2011) 74 *Modern Law Review* 555, 557.

[131] Commission's *Fourth Report* (2011) 12.   [132] Art 7(d).   [133] Art 3(2).

expectations concerning safety.[134] When the product does not meet these requirements of safety, however, there is no claim for compensation based on breach of safety. As regards medicines and other pharmaceutical products, there are no technical standards as such, only rules on procedural matters with respect to how to conduct clinical and medical research, as well as licensing authorization.

E. Conclusion

New health technologies, such as the examples provided in this chapter, may create new legal problems, or highlight old unresolved conflicts. Liability is a difficult topic to regulate through direct governance at EU level, given the diverse traditions at MS level. In order to bring about a greater uniformity in the law, a number of initiatives have been pursued, such as drafting non-binding principles[135] (so-called 'soft law') or establishing a binding common private law code. In any case, the Product Liability Directive may be inadequate to face the new problems posed by new health technologies, particularly as medical devices and medicinal products are unlike any other products.

This chapter sought to analyse the impact new health technologies have (and will continue to have) on EU product liability law, with particular reference to risks, markets, and rights. Such analysis revealed a lack of uniformity at MS level in relation to victims' rights to claim compensation as a result of suffering harm through the use of certain products that are regulated under particular product liability regimes, such as pharmaceuticals and human tissue products. This was highlighted through an examination of the development risk defence. Notwithstanding such lack of uniformity, however, it was shown that the market for new health technologies has not been affected as a result. In addition, reference was made to how risk has been interpreted in the context of the relationship between product safety and product liability legislation.

As regards rights, I would like to make one final observation. Throughout this chapter I have tried to highlight the impact governance may have on the right to compensation. The aforementioned lack of uniformity and the legal uncertainty it brings may impact upon one other right: namely, the right to seek health care services in another MS. Lack of understanding about how to make a complaint about medical treatment or how to obtain compensation may prove to be a barrier to obtaining medical treatment in another MS. Directive 2011/24/EU of the European Parliament and of the Council of 9 March 2011 on the application of patients' rights in cross-border health care states that in MSs where medical treatment takes place, there is a need to ensure that health care providers provide all relevant information to enable patients to make informed choices. This includes 'their insurance cover or other means of personal or collective protection with regard to professional liability', as well as providing information with regard to the mechanisms that are available for patients to 'seek remedies in accordance with the legislation of the Member State of treatment, if they suffer harm arising from the healthcare they receive.'[136] This raises a number of new questions: Does this information include information about the relevant product liability law? Would general information be enough or is more detailed information required? If so, how detailed must it be? Would patients seeking health care in another MS then be in a better position than local patients, who are not usually informed about such issues? Legal uniformity is not necessary, but legal certainty is. The lack of it may, in fact, hinder patients' rights.

---

[134] Art 3(3)(e) and (f).
[135] As suggested by ME Arbour, 'Compensation for Damage Caused by Defective Drugs: European Private Law between Safety Requirements and Free-Market Values' (2004) 10 *European Law Journal* 97, 101.
[136] Art 4(2)(b) and (c) of the Directive 2011/24/EU of the European Parliament and of the Council of 9 March 2011 on the application of patients' rights in cross-border healthcare [2011] OJ L88/45.

Govering the Spaces In-Between: Law and Legitimacy in New Health Technologies

Graeme Laurie

This contribution is concerned far more with the limits of law and legal intervention in the regulation of new health technologies than it is with any particular legal measure, response, or framework. It draws on the academic and field experiences of the author who has had the opportunity to engage with, and reflect on, the considerable regulatory challenges thrown up by the phenomenon of biobanking. Although biobanking is usually understood as a practice rather than a technology per se, its advent has generated many of the same questions raised by novel technologies about the role of European laws and legal regimes in dealing with uncertainty, risk, unknown future trajectories, and the implications of the same for individual rights. It is argued that the inherent nature of biobanking requires regulatory responses that are not easily accommodated by existing—or even future—legal mechanisms. Indeed, it is suggested that it is better not to talk of regulation at all in this context because of its association, at least in public understanding, with top-down, hard law, command and control responses. While this might be something of a caricature, these features are insufficient—and potentially unhelpful—in any regime applied to biobanks. Rather, it is advanced here that it is preferable to talk in terms of the need for appropriate governance mechanisms that are reflexive and adaptive to the particularities of these new practices and associated technologies, while acknowledging that reflexivity can also appear in some regulatory regimes. The point, however, is not a simple semantic one: it is driven by the need to design adaptive systems that can both respond to ever-changing features of biobanks and that can serve additional purposes when the limits of law are reached. Importantly, it is not novelty per se that poses the biggest challenge; it is a particular aspect, the uncertainty generated by the setting-up and operation of biobanks, that leads us to question the role and legitimacy of law in this context. The central argument is that law in general, including the gamut of laws that might be cast as 'European', can provide robust architectures and spaces within which these practices and technologies can be introduced and developed but legal regimes have little of value to contribute to the governance of the spaces in-between the foundations and pillars of these structures. Here—in the liminal spaces of certainty/uncertainty, protection/promotion, hype/reality, and promise/expectation—we require responsive governance mechanisms which are, in turn, driven by human ethical practices that can anticipate and respond effectively to the technical practices and developments as they take shape. This requires, in turn, that scientific and ethical developments co-evolve in mutually beneficial and durably effective ways.

I have argued elsewhere that the inadequate nature of the relationship between law and ethics in the new health technologies sector is revealed in particularly acute forms in the context of biobanks.[1] Biobanks are collections of human tissue and data brought together as a research resource; usually of considerable duration; sometimes with associated scientific research questions—such as the investigation of a particular condition or disease; but often with no particular research agenda. UK Biobank is an example of this last approach, being a collection of samples and data from 500,000 participants to be accessed in the future for the broad and yet-to-be-defined objective of 'health-related research'. The challenges are manifold not least because it is not possible to inform participants about possible or likely future uses of their samples and tissues and because it is not possible to know what kinds of applications for access will be forthcoming, from whom, from where, or for what ends. The prospective longitudinal nature of these entities makes it very difficult to plan a suitable regulatory environment. As a result, the adequacies of existing legal and ethical regimes to address these challenges are frequently called into question, not least whether approaches to consent to participate in medical research can sufficiently protect individuals' rights and interests and whether longer term uses, including commercial uses, can be appropriately controlled and in line with participants' original expectations about management of the resource.

While there is much existing literature and many assessments on the inadequacies of laws in responding to some of the core challenges of biobanks, it is often unquestioningly assumed that more law is the answer. I believe that we should challenge this assumption. There are, of course, two ways in which law might respond: (a) extension and/or revision of existing provisions in key areas such as consent, privacy, access etc., and (b) design and adoption of bespoke legal responses. As to the latter, some jurisdictions have legislated specifically for biobanks, such as Iceland (Act on Biobanks no 110/2000), Estonia (Human Genes Research Act 2000), Latvia (Human Genome Research Law 2003), Sweden (Biobanks in Medical Care Act 2002: 297), Norway (Act Relating to Biobanks 2003), Portugal (Law 12/2005, of 26 January, on personal genetic information, provisions on genetic databases), and Spain (Law 14/2007, of 3 July, on Biomedical Research, title on biobanks). As yet, there has been no EU attempt to intervene explicitly under the mantle of biobanking. Softer law options include the Council of Europe's Recommendation (2006)4 on research on biological materials of human origin and the OECD's Guidelines on Human Biobanks and Genetic Research Databases (2009). Yet it is not clear that such biobank exceptionalism is merited, particularly since the approaches are so diverse that they do not facilitate—and, indeed, might militate against—interoperability, which would at least be one sound scientific reason to seek some degree of harmonization through legal or quasi-legal intervention at various European levels. Furthermore, in the European Union (EU) context, it is not apparent that such interventions are legitimate on the commonly understood principles of subsidiarity and proportionality that underpin all EU legal measures, that is, the need to demonstrate that intervention is necessary, defensible relative to the risks and benefits, and likely to be more effective than EU Member States acting alone. There are, in fact, good reasons to question whether more law will result in a regulatory regime that is more effective in this context.

Part of the reason for this takes us back to the relationship between law and ethics in the health research context. Many of the contours of that relationship have been shaped by top-down regulatory responses that have distracted us from an appreciation of both

---

[1] G Laurie, 'Reflexive Governance in Biobanking: On the Value of Policy Led Approaches and the Need to Recognise the Limits of Law' (2011) 130 *Human Genetics* 347.

the limits of law and the potentially rich contribution of ethical engagement. This has left our regulatory environment impoverished as a result. In particular, the requirement of ethical review of scientific research protocols—driven in large part by the adoption of the Clinical Trials Directive 2001/20/EC—has failed to generate evidence that we now have a more ethically robust and defensible review system for science and research involving human participants. Rather, charging ethics committees through law to act as the gatekeepers of safe and effective research through a process of up-front, hypothesis-driven, risk-averse research approval has, arguably, led us to lose sight of the crucially important reflective element of ethical engagement. Inspectorate regulatory regimes, with a focus on institutional risk, encourage tick-box mentalities and promote a tendency towards systems of bureaucratic compliance over genuine engagement with ethical and social issues. Today's science and funding culture is not disposed to open-ended enquiry. It operates within an environment that mandates *ex ante* ethical approval and supports *ex post* sanction for failure to comply with an increasingly overwhelming body of bureaucracy. Let me be clear: this is not an argument in favour of a carte blanche culture of research regulation. It is instead a plea to consider whether our research management regimes operate as well as they might, given that questions of safety and efficacy that so dominate the realm of the clinical trial are not the sole or even primary considerations in other research endeavours such as biobanking. This is not to suggest that questions of safety and efficacy should not be addressed; rather, it is to propose that research regimes need to be complemented by other arrangements that are not driven by such considerations.

The clinical trial model of 'doing research' has often been lauded as the gold standard approach in scientific terms, albeit that this is not a position that goes unchallenged. It has heavily influenced and restricted both our legal and ethical thinking and has come to dominate the regulatory landscape. This too must be challenged with the objective of designing regulatory and, crucially, as I go on to elaborate, governance mechanisms that appropriately reflect the scientific objectives sought, adequately identify and protect participant interests, and also serve to promote the common good of supporting ethically sound, scientifically robust research. Underpinning all of this is the imperative to strive for proportionate governance and regulation, that is, not adding unnecessarily to regulatory burden and ensuring that what is in place is fit-for-purpose and remains so.

I suggest then that more regulation and more law in the biobanking context is not the answer. This is partly because we have sufficient existing legal measures and regimes to protect the core participant interests at stake—whether these be through the Data Protection Directive 95/46/EC (or the new draft Regulation COM(2012) 11 final), the Tissues and Cells Directives 2004/23/EC, 2006/17/EC, and 2006/86/EC, or broader appeals to Council of Europe human rights measures. These measures provide a legal architecture that identifies which rights and interests at stake, who deserves protection and how this should be achieved. In doing so, however, they create a legal edifice that is largely characterized by top-down, risk-averse, and protectionist models. This is not well suited to deliver appropriate and proportionate governance of the kind that can move us beyond concerns about risk and harm prevention and towards approaches that promote both scientific and participant interests in maximizing the outcomes from research. Moreover, when considering the challenges of the uncertainties generated by practices such as biobanks—equally about what research will be done and when this will occur—we come to realize the limits of law and many legal devices for their failure to deliver on these objectives. Two examples illustrate the point and demonstrate that what is required are suitable governance mechanisms that operate within the architectural and structural frameworks of existing laws and that assist in the careful judgements and ethical steering that are essential to ensure that research remains on course and that participants continue to trust the enterprise to which they have contributed.

Consent is a stalwart element of ethical and lawful health research regulation, albeit that it is not mandated in the context of research involving personal data. The Clinical Trials dynamic—and other sources such as data protection legislation (see Chapter 2)—would suggest, however, that when consent is sought it is *informed* consent that is the requisite standard. This requires that participants be fully informed about the nature, risks, consequences, and alternatives to participation. This is simply not possible in the biobanking realm—specific and explicit consent cannot be obtained. Rather, it is argued and increasingly accepted that *broad* consent to participate in biobanking is the most that can be achieved whereby participants agree to the broad proposition to contribute to a resource when its future uses remain undetermined. This is justified ethically by an ongoing commitment to keep participants informed as and when developments occur. If, however, we consider the current version of the Data Protection Regulation, draft Article 4.8 makes it clear that:

'...the data subject's consent' means any freely given specific, informed and explicit indication of his or her wishes by which the data subject, either by a statement or by a clear affirmative action, signifies agreement to personal data relating to them being processed.

This generates two important issues for biobank governance: first, consent cannot be the lawful basis for processing personal data in these projects; secondly, some other basis must be found or such projects are doomed. This particular legal view of consent is a very traditional view of 'informed consent' and raises the prospect of a reduced role for consent and one which is not live to the fact that people can agree to be informed after the fact about what is being done with their data and samples. As to other legitimate bases for processing data in biobanks, we are likely to see an increased role in appeals to public interest to justify lawful processing (see draft Articles 81 and 83). However, this begs further important questions: what counts as the public interest and how is this to be judged and monitored over time?

This brings me to my last point about the need to govern appropriately the liminal spaces in-between existing legal frameworks and within which biobanks must operate. I have suggested earlier that it is the uncertain nature of biobanking and new health technologies that raises most challenges for law and leads us to question its legitimacy. We have also seen that a key feature of any regulatory or governance regime must be its ability to remain fit-for-purpose over time. Law can often ossify our concerns at a particular moment in time, leaving legal regimes ill-equipped to respond to an ever-changing research environment. To address this I have argued elsewhere for systems of *reflexive governance* in biobanking (see n 1). Briefly, reflexive governance is both about in-parallel partnership in governance in the face of future uncertainty and the facilitation of mutual learning from experience. It requires ongoing ethical oversight of research and regular interaction with researchers to respond efficiently and effectively to challenges as and when they arise. An example of this in action is the UK Biobank Ethics and Governance Council which was created in tandem with the development of the scientific protocol. It has monitored and advised UK Biobank through set-up, recruitment, and now into its access phase. Many unanticipated issues have arisen along the way and evidence of its working is publicly available from its website: <www.egcukbiobank.org.uk>. Questions about what counts as public interest and how far participants should be informed are discussed and decided as the project develops. The practical contribution and added value of the approach is that it does not require bespoke legal intervention nor is it constrained by any such legal snapshot in time. It operates within the liminal spaces created by legal regulatory architectures and which generate as yet unresolved questions and unmet needs about how research should best proceed and remain live to participants' evolving expectations, hopes, and desires.

The effectiveness and legitimacy of such approaches can only be judged by their performance over time. That legitimacy is not, however, dependent on law and legal intervention through regulation, but rather on human ethical practices exercised within existing legal structures that are complemented by approaches such as reflexive governance.

The Promise of European Regulation of New Health Technologies in a Time of Ageing Populations

Belén Crespo Sánchez-Eznarriaga

When discussing health technologies, two aspects should be emphasized: their contribution to the improvement of personal and public health and their growing importance in the cost determination of all public health systems. The development of any European legislation on this subject should guarantee the safety and efficacy of these health technologies as well as facilitate innovation and rapid access to the market for their use as a health resource. Measures should be promoted that avoid inequities in access and patient availability as well as creating the development of competitiveness in a transparent setting. At the same time, there is a need to establish mechanisms that permit access to both clinical assessments identifying benefit-risk ratio and the evaluation of incremental cost-effectiveness, so as to understand the impact on health and the economy at the time of their authorization. This is necessary, regardless of whether the authorization should not be refused for economic reasons or that these aspects are assessed at the time of fixing prices or decision-making on reimbursement. In this sense, legislation should be transparent and foreseeable for the industry. It is equally necessary to incorporate citizens in decision-making on the use of resources, to consider the ethical aspects of the use of these technologies, and to respect the conditioning factors and specificities of each Member State.

Traditionally only medicines, medical devices, and medical and surgical procedures used in medical care have been considered as health technologies. However, organization systems within which medical care as well as the interventions of public health are provided, organization of health care, screening programmes, and health services or measures that have a possible impact on the health of populations or specific groups of people should be added. This approach would incorporate tools such as the technologies of health information and communications (TIC) and eHealth, a technological support in health care practice. These technologies compile information on citizens, their lifestyle habits and state of health, and on patients and their health interventions and will be determinant in the development of the future health model, since the possibilities of growth in health knowledge and its conditioning factors which may be derived from the exploitation of the compiled information is evident to all those concerned.

To broaden the framework is essential at this time when solutions are being sought to make health systems sustainable and efficient, and using these technological resources in an optimal manner is an integral part of these solutions. The health model should be directed towards the resolution of the problems derived from an aging population, which has been identified as the most important cause of the increasing health costs in countries of our environment. Together with this factor, chronic diseases which greatly affect quality of life and also place a burden on our health systems should be mentioned.

The challenge is to achieve that the elderly have an autonomous lifestyle in the best possible health conditions and that prevention prevails over treatment. The approach should be integral in order to be efficient and within this framework the combination of health technologies must occupy a prominent position. Nevertheless, their introduction should always be accompanied by economic assessments which demonstrate their cost-effectiveness. These assessments should bear in mind both their sole use, which is how they are going to be employed on most occasions, and their combined use. Although, until recently, the lack of economic assessment studies could be justified by the scarcity of information available on the use of health technologies, the recent incorporation of the technologies of health information and communications (TIC and eHealth) point to a promising future as regards having accessible and quality information available on health and the use of technologies. This will bring a decisive change in the knowledge of collective and individual health in coming years and, consequently, in the approach to health problems.

With regard to health technologies, a different level of legislative development is seen depending on whether the object is medicines or medical devices. In the case of medicines, and after more than forty-five years of European legislation, it can be confirmed that we have a highly harmonious and responsible system that functions and permits the introduction in the market of technologies of all types of medicinal product directed towards the promotion of health, prevention, diagnosis, and treatment of diseases in our population. Within this framework, medicinal products have an evolutionary and transparent legislation which contains the necessary tools to guarantee the quality, safety, and efficacy of the approved medicines. However, this same legislation is facing significant challenges in incorporating new technologies and therapies, some of which already exist (cell therapy, genetic therapy, and tissue engineering), whereas others are still emerging (nanomedicines and regenerative and personalized medicine) and are difficult to predict as regards their evolution and health results. To quote an example, the rapidity of genome sequencing makes it foreseeable that in the medium term we will have the genome identified for each individual. Obviously this will radically change the way in which medicines are prepared, targeted, and selected for treatments. A personalized medicine or one better adapted to each genetic profile will emerge and this will need new regulations as well as new health technologies which permit its development and lend support, having to respond, among other challenges, to management of the vast quantity of information produced.

In the case of medical devices, the legislation, although based on the same principles, is more liberal and its procedures are more open and less interventionist. This has its consequence in a greater variability in the model from country to country. Standing out as a paradigm are the accreditation structures, or in other words, the Notified Bodies whose development and judicial nature are of a different character across Europe, in some cases being public and in others private with very different results being produced. At the present time when the new European Union (EU) legislation is being prepared for medical devices, it is evident to all concerned that the crisis caused by PIP mammary implant fraud is going to play a determinant role in the approach to market regulation. One is able to venture that, without doubt, protection of citizens will be strengthened and there will be stricter and more transparent control mechanisms in this regulation.

The European system is appropriately structured and functions correctly and its network assessment model is efficient for all types of technologies. However, the present legislation available in health technologies does not include prior verification of their being effective when applied. For example, the loss of competitiveness of the EU in investigation and the scarcity of clinical trials when compared to other markets is a demonstrated fact. Also a reality is the question of whether the procedures being employed for the development of advanced therapies are appropriate for these products to reach the market and produce value as regards health results or whether we should act in a more proactive manner. Another example is to be found in the field of medicines and medical devices where the preoccupation is whether European legislation is providing an answer in terms of the safety of the products and raw materials emerging from a globalized world with different manufacturing quality standards. On another plane, voices have arisen requesting that the technologies authorized for the European market have an economic assessment measured in terms of incremental cost-effectiveness which is taken into account at the time of their approval, regardless of whether the decisions on pricing and reimbursement correspond to each Member State.

If this is so, and time and again the legislation does not cover expectations or is expensive in its application, then the question is why do we continue to prepare legislation on a theoretical plane and do not wish to introduce the economic assessment of results during the preparation of regulations. At this time of important economic crisis where the European health systems are revealing real problems of sustainability, the question arises of whether we should continue preparing legislation as regards health technologies in the same way. The most recent legislation on pharmacovigilance should be taken as an example. A new and highly responsible model has been designed but which implies in its application many resources with an additional elevated cost with regard to the model functioning up to now. In these times of economic crisis, its introduction could cause important economic dysfunctions in the Member States that have to meet a deadline for its fulfilment.

The regulation of the new health technologies should be equipped with agile mechanisms which promote and strengthen investigation and the introduction in the market of effective products and systems which allow Member States to meet the challenges arising from the aging population and the prevalence of chronic diseases. It is important to bear in mind that these technologies are often going to be used in combination in the same patient, and this should be duly considered. In the same way, the regulation of new health technologies should respond to an environment of a globalized world and should therefore adopt measures conducive to taking advantage of opportunities and avoiding risks, while fulfilling due guarantees for the citizens. Ethical factors and citizen participation in decision-making should play an important role.

In a context of economic crisis, it is expected that health technologies and their regulation should fulfil criteria of quality, safety, and efficacy as well as being effective and helping to maintain health systems. New technologies should be incorporated following an evaluation of their impact measured in terms of health and economic results. Mechanisms must be established to permit availability of scientific and economic assessments which identify the benefit–risk ratio and the health and economic impact of these technologies so as to introduce in the market those that contribute verifiable added advantages to the health of corresponding populations.

PART III

REGULATORY THEORY, REGULATORY INNOVATION, EUROPEAN LAW, AND NEW HEALTH TECHNOLOGIES

9

Risk, Legitimacy, and EU Regulation of Health Technologies

*Anne-Maree Farrell**

A. Introduction

The successful management of risks to public health has become an important way in which the EU seeks to enhance its legitimacy. This chapter explores the relationship between risk and legitimacy in the context of European Union (EU) regulation of health technologies. This will be done through an examination of EU-wide risk regulation regimes that have been established in relation to organs and blood,[1] pursuant to Article 168(4)(a) TFEU.[2] As health technologies, these human biological materials have been used to enhance or contribute to health through the prevention, diagnosis, or treatment of disease, as well as the alleviation of disability.[3] Indeed, blood has been described as

* An earlier version of this chapter was presented at a seminar held at the University of Nottingham in March 2010, which was part of the ESRC-funded seminar series *European Law and New Health Technologies* (RES-45-26-0764). I would like to thank the participants at this seminar for the feedback received, as well as Mark Flear, Tamara Hervey, Ron Peek, and Barbara Prainsack for their thoughtful and incisive reviews on subsequent drafts of the chapter. Part of the research for this chapter also draws on work done whilst in receipt of the ESRC research grant: *Risk Safety and Consent in Contemporary Blood Services in the UK: Perspectives from Sociology and Law* (RES-062-23-2741); and the University of Manchester Wellcome Strategic Programme: *The Human Body: its Scope Limits and Future*. The support of both the Wellcome Trust and the ESRC is gratefully acknowledged.

[1] In examining blood as a case study in this chapter, I focus solely on the risk regulation regime established under Directive 2002/98/EC of the European Parliament and of the Council of 27 January 2003 setting standards of quality and safety for the collection, testing, processing, storage and distribution of human blood and blood components and amending Directive 2001/83/EC, OJ L33 (Blood Directive). The Blood Directive establishes an EU-wide risk regulation regime in relation to 'human blood and blood components'. 'Blood' is defined as whole blood collected from a donor and processed either for transfusion or for further manufacturing (Art 3(a)); and 'blood component' is defined as a therapeutic constituent of blood (red cells, white cells, platelets, plasma) (Art 3(b)). I note that a separate regulatory regime has been established in relation to medicinal products derived from human blood and plasma pursuant to Directive 2001/83/EC of the European Parliament and of the Council of 6 November 2001 on the Community code relating to medicinal products for human use, OJ L311. A detailed examination of this regime is outside the scope of this chapter. For an overview of the interrelationship between the two regimes, see A-M Farrell, 'Is the Gift Still Good? Examining the Politics and Regulation of Blood Safety in the European Union' (2006) 14 *Medical Law Review* 155.

[2] Art 168(4)(a) TFEU (ex Art 152(4)(a) EC) provides for the adoption of minimum harmonization 'measures setting high standards of quality and safety of organs and substances of human origin, blood and blood derivatives; these measures shall not prevent any Member State from maintaining or introducing more stringent measures.' Pursuant to Art 168(7) (ex Art 152(5) EC), 'the measures referred to in paragraph 4(a) shall not affect national provisions on the donation or medical use of organs and blood.'

[3] They have been described as 'essential' health technologies, see World Health Organization, Essential Health Technologies <www.who.int/eht/eht_intro/en/index.html> accessed 14 May 2012.

underpinning the development of modern medicine in the 20th century.[4] Due to scientific and technological advances, their use in treating a variety of (chronic) medical conditions has expanded rapidly in recent years.[5] As a result of such developments, blood and organs are not easily categorized as either old or new technologies and should be viewed for present purposes as combining elements of both.

Both blood and organs have socio-cultural, scientific, and commercial value. In socio-cultural terms, they are inextricably linked to individual identity, as well as national identity in the case of blood.[6] Scientific and technological developments in the 20th century led to the greatly expanded use of such materials in clinical settings.[7] As a result, blood and organs acquired commercial value in both regulated and 'black' markets.[8] The multi-valuing of these human biological materials has led to ethical complexity, policy conundrums, and regulatory tensions in risk governance.[9] Policy and regulatory initiatives in relation to their use have tended to focus on their socio-cultural value to the detriment of fully acknowledging how market and exchange relations impact upon the assessment and management of risk. For example, the consequences of the failure to take account of the dynamics of the blood market contributed to a lack of appropriate national political and regulatory oversight of the risks posed by the Human Immunodeficiency Virus (HIV). In turn, this contributed to significant rates of infection with the virus in many European countries in the 1980s.[10]

As encapsulated in Titmuss's notion of the 'gift relationship',[11] voluntary, unpaid donation is a key principle underpinning policy and regulation of both blood and organs in the European context.[12] For the most part, their procurement and supply is

---

[4] For an overview, see D Starr, *Blood: An Epic History of Medicine and Commerce* (Alfred A Knopf 1998).

[5] Cellular therapies have been developed to treat a variety of diseases and conditions, including the use of haematopoietic (or blood-forming) stem cells to treat damaged tissue and/or cells, see M Strong, A Farrugia, and P Rebulla, 'Stem Cell and Cellular Therapy Developments' (2009) 27 *Biologicals* 103. Blood stem cells are excluded under the Blood Directive and are instead covered under Directive 2004/23/EC of the European Parliament and of the Council of 31 March 2004 on setting standards of quality and safety for the donation, procurement, testing, processing, preservation, storage and distribution of human tissues and cells, OJ L102 (Tissues and Cells Directive). A detailed examination of this Directive is outside the scope of this chapter. In relation to organs, techno-scientific developments have also led to greater recourse to the use of 'expanded criteria donation' (ECD), see A Cronin, 'Making the Margins Mainstream: Strategies to Maximise the Donor Pool' in A-M Farrell, D Price, and M Quigley (eds), *Organ Shortage: Ethics Law and Pragmatism* (CUP 2011). In addition, detailed consideration has been given to the use of animal organs for transplantation into human beings (xenotransplantation), see S Fovargue, *Xenotransplantation and Risk: Regulating a Developing Biotechnology* (CUP 2011).

[6] D Nelkin, 'Cultural Perspectives on Blood' in EA Feldman and R Bayer (eds), *Blood Feuds: AIDS, Blood, and the Politics of Medical Disaster* (OUP 1999); P Rabinow, *French DNA—Trouble in Purgatory* (Chicago UP 1999); C Waldby and R Mitchell, *Tissue Economies: Blood, Organs and Cell Lines in Late Capitalism* (Duke UP 2006).

[7] A-M Farrell, *The Politics of Blood: Ethics Innovation and the Regulation of Risk* (CUP 2012) 3–4.

[8] For an overview of the evolution of national and global markets in blood, see Starr (n 4); for an overview of the global trade in organs, see N Scheper-Hughes, 'The Global Traffic in Human Organs' (2000) 41 *Current Anthropology* 191.

[9] Farrell (n 7) 4.

[10] Farrell (n 7) 4.

[11] RM Titmuss, *The Gift Relationship: From Human Blood to Social Policy* (George Allen & Unwin 1970).

[12] Although the term 'voluntary, unpaid blood donation' will be used in this chapter, it is more formally referred to as 'voluntary, non-remunerated blood donation'. A widely accepted definition of the term in the case of blood, is that a donation should be considered voluntary and non-remunerated 'if the person gives blood, plasma or cellular components of his/her own free will and receives no payment for it, either in the form of cash or in kind which could be considered a substitute

organized on a local and/or national basis by government-sponsored or not-for-profit organizations.[13] Public trust is central to the functioning and success of what is viewed as a valued public service. As was highlighted in the fallout from HIV blood contamination episodes, the loss of public trust that occurred in the wake of revelations over the circumstances that led to such episodes can have significant adverse consequences with regard to maintaining adequate levels of donation to meet clinical needs. This is in addition to raising broader questions about the credibility of those with political, regulatory, and institutional responsibility for procurement and supply.[14] Against this background, the legitimacy of regulatory initiatives with respect to effectively managing risk becomes an important, albeit problematic, issue in terms of redressing the loss of public trust, as well as maintaining it.

B. Risk, Legitimacy, and EU Regulation

How best to deal with conflict which emerges around the use of health technologies has been recognized as a perennial challenge for regulators at both national and supranational levels.[15] This has impacted upon the extent to which claims can be made about the legitimacy of regulation involving such technologies, which may permit their use provided that certain standards or conditions are met.[16] In broad terms, legitimacy has been defined as 'a product of the way in which decisions are taken and the nature and quality of decisions'.[17] Specifically, it has been suggested that the legitimacy of regulatory norms and regimes should be assessed by reference to four criteria: constitutional; democratic; functional and performance-based; values and objectives-based. In relation to the first criterion, it is a question of whether fair and just procedures are in place, overseen by constitutionally established institutions. In relation to the second, there is a need to assess whether regulatory standards provide for participation, transparency, deliberation, and accountability. The third takes into account the use of expertise, as well as effectiveness and efficiency; and the fourth considers what the underlying rationale is for the regulatory regime.[18] In this chapter, it is the relationship between

---

for money. This would include time off work other than that reasonably needed for the donation and travel. Small tokens, refreshments and reimbursements of direct travel costs are compatible with voluntary, non-remunerated donations', see para 9(d) of 98/463/EC Council Recommendation of 29 June 1998 on the Suitability of Blood and Plasma Donors and the Screening of Donated Blood in the European Community, OJ L203.

[13] K Healy, *Last Best Gifts: Altruism and the Market for Human Blood and Organs* (Chicago UP 2006) 15–22; see also Farrell (n 7) 30–2.

[14] Farrell (n 7) 175.

[15] R Brownsword, *Rights Regulation and the Technological Revolution* (OUP 2008) 1–11, 160; J Black, 'Constructing and Contesting Legitimacy and Accountability in Polycentric Regulatory Regimes' (2008) 2 *Regulation & Governance* 137, 137–9; ML Flear and S Ramshaw (eds), 'Symposium: New Technologies, European Law and Citizens' (2009) 16(1) *MJECL*.

[16] For the purposes of this chapter regulation is defined as the 'sustained and focused attempt to alter the behaviour of others according to standards and goals with the intention of producing a broadly defined outcome or outcomes, which may involve mechanisms of standard setting, information gathering and behaviour modification' (see J Black, 'What is Regulatory Innovation?' in J Black, M Lodge, and M Thatcher (eds), *Regulatory Innovation: A Comparative Analysis* (Edward Elgar 2005) 11.

[17] C Scott, 'Governing without Law or Governing without Government? New-ish Governance and the Legitimacy of the EU' (2009) 15 *ELJ* 160, 160–1.

[18] D Casey and C Scott, 'The Crystallization of Regulatory Norms' (2011) 38 *JLS* 76, 87, drawing on the work of J Black and D Rouch, 'The Development of Global Markets as Rule-Makers: Engagement and Legitimacy' (2008) 2 *Law and Financial Markets Review* 218.

legitimacy and effectiveness covered by the third criterion that is the focus of particular attention in the examination of EU risk regulation involving blood and organs.

Although they may be considered separately, legitimacy and effectiveness should also be seen as interrelated issues where there is pronounced conflict over what values or principles should be taken into account in regulatory design and implementation.[19] Attracting sufficient support for a particular regulatory regime may prove to be difficult in such circumstances. Regulators may need to pursue different, albeit complementary, approaches with a view to generating support for a particular regulatory intervention. While acceptance of such an intervention by those to whom it is addressed is seen as important to enhancing its legitimacy,[20] this may remain an aspirational goal where there is entrenched opposition, particularly in relation to ethically divisive issues.[21] Where the nature of such opposition has its origins in ethical conflict over new technologies, then the legitimacy of the regulatory regime (whether in part or in full) is likely to remain problematic, and its effectiveness may be undermined as a result. In the circumstances, Brownsword has suggested that it is probably best to view regulatory effectiveness as a 'matter of degree', which will require evaluation at various points of the regulatory cycle to deal with matters of 'compliance and resistance, of correction and revision'.[22]

In recent years, conflict over the assessment and management of risk involving health technologies, as well as how best to ensure that regulation operates as an effective technique of legitimation in this context, has assumed a prominent place on the EU political agenda. This has occurred against a backdrop of ongoing concerns about the EU suffering from a 'democratic deficit', which was said to contribute to its lack of overall legitimacy.[23] Various academic analyses were offered as to whether and, if so, why the EU suffers from a legitimacy problem,[24] in addition to suggestions being made as to how to address the problem through improvements in decision-making processes, accountability mechanisms, and the effectiveness and efficiency of (regulatory) outputs.[25] This process of critical reflection was given further impetus in the wake of the political fallout from the BSE crisis in the late 1990s.[26] The political scandal that developed in the wake of this crisis provided a catalyst for the reform of risk governance processes at EU level. Such reforms included a reorganization of the way in which scientific and other forms of expert advice were provided.[27] A more sophisticated

---

[19] Brownsword (n 15) 10, 11.   [20] Casey and Scott (n 18) 88.

[21] Brownsword (n 15) 9–10. On the need to make use of differentiating legitimation strategies in the context of a plurality of constituencies, see I Ayres and J Braithwaite, *Responsive Regulation* (OUP 2002) 87.

[22] Brownsword (n 15) 11.

[23] A Føllesdal, 'Legitimacy Theories of the European Union' ARENA Working Papers WP 15/2004, 3 <www.sv.uio.no/arena/english/research/publications/arena-publications/workingpapers/ workingpapers2004/04_15.xml> accessed 10 April 2012.

[24] G Majone, 'Regulatory Legitimacy' in G Majone (ed), *Regulating Europe* (Routledge 1996); A Moravcsik, 'In Defence of the "Democratic Deficit": Reassessing Legitimacy in the European Union' (2002) 40 *JCMS* 603; A Føllesdal and S Hix, 'Where There is a Democratic Deficit in the EU: A Response to Majone and Moravcsik' (2006) 44 *JCMS* 533; C Bickerton, 'Europe's Neo-Madisonians: Rethinking the Legitimacy of Limited Power in a Multi-Level Polity' (2011) 59 *Political Studies* 659, 660; B Rosamond, 'Supranational Governance as Economic Patriotism? The European Union, Legitimacy and the Reconstruction of State Space' (2012) 19 *JEPP* 324.

[25] F Scharpf, *Governing in Europe: Effective and Democratic?* (OUP 1999) 9.

[26] E Vos, 'Overcoming the Crisis of Confidence: Risk Regulation in an Enlarged European Union' Working Paper (University of Maastricht 2004) 3; E Vos, 'EU Food Safety Regulation in the Aftermath of the BSE Crisis' (2000) 23 *Journal of Consumer Policy* 227.

[27] Specifically, advice has been sought from those with ethics expertise as a way of mediating ethics and risk-based concerns that have arisen in relation to the use of new (health) technologies with a view to finding an acceptable political compromise which would allow such initiatives to go forward,

approach was taken to the interpretation of the precautionary principle in the context of risk assessment, management, and communication.[28] Independent agencies were created to manage risk in specific policy sectors.[29] There was also increased resort to the use of more deliberative forms of participation in decision-making processes,[30] as well as a commitment to using a range of new governance mechanisms.[31] Successful risk governance across a range of health technologies became a touchstone for enhancing the EU's legitimacy, with regulation operating as the preferred technique of legitimation.

Majone has described the EU as having many of the hallmarks of the regulatory state, although it should be seen as operating in a different way to that seen at national level. It has some, but not all, of the features of statehood, with its main state-like activity being its power to engage in social and economic regulation.[32] Regulation is largely designed and monitored in the context of non-majoritarian decision-making processes, which are informed by the provision of expert advice and deliberative stakeholder participation, where appropriate. Majone views this approach as much more suitable for complex and plural polities such as the EU, rather than relying on mechanisms of 'direct political accountability'.[33] The EU has used its regulatory powers to expand its range of activities and level of control, as well as to enhance its legitimacy.[34] Notwithstanding such expansionist tendencies, the ability of the EU to ensure effective implementation and evaluation of its regulatory activities has nevertheless been circumscribed by a number of factors, including the need to take account of the principles of subsidiarity and proportionality;[35] limited financial and personnel resources; and weak control mechanisms with regard to the enforcement of regulation at Member State level.

One of the main drivers of the growth in EU regulation in recent years has been the perceived need to engage in more effective risk governance.[36] It has been suggested that the EU has a specific approach to risk regulation that is underpinned by a commitment to the promotion of the single market.[37] This is particularly apparent in the context of regulating risk involving the manufacture, supply, and movement of goods within the

---

see H Gottweis, 'Governing Genomics in the 21st Century: Between Risk and Uncertainty' (2005) 24 *New Genetics and Society* 175, 189; S Jasanoff, *Designs on Nature: Science and Democracy in Europe and the United States* (Princeton UP 2005) 201.

[28] Commission, Communication from the Commission on the Precautionary Principle, COM (2000) 1 final.

[29] See eg the European Food Safety Authority (EFSA) <www.efsa.europa.eu> accessed 8 June 2012.

[30] Jasanoff (n 27) 89; C Skelcher and J Torfing, 'Improving Democratic Governance through Institutional Design: Civic Participation and Democratic Ownership in Europe' (2010) 4 *Regulation & Governance* 71, 76.

[31] Commission, *European Governance: A White Paper*, COM (2001) 428 final.

[32] G Majone, 'The Rise of the Regulatory State in Europe' (1994) 17 *West European Politics* 77.

[33] Majone (n 24) 286; see also M Lodge, 'Regulation, the Regulatory State and European Politics' (2009) 31 *West European Politics* 280, 288–9.

[34] G Majone, 'The Rise of the Regulatory State in Europe' (1994) 17 *West European Politics* 77, 93–4.

[35] See Art 5, TEU.

[36] C Hood, C Scott, and R Baldwin, *The Government of Risk: Understanding Risk Regulation Regimes* (OUP 2001) 4. Regulating risk has also come to be seen as a key activity of the 'regulatory state' more generally, see M Moran, 'Understanding the Regulatory State' (2002) 32 *British Journal of Political Science* 391, 407.

[37] M Lee, *EU Regulation of GMOs: Law and Decision-Making for a New Technology* (Edward Elgar 2008) 6; V Heyvaert, 'Governing Climate Change: Towards a New Paradigm for Risk Regulation' (2011) 74 *Modern Law Review* 817, 822–5.

EU market, where concerns have been raised regarding health, environmental, or technological risks associated with their use.[38] Although risk regulation was traditionally employed to further the aims and objectives of the single market,[39] the political fallout from the BSE crisis led to a much greater expansion in its use to address broader concerns related to maintaining public trust and enhancing legitimacy.[40]

There has also been increased recourse to the use of new or more informal governance mechanisms by the European Commission (Commission) in risk governance processes. Such mechanisms are characterized by their open-endedness, flexibility, and voluntary approach and include codes of conduct, voluntary agreements, public-private partnerships, social dialogue, benchmarking, as well as more inclusive and deliberative forms of participation in policymaking processes, including the use of the Open Method of Coordination (OMC).[41] Although their usefulness and, indeed, their legitimacy has been the subject of critique by a number of academic commentators,[42] the Commission has continued to employ such mechanisms in an increasing diverse range of social policy sectors, including health.[43] In particular, the OMC has become the preferred new governance mechanism of choice in EU regulatory governance involving human biological materials. For this reason, more detailed mention is made of it here prior to examining its use in the following sections.

The underlying aim of OMC is to develop a non-legally binding consensus on policy goals, which may then be used to inform more direct political and/or substantive legal initiatives at some future date. It is said to permit a more flexible and participatory approach to the formation of policy involving a range of stakeholders through shared learning, benchmarking, best practices, and, if necessary, peer pressure to shift national policies towards mutually beneficial and agreed upon objectives. This is in contrast to the traditional command and control models more commonly employed at EU level.[44] Notwithstanding its growing popularity at EU level, the use of OMC has been criticized on the ground that there is little good quality empirical research

---

[38] V Heyvaert, 'Europe in a Climate of Risk: Three Paradigms at Play' *LSE Law Society and Economy Working Papers* 06/2010, 12, 16.

[39] E Fisher, *Risk Regulation and Administrative Constitutionalism* (Hart 2007) 210.

[40] Vos, 'Overcoming the Crisis of Confidence: Risk Regulation in an Enlarged European Union' (n 26) 7.

[41] S Borrás and A Ejrnæs, 'The Legitimacy of New Modes of Governance in the EU: Studying National Stakeholders' Support' (2011) 12 *European Union Politics* 107, 108.

[42] For a critical examination of various examples of new modes of governance at EU level, see G de Búrca and J Scott (eds), *New Governance and Constitutionalism in the EU and the US* (Hart 2006); S Borrás, 'Legitimate Governance of Risk at the EU Level? The Case of Genetically Modified Organisms' (2006) 73 *Technological Forecasting and Social Change* 61, 71; ML Flear and A Vakulenko, 'A Human Rights Perspective on Citizen Participation in the EU's Governance of New Technologies' (2010) 10 *HRLR* 661; M Dawson, *New Governance and the Transformation of European Law: Coordinating EU Social Law and Policy* (CUP 2011).

[43] T Hervey, 'The European Union and the Governance of Health Care' in G de Búrca and J Scott (eds), *New Governance and Constitutionalism in the EU and the US* (Hart 2006); T Hervey, 'The European Union's Governance of Health Care and the Welfare Modernization Agenda' (2008) 2 *Regulation & Governance* 103; ML Flear, 'The Open Method of Coordination on Health Care After the Lisbon Strategy II: Towards a Neoliberal Framing?' (2009) 13(1) *European Integration online Papers* <http://eiop.or.at/eiop/texte/2009-012a.htm> accessed 17 July 2012.

[44] J Scott and DM Trubek, 'Mind the Gap: Law and New Approaches to Governance in the European Union' (2002) 8 *European Law Journal* 1; S Borrás and K Jacobsson, 'The Open Method of Co-Ordination and New Governance Patterns in the EU' (2004) 11 *JEPP* 185, 188–9.

available pointing to its effectiveness in facilitating horizontal or vertical policy transfer or organizational learning.[45] Although its legitimacy as a mode of governance has been questioned, recently published research has suggested that there is a good deal of support among national stakeholders for the use of OMC processes in specific policy sectors.[46]

Notwithstanding such developments in risk governance at EU level, the decision as to whether to adopt a narrow or expansive approach to risk in specific policy sectors,[47] as well as how best to separate out science and politics in the context of risk governance, has proved problematic in practice. In a number of sensitive areas of EU governance, such as food safety,[48] the environment,[49] and the use of human biological materials, whether on their own or as part of a range of industrially engineered technologies,[50] the successful management of risks to public health has become a touchstone for enhancing public trust and promoting political credibility. It is for this reason that I argue in this chapter that effective risk governance of health technologies, such as blood and organs, involves moving beyond narrowly defined standard setting for quality and safety,[51] towards a broader approach that views risk as a socio-cultural construct that is shaped by public perception and a range of ethico-social concerns. It may require a political response that is driven by the need to enhance both public trust and regulatory legitimacy. This may result in the single market imperative operating as a dependent variable in order to attract sufficient support from relevant constituencies to ensure the adoption of, as well as adherence to, regulation.[52] Cultivating support for the adoption of such regulation may be buttressed by the use of new governance mechanisms, where appropriate.

Adopting this interpretation of risk, I further argue that if risk regulation involving health technologies is to operate as an effective technique of legitimation at EU level, then this should be assessed by reference to the following criteria: how risk is defined in the regulatory regime and its match with risk- and ethics-based concerns of relevant constituencies; whether the stated aims and objectives of the regulatory regime have been met following implementation; and what opportunities are available for facilitating transparency and evaluation about the functioning of the regime. In the next section, these arguments are explored in more detail through an examination of the EU risk regulation regimes involving blood and organs.

---

[45] E Szyszczak, 'Experimental Governance: The Open Method of Coordination' (2006) 12 *European Law Journal* 486, 496; V Hatzopoulos, 'Why the Open Method of Coordination Is Bad For You: A Letter to the EU' (2007) 13 *European Law Journal* 309, 326.

[46] K Armstrong, *Governing Social Inclusion: Europeanization through Policy Coordination* (OUP 2010); Borrás and Ejrnæs (n 41) 122–4.

[47] Lee has pointed out that the policy and regulatory construction of genetically modified food and related products as a risk problem at EU level has served to marginalize other socio-ethical or cultural concerns regarding their cultivation/use, see Lee (n 37) 18.

[48] M Kritikos, 'Traditional Risk Analysis and Releases of GMOs into the European Union: Space for Non-Scientific Factors?' (2009) 34 *European Law Journal* 405; M Weimer, 'Applying Precaution in EU Authorization of Genetically Modified Products—Challenges and Suggestions for Reform' (2010) 16 *European Law Journal* 624.

[49] Heyvaert (n 37).

[50] A-M Farrell, 'The Politics of Risk and EU Governance of Human Material' (2009) 16 *MJECL* 41.

[51] Lee has also observed the tendency towards adopting a narrow definition of risk based on safety in the context of EU regulation of technologies, rather than taking account of broader ethico-social problems created by the technology, see M Lee, 'Beyond Safety? The Broadening Scope of Risk Regulation' (2009) 62 *Current Legal Problems* 242.

[52] For the purposes of this chapter, the term 'relevant constituencies' includes Member States, national regulators (competent authorities), and stakeholder groups.

The concluding section of the chapter analyses the findings from such examination and offers some final comments on their broader implications for EU regulation of health technologies.

C. Regulating Blood

1. The Blood Directive

The blood risk regulation regime was established under the Blood Directive, which was adopted at EU level in January 2003. It was required to be implemented by Member States by February 2005.[53] The main objective of the Directive was to establish an EU-wide risk regulation regime which set minimum standards for blood quality and safety at key points in the donor-recipient chain. This was done in order to ensure a high level of human health protection.[54] Under the Treaty competence in Article 168(4)(a) TFEU, Member States are permitted to adopt more stringent measures in line with national priorities. National provisions dealing with blood donation are not affected by the regime.[55]

The Directive is directed primarily towards 'blood establishments' which include any structure or body that is responsible for any aspect of blood collection and testing.[56] Key standards which must be met include the appointment of a designated 'competent authority' to ensure the implementation of the Directive at national level,[57] as well as the appointment of a 'responsible person' to ensure its implementation within designated blood establishments.[58] To meet appropriate quality control standards, blood establishments must maintain appropriate documentation in relation to their operational, training, and reporting procedures,[59] as well as ensuring that there is a suitable level of data protection and confidentiality.[60] This is in addition to Member States being required to design and implement a haemovigiliance system in order to track adverse reactions and events arising out of the use of blood.[61] A key feature of the Directive is the focus on ensuring the quality and safety of blood donation. Specific Articles in the substantive part of the Directive deal with this aspect and include standard-setting in relation to donor information, examination, and eligibility, as well as testing requirements on donated blood. Standard-setting in relation to donor eligibility is seen as vital to managing risks to the blood system, particularly given the

---

[53] Blood Directive, Art 32(1).   [54] Blood Directive, Art 1.   [55] Art 168(7) TFEU.

[56] Note that hospital blood banks are excluded from the definition of blood establishments under Art 3(e). Art 6 states that only Arts 7, 10, 11(1), 14, 15, 22, and 24 of the Blood Directive apply to hospital blood banks.

[57] Blood Directive, Art 4(1).

[58] Blood Directive, Art 9.

[59] Blood Directive, Arts 11–12.

[60] Blood Directive, Art 24.

[61] Blood Directive, Arts 14–15. For further details in relation to technical requirements, specifications, and standards to be met in relation to traceability requirements and notification of serious adverse events and reactions, see Commission Directive 2005/61/EC having regard to Directive 2002/98/EC of the European Parliament and of the Council of 27 January 2003 setting standards of quality and safety for the collection, testing, processing, storage and distribution of human blood and blood components and amending Directive 2001/83/EC, OJ L256. In relation to a quality system for blood establishments, see Commission Directive 2005/62/EC of 30 September 2005 implementing Directive 2002/98/EC of the European Parliament and of the Council as regards Community standards and specifications relating to a quality system for blood establishments, OJ L256.

likely emergence of new infectious agents where no technology may yet exist to detect their presence in donated blood.[62]

Political conflict arose during the course of inter-institutional negotiations over the adoption of the Blood Directive with regards to whether voluntary, unpaid blood donation should be formally recognized within the risk regulation regime as the preferred method for sourcing national blood supplies. Such conflict had its origins in the long-standing stakeholder debate concerning the merits of voluntary, unpaid donation over paid donation on ethical, economic, and safety grounds.[63] Formal recognition of this method of donation in the substantive part of the Blood Directive would have been problematic for a number of Member States. For example, while Germany and Austria collect whole blood through voluntary, unpaid donation, they also permit plasma to be collected from paid donors, which is then used in the manufacture of products by the for-profit plasma products industry. Following the transmission of variant Creutzfeldt-Jakob disease (vCJD) through blood in the United Kingdom, arrangements were also made to source plasma used in a range of blood products administered to its citizens from paid donors in the USA.[64] This is against a background where well over 50 per cent of plasma from paid donors from the USA is used to source a range of blood products supplied on an EU-wide basis.[65]

The final text of the Blood Directive reflects the different strategies employed by EU decision-makers to facilitate a politically acceptable compromise on this issue. References to the importance of voluntary, unpaid blood donation for sourcing the EU blood supply, as well as its link to blood safety, are set out in the (non-legally binding) Recital to the Directive.[66] In contrast, Member States are simply 'encouraged' to take 'all necessary measures to ensure that blood is sourced from voluntary, unpaid blood donation' in the substantive (legally binding) part of the Directive.[67] Member States, which source their respective national blood supplies solely through this form of blood donation on a not-for-profit basis, are permitted to restrict or prohibit the importation of blood that does not accord with such arrangements, 'provided that the conditions of the Treaty are met'.[68]

The Blood Directive does not define what is meant by voluntary, unpaid blood donation, although it is suggested that the definition provided by the Council of Europe should be taken into account.[69] The absence of any binding definition provides for further flexibility with regard to what constitutes reimbursement (or payment) for blood donation. There is no direct reference to the reality of the blood market in the EU, save for the requirement that national donor identification systems should

---

[62] See Farrell (n 1) 171. Detailed technical requirements in relation to donated blood, including donor eligibility are set out in Commission Directive 2004/33/EC of 22 March 2004 implementing Directive 2002/98/EC of the European Parliament and of the Council as regards certain technical requirements for blood and blood components, OJ L91.

[63] For an overview of the arguments in favour of voluntary, unpaid blood donation, see Titmuss (n 12); Farrell (n 7) Chs 3–5.

[64] Farrell (n 7) 209.

[65] Farrell (n 7) 206.

[66] In Blood Directive, para 23, Recital, voluntary, unpaid blood donation is referred to as 'a factor which can contribute to high safety standards . . . and therefore to the protection of human health.'

[67] Blood Directive, Art 20(1).

[68] Blood Directive, Art 4(2). This means that national rules restricting movements of blood or blood components would be subject to proportionality scrutiny if challenged before national courts for non-compliance with Art 30 TFEU.

[69] Blood Directive, para 23, Recital.

ensure that blood imported from 'third countries' can be traced,[70] as well as the fact that the source material used in 'medicinal products derived from human blood or plasma products' (which are governed by Directive 2001/83/EC),[71] should comply with the quality and safety standards set out in the Blood Directive.[72]

Both Member States and the Commission have reporting obligations under the Blood Directive. Reports are to be provided by Member States to the Commission every three years in relation to measures taken to encourage voluntary, unpaid blood donation, with the Commission thereafter reporting to the Parliament and the Council on any further measures to be taken in this area.[73] In addition, three yearly reports are to be provided by Member States regarding their experiences in implementing the Directive, with the Commission thereafter reporting on the implementation of the Directive, in particular on measures relating to inspection and control, to a range of EU institutions, including the Parliament and the Council.[74]

2. Assessing Effectiveness

As mentioned at the beginning of this chapter, I have argued that the successful use of regulation as a technique of legitimation in the EU context to manage risk involving health technologies, such as blood and organs, should be evaluated by reference to its effectiveness. This was to be determined by reference to a number of criteria including how risk is defined in the regulatory regime and its match with risk- and ethics-based concerns of relevant constituencies; whether the stated aims and objectives of the regulatory regime have been met; and what opportunities are available for facilitating transparency and evaluation about the functioning of the regime. Turning to the first criterion, the risk regulation regime established under the Blood Directive defines risk in the field as simply a matter of standard-setting for quality and safety in relation to blood sourcing and supply issues. This mirrors the Treaty competence under Article 168(4)(a) TFEU. The catalyst for the creation of the competence had its origins in the political fallout from Member State HIV blood contamination episodes in the 1990s.[75] In the search for political credibility in the wake of such episodes, Member States were prepared to sanction a limited transfer of competence to EU level in relation to a matter of public health, so as to ensure that there was an EU-wide approach to setting minimum standards for blood quality and safety.[76]

In addition, persistent stakeholder conflict over whether voluntary, unpaid blood donation should be formally recognized as the preferred method for sourcing the EU blood supply in the Blood Directive created a highly charged political context, which provided an important backdrop to the approach taken to the design of the risk regulation regime. First, it led to a focus on an ethically principled approach embodied in the gift relationship in blood donation, as being vital to facilitating blood safety. Although there is clear public support for such an approach to blood donation in the

---

[70] Blood Directive, Art 14(1).

[71] Directive 2001/83/EC (n 1). As previously mentioned, this regulatory regime is not examined in this chapter. For a more detailed overview of the regime, see Farrell (n 1).

[72] Blood Directive, Art 31.

[73] Blood Directive, Art 20(2).

[74] Blood Directive, Art 26.

[75] A-M Farrell, 'The Emergence of EU Governance in Public Health: the Case of Blood Policy and Regulation' in M Steffen (ed), *Health Governance in Europe: Issues, Challenges and Theories* (Routledge 2005) 134.

[76] Farrell (n 1) 176.

EU context,[77] the extent to which it contributes to blood safety is contested. While the promotion of such an ethically principled approach may offer value in terms of enhancing the legitimacy of blood donation and supply, it has been argued that the effective management of risk in this context turns on a much more complex inter-relationship of epidemiological, scientific, market, and institutional factors.[78]

Secondly, a predominant focus on the sourcing and supply side of the blood system in the design of the risk regulation regime in the Blood Directive operated to the detriment of setting standards which could have incorporated a comprehensive vein-to-vein approach to risk management in the field.[79] Such a lop-sided approach also ignored the growing body of haemovigilance and other data that has identified the clinical setting in which the administration of blood takes place as posing a significant risk to patient-recipients.[80] Incorporating such an approach could have taken account of a number of ethically problematic issues involved in ensuring a safe and sufficient supply for blood recipients, as well as focusing on professional and institutional factors that may impact on whether optimum levels of safety are achieved in clinical settings.[81]

As part of its ongoing obligation under the Directive to submit reports to various EU institutions,[82] the Commission has concluded that its implementation has been satisfactory overall to date. Nonetheless, a number of problems remain. A few Member States continue to experience difficulties with regard to implementing aspects of the Directive, given under-developed institutional arrangements with respect to their national blood services.[83] In addition, further work still needs to be done in particular areas, including accreditation, licensing, and inspection of blood establishments, as well as the collection and analysis of data on adverse events and reactions to blood transfusion.[84] Stakeholders have also observed that the Commission could do more to clarify the interpretation of particular framework standards in the Directive, as well as allowing for more flexibility in the design and application of technical standards.[85]

In relation to the last two criteria for assessing effectiveness, the aims and objectives of the regulatory regime have largely been met in line with the narrow basis on which risk has been defined under Article 168(4)(a) TFEU. Regular evaluation has led to

---

[77] INRA Europe, *Europeans and Blood*, Eurobarometer 41.0 (European Commission 1995; European Opinion Research Group (EEIG), *Le don du sang*, Eurobaromètre spécial, 1883–4/Vague 58.2 (European Commission 2003).

[78] Farrell (n 7) Chs 3 and 8; see generally, Healy (n 13).

[79] J Stein, J Besley, C Brook, and others, 'Risk-Based Decision-Making for Blood Safety: Preliminary Report of a Consensus Conference' (2011) 101 *Vox Sanguinis* 277, 279.

[80] J-C Faber, 'The European Blood Directive: A New Era of Blood Regulation Has Begun' (2004) 14 *Transfusion Medicine* 257, 271; M Murphy, S Stanworth, and M Yazer, 'Transfusion Practice and Safety: Current Status and Possibilities for Improvement' (2011) 100 *Vox Sanguinis* 46, 46–52.

[81] Faber (n 80) 271.

[82] Blood Directive, Art 26(1) and (3).

[83] Commission, Report from the Commission to the Council, the European Parliament, the European Economic and Social Committee and the Committee of the Regions: First Report on the Application of the Blood Directive, COM (2006) 313 final; Commission, Communication from the Commission to the Council, the European Parliament, the Economic and Social Committee and the Committee of the Regions on the application of Directive 2002/98/EC setting standards of quality and safety for the collection, testing, processing, storage and distribution of human blood and blood components and amending Directive 2001/83/EC, COM (2010) 3 final.

[84] Commission, Meeting of the Competent Authorities on blood and blood components (Art 25, Directive 2002/98/EC), 12–13 April 2010, SANCO C6 TB/RP D(2010) 360180 Brussels.

[85] A Robinson, 'The European Union Blood Safety Directive and Its Implications for Blood Services' (2007) 93 *Vox Sanguinis* 122, 123–4.

adaptation of (technical) standards with a view to improving effectiveness in application. In addition, regulatory requirements under the Blood Directive with regard to periodic disclosure concerning implementation to a range of EU institutions, including the democratically accountable Parliament, have facilitated a necessary degree of transparency about its operation which contributes to the ongoing legitimacy of the regime. However, there are at least three interrelated aspects to the regulatory regime that may lessen its effectiveness in terms of facilitating legitimacy, as well as ensuring an optimum approach to risk governance in the field.

As mentioned previously, the narrow definition of risk which has predominantly focused on standard-setting in relation to blood sourcing and supply issues means that risk in the clinical setting, where blood is transfused, has been largely neglected. In addition, the effective management of future risks to the EU blood supply is likely to be compromised as a result of a failure fully to acknowledge the nature, scope, and diversity of the EU blood market, as the findings from national HIV blood contamination episodes have made clear.[86] The failure fully to acknowledge such market remains complicated by the continuing political salience attached to promoting voluntary, unpaid blood donation in the EU context. Since the adoption of the Blood Directive, the Commission has issued a number of reports on the approach taken to implementing voluntary, unpaid blood donation at Member State level. While most Member States have adopted measures in this regard, some continue to source their blood supplies from both paid and unpaid donors. In some Member States, individuals are paid for time off work due to donating blood, whereas in other Member States they are not. Expenses paid for attending to donate blood vary in amount and by category.[87]

The difficulties created by differing interpretations adopted by Member States in relation to sourcing national blood supplies were highlighted in the recent *Humanplasma* judgment. The Court of Justice found that Austria's legislative prohibition on the making of 'any payment whatsoever' in relation to blood to be used for transfusion was neither necessary nor proportionate with regard to the protection of public health. The Court observed that it was not clear that the receipt of financial compensation for blood donation necessarily created an increased risk for recipients given the specificity of current post-donation testing. In the circumstances, reimbursement of expenses, such as small tokens, refreshments, and payment for travel expenses connected with the donation were entirely compatible with voluntary, unpaid blood donation.[88] How best to reconcile ethico-social commitments to blood sourcing with market imperatives created by the reality of the EU blood market, as well as the single market more generally, is proving difficult for Member States. On this point, at least, the legitimacy of the EU risk regulation regime for blood quality and safety remains contested and is likely to remain so for the foreseeable future.

---

[86] Farrell (n 7) Chs 6, 8.

[87] Commission, Report from the Commission to the Council and the European Parliament on the promotion by Member States of voluntary, unpaid blood donations, COM (2006) 217 final; European Commission, Report from the Commission to the European Parliament, the Council, the European Economic and Social Committee and the Committee of the Regions. 2nd Report on Voluntary and Unpaid Donation of Blood and Blood Components, COM (2010) 138 final.

[88] Case C-421/09 *Humanplasma GmbH v Republik Österreich* [2010] ECR I-12869.

D. Regulating Organs

1. Organ Donation Directive

The EU risk regulation regime for organ donation and transplantation is established under what has become known as the Organ Donation Directive. It was adopted at EU level in July 2010 and was required to be implemented by Member States by the end of August 2012.[89] It is divided into four substantive chapters covering key aspects such as quality and safety standards for organs; donor and recipient protections in the transplantation process; the obligations of competent authorities, particularly with regard to information exchange; and the requirements for organ exchange with third countries, as well as European organ exchange organizations. Both Member States and the Commission have reporting obligations under the Directive. Member States are required to provide a report on the steps taken with regard to implementing the Directive, as well as experience gained in relation to such implementation by August 2013 and thereafter every three years.[90] In turn, the Commission is required to report to various EU institutions, including the Parliament, by August 2014 and every three years thereafter on the implementation of the Directive.[91] Unlike the Blood Directive, however, there is no specific reporting requirement in relation to action taken by Member States to encourage voluntary, unpaid donation. This is because it is the uncontroversial, default position for organ donation within the EU.

Chapter III of the Organ Donation Directive elaborates on the protections to be provided to organ donors and recipients in more detail than was seen in the earlier Blood Directive. Although it is made explicit that donation from both deceased and living donors should be voluntary and unpaid,[92] it is acknowledged that reimbursement of expenses associated with living organ donation including loss of income arising out of the donation is acceptable.[93] Emphasis is also placed on the not-for-profit procurement of organs,[94] as well as the need to avoid financial incentivization or the payment of benefits in relation to the use of living donors.[95] In this regard, advertising the need for, or availability of, organs with a view to financial gain or otherwise obtaining a comparable advantage, is considered to be unacceptable.[96] While it is acknowledged that consent requirements in respect of organ donation are a matter for Member States, the Directive makes clear that procurement of organs should not take place until they have been met.[97]

Particular emphasis is placed in the Directive on requirements to be met in relation to the management of risk involving living donors. Human rights concerns have been raised about this form of donation and its use is constructed narrowly in other international legal instruments.[98] Diverse approaches are taken to this form of organ donation as between Member States, with the United Kingdom having a much higher rate than

---

[89] Directive 2010/53/EU of the European Parliament and of the Council of 7 July 2010 on standards of quality and safety of human organs intended for transplantation, OJ L207.

[90] Organ Donation Directive, Art 22(1).

[91] Organ Donation Directive, Art 22(2).

[92] Organ Donation Directive, Art 13(1).

[93] Organ Donation Directive, Art 13(2).

[94] Organ Donation Directive, Art 13(4).

[95] Organ Donation Directive, Art 13(2).

[96] Organ Donation Directive, Art 13(3).

[97] Organ Donation Directive, Art 14.

[98] HDC Roscam Abbing, 'A Council of Europe Protocol on Transplantation of Organs and Tissue of Human Origin' (2002) 9 *EJHL* 63, 67.

Spain, for example.[99] In the Recital, it is acknowledged that living donors face particular 'physical, physiological and social' risks as a result of undergoing non-therapeutic medical treatment to remove a healthy organ for transplant into another.[100] In the substantive part of the Directive, Member States are required to take all necessary measures to ensure the highest possible protection of living donors in order to ensure the quality and safety of their organs for transplantation.[101] Emphasis is placed on the need to engage in careful selection of living donors by reference to their health and medical history, which should be undertaken by suitably qualified and competent professionals.[102] Records are also required to be kept in relation to organ donation by living donors, who should be monitored post-donation with respect to any risks and/or adverse reactions.[103]

While the Organ Donation Directive sets out a principled approach to guide organ donation and transplantation in the context of achieving a high level of quality and safety in the field, it is accompanied by a central focus on increasing organ procurement as a way of addressing the problems created by chronic organ shortage within the EU. The success of the Spanish model of organ donation and transplantation in increasing the rate of deceased organ donation is held out by the Commission and other key stakeholders as offering the best way forward towards increasing procurement rates in the EU.[104] Much of the policy discussions and consultation that took place prior to the adoption of the Organ Donation Directive focused on this issue,[105] as well as how best to embed it within the proposed risk regulation regime.

In the end, a multi-pronged approach was taken in the Directive. First, Member States are required to adopt and implement a set of 'operating procedures' which should establish a quality and safety framework covering key aspects of the organ donation and transplantation process.[106] Although this approach allows Member States a large degree of flexibility, the Directive nevertheless makes clear that the framework should include procedures covering identity verification of donors; consent requirements for organ donation; the completion of both organ and donor characterization; the traceability of organs; and the reporting of serious adverse events and reactions in the transplantation process.[107] Secondly, standard-setting with regard to personnel and institutions involved in organ donation and transplantation is broadly in line with key aspects of the Spanish model and is designed to ensure that all Member States establish institutional

[99] In the United Kingdom, 15.9 per cent of all renal transplants are from a living organ donor, compared to 5 per cent in Spain, see Council of Europe, Transplant Newsletter: International Figures on Organ Donation and Transplantation 2009, 15(1) 2010, 7.

[100] Organ Donation Directive, para 23, Recital. For an overview, see Robert Truog, 'The Ethics of Organ Donation by Living Donors' (2005) 353 *NEJM* 444.

[101] Organ Donation Directive, Art 15(1).

[102] Organ Donation Directive, Art 15(2).

[103] Organ Donation Directive, Art 15(3) and (4).

[104] R Matasanz and B Dominiquez-Gil, 'Strategies to Optimize Deceased Organ Donation' (2007) 21 *Transplantation Reviews* 177–88; MN Michel, 'Institutional Organisation and Transplanting the "Spanish Model"' in A-M Farrell, D Price, and M Quigley (eds), *Organ Shortage: Ethics Law and Pragmatism* (CUP 2011).

[105] See Priority Actions 1–5, Commission of the European Communities, Communication from the Commission. Action Plan on Organ Donation and Transplantation (2009–2015): Strengthened Cooperation between Member States, COM (2008) 819/3; A-M Farrell, 'Adding Value? EU Governance of Organ Donation and Transplantation' (2010) 15 *EJHL* 51, 56–66.

[106] 'Operating procedures' are described as 'written instructions describing the steps in a specific process, including the materials and methods to be used and the expected end outcome' (Organ Donation Directive, Art 3(p)).

[107] Organ Donation Directive, Art 4.

structures, as well as employing suitably qualified staff, who can work towards increasing organ procurement rates.[108] Finally, there are requirements for facilitating information exchange and networking as between national competent authorities, as well as between regional and EU organ exchange organizations, with a view to strengthening cooperation in the wake of implementation of the Directive and learning from best practice in the field.[109]

2. Assessing Effectiveness

At the time of writing, the Organ Donation Directive is still in the process of being implemented by Member States. Therefore, any assessment of the effectiveness of the regime is necessarily limited at this stage. However, three interrelated points can be made about the extent to which this regime is likely to be effective by reference to the criteria identified at the start of this chapter. In relation to the approach taken to defining risk, this Directive also has a similar format to that adopted in relation to the earlier Blood Directive. Although such format is grounded in the circumscribed Treaty competence in Article 168(4)(a) TFEU, the Commission recognized at an early stage that a different approach was needed in relation to managing risk- and ethics-based concerns of relevant constituencies,[110] which had its origins in the need to address the issues raised by chronic organ shortage within the EU.[111]

So what are the risk- and ethics-based concerns that have been raised by having to address the problem of organ shortage within the EU? There has long been a significant gap between supply and demand for organs in the EU context, with many patients dying while on national waiting lists for a suitable organ to be made available for transplantation.[112] What this has meant in practice is that transplant clinicians have been forced to be extremely selective about which patients are placed on waiting lists in the first place. In circumstances where few options may be available to individuals with end stage organ failure and who are on waiting lists, greater leeway has been allowed in relation to what constitutes an acceptable risk for such patients, as well as allowing significant discretion in the exercise of clinical judgement in relation to risks associated with organ transplantation in such circumstances.

In order to address the problem of organ shortage, some Member States have considered a range of options to increase organ procurement, such as permitting different forms of donation. This has included living organ donation, as well as what is known as expanded criteria donation (ECD) and non-heart-beating donation (NHBD). I have already briefly discussed the risk- and ethics-based concerns raised by the use of living organ donation, but such concerns also exist in relation to ECD and NHBD. In the former case, ECD involves making use of organs from (deceased) donors who would not be considered to be an optimum match for the recipient due to pre-existing illness or

[108] Organ Donation Directive, Arts 5, 6, 9, 12.
[109] Organ Donation Directive, Chs IV and V.
[110] Farrell (n 105) 53–6.
[111] Farrell (n 50) 62.
[112] Commission, Commission staff working document accompanying the proposal for a Directive of the European Parliament and of the Council on standards of quality and safety of human organs intended for transplantation and of the Commission action plan on organ donation and transplantation (2009–2015): Strengthened cooperation between Member States: Impact Assessment, SEC (2008) 2956, 9.

infection, and/or age at time of death.[113] In the latter case, NHBD involves making use of organs from a deceased donor who was diagnosed as dead by reference to cardiopulmonary rather than more acceptable neurological criteria (for example, brain stem death).[114]

Interestingly, although risk- and ethics-based concerns over what should be recognized as the preferred method for donation was a key point of conflict in relation to the Blood Directive, this proved uncontroversial in the Organ Donation Directive as voluntary, unpaid donation is the accepted default approach in the EU context (save for the reimbursement of limited expenses in the case of living organ donation). It was also uncontroversial that organ procurement should be conducted on a not-for-profit basis. Other areas where such concerns have been raised include what method of consent for organ donation should be adopted at national level with respect to increasing rates of procurement, as well as what criteria should be employed for allocating organs, both within and across Member States.[115] Notwithstanding lively and long-standing academic and policy debates in such areas,[116] the Commission appears to have opted not to tackle these particular concerns in any depth in the risk regulation regime that has been established under the Organ Donation Directive.

Nevertheless, there is evidence available to show that the Commission was prepared to acknowledge that a broader approach to risk governance was required in the field of organ donation and transplantation than was seen in the case of blood, in order to address concerns raised by the problem of organ shortage in the EU.[117] To this end, the Commission employed both traditional and new governance mechanisms in an attempt to achieve a consensus with relevant constituencies on the way forward with respect to managing such concerns. This has included the publication of a six-year action plan, which lists ten priority actions.[118] The action plan provides a road map for addressing these priorities and OMC processes are being used to realize them. It is hoped that the plan will offer a gradualist approach to strengthening cooperation, as well as facilitating cooperation, between Member States and key stakeholders in the field.[119] It includes employing OMC processes, such as the sharing of expertise, the identification of common objectives, the development of quantitative and qualitative indicators and benchmarks, and regular reporting on, and sharing of, best practices.[120] In support of the Commission's approach, regulatory impact assessments were also published in relation to the proposed Organ Donation Directive, which provided detailed analysis of the reasons for embarking upon such regulatory initiative. Such assessments enabled Member States and stakeholder groups to be better informed about the proposed design and implementation of the regulatory regime.[121]

---

[113] J Pascual, J Zamora, and J Pirsch, 'A Systematic Review of Kidney Transplantation from Expanded Criteria Donors' (2008) 52 *American Journal of Kidney Disease* 553–8.

[114] R Truog and F Miller, 'The Dead Donor Rule and Organ Transplantation' (2008) 359 *NEJM* 674.

[115] Farrell (n 105) 72–4, 77–8.

[116] For an overview, see A-M Farrell, D Price, and M Quigley (eds), *Organ Shortage: Ethics Law and Pragmatism* (CUP 2011).

[117] See Farrell (n 105) 68–9.

[118] Commission, Commission staff working document (n 112).

[119] Commission, Communication from the Commission to the European Parliament and Council. Organ Donation and Transplantation: Policy Actions at EU level, COM (2007) 275 final, 9–10.

[120] Commission Communication (n 119) 10.

[121] See eg Commission, Commission Staff Working Document: Accompanying Document to the Communication from the Commission to the European Parliament and Council: Organ Donation and Transplantation: Policy Actions at EU Level: Impact Assessment, SEC (2007) 704.

The use of new governance mechanisms by the Commission which was done with a view to developing consensus and facilitating adherence to the Organ Donation Directive, marked a break away from the approach it had taken in relation to the earlier Blood Directive. The question is to what extent this attempt has been effective at enhancing legitimacy among relevant constituencies. What evidence is currently available from the Commission points to a degree of formal acquiescence at least on the part of representatives of national competent authorities in relation to ensuring that the Organ Donation Directive is appropriately implemented in a timely manner at Member State level. Regular meetings are now held in Brussels between such representatives, where reports are presented on the progress towards implementation of the Directive; indicators and best practice in particular areas are examined; and working groups have been formed on specific issues, including cross-border organ exchange and living organ donation. It has been acknowledged that the adoption of the Directive has created an environment which facilitates cross-border synergies and research collaborations on organ donation and transplantation.[122] No doubt a clearer picture will emerge about the implementation process following the first reporting cycle by Member States and the Commission, which is due to be completed in 2014.

In the circumstances, there is currently limited information available in relation to assessing effectiveness of the risk regulation regime for organ donation and transplantation by reference to the remaining identified criteria. In relation to the second criterion (whether the stated aims and objectives of the regulatory regime have been met following implementation), there is a need to take account of the Treaty competence under Article 168(4)(a) TFEU. This is reflected in the Organ Donation Directive, which states that the aim is to establish common quality and safety standards in relation to the procurement, transport, and use of organs intended for transplantation to the human body throughout the EU. This is to be done in order to facilitate organ exchange for patients in need, as well as providing public reassurance that the same such standards are applied in all Member States.[123] Until the Directive is fully implemented at Member State level and the initial reporting cycle on implementation has been completed, it is currently difficult to assess whether such aims will be realized in practice. While not failsafe, reporting requirements are likely to operate as useful mechanisms for aiding transparency in ensuring that the aims and objective of the Directive have been achieved, as well as highlighting any particular issues which may be adversely impacting on full implementation of the risk regulation regime at Member State level. The potential therefore exists for risk regulation in the field to operate as a successful technique of legitimation, particularly in circumstances where new governance mechanisms continue to be employed to address issues of concern regarding implementation by relevant constituencies, such as regulators and key stakeholder groups.

E. Conclusion

This chapter examined the relationship between risk, legitimacy, and EU regulation of health technologies. It drew on a case study of risk regulation involving human

---

[122] Commission, Minutes of Third Competent Authority Meeting on Organ Donation and Transplantation, 26–27 September 2011 (Ref. Ares(2012)319456-19/03/2012, 10 January 2012), 3 <http://ec.europa.eu/health/blood_tissues_organs/docs/ev_20110926_mi_en.pdf> accessed 10 June 2012.

[123] Organ Donation Directive, paras 3, 6, 28, Recital.

biological materials, namely blood and organs. It was argued that risk should be viewed as a socio-cultural construct which is shaped by public perception and ethico-social concerns. Adopting such a construction involves recognizing that political responses to risk may be driven by the need to enhance public trust, as well as regulatory legitimacy. This may result in the single market imperative operating as a dependent variable in order to attract sufficient support from relevant constituencies for the adoption of, as well as adherence to, regulation. New governance mechanisms may also need to be strategically employed to bolster such support. By reference to the chosen case study, a number of criteria were used to assess the relationship between legitimacy and effectiveness including how risk was defined in the regulatory regime and its match with risk- and ethics-based concerns of relevant constituencies; whether the stated aims and objectives of the regulatory regime had been met; and what opportunities were made available for facilitating transparency and evaluation about the functioning of the regime.

An analysis of the two risk regulation regimes involving blood and organs revealed that how risk was defined and fed into regulatory governance was influenced by a combination of factors, including Treaty competence and how the multi-valuing of these human biological materials structured the political dynamics informing the design, adoption, and implementation of regulation. Although the single market imperative lies at the heart of much of the impetus for regulation at EU level, it operated as a dependent variable as EU decision-makers sought to negotiate an acceptable political compromise that would enable blood and organ risk regulation regimes to be adopted, as well as to facilitate adherence on the part of relevant constituencies. Finding such a way forward was vital with respect to facilitating the effectiveness and therefore the legitimacy of such regimes.

In relation to the latter two criteria, the evidence available in the relation to the Blood Directive revealed that the stated aims and objectives had largely been met. Risk had been narrowly defined in line with the Treaty competence and this had translated in practice to a lop-sided approach which had resulted in a focus on managing risk in relation to sourcing and supply issues rather than in clinical settings. This was likely to lessen the effectiveness of the risk regulation regime in practice and therefore the extent to which it was possible to realize the objective of providing a high level of human health protection. In relation to the third criterion, reporting obligations embedded in the Blood Directive had contributed to transparency in relation to the implementation process, facilitating evaluation of the functioning of the regime. While not failsafe, such requirements have provided valuable opportunities for enhancing regulatory legitimacy in what is a politically sensitive area of EU risk governance, where maintaining public trust is important. At the time of writing, the risk regulation regime established under the Organ Donation Directive is still in the process of being implemented at Member State level. Therefore, it is currently difficult to assess whether the opportunities afforded for transparency with regard to implementation of the regime are likely to be effective. What can be said is that similar reporting obligations exist as between the Blood and Organ Donation Directives. This augurs well in the short to medium term for facilitating transparency about how the Organ Donation Directive is operating in practice within the EU.

Undertaking an assessment as to whether the stated aims and objectives have been met in relation to the risk regulation regime established under the Organ Donation Directive is more complicated. It is clear that the Treaty competence under Article 168(4)(a) TFEU, on which the regulatory regime is based, is too narrow to accommodate the differential risk- and ethics-based concerns of relevant constituencies in the field. In contrast to the approach taken with the earlier Blood Directive, the Commission recognized such problems at an early stage and acknowledged that a broader approach to risk governance was required. To this end, it has pursued a number of strategies in order to facilitate consensus and adherence, as well as to increase regulatory legitimacy. Risk differentiation did take place due to the need to accommodate problems created by chronic organ shortage in the EU. This led to adaptation through the employment of a range of new governance mechanisms in order to manage such concerns and increase support from relevant constituencies for adherence to the risk regulation regime.

In a complex, multilevel governance environment such as the EU, risk governance involving health technologies has the potential to be politically sensitive, given the need to ensure a high level of public health protection in line with Treaty requirements. This is likely to be amplified where uncertainty arises about the nature and scope of risk in the context of innovation involving such technologies. What the findings from this chapter reveal, is that adopting a socio-cultural construction of risk enables not only quality and safety issues to be taken into account, but also ensures that risk and ethics-based concerns are factored into EU risk governance involving the use of such technologies. Although risk regulation may be grounded in a narrowly circumscribed Treaty competence, the use of new governance mechanisms may assist in managing such concerns through a process of differentiation and adaptation. This may facilitate greater adherence on the part of relevant constituencies to the regulatory regime once implemented, as well as enhancing its overall legitimacy.

10

Something Old, Something New, Something Borrowed: Emerging Health Technologies and the Continuing Role of Existing Regulations

Elen Stokes

A. Introduction

Describing a technology as 'new' has consequences beyond the interpretation of scientific and technological progress. It also plays an important role in determining how legal regulation interprets and progress responds to it. An existing technology may traditionally have been regulated in a particular way, whereas the emergence of a new variant may warrant a very different regulatory approach. There are numerous examples where the law distinguishes between 'old' and 'new' objects and scenarios of regulation, where new products or processes are set on a different regulatory path from old ones if they are deemed to be sufficiently new in degree or nature.[1] So significant are the prefixes 'new' and 'newly emerging' that within the regulatory literature there has developed a strand of scholarship focusing specifically on regulating new technologies.[2] The categorization of a technology or its applications as 'new' does not necessarily invite new regulatory responses, nor is there always or indeed anything substantively or inevitably 'new' about emerging technologies. Nonetheless, 'newness', it transpires, is an important focal point in the continuing debate about how best to manage the opportunities and challenges of technological development, even in instances where the presence of novelty is called into question, difficult to verify, or seemingly immaterial.

Given that a good deal of importance is attached to 'newness' in the regulation of science and technology, it is perhaps surprising that its meanings and implications have attracted relatively little attention in the legal and policy literature. This chapter begins

---

[1] See eg Regulation (EC) No 258/97 concerning novel foods and novel food ingredients [1997] OJ L43/1, Recital 2 and Art 3(4) on 'substantial equivalence'; historical examples include Council Directive 79/831/EEC of 18 September 1979 amending for the sixth time Directive 67/548/EEC on the approximation of the laws, regulations and administrative provisions relating to the classification, packaging and labelling of dangerous substances [1979] OJ L259/10, Art 13 which distinguishes between 'new' and 'existing' chemical substances.

[2] Good examples of this include MA Price, 'The Newness of New Technology' (2001) 22 *Cardozo Law Review* 1885; AJ Cockfield, 'Toward a Law and Technology Theory' (2003) 30(3) *Manitoba Law Journal* 383; A Cockfield and J Pridmore, 'A Synthetic Theory of Law and Technology' (2007) 8(2) *Minnesota Journal of Law, Science and Technology* 475; LB Moses, 'Why Have a Theory of Law and Technological Change' (2007) 8(2) *Minnesota Journal of Law, Science and Technology* 589; LB Moses, 'Recurring Dilemmas: The Law's Race to Keep Up with Technological Change' (2007) *Journal of Law, Technology and Policy* 239; LB Moses, Understanding 'Legal Responses to Technological Change: The Example of *In Vitro* Fertilization' (2005) 6(2) *Minnesota Journal of Law, Science and Technology* 505.

to unpack the role and interpretation of technological novelty in regulatory and policy debates at European Union (EU) level. Looking to the debate on nanotechnologies (introduced in Section B), it shows that the contours of 'newness' may be ill-defined and elastic but they are nonetheless considered to be important determinants of regulatory responses. Further still, there is a tendency in the legal and policy discourse, where it explicitly addresses the 'newness' or 'oldness' of a particular technology, to rely on a measure of novelty that focuses overwhelmingly on physical risks posed to human health or the environment. This chapter seeks to show that there are many more sites, in addition to those of risk, where newness emerges and is contested, negotiated, shaped by and capable of shaping, the regulatory environment. These 'other' sites assume more importance given the uncertainties surrounding new technologies, and this is particularly apparent in the case of nanotechnology. In the initial stages of a technology's development, when it is difficult to predict potential uses and effects, and policy choices have yet to be made, its regulatory fate is tied, in principle if not in practice, to broader considerations than simply the risk of harm.

One important consideration, explored in Section C, is the regulatory environment in which a new technology finds itself. Newness is as much about the specific attributes of a technology as it is about the capacity of the regulatory framework to deal with them. In the case of emerging uses of nanotechnology, the EU regulatory response is driven by arguments that there are already regulatory frameworks that could apply to its novel threats and opportunities. In other words, neither nanotechnologies nor their implications are 'new enough' to take them outside the remit of existing regulatory measures. Nanotechnologies do not, so the dominant policy position suggests, warrant a new regulatory approach or new regulatory provisions. Instead, they will inherit a raft of regulations in place long before nanotechnologies were introduced to the market.

Since newness (or lack thereof) seems to matter a great deal in decisions about regulating applications of technology, Section D explores the different contexts in which debates about newness come to the surface. It returns to the finding that, even though newness is made up of innumerable shades of grey, there is a tendency in the EU policy debate to focus almost exclusively on expert calculations of risk.[3] There are many reasons why this might be thought of as problematic, not least because it prioritizes risk issues when new technologies are often associated with extensive uncertainties and knowledge gaps. One problem stands out, however, as an under-explored feature of technology regulation, as highlighted by concluding remarks in Section E. Under the current approach to nanotechnologies, the propensity of regulators to default to existing regulations in the management of new technologies stems from certain assumptions about the content, nature, and workings of those regulatory provisions. Since those assumptions develop from long-standing regulatory frameworks and make up part of a deep-seated 'regulatory heritage', they are too often accepted without full and appropriate scrutiny.

B. Nanotechnologies

'Nanotechnology' comes from the Greek word 'nanos' meaning 'dwarf'. Often referred to as the 'small science', nanotechnology is a form of molecular engineering that enables

---

[3] For illustration, see M Lee, 'Risk and Beyond: EU Regulation of Nanotechnology' (2010) 35(6) *European Law Review* 799.

the manipulation of matter at a tiny scale. Typically materials are said to be on the 'nanoscale' if they have at least one dimension ranging from one nanometre (one billionth of a metre) to 100 nanometres.[4] To put this into perspective, a single human hair is enormous by comparison, measuring about 80,000 nanometres in width.[5]

The ability to design, alter, produce, and apply matter with nanoscale precision is commercially very attractive because it promises 'nothing less than complete control over the physical structure of matter'.[6] Moreover, it enables the development of advanced materials which have important and unique properties often not shared by the same materials, in bulk form. For instance, materials that are opaque in their conventional form can become transparent in nano form; likewise those that are insulators at bulk scale can become highly effective conductors when nano-sized; inert substances can become catalytic; and brittle materials can show signs of improved strength and resistance to fracturing. Their commercial potential is beginning to be realized and there is increasing optimism that nanomaterials will lead to significant advances in a number of fields including food, electronics, energy, agriculture, construction, personal hygiene, cosmetics, and health care. In the medical sector, nano-technologies and their derivatives are already used in the diagnosis and treatment of disease. Nanoparticles, for example, can be engineered in such ways as to enable the site-specific delivery of drugs.[7]

In terms of their regulation, one reason for singling out nanomaterials is their extremely small dimensions, which gives them a proportionately large surface area per unit mass. This can lead to an increase in reactivity, because more surface is available to react with other substances, and a corresponding increase in potential toxicity. For other nanomaterials, shape is more significant than size or surface chemistry as an indicator of potential hazardousness. Needle-shaped carbon nanotubes are of particular concern because of their heightened propensity, in certain contexts, to behave like harmful asbestos fibres.[8] Moreover, because of their dimensions, nanomaterials tend to be more mobile than larger particles of the same substance, meaning they may be more easily absorbed into and dispersed around ecosystems and the human body.[9] As yet, there is no conclusive evidence as to how nanomaterials might affect health or the environment; however, there are suggestions that certain varieties, in certain contexts, pose a plausible threat of harm. Some, not all, applications of nano-technology 'will present risks unlike any that we have encountered before'.[10] This is not to say that they will be necessarily more threatening, but it is conceivable that they will behave in previously unobserved and unexpected ways in the environment or living

---

[4] British Standards Institute (BSI), Vocabulary—Nanoparticles, Publicly Available Specification (BSI 2005) 71.

[5] Royal Society and Royal Academy of Engineering, Nanoscience and Nanotechnology: Opportunities and Uncertainties (Royal Society 2004) 5.

[6] FA Fiedler and GH Reynolds, 'Legal Problems of Nanotechnology: An Overview' (1994) 3(2) *Southern California Interdisciplinary Law Journal* 594, 599.

[7] For discussion, see SS Davis, 'Biomedical Applications of Nanotechnology—Implications for Drug Targeting and Gene Therapy' (1997) 15(6) *Trends in Biotechnology* 217.

[8] CA Poland and others, 'Carbon Nanotubes Introduced into the Abdominal Cavity of Mice Show Asbestos-Like Pathogenicity in a Pilot Study' (2008) 3 *Nature Nanotechnology* 423.

[9] For discussion, see House of Lords Science and Technology Committee, Nanotechnologies and Food, Vol II: Evidence (HL Paper 22-II, 2010) eg at 113 and 157.

[10] AD Maynard, *Nanotechnology: A Research Strategy for Addressing Risk* (Woodrow Wilson International Center for Scholars 2006) 8.

organisms, including humans.[11] Moreover, the possibility of difference does raises questions about some of the assumptions underpinning their regulation.

The problem, as it is construed by regulators, is that whilst we can begin to hypothesize about the unusual toxicity properties of carbon nanotubes,[12] for instance, or the capacity of some nanoparticles to cause DNA damage across cellular walls,[13] we are not yet in a position to articulate risks precisely. Even where there is initial evidence to indicate heightened hazardousness, it is unclear how this translates into risk because of the limited information currently available on properties and behaviour. The uncertainty in the area is profound. The problem is greater, however, than a simple lack of data. Policymakers also lack the methodological tools for measuring and assessing potential risks, and there is little consensus over the characteristics that determine toxicity profiles.[14]

C. Something Old: Existing Regulations

Ever since law and policy became preoccupied with issues of risk and technological innovation, there is one question that has defined the debate but has proved notoriously difficult to answer: Does new technology require new law?[15] In part, this difficulty is down to the sheer range of understandings of the term 'technology' making it difficult to ensure that consistency and meaning are not entirely lost.[16] For instance, 'technology' may be used to refer to tools and techniques, applied sciences, something that 'grows out of' science, end products, methods that achieve specific goals such as improved speed or efficiency, and solutions to technical problems. Bearing in mind the enormous variety of types and contexts in which technologies arise, it may be more appealing to think about legal and regulatory responses in narrower terms, such as those specific to particular branches of technology, like nanotechnology, biotechnology, or information technology. Indeed, legal disciplines show a similar tendency to break not only along doctrinal lines but along technological lines too (for example, medical law, cyber law).[17]

The context in which a technology arises can also contribute to problems of definition, since it may have different uses or implications from one setting to another. 'Nanotechnology', for example, is usually associated with complex engineering processes and the deliberate production or use of nanomaterials. Yet nanomaterials can also come into being naturally and unintentionally, and can have a diverse range of effects,

---

[11] Royal Commission on Environmental Pollution (RCEP), Novel Materials in the Environment: The Case of Nanotechnology (Twenty-seventh Report, Cm 7468, 2008) 14 and 57.

[12] See eg K Donaldson and CA Poland, 'Nanotoxicology: New Insights into Nanotubes' (2009) 4 *Nature Nanotechnology* 708; K Donaldson and others, 'Review: Carbon Nanotubes: A Review of Their Properties in Relation to Pulmonary Toxicology and Workplace Safety' (2006) 92(1) *Toxicological Sciences* 5.

[13] G Bhabra and others, 'Nanoparticles Can Cause DNA Damage Across a Cellular Barrier' (2009) 4 *Nature Nanotechnology* 876.

[14] See Section D2.

[15] D Friedman, 'Does Technology Require New Law?' (2001) 25(1) *Harvard Journal of Law & Public Policy* 71; for discussion also see R Brownsword, 'So What Does the World Need Now? Reflections on Regulating Technology' in R Brownsword and K Yeung (eds), *Regulating Technologies: Legal Futures, Regulatory Frames and Technological Fixes* (Hart 2008) 24–5 and 30–2.

[16] For discussion see ET Layton Jnr, 'Technology as History' (1974) 15(1) *Technology and Culture* 31; and Moses, 'Why Have a Theory of Law and Technological Change' (n 2) 591.

[17] Moses, 'Why Have a Theory of Law and Technological Change' (n 2) 594.

highlighting the importance of qualifying the terminology in some way. Volcanic dusts erupted into the atmosphere often comprise nano-particulate matter.[18] Similarly, viruses can be nano-sized, as can bacteria, fungi, and pollens.[19] So widespread is nano-scale matter in the natural world that it is claimed that '[e]very living thing is made of cells that are chock full of nanomachines ... Each one is perfect right down to the last atom.'[20] The principal focus for regulators is on manufactured nanomaterials, and for the most part the regulatory debate draws a distinction between natural and man-made varieties, however there are times when 'nanomaterial' is used without distinguishing between the two.[21]

Any attempt at the wholesale regulation of new technology, be that all new technologies or all of a particular branch of new technology, will inevitably be open to criticism for failing to recognize important nuances affecting the activities, relationships, and consequences of any one development. This is particularly true of 'ology' technologies, such as nanotechnology, biotechnology, synthetic biology, and information technology, which employ umbrella terms to capture the full range of applications and contexts of use. Regulatory debates have been similarly unable to resist the temptation to frame policy issues using broad, technology-specific categories. There are often good reasons for directing first-order policy questions at a technology rather than its specific uses, even if it is only to organize stakeholder discussion. At the same time, however, it may be problematic to assume that new technology requires blanket responses. A better approach, it has been suggested, is one which focuses on behaviour and functionality. In the case of nanotechnologies, it has been recommended that 'the relevant [regulatory] authorities should focus specifically on the properties and functionalities of nanomaterials, rather than size.'[22] The idea that regulation ought to be approached in terms of a product's inherent or physical characteristics rather than its mode of production finds support in other legal domains, such as international trade law.[23] The underlying concern in trade law is that measures based on production process, instead of product content, are likely to result in heavy-handed restrictions (on interjurisdictional trade in that context), but similar concerns are evident in relation to new technology regulation in the EU.[24]

Yet, notwithstanding the policy emphasis on case-by-case solutions, the regulation of nanotechnologies in the EU is still generally unwieldy and unresponsive to the challenges presented. As shall be seen later, a state of continuing uncertainty and contestation over the properties and functions of nanotechnology-enabled products can be seen to have two principal effects. First, perhaps counterintuitively, the regulatory debate has arguably become more, not less, focused on concrete evidence of risk. It is one thing to direct additional resources at reducing knowledge gaps, but it is another to persist with evidence-based policies taking little into account but the potential, albeit plausible,

---

[18] FJM Rietmeijer and IDR Mackinnon, 'Bismuth Oxide Nanoparticles in the Stratosphere' (1997) 102(3) *Journal of Geophysical Research* 6621.

[19] RCEP (n 11) 33.

[20] Richard Smalley, as quoted in KE Drexler, 'Nanotechnology: From Feyman to Funding' (2004) 24(1) *Bulletin of Science, Technology and Society* 21, 22.

[21] See eg Commission of the European Communities (CEC), Recommendation of 18 October 2011 on the Definition of Nanomaterial (2011/696/EU), para 2.

[22] RCEP (n 11) 64.

[23] See eg WTO Appellate Body Report, United States—Import Prohibition of Certain Shrimp and Shrimp Products, WT/DS58/AB/R, 12 October 1998.

[24] For discussion, see D Winickoff and others, 'Adjudicating the GM Food Wards: Science, Risk, and Democracy in World Trade Law' (2005) 30 *Yale Journal of International Law* 81.

threat of harm.[25] In these circumstances, a case can be made for adopting a broader interpretation of 'evidence' in the development of knowledge for policy, in the hope that it will result in richer and more 'authentic'[26] insights and outcomes. The difficulty, however, lies in dismantling the more deeply embedded concerns that opening up decision-making to non-risk issues and less disciplined ways of analysis will jeopardize the tractability, and hence the legitimacy, of conventional approaches to decision-making.[27] In relation to nanotechnologies, the dominant scientific-institutional model is proving difficult to overcome. A second and related consequence of uncertainty is that, without a sufficient degree of consensus around scientific knowledge claims, regulators are more likely than not to revert to pre-existing regulatory tools and techniques,[28] even if those tools and techniques are ill-equipped for dealing with technological change. This is arguably the most pronounced feature of the EU's regulatory response to nanotechnology. It is not unique to nanotechnology, however, and there are other examples where regulators respond in the first instance by defaulting to regulatory provisions that pre-date the technology in question. Cutting edge applications of synthetic biology, for instance, are not dealt with using specially tailored regulatory provisions but instead are managed using pre-existing frameworks designed to deal with biotechnologies more generally.[29] Similarly, the regulatory response to early recombinant DNA work was to rely on existing, generic legislation in areas of pharmaceuticals, veterinary medicines, dangerous chemicals, food additives, and animal foodstuffs.[30] That existing regulation is presumed to be sufficiently tolerant of technological change conveys little, if anything at all, about the suitability of those provisions as applied to new products and processes. It does, however, make it difficult to scrutinize existing regulations especially when their continued application to new technology is an unspoken assumption or even a foregone conclusion (discussed in Section E).

It also says something about the nature and expanse of the regulatory measures that are expected to cover and apply to new technologies, even if they were never designed with that in mind. Existing regulations are assumed to cover nanotechnology, it is argued, because they already have a broad remit and are geared up for issues of health and environmental risk. In the sectors where nanotechnologies are currently used, such as cosmetics, foods, medicines, construction, agriculture, and energy, regulatory coverage is extensive. The General Product Safety Directive,[31] for example, imposes an obligation on manufacturers and suppliers to place only safe products on the EU market.[32] It covers all products which are intended for, or likely to be used by,

[25] For a particularly illuminating discussion on the representation of uncertainty in a different context, that of climate change policy, see S Shackley and B Wynne, 'Representing Uncertainty in Global Climate Change and Policy: Boundary-Ordering Devices and Authority' (1996) 21(3) *Science, Technology & Human Values* 275, esp 281 where the authors cite Sir John Houghton, Chairman of the scientific assessment Working Group of the Intergovernmental Panel on Climate Change, who noted that 'the [quantitative] estimation of uncertainty is at the heart of the scientific method. . . . [e]ven when the uncertainties are large'.

[26] N Brown and M Michael, 'From Authority to Authenticity: The Changing Governance of Biotechnology (2002) 4(3) *Health, Risk & Society* 259.

[27] Shackley and Wynne (n 25).

[28] E Stokes, 'Demand for Command: Responding to Technological Risks and Scientific Uncertainties' (2013) 21(1) *Medical Law Review* (forthcoming).

[29] Royal Academy of Engineering, *Synthetic Biology: Scope, Applications and Implications* (RAEng 2009) 48.

[30] CEC, *Biotechnology in the Community* COM (83) 672 final/2-Annex, 74.

[31] Directive 2001/95/EC on general product safety, as amended [2002] OJ L11/4.

[32] Directive 2001/95/EC, Art 3.

consumers, except products already covered by sector-specific legislation applicable in areas such as cosmetic products, foodstuffs, and medicines. Sector-specific legislation contains similarly high standards of safety. Cosmetics, for instance, 'shall be safe for human health when used under normal or reasonably foreseeable conditions of use';[33] likewise food 'shall not be placed on the market if it is unsafe'.[34] Similar conditions of safety, even if they find expression in different regulatory tools, are set in the medical sector. Medicines and medical devices cannot be placed on the market unless and until they receive authorization, which in turn depends on whether they fulfil certain safety and quality requirements.[35]

The fact that existing legislation is comprehensive, in the sense that it covers general categories of product and imposes broad-brush conditions of safety, offers some explanation for the primacy afforded to old regulations in response to new technologies. It can also be explained by reference to the definitional breadth of current measures, meaning their tendency to avoid drawing any distinction between products on grounds of technological origin or particle size. Since regulations target products without regard to characteristics such as scale or mode of production, they are taken to apply to nanotechnology-enabled products in the same way as they apply to conventional-scale equivalents. In this regard, nanotechnologies can be described as being born into an inherited regulatory environment.[36] The Commission has drawn attention to the wide and overlapping remits of prior regulations by pointing out that '[v]irtually all product legislation imposes a risk assessment and the adoption of risk management measures. Nanomaterials are not excluded from this obligation.'[37] Although it noted that legislation may have to be modified as new information becomes available, the Commission was of the view that 'current legislation covers to a large extent risks in relation to nanomaterials and that risks can be dealt with under the current legislative framework.'[38] This finding has been made elsewhere, for example by the UK Medicines and Healthcare products Regulatory Agency (MHRA) which concluded that:

The existing regulations for medical devices require manufacturers to carry out an analysis of the risks associated with a medical device, to eliminate or reduce these where feasible, and to assess the balance of risks and benefits. Although the regulations for medical devices do not differentiate between medical devices that use nanotechnologies and those that do not, the MHRA is of the view that the existing regulations for medical devices and medicines are sufficiently broad in scope to cover risks associated with nanotechnology.[39]

These findings raise two observations. The first is that the policy debate is concerned, above all else, with issues of risk. This is not to say that risk issues ought to receive more cursory treatment, or that other factors should be shown the same type or degree of consideration. Rather, it highlights the possibility that regulatory decisions relating to nanotechnologies follow an unduly narrow path, given that nanotechnologies raise

---

[33] Regulation (EC) No 1223/2009 on cosmetic products [2009] OJ L342/59, Art 3.
[34] Regulation (EC) No 178/2002 laying down the general principles and requirements of food law, establishing the European Food Safety Authority and laying down the procedures in matters of food [2002] OJ L31/1, Art 14.
[35] See eg Council Directive 93/42/EEC of 14 June 1993 concerning medical devices [1993] OJ L169/1, Art 2.
[36] E Stokes, 'Nanotechnology and the Products of Inherited Regulation' (2012) 39(1) *Journal of Law and Society* 93.
[37] CEC, Communication on Regulatory Aspects of Nanomaterials COM(2008) 366 final, 6.
[38] CEC (n 37) 3.
[39] MHRA, <www.mhra.gov.uk/Howweregulate/Nanotechnology/index.htm>, accessed September 2011.

issues that are complex and evolving. There are many reasons for this particular trend, as documented in the substantial literature on cultures of expertise in decision-making, policy preferences for technical precision, and the presumed, but often mistaken, correlation between greater levels of scientific knowledge and better control and more trusted public authority.[40] Another is that, because 'risk' penetrates to the core of existing regulations (regulations that are now expected to cover new technological futures), it immediately becomes a natural focus of attention for regulatory questions on nanotechnologies.

A second observation is that, although the continued reliance on existing regulations, and all that that entails, might represent the dominant position in the EU, it is not universally accepted as the appropriate regulatory response. Many aspects of the nanotechnology debate, even if they are presented as irrefutable and unimportant, remain unsettled, contested, and still capable of leading to different regulatory approaches. As the following section seeks to show, the emergence of nanotechnology can indeed result in new concerns about risk but decisions about its regulation can pivot on a host of other factors besides. Some of these factors may well be accommodated by existing regulatory measures, while others may require a change of regulatory tack.

D. Something New: Emerging Nanotechnologies

1. What is New?

'Newness', it is said, 'is a quality that fits uneasily with law'.[41] The reason most commonly cited is that law is slow to keep up with the rapid pace of developments in science and technology.[42] But differing rates of change are not the only source of difficulty, since there are other factors that can act as frictional forces against responsive regulation, explored later. Whilst the policy discourse recognizes that there are no simple or straightforward solutions to new technology, it is still underpinned by the notion that all that is occurring at this early stage of nanotechnology's use is the development of new methods, better products, and potential, yet highly uncertain, risks.[43] As this section shows, transformation can be observed in many other senses too. By drawing attention to some of the other sites of newness, its aim is to highlight the variety issues with which policymakers have to contend.

Newness is perhaps most visible in a technology's products, processes, and designs. This is certainly true of technological developments in the past, when, for example, the introduction of the printing press, the steam engine, or the telegraph clearly bore the stamp of progress. Newness becomes less easy to spot where technological advance involves miniaturization or the manipulation of extremely small components (for example, nanotechnology; genetic modification) or, alternatively, where there are large-scale technological applications in geographically remote locations (for example, the hydraulic extraction of natural gas underground; off-shore wind farms). The flavour of my breakfast cereal may have recently improved thanks to the addition of nano-sized

---

[40] See eg S Jasanoff, *Science at the Bar: Law, Science, and Technology in America* (Harvard UP 1997), Ch 3; HM Collins and R Evans, 'The Third Wave of Science Studies: Studies of Expertise and Experience' (2002) 32(2) *Social Studies of Science* 235; B Wynne, 'Creating Public Alienation: Expert Cultures of Risk and Ethics on GMOs' (2001) 10(4) *Science as Culture* 445.

[41] Price (n 2) 1913.

[42] See eg the famous statement that the law marches ahead 'but in the rear and limping a little' Windeyer J in Mount *Isa v Pusey* (1970) 125 CLR 383, 395.

[43] Price (n 2) 1912.

flavour enhancers. I am unable to see the new nano-ingredients, and there is nothing on the packaging to indicate that I have bought a new type of product. It may taste a little better but it looks the same as the cereal I have always enjoyed. I may be reluctant, therefore, to describe it as a product of 'new' technology. Were its nano-ingredients to deliver significantly larger quantities of vitamins and minerals per spoonful, however, or give me a glowing complexion and glossy hair, I may be more inclined to think of it as noticeably different from, and hence 'newer' than, the less functional cereal I have eaten in the past. As certain qualities such as superiority and uniqueness become more apparent, it may matter less that nano-sized ingredients are invisible to the naked eye.

How we perceive technologies, even those that are invisible and intangible, is critical to how we respond, since human behaviour is reflective of what we believe or perceive to be true.[44] Politically, attitudes towards a technology can matter more than any of its intrinsic qualities given the known influence of perception on public trust and acceptability, for example. This is especially true in areas of high complexity and uncertainty, such as nanotechnology, where the effects can only be approximately estimated and are not determinate but depend on many social conditions and contingencies.[45] Familiarity, the research suggests, is an important variable affecting perception, as evidenced by the numerous studies showing that less familiar technologies are likely to be viewed more negatively than familiar, everyday technologies.[46] But even the literature that seeks to expose the foundational contingencies of perception can sometimes fall into the trap of thinking that diverse configurations of technology can be collapsed into binary opposites (for example, familiar/unfamiliar, known/unknown). The picture is far less coherent, involving multiple interactions and non-linear processes, resulting in what is described as the 'end of certainty'.[47]

2. How New?

The multivalency of new technology is further reflected in the idea that 'newness' is judged not only on the promise of technological futures but also on the fruits of technological pasts, since much depends on whether a technology is nominally or conceptually different from what has gone before. Thinking about the degree of newness can be particularly difficult in the case of converging technologies,[48] of which nanotechnology is one, which enable us to build on and make incremental (albeit profound) improvements to existing methods of research and development. Innovation may be described as evolutionary and continuous where it leads to the production of better but essentially similar products, for instance. Yet the lifecycle of those products may still be punctuated by more radical change, such as change resulting in new generations of products, re-branding, new users, new markets and new customers. Newness may be apparent in one aspect of nanotechnology (for example, more precise

---

[44] T Satterfield and others, 'Anticipating the Perceived Risk of Nanotechnologies' (2009) 4 *Nature Nanotechnology* 752.

[45] B Wynne, 'Uncertainty and Environmental Learning: Reconceiving Science and Policy in the Preventive Paradigm' (1992) 2(2) *Global Environmental Change* 111, 119–20.

[46] For discussion and further explanation in the context of nanotechnologies, see DM Kahan and others, 'Cultural Cognition of the Risks and Benefits of Nanotechnology' (2009) 4 *Nature Nanotechnology* 87.

[47] I Prigogine, *The End of Certainty: Time, Chaos, and the New Laws of Nature* (The Free Press 1997).

[48] MC Roco, 'Converging Technologies for Improving Human Performance: Integrating From the Nanoscale' (2002) 4(4) *Journal of Nanoparticle Research* 281.

manufacturing processes; products with novel functional properties; new waste streams) but not in others (for example, reliance on existing resources, skills, and knowledge; improved but very similar products). The intensity of technological change may also alter over time; technologies may begin by focusing on the adaptation, refinement, and enhancement of existing products or production methods but eventually become 'game changers' by redefining technological paradigms, products lines, markets, behaviours, and expectations.

Since aspects of newness exist conceptually on a continuum, it can be difficult to define products or processes of innovation as evolutionary or revolutionary, as incremental or radical, or as continuous or discontinuous. This is further compounded by the uncertainties and complexities that flow from the use of nanotechnologies, which entail uncertainty not only in projected consequences. There is technical uncertainty, for instance, in the sense that the characterization and assessment of some applications of nanotechnology suffer from inexactness. There is also methodological uncertainty owing to the lack of appropriate tools for characterizing, detecting, and monitoring the uses and implications of nanotechnology in certain domains. For some nanomaterials, risk assessment methods need to be further developed, validated, and standardized.[49] The problem extends to regulatory guidelines too which currently make 'very little reference to substances in particulate form'[50] making it difficult for regulators and regulatees to know which approach to testing should be followed. Methodological limitations are closely linked to epistemological uncertainty, because without sufficient information, it becomes difficult to 'to identify any generic rules governing the likely toxicology and ecotoxicology of nanoparticles in general'.[51] In the absence of data, it cannot be assumed that the nano-version of a chemical will have the same effects as its conventional chemical counterpart.[52] But epistemological uncertainty exists not only in the form of information gaps, which may be reduced over time as further research is conducted into known uncertainties, but also in the form of more fundamental contingency and indeterminacy.[53] These latter types present an even greater obstacle to credible risk assessment than our inability accurately to describe known aspects of nanotechnologies. They indicate areas of 'irremediable ignorance',[54] an inevitable by-product of increased policy commitments to clearly marked paths (for example, risk assessment, defined uncertainties),[55] which 'even in practice based on science, can no longer be expected to be conquered'.[56] Yet, the policy discourse on nanotechnology tends only to deal with uncertainty where, even though precise impacts are unknown, the parameters are relatively clearly drawn using established analytic models.

Notwithstanding the range of constitutive and interactional elements of nanotechnology and the abundant references to uncertainty in debates on its regulation, uncertainty in this context is narrowly framed in terms of 'uncertain impacts'

---

[49] Scientific Committee on Emerging and Newly Identified Health Risks (SCENIHR), Risk Assessment of Products of Nanotechnology, adopted 19 January 2009.

[50] SCENIHR (n 49).

[51] SCENIHR, Modified Opinion on the Appropriateness of Existing Methodologies to Assess the Potential Risks Associated with Engineered and Adventitious Products of Nanotechnologies, adopted 10 March 2006 after public consultation, 55.

[52] SCENIHR (n 51).

[53] H Hoffmann-Riem and B Wynne, 'In Risk Assessment, One Has to Admit Ignorance' (2002) 416(6877) *Nature* 123; SO Funtowicz and JR Ravetz, 'Science for the Post-Normal Age' (1993) 25(7) *Future* 739.

[54] D Collingirdge, *The Social Control of Technology* (Francis Pinter 1980).

[55] Wynne (n 45).

[56] Funtowicz and Ravetz (n 53).

or 'uncertain risks'. Risk is a useful device in that it organizes discussion and helps to produce terminological consistency in exchanges between policy actors. Its centrality in the debate also implies the relevance and authority of risk-based arguments over other approaches and agendas. The fact that there are still knowledge gaps does not undermine the potency and pervasiveness of risk-based arguments in respect of nanotechnology. Instead, it opens up space for conflict in which EU policy actors each advance arguments of risk in support of materially different policy options. Some argue, for instance, that it would be wrong to adopt a more stringent regulatory stance to nanotechnologies because it would involve reacting 'against imagined risks, merely because they are in something that is so small as to be difficult to identify, or even, dare I say, to understand.'[57] This sentiment is echoed in the argument that 'Where the Americans see opportunities, Europeans want first to protect themselves against any risk imaginable.'[58]

Others, by contrast, argue that the existence of potential risks, even if their likelihood and consequences are currently unknown, gives the green light to more interventionist protective measures, since '[w]e cannot simply allow these products to be put onto the market and tested on consumers; we cannot allow consumers to be treated as guinea pigs.'[59] In a similar vein, one policymaker states 'I am in favour of the precautionary principle and, hence, of a moratorium [on the use of nano in foodstuffs], since health risks have not been ruled out.'[60] For some, these risks are real: 'Coal dust is not hazardous, but nanoparticles in the form of carbon clusters cause serious brain damage in fish within 48 hours at concentrations as low as 0.5 ppm ... Our immune system is simply not adapted to cope with nanoparticles.'[61] For others, the issue is not about the tentative, even tenuous, illustration of risk but rather the ongoing state of uncertainty which, they argue, warrants a cautious response: 'Those who spurn precaution are not friends of nanotechnology.'[62] Current policy, it has been suggested, is anything but precautionary because '[a]t the moment, we are stepping on the gas of nanotechnology without first ensuring that we have emergency brakes or even knowing whether the steering is working.'[63]

The fact that risk continues to be uncertain propels policy arguments in opposite directions, on the one hand towards maintaining the regulatory status quo and, on

---

[57] European Parliament (EP) Debate No 4 of 28 September 2006, Giles Chichester, on behalf of the European People's Party–European Democrats.

[58] EP Debate No 4 of 28 September 2006, Robert Goebbels on behalf of the Party of European Socialists.

[59] EP Debate No 4 of 28 September 2006, Hiltrud Breyer Breyer on behalf of the Green Party/ European Free Alliance.

[60] EP Debate No 9 of 10 July 2010, Explanation of Votes, Robert Rochefort, in writing, on behalf of the Alliance of Liberals and Democrats for Europe. Note that this understanding of the precautionary principle is not universal and departs quite substantially from policy renditions (see eg CEC, Communication on the Precautionary Principle COM(2000) 1 final). For a fuller analysis of the spectrum of interpretations, and applications of the precautionary principle, see E Fisher, 'Precaution, Precaution Everywhere: Developing a Common Understanding of the Precautionary Principle in the European Community' (2002) 9 *Maastricht Journal of European and Comparative Law* 7; E Fisher, 'Opening Pandora's Box: Contextualising the Precautionary Principle in the European Union' in M Everson and E Vos (eds), *Uncertain Risks Regulated* (Routledge-Cavendish 2009) Ch 2; E Scotford, 'Mapping the Article 174(2) Case Law: A First Step to Analysis Community Environmental Principles' (2008) 8 *Yearbook of European Environmental Law* 1.

[61] EP Debate No 4 of 28 September 2006, Carl Schlyter, on behalf of the Green Party/European Free Alliance.

[62] EP Debate No 4 of 28 September 2006, David Hammerstein Mintz, on behalf of the the Green Party/European Free Alliance.

[63] EP Debate No 4 (n 62).

the other, towards the adoption of more restrictive market entry requirements for nano-enabled products. One policymaker comments: 'I see it as positively irresponsible that the Commission, even though it knows what is missing and is aware of the lack of any methodology for assessing the risks, wants to allow the marketing of consumer goods aimed at private citizens and their households, without the certainty of every risk having been removed.'[64] Naturally, it is impossible to say with absolute certainty that a substance or product is safe under all conditions of use, and any expectation of zero-risk is, usually, very quickly denounced in the policy pursuit of evidence-based deci-sion-making. This is reflected in the rhetoric and aspirations of the regulations, which emphasize how the governance of nano ought to be based on 'the best available scientific evidence',[65] and that the successful exploitation of nano 'needs a sound scientific basis'.[66] Here the conundrum is not whether regulatory responses ought to have any scientific footing at all; there is, after all, broad agreement at the policy level that an improved knowledge base can only improve the quality of decision-making (even if there is far less agreement as to what might constitute an appropriate regulatory response to that knowledge). Rather, the more troubling, but largely neglected, issue is how a policy of evidence-based management takes shape when the 'evidence' at stake is highly complex and hotly contested. As demands for clarity grow in both number and vigour, and new uncertainties continue to be uncovered, a space opens up where multiple considerations are entertained but where the discourse of risk monopolizes.[67]

Risk emerges from the discourse in other senses too. Here we see that policymakers are concerned not just with how to manage potential risks to health or the environ-ment, but also the risks of stifling growth and innovation and of failing to allay public concerns. '[W]e should avoid demonising this new technology, as has often happened in the past',[68] argued one policymaker, whilst another warned of market paralysis under an excessively cautious policy 'aimed at making people think that nanotechnologies are dangerous, because they manipulate the smallest particles—atoms and molecules'.[69] The focus of risk-based approaches on known and familiar risks means that they become 'locked in' to established analytical frameworks,[70] for instance. It also means that policymaking has a propensity to rehearse familiar rhetorics of risk and re-assert claims that public trust in regulatory decision-making depends, first and foremost, on the ability of regulations to prevent risk from materializing. Consequently, it is less open to the possibility of variation and evolution, over time and between contexts. It also marginalizes discussion about the political values and legitimate democratic concerns that underpin, inform, and are relevant to policy on nanotechnologies. That

---

[64] EP Debate No 4 of 28 September 2006, Hiltrud Breyer on behalf of the Green Party/European Free Alliance.

[65] JP Holden, CR Sunstein, and IA Siddiqui, 'Memorandum for the Heads of Executive Depart-ments and Agencies: Policy Principles for the U.S. Decision-Making Concerning Regulation and Oversight of Applications of Nanotechnology and Nanomaterials', adopted 9 June 2011, 4–5; see also HM Government, UK Nanotechnologies Strategy: Small Technologies, Great Opportunities, URN 10/825 (HMSO 2010).

[66] CEC, Communication: Towards a European Strategy for Nanotechnology COM(2004) 338 final, para 1.3

[67] For further discussion on the challenges of incorporating ethical expertise in nanotechnology regulation, see eg Lee (n 3).

[68] EP Debate No 15 of 6 July 2010, Horst Schnellhardt on behalf of the European People's Party–European Democrats.

[69] EP Debate No 4 of 28 September 2006, Robert Goebbels on behalf of the Party of European Socialists.

[70] R Baldwin and J Black, 'Really Responsive Regulation' (2008) 71(1) *Modern Law Review* 59, 66.

the debate gives short shrift to issues such as the acceptability of potential effects, imagined and promised futures, social purposes, needs, benefits, and priorities[71] reflects and reinforces the idea that they play only a peripheral role in regulatory decisions. Its ritualized focus on risk has attracted criticism:

What is absent, above all, is the willingness to consider concerns other than safety risks, not least the issue of whether or not new technologies are desirable, or issues to do with people's convictions about life in general. The benefits and possible adverse effects must first of all be considered, in order to prevent choices being made solely on the basis of economic value while the technology is still at an early stage in its development.[72]

This highlights the importance of problematizing, as opposed to presuming, values, meanings, and contexts. The starting point for the policy debate is often that the EU public is essentially wary about nanotechnologies and, unless potential risks are properly managed, such unease may quickly and irreversibly develop into unfounded fear.[73] So far there is little to support this assumption, and initial findings indicate that EU citizens are on the whole 'rather positive toward',[74] 'reasonably optimistic about'[75] and 'supportive of'[76] nanotechnology. Moreover, the results give a more nuanced account by showing, for instance, that applications of nanotechnology in some sectors, such as energy, are viewed more positively than in others, such as health and human enhancement[77] and food.[78] In the latter, there is an accompanying sense of dissatisfaction with the market motives of regulatory arrangements: 'Of course their aim is to get [nano-products] through, so how honest are they actually going to be? I mean, I know they're supposed to be but I wouldn't trust them.'[79]

The debate, as it is currently oriented, overlooks other new elements too, such as the impact of uncertainties on the ways in which information is generated and used. For example, in relation to nanotechnologies, information gaps appear to have two interesting effects. First, industrial actors are increasingly being relied upon by regulators to disclose information about applications of nanotechnology, even if this entails going beyond obligations contained in current regulatory frameworks. Manufacturers and suppliers of nanomaterials are encouraged to participate in voluntary reporting schemes so that regulators can collect data on current uses and be better able to design appropriate regulatory responses.[80] This outsourcing of informational responsibilities is

---

[71] CEC, Taking European Knowledge Society Seriously—Report of the Expert Group on Science and Governance to the Science, Economy and Society Directorate, EUR 22700 (DG for Research 2007).

[72] EP Debate, 28 September 2006, MEP Bastiaan Belder on behalf of the Freedom and Democracy Group.

[73] Council of the EU, 'Addendum to "I/A" Item Note' 12682/09 ADD 1 REV 1, 2.

[74] RV Burri and S Bellucci, 'Public Perception of Nanotechnology' (1998) 10(3) *Journal of Nanoparticle Research* 387, 389.

[75] CEC, Report on the European Commission's Public Online Consultation Towards a Strategic Nanotechnology Action Plan (SNAP) 2010–2015, 9.

[76] G Gaskell and others, 'A Report to the European Commission's Directorate-General for Research, Europeans and Biotechnology in 2005: Patterns and Trends, Final Report on Eurobarometer 64.3' (2006), available at <http://ec.europa.eu/research/biosociety/pdf/eb_64_3_final_report_second_edition_july_06.pdf>, last accessed December 2012, 19.

[77] N Pidgeon, 'Deliberating the Risks of Nanotechnologies for Energy and Health Applications in the United States and United Kingdom' (2009) 4 *Nature Nanotechnology* 95.

[78] See, generally, Food Standards Agency (FSA), *FSA Citizens Forums: Nanotechnology and Food* (FSA 2011).

[79] FSA (n 78) 23.

[80] Department for Environment, Food and Rural Affairs (Defra), UK Voluntary Reporting Scheme for Engineered Nanoscale Materials (Defra 2008); examples of reporting schemes in other jurisdictions include the US Environmental Protection Agency 'Nanoscale Materials Stewardship Program', and the Berkeley Municipal Code (amended through Ordinance No 6,960-NS January 2007), Chapter 6.95 of California Health and Safety Code, Title 15.

not in itself unusual given recent trends at EU level towards less state-led, more pluralistic forms of regulation,[81] but it does give private actors a different role in the regulatory process from the one envisaged under existing regulatory arrangements applicable to nanotechnology. Whilst there are strong efficiency arguments for taking advantage of private capacities and resources, it may come at a cost to other goals such as legitimacy and transparency. Whether or not that is the case, it does mean the emergence of new stakeholder roles and interactions, new expectations about the locus of responsibility for producing and assessing information, and new channels of communication that are not accounted for in the debate. New technologies, it is said, create:

shifts in the value of information, in the language used to describe information, in customs used to employ information, in expectations about how information will be used, and in norms that are applied to information and communication.[82]

Secondly, even though uncertainties can result in the dispersal of certain decision-making responsibilities, the official policy line is still that existing, state-promulgated measures take centre stage in regulating nanotechnologies. Under the current approach it is difficult to reconcile the argument that existing legislative provisions already cover nanotechnologies with other arguments deployed in the framing and attempted resolution of the regulatory problem. For example, a recurrent theme in the debate is the right of consumers to make informed decisions about the products they purchase, which emerges alongside a growing emphasis on individual responsibility for risk.[83] Indeed, uncertainties surrounding nanotechnologies could reasonably be expected to create a more level playing field in stakeholder dialogue and deliberation than is the case under current regulatory frameworks. We are all regulators now. This rather supposes, however, that along with the dispersal of regulatory responsibilities there is a corresponding shift in regulatory capacities, such as effective channels of communication and opportunities for engagement.[84] It is doubtful whether such channels and opportunities are available under the existing approaches.[85] Moreover, the presence of heightened uncertainties in the case of nanotechnologies, and new technologies generally, can in fact result in new and exaggerated demands for (state) control and (risk) certainty.[86]

3. New to Whom?

Finally, in determining a technology's newness, and hence its regulatory pathway, regard should also be had to the question to whom is the technology 'new'? A technology may be new to the world, to a jurisdiction or region, or to particular actors within a given territory. It may be new to a branch of industry, to a scientific community, to the market,

---

[81] See also E Fisher, 'The "Perfect Storm" of REACH: Charting Regulatory Controversy in the Age of Information, Sustainable Development, and Globalization' (2008) 11(4) *Journal of Risk Research* 541, particularly 548–51.

[82] ME Katsh, 'Law Reviews and the Migration to Cyberspace' (1996) 29(2) *Arkon Law Review* 115, 120.

[83] Better Regulation Commission (BRC), *Risk, Responsibility and Regulation—Whose Risk is it Anyway?* (BRC 2006).

[84] E Stokes, 'You Are What You Eat: Market Citizens and the Right to Know About Nano Foods' (2011) 2 *Journal of Human Rights and the Environment* 178.

[85] Stokes (n 84).

[86] Stokes (n 28).

to customers or to other stakeholders (for example, regulators, NGOs). Identifying how nanotechnologies are interpreted and, importantly, by whom can uncover other sites where regulatory responses are contested. This last point of conflict has less to do with applications of nanotechnology and more to do with the political power wielded by different EU institutions. It is about the tension between the Commission's stance that existing regulations are generally fit for purpose, and the newly waged campaigns led by the European Parliament—in particular its Committee on the Environment, Public Health and Food Safety (hereafter 'the Environment Committee')—for the introduction of new, nano-specific regulations.

Unlike the Commission[87] (and to some extent the Council[88]), the Parliament and its Environment Committee have been staunch supporters of regulatory amendment to reflect the fact the nanotechnologies may create new issues to which existing provisions are blind. The Commission, says the Environment Committee, has provided 'only a general legal overview' of current legislation which fails to consider the specific properties, uses, risks, and benefits of nanomaterials.[89] Moreover, the Environment Committee '[d]eplores the absence of a proper evaluation of the de facto application of the general provisions of Community law in the light of the actual nature of nanomaterials'[90] and does not agree with the Commission's findings that current legislation covers, in principle, the relevant risks relating to nanomaterials.[91] The Environment Committee goes further, arguing that all nanomaterials should be treated as 'new' substances for the purposes of regulation, which will make them subject if not to different regulatory provisions then to different techniques of assessment. Techno-logical newness, for the Environment Committee, translates into regulatory newness which, in turn, means the introduction of measures that distinguish between bulk and nano forms of material.

To date, nano-specific measures have been proposed on seven different occasions, in five product sectors (three proposals in the food sector, two in relation to electrical and electronic equipment, and one in each of the sectors for cosmetics and biocidal products). At the time of writing, four of these proposals have been adopted into legislation. Two new measures, relating to cosmetic products and foodstuffs, require that all products containing nanomaterials ingredients carry the label 'nano'.[92] Manu-facturers and suppliers of cosmetics are under an additional obligation to notify the Commission six months before placing products with nanomaterials on the market.[93] Other provisions, such as the one applicable to hazardous substances in electrical and electronic equipment, highlight the importance of taking into account the particular characteristics of nanomaterials in determining whether or not to restrict their market circulation, and encourage the substitution of nanomaterials for 'more environmentally friendly alternatives'.[94] The first nano-specific provision to be adopted in the EU,

---

[87] CEC (n 37).

[88] See eg Council of the EU, Proposal for a Regulation of the European Parliament and of the Council on cosmetic products (recast)—Preparation of an informal trialogue, 2008/0035(COD), p 3.

[89] EP, Resolution of 24 April 2009 on Regulatory Aspects of Nanomaterials P6_TA(2009)0328, para P.

[90] EP Resolution (n 89), para AA2.

[91] EP Resolution (n 89), para AA3.

[92] Regulation on cosmetic products (n 33) Art 2(1)(k); Regulation (EU) No 1169/2011 on the provision of food information to consumers [2011] OJ L304/18, Art 18(3).

[93] Regulation on cosmetic products (n 33) Art 16(3).

[94] Directive 2011/65/EU on the restriction of the use of certain hazardous substances in electrical and electronic equipment [2011] OJ L174/88, Recital 16.

relating to food additives, requires that a food additive that is already on the EU market but undergoes 'significant change in its production methods or in the starting materials used, or there is a change in particle size, for example through nanotechnology', will be treated as a new food additive and thus be subject to separate market entry controls.[95]

It is striking that all of these provisions are informational in character. Either they encourage the movement of information outwards from manufacturers/suppliers into the marketplace via product labelling, or they impose obligations on manufacturers/suppliers to report information inwards to a central regulatory authority.[96] Their collective focus on improving information flows can in part be explained by the policy debate which is alive with discussions of knowledge gaps and uncertainties. An explanation may also lie in the nature of the provisions themselves, for it is generally the case that there is an implicit assumption in policy discourses that information regulation is the most benign form of regulation.[97] The European Parliament and its Environment Committee are committed to changing provisions on nanotechnologies, and labelling and reporting requirements might well have offered the path of least resistance.

This is reflected in the European Parliament's approach to legislating on nanotechnologies. It will have been clear to the Parliament that the introduction of significant measures of nano-specific legislation on grounds of risk or functionality were likely to fail, particularly given the Commission's eagerness to promote trade in nanotechnologies and avoid unnecessary restrictive regulation.[98] Instead of arguing for more ambitious, overarching nano-specific legislation, therefore, the European Parliament has adopted a different tack, resorting to incremental, opportunistic, and ad hoc changes. This has played out through the insertion of provisions (for example, nano-labelling, nano-reporting requirements) into existing regulatory regimes. The Parliament cannot propose new legislation; hence, each of the new nano-specific provisions adopted were tabled by the Parliament's Committee as amendments to the Commission's original proposal. None of the Commission's original proposals contained any reference to 'nanotechnology' or 'nanomaterials'. These references were only subsequently introduced by the European Parliament on its first, or sometimes second, reading of the Commission's proposals, and were often among a raft of other amendments suggested by the Parliament.

What is interesting is that the European Parliament has targeted particular sectors (cosmetics, foodstuffs, hazardous substances, etc.) in which to introduce nano-specific amendments. These amendments are justified on a range of different grounds, including: '[c]onsumers might like to know whether a food has been produced by the use of nanotechnologies';[99] or 'consumers need transparent information to be able to make informed choices and purchases';[100] or '[t]here is currently little known about the

[95] Regulation (EC) No 1333/2008 on food additives [2008] OJ L354/16, Art 12.

[96] With the exception of Directive 2011/65/EU (n 94). However, the nano-specific provision in this Directive is contained only in a Recital.

[97] Even though information regulation can in fact be much more complex. For discussion see E Fisher, 'Transparency and Administrative Law: A Critical Evaluation' (2010) 63 *Current Legal Problems* 272; S Jasanoff, 'Transparency in Public Science: Purposes, Reasons, Limits' (2006) 69 *Law and Contemporary Problems* 21.

[98] CEC, *Communication on Nanosciences and Nanotechnologies: An Action Plan for Europe 2005–2009* COM(2005) 243 final, 2.

[99] EP, Report on the Proposal for a Regulation on Novel Foods, A6-0512/2008, Amendment 59.

[100] EP, Report on the Proposal for a Regulation on Novel Foods, Amendment 8.

health risks of nanotechnology';[101] or '[n]anomaterials have different characteristics to the same substances in a non-nanomaterial form'.[102] It may well be the case that the Parliament has chosen to exert legislative pressure in these particular sectors because nanotechnologies in those contexts bring into sharp focus the limited capacity of existing regulations to deal with issues of risk, uncertainty, societal consequences, public trust, ethics, and politics. But this tells us only part of the story. For the Parliament's Environment Committee, nanotechnologies are 'new' in many respects, but most importantly, they also offer a new opportunity for enterprising policymaking.[103]

E. Something Borrowed: Regulatory Assumptions

The aim of this chapter has been to highlight the dynamic, politically constituted nature of questions of 'newness'. Notwithstanding suggestions that it is difficult to disentangle new technologies from their broader context, the policy discourse still interprets and frames social questions along narrower lines of risk. Issues of risk are, of course, essential to regulatory decision-making, and the aim here is not to suggest that these be abandoned or replaced. Decisions need to be made, and there is a limit to the range of issues that can be taken into account if efficiency and expediency are to be achieved. Yet, current practices impose artificial closure on questions that are more open-ended than the process suggests.[104] This is particularly well illustrated by emerging technologies, which are often characterized by such high levels of uncertainty that it becomes more difficult to sustain policy commitments to risk assessment and proof of safety. Knowing what we do about the sometimes blinkered view of the current approach, for it has long been recognized in various fora, it is even more intriguing that the policy discourse should continue along the same tracks without any explicit reflection on its assumptions and routines.

One reason for maintaining the status quo is that it helps to reassert the authority and legitimacy of the current approach, and in so doing ensures stability and consistency in decision-making. Another, indirectly related, reason explored in this chapter, is that questions relating to the management of new technologies are inescapably framed and constituted by their regulatory heritage. Traditions in legal and regulatory policy-making will always be difficult to shake, not least because '[t]he development of law is imprisoned in the rhetoric of its prior existence'.[105] This is particularly so when new technologies are presumed to fall within the remit of existing regulatory provisions. New technologies, such as nanotechnologies, are not introduced into a legal vacuum[106] and so there is no requirement or expectation that policymakers will start afresh. Instead, nanotechnologies emerge into a regulatory environment already inhabited by legislation offering extensive public health, consumer, and environmental protection. Not only do nanotechnologies inherit the obligations contained in existing legislation, but they become subject to (or 'borrow') the assumptions and practices underpinning

---

[101] EP, Draft Report on the proposal for a regulation on food additives 2006/0145(COD), Amendment 19.

[102] EP, Draft Report on the proposal for a regulation concerning the placing on the market and use of biocidal products 2009/0076(COD), Amendment 44.

[103] See K Collins, C Burns, and A Warleigh, 'Policy Entrepreneurs: The Role of European Parliament Committees in the Making of EU Policy' (1998) 19(1) *Statute Law Review* 1.

[104] Wynne (n 45) 113.

[105] Price (n 2) 1913.

[106] In spite of some claims to that effect, see eg EP Debate No 4 of 28 September 2006, Hiltrud Breyer on behalf of the Green Party/European Free Alliance.

those provisions. This extrapolation of rules (for example, the obligation to ensure product safety) and traditions (for example, risk assessment) may be more difficult to apply where nanotechnologies throw up new and materially different risk, political, social, or ethical concerns.

A further consequence arises from new technologies being 'locked in' to existing regulations and ideas about newness. That is, when a new technology is introduced to a sector in which there is already expansive regulatory coverage, it is difficult to scrutinize existing regulatory provisions because this entails going against the great weight of history and policy expectation. Given that the regulation of nanotechnologies occurs by default, and is inflexibly and unconsciously dependent on prior rules, it becomes all the more difficult to challenge its application and appropriateness. Questioning existing regulations in these terms will also involve asking more fundamental questions about their essential qualities and commitments.

Even where existing regulatory regimes have been amended to include nano-specific provisions, the influence of existing regulatory and policy contexts continues to be felt. The focus of these amendments is on generating information and opening up routes for stakeholder communication (manufacturers-regulators; manufacturers-consumers), however they also place limits on the nature of that information (risk information; the label 'nano'). They are also subject to certain assumptions about how regulatory tools and techniques operate. For example, new nano-labelling requirements are founded on assumptions about the utility and effectiveness of information disclosure via a product's packaging. Labelling a product with a list of its ingredients promotes goals such as openness and transparency, yet it may do little to aid free choice unless meaning can be extracted. Nano-labelling requirements are also based on the assumption that the choice environment into which they are introduced is set up to offer tangible opportunities for free and informed decision-making. What is missing is an accompanying choice infrastructure, such as the provision of other user-information or opportunities for deliberation, on which nano-labelling measures can sit.

Nano-specific amendments are similarly constrained, therefore, by the legislative frameworks into which they are inserted. The interpretation of nanotechnologies as 'new' (politically 'new' for the European Parliament's Environment Committee) has undoubtedly contributed to the momentum behind new nano-specific legislation. Likewise, arguments that nanotechnologies are 'not new enough' have upheld the dominant policy view in the EU that they can be dealt with under existing regulatory regimes. This chapter has started to unpack the many ways in which newness may be construed and contested. It has also sought to remind that, as well as newness, an important determinant of a new technology's regulation is its policy past.

11

Science, Law, and the Medical-Industrial Complex in EU Pharmaceutical Regulation: The Deferiprone Controversy

John Abraham and Courtney Davis

A. Introduction

Logically, the production of pharmaceuticals in a society only makes sense for that society if they benefit health by being safe and effective to treat the illnesses for which they are prescribed. Publicly, at least, this is undisputed by all the major stakeholders, governments, pharmaceutical firms, patient groups, public health advocacy organizations, and the medical profession.[1] However, given that pharmaceutical companies have considerable commercial interests in marketing their drug products, it was gradually realized during the 20th century that industry scientists ought not to be the final arbiters of whether their firms' compounds were safe and effective due to conflict of interests.[2] Consequently, to inspire greater public confidence in the safety and effectiveness of pharmaceuticals, from the 1970s, all modern industrialized societies had established legislative provisions for pharmaceutical regulation. This raised the standards of drug evaluation that the industry had to meet, thereby bringing greater health protection to patients and the public. Yet, it must also be appreciated that such regulation was heavily shaped by consultation with the pharmaceutical industry, whose opposition was minimal. Indeed, the regulation also served to consolidate the hegemony of firms with superior techno-scientific standards of drug testing.[3] That included the European Union (EU) pharmaceutical regulatory system, whose presence gained a new prominence with the creation of the European Medicines Evaluation Agency (EMEA) in 1995, which had changed its name to the European Medicines Agency (EMA) by 2010.[4]

---

[1] J Abraham and C Davis, 'Interpellative Sociology of Pharmaceuticals: Problems and Challenges for Innovation and Regulation in the 21st Century' (2007) 19 *Technology Analysis & Strategic Management* 387.

[2] J Abraham, *Science, Politics and the Pharmaceutical Industry* (Routledge 1995); J Lexchin, 'The Pharmaceutical Industry and the Pursuit of Profit' in J Clare Cohen, P Illingworth, and U Schuklenk (eds), *The Power of Pills* (Pluto Press 2006) 11.

[3] J Abraham and G Lewis, *Regulating Medicines in Europe: Competition, Expertise and Public Health* (Routledge 2000); AA Daemmrich, *Pharmacopolitics: Drug Regulation in the US and Germany* (University of North Carolina Press 2004). MNG Dukes, *The Effects of Drug Regulation: A Survey Based on the European Studies in Drug Regulation* (MTP Press 1985); L Hancher, 'Regulating for Competition: Government, Law and the Pharmaceutical Industry in the UK and France' (PhD thesis, University of Amsterdam 1989); P Temin, *Taking Your Medicine: Drug Regulation in the US* (Harvard UP 1980).

[4] TK Hervey and JV McHale, *Health Law and the European Union* (CUP 2004).

This chapter is a case study of the controversy surrounding a thalassaemia drug, known as deferiprone, whose approval on to the EU market by the EMA, was appealed to what was then the European Court of Justice (ECJ, now the Court of Justice of the European Union (CJEU)) by one of the key clinical investigators of the drug, on grounds of safety and efficacy. However, perhaps unsurprisingly, given the transnational nature of the pharmaceutical industry, the story of the case takes us across the Atlantic to Canada where the drug was developed, though the legal aspects concerning clinical investigation explored in this chapter are similar in Canada and Europe. The purpose of the case study is to explore some of the interactions between law, science, and what Relman famously called, the 'medical-industrial complex', at various stages of controversy about drug technology.[5] In particular, it highlights the role of the law in constraining professional autonomy. In so doing, it also facilitates an examination of the roles of drug risks in clinical trials, the rights of stakeholders during the drug development process, such as those of pharmaceutical companies and clinical investigators, and the interaction between ethics and markets.

Within the social science and policy literature, discussions about pharmaceuticals and law are dominated by analyses of patenting and intellectual property rights, though political science and socio-legal studies are increasingly turning their attention to health law and the role of law in biomedical technology regulation.[6] In this chapter, we show how the law may be used by industry and what Majone has called 'the regulatory state' (regulatory agencies and the courts) to shape, limit, and close down scientific debate and professional autonomy pertaining to drug technology development.[7] It is a very different, and counter-balancing picture to the one drawn by some analysts of drug injury cases in medical controversy, such as Gabe and Bury, who portray the law as a challenge to scientific and regulatory authority causing amplification of uncertainty, fragmentation of expertise, and plurality of knowledge-claims.[8] Our analysis is also a reminder of the multi-faceted nature of professional autonomy in medicine, which should not be reduced to the view that doctors have too much autonomy, by reference solely to doctor-patient interactions.[9] For instance, the impact of the pharmaceutical industry and government drug regulatory agencies on the autonomy of the medical profession also needs to be considered.

In following the case since 2004 we have reviewed numerous reports and documents from the Canadian Association of University Teachers (CAUT), the College of Physicians and Surgeons of Ontario (CPSO), the then EMEA, the European Commission (Commission), the CJEU, the EU's expert Committee for Proprietary Medicinal Products (CPMP), and the University of Toronto-affiliated Hospital for Sick Children (HSC). In particular, we obtained and analysed the EMEA's European Public Assessment Report for deferiprone, which provided the official, published reasons for approving the drug on to the EU market. The pharmaceutical trade press and publications by the drug's manufacturer, Apotex, were also consulted. When necessary, key

---

[5] AS Relman, 'The New Medical-Industrial Complex' (1980) 303 *New England Journal of Medicine* 963.

[6] A-M Farrell, 'The Politics of Risk and EU Governance of Human Material' (2009) 16 *Maastricht Journal of European and Comparative Law* 41; ML Flear, 'The EU's Biopolitical Governance of Advanced Therapy Medicinal Products' (2009) 16 *Maastricht Journal of European and Comparative Law* 113.

[7] G Majone, *Regulating Europe* (Routledge 1996).

[8] J Gabe and M Bury, 'Halcion Nights: A Sociological Account of a Medical Controversy' (1996) 30 *Sociology* 447.

[9] E Freidson, *Professionalism* (Polity 2001).

parties to the controversy were interviewed. Our methodological approach is informed by empirical realism, rather than, say, actor-network theory, because our focus is on what institutional interests and politico-legal power do to knowledge-claims, rather than on how actors form beliefs.[10] We define law broadly to include use of litigation (including legal contracts), enforcement of regulations established in law, and the role of the courts in interpreting regulatory law.

B. The Compelling Nature of the Medical-Industrial Complex and its Legal Concomitants in Pharmaceutical Science and Markets

Scientific principles proposing the objective pursuit of truth, tested by open and public scrutiny by other scientists and experts, remain important bases for distinguishing between knowledge and mistaken/false beliefs. However, the assumption that those principles exhaust or are even fundamental to the practical work of scientists may often be an ideology, indeed mythology, of science, as much as a reality. In this section, we explain how the medical-industrial complex, together with its use of legally binding (contractual) agreements with medico-scientific experts involved in sponsored research gradually imposes itself on a biomedical scientific inquiry, initially driven by a desire to improve treatment for a relatively neglected group of patients in society, those with thalassaemia.

Thalassaemia is a blood disorder characterized by faulty production of haemoglobin made in the bone marrow for incorporation into red blood cells. In thalassaemia patients, red blood cells become fragile and break down, leading to severe anaemia without treatment. Thalassaemia is inherited via one or two recessive defective genes, resulting in thalassaemia-minor and thalassaemia-major, respectively. There are about 10,000 people with thalassaemia-major in the EU alone and as many as 30 million sufferers in India.[11]

In this chapter, we are concerned only with thalassaemia-major (hereafter 'thalassaemia'). To prevent thalassaemia patients dying from anaemia, they are treated with blood transfusions. However, successive blood transfusions cause a potentially toxic build-up of iron in the body (known as 'iron-loading') adversely affecting the liver and heart. Consequently, pharmaceuticals, known as chelating agents, are given to help the body to excrete the excess iron. Unfortunately, before the 1990s, the only standard treatment for iron-loading was by subcutaneous or intravenous infusion of the iron-chelating drug, deferoxamine, first introduced in 1963. Although biologically effective and relatively non-toxic, deferoxamine was far from the perfect treatment because patients needed to undergo such infusions for about eight to twelve hours several nights per week, which was unpleasant, costly, and prohibitively expensive for the poor without state health provision or health insurance.[12] Deferoxamine has also been associated with some cases of serious neurotoxicity and growth retardation.[13]

---

[10] J Abraham, 'Sociology of Pharmaceutical Development and Regulation: A Realist Empirical Research Programme' (2008) 30 *Sociology of Health & Illness* 869.

[11] VP Choudhry, 'Oral Deferiprone—Controversies on its Efficacy and Safety' (1998) 65 *Indian Journal of Pediatrics* 825; EMEA, European Public Assessment Report, CPMP 'Scientific Discussion' Ferriprox (deferiprone).

[12] SK Bichile, PJ Mehta, and SJ Paresh, 'Toxicity of Oral Iron Chelator L1' (1993) 41 *Journal of the Association of Physicians of India* 323; DG Nathan, 'Clinical Research: A Tale of Two Studies' (2003) 114 *Transactions of the American Clinical and Climatological Association* 219.

[13] S Di Vigiliis, M Cangia, and F Fran, 'Deferoxamine-Induced Growth Retardation in Patients with Thalassaemia-Major' (1988) 113 *Journal of Pediatrics* 661; NF Olivieri, JR Buncie, and E Chew,

Thus, the development of a safe and effective iron chelator that could be taken orally would offer great therapeutic benefit. Deferiprone was first synthesized in the early 1980s at Kings College, London, whose laboratories sold the rights to the UK government-owned British Technology Group. There, the drug showed initial signs that it might serve the desired therapeutic purpose.[14] Consequently, Dr Nancy Olivieri, a specialist in haematology and internal medicine at the HSC, affiliated to the University of Toronto, decided to organize a small trial with deferiprone in her clinic in 1988. After encouraging results from the first two years of a small pilot study, she discussed deferiprone with the US Food and Drug Administration (FDA), the world's largest and best-resourced drug regulatory agency with huge experience of drug development requirements. The FDA advised her that three studies should be performed before the drug could be approved on to markets, including longer term and larger randomized trials, which might necessitate the involvement of a pharmaceutical company.[15]

After designing such trials, Olivieri applied for funding to execute them from the Canadian Medical Research Council (CMRC), who declined to be sole sponsors, but indicated that it would be interested in a re-application under its university-industry programme. These events illustrate the endemic and pervasive presumption of industry involvement in pharmaceutical development, making alternatives to the medical-industrial complex nearly impossible for medical researchers. Evidently, the presumption of the complex in drug development existed in the minds of state-funded regulatory agencies and research councils, even before any actual involvement of pharmaceutical firms. It has also become an accepted convention of pharmaceutical science for many university managers. For instance, in 1997, the President of Johns Hopkins University insisted: 'to move your research forward, you've got to do partnerships with industry'.[16] As the UK Government had done for decades, by the late 1980s, the Canadian Federal Government had come to view transnational pharmaceutical companies as major vehicles for promoting economic growth, while the deficits were partly addressed by cutting federal funding for research.[17]

There is considerable evidence to suggest that academic and health care institutions hosting clinical research have been pursuing ever closer relationships. According to the US-based Pharmaceutical Research and Manufacturer's Association (PhRMA), between 1980 and 2003, overall research and development expenditures by US pharmaceutical companies increased from US$2 billion to US$33 billion.[18] During the 1990s, Canadian pharmaceutical firms' funding of clinical research grew to an annual spend of $624 million in 1998, while CMRC funding declined.[19] By 2001, clinical trial research expenditures in Canada totalled over $800 million.[20] In particular, Bekelman and others found that, between 1980 and 2002, in the USA, a quarter of

'Visual and Auditory Neurotoxicity in Patients receiving Subcutaneous Deferoxamine Infusions' (1986) 314 *New England Journal of Medicine* 869.

[14] Interview with Vice-President for Scientific Affairs, Apotex (12 September 2004).

[15] J Thompson, P Baird, and J Downie, 'The Olivieri Report: Independent Inquiry Commissioned by the Canadian Association of University Teachers' (James Lorimer 2001) 102–3.

[16] A Schafer, 'Biomedical Conflicts of Interest' (2004) 30 *Journal of Medical Ethics* 15.

[17] J Abraham, 'Partial Progress: Governing the Pharmaceutical Industry and the NHS, 1948–2008' (2009) 34 *Journal of Health, Politics, Policy and Law* 943; A Schafer, 'Biomedical Conflicts of Interest' (2004) 30 *Journal of Medical Ethics* 16.

[18] PhRMA, 'Pharmaceutical Industry Profile' (Pharmaceutical Research and Manufacturers of America 2004).

[19] RA Phillips and J Hoey, 'Constraints of Interest: Lessons at the Hospital for Sick Children' (1998) 159 *Canadian Medical Association Journal* 956.

[20] G DuVal, 'Institutional Conflicts of Interest: Protecting Human Subjects, Scientific Integrity, and Institutional Accountability' (2004) 32 *International and Comparative Health, Law and Ethics* 613.

biomedical investigators had industry affiliations.[21] Indeed, in the mid-1990s, the University of Toronto was negotiating a $20 million donation from the pharmaceutical firm, Apotex, towards the construction of a biomedical research centre and $10 million from the company for the university's affiliated hospitals.[22] Moreover, Robert Pritchard, then President of University of Toronto had lobbied the Canadian Government on behalf of Apotex about drug patent laws in a private letter to the Prime Minister.[23]

It was in this wider context of neo-liberalism and institutional relations that Olivieri met with Apotex, whose Vice-President was a former professor at the University of Toronto, to explore the possibility of the company supporting a deferiprone trial programme, in line with the advice she had received from the FDA and the CMRC. After initial concerns about whether deferiprone could be commercially viable, in 1993 Apotex decided that it was a worthwhile endeavour and agreed to co-sponsor the deferiprone trials with the CMRC.[24] The key trials became known as LA-01 (a two-year study comparing deferiprone with deferoxamine), LA-02 (a one-year non-comparative study), and LA-03 (a six-year compassionate use study). The company purchased the patent from the British Technology Group and asked Olivieri to accept a confidentiality clause as part of her contract.[25] This required her to keep secret all trial information up to three years after completion for LA-02, and a ban on publication until one year after completion regarding LA-01, unless disclosure was authorized by the firm

Table 11.1. Chronology of key events

1989	Olivieri synthesizes deferiprone
1993–5	Olivieri signs contract for deferiprone trials with Apotex, including confidentiality clauses
April 1995	Olivieri and others publish paper demonstrating 'favourable effect of deferiprone on iron balance'
July 1995	Some patients in LA-03 exhibit undesirable liver iron concentrations, indicating poor efficacy of deferiprone, so Olivieri requests a separate trial to investigate this, requiring patients to be informed of the negative results
September 1995	Olivieri advises Apotex of her obligation to inform HSC Research Ethics Board (REB) of adverse findings
February 1996	Apotex disputes loss of deferiprone efficacy during trials, refusing Olivieri permission to relay that claim to REB
May 1996	Olivieri informs REB and patients of her findings. Apotex terminates her trials and research sponsorship, telling her that disclosure of trial information without company approval would prompt legal action against her. Olivieri informs Apotex she intends to publish her findings
July 1996	Apotex's expert panel disagrees with Olivieri about deferiprone's efficacy
February–May 1997	Olivieri discovers liver toxicity/fibrosis in patients in LA-03. She informs REB and discontinues deferiprone use due to safety concerns

(continued)

[21] JE Bekelman, Y Li, and CP Gross, 'Scope and Impact of Financial Conflicts of Interest in Biomedical Research' (2003) 289 *Journal of the American Medical Association* 454.

[22] E Gibson, F Baylis, and S Lewis, 'Dances with the Pharmaceutical Industry' (2002) 166 *Canadian Medical Association Journal* 448.

[23] J Thompson, P Baird, and J Downie, 'The Olivieri Report: Independent Inquiry Commissioned by the Canadian Association of University Teachers' (James Lorimer 2001) 13. After Pritchard's conduct became public knowledge, he apologized to the university's executive committee for acting inappropriately.

[24] Interview with Vice-President, Scientific Affairs, Apotex (12 September 2004).

[25] Interview (n 24).

Table 11.1. Continued

September 1997	Olivieri expresses concerns to the University of Toronto about continuing conflict with Apotex
February 1998	Apotex applies to EMEA for marketing authorization in EU, including reports on LA-01, 02, and 03, but without Olivieri's signature
April 1998	Olivieri indicates to HSC that she cannot continue under prevailing conditions
August 1998	Olivieri and others publish findings about liver toxicity in *New England Journal of Medicine*
January 1999	Olivieri is fired from HSC. Later, her position is restored, her academic freedom affirmed, and she is promised legal support against Apotex
May 1999	CPMP recommend deferiprone's marketing authorization. Olivieri sends CPMP her concerns about the drug's safety and efficacy
June 1999	Marketing authorization decision-process is suspended pending CPMP's investigation of Olivieri's concerns
August 1999	Marketing authorization of deferiprone is granted
November 1999	Olivieri files for annulment of deferiprone's marketing authorization with European Court of Justice
March 2000	Commission, EMEA, and Apotex plead that Olivieri's case is inadmissible
April 2000	HSC refers disputes regarding Olivieri's clinical practice with deferiprone patients to CPSO
October 2001	CAUT report exonerates Olivieri, finding that the University of Toronto did not do enough to protect her academic freedom
December 2001	CPSO concludes that Olivieri acted in patients' interests, dismissing HSC's complaints against her
December 2003	European Court finds that Olivieri has no standing to challenge the Commission's decision regarding protection of public health

(see Table 11.1). There was no confidentiality clause pertaining to LA-03.[26] Although such restrictions on publication and data sharing were an assault on the ideals of science, within the medical-industrial complex, they were widespread and frequently passed without comment.[27] Between 1993 and 1995, Olivieri signed the contracts for these trials.

C. Controlling 'Acceptable' Discovery: Industrial Power, Ethics, and Legal Threat

In accordance with the scientific protocols of the deferiprone trials, iron-loading in the thalassaemia patients was assessed and monitored by regular liver biopsies, which were also used to evaluate the safety and efficacy of the iron-chelation therapy. The initial stage of the deferiprone trials conducted by Olivieri and sponsored by Apotex went well. Olivieri and others published early findings that deferiprone had a 'favourable effect' on the iron balance in patients.[28] However, later that year, Olivieri became

[26] CPSO, 'Complaints Committee Decision and Reason' (2001) 5.

[27] JE Bekelman, Y Li, and CP Gross, 'Scope and Impact of Financial Conflicts of Interest in Biomedical Research' (2003) 289 *Journal of the American Medical Association* 454; T Bodenheimer, 'Uneasy Alliance: Clinical Investigators and the Pharmaceutical Industry' (2000) 342 *New England Journal of Medicine* 1539.

[28] NF Olivieri, GM Brittenham, and D Matsui, 'Iron Chelation Therapy with Oral Deferiprone in Patients with Thalassaemia-Major' (1995) 332 *New England Journal of Medicine* 918.

concerned that some of the twenty-one patients on the long-term deferiprone trial, LA-03, were displaying adverse concentrations of iron in the liver. Initially, she deduced that, for six of these patients, deferiprone might be losing its efficacy, putting them at risk of iron overload, but by early 1996 this trend had increased to twelve patients.[29]

Olivieri requested permission from Apotex to establish a 'new' separate trial with patients for whom deferiprone's efficacy seemed to be sub-optimal, and informed the company of her obligation to report the negative efficacy outcomes encountered to both the HSC's Research Ethics Board and the particular patients affected. Upon reviewing the data, scientists at Apotex did not agree with Olivieri that deferiprone had been losing its effectiveness among a significant number of patients, though they accepted that this might be true for a few patients.[30] The firm, therefore, instructed her not to relay her view that the drug was losing efficacy to the Research Ethics Board.[31] While some patients were doing well on deferiprone from both a safety and efficacy point of view,[32] Olivieri reported findings that a significant proportion of trial subjects had iron concentrations in the liver above clinically desirable levels to the Board, who directed her to advise the patients of these risks. However, in May 1996, when she approached the patients to do this, Apotex terminated trials LA-01 and LA-03 and Olivieri's research contracts with the firm, including her involvement with LA-02. Moreover, the company warned her that all information obtained during the trial was to remain secret, otherwise legal action might be taken against her,[33] or as the vice-president of Apotex put it: 'We told her should she present information that is wrong that we are prepared to take action against her.'[34]

Olivieri's trials were terminated because she had broken an unwritten convention of the medical-industrial complex, namely to remain loyal to the sponsoring company. As the vice-president of Apotex put it, 'we had problems with her'.[35] This is clear from the letter sent to Olivieri by Apotex to explain the firm's decision to terminate the trials, which stated that Apotex 'could not justify Nancy as the Principal Investigator in studies of a drug she does not believe works'.[36] The company's vice-president later elaborated this perspective as 'if you [Olivieri] don't even believe that the drug is working, why do you want to even give it to those patients?'[37] Yet the supposed scientific methodology of the 'null hypothesis', with which clinical trials are designed, is precisely to test the validity of the assumption that the new therapy is no better than a placebo-control or an existing therapy as control. While the idealistic rationale of scientific methodology is to use clinical trials to discover whether or not new drugs are efficacious, evidently the convention of the medical-industrial complex is to prove that they are.

Apotex convened an expert panel to review Olivieri's claims about deferiprone and the data underpinning them. The firm reported that its panel unanimously disagreed

[29] J Thompson, P Baird, and J Downie, 'The Olivieri Report: Independent Inquiry Commissioned by the Canadian Association of University Teachers' (James Lorimer 2001) 124–31.

[30] Interview with Vice-President, Scientific Affairs, Apotex (12 September 2004).

[31] A Naimark, BM Knoppers, and FH Lowy, *Clinical Trials of deferiprone at the Hospital for Sick Children* (Hospital for Sick Children 1998).

[32] Interview with Nancy Olivieri, University of Toronto (28 June 2004).

[33] CPSO, 'Complaints Committee Decision and Reasons' (2001) 7; T Koch, 'Absent Virtues: The Poacher becomes Gamekeeper' (2003) 29 *Journal of Medical Ethics* 339.

[34] Despite these remarks, the company subsequently claimed it was 'invalid' to 'characterize the termination of Olivieri's contract as an attempt to stop her divulging her views'. See Correspondence, 'The Olivieri Case' (2003) 348 *New England Journal of Medicine* 861.

[35] Interview with Vice-President, Scientific Affairs, Apotex (12 September 2004).

[36] RA Phillips and J Hoey, 'Constraints of Interest: Lessons at the Hospital for Sick Children' (1998) 159 *Canadian Medical Association Journal* 956.

[37] Interview with Vice-President, Scientific Affairs, Apotex (12 September 2004).

with her conclusions about the drug's efficacy,[38] as did others researching the drug.[39] Subsequently, however, her interpretation was supported by other specialists and corroborated by research in Switzerland.[40] By that time, Indian medical researchers were also warning that 'due to the high frequency [25 per cent] of serious toxicity [immunologically-based arthralgia[41]] of deferiprone [among patients in Bombay], further trials, if any, should be carried out only in selected patients by applying strict criteria.'[42] Nonetheless, Apotex denied Olivieri consent to submit abstracts of her deferiprone research to the American Society for Haematology. The company also accused her of keeping incomplete trial information records,[43] and notified her that she was being removed from the steering committee of LA-02 for breaching contractual obligations, so denying her access to that trial's data and results.[44]

The underlying conflict between the norms of science publicly to present findings to the medical community and legal commitments to the company sponsoring the drug trials, had become explicit and intense. In this context, legal intervention promoted, and policed, convergence of medical knowledge-claims-making, rather than fostering plurality. Its role was to discourage medical specialists from publicly contesting techno-scientific interpretations that were consistent with the firm's commercial and institutional goals of progressing with development of its product, even if that meant threatening information-flows about drug safety and efficacy to the 'evidence-base' of medicine for the health system.[45]

D. Confronting Risks and Legal Constraint: Institutional Self-Interest versus Professional Autonomy

Despite the objections and legal warnings of Apotex, Olivieri presented her findings from LA-03 at the American Society for Hematology conference in Florida at the end of 1996. During 1997, she concluded that deferiprone was causing liver toxicity and accelerated liver fibrosis in some patients on LA-03, so she informed the patients and Research Ethics Board, and published an abstract in the journal, *Blood*, stating

---

[38] Interview with Medical Director, Apotex (12 September 2004).

[39] Correspondence (seven letters), 'Iron Chelation with Oral Deferiprone in Patients with Thalassaemia' (1997) 339 *New England Journal of Medicine* 1710; Correspondence, 'The Olivieri Case' (2003) 348 *New England Journal of Medicine* 861; CPSO, 'Complaints Committee Decision and Reasons' (2001) 8; F Tricta, G Sher, and R Loebstein, 'Long-term Chelation Therapy with the Orally Active Iron Chelator Deferiprone in Patients with Thalassaemia-Major' (6th International Conference on Thalassaemia and Haemoglobinopathies, Malta, 5–10 April 1997); Interview with Nancy Olivieri, University of Toronto (28 June 2004).

[40] Correspondence (seven letters), 'Iron Chelation with Oral Deferiprone in Patients with Thalassaemia' (1997) 339 *New England Journal of Medicine* 1710; P Tondury, A Zimmerman, and P Nielson, 'Liver Iron and Fibrosis during Long-term Treatment with Deferiprone in Swiss Thalassaemic Patients' (1998) 101 *British Journal of Haematology* 413.

[41] Pain in joints and muscle tissue.

[42] SK Bichile, PJ Mehta, and SJ Paresh, 'Toxicity of Oral Iron Chelator L1' (1993) 41 *Journal of the Association of Physicians of India* 323.

[43] Interview with Vice-President, Scientific Affairs, Apotex (12 September 2004).

[44] A Naimark, BM Knoppers, and FH Lowy, *Clinical Trials of Deferiprone at the Hospital for Sick Children* (Hospital for Sick Children 1998).

[45] LA Bero and D Rennie, 'Influences on the Quality of Published Drug Studies' (1996) 12 *International Journal of Technology Assessment in Health Care* 209; R DeVries and T Lemmens, 'The Social and Cultural Shaping of Medical Evidence' (2006) 62 *Social Science and Medicine* 2694; J Lexchin, KA Bero, and B Djulbegovic, 'Pharmaceutical Industry Sponsorship and Research Outcome and Quality' (2003) 326 *British Medical Journal* 1167.

that she had discontinued deferiprone in all patients due to safety concerns.[46] Nine months later, Olivieri and others published a major article detailing their findings of liver toxicity in patients taking deferiprone.[47] They reported that five of fourteen patients treated with deferiprone had progression of liver fibrosis, while none of the twelve patients treated with the control, deferoxamine, had such adverse effects.

Meanwhile, Apotex continued to claim that the drug was safe and effective and sought data from the HSC on patients who had received deferiprone on compassionate grounds. The firm also offered to provide new arrangements for Toronto patients to receive deferiprone if they did not wish to return to deferoxamine treatment. However, Olivieri rejected that proposal because she considered the safety monitoring procedures, which did not include liver biopsies, to be inadequate.[48] Subsequently, the firm questioned whether Olivieri had been meeting her obligations to provide data to regulatory authorities, but did not take legal action against her.[49]

Olivieri's determination to publish her work, despite legal threats from a powerful pharmaceutical company that could potentially damage her career, poses conceptual difficulties for over-socialized models of medical professionals as self-interested individuals protecting their status and dominance.[50] It also challenges over-contextualizing models of science in which experts are presented as instrumental creatures of their social context, discarding and adopting values according to what the situation demands.[51] While many scientists are, of course, determined to publish their work, they are often reported to adapt that strategy flexibly to maximize their own interests and career advancement. Olivieri's behaviour cannot be easily accounted for by such models, but reflected instead an 'objective'[52] value-commitment to professional autonomy and patient care, which was stable in the face of a changing context.

This is evident from the extent to which her material self-interest was placed in jeopardy by not relinquishing her value-commitments. From mid-1996 to early 1998, Olivieri sought support from the HSC and the University of Toronto. Initially, the HSC refused to supply her with legal assistance, though the Dean of the University's Faculty of Medicine asked Apotex to refrain from making legal threats.[53] According to Olivieri, neither the hospital nor the University of Toronto, 'both anticipating large donations from Apotex', supported her 'in fulfilling ethical obligations to patients or scientific obligations to the public'.[54] It was not until 1999 that the President of the University intervened directly by stating that 'gag orders' had 'no place in a University'.[55]

Olivieri complained about the close relationship between Apotex and the University of Toronto, including its affiliated hospitals, but was told that her complaints warranted

---

[46] CPSO, 'Complaints Committee Decision and Reasons' (2001) 9–12.

[47] NF Olivieri, GM Brittenham, and CE McLaren, 'Long-term Safety and Effectiveness of Iron Chelation Therapy with Deferiprone for Thalassemia-Major' (1998) 339 *New England Journal of Medicine* 417.

[48] J Thompson, P Baird, and J Downie, 'The Olivieri Report: Independent Inquiry Commissioned by the Canadian Association of University Teachers' (James Lorimer 2001) 177–204.

[49] A Naimark, BM Knoppers, and FH Lowy, *Clinical Trials of Deferiprone at the Hospital for Sick Children* (Hospital for Sick Children 1998).

[50] E Freidson, *Professionalism* (Polity 2001).

[51] S Jasanoff, *The Fifth Branch: Science Advisers as Policy-Makers* (Harvard UP 1990).

[52] By 'objective' here is meant not solely context-determined.

[53] D Spurgeon, 'Trials Sponsored by Drug Companies' (1998) 316 *British Medical Journal* 618.

[54] D Spurgeon, 'Report clears Researcher who broke Drug Company Agreement' (2001) 323 *British Medical Journal* 1085.

[55] V Di Norcia, 'The Olivieri Report' (2003) 9 *Science and Engineering Ethics* 129.

no action.[56] In April 1998, Olivieri indicated by letter to the HSC administration that she could not continue under the prevailing work pressures. One month after Olivieri published her concerns about deferiprone's liver toxicity in some patients in the *New England Journal of Medicine*, the HSC Board of Trustees set up an inquiry into the dispute about Olivieri's deferiprone trials, which absolved the HSC of any responsibility for the dispute and included an investigation into the mistaken[57] notion that she had not reported her concerns about the drug's liver toxicity to the HSC Research Ethics Board.[58] In other words, the initial response of her employers at the HSC and the University of Toronto was to assume that she was the source of the difficulties. Initially, at least, that seemed to be a less costly approach to those institutions than entering into confrontation with a transnational pharmaceutical company.

The HSC interpreted Olivieri's admission of unacceptable pressures from the deferiprone dispute as a letter of resignation—an action regarded by Olivieri as constructive dismissal. In January 1999, Olivieri was fired from her position as Head of the Haemoglobinopathy Research Programme at the HSC, though later in the month, in the aftermath of widespread professional protest receiving media coverage, the HSC agreed to re-instate her, affirmed her academic freedom, and offered financial support if Apotex litigated against her.[59]

This shows the complexity of professional autonomy and how precarious its protection is within the medical-industrial complex, especially when powerful pharmaceutical firms are willing to use the law in ways that constrain such autonomy. It is not simply a matter of pressure from the drug manufacturer on the investigating clinical scientist; the roles of the hospital and/or university are also crucial. When conflict emerges over drug technology development, whether the university/hospital place allegiance with the professional autonomy of its clinical investigator or with the maintenance of a good relationship with the pharmaceutical manufacturer may be a finely balanced judgement based on which political forces (including industrial legal power and the determination of the clinical scientist) might cause least damage to institutional reputations and interests. That calculation is itself determined by where the law stands.

E. The European Regulatory State and the Limits of Scientific Pluralism under the Law

While Olivieri was exonerated in Canada, Apotex continued its plans to market deferiprone outside North America. Between 1987 and 1998, deferiprone was evaluated in seventeen countries at thirty-two clinical centres.[60] From 1994 it was marketed

---

[56] E Gibson, F Baylis, and S Lewis, 'Dances with the Pharmaceutical Industry' (2002) 166 *Canadian Medical Association Journal* 448.

[57] Subsequently, the HSC admitted it made mistakes. See T Koch, 'Absent Virtues: The Poacher becomes Gamekeeper' (2003) 29 *Journal of Medical Ethics* 337; The external independent CPSO inquiry dismissed complaints about Olivieri, concluding: 'Dr Olivieri ceased to administer [deferiprone] in a timely and expedient way, which was in the best interests of her patients . . . [and] Dr Olivieri promptly set up meetings with her patients and informed clinical personnel.' See CPSO, 'Complaints Committee Decision and Reasons' (2001) 16.

[58] CPSO, 'Complaints Committee Decision and Reasons' (2001) 12–16; V Di Norcia, 'The Olivieri Report' (2003) 9 *Science and Engineering Ethics* 127; D Spurgeon, 'Canadian Case Questions Funding' (1999) 318 *British Medical Journal* 77.

[59] J Thompson, P Baird, and J Downie, 'The Olivieri Report: Independent Inquiry Commissioned by the Canadian Association of University Teachers' (James Lorimer 2001) 225–70, 505–8.

[60] VP Choudhry, 'Oral Deferiprone—Controversies on its Efficacy and Safety' (1998) 65 *Indian Journal of Pediatrics* 825; AV Hoffbrand and B Wonke, 'Iron Chelation Therapy' (1997) 242 (suppl 740) *Journal of Internal Medicine* 37.

extensively in India by the local pharmaceutical company, Cipla, with the approval of the Indian Department of Health.[61] Indeed, by 2005, the drug had been approved on to the market in twenty-nine countries, mainly in Asia and Europe, but never gained approval in the USA or Canada.[62] In this section we focus on its approval on to the European market. We consider how EU law, in the form of regulations and the courts, weighed the importance of clinical investigators compared with drug manufacturers when in dispute over whether the technology should be approved. That necessitates an understanding of the evidence about deferiprone considered by the regulators.

On 6 February 1998, Apotex submitted an application to the then EMEA for consideration under the supranational centralized procedure to obtain approval to market deferiprone throughout the EU—known as 'marketing authorization'.[63] According to the regulations, 'all information which is relevant to the evaluation of the medicinal product concerned shall be included in the application, whether favourable or unfavourable to the product', including 'the particulars of each clinical trial to allow an objective judgement to be made' and a 'final report signed by the [clinical] investigator'.[64] However, under Article 13(2) of the relevant regulations, in 'exceptional circumstances', when the manufacturer/applicant can show inability to provide comprehensive data, a marketing authorization may be granted if 'in the present state of scientific knowledge comprehensive information cannot be provided'.[65]

The EMEA's expert scientific committee, the CPMP, reviewed the techno-scientific data provided by Apotex. The clinical trial data submitted in support of the efficacy and safety of deferiprone comprised three trials, involving 247 patients in total. These were LA-01, LA-02 (followed up as LA-06), and LA-03. Trial LA-01, for which Olivieri was the principal clinical investigator, was an 'open' (non-blinded), two-year study comparing thirty-five patients taking deferiprone with thirty-six patients receiving deferoxamine. The original hypothesis to be tested in this study was that the efficacy of deferiprone was within 20 per cent of the efficacy of deferoxamine as measured by iron concentration in the liver. However, according to the CPMP, 'this hypothesis could not be tested' partly due to 'poor compliance with study procedures'.[66] Nevertheless, based on measuring serum ferritin,[67] the results of this trial were that, on average, hepatic iron concentrations in deferiprone-treated patients increased more than in deferoxamine-treated patients.[68] In other words, deferiprone was less effective than deferoxamine. As Porter detailed:

At the end of two years, hepatic iron was in the optimal target range in only 7% of deferiprone-treated patients compared with 64% of those randomized to deferoxamine, even though

---

[61] EMEA, European Public Assessment Report, CPMP 'Scientific Discussion' Ferriprox (deferiprone).

[62] C Dyer, 'Whistleblower Vows to Fight On' (2004) 328 *British Medical Journal* 187; J Hoey and AM Todkill, 'The Left Atrium' (2005) 173 *Canadian Medical Association Journal* 914.

[63] EMEA, European Public Assessment Report, 'Background Information on the Procedure' Ferriprox (deferiprone) 1.

[64] Council Regulation (EEC) 2309/93 of 22 July 1993 laying down Community procedures for the authorization and supervision of medicinal products for human and veterinary use and establishing a European Agency for the Evaluation of medicinal products [1993] OJ L214/1.

[65] Council Regulation (EEC) 2309/93, Annex, part 4.

[66] EMEA, European Public Assessment Report, CPMP 'Scientific Discussion' Ferriprox (deferiprone) 7.

[67] A complex of iron and protein found mainly in the liver and spleen, and the principal form in which iron is stored in the body.

[68] EMEA, European Public Assessment Report, CPMP 'Scientific Discussion' Ferriprox (deferiprone) 7.

treatment compliance in the deferiprone group was superior (90%) to that in the deferoxamine group (70%). The study was discontinued in 1996 because of disagreements between Apotex and the clinical investigators.[69]

Trial LA-02 was a one-year, non-comparative study of 187 patients receiving solely deferiprone treatment. The CPMP reported that deferiprone seemed to prevent any rise in hepatic iron concentration during the trial, and that, for patients starting with heavy iron-loading, the drug seemed progressively to decrease the concentration over time. However, twenty-five patients had to be withdrawn from the trial, presumably due to toxicity or lack of efficacy.[70] LA-03 was a long-term, six-year trial based on compassionate use of the drug in just twenty-five patients, which seemed to show some decrease in serum ferritin in the first two years, but not thereafter.[71] The CPMP concluded that 'because of the deficiencies in the comparative study [LA-01], the only data available for assessment of efficacy are uncontrolled.'[72] Indeed, four years later, Nathan confidently asserted:

It is to be emphasized that to this day, we do not know the actual status of deferiprone in therapy. Several investigators remain supportive of the drug, but a randomized prospective phase 3 trial to compare its efficacy with the standard deferoxamine has never been performed. The published reports of the drug are all uncontrolled and highly suspect.[73]

Apotex, however, contended that in the five years since 1999, evidence showed that deferiprone was 'probably more effective than deferoxamine in removing iron from the heart'.[74]

At the time of the CPMP's review of deferiprone, several studies were already published challenging the firm's view. These suggested that the drug was less effective than deferoxamine or even ineffective in a substantial proportion of patients even at doses above which toxicity might be expected.[75] The Committee was clearly aware of some, if not all, of these studies in reaching its conclusion.[76]

For the CPMP, the most important adverse reactions to deferiprone were agranulocytosis[77] and neutropenia[78] at incidences of 1.2 per cent and 6 per cent, respectively. However, because deferoxamine therapy posed many difficulties, including some of its own toxicities, the Committee decided that deferiprone's risks were acceptable given that the drug would be approved as a second-line treatment only for patients unresponsive to, or intolerant of, deferoxamine therapy.[79]

---

[69] JB Porter, 'A Risk-benefit Assessment of Iron-chelation Therapy' (1997) 17 *Drug Safety* 417.

[70] EMEA, European Public Assessment Report, CPMP 'Scientific Discussion' Ferriprox (deferiprone) 7.

[71] EMEA (n 70).

[72] EMEA (n 70) 10.

[73] DG Nathan, 'Clinical Research: A Tale of Two Studies' (2003) 114 *Transactions of the American Clinical and Climatological Association* 223.

[74] Interview with Vice-President, Scientific Affairs, Apotex (12 September 2004).

[75] AV Hoffbrand and B Wonke, 'Iron Chelation Therapy' (1997) 242 (suppl. 740) *Journal of Internal Medicine* 37; AV Hoffbrand, F AL-Refaie, and B Davis, 'Long-term Trial of Deferiprone in 51 Transfusion-dependent Iron Overloaded Patients' (1998) 91 *Blood* 295; P Tondury, A Zimmerman, and P Nielson, 'Liver Iron and Fibrosis during Long-term Treatment with Deferiprone in Swiss Thalassaemic Patients' (1998) 101 *British Journal of Haematology* 413.

[76] EMEA, European Public Assessment Report, CPMP 'Scientific Discussion' Ferriprox (deferiprone) 10.

[77] A potentially life-threatening disorder in which bone marrow fails to produce enough white blood cells to counteract infections.

[78] An abnormally low number of white blood cells.

[79] EMEA, European Public Assessment Report, CPMP 'Scientific Discussion' Ferriprox (deferiprone) 8–11.

In January 1999, the CPMP formed the opinion that marketing authorization of deferiprone, under the tradename, Ferriprox, should be approved for marketing within the EU, and advised the EMEA and the Commission accordingly.[80] However, before the Commission translated this advice into a regulatory decision, Olivieri sent letters in April and May 1999 to the EMEA and members of the CPMP. In these letters Olivieri presented scientific grounds on which she based her opinion that marketing of deferiprone would increase the risk of premature death to those taking it, due to the drug's hepatic and cardiac toxicity, especially progression of liver fibrosis. She also presented her finding that, in 32 per cent of patients treated with the drug, iron overload affecting the heart became worse. In those letters she also set out her version of events regarding her dispute with Apotex and the premature termination of LA-01. Consequently, the Commission suspended the normal regulatory process to allow the CPMP to consider the new safety information and to receive further responses from Apotex.[81]

The CPMP formed an expert group to review evidence about deferiprone's safety further. The expert working group acknowledged an unresolved controversy over liver fibrosis associated with deferiprone, but was swayed by the argument that it was to be used as a treatment of last resort for those patients who could not take deferoxamine, and that consequently it was worthwhile to manage the drug's risks.[82] In June 1999, following the recommendation of its expert group, the CPMP recommended that marketing authorization should be granted under 'exceptional circumstances' legislation.[83] Additional measures were demanded, such as labelling informing physicians of inconclusive risks of liver fibrosis and monitoring for it in subpopulations of patients, as well as requiring that Apotex provide detailed sales figures for each Member State to ensure that deferiprone's prescription really was restricted to second-line use.[84] The EMEA also forced the company to investigate further Olivieri's concerns about deferiprone's effect on cardiac function,[85] though she did not consider that the studies conducted on this matter were sufficient.[86]

Nonetheless, the CPMP concluded that 'there is still doubt that deferiprone may worsen hepatic fibrosis' because trial results on the matter conflicted.[87] Four years later, such doubt seemed to remain as Nathan commented that deferiprone's 'toxicity is uncertain and a matter of considerable debate'.[88] The US regulatory agency, the FDA, were also not convinced about the drug's safety, even in 2004, and demanded further toxicity studies before even considering it for approval on to

[80] EMEA, European Public Assessment Report, 'Background Information on the Procedure' Ferriprox (deferiprone) 2.

[81] Case T-326/99 *Fern Olivieri v Commission of the European Communities and the European Agency for the Evaluation of Medicinal Products, supported by Apotex Europe Ltd*, ECR II-06053 paras 24–30, 84.

[82] Interview with Member of Expert Working Group (28 September 2004); Interview with Nancy Olivieri, University of Toronto (28 June 2004).

[83] EMEA, European Public Assessment Report, 'Background Information on the Procedure' Ferriprox (deferiprone) 2.

[84] Case T-326/99 *Fern Olivieri v Commission of the European Communities and the European Agency for the Evaluation of Medicinal Products, supported by Apotex Europe Ltd*, ECR II-06053 paras 32–4.

[85] Interview with Vice-President, Scientific Affairs, Apotex (12 September 2004).

[86] Interview with Nancy Olivieri, University of Toronto (28 June 2004).

[87] EMEA, European Public Assessment Report, CPMP 'Scientific Discussion' Ferriprox (deferiprone) 9–10.

[88] DG Nathan, 'Clinical Research: A Tale of Two Studies' (2003) 114 *Transactions of the American Clinical and Climatological Association* 231.

the US market.[89] This was despite Apotex's claim that post-marketing studies outside North America showed that deferiprone protected the heart more than deferoxamine.[90] In August 1999, the Commission accepted the CPMP's advice, permitting deferiprone marketing across the EU.[91]

In November 1999, Olivieri challenged that regulatory decision in what was then known as the ECJ on the grounds that it was flawed and not in the interests of public health. The Commission and the EMEA, supported by Apotex, asserted that her challenge was inadmissible.[92] Olivieri argued that the regulatory decision-making process was flawed because she was the only person who could guarantee the authenticity of certain clinical trial reports on which the marketing authorization was based, yet those reports did not bear her signature. However, the ECJ found that Olivieri's challenge was inadmissible because the CPMP had taken account of all information she wished to provide about deferiprone within the techno-scientific aspect of the regulatory process. For the ECJ, Olivieri's right to intervene in the process, with respect to the protection of public health, ended after that stage.[93] The ECJ took this view partly because of the narrow design of the EU drug regulatory framework, which created a bilateral procedure between Apotex and the EMEA/Commission regarding marketing authorization.

Consequently, Olivieri's objections to the approval of deferipone on to the EU market could not be tested in court. On the ECJ's ruling, within EU pharmaceutical regulation, only its regulatory apparatus had the authority to decide where the interests of public health lay. Citizens could attempt to influence the regulatory state's determination of the public interest, but once such a determination was made it could not be challenged by citizens, unless the patients themselves wished to claim a violation of their rights. The supranational system permitted no judicial review of substantive techno-scientific issues underpinning regulatory decisions in this context. Regarding medical professional autonomy, the case implied that the regulatory-industrial relationship is privileged to the exclusion of the clinical investigator. In this respect, EU law constrains pluralism of medical expertise and serves to limit fragmentation of scientific knowledge-claims beyond the industry-regulator relationship.

F. Discussion and Conclusion

Our investigation of the deferiprone case shows the almost irresistible nature of pharmaceutical industry involvement in drug technology development in modern industrial societies, even for medical scientists and professionals who are motivated by therapeutic advance for patients and public health, rather than career or commercial goals. The consequent reality of the socio-legal conventions of science in the medical-industrial complex may be far removed from ideal scientific principles. This has been insufficiently appreciated in popular and sociological representations of medical controversies, not least because when they have examined the involvement of the

---

[89] Interview with Vice-President, Scientific Affairs, Apotex (12 September 2004); Interview with Nancy Olivieri, University of Toronto (28 June 2004).

[90] Interview with Vice-President, Scientific Affairs, Apotex (12 September 2004).

[91] EMEA, European Public Assessment Report, 'Background Information on the Procedure' Ferriprox (deferiprone) 2.

[92] Case T-326/99 *Fern Olivieri v Commission of the European Communities and the European Agency for the Evaluation of Medicinal Products, supported by Apotex Europe Ltd*, ECR II-06053 paras 49–65.

[93] Case T-326/99 *Fern Olivieri v Commission of the European Communities and the European Agency for the Evaluation of Medicinal Products, supported by Apotex Europe Ltd*, ECR II-06053 paras 66–98.

pharmaceutical industry in science, the focus has often been on how actors construct their beliefs, rather than on how those beliefs relate to scientific evidence and decision-making by key institutions, such as regulatory agencies and the courts.

Moreover, loss of professional autonomy in the medical-industrial complex is connected to the politics of how medical science ought to be conducted, together with the extent to which the law reinforces the influence of various stakeholders. It is also important to emphasize the significance of legal *threat* in the context of drug technology development. Even if a firm's legal right to suppress a clinician's knowledge-claims is never tested in court, the mere existence of the threat may shape what is known, or at least when evidence becomes known, to the wider biomedical scientific community. This is a far cry from the classical sociological models of academic science with their preoccupations with 'paradigm' shifts and 'disinterestedness'.[94] Although the existence of legal threat did not prevent Olivieri from pursuing legal and professional avenues open to her, it affected the timing of knowledge-claims, as she had to negotiate its institutional ramifications. Furthermore, it is not difficult to imagine that other less determined individual medical scientists might simply be intimidated into withdrawing from controversy.

Our case study supports the rather depressing findings of Rhodes and Strain that academic establishments may regard medical specialists who conflict with industry as undermining academic institutional interests due to: possible forfeiture of industry support/grants amounting to financial loss; potential decline in prestige from losing industry support; fear of negative publicity; and the threat of industry litigation requiring a costly defence.[95] Consequently, with industry funding, instead of jealously protecting academic freedom and intellectual openness, university administrations may become hospitable to the censorship and non-disclosure found in the commercial sector.[96] As implied by Flear, such neo-liberal developments point to the need for a hitherto neglected political economy of medicine in academic institutions relating them and their medical specialists to the interests of industry and public health, especially in the EU, rather than to abstract normative ideal-types of the academy and scientists.[97]

Many previous discussions of litigation in medicine and pharmaceutical controversies have concentrated on how legal interventions represent challenges to medical expertise and autonomy from increasing consumer/patient rights—challenges which fracture medical expertise.[98] The deferiprone case indicates that a more expansive conceptualization of the role of the law in medical disputes is required. In this case, legal interventions did indeed serve to threaten and limit medical autonomy, but not by fracturing medical expertise and increasing its contestability. On the contrary, legal intervention sought to terminate, ultimately successfully, contestation and to funnel medical expertise into a consensus, first shaped by the drug manufacturer and then by the regulatory apparatus. This implies that while litigation by those outside the

[94] TS Kuhn, *The Structure of Scientific Revolutions* (University of Chicago Press 1962); RK Merton, 'Science and the Social Order' in NW Storer (ed), *The Sociology of Science* (University of Chicago Press 1938); RK Merton, 'The Normative Structure of Science' in NW Storer (ed), *The Sociology of Science* (University of Chicago Press 1942).

[95] R Rhodes and JJ Strain, 'Whistle-blowing in Academic Medicine' (2004) 30 *Journal of Medical Ethics* 35.

[96] A Schafer, 'Biomedical Conflicts of Interest' (2004) 30 *Journal of Medical Ethics* 8.

[97] Flear (n 6).

[98] R Dingwall, P Fenn, and L Quam, *Medical Negligence* (Centre for Socio-Legal Studies 1991); J Gabe and M Bury, 'Halcion Nights: A Sociological Account of a Medical Controversy' (1996) 30 *Sociology* 447.

practising profession may be legitimately conceptualized as a challenge to medical autonomy, its consequences for medical expertise (for example, fragmentation versus closure) are context-dependent upon the goals of the interests involved. Legal interventions in drug controversies are not necessarily drivers of fragmentation or pluralism of medical expertise, they may be levers of consolidation and marginalization instead, especially if employed by industry and/or the state.

Moreover, the ruling of the then ECJ, previously referred to, asserts that once the decision-making process by the EU's supranational drug regime is complete, no citizens other than the manufacturer have standing to challenge whether the decision was in the interests of public health. In particular, this includes the clinical investigator responsible for the medical management of the trials submitted to the EU drug regulatory agency. EU law presumes that the supranational regulatory regime has the ultimate authority to decide what is in the interests of public health and it need not be publicly accountable in the courts for that decision even if the validity of the underpinning evidence is challenged by the absence of signatures of clinical investigators. A doctor centrally involved in drug development with patients, it seems, may not legitimately launch a legal challenge against a regulatory decision by claiming that the regulator has failed to uphold its legal duty to protect the health interests of those patients. Consistent with 'neo-liberal corporate bias', in this respect, the EU's regulatory regime, in consultation with the drug manufacturer, determines what is in the interests of the clinical investigator's patients and public health, rather than the doctor.[99]

The deferiprone case appears to leave open the possibility in the EU that a pharmaceutical firm could legally terminate trials if it believed that the clinical investigator was going to interpret emerging results in ways not to the company's liking. Evidently, medical autonomy is precarious because of the power of industry and the state. Specifically, in such controversies, the professional autonomy of medical specialists and the interests of public health may be in peril if they are not consistent with the perspective of the regulatory regime both in terms of legal provisions and technical evaluation. Finally, our case study highlights that the production and maintenance of medical knowledge about pharmaceuticals is not merely the outcome of laboratory science, it also involves, to varying degrees, the socio-political and socio-legal dimensions of the 'medical-industrial complex', the regulatory state, and the courts.

Regarding improvements to EU drug law and regulatory measures that might be considered in drawing lessons from this case, it would be desirable to permit more extensive rights to third parties wishing to challenge drug regulatory decisions in the courts, as occurs in the USA. Such third parties may be clinical investigators, but they may also be citizen groups, such as the Public Citizen Health Research Group in the USA. As the United Kingdom and other countries embark on reflective debates about how to limit private funding of political parties in order to protect the integrity of the political process, so a similar high-profile political debate needs to take place regarding commercial funding of biomedical research in relation to its scientific and ethical integrity. We make no specific recommendations in this respect, other than to comment that there is a pressing need for governments to formulate public interest regulation of the medical-industrial complex, so that the law in this field may be deployed in the interests of public health, where it belongs, rather than in threats to clinical scientists or exclusionary judgments.

[99] J Abraham and G Lewis, 'Citizenship, Medical Expertise, and the Capitalist Regulatory State in Europe' (2002) 36 *Sociology* 67.

12

The Governance of Therapeutic Nanoproducts in the European Union—A Model for New Health Technology Regulation?

Bärbel Dorbeck-Jung

A. Introduction

In the past five years nanomedical applications have been promoted worldwide as highly promising new health technologies to cope with unmet causes of mortality and morbidity of the population. Nanomedicine has the goal to provide cost-effective novel therapies and diagnostics using the expanding possibilities of nanotechnologies.[1] Although nanomedicine is still in its infancy, it is advancing rapidly. A growing number of nanomedical products, including nano-pharmaceuticals and diagnostic techniques for the rapid detection of leukemia based on nanotechnologies, have already been granted approval by regulatory agencies such as the European Medicines Agency (EMA) and the US Food and Drug Administration (FDA) and have entered the market place in certain jurisdictions.[2] Cancer, Parkinson's, and Alzheimer's are diseases for which therapeutic products are being developed. Research efforts are particularly intensive with regard to new methods and tools for diagnostics, screening and imaging, as well as to drug development, drug delivery, tissue engineering, medical implants, and gene therapy.[3]

Nanomedicine poses a large range of challenges to European medical product regulation. A crucial challenge is the uncertainty about the scientific and technological development and its effects. There is insufficient knowledge about the benefits of nanomedical products and the paths of technological development, and the characteristics and behaviour of nanomaterials, are not well known.[4] Knowledge gaps in relation

---

[1] European Technology Platform Nanomedicine (ETPN), 'Roadmaps in Nanomedicine Toward 2020' (2009) 6 <www.etp-nanomedicine.eu/public> accessed 10 April 2012.

[2] V Wagner and others 'The Emerging Nanomedicine Landscape' (2006) 24(10) *Nature Biotechnology* 1211; OC Farokhzad and R Langer, 'Nanomedicine: Developing Smarter Therapeutic and Diagnostic Modalities' (2006) 58 *Advanced Drug Delivery Reviews* 1456; EMA, '1st International Workshop on Nanomedicines 2010', Summary Report, EMA/538503 (2010).

[3] M Ferrari and others 'Nanomedicine and Society' (2009) 85 *Clinical Pharmacology & Therapeutics* 466.

[4] European Science Foundation (ESF), 'Forward Look on Nanomedicine', Strasbourg Cedex (2005) <www.esf.org/publications/214/Nanomedicine.pdf> accessed 10 April 2011; European Group of Ethics in Science and New Technologies (EGE), Opinion on the Ethical Aspects of Nanomedicine (Brussels: European Commission 2007); Scientific Committee on Emerging and Newly Identified Health Risks (SCENIHR), 'Opinion on the Appropriateness of the Risk Assessment Methodology in Accordance with the Technical Guidance Documents for New and Existing Substances for Assessing the Risks of Nanomaterials' (DG Health and Consumers 2007); Royal Commission on Environmental Pollution (RCEP), Novel Materials in the Environment: The Case of Nanotechnology (2008) <www.rcep.org.uk/reports/27novel%20materials/documents/NovelMaterialsreport_rcep.pdf> accessed 10 April 2012; M van Zijverden and AM Sips (eds), *Nanotechnology in Perspective: Risks for Man and the Environment*

to the toxicological aspects of nanomaterials and their implications for health and environment pose crucial challenges to safety regulation; other regulatory challenges refer to certain characteristics of nanomedical products, as well as to changing research, development, and manufacturing processes in the medical products sector. Upcoming nanomedical products are said to display distinct characteristics such as the complexity of clinical use and multifunctionality, as well as the integration of different areas of nanomedicine and technology subsets from drugs to medical devices and human material ('combined products'). In the case of combined products, it can be unclear which regulatory regime applies.[5] Changes in the medical products life cycle include a shift from the product marketing stage to the research and development cycle.[6] Since nanomedical research and development is mainly undertaken by small and medium sized companies with limited resources, another regulatory challenge is to facilitate their innovative activities prudently.

European governance of nanomedicine is a particularly interesting example of new health technology regulation, because of the use of new governance modes and its multilevel character. The spirit of experimentation, learning, and interdisciplinary and international collaboration that governs the regulatory arena provides us with rich regulatory lessons.[7] This chapter analyses the governance responses of European regulators to the challenges nanomedical products are posing. The aim is to explore the lessons that can be learned from the European nanomedical governance activities to regulate new health technologies. The lessons refer to the question how safe and beneficial health technology innovation can be effectively supported by regulation. We assume that effective regulation requires comprehensive regulatory regimes, appropriate methods of governance, and capable regulators.[8] To reduce the complexity of the

(RIVM 2008); NIOSH, National Institute for Occupational Safety and Health, 'Approaches to Safe Nanotechnology' (NIOSH 2009) <www.cdc.gov/niosh/docs> accessed 10 April 2012.

[5] BR Dorbeck-Jung, 'Governing Nanomedicine: Learning from Regulatory Deficiencies of European Medical Technology Regulation' (2009) XXV 94 *Politeia* 41; J D'Silva and G van Calster, 'Taking Temperature—A review of European Union Regulation in Nanomedicine' (2009) 16 *European Journal of Health Law* 249; N Chowdhury, 'Regulation of nanomedicines in the EU: distilling lessons from the paediatric and the advanced therapy medicinal products approaches' (2010) 5(1) *Nanomedicine* 135; J D'Silva and DM Bowman, 'The Regulation of Nanomedicine' in R Hunter and V Preedy (eds), *Nanomedicine in Health and Disease* (Science Publishers 2011).

[6] R Gaspar, 'Therapeutic Products: regulating drugs and medical devices' in G Hodge, D Bowman, and A Maynard (eds), *International Handbook on Regulating Nanotechnologies* (2010) 291, 293. By product life cycle we understand all pre-marketing, marketing, and post-marketing activities, see E Kaufer, 'The regulation of new product development in the drug industry' in G Majone, *Deregulation or Re-regulation? Regulatory reform in Europe and the United States* (Pinter 1990) 155.

[7] BR Dorbeck-Jung and others, 'Governing Nanomedicine: Lessons from within, and for the EU medical technology regulatory framework', Guest Editors Introduction (2011) 33(2) *Law and Policy* 215.

[8] The assumption is based on the idea that regulation is effective when certain policy goals are achieved (H Opschoor and K Turner, *Economic Incentives and Environmental Policies: Principles and Practice* (Kluwer Academic Publishers 1994)). A basic requirement is that regulation covers all subjects that are essential to achieve the policy objectives (BR Dorbeck-Jung, 'How can Hybrid Nanomedical Products regulation cope with wicked Governability Problems?' in M Goodwin and others (eds), *Dimensions of Technology Regulation* (WLP 2010)). Effectiveness depends also on whether the regulated parties are willing to follow the rules (T Havinga, 'Private Regulation of Food Safety by Supermarkets' (2006) 28 *Law & Policy* 515; SI Karlsson-Vinkhuyzen and A Vihma, 'Comparing the Legitimacy and Effectiveness of Global Hard and Soft Law: An Analytical Framework' (2009) 3 *Regulation & Governance* 400). Certain governance modes like co-regulation and self-regulation are said to stimulate the willingness to comply (Halpern, 'Hybrid design, systemic rigidity: Institutional dynamics in human research oversight' (2008) 2 *Regulation & Governance* 8; N Gunningham, 'The New Collaborative Environmental Governance. The Localization of Regulation' (2009) 36(1) *Journal of Law and Society* 145; A Héritier and M Rhodes (eds), *New Modes of Governance in Europe* (Palgrave Macmillan

investigation, the particular focus will be the therapeutic area of nanomedicine. In this area, product marketing is developing rapidly, regulatory problems are being explored and governance responses are emerging.[9] The central research question of the chapter is: What can the regulation of new health technologies learn from the European governance activities related to therapeutic nanoproducts? To answer this question, the potential benefits and risk of therapeutic nanoproducts will be discussed in the first section. The second section explores regulatory problems that are induced by the challenges of nanotherapeutic development. The third section deals with governance activities that have been employed in the European Union to control therapeutic nanoproducts. Thereafter, in the fourth section the governance responses will be analysed. The analysis is guided by three questions: first, whether existing European medical product regulation is comprehensive enough to control therapeutic nanoproducts; secondly, whether regulatory modes seem to be effective to cope with the regulatory challenges; and, thirdly, whether regulators have the capacity to control these products. The analysis leads to tentative conclusions on the lessons the regulation of new health technologies can learn from EU attempts to govern therapeutic nanoproducts.

The exploration of regulatory problems and governance responses builds on a social constructivist approach that has been developed in socio-legal theory.[10] According to this approach, basic concepts of inquiry are: the relevant regulatory structure (rules, principles, and significant regulatory actors); the ideas and beliefs of regulatory actors in relation to regulatory problems and their capacity to regulate, as well as their inter-actions to comply with existing regulations or to modify them. By 'significant regulatory actors' I refer to institutional players and stakeholder groups that exert influence on the regulatory activities in relation to the product life cycle. The significance of these actors lies not only in their actual influence on the regulatory process but also in their position and, therefore, their ability to influence debates and discussions on this issue in the future. The investigation relies on three data sources: legal, policy, and scientific documents; interviews; and observation. The description of the nanomedical markets and the effects of nanomedical products is based on the relevant policy and scientific documents. The specification of regulatory problems and governance activities builds on all three data sources. It includes legal documents related to European medical product regulation, scientific literature, and policy documents with information on regulatory problems and strategies. It builds on twelve in-depth semi-structured

2011); M Rhodes and J Visser, 'Seeking Commitment, Effectiveness and Legitimacy: New Modes of Socio-Economic Governance in Europe' in A Héritier and M Rhodes (eds), *New Modes of Governance in Europe* (2011) 104). When the consequences of certain developments like nanomedicine are complex and uncertain the capacity of regulators to respond adequately to emerging structures is particular important (J Black, 'Constructing and contesting legitimacy and accountability in Poly-centric regulatory regimes' (2008) 2 *Regulation & Governance* 137; BR Dorbeck-Jung and others, 'Contested Hybridization of Regulation: Failure of the Dutch Regulatory System to Protect Minors from Harmful Media' (2010) 4 *Regulation & Governance* 154).

[9] R Gaspar, 'Regulatory Issues Surrounding Nanomedicines: Setting the Scene for the Next Generation of Nanopharmaceuticals' (2007) 2(2) *Nanomedicine* 143; Gaspar (n 6); R Gaspar and R Duncan, 'Polymeric Carriers: Preclinical Safety and the Regulatory Implications for Design and Development of Polymer Therapeutics' (2009) 61(13) *Advanced Drug Delivery Reviews* 1220; C Altenstetter, 'Medical Device Regulation. The Myths and Facts about Patient Safety' (2011) *Law and Policy* 227; BR Dorbeck-Jung and N Chowdhury, 'Is the European medical products authoriza-tion regulation equipped to cope with the challenges of nanomedicines?' (2011) 33(2) *Law and Policy* 276.

[10] Dorbeck-Jung and Chowdhury (n 9).

interviews with significant regulatory actors.[11] In addition to interviews, the author observed and analysed the discussions at relevant meetings and conferences at the EMA, the European Commission, the European Technology Platform Nanomedicine, and other nanomedical scientific associations.[12]

B. Nanomedicine: Markets, Benefits, and Risks

1. Nanomedicine(s): Revolutionizing Health Care?

Nanomedicine is defined as 'the science and technology of diagnosing, treating and preventing disease and traumatic injury, of relieving pain, and of preserving and improving human health, using molecular tools and molecular knowledge of the human body'.[13] Nanomedicine includes the areas of diagnostics, therapeutics, and regenerative medicine.[14] In this taxonomy, the therapeutics area of nanomedicine is divided into 'nanopharmaceuticals' and 'nano-enabled devices'. Therapeutic nanoproducts are not yet a clearly defined group of products: they refer to innovation in drug delivery and medicines based on the use of nanoparticles of the active ingredient. Nanoparticles can also be used as a carrier material or porous material from which the active ingredient is released in a controlled manner. Nanopharmaceuticals are used as delivery systems for biological pharmaceuticals.[15] In the introduction, certain diseases were mentioned for which therapeutics products are being developed.

A survey stated in 2006 that there were twenty-three nanoscale drug-delivery systems worldwide, which had already been launched in the market.[16] Very recently forty nanomedical products were identified that completed the journey from lab to clinical use.[17] To date, eighteen nanopharmaceuticals are on the European market.[18] US reports have suggested that the number of nanomedicines authorizations by the FDA stands at between twelve and eighteen, and that there are several new products in the pipeline to be commercialized in the near future. The FDA also identified drug delivery and *in vivo* imaging as the most active areas. In the field of drug delivery, dozens of products are in development. Estimates indicate that by 2015 about half of drug delivery systems will be based on nanotechnology.[19] Major breakthroughs in medical applications of nanotechnologies are said to be in the areas of smart drug delivery systems, bio-diagnostics and early discovery of diseases, improved implants,

---

[11] Twelve interviews were held between May to September 2009 (eight in person, three on the phone, and one by email). The topics referred to the definition of nanopharmaceuticals, regulatory problems the respondents have experienced with regard to the marketing of nanomedicines, and regulatory responses, see Dorbeck-Jung and Chowdhury (n 9). All regulatory actors we interviewed are key representatives of a company, regulatory bodies, or scientific advisory bodies. In this context, 'key' means that the respondent has been involved in the marketing of nanomedicines or in the consultation on nanomedicinal regulation. We interviewed three representatives of pharmaceutical companies that have marketed nanomedicines. Interviews were also held with two representatives of the EMA, representatives of three national medicines evaluation bodies, one representative of the European Scientific Committee on Emerging and Newly Identified Health Risks (SCENIHR), one representative of the European Group on Ethics in Science and New Technologies (EGE), one representative of the European Technology Platform Nanomedicine (ETPN) and one representative of the New & Emerging Technologies (N&ET) Working Group to the European Medical Devices Expert Group.

[12] The empirical research took place from May 2009 to October 2011.

[13] See ESF (n 4); Nanotechnologies mean the design, characterization, production, and application of structures, devices, and systems by controlling shape and size at the nanometre scale where properties differ significantly from those at larger scale (EMA, 'Nanotechnology-based Medicinal Products for Human Use', Reflection Paper EMA/CHMP/79769 (2006)).

[14] See ETPN (n 1).   [15] Gaspar (n 6) 296.

[16] Wagner and others (n 2).   [17] Duncan and Gaspar (n 9) 1.

[18] See n 2.   [19] Zijverden and Sips (n 4).

visualization of cells, tissues, or organs, and targeting tissues and organs for regeneration and repair. Rutledge Ellis-Behnke, an eminent neuroscientist, speaks of the 'nanomics revolution'. He is convinced that this revolution goes far beyond manipulating living tissue. At a workshop of the European Medicines Agency in September 2010, Ellis-Behnke argued: '*The nanomics revolution* delves into *molecular manipulation* that will change what we wear and how we live... Tissue engineering is no longer taking a cell, placing it in a particular scaffold, putting it back in the body and hoping that everything will reconnect and function properly. It is the ability to *influence* an environment either by adding, subtracting or manipulating that environment to allow it to be more conducive for its purpose.'[20]

2. Potential Benefits

Therapeutic nanoproducts are currently regarded as one of the most promising fields of nanomedicine. At the EMA 2010 Workshop, Philippe Martin, Directorate General for Health and Consumers of the EU formulated the mission statement of nanomedicines as 'to contribute to the delivery of effective, safe, and affordable treatments to patients, using the fundamental, flexible, and multi-functional approaches made possible by nanoscience and nanotechnologies and to contribute to sustainable economic growth directly, by improving public health, and, more generally, by generating reliable revenue streams worldwide, while benefiting form a robust legislative framework and taking advantage of an environment favourable to innovation.'[21] Earlier, the European Science Foundation stated that the scientific integration between emerging technologies, and the ability to benefit from converging sciences, raises the possibility of bringing better medicines faster to the market and looking at improved ways to solve previously unmet clinical needs.[22]

The great strength of nanomedicines is said to lie in the controlled release system.[23] The effectiveness of the drug can be increased by the modification of the surface of nanoparticles. Nanodrugs are expected to make a positive contribution to the prevention, diagnosis, and treatment of diseases such as cancer, infections, auto-immune diseases, and inflammations. They may also be suitable for treating diseases that at present can only be treated with drugs that have many adverse effects. It is expected that nanomedicines will have fewer adverse effects because the drug can be more accurately targeted at its destination and because a reduced amount of the drug will have to be

---

[20] EMA (n 2) 7.

[21] This statement corresponds to the main policy goals of the European medical product regulation system, which are: a high level of public health protection, timely access to new medical products, harmonizing the internal market of pharmaceuticals, and coherence and transparency of the procedures. See COM (2001) 606 final, Report of the Commission on the basis of Article 71 of Regulation (EEC) No 2309/93, 10–13. More generally, according to the theory of public technology regulation, basic regulatory jobs are to support beneficial technological development, to create trust, and to protect constitutionally recognized interests, see F van Waarden, *Regulation, Competition and Innovation* (Dutch Advisory Committee on Technology Policy 1996); D Vogel, 'The New Politics of Risk Regulation in Europe', *CARR Discussion Paper* (LSE 2001); P Newell, *Biotechnology and the Politics of Regulation*. Working Paper No 146 (Institute of Development Studies 2002); J Kent and others, 'Towards Governance of Human Tissue Engineered Technologies in Europe: Framing the Case for a New Regulatory Regime' (2006) 73 *Technological Forecasting and Social Change* 41; BR Dorbeck-Jung, 'What Can Prudent Public Regulators Learn from the United Kingdom Government's Nanotechnological Regulatory Activities' (2007) 1 *Nanoethics* 257.

[22] ESF (n 4).   [23] Zijverden and Sips (n 4).

administered. Many drugs that have failed due to solubility issues in the past may show efficacy without side effects, if delivered in a targeted molecular form.[24] The use of nanotechnology in medicines itself is seen as a risk minimization measure, for example allowing for more controlled application of toxic drugs via delivery systems using nanomaterials.[25]

3. Potential Risks

Analyses of the scientific committees of the EU, its Member States, the USA, and the OECD have concluded that there are still many knowledge gaps about the risks of nanomaterials to humans and the environment.[26] These risk studies distinguish between free nanoparticles that are released into the body or the environment and fixed nanoparticles. The toxicological risks of free nanoparticles depend on material properties, exposure route, and dose.[27] The small size of nanoparticles results in a relatively large surface area which is accompanied by an increase in surface activity. This may or may not lead to increased reactivity towards cells and organs and the environment, resulting in toxic responses.[28] To date, toxicological studies have indicated that free nanoparticles might penetrate through blood and brain barriers, or remain lodged in capillaries.[29] Research has shown that nanoparticles of less than 100 nanometres can enter cells, less than 40 nanometres they can enter the cell nucleus, and less than 35 nanometres they can pass the blood brain barrier.[30] These particles could also have an impact on the immune system and be consumed by macrophages. Another risk challenge is related to uncertainties about the biocompatibility of medical products/materials in which nanoparticles have been used.[31]

With regard to nanomedicines, a potential safety risk is the lack of a way to measure the amount and duration of the drug delivery release of new nanomedicines.[32] Furthermore, the use of nanotechnologies that eliminate the blood brain barrier may lead to safety problems in therapeutics that are based upon having an intact barrier to prevent entrance into the brain. Compared to medicines that do not use nanomaterial, a potential risk lies in a different distribution of the particles in the body. If nanopharmaceuticals gain access to tissues normally bypassed by larger particles, the question arises whether they could have detrimental effects on cellular and tissue

---

[24] EMA (n 2) 7.   [25] EMA (n 2) 21.

[26] SCENIHR (n 4); Zijverden and Sips (n 4); EC, 'Nanosciences and Nanotechnologies: An Action Plan for Europe 2005–2009: First Implementation Report 2007–2009', COM(2007) 505 final.

[27] RE Geertsma and others, *New and Emerging Medical Technologies: A Horizon Scan of Opportunities and Risks* (RIVM 2007) <www.rivm.nl/bibliotheek/digitaaldepot/New_emerging_medical_technologies.pdf>.

[28] RD Handy and others, 'The Ecotoxicology of Nanoparticles and Nanomaterials: Current Status, Knowledge Gaps, Challenges and Future Needs' (2008) 17 *Ecotoxicology* 315.

[29] A Nel and others, 'Toxic Potential of Materials at the Nanolevel' (2006) 311 *Science* 622; M Kandlikar and others, 'Health Risk Assessment for Nanoparticles: A Case for Using Expert Judgement' (2007) 9 *Journal of Nanoparticle Research* 137; C Poland and others, 'Carbon nanotubes introduced into the abdominal cavity of mice show asbestos-like pathogenicity' (2008) 3 *Nat Nanotechnol* 423; MJ Osmond-McLeod and others, 'Durability and Inflammogenic Impact of Carbon Nanotubes Compared with Asbestos Fibres' (2011) 8(15) *Particle and Fibre Toxicology*.

[30] M Lundqvist and others, 'Nanoparticle Size and Surface Properties Determine the Protein Corona with Possible Implications for Biological Impacts' (2008) *PNAS* 105; A Salvati and others, 'Experimental and Theoretical Approach to Comparative Nanoparticle and Small Molecule Intracellular Import, Trafficking, and Export' (2010) *Molecular Biosystems*.

[31] See Zijverden and Sips (n 4).   [32] EMA (n 2) 7.

functions. Another potential safety risk refers to immunomodulation resulting from the medicinal products and their delivery carrier system. There is not enough meaningful data available to support a critical analysis of safety before moving to clinical use.[33] When nanoparticles are fixed in, or on, a device, health risks are indicated only if they are released due to, for example, a chemical reaction.

C. Regulatory Problems

1. Comprehensive Regulation/Regulatory Gaps

a. Existing regulation

To understand the regulatory problems that therapeutic nanoproducts are posing, we first need an overview of the existing regulation. In the EU, no specific rules have been established with regard to therapeutic nanoproducts: rather, the current regulatory system of medical products is applicable. This system is composed of two main regimes (medicinal products and medical devices) which have specific or additional provisions for specific applications. Due to the broad scope and the variety of regulatory activities, as well as the forms and levels of regulation, the regulatory system under which therapeutic nanoproducts fall is very complex. It covers the whole product life cycle: the stages of research and development, and marketing (including manufacturing) and post-marketing controls (including vigilance and waste disposal). Regulatory activities related to these stages include rule-setting, implementation, oversight, and enforcement.[34] Competent bodies are EU and national institutions. Forms of regulation include legislation ('hard law') and guidance rules and standards ('soft regulation'[35]). With regard to 'hard law', general European drugs legislation[36] applies to all therapeutic nanoproducts that are classified as medicinal products.[37] In addition, where therapeutic

---

[33] Gaspar (n 6) 304.

[34] C Scott, 'Private regulation of the Public Sector: A Neglected Facet of Contemporary Governance' (2002) 29 *Journal of Law and Society* 56.

[35] By soft law we understand rules that although not legally binding are effective in regulatory practice, see L Senden, *Soft Law in European Community Law* (Hart 2004). In the field of medical products, examples of soft regulations are: the Committee for Advanced Therapies (CAT) 2009 Scientific guideline on the minimum quality and non-clinical data for certification of advanced therapy medicinal products (EMEA/CAT/486831/2008), the EC 2006 guideline on the definition of a potential serious risk to public health (2006/C 133/05), the 2006 Committee for Medicinal product for Human Use (CHMP) Guideline on the environment risk assessment of medicinal products for human use (EMEA/CHMP/SWP/4447/00), the EMA guideline on scientific aspects and working definitions for the mandatory scope of the centralized procedure, and the 2005 EC guideline on the packaging information of medicinal products for human use. Safety, quality, and efficacy standards for drugs are usually made by the International Conference on Harmonization of Technical Requirements for the Registration of Pharmaceutical for Human Use (ICH). In the ICH, the European Pharmaceutical Association, the EMA, the FDA, and the Japanese Competent Authority are participating. Another example of soft regulation is the 2007 Recommendations of the N&ET Working Group to the European Medical Devices Expert Group <http://ec.europa.eu/enterprise/newsroom/cf/_getdocument.cfm?doc_id =3168> accessed 10 April 2012.

[36] The general drugs regulation is mainly composed of Directive 2001/83/EC; Regulation EC/726/ 2004, and the Directives 2001/20/EC (Good Clinical Practice), 2003/94/EC (Good Manufacturing Practice), 2005/28/EC (Good Clinical Practice—investigational medicinal products).

[37] A *medicinal product for human use* is defined as any substance having properties for treating or preventing diseases in human beings or that may be used in or administered to human beings with a view to restoring, correcting, or modifying physiological functions by exerting principally a pharmacological, immunological, or metabolic action (Art 1(1b2)), Directive 2004/27/EC.

nanoproducts are characterized as advanced therapies medicinal products (ATMPs[38]), additional provisions apply (Regulation EC/1394/2007). This is also the case with medicinal products for paediatric use (Regulation EC/1901/2006) and orphan drugs (Regulation EC/141/2000). Furthermore, where medical devices[39] use nanomaterials, medical devices regulation may apply.[40]

Therapeutic nanoproducts can also fall under Regulation (EC) No 1907/2006 on the Registration, Evaluation, Authorization and Restriction of Chemical Substances (REACH). Substances to which the REACH definition applies and which are used in the manufacturing process can be subject to the REACH obligations.[41] In the case of substances that are explicitly employed in pharmaceuticals and medical products, some exemptions are made. In all cases, the regulatory obligations pertaining to information disclosure and acceptable use apply. Furthermore, to activities of science, development, and manufacturing of therapeutic nanoproducts, a large body of regulation on occupational health and safety applies. The rules of the regulatory systems related to medical products and to occupational health and safety are set at all regulatory levels (including the international level). They are implemented at the European level and at the level of the Member States. Rule enforcement is a primary competence of the Member States. To reduce the complexity of the investigation, the focus of this chapter will be the European medical product regulation system.

Regulatory gaps arise when existing rules do not cover essential subjects of new health technology development, when the guiding principles of this system are no longer appropriate, and when the existing rules are not adequate to provide for a high level of public health protection, timely access to new medical products, and beneficial product innovation. These issues will be examined in the next section.

Unregulated issues

In the regulatory debate on therapeutic nanoproducts, two main unregulated issues are mentioned: the lack of a legal definition of nanomaterials and nanomedicine, and the possibility that new developments of therapeutic nanoproducts are not covered by the European regulation system. Definitions are important as 'they assist in establishing the subject matter and scope of what is to be regulated'.[42] With the expected increase in the applications of nanotechnology in medicine, it has been argued that there is now an urgent need in the EU to identify what can be considered as a nanomaterial by clear unequivocal descriptions. According to Bergeson and Aauer, this need comes from the

---

[38] *Advanced therapies medicinal products* mean any medicinal products for human use that include gene therapy medicinal products, somatic cell therapy products, and tissue engineered products (Art 2, Regulation 1394/2007/EC).

[39] *Medical device* means any instrument, apparatus, appliance, software, material, or other article, whether used alone or in combination, together with any accessories, including the software intended by its manufacturer to be used specifically for diagnostic and/or therapeutic purposes and necessary for its proper application, intended by the manufacturer to be used for human beings for diagnostic or other purposes (Art 1(1), Directive 2007/47/EC). It achieves its principal intended action in or on the human body by mechanical means.

[40] Medical devices regulation contains Directives for active implantable devices (90/385/EEC), medical devices (93/42/EEC), and *in vitro* medical devices (98/79/EC). At present, it is the subject of a recast procedure that is expected to be finalized in 2012.

[41] D'Silva and Van Calster (n 5) 261.

[42] D M Bowman and others, 'Defining Nanomaterial for the Purpose of Regulation with the European Union' (2010) 2 *European Journal of Risk Regulation* 115. Cf Chapter 4 in this collection.

uncertainty regarding the safety evaluation and risk assessment of nanomaterials.[43] In October 2011, the European Commission adopted a Recommendation on the definition of nanomaterial.[44] The Recommendation has been widely welcomed, but also largely criticized.[45]

'Nanotheranostics'[46] are one type of new product that may not be covered by the existing regulatory regimes: these products combine facilities for diagnosis and therapy. Other challenging developments are the enrichment of the immunological, metabolic, and pharmacological function of products by novel and additional physical/chemical dimensions that are linked to how cells 'see' and 'respond' to properties of nanomaterials.[47] Since both developments are at a very early stage, it is not yet clear whether they will lead to regulatory gaps.

b. Inappropriate guiding principles

According to the literature, policy documents, and interviews, therapeutic nanoproducts challenge the principle of regulatory classification that guides the application of regulatory regimes. The European medical products regulation system departs from the idea that medical products are classified according to the *principal mode of action*. In the case of pharmaceuticals and ATMPs, the principal mode is pharmacological, immunological, or metabolic, while medical devices principally act by mechanical means.[48] This means, for example, that therapeutical nanoproducts with a principal mechanical action and a secondary pharmacological action are brought under the medical devices regulation regime. The doctrine of the principal mode of action, however, does not apply to ATMPs. Regulation 1394/2007 is a *lex specialis*. Combined advanced therapy medicinal products are always subject to the general pharmaceuticals regulation and the specific ATMP provisions. According to regulators and companies, a specific classification problem is that the principal mode of action may be difficult to determine in therapeutic applications using nanomaterials. Given the complex mechanism of action therapeutic nanoproducts are exhibiting, the regulatory principle of the principal mode of action is regarded as being too simplistic. Nanomedical applications seem also to challenge the *internal* logics of the medical product regulation regimes. For example, the commercialization of more advanced and sophisticated nanodevices that offer a range of different applications, while using various materials and coatings, is likely to blur the distinction the medical devices system makes between a medical device and an *in vitro* device which are regulated by different Directives and different harmonized standards.[49] As a consequence, it is questionable whether the generally accepted approach to treat such products primarily as *in vitro* devices is appropriate. Respondents from companies report that there is much uncertainty about the applicable regulatory regime in the case of combined products.[50] Since the requirements of the two regimes

---

[43] L Bergeson and C Auer, 'Nano Disclosures: Too Small to Matter or Too Big to Ignore?' (2011) 25(3) *Natural Resources & Environment* <www.actagroup.com/other_pdfs/00070483.pdf>.

[44] Commission Recommendation of 18 October 2011 on the definition of nanomaterial (2011/696/EU) OJ L275/38.

[45] See <http://2020science.org/2011/10/18/ec-adopts-cross-cutting-defintion-of-nanomaterials-to-be-used-for-all-regulatory-purposes/> accessed on 2 May 2012.

[46] Gaspar (n 6) 311.

[47] EMA (n 2) 25.

[48] See the definitions in nn 10 to 12.

[49] D'Silva and Bowman (n 5); J D'Silva, 'What's in a Name?—Defining a "Nanomaterial" for Regulatory Purposes in Europe' (2011) 4 *European Journal of Risk Regulation* 420.

[50] Dorbeck-Jung and Chowdhury (n 9).

are different, and borderline products are expected to increase, many commentators emphasize that there is a serious classification problem that has to be resolved soon.[51]

A further challenge concerns the *benefit-risk balance* principle which guides the evaluation of medical products in the context of marketing controls. According to the interviews, the European rules concerning the authorization of medicinal products for human use—the methodology of the current regime of drugs evaluation with its case-by-case risk-benefit balance approach—is robust enough to address nano-medicines.[52] Companies and competent bodies have not experienced specific nano-related problems in the market authorization process of nanomedicines. To date, evaluation bodies have treated nanopharmaceuticals as conventional products. Interesting examples of how the EMA is assessing nanomedicines are provided by the European Public Assessment Reports (EPAR) of the drugs Abraxane,[53] Mepact,[54] and Rapamune.[55] Referring to the evaluation process of the eighteen nanomedicines that have gone through the centralized authorization procedure, the EMA concludes that the benefit-risk balance principle is appropriate for nanoproducts.[56] Despite the complexity, the submitted quality, safety, and efficacy data were sufficient to support the assessment of benefit-risk balance. The Agency thinks that the current risk management framework is flexible enough to accommodate the specific risks of therapeutic nanoproducts.

In this context, competent bodies emphasize that the European evaluation system does not take a 'zero risk approach'. As long as the product meets its intended purpose and the benefit–risk balance is positive, the product will be licensed. In this context, one of our interviewees, a representative of an authorization body, notes that the benefits mentioned by the applicant of a market authorization are not taken for granted: they are carefully assessed on the basis of mortality studies and data on the quality of life. Competent bodies and companies report that the measurement of the benefits depends on the kind of disease and on whether the product seems to fulfil unmet health needs. As one of them put it: 'In cancer we accept a larger risk than in the case of headaches. In the case of headache we already have so many products. Therefore, the new product will have to pass higher standards of safety.' This is also the experience of the companies that were interviewed. For instance, one of the respondents noted that cancer drugs that contain nanoparticles were approved before all effects (including toxicity) were entirely investigated because of the high benefits that were expected.

c. Implementation problems

All commentators agree that regulatory problems arise in the implementation of the existing framework of European medical products regulation. Most of them think that the existing guidance on safety, quality, and efficacy standards is not adequate: they call for nano-specific standards. In the discussion of these regulatory problems, the relation with scientific problems of measurement and risk assessment is emphasized. Specific guidance on safety, quality, and efficacy for therapeutical nanoproducts requires reliable

---

[51] Dorbeck-Jung (n 5); D'Silva and Van Calster (n 5); Chowdhury (n 5); Dorbeck-Jung and Chowdhury (n 9); D'Silva and Bowman (n 5); Duncan and Gaspar (n 9).
[52] EMA (n 2); Dorbeck-Jung and Chowdhury (n 9).
[53] EPAR EMA/274989/2010 2/3TAbraxane EMA/274989/2010.
[54] EPAR EMA/475879/2010 2/3Mepact EMA/475879/2010.
[55] EPAR EMA/281788/2010; EMEA/H/C/273.
[56] EMA (n 2) 21.

testing methods. These testing methods have not yet been developed because of the 'nanosize' and the unique behaviour of nano-systems in biological structures. The levels of nanopharmaceuticals in blood and tissues are difficult to measure.[57] Safety regulation cannot be updated, because the risks cannot yet be determined. Existing risk assessment criteria rely on mass metrics. They do not yet cover agglomeration, particle size, shape, and surface reactivity which are essential for the risk evaluation of nanomaterials.[58] The available methods are said not to be appropriate to the mass balance and not to distinguish between discrete nanopharmaceuticals and aggregates. Furthermore, the immunological heterogeneity is said to be a critical hurdle for safety evaluation.[59] It is said that the existing guidelines are not tailored to assess the immunosuppressive potential of nanomedicines. The specificities and modalities of the immunotoxicity evaluation of nanomedicines remain to be fully characterized and validated for regulatory responses. Scientific problems of measurement and risk assessment also induce challenges to the environmental impact analysis which is mandatory for medicinal products.[60] In this field, knowledge is still limited. Test guidelines on the fate and effects of substances in the environment have to be adapted to specific nanomaterial needs. According to ecotoxicologists, adaptation is complicated because of the wide variety and diversity of nanoparticles that are used in nanomedicine applications.[61] The environmental impact analysis of therapeutic nano-products is regarded as an important regulatory problem.[62]

2. Governance Methods

For more than ten years, European law has been discussed as a system of governance.[63] The language of governance is used to explain a range of processes and practices that have a normative dimension but do not operate primarily through a formal hierarchical mechanism of traditional command-and-control legal institutions.[64] Sources of EU law include 'hard' or binding legal measures (such as Regulations, Directives, and Decisions), but also a variety of measures of 'soft' or non-binding law (such as Recommendations and guidance), which though lacking formal legal force, may nevertheless have significant effects in practice. The governance of health care in the EU involves a large variety of methods including traditional hierarchical legislation and non-hierarchical policy coordination which focuses on mutual learning within networks, through the use of information-gathering, knowledge dissemination, standard-setting, benchmarking, and monitoring.[65] Governance equally involves, Hervey and Vanhercke note, the introduction of governance mechanisms (such as broad consultation) within legislation.

In the European medical products regulation system, we find a large number of combinations of traditional hierarchical legislation and soft regulation. The pharmaceuticals regime primarily follows the traditional legislative approach ('old style' harmonization), while the medical device regime uses the so-called 'new' approach. The new approach means that, at the EU level, minimum requirements for health and safety

---

[57] See Gaspar (n 6) 305.   [58] See Handy and others (n 28).   [59] EMA (n 2) 12.
[60] See Annex II, Directive 2001/18/EC.
[61] EMA (n 2) 22.
[62] Gaspar (n 9) 143.
[63] TK Hervey and JV McHale, *Health and Law in the EU* (CUP 2004).
[64] G de Búrca, and J Scott (eds), *Law and New Governance in the EU and the US* (Hart 2006).
[65] TK Hervey and B Vanhercke, 'Health Care and the EU: the Law and Policy Patchwork' in E Mossialos and others (eds), *Health Systems Governance in Europe* (CUP 2010) 105.

are set and non-state corporate actors are involved in the regulatory process by the elaboration of 'European industry standards'.[66] In recent years, private actors have increasingly been involved in lawmaking[67] and implementation[68] processes. Indeed, referring to a recent definition of governance,[69] European medical products regulation can be understood as a system of 'co-production' of norms and public goods where the co-producers are different kinds of actors. As will be shown later in the discussion of governance responses, co-production seems to be the dominant method to accommodate the 'newness' of therapeutic nano-products.[70]

3. Problems of Regulatory Capacity

Earlier we saw that regulators are confronted with a large range of technological, scientific, normative, conceptual, and institutional uncertainties. Commentators agree that nanomedicine poses challenges to the expertise of regulators and to their ability to balance technological benefits against risks. Regulation is based on evidence. Regulators are required constantly to update their knowledge on the technological development and the (potential) performance of regulation. Nanomedicine puts pressures on the capacity of regulators to keep pace with developments of (nanomedical) science, new applications, and risk assessment. According to the interviews, some national competent bodies doubt whether they have the expertise to evaluate the safety, quality, and efficacy of therapeutic nano-products at their disposal. The increasing combination of various kinds of medical products and functions within nanomedicine engender a couple of particular challenges. For instance, regulators have to be equipped to evaluate not only molecules but also integrated systems with additional and novel dimensions as well as properties beyond classical immunological, pharmaceutical, and metabolic functions.[71] Reviews of the regulatory supervision in the field of medical devices question the competences of the notified bodies that are charged with the assessment and authorization of these borderline products.[72] Lacking regulatory capacity may also be a problem for small and medium size companies (SMEs). Large companies can rely on the expertise of their regulatory affairs department, while SMEs have to call in consultants and face expense they cannot afford. Since many therapeutic nano-products are being developed by SMEs, their lack of regulatory expertise may inhibit the marketing of beneficial innovative products.

Considering regulatory problems of therapeutic nano-products, we observed that there are regulatory gaps and difficulties in classifying the new products according to the existing regulatory principles, as well as implementation problems and lack of regulatory knowledge. In the next section, the governance responses to these regulatory problems will be explored. Referring to Bartolini's definition[73] and to the relevant

---

[66] Hervey and MacHale (n 63) 57.

[67] An interesting example is the process of the ATMP Regulation (see A Faulkner and others, 'Purity and the Dangers of Regenerative Medicine: Regulatory Innovation of Human Tissue-Engineered Technology' (2006) 63 *Social Science & Medicine* 2277).

[68] eg medical devices are approved ('notified') by private and public bodies. Patient organizations participate in the scientific committee that advises on the approval of ATMPs.

[69] S Bartolini, 'New Modes of European Governance: An Introduction' in A Héritier and M Rhodes (eds), *New Modes of Governance in Europe* (Palgrave 2011) 1.

[70] See also Chapter 10 in this collection.

[71] EMA (n 2) 5.

[72] CM Herndorn, 'Iontophoretic Drug Delivery System: Focus on Fentanyl' (2007) 27(5) *Pharmacotherapy* 745; D'Silva (n 49).

[73] See Bartolini (n 69) 8.

policy rationales, governance responses are related to the co-production of regulation that serves to achieve product safety, quality, and efficacy, as well as beneficial nanotherapeutic innovation. Setting the scene for the ongoing governance activities, the section starts by describing the involved stakeholders, significant actors, and main governance initiatives.

D. Governance Responses

1. Significant Actors and Governance Initiatives

In governance activities that aim at coping with the regulatory problems of therapeutic nano-products, four different categories of stakeholder are involved: first, technology suppliers; secondly, technology users; thirdly, regulators; and fourthly, other groups (for example, insurances and civil society).[74] In practice, *significant regulators,* which have been actively involved in governance initiatives, are: the EMA, the European Commission (DG Health and Consumers), its Scientific Committee on Emerging and Newly Identified Health Risks (SCENIHR), the European Working Group on New and Emerging Technologies in Medical Devices (N&ET Working Group), the European Technology Platform Nanomedicine (ETPN), and the European Foundation for Clinical Nanomedicine (CLINAM).

Within this group, the EMA and DG Health and Consumers have undertaken the most regulatory activities. In 2005, the EMA launched the Small and Medium Size Enterprises Office.[75] SMEs that develop therapeutic nano-products can contact the Office for financial support and scientific and regulatory advice. The EMA reflection paper on nanotechnology-based medicinal products for human use which was published in 2006 can be regarded as the first specific governance activity in relation to nanomedicines.[76] In the same year, regulators from the EU, USA, Canada, and Australia started an international observatory. In 2009, the EMA Committee for Medicinal Products for Human Use (CHMP) established an ad hoc expert group on nanomedicines. This group includes selected experts from academia and the European regulatory network of the competent authorities. It supports the Agency's activities by providing specialist input on new scientific knowledge. The group contributes to the review of guidelines with respect to nanomedicines, as well as to the Agency's discussion with international partners. In the same year, a regulators' conference on nanomedicines was held at the FDA. At this conference the organization of an international workshop was agreed. The workshop was held in September 2010 at the EMA. Very recent initiatives of the EMA can be found in the Work Programme 2011 which notes that the Agency will have to address new challenges in fields like nanotechnologies, personalized medicine, borderline products, and other complex areas, such as the combination of medicines and medical devices as single integral products, leading to further reflection on the criteria to address borderline issues.[77] DG Health and Consumers organizes annual conferences on the safety of nanotechnologies which include nanomedical applications. Another active regulator is the N&ET Working Group which issued recommendations related

---

[74] See EU-OSHA, 'European Agency for Safety and Health at Work Literature Review', Workplace Exposure to Nanoparticles (2008) edited by J Kosk-Bienko, 9.

[75] See <www.ema.europa.eu/ema/index.jsp?curl=pages/regulation/general/general_content_000059. jsp&mid=WC0b01ac05800240cc&jsenabled=true> accessed 14 April 2012.

[76] See EMA CHMP/79769.

[77] See EMA/MB/482208/2010.

to nanotechnologies in medical devices in 2007.[78] Furthermore, the European Group of European Group on Ethics in Science and New Technologies (EGE) addressed regulatory problems in its 2007 Opinion on nanomedicine.[79]

Other *potentially* significant actors like doctors' and patients' organizations, the ICH, the European Directorate for the Quality of Medicines and Health Care (EDQM at the Council of Europe), and the World Health Organization have not yet been actively involved in regulatory governance activities related to therapeutic nanoproducts. According to the interviews and conference debates, the absence of these stakeholders can be explained by lack of expertise and financial resources, as well as by other policy priorities. In addition, two representatives of a national competent body noted that their organization is not active because they do not want to contribute to regulatory hype in terms of creating a specific regulatory framework which, in their view, is not necessary. In its proposed Road Map to 2015 the EMA emphasizes the growing importance of the structural involvement of patients and health care professionals in its activities.[80]

2. Governance Activities to Fill Regulatory Gaps

In the past years, various governance activities have been employed to prepare regulatory changes. To cope with the lack of a definition of nanomedicine, the EMA's Scientific Committee proposed a definition in 2006.[81] The definition is related to the European Science Foundation's ideas. The CHMP defined nanomedicine as 'the application of nanotechnology in view of making a medical diagnosis or treating or preventing diseases. It exploits the improved and often novel physical, chemical and biological properties of materials at nanometre scale.' In October 2011, the European Commission adopted a Recommendation on the definition of nanomaterial.[82] A legal definition is still lacking.

The EMA CHMP Reflection Paper (2006) can be regarded as a first governance response to potential regulatory gaps related to nanomedicines. The conclusions of the paper clarify that the creation of the Innovation Task Force was the next step to deal with regulatory problems of novel products. The governance activities of this Task Force and other platforms like the ad hoc expert group on nanomedicines, the SME Office, the international observatory, meetings with other regulatory bodies and industry, and the 2010 EMA Workshop include the coordination of scientific and regulatory competence, the collection of scientific knowledge and regulatory experience, as well as early dialogue with applicants, international exchange, and the support of innovative SMEs.

At the 2010 Workshop, the aim of the present governance activities was summarized by the Head of the EMA Unit Human Medicines and Development as follows: 'The regulatory bodies need to be prepared for the timely introduction of safe and efficacious nanomedicines of a high quality, as nanotechnologies bring not only opportunities to improve current treatments but also the potential to change the way we approach healthcare and diseases.'[83] One conclusion of the workshop was that pooling of knowledge and expertise at a global level and across disciplines is required to

---

[78] See n 35.   [79] See EGE (n 4).

[80] EMA, 'The European Medicines Agency Road Map to 2015: The Agency's Contribution to Science, Medicines, Health', *Draft for Public Consultation* EMA/299895/2009.

[81] See n 13.   [82] See n 44.   [83] EMA (n 2) 3.

cope with the challenges of nanomedicines. Another conclusion was that regulatory action requires more knowledge on scientific development of nanomedicine and its regulatory implications. Until science has elucidated the remaining gaps, the EMA proposed to keep following the case-by-case approach along the development process depending on the therapeutic indications considered.

At present, regulatory standardization of therapeutic nanoproducts is not yet regarded as an appropriate route. Evaluating the workshop, the EMA concluded that platforms for continued dialogue on emerging science and on the needs of patients and expectations are required in order to keep abreast of scientific progress and to provide a regulatory environment suitable for scientific innovation to the benefit of patients. The evaluation indicates that governance lessons can be learned from the underpinnings of the risk-benefit balance of approved nanomedicines.[84] It notes that the Risk Management Plan that is required for all new active substances or any other 'high-risk' products is of particular interest to show how nanopharmaceuticals are evaluated. With regard to the environmental impact assessment, the EMA will set up common instructions and training for users.

As regards the lack of nano-specific safety, quality, and efficacy standards, a remaining problem is that evidence on the benefits and risks of therapeutic nano-products has not yet been provided. However, according to the principles of the European medical products system, this does not mean that regulators have to wait for product marketing. The approved nanomedical products indicate that market authorization can also be obtained in cases of uncertain effects when a *balance* between the benefits and risks of therapeutical nano-products can be proved on the basis of existing safety, quality, and efficacy standards. In this context, the question arises whether it would be helpful to establish provisional and experimental standards on the basis of the experience that has already been gained with the authorization of therapeutic nano-products, or whether it would be more prudent to wait for more evidence and to use the existing safety, quality, and efficacy standards on a case-by-case approach. It is likely that provisional standards provide certainty that may stimulate industrial investment into nanomedicine. However, as research on benchmarks for the reduction of exposure to nanomaterials in the workplace indicates, provisional standards tend to be treated as robust guidance.[85] As a consequence, a false sense of certainty and stability may emerge that impedes precautionary measures. Regarding these undesirable side effects, as well as the existing knowledge gaps and political issues, the preparatory governance strategy and activities that have been set out mainly by DG Health and Consumers together with the EMA seem to be appropriate.

3. Adaptation of the Regulatory System

At present regulatory responses are at a preliminary stage. To date, the regulatory gaps have not yet been filled and the principle of the primary mode of action has not been adapted to the complexities of existing and expected therapeutic nano-products.

---

[84] EMA (n 2) 21.

[85] An explorative case study on the use of provisional benchmarks to limit exposure to nanomaterials in the workplace in the Netherlands and Germany indicates a tendency of expectations on regulatory certainty (BR Dorbeck-Jung 'Soft regulation and responsible nanotechnological development in the European Union: Regulating occupational health and safety in the Netherlands' (2011) 2 *European Journal of Law and Technology* 1). Regulatees tend to expect that a use of provisional benchmarks provides the certainty that they are on the safe side. As a consequence, they may not take necessary additional measures to protect employees. To exclude a false sense of certainty, German regulators do not use these provisional benchmarks that have been developed by a German organization.

Governance activities are still focusing on the collection and integration of scientific and regulatory expertise. The existing regulatory regimes are intensively tested to assess whether they are 'nano-proof'. One interesting example is the broad use of the definition of 'advanced therapies medicinal products' to novel therapeutic products. If a broad interpretation will be accepted in regulatory practice the classification problem could be (at least partly) solved. The ATMP regulations would then apply to almost all therapeutic nano-products. As a consequence, European medical products regulation would move in the direction of a convergence of the pharmaceuticals and medical devices regimes, which would be guided by the medicinal products regulatory approach. Such an integration of the two regulatory regimes is stimulated by evaluation and revision of European medical devices regulation.

According to the European Commission, experience indicates that the current regime does not always offer a uniform level of protection of public health in the EU. It is criticized as being too fragmented, difficult to follow, and fraught with national variation. As the Commission notes: 'New and emerging technologies have challenged the current framework, highlighting gaps and pointing to a certain scarcity of expertise. In addition, in recognition that the medical devices market is a global one, to keep European industry competitive, the EU regime needs to further converge on the "global model".'[86] In this context, the Commission points to a recent draft report on the possible way forward in converging the regulatory frameworks of combination products internationally.[87] In the current recast procedure of the medical devices Directives, the harmonization of medical devices and pharmaceuticals regulation with regard to combined products is an issue in the context of a proposal to set up a supra-Directive borderline committee.[88]

Currently, the EMA seems to focus on the optimization of existing guidance rather than on developing new requirements for nanomedicines. Various combinations of diagnostics, medical devices, and medicinal products are brought under the scope of the ATMP Regulation.[89] However, an adaptation of the risk management plan including novel designs of trials and additional risk minimization measures is expected. In this context, the Agency notes that the current risk management framework is flexible enough to accommodate the specific risks of nanomedicines.[90] In the present situation, continuous strengthening of the regulatory networks including European, national, and international stakeholders, as well as ongoing knowledge collection, sophistication of regulatory methods, and systematization of experience with therapeutic nano-products seems to be the most prudent governance action. It is striking, however, that these activities are taking place in different networks (medical devices and medicinal products) that do not seem to be well connected: the regulatory bodies for medical devices do not have an active role in the governance activities of

---

[86] European Commission, 'Commission Staff Working Paper. Situation in the Different Sectors' COM (2011a) 588 final, 355.

[87] The report has been issued by an international regulatory ad hoc Task Force on combination products, composed of the Members of the Global Harmonization Task Force for medical devices (GHTF) and of representatives of the ICH for the pharmaceutical products.

[88] See <http://medicaldeviceslegal.com/2011/03/30/update-on-eu-medical-devices-recast-regarding-combination-products/> accessed 14 April 2012.

[89] See on this issue, VN Uversky, AV Kabanov, and YL Lyubchenko, 'Nanotools for Megaproblems: Probing Protein Misfolding Diseases Using Nanomedicine Modus Operandi' (2006) 5(10) *Journal of Proteome Research* 2505.

[90] See n 2.

the medicinal products evaluation bodies on nanomedical products and vice versa. Lack of collaboration in this respect may be detrimental to the regulation of combination products.

The exploration of regulatory problems indicates that the existing regulatory regimes of pharmaceuticals and medical devices are comprehensive enough to accommodate therapeutic nano-products. A specific new regulatory regime for nanomedical products does not seem to be required. The enduring existence of regulatory gaps raises the question whether the European governance responses to the challenges of therapeutic nano-products are appropriate. Regarding the classification principle, it is not clear whether the path of a broad interpretation of 'advanced therapies medicinal products', which would induce a general application of the medicinal products regulation, would be accepted within the EU. The proposal to set up a supra-Directive borderline committee that has been made in the medical devices recast procedure is pointing in another direction. Probably the EMA has to wait before introducing a new classification principle until the recast procedure is finalized.

4. Governance Approach

The governance approach that has emerged to guide therapeutic nano-products can be characterized as incremental regulatory innovation.[91] Governance activities are guided by successive changes with a focus on preparatory governance based on learning and other methods of new governance. If the political debate on therapeutic nano-products leads to a convergence of the medical devices and the pharmaceuticals regimes, incremental innovation may be followed by progressive regulatory innovation. Systemic and transformative changes, however, will largely depend on changes in the medical products industry and further nanomedical development. Certain trends of disruptive change have been indicated. One is the general trend of delocalization of production facilities and outsourcing. As a consequence, manufacturing regulation is said to be increasingly subject to global cooperation, implementing common requirements for good manufacturing practice and quality management systems. As one influential expert put it: 'Basic science and regulatory sciences (mostly pharmaceutical sciences, including manufacturing science, safety sciences and clinical pharmacology) will tend to be more integrated in the near future, helping to establish adequate platforms for assessing risk (namely through validated biomarkers) and improved management of access to innovative technologies in specific stages.'[92] Another trend is the focus on a fast translation of product development to practice. This may require an adaptation of pre-marketing regulation. Considering these trends and the unresolved regulatory problems of therapeutic nano-products, it seems that European regulators of new health technologies will have extremely exciting times in the coming years.

---

[91] I refer to Black's definition of regulatory innovation as 'the use of new solutions to address old problems, or new solutions to address "new" (or newly constructed) problems' (J Black and others (eds), *Regulatory innovation—A Comparative Analysis* (Edward Elgar 2005) 15). Black highlights that regulatory innovations are second- or third-order changes in the performance of regulatory functions, institutional structures, and organizational processes which have an impact on the regulatory regime.

[92] Gaspar (n 6) 312.

E. Conclusion

What, then, are the lessons of all of this for the regulation of new health technologies? The analysis of governance responses to regulatory problems of therapeutic nano-products leads to the following tentative lessons:

Uncertain risks and benefits call for a preparatory and collaborative mode of regulation.

The governance activities of the European Medicines Agency and DG Health and Consumers related to therapeutic nan-oproducts are an interesting example of responsive preparatory governance. They show that regulators do not need to wait when risks and benefits are uncertain. They can establish a sophisticated regulatory network with experts and other stakeholders to obtain insights into the properties and effects of existing and coming products.

Effective preparation of regulatory adaptation requires ongoing extension and integration of regulatory networks.

The ongoing extension and sophistication of the EMA's regulatory network and its body of regulatory science shows how regulation can be proactively prepared. The lack of active and integrative collaboration with the medical devices network, however, seems to be problematic when it comes to new regulation for combination products. Prudent regulators are recommended to seek more collaboration with core regulatory partners and to focus on co-regulation. In cases of conflicting interests, efforts to negotiate regulatory changes can be crucial.

Prudent regulators focus primarily on a case-by-case approach using the benefit-risk balance principle.

The approval of nanomedical products in the European Union indicates that the guiding benefit-risk balance principle is robust enough to accommodate the marketing of therapeutic nano-products. Regarding the specification of safety, quality, and efficacy standards for new health technologies, the use of a case-by-case approach seems to be adequate until robust scientific knowledge has been provided. Since provisional standards may lead to a false sense of certainty, regulators are recommended not to focus on regulatory experimentation.

Adaptation of regulation should be embedded in changes of the research, policy, and industrial environment.

The analysis of governance activities related to therapeutic nano-products indicates two trends of disruptive changes in health research, health policy, and the medical products industry that seem to be relevant for the regulation of all new health technologies. These are, first, the globalization of manufacturing activities and, secondly the focus on a fast translation of research and development to practice. To cope with these changes, prudent regulators are recommended to pay specific attention both to the internationalization of manufacturing regulation and to the adaptation of pre-marketing controls.

Regulating Embryo Research

Emily Jackson

Within Europe, there is no consensus on how research on embryos should be regulated. The diversity of views on the moral status of the embryo means that, as with abortion, European countries have a wide margin of appreciation when deciding whether or when to permit scientists to carry out research on human embryos. Of course, there have been attempts to frame Europe-wide general principles, such as those contained in the Convention on Human Rights and Biomedicine. In relation to embryo research, Article 18 of the Convention simply states that: 'Where the law allows research on embryos *in vitro*, it shall ensure adequate protection of the embryo.' Not only does this suggest that states are free to decide whether to allow research on embryos at all, but also, given that embryos are necessarily destroyed after research has taken place, the meaning of 'adequate protection' is opaque, at best. It could therefore be argued that the Convention, in practice, offers minimal guidance on the content of any laws regulating embryo research. Article 18 §2 purports to prevent the creation of embryos for research purposes and, in part due to its inconsistency with the UK legislation which does permit the creation of embryos for research, the United Kingdom is not a signatory to the Convention.

Unlike research on animals and research involving human subjects, embryo research is not regulated throughout the European Union (EU) via the transposition of European Directives.[1] Of course, this does not mean that EU law is irrelevant to embryo research. The European Court of Justice has recently ruled that human embryonic stem cell lines cannot be the subject of patent protection,[2] and the EU Tissues and Cells Directive[3] clearly affects how much donors of eggs and sperm can be compensated in return for their donation.

But the fundamental question of whether or in what circumstances embryo research should be permitted has been left to individual states' discretion. In some countries, like Germany, the rules are restrictive; in others, like Ireland, they are unclear. The United Kingdom, on the other hand, has the most long-standing and one of the most liberal statutory regimes in the world. I have been a member of the UK's regulatory authority, the Human Fertilisation and Embryology Authority (HFEA) for nine years, and this short commentary is intended to provide a brief personal overview of some of the challenges faced by the HFEA in recent years.

At the outset, one of the most obvious difficulties, from the regulator's point of view, is that science moves quickly, whereas amending primary legislation is a laborious process, which inevitably happens relatively infrequently. In the United Kingdom, the Human Fertilisation and Embryology Act 1990 has been amended by Parliament twice

---

[1] Animals in Research Directive 2010/63/EU [2010] OJ L276/33 and EU Clinical Trials Directive 2001/20/EC [2001] OJ L121/34.

[2] Case C-34/10 *Brüstle v Greenpeace* (2011).

[3] Directive 2004/23/EC [2004] OJ L102/48.

since it came into force over thirty years ago, and while it has stood the test of time remarkably well, there have been occasions when, first, its wording has led to a lack of clarity over whether a new technique fits within the statutory scheme and, secondly, when what it means to say that the use of embryos is 'necessary' has had to be reevaluated in the light of scientific developments.

When it debated the Act in 1990, Parliament assumed that the principal reason why scientists would wish to carry out experiments on embryos would be to refine and improve treatments involving embryos, such as IVF and pre-implantation genetic diagnosis. Because abnormal embryo development is thought to be implicated in some cases of miscarriage, it was also thought that embryo research might lead to a better understanding of the causes of miscarriage. Since some methods of contraception involve disrupting the implantation of fertilized eggs, it was additionally believed that research on embryos might be helpful when developing new methods of contraception. In order to accommodate all these potential uses of embryo research, the 1990 Act set out five statutory purposes, including promoting advances in the treatment of infertility; increasing knowledge about the causes of miscarriage; developing more effective techniques of contraception; and developing methods for detecting the presence of gene or chromosome abnormalities in embryos before implantation.[4]

Research can only receive a licence from the HFEA if the Licence Committee, with advice from expert peer reviewers, judges that it is 'necessary or desirable' for one of the statutory purposes and, additionally, that the use of embryos is necessary. This at first sight rather confusing wording—that the research should be 'necessary *or desirable*' (for a statutory purpose) and also that it should be 'necessary' (to use embryos)—in fact captures the idea that it may be sufficient that it is 'desirable' to carry out the particular research project, since the bar would be set unfeasibly high if the research itself had to be necessary in order to understand miscarriage, for example. Since the outcome of research is, by definition, not yet known, it would be difficult to hold scientists to a 'this research must be necessary' test. On the other hand, it does have to be necessary to use embryos in the research. To put it bluntly, if scientists could carry out the proposed research project equally well using mice, then they cannot receive a licence to use human embryos in research.

Pressure was exerted on these statutory purposes following the publication of a paper in 1998, in which researchers at the University of Wisconsin explained how they had, for the first time, derived and cultured a human embryonic stem cell line.[5] In order to carry out this sort of research in the United Kingdom, a licence from the HFEA would be necessary, but stem cell research does not appear to fit within any of the original statutory purposes. The principal reason why scientists are interested in carrying out research involving human embryonic stem cells is because they are pluripotent, that is they are capable of differentiating into different types of tissue. The hope is then that stem cells might be used to create new tissue, which could be used to repair damaged tissues or organs. This has nothing to do with improving fertility treatments, or better understanding of miscarriage, or improving contraceptive techniques. Under the Human Fertilisation and Embryology Act 1990, embryonic stem cell research would not appear to be licensable, since it is not 'necessary or desirable' for one of the original five purposes.

---

[4] Human Fertilisation and Embryology Act 1990, Sch 2(3)(2).
[5] JA Thomson and others, 'Embryonic Stem Cell Lines Derived from Human Blastocysts' (1998) 282 *Science* 1145.

Fortunately, the drafters of the 1990 Act had attempted to 'future proof' this particular part of the legislation, and the statute also specified that 'such other purposes as may be specified in regulations' could be added to the statutory purposes for which embryo research can be licensed. As a result, this part of the legislation could be updated more quickly than if primary legislation had been necessary. Three further research purposes were added by the Human Fertilisation and Embryology (Research Purposes) Regulations 2001, in order to include the purposes of stem cell research. Once these came into force, a licence could also be issued for research that was necessary or desirable for the purposes of increasing knowledge about the development of embryos and/or increasing knowledge about serious disease and/or enabling any such knowledge to be applied in developing treatments for serious disease.

I joined the HFEA in 2003, so the expansion of the research purposes predates my membership. Just before I became a member, a further issue had emerged. Section 1(1) of the Human Fertilisation and Embryology Act 1990 appeared to contain a statutory definition of the word 'embryo': 'In this Act, except where otherwise stated—embryo means a live human embryo where fertilisation is complete . . .' It was these latter words 'where fertilisation is complete' that posed a problem following the announcement, in 1997, that Dolly the sheep had been created through a process known as cell nuclear replacement (CNR), or cloning. In order to create Dolly, the nucleus had been removed from a sheep's egg, and a cell taken from an adult sheep had been inserted into this denucleated egg, with an electric current being used to trick it into beginning the process of cell division.

This process undoubtedly leads to the creation of embryos, but it does not involve fertilization. At first sight, then, it looks as though it does not fall within the statutory definition in section 1 of the Act. This was not because the statute's drafters had not anticipated the possibility of cloning; rather, they had assumed it would be possible only using already fertilized eggs. In 2002, this apparent gap between the statute's wording and the procedure involved in Dolly's creation was the subject of a judicial review action brought by Bruno Quintavalle, on behalf of the Pro-life Alliance. His claim was that the definition of 'embryo' in the 1990 Act did not cover embryos created by CNR. This would mean that human embryos created through this process lay outside the HFEA's regulatory remit and would therefore be almost completely unregulated within the United Kingdom. Essentially, if Bruno Quintavalle was right, it would have been lawful to clone a human being in your garden shed.

Quintavalle succeeded at first instance, leading the government to pass emergency legislation banning reproductive cloning. But the government appealed successfully to the Court of Appeal, and the House of Lords subsequently dismissed Quintavalle's appeal.[6] The gist of the House of Lords' judgment was that the Act had not, in fact, offered a special definition of the word embryo, which was instead an ordinary word of the English language. Indeed, section 1 would be a rather odd 'definition' since it effectively says 'an embryo is . . . an embryo'. We don't normally define words by using the word itself. To use an analogy, if we were to pass a piece of legislation regulating the treatment of tables, we would not say: 'for the purposes of this Act, a table is a round table that is made out of wood'. That doesn't define the word table, rather it takes for granted the meaning of the word table, and instead tells us *which sort of table* is to be regulated. If you didn't know what a table was, this definition wouldn't help you, other than alerting you to the fact that *some* tables are round and made out of wood.

---

[6] *R (on the application of Quintavalle) v Secretary of State for Health* [2003] UKHL 13.

In the same way, section 1 is simply specifying the *type* of embryo which is covered, namely that it must be live and human. A cloned human embryo is undoubtedly a live, human embryo and hence is covered by the regulatory regime. The Lords were also undoubtedly influenced by the fact that Parliament's intention was for the regulatory scheme to be comprehensive: in Lord Bingham's words, 'there was to be no free for all'.

Section 1(1) was subjected to further pressure a couple of years later. This time it was not the words 'when fertilisation is complete' that were the issue, but the more basic and prosaic word 'human'. One of the reasons why cell nuclear replacement was such an exciting development was that it was thought that, taken together with the extraction of stem cell lines from embryos, these processes might lead to a whole new sort of regenerative medicine. Grossly simplified, it would work something like this. A cloned embryo would be produced using a patient's skin cell, say, and then a stem cell line could be extracted and 'tricked' into differentiating into whatever replacement tissue the patient might need. If I need new heart tissue, say, my skin cell could be inserted into a denucleated egg in order to produce a cloned embryo, from which stem cells could be extracted and persuaded to grow into new heart tissue which—unlike a conventional heart transplant—would not be rejected because it would be 'my' tissue. If this worked, it would undoubtedly be an extraordinary medical breakthrough—the organ shortage, for example, might disappear—but, for reasons which are still not properly understood, in practice it has proved rather difficult to extract stem cell lines from cloned embryos.

The process of cell nuclear replacement is dependent upon scientists having access to eggs which can be denucleated so that the patient's skin cell, or whatever other cell is used, can be inserted into it (although it should be noted that in 2011, it appeared that complete denucleation might be part of the problem).[7] Access to human eggs depends upon women specifically donating them to research, and although there may be some women willing to do this, the discomfort and inconvenience of egg donation means that human eggs are inevitably in short supply. Some scientists therefore argued that while this line of inquiry is still at the 'basic research' stage, it would be more sensible to essentially practise the processes of cell nuclear replacement and stem cell extraction using animal eggs. Cow eggs, for example, can be readily obtained from abattoirs; there would be no intention to experiment on the cows, just to use what would otherwise be treated as waste material.

Could such research receive a licence from the Human Fertilisation and Embryology Authority? Given that—for the purposes of the Act—'an embryo is a live human embryo where fertilisation is complete', would an embryo created using a denucleated cow egg and human nuclear DNA be considered human, or not? In 2007, following an intensive public consultation exercise, the HFEA decided that because these embryos contain a full nuclear human genome, they too are both live and human, and hence covered by regulation, which was, as the House of Lords had held in *Quintavalle,* intended to be comprehensive.

The HFEA's Research Licence Committee issued the first two licences for research projects which intended to use animal eggs to create admixed embryos in January 2008, and a third one was licensed a few months later. These decisions were subsequently the subject of another application for judicial review, this time from Comment on Reproductive Ethics (a pro-life pressure group chaired by Josephine Quintavalle) and the

---

[7] S Noggle and others, 'Human Oocytes Reprogram Somatic Cells to a Pluripotent State' (2011) 478 *Nature* 70.

Christian Legal Centre. This judicial review application was superseded by the passage of the Human Fertilisation and Embryology Act 2008, which amended the 1990 Act and specifically permitted the creation of what the Act describes as human admixed embryos. In *R (on the application of Quintavalle and CLC) v HFEA*,[8] Dobbs LJ held that the HFEA's legal advice—that it should take a cautious approach and treat such embryos as human in order to ensure that they are regulated—was in accordance with the spirit and purpose of the 1990 Act. She also noted that Parliament had made its intention in relation to hybrid embryos clear, and that it would be pointless to strike down licences that would simply have to be reissued when the amending statute came into force.

More recently, pressure has been exerted on a different word in the statute, namely the requirement that the use of embryos is 'necessary'. For two reasons, it could be argued that, in relation to stem cell research, the bar has been raised and that it is more difficult to establish the necessity to use human embryos today than it was ten years ago.

First, scientists have had remarkable success in inducing adult cells to act in the same way as embryonic stem cells, that is, it looks as though they can be induced to become pluripotent.[9] If a proposed stem cell research project could be carried out on induced pluripotent stem cells (iPS), rather than embryonic stem cells, then it would not be possible to establish that the use of embryos is *necessary*. Because pluripotency is induced in adult cells with the help of viral factors, cells derived in this way would not be straightforwardly suitable for clinical use. Indeed, most scientists believe that human embryonic stem cell research and research on iPS cells should continue in parallel, and that both continue to be necessary in order to make progress towards the availability of stem cell therapies for the treatment of a wide variety of conditions.

Nevertheless, the Research Licence Committee's statutory duty to license research involving embryos only when the use of embryos is necessary, has required it to ask a further question when making licensing decisions: namely, could this research be carried out using iPS cells. Peer reviewers are now specifically asked to express a view on this point, and if the research project could equally well be carried out using iPS cells, necessity has not been established, and a licence could not be issued.

The second development which has exerted pressure on the necessity requirement is the UK Stem Cell Bank which now contains eighteen stem cell lines which are available for use by other scientists, with many more awaiting approval. As the number of stem cell lines deposited in the bank grows, a scientist who wishes to carry out research using human embryonic stem cells will be increasingly unlikely to have to create their own embryonic stem cell line. If it is possible to apply to use a suitable stem cell line that has been deposited in the bank, then it is not necessary to use embryos in order to create a new stem cell line. If the use of embryos is not necessary, a licence cannot be issued.

Once again, this means that a new question must be added to the Research Licence Committee's deliberations. In an application to carry out human embryonic stem cell research, the Research Licence Committee must ask whether it would be possible to carry out the research project using stem cell lines which have been deposited in the UK Stem Cell Bank. Only if the answer to this question is 'no'—perhaps because the researchers wish to create a disease-specific cell line for a disease which is not among those represented in the bank—could a licence be issued. This issue has arisen in one

---

8 [2008] EWHC 3395 (Admin).

9 K Takahashi and S Yamanaka, 'Induction of Pluripotent Stem Cells from Mouse Embryonic and Adult Fibroblast Cultures by Defined Factors' (2006) 126 *Cell* 663.

case, in which the Research Licence Committee refused an application for a licence on the ground that it could not be satisfied that it would be impossible to use existing stem cell lines in the particular drug toxicology research project. A preference to create a new line, free from third party entanglements, did not amount to a necessity to do so, and the application was refused.[10]

Before I was appointed to chair the Research Licence Committee (RLC), the HFEA's Licence Committees dealt with both treatment and research licences. The decision to set up a specialist committee to issue only research licences was, in my view, a wise move in the interests of both consistency of decision-making and the development of expertise. When I left the HFEA in 2012, I had chaired the RLC for seven years, during which it has been interesting to observe shifts in its workload. In its early years, most applications to the RLC were to carry out stem cell research. More recently, not only have the number of applications to carry out stem cell research diminished, but across the board, there are fewer applications for new projects. A combination of diminished funding opportunities and the existence of the functioning UK Stem Cell Bank mean that licensing embryo research—while undoubtedly still a vitally important role—is no longer the extremely time-consuming one it was six years ago.

The relative lack of activity in this sector is one reason why I consider that the Coalition Government's announcement that it intended to divide up the HFEA's functions—with treatment going to the Care Quality Commission and embryo research to the new Health Research Authority—was unwise. Expecting an entirely new body to acquire the necessary expertise to regulate an especially complex and controversial type of research, when an existing regulator can straightforwardly continue to regulate the few centres which continue to carry out embryo research, seems to me to be a waste of resources.

There are also good reasons for keeping the regulation of embryo research and the regulation of the treatment which creates the embryos used in that research together. Separating them misses the essential point that embryo research and IVF treatment generally involve exactly the same embryos: almost all of the embryos used in research were originally created with the intention that they should be used in the patients' fertility treatment. The couples who agree to donate embryos which are not suitable for use in their treatment to research do so when they are patients, during the consent process in which they give their consent to IVF treatment. With two regulators, that consent process would have to be regulated by two different bodies, which might impose different standards or have different requirements.

More importantly still, there are issues which arise at the intersection of treatment and research. Hypothetically, if a centre were to adopt a policy that it will only freeze embryos for patients if they have a minimum of four spare grade A embryos, then a couple which have three spare grade A embryos will be unable to freeze those embryos for their future use, and if they are asked whether they would be willing to donate those embryos to research, they may be likely to say yes. This is unfair on the patients, however, whose wish to have a baby should always take priority over the researchers' desire for embryos to use in research. The freezing policy in the treating centre is then of critical importance to the ethical acceptability of the process through which people give their consent to donate embryos for research, but this might be missed by a treatment inspectorate, which is not concerned with research, and by a research inspectorate, which is not concerned with treatment.

---

[10] Minutes available at <www.hfea.gov.uk>.

Whichever body is responsible for the licensing of embryo research in the United Kingdom in the future, one thing is certain: there will be unforeseen scientific developments which will put pressure on the statutory framework. Developments within the EU may also have a role to play—the non-patentability of embryonic stem cell lines may have implications for researchers in the United Kingdom, for example. But the core regulatory business of the HFEA—namely licensing embryo research within the United Kingdom—whether it is done by the Health Research Authority or by the HFEA, will continue to be exceptionally challenging and controversial. There will always be people who think embryo research is wrong, and there will always be scientists who resent the bureaucracy and intrusiveness of regulation. Somewhere between these extremes, regulators have to steer a difficult course which takes seriously both the specialness of the human embryo and the importance of scientific progress. There will never be agreement on exactly what that course should be, but having been involved in steering it has been the most enormous privilege.

PART IV

NEW TECHNIQUES FOR RESEARCHING EUROPEAN LAW AND NEW HEALTH TECHNOLOGIES

13

Taking Technology Seriously:
STS as a Human Rights Method

Thérèse Murphy and Gearóid Ó Cuinn*

A. Introduction

This chapter is an experiment; to be specific, it is an experiment in human rights method. It takes two new-health-technology cases from the European Court of Human Rights,[1] widely seen as the premier international human rights court, and it sets about reading them differently. By this we mean, it reads the cases not in the law way but rather in the style of science and technology studies (STS).

We will not try to explain STS as that would be a chapter in itself (and it would not be an easy chapter to write either). But, by way of a crude outline, we will say the following: STS, a relatively young academic field, crystallized from the 1970s onwards, although it has roots reaching back to the inter-World War years.[2] Today it encompasses a range of scholarly perspectives and, as a result, a range of methods and organizing ideas—including both Sheila Jasanoff's empirical comparative work around concepts such as co-production, sociotechnical imaginaries, and, latterly, bioconstitutionalism,[3] and Bruno Latour's actor-network theory.[4] Amidst this diversity, science and technology provide the common ground, and two questions attract a lot of attention: first, how do science and technology inscribe our lives and livelihoods? Secondly, how do society and culture, in turn, impact upon the development of science and technology?

We do need to explain what we mean when we say 'STS as a human rights method' and, given the range of STS, what we mean when we say we are going to read in the 'style of STS'. 'Reading cases the law way' and 'human rights method' need explanation too. We shall start with the latter. To speak of reading cases the law way is, in part, a fiction; there is more than one way—a critical legal scholar reads in a particular way, a doctrinalist in another. How a lawyer reads relates to her reason for reading: is she,

* Earlier versions of this paper were presented at the University of Manchester, the University of Hannover, and Kings College London: the feedback received helped to shape the final paper. Our thanks to Emilie Cloatre, Mark Flear, David Fraser, Tamara Hervey, Bettina Lange, Sheelagh McGuinness, Sally Sheldon, and Noel Whitty for incisive reviews. We also want to acknowledge the ESRC (RES-451-26-0764) which supported the seminar series for which this paper was written.

[1] Hereinafter 'the Strasbourg Court', reflecting the city in which the Court has its home, or simply 'the Court'.

[2] Origins stories are always controversial; however, some within STS cite Thomas Kuhn's study, *The Structure of Scientific Revolutions* (University of Chicago Press 1962) as an important jumping-off point.

[3] See, respectively, S Jasanoff (ed), *States of Knowledge: The Co-Production of Science and Social Order* (Routledge 2004); S Jasanoff and S-H Kim, 'Containing the Atom: Sociotechnical Imaginaries and Nuclear Power in the US and Korea' (2009) 47 *Minerva* 119; S Jasanoff (ed), *Reframing Rights: Bioconstitutionalism in the Genetic Age* (MIT Press 2011).

[4] See eg B Latour, *Science in Action: Following Scientists and Engineers through Society* (Harvard UP 1987).

for instance, looking to piece together an appeal, or is she reading with an eye to rewriting the judgment (rewriting it as, say, a feminist judgment[5])? At the same time however there is, it seems, something shared; something shared through legal education—a way of reading that extracts, or knows how to extract, the facts, the issue, the decision, and the reason for that decision. It might be too much to call this reading cases 'the law way', but it would be foolish to ignore it.

We, of course, are setting out to read cases differently. This sounds like something that should appeal to human rights lawyers: the topic of human rights seems almost to mandate interdisciplinary inquiry. On the other hand, human rights lawyers, like lawyers more generally, tend to be steeped in the formalities or technicalities of law. More than this, there can be a core commitment to these technicalities; a commitment to *using* them. One reason for this is that the technicalities of law do sometimes work in the interests of marginalized groups. Mimicking the technicalities has been a strategy too: as, for instance, in the Tokyo Women's International War Crimes Tribunal where an alliance of NGOs, activists, and academics constructed a quasi-legal process, a 'people's court' which was presided over by four 'judges' who produced a lengthy and rigorous 'opinion', all with the aim of bringing moral judgement to the perpetrators of wartime sexual slavery.[6] More recently, Karen Knop and others have recommended '*theorizing* through [legal] technique'[7]—which is a fascinating idea, not least because technique is widely seen as the stronghold of doctrinal lawyers not legal theorists.

All of this makes it difficult, however, to think about reading cases differently. And to read cases differently via STS—to see STS as a *human rights method*—seems more difficult still. Human rights method, at least for lawyers, needs to be enabling, and it might be hard for lawyers to think of STS in that way. STS does not say what ought to be, and it does not pursue usefulness in any conventional sense.[8] Variants such as Latour's actor-network theory, with its thick ethnographic approach to particular networks of human and non-human actors, seem more challenging still.[9] Human rights lawyers will surely ask: how does one instrumentalize that?[10]

B. STS *à la Carte*

So, two challenges lie ahead: first, STS might not be value-added—reading cases STS-style might not be different enough from (at least some) law ways of reading cases.

---

[5] See eg R Hunter, C McGlynn, and E Rackley (eds), *Feminist Judgments: From Theory to Practice* (Hart 2010), which includes chapters by Sonia Harris-Short and Sally Sheldon on *Evans*, one of the cases we shall be discussing. This method is becoming part of human rights too: see E Brem (ed), *Diversity and Human Rights: Rewriting Judgments of the ECHR* (CUP 2012).

[6] Women's International War Crimes Tribunal for the Trial of Japan's Military Sexual Slavery, case no PT-2000-1-T (4 December 2001), The Hague <www1.jca.apc.org/vaww-net-japan/english/womenstribunal2000/judgement.html> accessed 25 June 2012.

[7] K Knop, R Michaels, and A Riles, 'From Multiculturalism to Technique: Feminism, Culture, and the Conflict of Laws Style' (2012) 64 *Stanford Law Review* 589, 589 emphasis added.

[8] Proposing a 'more "serviceable STS" that retains its critical and independent perspective on science', see A Webster, 'Crossing Boundaries: Social Science in the Policy Room' (2007) 32 *Science, Technology & Human Values* 458.

[9] See however A Riles, *The Network Inside Out* (University of Michigan Press 2000); R Levi and M Valverde, 'Studying Law by Association: Bruno Latour Goes to the Conseil d'Etat' (2008) 33 *Law & Social Inquiry* 805, providing an overview of its potential interest for sociolegal scholars.

[10] On instrumentalization, see A Riles, 'Anthropology, Human Rights, and Legal Knowledge: Culture in the Iron Cage' (2006) 108 *American Anthropologist* 52.

Secondly, STS might be too different, too different to be seen by lawyers as a human rights method. STS will, of course, have its own views on being, or not being, a human rights method, and on whether and how to read cases.[11] Indeed, the diversity within STS makes it likely that there will be a full spectrum of views on these points. It also means we need to explain what we mean when we say are going to read 'in the style of STS'.

Our STS is *à la carte*. Above all, it is about asking STS-type questions; questions traditionally asked within STS but asked far less, or not all, within human rights law. To frame our experiment we shall be concentrating on three questions. The first is: how has the European Court of Human Rights represented new health technologies? We start from the position that these representations matter; that they have effects—effects that run wide and deep, far beyond the resolution of individual disputes. Most obviously, they help to stabilize particular technologies as human rights friendly (or not), as regulable by law (or not) and, as we shall see, as real, realizable, or important to realize (or not). In STS parlance, these representations help to produce technology; they are part of the 'co-production', the mutually constitutive interactions, of science and technology and law. These representations also help to produce the question of whether there is, could, or should be a field called 'European law and new health technologies' (though that is also true of both this book and STS scholarship itself[12]).

Our second question asks: how has the Court represented those at the heart of the new-health-technology disputes that have come before it? Here we are interested not in the contracting states that find themselves before the Court accused of violating one or more Convention rights,[13] but rather the individuals and couples who have taken their cases all the way to Strasbourg, the city where the Court has its home. In the lexicon of STS, governmentality, and anthropology, these individuals and couples are 'moral pioneers', 'biological citizens', or part of 'biosociality'.[14] This trilogy of terms captures the way that science and technology, actual and promised, are affecting individuals and families and, in turn, are being affected by them. It aims, above all, to capture the ways that science and technology are negotiated, not simply imposed on us. Here, of course, we are not engaged in the ethnographic, bottom-up inquiry that is standard in studies of biological citizenship: we are reading cases. But, by offering access to an *institutional* account of biological citizenship, our case-reading can be seen as a supplement to those studies. To provide that supplement, we shall be asking: what is the Court's account of who a biocitizen is? Does the Court, for example, posit one universal biocitizen? Or is it populating Europe with different biocitizens?

Our third and final question will take us to states, specifically to states as law-makers, and to the Court itself. It asks: how does the Court represent the capacity of law? Specifically, what does the Court see as the characteristics of 'good law', and thus good state practice, in the arena of new health technologies? Related to this, how

---

[11] Practices of document production and adjudication have been looked at with ANT: see in particular B Latour, *La fabrique du droit: une ethnographie du Conseil d'État* (La Découverte 2002); M Valverde, *Law's Dream of a Common Knowledge* (Princeton UP 2003).

[12] As regards the latter, see eg J Dratwa, 'Representing Europe with the Precautionary Principle' in Jasanoff (2011) (n 3).

[13] The European Convention for the Protection of Human Rights and Fundamental Freedoms 1950, ETS 5.

[14] See, respectively, R Rapp, *Testing Women, Testing the Fetus: The Social Impact of Amniocentesis in America* (Routledge 2000); A Petryna, *Life Exposed: Biological Citizens after Chernobyl* (Princeton UP 2002), and N Rose and C Novas, 'Biological Citizenship' in A Ong and SJ Collier (eds), *Global Assemblages, Politics and Ethics as Anthropological Problems* (Blackwell 2005); P Rabinow, 'Afterword' in S Gibbon and C Novas (eds), *Biosocialities, Genetics and the Social Sciences* (Routledge 2007).

does the Court see its own role in a 'good law' set-up? Also, how are its tools—say, the margin of appreciation—being shaped by science and technology? And how, in turn, are these tools shaping science and technology, national practices, and human rights law?

C. STS as a Human Rights Method?

Having explained what we are going to do, we need to explain why. Why *this* experiment? Why think about STS as a *human rights method*? It is not, we admit, a proposal that is likely to arouse enthusiasm. For starters, method is thoroughly dull-sounding; human rights method more so—who would choose to look at method when human rights provide opportunities to examine and, more importantly, to affect the workings of power, empowerment, and accountability? Practitioners of STS may raise eyebrows at our experiment too. They may say that their tools are just that—theirs, not ours. There may also be concern that something, something important, is going to get lost in translation. There may even be claims of hubris; claims that we are annexing STS, attempting to make it part of human rights method, a terrain where lawyers have long held sway.

To be clear: our experiment is not a power-grab. It is rooted in curiosity, not in colonization (albeit that lawyers tend to instrumentalize everything).[15] Moreover, we believe this curiosity is timely. It is true that lawyers have been the sovereigns of human rights, and of human rights method, but that is changing: there are now movements within and outwith legal scholarship providing evidence of this. Human rights lawyers, for their part, are increasingly interested in human rights method, their own and that of others.[16] Meanwhile, non-lawyers—notably, anthropologists, sociologists, and political scientists—have been studying the methods of human rights lawyers,[17] and they have also been studying human rights through their own methods.[18] Independently of this, STS has been on the rise in legal circles.[19] In addition, both rights 'as law' and rights more generally have been acquiring a higher profile in STS, not least because of the arrival of 'bioconstitutionalism'—a term crafted by Sheila Jasanoff and others to capture how today's science and technology have been changing relations between life and law.[20]

These different movements are, in part, why we chose this experiment. Mostly, however, we chose it because we have been disappointed by the international human rights law encounter with new health technologies. We accept that technology as a threat to human rights, and rights to technology as a threat to human dignity, are popular themes in the media and beyond. We accept too that there has been a minor

---

[15] Riles (n 10). For discussion in a new technologies and human rights context, see T Murphy, 'Technology, Tools and Toxic Expectations' (2009) 2 *Law, Innovation and Technology* 181.

[16] See eg T Murphy, *Health and Human Rights* (Hart 2013); LE White and J Perelman (eds), *Stones of Hope: How African Activists Reclaim Human Rights to Challenge Global Poverty* (Stanford UP 2011).

[17] See eg SE Merry, *Human Rights and Gender Violence: Translating International Law into Local Justice* (Chicago UP 2006).

[18] See eg BA Simmons, *Mobilizing for Human Rights: International Law in Domestic Politics* (CUP 2009).

[19] See eg A Faulkner, B Lange, and C Lawless (eds), 'Special Issue: Material Worlds: Intersections of Law, Science, Technology, and Society' (2012) 39 *Journal of Law and Society* 1; M Valverde, R Levi, and D Moore, 'Legal Knowledges of Risk' in Law Commission of Canada (ed), *Law and Risk* (UBC Press 2005).

[20] Jasanoff (2011) (n 3).

flurry of international human rights lawmaking on new health technologies. And also that access to medicines—most of all access to antiretrovirals—seems like a human rights success story of recent years.[21]

Yet, access to medicines apart, it feels as if the really interesting work on new health technologies is happening elsewhere. So, for example, feminist scholarship, governmentality studies, law and society, medical anthropology, scholarship in the field of technology regulation, and, of course, STS (with all its various subfields) seem a great deal more engaged and engaging, and a great deal more reflexive, than their international human rights law counterpart.[22] The latter, by contrast, seems in short supply and, where it is present, mired in grand expectations. It focuses above all on law being applied to technology; on the force of law as prohibiting or enabling, on law's capacity to protect and promote (whether that be protecting and promoting new health technologies, or the rights and dignity of individuals where these are seen to be threatened by such technologies, real or potential).

There is lots of talk of limits—of law acting as a limit, and of the limits of law—but, by and large, little else. Where, for example, are the human rights lawyers writing on biological citizenship and how, if at all, human rights—as law, and as discourse—produces such citizens? In other contexts, human rights have been cast as the 'sole approved discourse of resistance'.[23] Is that, we wonder, true of new health technologies too? How, for instance, do scientists and scientific societies see human rights? Do they see them as producing a particular type of science, a particular type of scientist, and a particular type of (open access) publishing? Sheila Jasanoff has argued that Britain's scientific community sees bioethics 'first and foremost as a device for safeguarding space for research':[24] are human rights seen in the same way or differently, and why is that? Also, to what extent do the positions of scientists and scientific societies parallel those of the national cultures in which they work? The 'cross-borderness' of contemporary scientific practice could well be an important counter-influence here, shaping not just scientists' perceptions of law but also its own forms of 'soft law' as an offshoot of the very arrangements and actions that are needed for international scientific collaboration to function at all.[25]

Where, too, is the work on the standing of human rights—as law, and as a discourse—vis-à-vis other legal and non-legal ways of governing new health technologies? Law-wise, the interesting questions include whether human rights law is perceived differently to, say, criminal or intellectual property law, and whether domestic human rights law is treated differently to its international counterpart. Where is the human rights law research on this? Similarly, where is the research reflecting on

---

[21] Murphy (n 16) ch 4.

[22] Examples of such work by legal scholars include R Brownsword and M Goodwin, *Law and the Technologies of the Twenty-First Century* (CUP 2012); SS Silbey and P Ewick, 'The Architecture of Authority: The Place of Law in the Space of Science' in A Sarat, L Douglas, and M Umphrey (eds), *The Place of Law* (University of Michigan Press 2003); I Karpin, 'The Uncanny Embryos: Legal Limits to the Human and Reproduction without Women' (2006) 28 *Sydney Law Review* 599; A Pottage, 'The Socio-Legal Implications of the New Biotechnologies' (2007) 3 *Annual Review of Law and Social Science* 321.

[23] B Rajagopal, *International Law from Below: Development, Social Movements and Third World Resistance* (CUP 2003).

[24] S Jasanoff, *Designs on Nature* (Princeton UP 2005) 187.

[25] For discussion of this phenomenon, see MT Mayrhofer and B Prainsack, 'Being a Member of the Club: The Trans (Self-) Governance of Networks of Biobanks' (2009) 12 *International Journal of Risk Assessment and Management* 64.

why, policy-wise, bioethics has been the 'go to' discipline for contributory expertise?[26] To be clear: we are not proposing a play for power—finding a way to oust bioethics so that human rights law can take its place. Instead, we are interested in how bioethics' status is made and remade, and how that affects science and technology, human rights and human rights law, and bioethics itself. We read Noelle Lenoir's comment 'Bioethics—it is everything that Europe is about'[27] and we are intrigued. Europe's identity for us is much more strongly legal than bioethical. 'Legal Europe' or indeed 'political Europe' we can grasp;[28] 'bioethical Europe', by contrast, is an enigma.[29]

Formulations such as 'ethics and rights' (as in UNESCO's 2005 Universal Declaration on Bioethics and Human Rights), 'ELSI' (ethical, legal, and social implications), and 'sensitive moral or ethical issues' (as used by the Strasbourg Court) are popular, but here too we feel that interesting and important questions are being elided—such as how does a bioethically managed advisory group treat legal knowledge and, indeed, legal experts where they form part of its membership? Equally, is the treatment of human rights similar across the range of 'regulatory ethics',[30] including academic, clinical, corporate, and 'public bioethics'?

For a range of reasons, then, this experiment with STS as a human rights method seemed worthwhile. So too did the focus on the European Court of Human Rights: the Court is the institutional core of human rights law in Europe, a region widely seen as distinctive in its engagement with new technologies and as more robust than others in its systems for protecting human rights. Admittedly, we did have doubts when a search on HUDOC, a database of judgments and admissibility decisions, threw up far fewer cases on new health technologies than we expected.[31] Where were Europe's biocitizens? Were their cases wending their way to Strasbourg (in a system plagued by delay), or is European human rights law peripheral to European biosociality?

Fortunately, there was a small cluster of cases on assisted reproductive technologies (ARTs) and from these we selected two: *Evans v United Kingdom*[32] and *SH and Others v Austria*.[33] We didn't, to be honest, spend time thinking about how STS would do case

---

[26] For one bioethicist's reflections on the dynamic of rights/bioethics, see Chapter 14 in this collection. Insight might also be gained from the selection made by the research division of the ECtHR in 'Research Report: Bioethics and the Case-law of the Court' (Council of Europe/European Court of Human Rights, 2012) <www.echr.coe.int> (Case-law–Case-Law Analysis–Research Reports): the report addresses reproductive rights (prenatal diagnosis and the right to a legal abortion), medically assisted procreation, assisted suicide, consent to medical treatment or examinations, ethical issues concerning HIV, retention of biological data by the authorities, and the right to know one's biological identity.

[27] N Lenoir, 'Biotechnology, Bioethics and Law: Europe's 21st Century Challenge' (2006) 69 *Modern Law Review* 1, 1.

[28] Within which one could include what Christian Joerges labels 'Europeanization through de-legalisation': see 'Integration through De-legalisation? An Irritated Heckler' (2007) European Governance Discussion Paper No N-07-03.

[29] Ethics and the 'ethical' do, of course, play a significant role in European critical and social theory.

[30] D Callahan, 'Why America Accepted Bioethics' (1993) 23 *Hastings Center Report* 8, 8.

[31] <www.echr.coe.int>. For a full report, see T Murphy and G Ó Cuinn, 'Works in Progress: New Technologies and the European Court of Human Rights' (2010) 10 *Human Rights Law Review* 601.

[32] See *Evans v United Kingdom* (2006) 43 EHRR 21 (Chamber); *Evans v United Kingdom* [GC] (2008) 46 EHRR 34. At the domestic level there were judgments from the High Court of England & Wales (*Evans v Amicus Healthcare Ltd and others* [2003] EWHC 2161 (Fam)) and, on appeal, the Court of Appeal (*Evans v Amicus Healthcare Ltd and others* [2004] EWCA (Civ) 727). The (then) UK House of Lords declined leave to appeal: thus, having exhausted domestic remedies, it was open to Evans to take her case to Strasbourg.

[33] *SH and Others v Austria* (2010) 52 EHRR 6 (Chamber); *SH and Others v Austria* App no 57813/00 (Grand Chamber [GC], 3 November 2011). At the time of writing, judgment had not been

sampling: that is an interesting question but we had so little material to work with that it did not arise. In what follows we track how *Evans* and *SH and Others* frame, first, new health technologies, secondly, biocitizenship, and, finally, law itself. Thereafter we set down some first thoughts on STS as a human rights method. We begin, however, with a traditional, or 'disciplined', version of the basics of the two cases: namely, the facts, the issue before the Court, the decision, and how the Court reasoned its way to that decision. We begin, in other words, with the 'lawyers' quartet'.

D. A Tale of Two Cases

What if a woman and a man create and then store embryos but at a later point disagree about their use for treatment purposes? Should a human rights court proceed on the basis that there is a right of veto and, if so, should women and men be given equal rights of veto? The European Court of Human Rights had to consider these issues in *Evans*, a case concerning six embryos stored in the United Kingdom in accordance with the provisions of the relevant legislation, the Human Fertilisation and Embryology Act 1990 (the 1990 Act). For the applicant, Natallie Evans, these embryos were the only chance to try for a child who would be genetically related to her. The embryos had been created, using Evans's eggs and the sperm of her then-fiancé, Howard Johnston, before she underwent cancer treatment that destroyed her fertility.

Johnston triggered the dispute when, following the end of his relationship with Evans, he refused consent to the continued storage or use of the embryos: under the 1990 Act, this meant that the embryos had to be destroyed.[34] Evans responded by challenging that law on a range of grounds: here we focus exclusively on her human rights claims[35]—her claims, in other words, that the 1990 Act was not compliant with the European Convention on Human Rights (ECHR). At the outset there were four such claims: first, that the six frozen embryos were entitled to protection under Articles 2 and 8 of the ECHR; secondly, that the consent provisions of the 1990 Act violated her rights to respect for private life and family life under Article 8 because they did not permit her to proceed to treatment with the embryos without the agreement of Johnston; thirdly, and relatedly, that these provisions violated her Article 12 right to marry and found a family; and, finally, that these provisions were discriminatory and thus contrary to Article 14 of the ECHR read in conjunction with Article 8.

Four courts considered the case—the High Court and Court of Appeal in England, and then both the Chamber and Grand Chamber of the Strasbourg Court—and all four decided against Evans (though there were dissenting opinions in both the

---

delivered in *Costa and Pavan v Italy* App no 54270/10 (Chamber, 28 August 2012), a case concerning a married heterosexual couple who were legally prohibited from accessing IVF and pre-implantation genetic diagnosis (which they wanted in order to avoid passing cystic fibrosis to any further offspring) even though Italian law permitted abortion where a foetus showed symptoms of this illness. That inconsistency in Italian law led the ECtHR to conclude that the interference with the applicants' rights to private and family life was disproportionate. Also, at the time of writing, *Knecht v Romania* App no 10048/10 (communicated 8 July 2010), a case concerning seizure of frozen embryos, was pending before the Court.

[34] The Human Fertilisation and Embryology Act 2008 introduced a range of changes to the 1990 Act. One of these, a 'cooling off' period, bears the mark of *Evans*: its introduction means there can be no immediate destruction of stored embryos following a disagreement as to their future disposition.

[35] A full account of the co-production of law and technology would require a study of the other branches of legal knowledge that were, or might have been, deployed in *Evans*. Other possible rights claims would need to be considered too.

Chamber and Grand Chamber). The argument centred on Articles 8 and 14: the other claims, concerning Articles 2 and 12 respectively, were either disposed of swiftly or, latterly, abandoned by the applicant. Evans's core argument was that the consent provisions of the 1990 Act violated her right to respect for private life under Article 8. But Johnston too had a right to respect for private life and if Evans proceeded to treatment he could find himself being made a genetic father against his wishes. Evans's position, however, was that '[s]he was the primary figure in reality, and should be so in law'.[36] She insisted that the aims of the 1990 Act could be as well, or better, served by allowing the man's withdrawal of consent to be overridden in exceptional cases, or by allowing gamete providers to give an irrevocable consent at the point of fertilization.[37] Thus her argument was that the law, as it stood, was not 'necessary in a democratic society'; specifically, its insistence on a bright line—permitting of no exception in hard cases, and thus no balancing of the interests concerned—rendered it unfair and disproportionate.

The Article 14 claim, concerning discrimination, came attached to the Article 8 one. This will sound strange to those who are not familiar with the ECHR: in reality, however, 'conjunction' is required by the language of Article 14. That Article does not provide a general guarantee of equal treatment without discrimination; it is simply a guarantee against discrimination in the enjoyment of the substantive rights and freedoms set forth elsewhere in the Convention. Evans invoked Article 14 in conjunction with Article 8 to argue that, because of the 1990 Act, she and other infertile women seeking to implant frozen embryos against the wishes of the genetic father were treated differently to fertile women. Specifically, women who conceived through intercourse, rather than IVF, could determine the future of an embryo from the moment of fertilization.

So, how did the Grand Chamber of the Strasbourg Court, the final court of appeal, respond to these claims? On the Article 14 point it decided against Evans simply by referring back to its reasons for deciding against her under Article 8: those reasons, it said, would afford a reasonable and objective justification for any difference in treatment. As regards Article 8, the Court accepted, first, that the right to respect for the decision to become a parent 'in the genetic sense'[38] fell within the scope of that Article's right to respect for private life. This meant that Article 8 was engaged. However, Johnston had an Article 8 right too; a genetic parent's right to decide against becoming a parent. Thus there was a conflict of Article 8 rights and, in the Court's words, each person's interest was 'entirely irreconcilable with the other's'.[39] There were also wider, public interests to be taken into account. Two such interests were nominated by the Court: first, the impugned provisions upheld the principle of the primacy of consent and, secondly, their 'bright-line', or no-exceptions approach, promoted legal clarity and certainty.[40] This meant that the question to be resolved was whether the provisions 'as applied in the present case struck a fair balance between the competing public and private interests involved'.[41]

Before answering this, the Court addressed the margin of appreciation to be afforded to the state in assessing whether Article 8 had been violated. It concluded that the

---

[36] C Morris, '*Evans v United Kingdom*: Paradigms of Parenting' (2007) 70 *Modern Law Review* 992, 995.

[37] *Evans* (Chamber) (n 32) para 51.

[38] *Evans* [GC] (n 32) para 72. See also *Dickson v UK* [GC] (2008) 46 EHRR 41.

[39] *Evans* [GC] (n 32) para 73.

[40] *Evans* [GC] (n 32) para 74.   [41] *Evans* [GC] (n 32) para 76.

margin had to be a wide one, giving two reasons for this: first, there was no European consensus on how to regulate the matter in issue; and, secondly, 'the use of IVF treatment gives rise to sensitive moral and ethical issues against a background of fast-moving medical and scientific developments.'[42] The next move made by the Court, its penultimate one, was to say that the impugned provisions were clear and had been brought to the attention of Evans: moreover, Evans, like Johnston, had signed the consent forms required by the law. All that remained was the fair balance question and, as we know, this went against Evans: the Court said that the no-exceptions approach of the impugned provisions served public interests that were both legitimate and consistent with Article 8, and as regards the competing private interests, it could see no reason for ranking Evans's interest above that of Johnston.

Our second case, *SH and Others v Austria*, came before the Court within a year of the Grand Chamber's decision in *Evans*.[43] It too was heard by both chambers, and like *Evans* it concerned a challenge to an ART law. The applicants, two married couples, alleged that provisions of Austria's Artificial Procreation Act prohibiting heterologous techniques for IVF (that is, techniques using donor eggs or sperm) violated their rights under Article 8, and under Article 14 in conjunction with Article 8. Neither couple could conceive a child without access to such techniques: the first and second applicants, SH and DH, required sperm donation for IVF, and the third and fourth, H E-G and MG, required egg donation. Three courts considered their case—Austria's Constitutional Court and, later, the Chamber and Grand Chamber of the Strasbourg Court. They lost before the Constitutional Court, succeeded before the Chamber which concluded that there had been a violation of Article 14 in conjunction with Article 8, but lost again before the Grand Chamber where the argument centred on whether the prohibition of egg and sperm donation under Austrian law was in breach of Article 8.[44]

The applicants had argued that there was now a consensus amongst the contracting states that egg and sperm donation should be allowed. They also argued that the special importance of the right to found a family and the right to procreation meant that states enjoyed no margin of appreciation at all in regulating these issues. Austria's ban on heterologous techniques was, they said, a direct interference with their rights under Article 8(1); moreover, it could not be justified under Article 8(2) as it was neither necessary in a democratic society nor proportionate. Indeed, without the ban, the treatment they needed 'would have been a common and readily available medical technique'—a technique that had made 'considerable progress over the previous years and had become far more reliable than in the past'.[45] Moreover, Austria could offer no sound argument in support of the ban: the risks it saw as being associated with the technique—notably, exploitation of female donors and the creation of unusual family relationships with potentially adverse effects on child welfare—were either unconvincing or manageable via regulation. It was also, they said, 'incoherent and illogical'[46] for Austria to permit sperm donation in relation to insemination but then prohibit both sperm and egg donation for IVF.

In the Grand Chamber, the Court began by acknowledging that the applicants and the Austrian Government did agree on one point: Article 8 applied here. The Court

---

[42] *Evans* [GC] (n 32) para 81.
[43] The application was lodged in 2000 but it was 2007 before the admissibility decision.
[44] The Grand Chamber found there was no cause for a separate examination of the facts from the standpoint of Art 14 read in conjunction with Art 8.
[45] *SH* [GC] (n 33) para 56.   [46] *SH* [GC] (n 33) para 59.

endorsed this, saying that it considered 'that the right of a couple to conceive a child and to make use of medically assisted procreation for that purpose is also protected by Article 8, as such a choice is an expression of private and family life.'[47] The Court noted that in the last decade or so 'many developments in medical science have taken place to which a number of Contracting States have responded in their legislation', describing this as a shift from an earlier period when 'generally speaking, the law appeared to be in a transitional stage'.[48] It insisted, however, that the issue was not whether the Austrian prohibitions 'would or would not be justified today',[49] but rather whether they were Convention-compliant in the late 1990s, the point at which they were considered by the Austrian Constitutional Court.

In addressing this issue, the Court framed the case as one involving an interference with the applicants' rights to respect for their family life under Article 8(1) and proceeded to examine whether that interference could be justified under Article 8(2). Its particular focus was whether the prohibitions could be said to be 'necessary in a democratic society'. For the same reasons as it had given in *Evans*, the Court determined that the margin of appreciation to be afforded to the state must be a wide one. Moreover, this margin extended both to the state's decision to intervene in the area and to the rules it laid down to achieve a fair balance between competing public and private interests. The Court did find what it called an 'emerging European consensus' towards allowing gamete donation for IVF, but argued that this did not 'decisively narrow' the wide margin: the emerging consensus was not 'based on settled and long-standing principles established in the law of the member states'—it simply reflected a 'stage of development within a particularly dynamic field of law'.[50] In this way, the Court reached what it saw as the key question: did the impugned provisions of the Artificial Procreation Act strike a fair balance between the competing interests of the state and the applicants? In answering this, the Court concluded that the situation of SH and DH ('couple H'), who required IVF with the use of donor eggs, and that of H E-G and MG ('couple G'), who required IVF with donor sperm, ought to be examined separately.

Couple H's plans had been blocked by the Act's ban on egg donation—a ban that covered not just their situation, IVF with donor eggs, but any use of donor eggs in assisted procreation. Such a ban, the Court said, could not be grounded simply in moral considerations or social acceptability: a complete ban would only be Convention-compliant if it had been 'shaped in a coherent manner', allowing 'the different legitimate interests involved to be adequately taken into account'.[51] Responding to Austria's claims that egg donation carried both a risk of harm to women (especially the donors) and a risk of unusual family relations given the splitting of motherhood involved in IVF using donor eggs, the Court noted that Austrian law already addressed the former at least in part and that further measures could be adopted for the purposes of risk-minimization. Ultimately, however, it took the view that the ban did not exceed Austria's wide margin of appreciation.

Couple G required donor sperm not donor eggs. The Artificial Procreation Act permitted the use of such sperm for *in vivo* fertilization, but barred its use for IVF. Couple G argued that this made no sense: moreover, some of the arguments raised

---

[47] *SH* [GC] (n 33) para 82.   [48] *SH* [GC] (n 33) paras 83–4.

[49] *SH* [GC] (n 33) para 84.

[50] *SH* [GC] (n 33) paras 96–7. These arguments face strong criticism in the joint dissenting opinion, paras 4–6.

[51] *SH* [GC] (n 33) para 100.

by the government in defence of the prohibition on egg donation clearly had no relevance outside that context. The Grand Chamber accepted the latter point, but went on to decide against the applicants: as regards the ban on sperm donation for IVF the Austrian legislature, at the relevant time, had not exceeded the margin of appreciation afforded to it. In the Court's view, the law's different treatment of sperm donation for *in vitro* fertilization than for *in vivo* conception was simply evidence of 'the careful and cautious approach adopted by the Austrian legislature in seeking to reconcile social realities with its approach of principle in this field.'[52] More generally, the 'basic concerns' relied on by the government to justify the ban on egg donation had purchase in this context too:

[T]he intervention of third persons in a highly technical medical process was a controversial issue in Austrian society, raising complex questions of a social and ethical nature on which there was not yet a consensus in the society and which had to take into account human dignity, the well-being of children thus conceived and the prevention of negative repercussions or potential misuse.[53]

E. The Cases Retold

1. Representing New Health Technologies

Let's now proceed to reading the two cases STS-style; to what legal doctrinalists might call the 'undisciplined' reading. As noted earlier, we shall use three questions to structure our reading: how did the Court represent, first, the new health technologies at the core of these two cases; secondly, biological citizenship; and, thirdly, the capacity of law?

As regards the first of our questions, both *Evans* and *SH and Others* bear the mark of other new technology cases: for the Court, IVF, like new technologies more generally, is 'fast-moving', 'subject to particularly dynamic development in science'. The Court, to our knowledge, has never defined 'new technologies'. It speaks instead of technologies undergoing 'rapid development',[54] of the technology available for use . . . continually becoming more sophisticated'.[55] Technological development has not, however, been treated as an intrinsically benign phenomenon. In *S and Marper v United Kingdom*, having noted the 'rapid pace of developments in the field of genetics and information technology', the Court said that it could not 'discount the possibility that in the future the private-life interests bound up with genetic information may be adversely affected in novel ways or in a manner which cannot be anticipated with precision today.'[56] It also issued a warning to technology-hungry states, emphasizing that the take-up of technologies such as DNA databases in the criminal justice sphere must not lead to Article 8 becoming 'unacceptably weakened'.[57]

Of course, for the applicants in *SH and Others* the technology they had been barred from taking-up was not 'new': it was, they argued, a 'common and readily available medical technique which had made considerable progress over the previous years and had become far more reliable than in the past.'[58] The dissenting judges echo this view, opening their joint opinion with a reference not to 'artificial procreation' but rather to medically assisted procreation, to which they then apply the acronym 'MAP'. For these judges, what *was* artificial was the decision of the Grand Chamber to restrict its

---

52 *SH* [GC] (n 33) para 114.   53 *SH* [GC] (n 33) para 113.
54 *KU v Finland* (2009) 48 EHRR 52, para 22.
55 *Kruslin v France* (1990) 12 EHRR 547, para 33.
56 *S and Marper v United Kingdom* [GC] (2009) 48 EHRR 50, para 71.
57 *S and Marper* (n 56) para 112.   58 *SH* [GC] (n 33) para 56.

examination to the situation that prevailed in 1999, not least because—as the Grand Chamber itself clearly acknowledged—the European consensus on gamete donation 'has evolved considerably'.[59] Furthermore, in their view, even in 1999, the data did 'mainly support'[60] the existence of a consensus on gamete donation. Also, given that both the Austrian Government and the Grand Chamber had emphasized that couples could go abroad for the treatment, and have maternity and paternity recognized by Austrian law, what precisely was so 'new' about this technology that it needed to be banned 'at home'?

SH and Others also offers a framing of 'combination' treatment. Recall that for two of the applicants, couple G who needed access to donor sperm for the purposes of IVF, Austria's law made no sense: it permitted both IVF for couples using their own gametes and *in vivo* fertilization using donor sperm, but it barred the treatment they needed. Why was a combination of the two techniques prohibited when, taken in isolation, they were allowed? Couple G found support in the Chamber; it said that any such prohibition 'required particularly persuasive arguments'. The only argument it could find was that *in vivo* artificial insemination 'had been in use for some time, was easy to handle and its prohibition would therefore have been hard to monitor.'[61] But the efficient policing of prohibitions could not, it said, outweigh the private life interests of couple G and justify the ban. However, as noted earlier, the Grand Chamber reversed this, avoiding any framing of the technique as a combination and describing the difference in treatment as evidence of Austria's 'careful and cautious' approach. Sperm donation for *in vivo* fertilization was, it said, a 'technique which had been tolerated for a considerable period [before the Act] and had become accepted by society.'[62]

For Natallie Evans, the problem was not acceptability or unacceptability of medically assisted procreation but availability: at the time she was diagnosed with ovarian cancer, egg freezing was just being established as a clinical procedure. The High Court noted that the technique 'was very much in its infancy and far removed from standard medical practice';[63] the Court of Appeal, for its part, noted that egg freezing 'was not an option'.[64] Indeed, throughout the proceedings, egg freezing was simply, as the Grand Chamber put it, 'not performed':[65] despite being an integral part of IVF's viability as a treatment, it remained unexamined by the courts. It was merely a banal part of IVF; as STS would say, it was black-boxed—IVF remained intact as an input-output device,[66] 'gametes in-embryos out', its complexity not factored in the courts' reasoning. STS would open this black-box, so let's now follow suit.

Evans told the Court of Appeal that at the ART consultation, attended by Johnston and herself immediately after receiving news of her cancer, she had raised the option of egg freezing:

I asked whether it was possible simply to have my eggs frozen. [The consultant] replied that they did not carry out that procedure . . . At this point Howard told me not to be stupid and that there was no need for that. He told me that he loved me, that we would be getting married and having a

---

[59] *SH* [GC] (n 33) joint dissenting opinion at para 5.
[60] *SH* [GC] (n 33) joint dissenting opinion at para 10.
[61] *SH* [GC] (n 33) para 111, summarizing the view taken in the Chamber.
[62] *SH* [GC] (n 33) para 114.
[63] *Evans* (EWHC) (n 32) para 60. There were, the High Court noted, 'no reported pregnancies in the UK resulting from it'.
[64] *Evans* (EWCA) (n 32) para 307.
[65] *Evans* [GC] (n 32) para 15.
[66] See B Latour, *Pandora's Hope: Essays on the Reality of Science Studies* (Harvard UP 1999).

family together. I said, 'But what if we split up?' Howard told me that we were not going to and that I should not be such a negative person.[67]

So, had egg freezing been available, there might have been an interpersonal bar on its use: 'love' meant there 'was no need for that [procedure]'. At the time there might also have been a legal bar: section 13(5) of the 1990 HFE Act which required licensed providers to take account of 'the welfare of any child who may be born as a result of treatment services (including the need of that child for a father).'[68] The pursuit of egg freezing, or of the use of donor sperm to create embryos, might have cast doubt on the durability of Evans's relationship with Johnston and brought this section into play.

Essentially, the freezing technology was portrayed as not being technically advanced enough to accommodate eggs but it also enrolled a legal prohibition of sorts. Might that prohibition be part of the reason why egg freezing was not technically advanced? And did the equivalence of the egg and the sperm elsewhere in the 1990 Act play a part too, generating a presumption of *gamete equality*? Schedule 3 to the Act, which deals with storage, consistently refers to 'gametes': paragraph 8(1), for example, ignores the fact that women were in no position to freeze eggs by referring to the fact that a *'person's* gametes' must not be kept in storage without an effective consent by that person. From this legislation a code of practice was developed to guide clinics: the edition published at the time of Evans's treatment referred to the storage of 'gametes or embryos' and did not acknowledge the technical gaps surrounding male and female cells.[69] Similarly, the Warnock Report, which preceded the legislation, referred to *people* storing their gametes.[70]

Symmetry between male and female gametes also flowed through the paperwork associated with the 1990 Act. Consider, for example, that Evans and Johnston gave their consent by ticking boxes on 'structurally identical'[71] forms. Her form 'essentially replicated that signed by [Johnston]'[72] except that hers contained 'the necessary substitution of sperm for eggs'.[73] This legal artefact would be examined closely by the courts. It induced what the joint dissenting opinion in the Grand Chamber calls a 'formal contractual approach',[74] permitting the majority to take a particular direction—one where male and female gametes were equivalent genetic packages that delivered the right to be, and not to be, a genetic parent. In other words, it created genetic commensurability and established Evans and Johnston as persons of equal standing.

Moreover, both in the Warnock Report and subsequently, *embryos*, rather than the gametes used to produce them or the techniques for storing such gametes, occupied centre-stage. This reflected what was going on in laboratories at the time. Initial animal studies suggested that egg freezing might induce chromosomal abnormalities,[75] which

---

[67] *Evans* (EWCA) (n 32) paras 22–3.
[68] The amendment of the Act in 2008 removed reference to 'including the need of that child for a father'.
[69] Human Fertilisation and Embryology Authority, 'Code of Practice' (4th edn July 1998) <www.hfea.gov.uk/docs/4th_Edition_Code_of_Practice_1998–07.pdf> accessed 20 May 2012.
[70] M Warnock, *A Question of Life: The Warnock Report on Human Fertilisation and Embryology* (Basil Blackwell 1985).
[71] *Evans* (EWCA) (n 32) para 81.
[72] *Evans* [GC] (n 32) para 16.
[73] *Evans* (EWCA) (n 32) para 81.
[74] *Evans* [GC] (n 32) joint dissenting opinion at para 10.
[75] See eg M Magistrini, 'Effects of Cold and of Isopropyl-N-Phenylcarbamate on the Second Meiotic Spindle of Mouse Oocytes' (1980) 22 *European Journal of Cell Biology* 699; J Van Blerkom and P Davis, 'Cytogenetic, Cellular and Developmental Consequences of Cryopreservation of Immature and Mature Mouse and Human Oocytes' (1994) 27 *Microscopy Research and Technique* 165.

both precipitated a voluntary moratorium on clinical oocyte cryopreservation[76] and led Warnock to recommend that egg freezing and storage should not be licensed 'until research has shown that no unacceptable risk is involved'.[77] However these results were linked to research that prioritized the study of *embryos*. Studies on egg freezing were under-funded and slow to produce reliable results as they were typically tied to 'poor quality and immature' ova left over from IVF activities.[78] These sub-standard eggs fared poorly, especially as they were being subjected to storage conditions developed to suit embryos. While further research would eventually accommodate egg freezing, the momentum of both policy and science lay with producing and storing embryos.[79] Egg freezing later became more attractive as the ethical and legal complications associated with storing embryos were revealed through practice.[80] This eventually boosted research and the success of oocyte storage (which began to materialize around the time Evans came to court). It was found that, among other things, simple variations in the concentrations of and exposure time to sugars and other cryoprotectants dramatically increased the post-thaw viability of the egg.[81] Hence, the social context was instrumental in shaping the outcome of these studies; it was not merely the case that egg freezing reached the limits of technology and was 'not available'—rather, it was relegated or even neglected because of an ethico-legal order focused on embryos.

In describing how cryopreservation in IVF came into practice, we can see that symmetry between Natallie Evans and her partner existed only on paper. This equivalence derived from scientific representations depicting an equal contribution by gametes and a legal order focused on the embryo: an object that also inscribed an equivalence between male and female gametes. Thus, the scientific and legal orders were mutually constitutive. Other aspects of the law, consent forms, and clinic consultations subsequently helped to stabilize or 'produce' this understanding of IVF which required the silencing of certain inequalities between male and female cells as regards cryopreservation. Consent, a moral programme, became the 'passage point' for the operation of the technology—and written into this programme is the equivalence of male and female for artificial fertilization while ignoring a gender bias in cryopreservation.

By decentring the analysis towards the technology—by reading STS-style—we reveal the impact of law's representation of IVF and how uneven the playing field was before the Court was asked to consider categories of persons for the purposes of Article 14 (father/mother, fertile/infertile, assisted/non-assisted). Although the 1990

---

[76] MJ Tucker, 'The Freezing of Human Oocytes', Georgia Reproductive Specialists <www.ivf.com/freezing.html> accessed 25 June 2012. The moratorium began to lift in the mid-1990s.

[77] Warnock (n 70) para 10.2. Egg freezing became a licensable activity just months before Evans walked into the fertility clinic: HFEA, 'The Storage and Use of Frozen Eggs', chair's letter CH(00) 0630 (30 April 2000) <www.hfea.gov.uk/2709.html> accessed 25 June 2012.

[78] S al-Hasani and others, 'Cryopreservation of Human Oocytes' (1987) 2 *Human Reproduction* 695.

[79] N Koutlaki-Kourti, 'Human Oocyte Cryopreservation: Past, Present and Future' (2006) 13 *Reproductive BioMedicine* 427.

[80] Koutlaki-Kourti (n 79); R Fabbri and others, 'Human Oocyte Cryopreservation: New Perspectives Regarding Oocyte Survival' (2001) 16 *Human Reproduction* 411. D Edgar and D Gook, 'A Critical Appraisal of Cryopreservation (Slow Cooling Versus Vitrification) of Human Oocytes and Embryos' (2012) 18 *Human Reproduction* 536 note: 'there has been a resurgence of interest in cryopreservation of oocytes. This was driven by a desire to preserve fertility potential in young women undergoing gonadtoxic treatments and also by restrictive legislation which prevented embryo cryopreservation in some countries, but has found other applications in areas such as oocyte donation.'

[81] Fabbri and others (n 80); R Fabbri and others, 'Technical Aspects of Oocyte Cryopreservation' (2000) 169 *Molecular and Cellular Endocrinology* 39.

Act was somewhat future-proofed, as Warnock anticipated that egg freezing would eventually occur, it was shaped by a faith in technological progress that had yet to materialize fully when Evans entered the clinic. The technology did not behave in a way that was expected and the consent procedures silenced other elements that were sucked into the process, such as Johnston's assurances of love, obstacles to egg freezing at another clinic or using donor sperm, and the termination of Evans's prospects of genetic parenthood.

2. Representing Biological Citizenship

Prompted by the law's identikit treatment of freezing technologies for eggs and sperm, we are now going to ask: how, if at all, *was* difference constructed by the Court in *Evans* and, later, in *SH and Others*? We are interested here not in the technologies themselves, but rather in the individuals and groups—the biological citizens—produced by these judgments. Thus we are interested in questions such as: is the Court prescribing a distinctly European biocitizen? Does biocitizenship, as produced by the Court, take a particular form and, if so, with what effects?

A preliminary note: reasoning about difference is not as natural as it sounds for a human rights court—in fact, what counts as a relevant difference, and how any such differences are to be treated, has long been tough terrain for human rights law. Part of the reason for this is that law has played a part in the construction of difference, which means that it too is accountable for the harms that have flowed from being labelled 'different'. Human rights law is sometimes seen as the antidote to these failings; by institutionalizing and internationalizing rights, natural difference can be recognized, respected, and protected through the law. But, as STS scholars and at least some human rights lawyers will testify, 'natural difference' has not become a pre-given, and law itself continues to be one of the forces producing what we think of as natural and what we think of as different.[82]

Asking a human rights court to rule on difference in a *new health technology* case may be more complicated again—especially if the court in question is Europe's human rights court, founded in the wake of the Second World War and the legacy of Nazi medical experimentation.[83] True, the Strasbourg Court speaks of IVF as 'fast-moving', orienting us towards the future and everything that comes with that—including preparedness, possibility, and responsibility. More generally, anticipation often seems like the defining quality of good lawmaking in the new health technology field. Yet the past is neither excluded nor excludable. Moreover, international human rights law has a more powerful origins story than most. Origins cascade through it; to use Elen Stokes's term, 'regulatory heritage' is all about in human rights law.[84]

Turning now to the cases and their biocitizens, let's start with *Evans* where, in essence, Natallie Evans's claim was that biocitizens are not all the same, and that ART law—if it is to be rights-compliant—needs to make provision for this. Specifically, a rights-respecting ART law would either parallel the law on unassisted reproduction, installing women as the primary decision-makers after the point of fertilization, or it

---

[82] See eg M Minow, *Making All the Difference: Inclusion, Exclusion, and American Law* (Cornell UP 1990); D Herman, *An Unfortunate Coincide: Jews, Jewishness and English Law* (OUP 2011).

[83] GJ Annas and MA Grodin (eds), *The Nazi Doctors and the Nuremberg Code: Human Rights in Human Experimentation* (OUP 1995).

[84] See Chapter 10 in this collection. For a history of the ECHR, see E Bates, *The Evolution of the European Convention on Human Rights* (OUP 2010).

would set up a scheme for the assessment of competing interests in individual cases—a scheme that would be able to take notice of Evans's 'greater physical and emotional expenditure during the IVF process, and her subsequent infertility'[85] and thus give her rights precedence. Put differently, for Evans, if ART law was to be rights-respecting, it had to distinguish between women and men gamete-providers.[86]

As we have seen, the Court did not agree with Natallie Evans. It never got into the detail of her claim that treating her differently to a fertile woman was discrimination, however it did observe that there was 'an essential difference' between IVF and fertilization through sexual intercourse: namely, '[t]he fact that it is now technically possible to keep human embryos in frozen storage' means that, with IVF, time may lapse between the creation of the embryo and its implantation in the uterus. It also observed that the delay, or lapse of time, may be substantial and went on to say that it is 'legitimate—and indeed desirable—for a State to set up a legal scheme which takes this possibility of delay into account.'[87] Hearing this, Natallie Evans might well have wanted to counter-argue that with fertilization through sexual intercourse there is also a lapse of time before implantation; a lapse of time during which a woman might take emergency or 'morning after' contraception. Would the Court have responded by differentiating between delay and the possibility of *substantial* delay?

But Natallie Evans didn't just argue that she should be treated in the same way as a fertile woman; she also argued that a rights-respecting ART law would allow a woman like her to be treated differently to a man like Johnston. The Court gave short shrift to this, echoing a view expressed in all three of the lower courts.[88] That view was at its most explicit in the English High Court, where the judge Wall J gave the following stamp of approval to the law's equal treatment of women and men:

It is not difficult to reverse the dilemma. If a man has testicular cancer and his sperm, preserved prior to radical surgery which renders him permanently infertile, is used to create embryos with his partner; and if the couple have separated before the embryos are transferred into the woman, nobody would suggest that she could not withdraw her consent to treatment and refuse to have the embryos transferred into her. The statutory provisions, like Convention Rights, apply to men and to women equally.[89]

We are conscious that it would be easy to get in a tangle here. But, very tentatively, let's try to think a little more about the right to be, and not to be, a genetic parent. In particular, where biological citizenship is figured as *genetic* citizenship, is human rights likely to end up at odds with itself as it tries to configure genetic, gestational, and legal parenthood in human rights terms? More particularly, will the right to be, and not to be, a genetic parent leave human rights working at cross-purposes with itself?

For Evans and her legal team, it must have seemed a good start when the Strasbourg Court confirmed that the right to be a genetic parent fell within Article 8. This signalled that there was a case to be argued. But was it also a problem: doesn't law generally frame female parenthood as more *gestational* than genetic? And hasn't fatherhood become the genetic-weighted form of parenthood in law, amidst the rise of paternity testing and

[85] *Evans* [GC] (n 32) para 80.

[86] For discussion, see S Sheldon, 'Gender Equality and Reproductive Decision-Making' (2004) 12 *Feminist Legal Studies* 303.

[87] *Evans* [GC] (n 32) para 84.

[88] *Evans* [GC] (n 32) para 80; *Evans* (Chamber) (n 32) para 66; *Evans* (EWCA) (n 32) para 67; *Evans* (EWHC) (n 32) para 320.

[89] *Evans* (EWHC) (n 32) para 320.

displacement of the presumption of legitimacy,[90] and also the trend towards keeping genetic fathers in their children's lives post-divorce (both financially and in other ways too)?[91] Put differently, in law's 'sexual family'[92] is there a counter-intuitive quality to a woman's right to be a genetic parent and, equally, an expansive aspect to genetic fatherhood? In what follows, we look more closely at these questions.

In life, motherhood—and fatherhood too—are crafted in all sorts of ways.[93] In law, by contrast, there are rules (albeit a proliferating set of rules). One such rule, widely followed, is that the woman who gives birth to the child is its mother: legally, motherhood is written on the body *not* in the genes. Indeed in *SH and Others*, the Austrian Government sought to defend its ban on using third party ova in ART partly by reference to the harm of 'split motherhood', a term it uses to describe the situation where one woman provides the ovum and the other carries the child. Split motherhood, the Austrian Government said, is a threat both to child welfare and to the principle of the law that the woman who gives birth is the legal mother.[94] Initially the Grand Chamber seemed to hesitate about this framing, pointing to the law's apparent ability to regulate adoption. Its conclusion, however, was that split motherhood through adoption 'differs significantly' from split motherhood through ART: the latter, it concluded, 'has added a new aspect to this issue'.[95]

True, the Court did nudge Austria to keep its ART law under review and it also seemed to suggest that ART's split motherhood could be handled legally. But we should not assume that any such attempt would recognize the genetic element. Take the UK's Human Fertilisation and Embryology Act 2008 (amending the 1990 statute of the same name), which ushers in a new form of legal parenthood for women, mainly to follow through on the recognition of civil partnerships which happened a few years earlier. This new form of parenthood is called agreed female parenthood and, for our purposes, what is interesting about it is that it *cannot* be acquired through a genetic link. Thus, today in the United Kingdom both legal motherhood (acquired by giving birth to the child) and female parenthood (acquired on the basis of an agreement with the legal mother which meets statutorily prescribed conditions) are officially non-genetic. Moreover, the law takes the time to say this explicitly.[96]

But what of Howard Johnston and the men in *SH and Others*? Can it be said that genetic citizenship, as framed by the Strasbourg Court, is father-friendly? In *Evans*, the right to be, and not to be, a genetic parent brought forced fatherhood into view— forced fatherhood as a *human-rights wrong*. This right not to be a genetic father also seemed to pluralize very easily, seguing into a considerably fuller bodied fatherhood. This genetic father was no mere 'father figure'. In the Grand Chamber, as in the lower

---

[90] Whereby the law treated a child born to a married woman as the legitimate offspring of her husband.

[91] C Smart and B Neale, *Family Fragments?* (Polity 1999); R Collier and S Sheldon, *Fragmenting Fatherhood: A Socio-Legal Study* (Hart 2008).

[92] M Fineman, *The Neutered Mother, the Sexual Family and other Twentieth Century Tragedies* (Routledge 1995). Using Fineman, see J McCandless and S Sheldon, 'The Human Fertilisation and Embryology Act (2008) and the Tenacity of the Sexual Family Form' (2010) 73 *Modern Law Review* 175.

[93] See eg H Ragone, *Conception in the Heart: Surrogate Motherhood in America* (Westview 1994); as its title suggests this study of surrogacy shows how conception can occur 'in the heart'.

[94] The Italian Government, an intervener in the case, went further still: 'to call maternal filiation into question by splitting motherhood would lead', it said, 'to a weakening of the entire structure of society': *SH* [GC] (n 33) para 73.

[95] *SH* [GC] (n 33) para 105.

[96] See further McCandless and Sheldon (n 92).

courts, we are told that Johnston's 'clear position was one of fundamental rather than purely financial objection', and Evans's promise to make no claims on him as a father seems to have had no influence at all on the proceedings.[97]

In this respect *Evans* feels very different to earlier European law cases involving genetic fathers, rights, and reproduction. Consider, for example, the case of Mr Paton whose attempt to prevent his estranged wife from having an abortion made no headway at Strasbourg.[98] Switching to EU law, there is the case of Diane Blood and her husband, Stephen, from whom sperm had been taken by means of electro-ejaculation whilst he was in a coma with fatal meningitis.[99] The Bloods had been trying for a child prior to Stephen's sudden illness; at the same time, however, his sperm was taken without his consent. Ultimately, because of the influence of EU law, his wife, Diane, was given permission to export it to Belgium to avail of ART there. She went on to have two children using her late husband's sperm: she also succeeded in having the law changed so that, in cases like hers, the genetic father's name could appear on the child's birth certificate.

An STS-way of reading requires that we ask: who are the biocitizens emerging from these earlier cases? And in what ways might they differ from biocitizens who have the right to be, and not to be, a genetic parent? For instance, does Mr Paton emerge more as a *husband* (in a deteriorating marital relationship) than a genetic father? And does the *Paton* case frame the pregnant biocitizen as a unique rights holder, at least with respect to the decision to be, or not to be, a gestational parent (albeit that this is subject to the state's regulation of abortion)? In similar vein, does the *Blood* case suggest that widows may be another European biocitizen? Would, or should, *widowers* be accorded equal treatment? If we broaden the frame there are obviously other questions too, including what kind of citizens would the Blood children have been had their mother not campaigned for a change in the law on birth certificates, and how might the right to be, and not to be, a genetic parent affect gay men?

These questions of gender difference and European biocitizenship were also present in *SH and Others*. Recall that the Austrian Government insisted not just that donated gametes were different but that donated eggs, in particular, merited different treatment in order to avoid not just problems with 'split motherhood' but also the risk of exploitation and humiliation of women, especially those from economically disadvantaged backgrounds.[100] By introducing 'harm to women' in this way Austria was making a familiar legal move, albeit one that still has the capacity to surprise.[101] Here what interests us is how 'harm to women' framed the biocitizens emerging from *SH and Others*. Three points need to be made. First, the case's most fully formed biocitizen is the egg donor. The Austrian Government framed her as both 'at risk' and 'a risk' (she facilitates 'split motherhood', which in turn threatens both the welfare of

---

[97] The relationship between the right to be (and not to be) a genetic parent and moves to privatize dependency, ie, to shift financial responsibility for children from the state, merits ongoing study.

[98] *Paton v United Kingdom* (1980) 3 EHRR 408. In *M v The Netherlands* (1993) 74 DR 120, where a sperm donor sought to invoke the right to respect for family life protected by Art 8 ECHR, the (now defunct) European Commission on Human Rights expressed the view that where a man had donated sperm only to enable a woman to become pregnant through artificial insemination, that alone did not give him a right to respect for family life with the child.

[99] *R v Human Fertilisation and Embryology Authority, ex parte Blood* (1997) 2 All ER 687 (CA).

[100] *SH* [GC] (n 33) para 101. On this point, there was also argument concerning the welfare of the child.

[101] See eg *Gonzales v Carhart* 550 US 124 (2007) wherein the US Supreme Court invoked the regret of some women for their past abortions as a reason to uphold a federal law criminalizing a partial-birth abortion procedure.

the child and the law). Although the Court upheld Austria's prohibition on egg donation as Convention-compliant, it did not seem convinced by these arguments. Noting the applicants' point that Austrian law already barred donor remuneration, it suggested that the legislature 'could theoretically devise and enact further measures or safeguards to reduce the risk attached to ovum donation as described by the Government.'[102] Law, it seems, can be counted on to handle 'harm to women'.

Secondly, at this juncture, the Court's preferred egg donor seems to be the unpaid one: she makes for a better biocitizen than her counterparts.[103] But the picture complicates towards the end of the judgment, where the Court emphasizes that couples like the applicants have the option to go abroad for treatment and then have their parental status recognized at home in Austria.[104] We now have the egg donor 'at home' and her counterpart abroad—and, notably, the Court makes no mention of the risks for, or of, the latter. Why is it that neither Austria nor the Court seems concerned about 'cross-borderness'[105]—about either those who are 'abroad', whether in Europe or elsewhere, or those who are going abroad?[106] And if such concerns were to develop, exactly how far should they extend: should they include the rights of 'relative strangers'[107]—a donor's parents, say, or donor-conceived half siblings?

Thirdly, and finally, the Court in *SH and Others* makes no effort to distinguish egg donors from sperm donors. Having reviewed the harm to women arguments at length, it simply binds the treatment of third party sperm to that of eggs. Yet again, equal treatment is deemed Convention-compliant: both donor eggs and donor sperm involve 'the intervention of third persons in a highly technical medical process', thereby giving rise to 'sensitive moral issues'.[108]

There are undeniably difficult questions here. We will not try to resolve them; instead, we want to revert to one of our own original questions—is reading in the style of STS value-added? Equality and difference are clearly core concerns for human rights; moreover, even if a human rights reading might not have proceeded in the manner described, a feminist or socio-legal reading might well have. On the other hand, biocitizenship is not a concept from legal feminism or socio-legal studies, and reading cases with biocitizenship in mind does seem to spark fresh thinking. In particular, it encourages us to ask: what is being sanctioned by the Strasbourg Court and, more generally, what might be the effects of rights-based biocitizenship?

We tracked biological citizenship manifesting in genetic form—in one particular genetic form via the Court's addition of the right to be, and not to be, a genetic parent to the ECHR's right to respect for private and family life. We used this to raise questions about new forms of inequality. We also, albeit briefly, raised questions about harm and the law. We could have raised other questions, including law's treatment of

---

[102] *SH* [GC] (n 33) para 105.

[103] See relatedly C Waldby and M Cooper, 'From Reproductive Work to Regenerative Labour: The Female Body and the Stem Cell Industries' (2010) 11 *Feminist Theory* 3.

[104] *SH* [GC] (n 33) para 114.

[105] For elaboration of this concept in a different NHT context, see JY Zhang, C Marris, and N Rose, 'The Transnational Governance of Synthetic Biology: Scientific Uncertainty, Cross-Borderness and the "Art" of Governance': BIOS Working Paper No 4 (2011) <www.kcl.ac.uk.sshmm> accessed 25 June 2012.

[106] On the latter, see the discussion of *A, B and C v Ireland* in Chapter 17 of this collection.

[107] We borrow this phrase from a project underway at the Morgan Centre at the University of Manchester <www.socialsciences.manchester.ac.uk/morgancentre/research/relative-strangers> accessed 25 June 2012.

[108] *SH* [GC] (n 33) para 113.

'second thoughts'.[109] In *SH and Others*, for instance, the Court seems to direct Austria to have second thoughts. In *Evans*, by upholding the 1990 Act as Convention-compliant, it endorses the statute's treatment of second thoughts in the field of ARTs. One question that arises is: are the second thoughts of biocitizens—or more particularly biocitizens in a *reproductive* context—treated differently to second thoughts in other contexts?

Rights-based biocitizenship sparks other questions too. Saying that human rights gives its backing to truth-telling seems far too simplistic in an era marked by the rise of the right to know one's genetic identity: is it time perhaps to talk about *rights-based* secrets and lies, not just rights-based truth telling? Are *family* secrets and lies—say, keeping the fact of donor conception from a child—akin to other secrets and lies that the law seeks to expose? Why should law decide that genetic truth is good for families? What sort of family is that likely to produce?[110] Moreover, what precisely is the overarching frame here: is it secrecy, family secrecy, or what might be called 'repro-secrecy'? More broadly, are our two cases about the geneticization of rights and the effects of that, or about new health technologies, or perhaps about reproduction?[111] These are fascinating questions of classification and its consequences, and they deserve serious study.

3. Representing Law

We have reached our third and final batch of questions: how does the Court represent the capacity of law? What does it prescribe as the characteristics of 'good law'? How does it see its own role, and how are its own technologies—notably, the European consensus and the margin of appreciation—shaping and being shaped by new health technologies?

Reading the cases with these matters in mind, what struck us most was the Court's faith in law. Generally speaking, new health technologies produce calls for more law and, from others, for less law. There tends to be lots of talk of law acting as limit and, equally, lots of talk of the limits of law. The Court pursues a different line. ARTs may be 'fast moving', and across Europe medically assisted procreation may be 'regulated in detail in some countries, . . . regulated only to a certain extent in others and in some other countries not at all',[112] but, for the Court, law has not been outpaced: ART is an area that is subject to a 'particularly dynamic development'[113] not just in science, but also in law (accepting, however, that this double dynamism makes it 'understandable that the states find it necessary to act with particular caution'[114]).

Indeed, as we have seen, the Court has evolved Article 8 to encompass the right to be, and not to be, a genetic parent. Moreover, although it found against the applicants in *SH and Others*, its attitude towards risk-minimization via law seems robust. In its view,

---

[109] For this phrase, see S Appleton, 'Reproduction and Regret' (2011) 23 *Yale Journal of Law & Feminism* 255.

[110] See further C Smart, 'Law and the Regulation of Family Secrets' (2010) 24 *International Journal of Law, Policy and the Family* 397; I Turkmendag, 'The Donor-conceived Child's "Right to Personal Identity": The Public Debate on Donor Anonymity in the United Kingdom' (2012) 39 *Journal of Law and Society* 58. For a summary of the ECtHR's case law on the right to know one's biological identity, see Council of Europe (n 26) 44–50.

[111] Or indeed about sex/no-sex distinctions: see eg Appleton (n 109) who argues that, as regards the USA, respect for choices is far more prevalent in non-sex cases.

[112] *SH* [GC] (n 33) para 95.

[113] *SH* [GC] (n 33) para 118.   [114] *SH* [GC] (n 33) para 103.

the various risks raised by the Austrian Government in defence of the prohibition on gamete donation for IVF either had been addressed by law or could be.[115] Its only concession was to the risk of 'unusual family relations', where it noted that split motherhood added a 'new aspect' not present in the adoption context (the latter being an arena with a 'satisfactory legal framework'[116]).

The Court does more in these cases, however, than profess faith in the capacity of law: it also produces a cluster of preferred qualities of this law (even if, at the same time, it accords each state a wide margin of appreciation). In *Evans* it was declared 'legitimate—and indeed desirable'[117] for a state to set up a legal scheme recognizing the possibility of delay between fertilization and implantation produced by IVF.[118] The principle of the primacy of consent was also highlighted. As was the case with legal clarity and certainty, consent was framed as a public interest that a legislature ought to weigh in any fair balance between private and public interests.[119] There was evidence too of the Court's preferred approach to law 'in the making': Austria's legislature was applauded for an approach that was 'careful and cautious', and as regards the United Kingdom it was 'relevant' that the 1990 Act was 'the culmination of an exceptionally detailed examination of the social, ethical and legal implications of developments in the field of human fertilisation and embryology, and the fruit of much reflection, consultation and debate.'[120]

Choosing a complete ban or, as in *Evans*, a bright-line rule is not necessarily a sign of 'bad law'. True, in *SH and Others* the Court said that moral and social concerns in a sensitive domain like artificial procreation are not in themselves a justification for a complete ban on specific techniques such as egg donation.[121] At the same time, however, its decision in that case upholds two absolute prohibitions: one on egg donation; the other on sperm donation for the purposes of IVF. Similarly, in *Evans* the challenge to the 1990 Act's bright-line stance on consent fell on deaf ears: for the Court, the bright-line had the advantage of legal certainty and clarity, and avoided ad hoc balancing exercises.

But good law is also regularly reviewed law; it is law that is subject to 'thorough assessment', 'taking into account the dynamic developments in science and society'.[122] Thus although Austria's ban on gamete donation for IVF, devised in the early 1990s, did pass muster in *SH and Others*, there was a shot across its bow from the Court:

> Even if it finds no breach of Article 8 in the present case, the Court considers that this area, in which law appears to be continuously evolving and which is subject to particularly dynamic development in science and law, needs to be kept under review by the Contracting States.[123]

Relatedly, the *wide* margin of appreciation emerges from *SH and Others* as a legal technology with a latent expiry date. It is for the Court to determine both the margin

---

[115] The Chamber judgment, *SH* (Chamber) (n 33) para 76, identifies ethics as a potential regulatory tool.

[116] *SH* [GC] (n 33) para 105.

[117] *Evans* [GC] (n 32) para 84.

[118] *Evans* [GC] (n 32) para 85.

[119] *Evans* [GC] (n 32) para 74.

[120] *Evans* [GC] (n 32) para 86; *Evans* (Chamber) (n 32) para 63. For more on how rights produce the 'responsible state', see Chapter 3 in this collection at Section F.

[121] *SH* [GC] (n 33) para 100.

[122] *SH* [GC] (n 33) para 117.

[123] *SH* [GC] (n 33) para 118. For analysis of Austrian's stance on reproductive medicine, see B Prainsack and R Gmeiner, 'Clean Soil and Common Ground: The Biopolitics of Human Embryonic Stem Cell Research in Austria' (2008) 17 *Science as Culture* 377.

and the criteria that count towards it: at present the latter include both circumstances 'where a particularly important facet of an individual's existence or identity is at stake'[124] (which ought to narrow the margin in an ART case) and the absence of consensus within the member states of the Council of Europe, 'either as to the relative importance of the interest at stake or as to the best means of protecting it, particularly where the case raises sensitive moral or ethical issues' (which will work to broaden the margin). Mostly the Court has insisted that such a consensus has to be 'found' before it will narrow the margin of appreciation.[125] *SH and Others*, however, suggests what might be called a new consensus on the 'European consensus': to the dismay of the four dissenting judges,[126] the majority added 'emerging consensus' to the established roster of 'consensus' or 'no consensus'. In the view of the majority, there will be an emerging European consensus where there is '*not yet* clear common ground' between the contracting states; an emerging consensus is not based 'on settled and long-standing principles established in the law of the member states but rather reflects a stage of development within a particularly dynamic field of law.'[127]

Thus dynamism seems to emerge from this case as the overriding characteristic of both the law and the science and technology of gamete-use. That characteristic, in turn, produces its own 'rights technology': for the Grand Chamber, when both law and science are particularly dynamic, the Court needs its own hope technology—the 'emerging European consensus', a tool that seems to embody not just the Court's faith in law but, uncannily, a sort of 'not yet' sensibility that is familiar from both ARTs and science and technology more generally.

Here, as in the earlier sections, we want to conclude by considering whether reading in the style of STS has been value-added. What does the STS angle contribute in opening up our understanding of how law is represented? For starters, it encourages us to track representations; that would not be part of all forms of legal inquiry but seems particularly useful in light of the fact that the stance within law tends to be either 'more law' or 'less law'. Secondly, a more full-bodied STS might well be more value-added, focusing, for example, on the material artefacts that form part of the operation of the Court—say the circulation of files—and how if at all this differs from domestic courts or, indeed, non-human rights courts.[128] Thirdly, reading in the style of STS does however attune us to what Jasanoff and Kim call 'sociotechnical imaginaries'. This STS concept 'builds in part on the growing recognition that the capacity to imagine futures is a crucial element in social and political life.'[129] We see the Court as an important passage point for *European* sociotechnical imaginaries, producing not just its own imaginary (by means, say, of the European consensus) but also having a more indirect influence on imaginaries within individual Council of Europe states and, potentially, further afield too. In *SH and Others*, for instance, it found no violation of the Convention but it directed the Austrian Government to undertake

---

[124] *Evans* [GC] (n 32) para 77.

[125] cf *Goodwin (Christine) v United Kingdom* [GC] (2002) 35 EHRR 447. See further Chapter 3 in this collection.

[126] In *SH* [GC] (n 33) the joint dissenting opinion denounces it as an 'unprecedented step of conferring a new dimension on the European consensus and applies a particularly low threshold to it, thus potentially extending the States' margin of appreciation beyond limits' (para 8).

[127] *SH* [GC] (n 33) para 96. The 'emerging consensus' has appeared in non-health technology cases too: see eg *Beard v United Kingdom* (2001) 33 EHRR 442.

[128] See eg T Scheffer, K Hannken-Illjes, and A Kozin, 'How Courts Know: Comparing English Crown Court, US-American State Court, and German District Court (2009) 12 *Space & Culture* 183.

[129] Jasanoff and Kim (n 3) 122.

a review of ART legislation. Austria may do as directed or it may resist doing so: either way, the Strasbourg Court is playing a part in the production of Austria's socio-technical imaginary. The Court's own mode of producing imaginaries is interesting too. For instance, how precisely does it 'know' that a European consensus is emerging?

F. Conclusion

Having now read our two cases in two different ways—in one particular law way, and in the style of STS—what have we learned? Two points stand out. First, reading cases differently is not easy; doubts creep in. Will this reading be different enough to be recognizably STS? Equally, might it be so different that human rights lawyers will simply disengage?

On the other hand—and this is our second point—reading our cases with STS was surprisingly enabling. Critics argue that human rights lawyers spend too much time on rights as *law*, that we have cabined rights in a 'juridical cage'.[130] Other critics argue that all of us, lawyer and non-lawyer alike, spend too much time on rights; that even those who oppose rights engage in rights talk by seeking to draw boundaries between what is and what is not a legally protected right. Yet, reading our two cases with STS felt like looking afresh at rights-as-law talk. Most important of all, it freed us from the standard fare of law and limits.

True, reading in the style of STS was not always value-added. In places, what we extracted was akin to what might be expected from a socio-legal, feminist, or critical legal reading. On the other hand, however, STS does prompt a greater, more sustained focus on science and technology than has been common in any of those fields. Furthermore, STS clearly offers far more than questions that can be used to read cases. The questions we used to read cases could also be used in other ways too—ways that might help lawyers to describe how human rights law is being made or remade by new health technologies, and how new health technologies are being made or remade by human rights law. To explain what we mean by this, we close with two examples.

Biocitizenship is not produced by the Strasbourg Court alone. The small number of cases in our sample drives home this point (although the presence of three interveners in *SH and Others* suggests that it will be important to track not just individual biocitizens but also what might be called 'organized biocitizenship').[131] We wonder if a similar phenomenon exists across Europe's courts. If it does, should that be taken as evidence that Europe's biocitizens are political actors rather than litigious ones (and relatedly that they do not see law, or at least legal adjudication, as political)? Or is it the branch of law that is influential—would intellectual property, for example, throw up more cases? Relatedly, within human rights law, to what extent does the right at issue, or the stance of a particular court on that right, influence the decision to turn towards adjudication?[132]

Secondly, as with biocitizenship, law or legal knowledge about new health technologies is not produced only by the Strasbourg Court. Other courts, and lawmaking

---

[130] A Sen, 'Elements of a Theory of Human Rights' (2004) 32 *Philosophy & Public Affairs* 315, 319.

[131] See also Council of Europe (n 26) 4 noting that 'complex [bioethical] issues are increasingly being raised before the European Court of Human Rights, and we can perhaps expect more applications touching subjects such as gene therapy, stem cell research and cloning in the future.'

[132] eg the ECtHR's stance on Art 2 ECHR and the human embryo, on which note the pending case of *Knecht v Romania* (n 33).

bodies, are playing a part too.[133] And, as we pointed out earlier, it is also be important to recognize other ways of 'knowing' new health technologies.[134] European law on new health technologies is not being made only by lawyers, but also by non-lawyers—not least by organizations charged with 'public bioethics', and by scientists, as they make choices about how to understand what law is, what it is not, and what it requires.

[133] Arguing for a 're-vitalization of the independent capacities and powers of national authorities that must act independently with a view to securing the rights and freedoms of the ECHR', see J Christoffersen, 'Individual and Constitutional Justice: Can the Power Balance of Adjudication be Reversed?' in J Christoffersen and RM Madsen (eds), *The European Convention on Human Rights* (OUP 2011) 182.

[134] See relatedly B Prainsack and M Kitzberger, 'DNA Behind Bars: Other Ways of Knowing Forensic DNA Technologies' (2009) 39 *Social Studies of Science* 51, exploring how, for prisoners, forensic DNA technologies assumed the role of 'institutionalized memories of their delinquency'. See also B Prainsack and H Machado, *Tracing Technologies* (Ashgate 2012).

14

Novel Rights-Based Approaches to Health Technologies

*Richard Ashcroft**

A. The Normative Governance of Biomedicine in Europe: Many Frameworks, No Framework, an Emerging Framework?

The governance of new health technologies is something which has attracted the attentions of European courts and lawmakers, and policymakers more generally, quite frequently.[1] One of the central difficulties for their considerations has been the lack of a consistent, shared normative basis for evaluation of regulation of such technologies. If we reflect on the range of issues calling for governance at the European level, some of the reasons for this lack quickly become apparent. Abortion, stem cell (especially embryonic stem cell) research, animal experimentation, physician-assisted suicide, *in vitro* fertilization, HIV testing and surveillance, regulation of herbal remedies and vitamin supplements, cross-border treatment referrals... The first problem is obvious: even within individual states there may be little social or moral consensus over the permissibility, utility, or legitimacy of a given technology, or a given application of that technology. A weaker or stronger consensus may emerge or have emerged, either about the acceptability of the technology and its applications as such, or about the governance and regulatory frameworks controlling uses of the technology and its applications. But not only may this consensus vary from country to country across the region, for political, social, cultural, professional, institutional, or religious reasons, such that a 'European' consensus may be even less apparent than a national one, it is also the case that the legitimacy of a European governance framework may be less, or more fragile, than that of any particular national framework.[2] There are various reasons for this: first, if the legitimacy of a framework is as weak as its weakest element, then if the legitimacy of a European framework depends upon the legitimacy of contributing states' frameworks, the legitimacy of the European framework can be expected to be as

* This chapter reproduces a substantial, edited portion of a previously published article: RE Ashcroft, 'The Troubled Relationship Between Human Rights and Bioethics', Ch 3, pp 31–51, in MDA Freeman (ed), *Law and Bioethics: Current Legal Issues, vol 11* (OUP 2008). This material is reproduced by permission of the publisher. I am particularly grateful to Mark Flear, Tammy Hervey, and Thérèse Murphy for their advice and assistance in the preparation of this chapter, and to Kenneth Armstrong for invaluable preliminary discussions. All errors are my own.

[1] For discussion, see eg JV McHale and TK Hervey, *Health Law and the European Union* (CUP 2004); D Beyleveld and R Brownsword, *Human Dignity in Bioethics and Biolaw* (OUP 2005); E Mossialos, G Permanand, R Baeten, and TK Hervey (eds), *Health Systems Governance in Europe* (CUP 2010); and now R Brownsword and M Goodwin, *Law and Technologies of the Twenty-First Century* (CUP 2012).

[2] For a fascinating political and historical overview of this issue see P Anderson, *The New Old World* (Verso 2009) and for a more detailed discussion of institutions and governance see K Armstrong, *Governing Social Inclusion: Europeanization through Policy Coordination* (OUP 2010).

weak, if not weaker, than the weakest legitimacy framework of all contributing states. Secondly, there may be independent reasons why the legitimacy of the European framework is weaker than that of national frameworks, to do with the perceived 'democratic deficit' of the European Union (EU), or the structure of the Council of Europe (CoE) as a council of states, not citizens, or the perception of the European Courts (both the European Court of Human Rights (ECtHR) and the Court of Justice of the EU (CJEU)) as being remote from democratic control and oversight.[3]

Mention of these particular institutions brings me to my second reason for a lack of a common normative framework for governance of new health technologies: the restricted competence of the various European institutions. As is well known, the EU has a variety of competences in specific sectors, including public health, product safety, open market provisions concerning the free movement of goods and services and of consumers within the EU, and social rights provisions concerning the free movement of workers. Taking abortion as an instance, there is no EU competence to regulate abortion as such across the Union; although there are a range of legal rights to travel, receive, and dispense information about abortion services[4] and so on protected by open market provisions. The third reason why there is a lack of a common normative framework is the fragmentation of European governance itself. Apart from the obvious fact that the primary actors in regulation and governance are and will likely remain the sovereign nation states of the European region, the supranational and international institutions of the region are diverse, with diverse constitutions, competences, memberships, and geographical scope. The powers, memberships, and relationships among the EU, the CoE, and various technical agencies such as the European Patent Office (EPO) or the regional office of the World Health Organization are complex. To take just one example, governance of embryonic stem cell research crosses the competence of Member States, the EU institutions, the CoE as policymaking forum and through the ECtHR, the EPO, and so on.[5]

In sum: there are many reasons why a single European normative framework for health technologies is lacking. However, in one sense a consensus is emerging around a framework, albeit at rather an Olympian level remote from practical policymaking. Consistent with other trends in EU constitutional strategy, and drawing on long-standing work of the CoE, a consensus seems to be emerging around the development of a normative framework of human rights. From the adoption of the Convention for the Protection of Human Rights and Dignity of the Human Being with regard to the Application of Biology and Medicine: Convention on Human Rights and Biomedicine (the Oviedo Convention) in 1997, and its subsequent protocols on Cloning (1998), Transplantation (2002), Biomedical Research (2005), and Genetic Testing for Health Purposes (2008), the CoE has been very active in developing a normative framework for biomedicine which quite deliberately and explicitly evolves from the 1950 Convention for the Protection of Human Rights and Fundamental Freedoms (the European Convention on Human Rights, or ECHR).[6] Meanwhile, the EU's evolving jurisprudence on human rights led up first to the proclamation in 2000 of its Charter of Fundamental Rights of the European Union and more recently the ongoing negotiations

---

[3] A helpful brief overview of the debate here is: K Dzehtsiarou and A Greene, 'Legitimacy and the Future of the European Court of Human Rights: Critical Perspectives from Academia and Practitioners' (2011) 12 *German Law Journal* 1707.

[4] Case C-159/90 *SPUC v Grogan* [1991] ECR I-4865. See R Lawson, 'The Irish Abortion Cases: European Limits to National Sovereignty?' (1994) 1 *European Health Law Journal* 167.

[5] A Plomer, 'After *Brüstle*: EU Accession to the ECHR and the Future of European Patent Law' (2012) 2 *Queen Mary Journal of Intellectual Property* 110.

[6] See generally Chapter 3 in this collection.

for accession of the Union as such to the CoE, which would commit the Union to adoption of the ECHR as a binding instrument forming part of EU law.[7] Within the EU, therefore, there is good reason to see a human rights framework as an emerging normative framework for the Union. Moreover, because the CoE's evolving human rights framework details norms for biomedicine, it is plausible to think that insofar as the Union develops a governance framework for life sciences and medicine within its defined areas of competence, it will draw increasingly on the CoE's approach. This would not be surprising, given that all EU Member States are also CoE Member States: but the impact on citizens and Member States will be all the greater than at present not so much because of the authoritative and directly binding nature of CJEU judgments (in contrast with the judgments of the ECtHR, which certain states party to the Convention seem quite happy to overlook as it suits them), but because of the supranational and coordinated nature of European policymaking, its wide scope, the density of its regulatory structures, interconnections between key national actors through common European institutions and cooperative procedures, and the consequent ability of EU law and regulatory practice not only to penetrate into national legal orders, but also to affect practice.

Grant that the development of a human rights-based framework for biomedicine within the EU institutions will be translated across from the CoE, and that there may be some form of jurisprudential convergence between the CJEU and the ECtHR: what would this imply for the structure, shape, and content of the governance of biomedicine in Europe? A brief answer might go: not very much. If we consider how little the Oviedo Convention has been invoked in the ECtHR, and how no application to that Court may be founded on the breach of a claim of an Oviedo Convention right alone, but must instead claim a breach of a right granted by an article of the ECHR, we might well conclude that whatever the diplomatic uses of the Oviedo Convention, it will have little role in litigation or policy formation even when translated into the EU context. Moreover, there is the vexed question of the relationship of this arguably minor, but nonetheless formal and concrete, set of legal rules to the arguably more influential, but informal, role played by bioethics in EU policymaking.

I will explore the tensions between bioethics and human rights in more detail later. In the context of this discussion of a developing normative framework for European governance of biomedicine, and the institutionalization of a human rights approach, it is important to describe very briefly the way in which bioethics has been used within the EU institutions.[8] First, from the late 1980s onwards, bioethics has been developed as a language to shape EU policy especially in its scientific and technological research and development agenda for the region. Bioethics has been adopted within the European Commission as a sort of 'horizon scanning' device, for ascertaining what the ethical, legal, social, and policy issues particular technologies, from mass data processing to nanotechnology, may throw up as risks (and sometimes opportunities) for developing technologies. The main vehicle for this type of work is the European Group on Ethics, which is an advisory committee to the European Commission, established in 1991, with a mandate renewed every five years by Decision of the Commission.[9] Secondly, bioethics has had a curious hybrid role as both formal academic research, supported

---

[7] The EU's accession to the CoE is required under Article 6(2) TEU. See, for an introduction to the issues, P Craig and G de Búrca, *EU Law: Text, Cases, and Materials* (OUP 2011) 362–407. See also Plomer (n 5), and more generally P Alston (with M Bustelo and J Heenan) (ed), *The EU and Human Rights* (OUP 1999) and D Ehlers (ed), *European Fundamental Rights and Freedoms* (De Gruyter Recht 2007).

[8] See B Salter, 'Bioethics, Politics and the Moral Economy of Human Embryonic Stem Cell Science: The Case of the European Union's Sixth Framework Programme' (2007) 26 *New Genetics and Society* 269.

[9] <http://ec.europa.eu/bepa/european-group-ethics/index_en.htm> accessed 12 July 2012.

by research grants made by the Commission under its several Framework Programmes, and as a kind of cultural politics. Research projects, fellowships, and networks have been supported by the Commission in ways which both promote bioethics as a research activity in its own right, and as a kind of mixed 'ELSI' (ethical, legal, and social issues) and 'Public Understanding of Science' or 'Public Engagement with Science' activity which supports and enables scientific research and translation into technological application, and thirdly as a means of bringing together scientists and others from different countries across the Union, active in bioethics and cognate fields, to promote better awareness and understanding of each others' work—with a not-so-subtle motivation that this may promote European convergence on values and forms of argumentation.

Given these plural roles of bioethics within the EU institutions (primarily, as noted, the Commission), we might have expected to see more explicit acknowledgement of an 'emergent 'European bioethic' (sic) within the Union's decision-making processes and jurisprudence.[10] In fact, for three important reasons, this has not happened. First, for constitutional reasons the adoption of a common set of values and principles of ethics has rarely, if ever, been attempted within the EU polity—for a much more dramatic example, consider the debate over whether reference could or should be made to Europe's historical identity as Western Christendom during the EU Constitution debates. Secondly, while bioethics has been useful as a set of soft guides to problem definition, norm specification, and rule interpretation, it has lacked the practical 'form of life', interpretive practices, or cross-institutional and cross-national legitimacy of formal legal rules; and where coordination of Union activities or promulgation of policy or principle has been necessary, law has tended to be the formal tool which predominates. Thirdly, and perhaps most important in practice, the overarching principle of subsidiarity governing coordination of activities and policy-formation within the Union implicitly recognizes, amongst other things, norm and value plurality between Member States, such that save in a few highly technical areas (the regulation of clinical trials of medicinal products, for instance) where prior consensus on core principles is established, disagreement on bioethical principles is almost to be assumed. After all, though the European Community was founded amongst other things to make war between European states less likely, the mechanism chosen to bring that result about was peaceful commerce, rather than the development of a common philosophy or ethic or civil religion.

One qualification is needed to this claim that bioethics has not become deeply embedded in policymaking, and that there is not (or at any rate not yet) an emergent 'European bioethic'. The place of the 'precautionary principle' must be acknowledged as an important general principle of EU law and policy. I can only make some very general observations about it here. First, it must be acknowledged that it is a principle of EU *law*, being mentioned specifically in Article 191(2) TFEU as a principle of environmental protection; and Article 11 TFEU requires environmental protection to be integrated into all EU policies. Thus, it is arguable that the precautionary principle must be applied in health care and health technology regulation and policy. This

---

[10] For one more than usually quixotic attempt to develop such a bioethic, which illustrates both the nature of the enterprise and the kind of work being done in the 1990s under the auspices of the European Commission's framework programmes in bioethics, see <http://ec.europa.eu/research/biosociety/pdf/final_rep_95_0207.pdf>, the final report of a project which ran between 1995 and 1998 on 'Basic Principles in European Bioethics and Biolaw', led by Professor Peter Kemp of the University of Copenhagen. I wrote a philosophical critique of this, published as RE Ashcroft, 'El papel de la autonomía en la ética médica' (The role of autonomy in medical ethics) (2000) 5 *Perspectivas Bioéticas* 91 (in Spanish).

granted, however, we have room for scepticism about its status as an ethical principle. First, in the EU context, it is clearly articulated as a principle of risk management, rather than as a principle of ethics. While ethics and risk management overlap, they are not synonymous. Secondly, and much more seriously, there are serious conceptual and normative problems in interpreting and applying the precautionary principle, and there is far from a consensus on the meaning, scope, and application of the principle, in law or ethics.[11] The policy conversation of the EU is developing the principle, and the similarly contested concept of solidarity, but as yet it lacks a commonly understood meaning, and still less as commonly accepted normative force.[12]

Now that we can see some of the reasons why bioethics has been useful in the development of European policy and research, but nevertheless not a dominant feature of the European policy landscape, we can begin to consider the relationship between human rights and bioethics. In what follows, I will approach the *European* dimension of this debate rather obliquely. It must be acknowledged that there are a lot of 'bioethical' cases in ECHR jurisprudence. My belief—which I think can be supported, but which I do not set out to document here—is that 'bioethical' cases are rendered in one of two ways by the ECtHR: they are either translated into 'classical' human rights cases which fit more neatly with the main lines of development of Convention jurisprudence (for example, protection of private and family life, access to justice, the proper constitutional limits on state power, etc.) or they are deemed to fall within the notorious 'margin of appreciation' wherein a state party to the Convention may legitimately make its own interpretation of what a Convention right requires, provided that this is open to democratic scrutiny within that state. The Court has been very slow to develop a bioethical jurisprudence of its 'own', even since the adoption of the Oviedo Convention. Therefore, my tack is to look more abstractly at the debates over the relationship between human rights and bioethics which arose in the context of the development and proclamation of UNESCO's Universal Declaration on Bioethics and Human Rights 2005 (UDBHR). Whereas the Oviedo Convention has attracted relatively little attention from bioethicists (though the academic legal community has paid it more notice), the UDBHR has been widely discussed, and I think it provides a useful case study for thinking about the limits of bioethics—and human rights—which may be instructive in the developing European context.

B. Bioethics and the Universal Declaration on Bioethics and Human Rights[13]

On the face of it, the Declaration was a consolidation of previously adopted positions and statements of a wide range of international bodies, and followed a trend of the adoption of international declarations and conventions such as UNESCO's

---

[11] The definitive overview is now C Munthe, *The Price of Precaution and the Ethics of Risk* (Springer 2011).

[12] Roger Brownsword is particularly prominent in seeking to flesh out what the precautionary principle should mean, and its place in rights-based thinking about technology and society. See his *Rights, Regulation, and the Technological Revolution* (OUP 2008). My point here is an empirical one about the current state of EU policymaking and institutions, rather than theoretical and normative. But my sympathies regarding the precautionary principle are with Munthe's scepticism. On solidarity, see B Prainsack and A Buyx, *Solidarity: Reflections on an Emerging Concept in Bioethics* (Nuffield Council on Bioethics 2011).

[13] The following section is taken, with some editing, from RE Ashcroft, 'The Troubled Relationship between Bioethics and Human Rights' in MDA Freeman (ed), *Law and Bioethics: Current Legal Issues, vol 11* (OUP 2007) 31, specifically the section from 32–8.

International Declaration on Human Genetic Data (2003), Universal Declaration on the Human Genome and Human Rights (1997), and the CoE's Oviedo Convention on Human Rights and Biomedicine (1997). In addition to the international organizations, influential non-governmental organizations such as the World Medical Association had promulgated authoritative guidance on medical ethics and human rights (such as the latter's periodically revised Declaration of Helsinki on the ethics of research on human subjects). Yet the UNESCO Declaration, in both its draft and final forms, was widely criticized, or even derided, in the bioethics literature.

In October 2003, UNESCO was mandated by its Member States to draw up a declaration of fundamental principles in the field of bioethics.[14] A draft declaration was published in early 2005 and attracted considerable academic discussion (for a sample, see a special issue of *Developing World Bioethics* devoted to the draft, introduced in an editorial by Willem Landman and Udo Schüklenk, in 2005). This draft went through considerable amendment when considered by the national representatives to UNESCO, and the finalized Declaration was adopted 'unanimously and by acclamation' by UNESCO on 19 October 2005.

The Declaration has a long preamble of reflecting, recognizing, recalling, and noting clauses, linking it to the major international and regional human rights instruments, and to the research ethics guidelines of the World Medical Association (WMA) and the Council for the International Organizations of Medical Sciences (CIOMS). As such, the Declaration is clearly intended to be taken as a further contribution to this genre of international law and human rights. The problems framing the preamble are, on the one hand, expanding access to scientific, technological, and medical advances on a more equitable basis worldwide, while on the other controlling scientific and technological change and its impact on human rights and human dignity. While the focus is on human-related research, the Declaration notes the importance of the environment or biosphere, and the welfare of animals. It also notes the importance of groups such as families and communities, the fact of cultural diversity, and the economic differences between developing and developed world countries.

The Declaration in its main part is divided into General Provisions stating the aims and addressees of the Declaration (Articles 1 and 2), Principles (Articles 3 to 17), guidance on the Application of the Principles (Articles 18 to 21), guidance on Promotion of the Declaration (Articles 22 to 25), and Final Provisions relating to the relationship between principles in the Declaration and limitations on their scope (Articles 26 to 28).

The content of the principles is a mixture of statements of moral principle and statements which have the form of human rights familiar from older human rights declarations and treaties. We can find three broad classes of statement in the Articles. First, there are statements of principle, for example, Article 13 reads: 'Solidarity among human beings and international cooperation towards that end are to be encouraged'. Secondly, there are prescriptive statements similar in form to classical human rights proclamations. For instance, Article 11 reads: 'No individual or group should be discriminated against or stigmatized on any grounds, in violation of human dignity, human rights and fundamental freedoms.' Thirdly, there are what we could call articulating norms, bridging the gap between statements of principle and human rights norms. For instance, Article 3 subsection 1 reads: 'Human dignity, human rights and fundamental freedoms are to be fully respected'. This sort of Article underlines the

---

[14] HTM Ten Have, 'The Activities of UNESCO in the Area of Ethics' (2006) 16 *Kennedy Institute of Ethics Journal* 333.

difference between this Declaration and other human rights instruments. Some of these statements of principle are prior to rights statements (thus, Article 5 is a principle of respect for autonomy, which would then be cashed out in specific rights assignments). Others are interpretative statements indicating how human rights norms are to be understood and applied (Article 6 on consent in medicine and scientific research can be taken this way). Moreover, there is a wide range of degrees of specificity and of prescriptiveness in the Articles. Article 7 gives a very detailed specification of the protection of individuals who lack capacity to consent to participation in research or to medical treatment, whereas Article 10 gives a very abstract principle of equality ('The fundamental equality of all human beings in dignity and rights is to be respected so that they are treated justly and equitably'), and Article 16 is both abstract and only minimally prescriptive ('The impact of life sciences on future generations, including on their genetic constitution, should be given due regard').

The Declaration is therefore a complex hybrid in form, and was the outcome of a political process. As such, it can hardly be expected to be either intellectually coherent or a particularly fine example of the legal draftsman's art. Yet coherence is not necessarily a desideratum for a statement of principles, as long as a minimum internal consistency is achieved.[15] As Professor Henk ten Have, Director of UNESCO's Division of Science and Technology, puts it:

The Declaration on Bioethics aims to determine those principles in the field of bioethics that are universally acceptable, in conformity with human rights as ensured by international law. It does not pretend to resolve all the bioethical issues presently raised and that evolve every day. Rather, its aim is to constitute a basis or frame of reference for states wishing to endow themselves with legislation or policies in the field of bioethics. It also aims, as far as possible, to inscribe scientific decisions and practices within the framework of a certain number of general principles common to all. And it aims to foster dialogue within societies on the implications of bioethics and the sharing of knowledge in the field of science and technology.

Further:

... it anchors the principles it endorses in the rules that govern respect for human dignity, human rights, and fundamental freedoms. By drawing on the 1948 *Universal Declaration of Human Rights*, it clearly enshrines bioethics in international human rights law in order to apply human rights to the specific domain of bioethics.

Beyond these practical and legal aims, ten Have goes on to say that:

The Declaration on Bioethics ... reiterates the need to place bioethics within the context of reflection open to the political and social world. Today, bioethics goes far beyond the codes of ethics of the various professional practices concerned. It implicates reflection on the evolution of society, indeed world stability, induced by scientific and technological developments. The Declaration on Bioethics paves the way for a new agenda of bioethics at the international level.[16]

---

[15] This makes for an interesting interpretive debate. If principles are, on the face of it, in contradiction, how far should we construe them as mutually consistent? Or do we take the interpretative work here as a question of balancing principles which are taken to be in tension rather than in logical contradiction? Or do we instead convict the statements in the text as in actual contradiction, and a sign of poor drafting? Bioethicists are inclined, I think, to the last approach, whereas human rights advocates, especially those with legal training, would prefer the more charitable construction approaches.

[16] Ten Have (n 14) 341.

Given these various aims it is unsurprising that the Declaration is as complex as it is, even were its process of preparation purely scholarly and not a political process of intergovernmental negotiation.

Ten Have's account of the purposes of the Declaration gives us an important insight into the controversies which greeted the publication of the draft Declaration and then the adoption of the finalized version itself in the course of 2005. Does the Declaration codify best practice? Or international consensus only? Or interpret higher order human rights norms for this specific context? Or declare a new agenda somewhat ahead of current policy and state practice? Is it mainly addressed to states currently lacking bioethical law and regulation, or does it also speak to states in the bioethical vanguard but whose practice departs from this policy, or to the community of states taken altogether? More fundamentally, how does it situate bioethics with respect to human rights law, doctrine, and practice? Does bioethics precede human rights (for instance, by giving it a philosophical foundation or a specification of which entities have human rights) or provide a language for application of human rights to concrete problems at a level of specificity greater than human rights norms can address? Or, more ambitiously, does the Declaration intend to make human rights into the master language for doing bioethics?

This complexity or perhaps opacity has been taken by some commentators in the way ten Have hopes, as opening a new agenda for international bioethics. Thus Mônica Serra, a Brazilian bioethicist, while noting some weaknesses (the absence of any statement on animal welfare or rights and the vagueness of its principles regarding the future of the environment) praises the UDBHR's breadth, its awareness of the way bioethical concerns should range from nanotechnology and cloning through to access to clean water and the need to improve global health equity. And at a political level, she finds most hope in the way the Declaration was shaped by the representatives of the developing countries, to whom she attributes the extension of the scope of the Declaration beyond advanced biomedicine to social and environmental bioethics. On the one hand, the UNESCO process gave equal weight to all Member States' representations (or, if not equal weight, at least some weight). On the other hand, by actively promoting consensus on the Declaration, it avoided division between the developed and developing countries.[17] This could be contrasted with (for instance) the revisions of the Declaration of Helsinki and the CIOMS guidelines on international biomedical research, which were produced and steered almost exclusively by first world bioethicists and researchers, with developing world views presented reactively.[18]

Japanese bioethicists Atsushi Asai and Sachi Oe argue that the UDBHR can be seen as an 'up-to-date compendium of bioethical knowledge' and moreover that 'the world would be a better place for everyone to live, if human beings would become aware of the serious implications of every sentence in *UDBHR* and acquire the habit of making all possible efforts to identify ethical action in the midst of the mutually conflicting norms and principles.'[19] They acknowledge the philosophical weaknesses of the Declaration but hold that this not the important point about it, which is that it represents

---

[17] M Serra, 'UNESCO has Given Bioethics a Human Face' (2005) Scidev.net, 1 December 2005 <www.scidev.net/content/opinions/eng/unesco-has-given-bioethics-a-human-face.cfm> accessed 11 December 2007.

[18] RJ Levine, S Gorovitz, and J Gallagher (eds), *Biomedical Research Ethics: Updating International Guidelines—A Consultation* (CIOMS 2000); U Schüklenk and RE Ashcroft, 'Background Report: International Research Ethics' (2000) 14 *Bioethics* 158.

[19] A Asai and S Oe, 'A Valuable Up-To-Date Compendium of Bioethical Knowledge' (2005) 5 *Developing World Bioethics* 216, 218.

a call to live a more ethical life and to practise ethical reflection in the face of problems and contradictions of principle. Interestingly they take it to be as much addressed to private individuals as to scientists, professionals, and states. Writing from South Africa and the USA, respectively, Loretta Kopelman and Ruth Macklin, while again noting conceptual and drafting weaknesses, praise the Declaration as both internationally authoritative and clear in its rejection of cultural relativism: by framing the bioethical issues in the human rights structure, a clear rejection of female genital mutilation is marked, for instance.[20] Macklin highlights for particular praise Article 21, which requires states to hold their nationals *and other private non-state actors* responsible for their activities overseas under the Declaration's principles. This Article is of particular importance both for multinational clinical trials, a matter of heated debate over the past ten years, and for so-called 'bioethical tourism', where researchers search for the regulatory regime least restrictive of their proposed research (a particularly problematic issue in regard to assisted human reproduction, for example).[21]

However, even these positive readings of the Declaration are not unequivocal in their support for it, and the balance of academic commentary on the Declaration has been critical. Criticisms include charges that the Declaration involves a narrowly Western view of human rights[22] and a narrowly intellectual approach to human rights which misunderstands and overlooks inequalities in wealth, gender oppression, and the exclusion of the voices of the poor and vulnerable from participation in political processes nationally and internationally.[23] To that extent, one could say that the Declaration is no better and no worse than other human rights instruments since 1948, and that these criticisms are hardly specific to this most recent Declaration. On the other hand, its recency may make these charges (if valid) more rather than less serious, since it must have been framed in full awareness of these criticisms' general import.

These criticisms can be considered as *Ideologiekritik* addressed to the social, economic, and cultural conditions of production of the Declaration and the way it arguably mystifies its objects and the processes which support and sustain its effects. Another more directly political criticism of the Declaration points to the way in which it was drafted and adopted. Several commentators question why UNESCO, rather than the World Health Organization, was charged with this task, given the different work of the two organizations and their greatly differing statuses and reputations internationally.[24] More seriously, they criticize the way the draft was finalized by negotiation between 'experts' from UNESCO's Member States' governments, most of whom had no credentials *as bioethicists*, and which process, by its unavoidably political character,

---

[20] LM Kopelman, 'The Incompatibility of the United Nations' Goals and Conventionalist Ethical Relativism' (2005) 5 *Developing World Bioethics* 234; R Macklin, 'Yet Another Guideline? The UNESCO Draft Declaration' (2005) 5 *Developing World Bioethics* 244.

[21] See Chapter 17 in this collection, for views on 'reproductive tourism' from would-be parents; G Pennings, 'Reproductive Tourism as Moral Pluralism in Motion' (2002) 28 *Journal of Medical Ethics* 337.

[22] J-B Nie, 'Cultural Values Embodying Universal Norms: A Critique of a Popular Assumption about Cultures and Human Rights' (2005) 5 *Developing World Bioethics* 251.

[23] MC Rawlinson and A Donchin, 'The Quest for Universality: Reflections on the Universal Draft Declaration on Bioethics and Human Rights' (2005) 5 *Developing World Bioethics* 258.

[24] H Wolinsky, 'Bioethics for the World' (2006) 7 *EMBO Reports* 354; W Landman and U Schüklenk, 'From the Editors: UNESCO "Declares" Universals in Bioethics and Human Rights—Many Unexpected Universal Truths Unearthed by UN Body' (2005) 5(3) *Developing World Bioethics* iii; J Williams, 'UNESCO's Proposed Declaration on Bioethics and Human Rights—A Bland Compromise' (2005) 5 *Developing World Bioethics* 210.

bore no relation to the standard practice of bioethical analysis and debate. These criticisms are a little odd, partly because 'bioethics' is not a profession and there are no credentials agreed upon to entitle someone to call themselves a bioethicist, but mainly because there is not and never could be an international process which was left entirely to the technical experts of all nations.[25] The nearest case to this suggested way of producing guidelines would be the revision of the Declaration of Helsinki by the WMA—which in its turn has been strongly criticized (often by some of the same people criticizing UNESCO for its lack of academic rigour) for the lack of openness and technocratic character of its decision-making.

Leaving aside the ideological and political critique of the Declaration, most criticisms it has faced are intellectual and complain about vagueness, poor drafting, contradictions between principles, inadequate attention to social and environmental issues, lack of specificity or prescriptiveness, imposition of a consensus view where an issue remains open or controversial, banality, importation of problematic concepts (for instance, human dignity), and so on.[26] Some commentators have difficulty making any sense of the relationship between bioethics as a practice (a way of thinking about moral problems) and bioethics as represented in the Declaration (a list of principles), and the relationships between those principles and human rights.[27] Most seriously, it is alleged by several commentators that the Declaration simply fails to understand the field it proposes to regulate, a claim which is urged with particular force by those who have an interest in public health and health equity. Michael Selgelid, for instance, argues that the Declaration privileges liberty in an unreflective way, thus downplaying substantive (rather than merely formal) equality and the role of collective action, backed by coercive sanction, in infectious disease control and in measures designed to promote health equity.[28] Given all of these criticisms, these commentators might be pleased to find that the Declaration lacks legal force or enforcement mechanisms—but, indeed, this is also a commonly levelled criticism. The Declaration merely 'invokes' principles and human rights, lacking any of the legal or moral punch of earlier Declarations and binding treaties and conventions.[29]

The issue is not the merit or otherwise of these criticisms, but rather the signal they give of the mutual incomprehension of those who, on the one hand, drafted or supported the Declaration as bringing together human rights and bioethics agendas and agreeing a common framework of principles and approach to further policy and legislation, and those who criticize the Declaration for its intellectual, ideological, and political inadequacies. I claim that what this debate demonstrates is that rather than the

---

[25] D Benatar, 'Bioethics and Health and Human Rights: A Critical View' (2007) 32 *Journal of Medical Ethics* 17.

[26] D Benatar, 'The Trouble with Declarations' (2005) 5 *Developing World Bioethics* 220; M Häyry and T Takala, 'Human Dignity, Bioethics and Human Rights' (2005) 5 *Developing World Bioethics* 225; M Selgelid, 'Universal Norms and Conflicting Values' (2005) 5 *Developing World Bioethics* 267; J Williams, 'UNESCO's Proposed Declaration on Bioethics and Human Rights—A Bland Compromise' (2005) 5 *Developing World Bioethics* 210; H Wolinsky, 'Bioethics for the World' (2006) 7 *EMBO Reports* 354; CC Macpherson, 'Global Bioethics: Did the Universal Declaration on Bioethics and Human Rights Miss the Boat?' (2007) 33 *Journal of Medical Ethics* 588.

[27] Benatar (n 25).

[28] M Selgelid, 'Universal Norms and Conflicting Values' (2005) 5 *Developing World Bioethics* 267; An irony here is that bioethics is itself often charged with this sort of individualism by human rights advocates. See eg P Farmer and N Gastineau Campos, 'New Malaise: Bioethics and Human Rights in the Global Era' (2004) 32 *Journal of Law Medicine and Ethics* 243.

[29] MC Rawlinson and A Donchin, 'The Quest for Universality: Reflections on the Universal Draft Declaration on Bioethics and Human Rights' (2005) 5 *Developing World Bioethics* 258.

Declaration bringing bioethics and human rights discourses and practitioners together, it in fact forced them to confront their differences.

C. From Paris to Brussels via Strasbourg: UNESCO to the EU

What can we learn from the UNESCO UDBHR debate in looking again at the CoE's Oviedo Convention? If we were to transpose the Oviedo Convention from its rather minor role as a persuasive authority in the interpretation of the ECHR, to a rather more important role as a guiding set of principles for the governance of biomedicine within the EU, what does the 2005 debate tell us? Before we can answer that question we must note some important differences between the two instruments. First, as the critics of the UDBHR note, rather emphatically, the UNESCO Declaration is no more a binding legal instrument than was its ancestor the Universal Declaration of Human Rights. As with the Universal Declaration of Human Rights, if the UDBHR is to acquire anything more than minimal force, an instrument or instruments with the force of a treaty would be required (as the International Covenant on Civil and Political Rights 1966 and International Covenant on Economic, Social and Cultural Rights 1966 translated the Universal Declaration from statement of principles to justiciable legal instruments). As it stands, the UDBHR compels nothing, and encourages at most. On the other hand, as its defenders argue, the UDBHR has merit as a statement of internationally agreed principles and standards, which can be implemented piecemeal into domestic legislation and eventually binding international agreements; and, moreover, the soft law processes developing through 'progressive realization' have a useful persuasive and coordinating role. So one lesson from the UDBHR for the EU may be that the most effective way to allow the Oviedo Convention to acquire force would be to emphasize the role it can play in the 'open method of coordination' and 'networked governance'. There is more than one way to achieve harmonization of activities towards common European goals; and hard law is only one, and need not be assumed a priori to be the most effective.[30] It would not be necessary to strengthen the Oviedo Convention's formal legal status in order for its status as a tool of policy coordination to rise.

Another lesson of the UDBHR debate is that even where bioethical principles are taken up directly into a human rights instrument, they do not become or remain immune to criticism. Setting aside the criticisms of human rights from philosophers who do not believe that the rights concept is intelligible or defensible, we still have to acknowledge that most of the principles articulated in the UDBHR are beset with interpretive difficulties, both on their face and in terms of their interrelationships.[31]

---

[30] See Armstrong (n 2). To be clear: the UDBHR is 'softer' law than the Oviedo Convention, in that the Convention is a formal treaty. But the Oviedo Convention is 'softer' than the ECHR, both because it can ground no application to the ECtHR in its own right, and because it has been signed and ratified by only a portion of Member States of the CoE, with notable non-signatories including the United Kingdom, the Republic of Ireland, and the Federal Republic of Germany. France has signed, but not ratified, the Oviedo Convention. The table of signatures and ratifications is here: <http://conventions.coe.int/Treaty/Commun/ChercheSig.asp?NT=164&CM=8&DF=11/2/2007&CL=ENG> accessed 17 July 2012.

[31] The argument that the rights concept is indefensible is normally traced back to Bentham. See J Waldron, *Nonsense Upon Stilts: Bentham, Burke and Marx on the Rights of Man* (Routledge 1987). The contemporary philosophical debate acknowledges that positive *legal* rights exist, even if the concept of *moral* rights is problematic. The difficulty such philosophers have is in deriving a set of *human* rights which have the form of legal rights but which normatively transcend the set of positive rights any legal system happens to accord its subjects from time to time and place to place. A valuable contribution to

Now, obviously this is also true of the principles in the ECHR. But in the latter Convention, its drafting ensured that its terms of art inherited an interpretive canon familiar to working lawyers in the jurisdictions of the states party to the Convention, be they specialists in 'municipal' or 'international' law. The same may not be true of bioethical principles. This, arguably, does not matter: whereas with a formal legal instrument the interpretation of that instrument is a matter of legal expertise, and in the end judicial decision, the interpretation of the UDBHR as a tool for shaping policy is not so much a matter of strict interpretation but rather one of diplomacy and administration. The Oviedo Convention has a hybrid character, both as a legal instrument to which reference is made in the ECtHR, and in future in the ECJ, and as a policy-shaping guideline suitable for looser and more flexible interpretation. Difficulty may arise, however, where the application of the Oviedo Convention in policymaking is open to challenge before the ECJ. Which reading—the 'lawyerly' reading or the 'policymaker's'—should take priority? We have to acknowledge that the Oviedo Convention, and to some extent the UDBHR, are trying to do two different things at once. On the one hand, they are trying to give flesh and detailed articulation *in the context of biomedicine* to well-settled principles of extant human rights law. They aid in the interpretation of those principles. Call this the *interpretive* reading of the 'junior' conventions (the Oviedo Convention and the UDBHR). On the other hand, they are trying to supplement extant human rights principles with principles specific to their given domain, which were either not yet consensually accepted at an earlier date, or perhaps not yet salient at that earlier date, but which are on the same footing as the principles of earlier binding human rights instruments as universal binding norms. Call this the *protocol* reading: they expand the scope of agreed human rights norms, rather than simply spelling out, illustrating, or explaining them. It is not always clear which reading of the junior conventions in the biomedical field ought to be preferred. Arguably, since the Oviedo Convention has neither the range of signatures nor the ratifications of the ECHR, and remains persuasive only, with rather few citations, the interpretive reading is better attested in practice. Yet if the Oviedo Convention is to be taken into EU law and policy, the utility of doing so is better supported by taking the protocol reading. Whether it is granted that status depends on whether the Member States of the Union would find it useful to have it used in that way, as well as on whether those Members States of the Union which have yet to sign (or have signed but not yet ratified) the Oviedo Convention now do so.

One attractive reason for this course—making use of the Oviedo Convention as a normative basis for the regulation of biomedicine within the Union—is the sheer complexity of extant Union law governing biomedicine. The intellectual difficulty of understanding how to translate an interesting discovery in stem cell biology via technology developments involving novel techniques in tissue engineering into the clinic is such as to make one wonder whether the law is quite as complex as the science itself.[32] The EU Charter of Fundamental Rights has relatively little application to human rights in biomedicine, save in respect of real property rights in biological materials and intellectual property rights over inventions arising from the use of such

---

this debate and summary of its major features is J Tasioulas, 'Taking Rights Out of Human Rights' (2010) 120 *Ethics* 647.

[32] J Kent, *Regenerating Bodies: Tissue and Cell Therapies in the Twenty-First Century* (Routledge 2012).

materials.[33] Similarly, as I proposed earlier, the ECtHR has tended not to develop its bioethical jurisprudence very far from its classical civil and political rights remit, relying to a considerable extent on its 'margin of appreciation doctrine' and supervising procedural fairness rather than fundamental principles, in most cases. However, once the EU completes its accession to the ECHR, it acquires an obligation to make policy and law consistent with Convention rights. In the field of biomedicine this might best be fulfilled by shaping its policy in the field of biomedicine with the Oviedo Convention as the normative framework.

This would have two signal advantages: the first is that it tackles the 'democratic deficit' problem which is highlighted in the margin of appreciation jurisprudence. Where the Strasbourg Court is often content to remit certain issues to states party to the ECHR, it can only confidently do so when the state is able to argue, as in *Evans v United Kingdom*, that it has subjected the legal rule under challenge to careful consultation and parliamentary scrutiny.[34] It is at least questionable whether, if the Strasbourg Court had to decide an issue, which, were it to come from a common-or-garden state party, would be handled under the margin doctrine, it would feel able to do so in the same way if the application were against the EU as respondent party. This question arises from the status of the European Parliament as only a relatively weak mechanism for democratic scrutiny of EU policy and legislation, and a similarly weak democratic control over the actions of the Council of Ministers via Member State parliaments. If the EU argued that its policy was formed through application of the Oviedo Convention, this problem might disappear. Instead, the issue would become one of whether the EU had interpreted the Oviedo Convention appropriately.

The second advantage might point in exactly the opposite direction. Suppose the Strasbourg Court did not follow this line of reasoning, and held that an EU policy had not received sufficient public scrutiny, whatever formal reference it might have made to the Oviedo Convention. This might have the pleasing result of requiring the Union to give a greater role to the European Parliament in scrutinizing policies, at least insofar as they bear on biomedical governance affairs. While EU policy is shaped through a myriad of intergovernmental contacts, policy networks, and the wide range of tools available in the Open Method of Coordination, it is questionable whether any of these mechanisms have the same kind and degree of accountability and legitimacy as has parliamentary democracy. Reflecting again on *Evans v United Kingdom*, it is doubtful whether the UK's arguments that the policy embodied in the Human Fertilisation and Embryology Act (1990) fell securely within the margin of appreciation but for the combination of extensive consulation *and* parliamentary scrutiny and debate that led to legislation.

---

[33] Plomer (n 5) Data protection rights are also important in connection with biobanks and DNA sample collections. The evolving jurisprudence here is arguably a development of human rights protection in the context of personal privacy and civil liberties. A consistent theme in the law and policy of biological sample collections is the incommensurability of world-views between biomedical researchers, who see controls on the use of such collections as undermining research and endangering public health and well-being, and civil libertarians, who see such collections as extensions of state surveillance over the individual. Compare and contrast the reasoning in *S and Marper v United Kingdom* [2008] ECHR 1581 and *R (ex parte Source Informatics) v Department of Health* [1999] All ER (D) 563, where the former case is concerned with civil liberties, police powers, and forensic DNA collections, and the latter is concerned with legitimate (albeit commercial) use of data for research purposes.

[34] *Evans v United Kingdom* [GC] (2008) 46 EHRR 34; G Letsas, *A Theory of Interpretation of the European Convention on Human Rights* (OUP 2009). On the Court's handling of *Evans*, see also Chapter 13 in this collection.

This chapter has necessarily been essayistic and speculative in character. We simply do not know how the European governance of biomedicine will evolve; we do know that current trends, if they continue, will lead to a greater reliance on human rights norms and forms of argument, in biomedicine as elsewhere in governance. We do not know how the available human rights norms at EU, CoE, UNESCO, or other international levels will be applicable or applied to this problem of norm deficit. It is reasonable to think that just as intellectual property regimes have been forced to address challenges from human rights activist movements, and the conflict of norms which arises where intellectual property norms, trade norms, and human rights norms are brought face to face, the same may well apply in complex and interesting ways once the human rights legal framework is brought in, in full, to EU governance on EU accession to the ECHR.[35] Another issue we do not fully understand at this stage is the way in which existing EU mechanisms for discussing 'bioethical' issues will converge either in institutional form, or intellectual content, with the emerging human rights framework.[36]

The development within the EU institutional and legal framework of a language of bioethics has been a slow but continuous process over the past twenty-five years. Similarly, the development of an EU approach to human rights, both in the guise of its own fundamental rights discourse and in foreign policy, has been evolving for many years. The convergence of these two trends, under the influence of the planned accession of the EU to the ECHR, opens up some fascinating possibilities for the reshaping of the regulation of biomedicine in the EU and, indeed, for the functioning of its institutions. A fusion of these two trends may allow for a more transparent debate, in public, in policymaking and in the courts, than is currently actual or possible. It may allow a greater degree of common commitment to normative goals across the range of EU health and health technology policy. And it may facilitate the translation of bioethical concerns and values into policy in ways which can be secured or challenged with more robust tools of legal norm interpretation and enforcement. On the other hand, as we saw with the UDBHR, the outcome of this process may well be weak and vague. Or it may be that, as with the Oviedo Convention, a stronger outcome is possible but it cannot (yet) achieve adoption by all states within the CoE system. An ethical framework for the regulation of new health technologies is necessary. The current European legal framework is excessively complex, in part because it is a patchwork of EU, CoE, and domestic legislation, and in part because in the absence of a common value framework a piecemeal technical framework has evolved to handle specific problems while leaving broader purposive questions unasked or unanswered. The open questions therefore are (a) would adoption by the EU legislators of the CoE's human rights-based approach resolve the overall unclarity here?; (b) would the outcome of such adoption be any clearer than the present patchwork or will we be in the same position of uncertainty as we are currently vis-à-vis the precautionary principle? And (c) is it better to have a vague framework, or no framework?

[35] H Hestermeyer, *Human Rights and the WTO: The Case of Patents and Access to Medicines* (OUP 2007).
[36] RE Ashcroft, 'Could Human Rights Supersede Bioethics?' (2010) 10 *Human Rights Law Review* 639.

15

Sociotechnical Innovation in Mental Health: Articulating Complexity

Martyn Pickersgill

A. Introduction

The use of innovative technology within psychiatry and psychology has often provoked complex and sometimes acrimonious discussion of law and ethics—as the histories of electro-convulsive therapy and psychopharmaceuticals remind us all too well.[1] The stories of these techniques underscore the great degree to which the mental health professions, and the innovations they give rise to and which function within them, are inherently social. Institutional and political interests, norms, and expectations, shape the acceptance and resistance of technology as well as stimulate further sociotechnical change (including shifts in law and other forms of governance).[2] In this chapter, I seek to cast fresh light on the social dimensions of innovation, health, and regulation through exploring the web of associations constitutive of and engendered by one particular technology: the Diagnostic and Statistical Manual of Mental Disorders (DSM). Popularly known as 'the bible' of psychiatry, the DSM is the official list of psychopathologies recognized by the American Psychiatric Association (APA). The case of the DSM provides an important platform from which the production and circulation of ethics, rights, and risks within psychiatry can be observed, and demonstrates the centrality of 'mundane' technologies (diagnostic handbooks, clinical practice guidelines, and quality of life indicators) in the networks that produce and sustain more 'novel' biomedical produces and devices, as well as how (biomedical) developments outside Europe can have major transformative effects on European life. Such issues are crucial to explore within socio-legal studies and medical sociology.

In what follows, I discuss the social dimensions of innovative health technologies broadly, before detailing the development and reception of the seminal third edition of the DSM—the DSM-III—which was released by the APA in 1980.[3] The former task is necessary in order fully to flesh out the conceptual tools and empirical findings that I implicitly and explicitly draw upon in this analysis (and which may be of interest to legal scholars addressing important normative questions about regulation and governance). In discussing the DSM-III, I focus especially on one particular diagnostic category: antisocial personality disorder (ASPD). Personality disorders are 'the Achilles' heel of psychiatry' and 'the bane of law'; here, I show how these constructs are embroiled with mental health research, policy, and practices—and, hence, illustrate

---

[1] D Healy, *The Creation of Psychopharmacology* (Harvard UP 2002); E Shorter and D Healy, *A History of Electoconvulsive Treatment in Mental Illness* (Rutgers UP 2007).

[2] cf A Hedgecoe and P Martin, 'The Drugs Don't Work: Expectations and the Social Shaping of Pharmacogenetics' (2003) 33 *Social Studies of Science* 3.

[3] APA, *Diagnostic and Statistical Manual of Mental Disorders* (3rd edn, APA 1980).

how an innovation like the DSM-III can itself effect a range of innovative socio-technical practices across a range of domains.[4] The DSM-III, rather than later editions of this handbook, is the primary (but not exclusive) object of concern by virtue of the disproportionate influence of this volume on science, medicine, and subjectivity internationally. In the years when DSM-I and -II reigned, it would have been hard to imagine the import of DSM-III; conversely, the authority of DSM-IV owed much to the ubiquity of its predecessor.

This chapter is different from the other contributions to this collection, in that its aim is not, in fact, to provide a specific analysis of the role of a new technology in European law. Rather, it instead feeds into such issues through its intention to render problematic the terms under which these debates play out, and hence ultimately seeks to take regulatory discourses into, as yet, unchartered territories. European institutions, including the European Union (EU), are increasingly orientating themselves towards the legal and regulatory challenges that new technologies are deemed to introduce; indeed, even the European Court of Human Rights has an interest in these issues.[5] Yet, the relationship of the EU with innovation is ambiguous: even as moves are made to interrogate the ethical implications of new science and technology, the very same actors and networks involved can serve to implicitly endorse them.[6] Important parallels can be made with the EU's efforts to promote citizen participation in governance in ways that can paradoxically act to disempower them.[7] Innovation, it seems, is often regarded as a common good—and if some resist then governance regimes that reposition it as such are seen as being required. National law and policy may, on occasion, also come to be shaped, challenged, or rendered impotent by, for instance, EU law; this has been made vividly clear in regard to the use of and access to health technologies.[8] Clearly, then, there is a need to engage with not only specific technologies and particular regulatory frameworks, but also with the concepts that animate and direct debates in these arenas.

In focusing on a less obviously sensational technology, this chapter seeks to focus attention on social, legal, and ethical issues that might otherwise go unnoticed by lawyers and other regulators. In so doing, I implicitly seek to recontextualize innovation, and indeed regulation more broadly. 'Innovation' is here understood to be an alignment of tools and practices that occurs within a dynamic matrix of ethics, wider social norms, markets, and politics. 'Regulation' can be understood not solely as a set of authoritative rules or directives (such as formalized laws), but also a range of socio-technical practices that shape institutions and subjectivity either deliberately or otherwise. Thus, my account deliberately diverts attention away from the specific biomedical risks that innovative health technologies might present patients, and the ways through which these are governed by law, and seeks instead to bring broader societal concerns more sharply into focus. It is hoped that in so doing this analysis may orientate the reader towards some of the unanticipated and diffuse effects of innovative health

---

[4] DN Greig, *Neither Bad Nor Mad: The Competing Discourses of Psychiatry, Law and Politics* (Jessica Kingsley Publishers 2002) 108.

[5] T Murphy and G Ó Cuinn, 'Works in Progress: New Technologies and the European Court of Human Rights' (2010) 10 *Human Rights Law Review* 601.

[6] H Busby, T Hervey, and A Mohr, 'Ethical EU Law? The Influence of the European Group on Ethics in Science and New Technologies' (2008) 33 *European Law Review* 803.

[7] ML Flear, '"Together for Health"? How EU Governance Undermines Active Biological Citizenship' (2008) 26 *Wisconsin International Law Journal* 368; ML Flear and A Vakulenko, 'A Human Rights Perspective on Citizen Participation in the EU's Governance of New Technologies' (2010) 10 *Human Rights Law Review* 661.

[8] TK Hervey and JV McHale, *Health Law and the European Union* (CUP 2004).

technologies that are often unheeded (especially in anticipatory governance) but which may nevertheless demand our examination.

In large part, my intent, then, is to begin to chart some of the *complexity* inherent in the articulations between health, technology, and innovation. As Mol and Law define it, a situation is complex 'if things relate but don't add up, if events occur but not within the processes of linear time, and if phenomena share a spare but cannot be mapped in terms of a single set of three-dimensional coordinates.'[9] This definition is itself not transparent, but it directs our analytic gaze to the fact that complex situations are rarely easily factorialized into causative processes and bounded effects. Instead, entities and the sociotechnical networks they are embedded within interact in multiple ways that are not readily made captive by scholars: complex situations are the outcome of ongoing processes of co-production between the material and the semiotic.[10] In this chapter I therefore emphasize the dynamic relationship between mental health, biomedical innovation, and law and regulation, and the ways in which they shape and perhaps form one another.

1. The DSM

First released in 1952, the DSM had no more than subtle effects on the work of US psychiatrists. However, the 1980 third edition (DSM-III) profoundly transformed psychiatric theorization, funding, research, and treatment, as well as the subjective experience of the individuals who came to be classified with one of its labels. Furthermore, the sociotechnical innovation that the DSM-III at once represented and further activated was not restricted to the USA; rather, its effects were felt internationally, particularly within Europe. For instance, professional bodies such as the Royal College of Psychiatrists in the United Kingdom soon adopted the text and its theoretical underpinnings within psychiatric education and practice, introducing its innovative potential to British biomedical and cultural contexts.

The adoption of the DSM-III was facilitated by the lack of formal regulation governing its use both nationally and at the European level, for instance by the EU. It was beyond the regulatory purview of bodies charged with governing the safety and efficacy of medical devices and pharmaceuticals, and the only barrier to its use was the prohibitive cost of purchasing it. Whilst the text itself highlighted the risk of its categories being used by those unschooled in psychiatry, as a book the DSM-III could be bought and sold as any other. Accordingly, the manual came to be at home in the offices and laboratories of a range of actors, including those beyond psychiatry (for example, molecular geneticists and psychologists), and its terminology came to have traction outside the mental health professions (for example, education). The success of the DSM-III in turn innovated the creation of subsequent editions, with the next, fifth edition—the DSM-5—due in 2013. More importantly, the diagnostic categories it contained were performative; they became part of and further stimulated clinically and culturally significant forms of praxis, such as novel scientific research and legal innovations.

Innovative health technologies, like the DSM and the diagnostic categories it contains, have a social life (which affects their regulation, and impacts upon law and governance). They have histories, and exist in a network of inter-dependent relations

---

[9] A Mol and J Law, 'Complexities: an introduction' in J Law and A Mol (eds), *Complexities: Social Studies of Knowledge Practices* (Duke UP 2002) 1.

[10] cf S Jasanoff, 'Ordering Knowledge, Ordering Society' in S Jasanoff (ed), *States of Knowledge: The Co-Production of Science and Social Order* (Routledge 2004).

with other sociotechnical objects and practices. Such networks enable the mobility of technologies, between countries, and between the courts, the policy room, the laboratory, and the clinic. Innovative health technologies are not just enmeshed within clinical life, but are part of society more broadly—and should be regulated accordingly. This active social life relies upon, supports, and animates existing and novel material-semiotic entities: diagnostic practice, drug development, legal precedent, and so on. In turn, these feedback and (re)shape the innovation itself. In the next section, I discuss some of the existing (predominantly) sociological work relating to this point, which sets the scene for a more focused analysis of the DSM.

B. Health, Technology, and Society

As assemblages of interacting institutional, material, and symbolic elements that reciprocally shape one another, 'health', 'technology', and 'society' can be understood to be material-semiotic hybrids that exist through mutually constitutive relationships. Accordingly, analytic purchase on any one of these categories might more firmly be sought by considering these relations. Sociological studies of biomedical innovations have rendered this relationality into sharp relief. In everyday life, health, technology, and society intermingle in almost tangible ways, as evidenced in particular through concerns around the ubiquity of pharmaceuticals.

As with technology more broadly, health innovations are formed through complex processes that are at once political, gendered, and classed, and involve actual and imagined users in as much as technologists themselves.[11] In spite of widespread appeals to 'innovate' within biomedicine and elaborate funding strategies designed to support this, innovation is therefore not an unproblematic process. Aside from the obvious technical issues involved, 'bringing a technology into existence' is, as sociologist Adam Hedgecoe reminds us, a 'complicated and fraught process' wherein the social is 'central'.[12]

In particular, (prospective) innovation within biomedicine may engender considerable public and regulatory unease.[13] Such disquiet can have diverse effects on the governance of biomedicine by law and policy, and hence on the scope and nature of the technologies that may result from it. Formal mechanisms of governing scientists and engineers likewise interact with their own personal and professional ethical and social norms, further impacting on the ways in which investigations are progressed and the kinds of studies that are undertaken.[14]

---

[11] D MacKenzie and J Wajcman (eds) *The Social Shaping of Technology, Second Edition* (Open UP 1999); R Williams and D Edge, 'The Social Shaping of Technology' (1996) 25 *Research Policy* 865; L Winner, 'Do Artefacts Have Politics?' (1980) 109 *Daedalus* 121; S Woolgar, 'The Turn to Technology in Social Studies of Science' (1991) 16 *Science, Technology & Human Values* 20; S Woolgar, 'Configuring the User: The Case of Usability Trials' in J Law (ed), *A Sociology of Monsters: Essays on Power, Technology and Domination* (Routledge 1991).

[12] A Hedgecoe, *The Politics of Personalised Medicine: Pharmacogenetics in the Clinic* (CUP 2004) 28.

[13] N Brown, A Faulkner, J Kent, and M Michael, 'Regulating Hybrids: "Making a Mess" and "Cleaning Up" in Tissue Engineering and Transpecies Transplantation' (2006) 4 *Social Theory and Health* 1; A Faulkner, I Geesink, J Kent, and D Fitzpatrick, 'Tissue-Engineered Technologies: Scientific Biomedicine, Frames of Risk and Regulatory Regime-Building in Europe' (2008) 17 *Science as Culture* 195; J Kent and N Pfeffer, 'Regulating the Collection and Use of Fetal Stem Cells' (2006) 332 *British Medical Journal* 866; S Wright, *Molecular Politics: Developing American and British Regulatory Policy for Genetic Engineering, 1972–1982* (Chicago UP 1994).

[14] M Pickersgill, 'The Co-Production of Science, Ethics and Emotion' (2012) *Science, Technology & Human Values* 579.

This is not, of course, to say that regulators are necessarily acting to limit innovation in any kind of quantitative way. Rather, regulation may effect a qualitative shift in the kinds of health technologies that come to be developed. Furthermore, in responses to various claims that there is an innovation 'crisis'—particularly in regards to the pharmaceutical industry—regulation can itself be employed to support and encourage innovation. For instance, regulatory bodies such as the European Medicines Agency are increasingly reconfiguring themselves from 'guardians' of public health into stewards that play 'a key role in promoting innovation'.[15] In so doing, the EU simultaneously contributes to the promotion of the diagnostic standards which detail the disease constructs that pharmaceuticals purport to treat. In the case of the DSM, this may contribute to its reification as an innovative health technology through indirectly facilitating drug innovation.

Promissory discourse plays an important role in efforts to realize the potential of new and imagined therapies for biomedical practice, wherein institutional and material expectations are 'intimately entwined'.[16] Indeed, it may be that regulatory practices themselves help to enjoin the crystallization of speculation and anticipation about the future into specific, articulable expectations.[17] Translating new health technologies into clinical practice is thus far from simple: technologies 'do not simply arrive in the health market'—this itself 'has to be created, and clinicians and patients, regulatory agencies and health authorities all have to see them as of value'.[18]

This draws our attention to the fact that innovative health technologies are rarely regarded as 'simply good or bad—as if they were absolute standards. Rather they are better or worse': health professionals compare innovations with the tools they already have at their disposal, in terms of multiple dimensions of risk, likely patient compliance, long-term efficacy, cost, and so on.[19] Such comparisons enable a technology to be considered in terms of clinical utility; this is an aspect of innovation that is inherently relational and specific to the sociotechnical milieu within which the object in question is situated, as well as to the epistemological and ontological assumptions and norms operative therein. Usefulness is not simply about clinical benefit, therefore, but also relates to a 'clinician's view of their social and ethical duty towards an individual patient and their family'—that is, on an individual assessment of their duty of care.[20] It is also about the degree to which an innovation 'can be translated into the more everyday world of the technology users'—how well it aligns with current practice and is constructed as being, in the idiom of Clarke and Fujimura, the 'right tool for the job'.[21]

---

[15] SJ Williams, P Martin, and J Gabe, 'The Pharmaceuticalisation of Society? A Framework for Analysis' (2011) 33 *Sociology of Health & Illness* 710, 715; C Davis and J Abraham, 'Desperately Seeking Cancer Drugs: Explaining the Emergence and Outcomes of Accelerated Pharmaceutical Regulation' (2011) 33 *Sociology of Health & Illness* 731.

[16] SP Wainwright, C Williams, M Michael, B Farsides, and A Cribb, 'From Bench to Bedside? Biomedical Scientists' Expectations of Stem Cell Science as a Future Therapy for Diabetes' (2006) 63 *Social Science and Medicine* 2052, 2062.

[17] R Tutton, 'Promising Pessimism: Reading the Futures to be Avoided in Biotech' (2011) 41 *Social Studies of Science* 411.

[18] A Webster, 'Innovative Health Technologies and the Social: Redefining Health, Medicine and the Body' (2002) 50 *Current Sociology* 443, 451.

[19] A Mol, 'Cutting Surgeons, Walking Patients: Some Complexities Involved in Comparing' in Law and Mol (n 9) 218.

[20] Hedgecoe (n 12).

[21] Webster (n 18) 443; A Clarke and J Fujimura (eds), *The Right Tools for the Job* (Princeton UP 1992).

This is a point that may be lost in attempts to regulate to encourage the employment of one tool or technique over another. More generally, the polyvalence of 'clinical benefit' and the imperative of clinical usefulness raise questions about the effectiveness of regulatory regimes that attempt to capture utility in terms of efficacy that reduce this to, for instance, the material properties of an innovation (be it a drug or other form of innovation), rather than understand it as a dynamic concept that can only really be understood in terms of how a new technology may come to be embedded within the sociotechnical world of the clinic.

If a new health technology does become operative within the clinic, it may go on to have effects far beyond those initially conceived. This is a direct consequence of the web of interactions between institutions, tools, and users that constitute the 'context' within which the innovation is implemented. Technologies interact with, mediate, and form social relationships and conceptions of selfhood. Within medicine, innovative tools and techniques may transform our understandings of the human body and the nature of normality and pathology. Such transformations in the regimes of knowledge and normativity help to reshape shape research trajectories, expectations about medical futures, and, thus, the innovation pathway itself.[22]

Technologies 'can indeed be constitutive of new social dynamics, but they can also be derivative or merely reproduce older conditions.'[23] This is as a consequence of the fact that social values are embedded in tools and techniques: artefacts have politics.[24] Ideas about the correct use of a technology are literally built into innovations; these imply particular views of who counts as an appropriate user, and hence imaginaries of society more broadly are materialized. This is commonly referred to as the 'inscription' of technological objects, whereby the result is that users are enjoined to follow particular scripts when using the technology—though users may well find ingenious ways of rewriting these.[25]

Accordingly, though innovation, health, and society may be shaped through regulatory processes, technology can also act as a form of regulation in its own right since it forces certain kinds of human behaviour whilst removing the conditions of possibility for others—including through shaping the law itself.[26] In medicine as elsewhere this may be problematic, since although 'technology can have profound regulatory effects', it often lacks 'the safeguards built into democratic systems of rule-making and enforcement'.[27] One form of innovation that often tends to exert regulatory effects within biomedicine is the humble clinical standard. Standardization can be usefully regarded as 'the process of rendering things uniform', whilst a standard is both the 'mean and outcome' of this.[28] Accordingly, clinical standards include design standards,

[22] P Martin, 'Genes as Drugs: The Social Shaping of Gene Therapy and the Reconstruction of Genetic Disease' (1999) 21 *Sociology of Health & Illness* 517; K Wailoo, *Drawing Blood: Technology and Disease Identity in Twentieth-Century America* (Johns Hopkins UP 1997).

[23] S Sassen, 'Towards a Sociology of Information Technology' (2002) 50 *Current Sociology* 365, 365.

[24] Winner (n 11).

[25] M Akrich, 'The De-scription of Technical Objects' in WE Bijker and J Law (eds), *Shaping Technology/Building Society: Studies in Sociotechnical Change* (MIT Press 1992).

[26] T Dant, 'Material Civilization: Things and Society' (2006) 57 *British Journal of Sociology* 289; J Johnson [B Latour], 'Mixing Humans and Non-Humans Together: The Sociology of a Door-Closer' (1998) 35 *Social Problems* 298; H Landecker, 'Between Beneficence and Chattel: the Human Biological in Law and Science' (1999) 12 *Science in Context* 203.

[27] K Yeung and M Dixon-Woods, 'Design-Based Regulation and Patient Safety: A Regulatory Studies Perspective' (2010) 71 *Social Science and Medicine* 502, 503.

[28] S Timmermans and M Berg, *The Gold Standard: The Challenge of Evidence-Based Medicine and Standardization in Health Care* (Temple UP 2003) 24.

performance standards, and terminological standards, the latter of which would include diagnostic manuals (such as the DSM) that collect together lists of diseases and define their nature.[29] Today, they are ubiquitous within 'Western' medicine.[30]

Though complex to produce, standards act as a vital form of infrastructural support to medical practice—and indeed to professional work and social life more broadly.[31] Within research, they act as 'a collective good, or necessary evil, that will provide scientists with comparable data and thus the basis on which to make general claims'.[32] As such, they are 'necessary for knowledge communication, research collaboration, and consistent diagnosis in an increasingly globalized world'.[33] In clinical practice, standards manage uncertainty and direct the medical gaze, rendering complex decision-making around treatment and diagnosis comprehensible, accountable, and legitimate.[34] In the words of Timmermans and Berg, the 'implementation of clinical practice guidelines or novel nomenclatures generates action and creates new forms of life'.[35] Standards, then, do not simply *regulate* biomedical work—they *transform* it.

In this way, we might understand standards as a form of technology—and, indeed, law and formalized ethical systems as well.[36] Technology might best be defined here as an artefact that enables symbolic or material change. Standards may thus emerge through processes of innovative research, but they are also agents of innovation: they can stimulate new ways of working, new kinds of professional relationships, new institutional and regulatory orders, and the production of new knowledge. Obviously, though, standards do not necessarily and always lead to radical change. As a technology, the effects of innovative standards on (mental) health practice may be marginal—as the discussion earlier on the problems of translation indicates.[37] Furthermore, whilst standards may seek to discipline the ontology of pathology and render it more amenable to research and clinical intervention, contestation may remain—perhaps especially in mental health.[38] However, subtle changes may have profound consequences, and some clinical standards within psychiatry and psychology have resulted in major effects in the ways in which health and subjectivity are imagined and made governable.

One of the most important and influential of such standards is the DSM. As a health technology, it is at once an example of innovation and a tool with which to innovate. As we will see, it has had diverse effects on the ways in which mental health is theorized,

---

[29] Timmermans and Berg (n 28) 25.

[30] G Weisz, A Cambrosio, P Keating, L Knaapen, T Schlich, and VJ Tournay, 'The Emergence of Clinical Practice Guidelines' (2007) 85 *Millbank Quarterly* 691.

[31] T Moreira, C May, and J Bond, 'Regulatory Objectivity in Action: Mild Cognitive Impairment and the Collective Production of Uncertainty' (2009) 29 *Social Studies of Science* 665.

[32] L Eriksson and A Webster, 'Standardizing the Unknown: Practicable Pluripotency as Doable Futures' (2008) 17 *Science as Culture* 57, 59.

[33] CD Wylie, 'Setting a Standard for a "Silent" Disease: Defining Osteoporosis in the 1980s' (2010) 41 *Studies in the History and Philosophy of Biological and Biomedical Sciences* 376.

[34] GC Bowker and SL Star, *Sorting Things Out: Classification and its Consequences* (MIT Press 1999).

[35] Timmermans and Berg (n 28) 23.

[36] Pickersgill, 'Standardising Antisocial Personality Disorder: The Social Shaping of a Psychiatric Technology' (2012) 24 *Sociology of Health & Illness* 544.

[37] M Barley, C Pope, R Chilvers, A Sipos, and G Harrison, 'Guidelines or Mindlines? A Qualitative Study Exploring what Knowledge Informs Psychiatrists' Decisions about Antipsychotic Prescribing' (2008) 17 *Journal of Mental Health* 9.

[38] L Knaapen and G Weisz, 'The Biomedical Standardization of Premenstrual Syndrome' (2008) 39 *Studies in the History and Philosophy of Biological and Biomedical Sciences* 120.

researched, and treated, with broad implications for the regulation of biomedicine and the governance of everyday life—including the marketing of medications, the risks associated with these, the rights of the consumer, and the legal administration of those ascribed with DSM disorders.

C. Ordering Disorder

The first edition of the DSM is widely held as emerging from a concern within the APA regarding the 'nosological confusion, proliferation of nomenclatures, and shift towards psychodynamic and psychoanalytic concepts' that characterized US psychiatry in the post-war era.[39] An important moment in mental health, the release of this manual nevertheless provoked far less attention than subsequent revisions; the DSM-II, published in 1968, was far more widely heralded (and sometimes critiqued). One aim of the new text was to complement, if not directly challenge, the authority of the World Health Organization's International Classification of Diseases: DSM-II was viewed by some in the APA as representing 'a significant advance toward the use of a standard international classification system to facilitate the exchange of ideas among psychiatrists of all countries'.[40]

As the DSM-I and, in particular, the DSM-II began to find traction within psychiatry and mental health more widely, broader shifts were occurring within the landscape of US psychiatric theory, research, and practice. In particular, gradual moves from psychoanalytic to more somatic styles of thought were taking place. These were supported by the activities of the major funding and research agency, the National Institute of Mental Health (NIMH), whose attention came to be increasingly fixed upon the sponsorship of more 'scientific' biological work and training. Nevertheless, the NIMH continued to fund investigations that took psyche and society as their focus. Such heterogeneity on the part of this premier biomedical funding body was reflected within the aetiological accounts of individual psychiatrists.[41] When articulating the potential causes and treatments for mental disorder, these professionals' writings in key journals were highly eclectic. In so doing, they built models of disease that drew upon a wide range of biological, psychological, and environmental or social 'factors'.

Heterogeneous approaches to mental health did not, however, prevent either the fall of certain perspectives, or the rise of others. As noted earlier, from the mid-20th century onwards psychoanalysis began—slowly but surely—to lose support in the USA whilst discourse regarding the bodies of the mentally ill became re-energized. As the 1980s began, this turn towards what many called 'biological psychiatry' was markedly evident. Somatic approaches were deemed more scientific than psychoanalytic perspectives, and attracted considerable funding and prestige. This reconstitution of psychiatry as a justifiable division of US biomedicine was, in part, stimulated by attacks on the legitimacy of the expertise psychiatrists professed to possess. It was also animated by the development, decreasing expense, and proliferation of genetic and neuroscientific technologies that lent themselves well to the investigative aims of those who sought to study psychopathology 'scientifically'. Such a shift was both reflected in and furthered

---

[39] GN Grob, 'Origins of DSM-I: A Study in Appearance and Reality' (1991) 148 *American Journal of Psychiatry* 421, 428.

[40] RL Spitzer and PT Wilson, 'A Guide to the American Psychiatric Association's New Diagnostic Nomenclature' (1968) 124 *American Journal of Psychiatry* 1619, 1619.

[41] M Pickersgill, 'From Psyche to Soma? Changing Accounts of Antisocial Personality Disorders in the American Journal Psychiatry' (2010) 21 *History of Psychiatry* 294.

by the release of a new APA nosology—a very different kind of technology—in 1980: the DSM-III.

The development of the DSM-III was led by Columbia University psychiatrist Robert Spitzer, and the work of the DSM-III Task Force was marked by a series of complex negotiations that belied the 'objective' nature of the psychiatric technology it sought to develop. In particular, many felt that Spitzer and colleagues intended to implicitly introduce a more somatic focus to psychiatry through the DSM-III—an aim that did not go unchallenged by psychoanalysts. One point of controversy was the proposed removal of the concept of 'neurosis'.[42] Though psychoanalysts had traditionally been relatively unconcerned with diagnostic categories, neuroses were fundamental to their theoretical frameworks: omission from the new DSM would thus be a serious affront. Consequently, psychoanalysts sought to reshape the processes of innovation underlying the emerging technology of the DSM-III, mobilizing against Spitzer and his committee. Spitzer was nevertheless successful in 'curing' the DSM of neurosis, and in largely removing from this new technology any circuits that enabled psychoanalytic power still to flow.

Instead of privileging the psychosocial, the DSM-III was therefore structured by more biological assumptions—though Spitzer himself denied that the manual was 'covertly committed to a biological approach to explaining psychiatric disturbance'.[43] Regardless, with the DSM-III Spitzer helped to orientate the professional focus of US mental health professionals towards a more biological, 'scientific' psychiatry.[44] Moreover, the empirical research drawn upon in the development of this new diagnostic technology helped to justify the notion that the disorders it listed were discrete and observable natural kinds, contributing to diminishing the claims of critics who thought mental illness nothing but a myth.[45]

The DSM-III was especially important in helping to make the study of psychopathology what Fujimura might call a more 'do-able' problem: using this innovative standard, mental illness could be characterized, categorized, interrogated, and manipulated.[46] Articulated through experimental paradigms and large-scale pharmaceutical studies, the DSM-III disorders were made real. The DSM-III was salient in furthering the 'technosomatic shift' in psychiatry: an increased emphasis on the bodies of the mentally ill, and on technologies such as neuroimaging techniques to visualize these.[47]

As Mol has shown for arterial disease, the technologies through which disease is pictured by physicians (for example, via X-ray, using angiograms, or through observation in the clinic) informs the treatments that are prescribed for it.[48] In the case of mental health, new methods of visualizing the brains of individuals with attention deficit disorder, schizophrenia, and a range of other disorders, contributed to rendering treatments that acted directly upon the soma more legitimate and desirable. Yet, such images did not directly indicate what kinds of therapeutic innovations were necessary, nor could they answer more profound questions about the ontology of the disease itself.

[42] R Mayes and AV Horwitz, 'DSM-III and the Revolution in the Classification of Mental Illness' (2005) 41 *Journal of the History of the Behavioral Sciences* 249.

[43] RL Spitzer, 'Values and Assumptions in the Development of DSM-III and DSM-III-R: An Insider's Perspective and a Belated Response to Sadler, Hulgus, and Agich's "On values in Recent American Psychiatric Classification"' (2001) 189 *Journal of Nervous and Mental Disease* 351, 351.

[44] Mayes and Horwitz (n 42).

[45] Mayes and Horwitz (n 42).

[46] J Fujimura, 'Constructing "Do-able" Problems in Cancer Research: Articulating Alignment' (1987) 17 *Social Studies of Science* 257.

[47] Pickersgill (n 41).   [48] Mol (n 19).

Rather, what came often to occur was a co-production of the disorder and its treatment.[49]

In regards to the effects of the APA manuals on psychiatry and psychology internationally, although some clinicians drew attention to the limitations of the DSM-III many others appeared to take the innovative diagnostic technologies it contained to be established frameworks that were more than acceptable for application within research and practice. Not everyone, of course, was happy about the increased 'Americanization' of mental health, 'medicalization' of burdens of everyday life, and positioning of pharmaceuticals as 'fixes' for these.[50] In spite of these caveats it is nevertheless clear that, to a significant degree, European psychiatry and psychology came to be closely aligned with the USA in terms of nomenclature from the late 20th century onwards—with the wide circulation of the DSM-III playing a vital role in this shift.

D. Pathological Antisociality and the Social Life of Antisocial Personality Disorder

In this section, I move away from analysing the DSM-III in general towards the examination of one specific diagnostic innovation contained therein: antisocial personality disorder (ASPD), a terminological standard aimed at capturing pathological antisociality. First introduced into the psychiatric vocabulary in the 1970s, ASPD is used to categorize individuals who are considered to have a pervasive disregard for the rights and feelings of others. This might entail the violation of social and legal norms, underpinned by a lack of empathy and concern for the safety of self and others, and an excess of recklessness and aggressiveness. Since its introduction, discourse centring on ASPD has been voluminous and sometimes fractious within US and European psychiatry. Today, the diagnosis remains salient for mental health practitioners internationally, with discussions about its validity ongoing—not least as a consequence of the writing of a new DSM and the anticipatory debate this has impelled. In order to more fully account for the impact of this technology, I first chart how the mental health professions 'managed' antisocial behaviour prior to the introduction of ASPD.

Personality disorders have a long history within psychiatry, with categories such as psychopathic personality disorder (psychopathy) dating back to the 19th century.[51] In US psychiatry, both psychopathy and sociopathic personality disorder (sociopathy) have played important roles as diagnostic labels for the concept of antisociality that psychiatrists have considered their concern. The sociopathy construct was associated primarily with social deviance, and used by psychiatrists to refer to antisocial individuals. It appeared in various forms within the first and second editions of the DSM (DSM-I and -II), although these differences tended to be elided when the diagnosis was invoked in contributions to practitioner journals. Psychopathy, on the other hand, was never an 'official' diagnosis. Nevertheless, in spite of its absence from the APA nomenclature, this construct played a prominent role in

---

[49] N Rose, 'Neurochemical Selves' (2003) 41 *Society* 46.

[50] A Lakoff, *Pharmaceutical Reason: Knowledge and Value in Global Psychiatry* (CUP 2005); S Lloyd, 'The Clinical Clash over Social Phobia: The Americanization of French Experience?' (2006) 1 *BioSocieties* 229; S Scott, 'The Medicalisation of Shyness: From Social Misfits to Social Fitness' (2006) 28 *Sociology of Health & Illness* 133.

[51] GE Berrios, 'European View on Personality Disorders: A Conceptual History' (1993) 34 *Comprehensive Psychiatry* 14; H Werlinder, *A History of the Concepts. Analysis of the Origin and Development of a Family of Concepts in Psychopathology* (Almqvist and Wiksell International 1978).

discussions of antisocial personality, appearing, for instance, in articles within leading publications such as the *American Journal of Psychiatry*. Gradually, the concept came to be associated primarily with the ideas of US psychiatrist Hervey M Cleckley, and, following conceptual innovation in the 1970s, with the prominent Canadian psychologist Robert Hare.

Psychopathy remains prominent within clinical, scientific, and popular cultures, and those characterized as psychopaths continue to prove compelling to a variety of publics in the USA and Europe.[52] In spite of its lack of official standing within psychiatry, the category is nevertheless a long-standing and well-known measure of personality pathology within the discipline of psychology, where much of the research and theorization relating to psychopathy is undertaken. Moreover, despite not featuring in the DSM as such, ideas associated with the category are embedded within many of the formulations of pathological antisociality that have appeared in this manual over the last sixty years; the ambiguous category of psychopathy has thus continued to resonate through clinical, scientific, and popular discourse, profoundly shaping the later development of diagnostic criteria associated with antisocial behaviour.[53] Furthermore, many mental health professionals regard psychopathy as broadly similar to DSM diagnoses that seek to capture antisocial behaviour.

Within Europe, psychiatrists had likewise long been concerned with personality disorders relating to antisocial behaviour. However, without the DSM and the diagnostic innovation it enjoined, psychiatrists had fewer categorizations available to employ in order to describe individuals who were deemed to exhibit pathological forms of antisociality; for many years, discourse revolved almost exclusively around psychopathy. In the United Kingdom, for instance, as in the USA, psychopaths were viewed as manifestly antisocial, and a wide variety of aetiological models were put forward to explain the development of their personality disorder. However, in general, UK framings of psychopathy in the mid-20th century resonated more with somatic than psychic perspectives. This was a marked contrast to US aetiological accounts, which tended to be situated in a psychoanalytic rubric even as they drew on somatic ideas.

This disjuncture is less surprising when we bear in mind broader psychiatric discourse in the USA and the United Kingdom. In both countries, developmental narratives for antisociality reflected the dominant approaches of each nation's psychiatry. For the most part, UK practitioners tended to be orientated more explicitly towards biology and materialist conceptions of mental disorder than their counterparts across the Atlantic. In neither case, though, were these broader trends hegemonic, allowing the proliferation of diverse models, understandings, and practices. Furthermore, if British mental health professionals and their colleagues in the USA were alike in producing diverse articulations of psychopathy, they were similar too in their frustration with the ambiguity of this category. However, here, too, there were key differences. Whilst contributors to US journals lamented the lack of clarity regarding what precisely the classification of psychopathy referred to, psychiatrists and commentators in the United Kingdom more frankly admitted their ignorance.

---

[52] eg J Blair, D Mitchell, and K Blair, *The Psychopath: Emotion and the Brain* (Blackwell Publishing 2005); J Clarke and A Shea, *Psychopaths: Inside the Minds of the World's Most Wicked Men* (John Blake 2004); B Oakley, *Evil Genes: Why Rome Fell, Hitler Rose, Enron Failed, and My Sister Stole My Mother's Boyfriend* (Prometheus Books 2007); J Ronson, *The Psychopath Test: A Journey Through the Madness Industry* (Picador 2011).

[53] Pickersgill (n 36).

These concerns became acute as a consequence of the legal role the category played. The 1959 and 1983 Mental Health Acts of England and Wales both included and loosely defined the category of 'Psychopathic Disorder', which was viewed as approximately equivalent to the clinical term psychopathy. In the United Kingdom, the lack of consensus on psychopathy thus had significant legal implications and, therefore, social and ethical consequences. These issues were not irrelevant to US psychiatrists and lawyers; however, in the United Kingdom, the frank admissions of ignorance regarding psychopathy by even very senior commentators led to the clinical and legal uncertainties associated with the disorder being seen as particularly problematic. What was psychopathy, and who were psychopaths? How could the disorder be reliably recognized? More importantly, how could this identification be achieved legitimately, without falling into the trap of explaining both psychological and social deviancy using the terms of the other? There was no consensus regarding any of these questions. The ambivalences, uncertainties, and frustrations occasioned by pathological antisociality thus endured into the mid-late 20th century.

1. Introducing ASPD

Things began to change, however, in the 1980s, when the popular DSM-III formalized ASPD (the original criteria for which were written by the Personality Disorder Advisory Committee headed by Robert Spitzer himself). Operating as part of the broader political ecology of the DSM-III, this was not a committee of equals. Rather, some voices were allowed to achieve greater volume than others; conversely, some members, though ostensibly vocal, were effectively silenced.[54] A complex tangle of personal and professional associations could be discerned as operative within the Committee, the dynamics of which reflected and informed the kinds of expertise deemed by Spitzer to be legitimate. In particular, the Committee included prominent sociologist Lee N Robins, highly regarded for her work on sociopathy. Robins had long-standing ties to Spitzer, whose empiricist sensibilities aligned well with her own behaviourist inclinations. Her influence on ASPD was markedly apparent, the criteria of which relied heavily on the identification of specific antisocial behaviours (such as stealing and promiscuity).

Rather than psychopathy, ASPD continued to be used in the revised edition of the DSM-III released in 1987 (the DSM-III-R). It also appeared in the later DSM-IV, published in 1994, and, indeed, in its revised version, DSM-IV-TR, published in 2000. Though the next iteration of the APA diagnostic manual looks set more explicitly to engineer a rapprochement between ASPD and psychopathy, the former category has been very successful in terms of the research, policy, and clinical attention it has attracted.

Despite a rapid uptake, the ASPD diagnostic was not without its problems, however; its validity and conceptual underpinnings were debated in both the United Kingdom and, especially, the USA. As a form of diagnostic innovation, some controversy also formed around ASPD. In particular, the closeness of ASPD to everyday understandings of social deviancy was construed as a matter of concern, underscoring the enduring ontological uncertainties associated with personality disorder. Anthropologist Nuckolls has argued that ASPD has a history that represents 'values strongly congruent with familiar cultural stereotypes', such as 'the "independent" male'.[55] Accordingly, we should perhaps not be surprised that mental health professionals themselves are

---

[54] C Lane, *Shyness: How Normal Behavior Became a Sickness* (Yale UP 2007).
[55] CW Nuckolls, 'Toward a Cultural History of the Personality Disorders' (1992) 35 *Social Science and Medicine* 37.

aware of the risks and tensions of using ASPD to label the bad behaviour of some individuals, especially men, as a form of psychological dysfunction.

Furthermore, there has been what is sometimes acrimonious debate regarding whether ASPD and psychopathy can be taken to be synonymous constructs.[56] One trope within the mental health literature on this subject holds that ASPD is associated with impulsive and aggressive behaviour, whereas for psychopathy the nature of antisociality may be quite different (for example, property crime rather than assault), indicating more premeditation.[57] In turn, some investigators regard these different types of antisocial behaviour as reflected in distinct forms of aggression—reactive versus impulsive variants—that are underpinned by separate neurobiological pathways.[58] Universal agreement on this matter remains lacking, however.

The question itself—are ASPD and psychopathy 'the same'?—is one that has implications that pervade forensic mental health. That it is an epiphenomenon of the diagnostic innovation that produced the former construct in no way diminishes its import; rather, this epiphenomenal aspect precisely illuminates the unanticipated effects of innovation in regards to the creation of new forms of social and clinical life, and the simultaneous production of novel normative dilemmas. In other words, the fact that a debate emerges in part as a consequence of an innovation does not mean that it lacks salience to the analyst—to dismiss contestation as 'merely' an (inevitable) result of the introduction of innovative technologies would be to miss the extent to which these can transform the very clinical and political contexts within which they have come to be embedded, and enjoin new questions about rights, risks, and responsibilities.

In particular, the lack of a consensus regarding the relationship between ASPD and psychopathy results in much uncertainty on the part of those who research and treat these disorders.[59] This in and of itself has ethical significance; for instance, when an individual is labelled with (for example) ASPD, and is treated by different individuals throughout their 'career' within mental health services. Whilst some professionals may take ASPD and psychopathy to be roughly isomorphic, others believe firmly that these are distinct disorders and that psychopathy is 'worse' than ASPD. The therapeutic and judicial implications of this disagreement multiply when we take into account the fact that some mental health professionals consider psychopathy to be resistant to treatment. Access to services may thus become compromised, potentially mid-way through an individuals therapeutic journey. Recommendations for release dates from prison can, in some circumstances, also be affected by what diagnostic labels an individual has attracted, and what is the perceived relationship between these and criminal recidivism. The rights of an individual understood as pathologically antisocial thus relate closely to what specific diagnostic label they are ascribed with. Unfortunately, practice guidelines seem only to further complicate the ontological and normative issues at stake.[60]

[56] eg BA Arrigo and S Shipley, 'The Confusion over Psychopathy (I): Historical Considerations' (2001) 45 *International Journal of Offender Therapy and Comparative Criminology* 325; RD Hare, SD Hart, and TJ Harpur, 'Psychopathy and the DSM-IV Criteria for Antisocial Personality Disorder' (1991) 100 *Journal of Abnormal Psychology* 391; JRP Ogloff, 'Psychopathy/Antisocial Personality Disorder Conundrum' (2006) 40 *Australian and New Zealand Journal of Psychiatry* 519.

[57] eg JI Warren and SC South, 'Comparing the Constructs of Antisocial Personality Disorder and Psychopathy in a Sample of Incarcerated Women' (2006) 24 *Behavioral Sciences and the Law* 1.

[58] eg RJR Blair, 'Neurocognitive Models of Aggression, the Antisocial Personality Disorders, and Psychopathy' (2001) 71 *Journal of Neurology, Neurosurgery, and Psychiatry* 727.

[59] M Pickersgill, '"Promising" Therapies: Neuroscience, Clinical Practice, and the Treatment of Psychopathy' (2011) 33 *Sociology of Health & Illness* 448.

[60] MD Pickersgill, 'NICE Guidelines, Clinical Practice and Antisocial Personality Disorder: The Ethical Implications of Ontological Uncertainty' (2009) 35 *Journal of Medical Ethics* 668.

For mental health professionals, scientists, and policymakers, the ambiguous relationship between ASPD and psychopathy is far from the only uncertainty associated with the former construct. Regarded as a global personality dysfunction, rather than a discrete disorder that, like schizophrenia or depression, is associated with certain dysfunctions of cognition or affect, the ethical and clinical basis for the position of ASPD and other personality disorders as objects of psychiatric concern has been repeatedly considered and negotiated.[61] Though today there is, generally, agreement that conditions like ASPD legitimately come within the purview of psychiatry and psychology, personality disorders are not usually considered mental illnesses, in part due to their global nature but also as a consequence of their endurance and pervasiveness within an individual.[62] This has major implications for services for personality disorder in general, and ASPD in particular. Who should take responsibility for them, where these should be located, how much money should be invested in them, who should be allowed access, and what they should look like remain pressing political and clinical questions that are difficult to answer.

What is clear, however, is that a large number of individuals meet the criteria for ASPD, and that these individuals are primarily men. This is evidenced by, for example, a survey conducted by the UK Office for National Statistics in the late 1990s, which found that 63 per cent of males on remand, 49 per cent of males sentenced, and 31 per cent of all female prisoners met the DSM criteria for ASPD.[63] Individuals living under the label of ASPD thus straddle the boundaries between normality and pathology, criminology and mental health. To what extent does personality disorder simply represent an extreme of 'normal' social deviancy? Are those characterized with ASPD 'mad' or 'bad'? Does it even make sense to frame debates this way? To what extent are criminal offenders with a personality disorder responsible for their actions, and what are the implications of this for their management? In terms of policy, should offenders diagnosed with personality disorder come under the remit of the Department of Health or the Home Office? Should they be managed within prisons or hospitals? To what extent does the DSM category of ASPD construct the riskiness of the individual that the criteria aim to capture? The questions multiply, but consensus around answers remains lacking, even as policies are necessarily made and implemented.

One response to these perhaps intractable questions has been to further research into pathological antisociality, and in ways that are acceptable within the limits set by the dominant epistemological norms of mental health (themselves tightly bound to the kinds of investigations the DSM enables). If, from the 1980s, professionals and patients in the USA were increasingly framing disorders such as schizophrenia and depression in biological terms, psychiatrists and psychologists in the United Kingdom (and elsewhere in Europe) were also moving further towards technosomatic approaches to the study and management of mental illness. The new DSM-III diagnostic ASPD, alongside a novel psychometric test called the Psychopathy Checklist (developed by Canadian psychologist Robert Hare), allowed biomedical investigations of personality disorder to become more standardized and, therefore, 'scientific'. This was particularly important for UK mental health professionals, many of whom had long been frustrated with the diverse

---

[61] N Eastman and B Starling, 'Mental Disorder Ethics: Theory and Empirical Investigation' (2006) 32 *Journal of Medical Ethics* 94.

[62] RE Kendell, 'The Distinction Between Personality Disorder and Mental Illness' (2002) 180 *British Journal of Psychiatry* 110.

[63] N Singleton, H Meltzer, and R Gatward, *Psychiatric Morbidity Among Prisoners in England and Wales* (HMSO 1997).

understandings of and management practices for these conditions. These issues were increasingly pressing following the introduction of a new Mental Health Act in 1983. The 'culmination of a vigorous reforming campaign' articulated 'in terms of rights', the Act included new criteria for the management of offenders categorized with an antisocial personality disorder.[64]

Subsequently, as a consequence of its prevalence and perceived costs to society, ASPD has reached new prominence within the United Kingdom. Specifically, this has been in relation to the drafting of controversial mental health legislation referring explicitly to personality disorder.[65] In 1999, plans began to ferment regarding the reformation of the 1983 Mental Health Act of England and Wales. Whilst the inclusion of the ambiguous category of psychopathy within English and Welsh mental health law had long led to various debates about personality disorders, legislative scrutiny of these conditions was especially marked from 1999 to 2007. Here, again, 'rights' came to the fore; in particular, a number of debates played out regarding the extent to which proposals to change the 1983 Act were congruent with the European Convention on Human Rights.[66]

Others have analysed this issue more fully, what is of interest to us here is the great extent to which the individual diagnostic technologies (such as ASPD) contained within the DSM are the terms operationalized within such discourse.[67] In effect, by the close of the 20th century it became remarkably difficult—if not impossible—for UK legal discourse on mental health not to engage (at least in part) with US diagnostic technologies. In so doing, the DSM was embroiled within the very process of lawmaking—and as such its legitimacy was further amplified. Today, 'rights' and the DSM continue to relate with one another in complex ways within discourse on (inter)national public mental health: the deployment of diagnostic categories contained within the DSM and the use of psychopharmaceuticals co-produced with them are at once regarded as having the potential to compromise autonomy, whilst at the same time the right to be treated for mental health conditions is articulated in the same terms.

Let us return, though, to England and Wales, and the 1990s. As moves to reform the 1983 Act advanced, issues concerning the 'treatability' of personality disorder were placed in the foreground of the mental health landscape. This was specifically in relation to a drive by the Home Office and the Department of Health to push forward a controversial new policy for mentally disordered offenders. Part of this entailed the proposed removal of the so-called 'treatability test' from the existing Act. This 'test' was a clause restricting compulsory detention of individuals (including convicted offenders) within NHS facilities to only those individuals whose mental disorder was considered treatable. Individuals with personality disorders associated with antisocial behaviour (for example, ASPD and psychopathy) had long been held to be untreatable by many psychiatrists and psychologists; as such, under the Mental Health Act 1983, individuals living under

---

[64] N Rose, 'Unreasonable Rights: Mental Illness and the Limits of Law' (1985) 12 *Journal of Law and Society* 199, 199.

[65] D Pilgrim, 'New "Mental Health" Legislation for England and Wales: Some Aspects of Consensus and Conflict' (2007) 36 *Journal of Social Policy* 79. See also: N Manning, 'Actor Networks, Policy Networks, and Personality Disorder' (2002) 24 *Sociology of Health & Illness* 644; D Pilgrim, 'Disordered Personalities and Disordered Concepts' (2001) 10 *Journal of Mental Health* 253; M Pickersgill, 'How Personality became Treatable: The Mutual Constitution of Clinical Knowledge and Mental Health Law' (in press) Social Studies of Science.

[66] For work on the work of European law in framing engagements with technologies, see Murphy and Ó Cuinn (n 5).

[67] eg G Norris, 'Offenders, Deviants or Patients? Human Rights and the Incarcerated Offender' in M Odello and S Cavandoli (eds), *Emerging Areas of Human Rights in the 21st Century: The Role of the Universal Declaration of Human Rights* (Routledge 2011).

the label of an untreatable personality disorder (but no other form of mental disorder or learning disability) who had committed a crime were more often detained within prisons than hospitals.

In the late 1990s, as part of the process of forming new mental health policy, the UK Government asked why mentally disordered offenders considered to be 'untreatable' could not, in future, be held within High Secure Hospitals. By removing the treat-ability test from the Mental Health Act, the government would be able legally to detain personality disordered offenders within hospitals—potentially, given further restric-tions on the release of patients, such individuals could be detained indefinitely. In this way, some of the key policy questions regarding personality disorder had the potential to be resolved. However, mental health stakeholders of all kinds were incensed by these proposals, and, in large part as a consequence of their vigorous lobbying, the treatability test was modified rather than abandoned in the resulting 2007 Mental Health Act of England and Wales. To an extent, this was sold as an ethical imperative: individuals diagnosed with ASPD would no longer have their right to treatment compromised.

Associated with these legislative developments was a massive increase of public spending on and infrastructural development for personality disorder services and research from institutions like the Medical Research Council, the Department of Health, and the Home Office. By doing so, and, more generally, by bringing issues of treatability into the foreground, the government helped to create a new discursive space within which those clinicians who had long believed that personality disorders were treatable could articulate their views. Consequently, the voices of those profes-sionals advocating treatment for conditions like ASPD increased in number and volume. Opinion gradually shifted: personality disorder started to become regarded as treatable. Implicitly, personality was thus shown to be plastic, mouldable through clinical intervention. Law, then, or more accurately the social and scientific develop-ments animated by it, profoundly shaped understandings of the concept of ASPD—a concept introduced by an innovative psychiatric technology aimed at identifying it in individuals—just as ASPD itself impacted on the development of mental health law.

2. Ontology and Treatment

Some of the aforementioned funds earmarked for research into personality disorder were invested in neuroscientific studies on ASPD and psychopathy. Although the body of neurologic research into these conditions is slimmer than that of other areas (for example, epidemiological and psychotherapeutic investigations), models of personality disorder that imply a neurobiological aetiology are increasingly prominent and appar-ent in, for instance, Department of Health guidelines.[68] Neuroscience researchers are occupying positions of influence within clinical and policy arenas, and from them advocating ever greater shifts to integrate neurobiology with personality disorder research and practice.[69] Such calls are occurring as part of a wider move within psychiatry to reformulate psychopathological taxonomy along neurobiological lines.[70]

[68] National Institute for Mental Health in England (NIMHE), *Personality Disorder, no longer a diagnosis of exclusion* (2003) <www.dh.gov.uk/en/Publicationsandstatistics/Publications/Publications PolicyAndGuidance/DH_4009546>.
[69] eg R Hare, 'Forty Years aren't Enough: Recollections, Prognostications, and Random Musings' in H Herves and JC Yuille (eds), *The Psychopath: Theory, Research, and Practice* (Lawrence Erlbaum Associates 2007).
[70] eg SE Hyman, 'Can Neuroscience be Integrated into the DSM-V?' (2007) 8 *Nature Reviews Neuroscience* 725.

Yet, ASPD is by no means a thoroughly 'neurologised' concept. Neuroscientists investigating ASPD and other personality disorders, such as psychopathy, frame these conditions as complex and opaque. They are considered to develop through the interrelations of adverse genetic and environmental conditions, which condense into specific dysfunctions within the brain. Thus, the brain at once mediates the network of heterogeneous entities that interact to produce personality disorder, whilst also acting as a key node within that network, evidencing its effects through cerebral structure and function. Significantly, as a consequence of this multimodality, some neuroscientists assert that psychotherapy is potentially more efficacious than psychopharmacology in the management of personality disorder.[71] It is clear, then, that ASPD and psychopathy are painted as biopsychosocial conditions even by specialists in their somatic aspects.

The 'traditional' construal of personality disorders as complex, multi-faceted conditions thus persists; ASPD continues to be framed in diverse biological, psychological, and environmental terms, with individual professionals placing a different emphasis on each of these 'components'. Accordingly, whilst we might conclude that there has been (at least implicit) agreement internationally that ASPD is a 'biopsychosocial' disorder, there has been no firm consensus on the specific contributions of each of these factors, or on the exact mechanisms of development.

In terms of the aetiology of and treatment options for personality disorder, the views of today's clinicians resonate with those of many scientists. However, whilst neuroscience is deemed to hold therapeutic promise, it is not currently thought clinical useful. The claims of neuroscience may even be ignored if health professionals consider them antagonistic to clinical aims. Accordingly, neuroscience has not, through the generation of incontestable and objective knowledge, contracted the body of narratives available to clinicians to describe the development of ASPD. Instead, it has expanded it: neuroscience complicates further the ontology of ASPD by providing new ways through which the disorder can be articulated, and, as a contested area of research, creates a focal point around which such discourses can revolve.

This has implications for the governance of individuals meeting the criteria for disorders of sociality: if ASPD is an opaque condition characterized by uncertainty then a 'medical model' for severe antisocial behaviour is more easily challenged, underscoring the importance of the questions raised earlier regarding where, exactly, criminals who meet the criteria for ASPD should be ensconced and who has the legitimate right to hold them there—the health or the criminal justice system? And what about therapeutic innovation: how should mental health researchers proceed to develop appropriate therapies for a disorder when they are not sure what causes it?

However, when we examine this second problematic more closely we can see that it is not as intractable as we might initially conclude. Just as the law has long made allowances for the fact that forensic mental health patients tend to transgress the boundaries of both juridical and medical realms, so too have psychiatry and psychology traditionally proceeded very well in treating disorders that have uncertain aetiologies. For ASPD, and personality disorder more broadly, a lack of clear causal mechanism (and an ongoing uncertainty regarding whether the category can even be considered a discreet and legitimate 'disorder') has, in some ways, impeded therapeutic progress; for instance, there are no drugs specifically indicated for the treatment of ASPD, and given its complex ontological status it is perhaps unlikely that any pharmaceuticals will emerge. Indeed, in the United Kingdom, the National Institute for Health and Clinical

---

[71] Pickersgill (n 59).

Excellence (NICE) is remarkably clear about what it thinks about the role of drugs in managing ASPD, stating: 'Pharmacological interventions should not be routinely used for the treatment of antisocial personality disorder or associated behaviours of aggression, anger and impulsivity.'[72]

In practice, psychiatrists and psychologists go about treating ASPD in different ways, according to the ontological imaginaries they use to understand the disorder. Furthermore, as a consequence of the complex legal situation that emerged following the 2007 Mental Health Act of England and Wales, mental health practitioners were impelled to innovate. Accordingly, a range of therapies became widely regarded as (relatively) effective in treating personality disorder. Today, the kinds of treatments employed by clinicians working with those diagnosed with ASPD or other personality disorders are commonly psychotherapeutic techniques such as Dialectical Behaviour Therapy (DBT), often coincident with drug therapies to 'enable' the success of the psychotherapy through treating co-morbid disorders with which ASPD is often associated (for example, depression).

Such treatment programmes are commonly imagined and implemented within specially protected units (so-called Dangerous and Severe Personality Disorder, or DSPD, Units) within already high-secure facilities such as Broadmoor and Rampton Hospitals. A consequence of the political will to govern more effectively personality disorder that was so powerful in the early years of this century, these ambiguous institutions intersect the health and criminal justice systems. In so doing, they exemplify the long-standing tensions between policy and practice regarding whether ASPD is a psychiatric condition or a particularly acute form of 'normal' social deviancy. By acting as innovative 'treatment' centres for personality disorder, the DSPD Units have the potential to dissolve some of these tensions, and more firmly situate ASPD and similar conditions within a medical rubric. More profoundly, in trialling new ways of managing individuals with personality disorder, DSPD Units experiment with new ways of framing these conditions. In effect, they are what might be called 'laboratories of ontology', reconstituting what it is to have a disordered personality by shaping ideas about what these conditions are and how they might be acted upon.

More recently, the kinds of authoritative knowledge that health technologies such as ASPD specifically and the DSM in general enable biomedical investigators to produce have led to new speculation about their further potential uses in the innovation of law and policy. Some scientists have argued, for instance, that 'neuroimaging data could possibly inform questions of culpability, likelihood of future offense [sic] and prospects for rehabilitation'.[73] In response, members of the legal community have raised concerns that neurobiological research on antisociality and violence may 'be utilized to "prove" poor parenting' and 'to "predict" future criminality', with obvious ethical

---

[72] National Institute for Health and Clinical Excellence (NICE), *Antisocial Personality Disorder: Treatment, Management and Prevention, NICE Clinical Guideline 77* (2009), 28. Available at <www .nice.org.uk/nicemedia/pdf/CG77NICEGuideline.pdf>. The National Institute for Health and Clinical Excellence provides independent advice and recommendations to the National Health Service for England and Wales regarding drugs, devices, and other forms of interventions for a range of medical and public health issues; see R Steinbrook, 'Saying no isn't NICE—The Travails of Britain's National Institute for Health and Clinical Excellence' (2008) 359 *New England Journal of Medicine* 1977. NICE has no formal jurisdiction in Northern Ireland and Scotland, though its advice is commonly taken up in those countries.

[73] M Koenigs, A Basin-Sommers, J Zeier, and JP Newman, 'Investigating the Neural Correlates of Psychopathy' (2011) 16 *Molecular Psychiatry* 792, 792.

implications regarding the rights of already marginalized individuals.[74] As technologies such as the DSM and other standards such as the Psychopathy Checklist stimulate further innovative biomedical research, then, speculation continues about the ways in which the law itself and other institutions may change in order to regulate more effectively the care and treatment of the mentally ill. At the same time, debates about the legitimacy of these possible shifts play out—potentially looping back and impacting upon the social and technical actants in the networks through which they might occur. In effect, new health technologies thus do not simply stimulate new research which may intersect with legal matters: they play a role in shaping wider forms of social and technical developments that relate to each other in multiple and multi-layered ways. Law and regulation, technology and innovation, and mental health and subjectivity continue to complicate one another.

E. Conclusion

In this chapter I have interrogated the ways in which, in an era of costly, high-tech biomedical apparatuses and treatments, a simple book has acted—and continues to act—as an innovative health technology: one that radically recalibrated not only the mental health professions but contributed to the reshaping of law, science, and everyday life on an international scale. In decentring the novel and refusing an understanding of 'innovation' based solely on the claims of prominent scientists, clinicians, and institutions, I have instead highlighted alternative forms of innovative biomedical tools and techniques that have far-reaching effects on practice and regulation, stimulate new forms of experimental, clinical, and social life, and reshape subjectivities in Europe and worldwide.

One function of both law and technology is to reduce complexity; to make life run more smoothly, so as to order the natural and the social and more effectively govern interactions at both macro and micro scales.[75] Yet, as we have seen here, it is precisely through the interaction between law and biomedical innovation (especially in the form of the humble clinical standard) that the complexities of mental health are multiplied. Whilst regulation is commonly seen as a barrier to innovation, in the case of the mental health law and practice we can see how in fact it is important to understand socio-legal discourses and institutions as drivers: they can and do impel radical change in treatment, profoundly recasting the ontologies of the subjects they seek to habilitate. In the process, new questions about the administration and treatment of those deemed mentally ill, and the use of diagnostic and therapeutic innovations in relation to this, must be asked. In the case of controversial categories such as antisocial personality disorder, these may prove difficult to answer in ways that prove durable, legitimate, and ethical.

Let us assume, just for a moment, that ASPD is an unproblematic mental disorder that does need to be treated. But what does this mean? In her analysis of the competing philosophies of nature that structure debate regarding endangered species, sociologist Thompson shows that 'that idea that a species should be "saved" is not nearly as transparent as it first appears'.[76] Rather, multiple questions lurk beneath the

---

[74] C Walsh, 'Youth Justice and Neuroscience: A Dual-Use Dilemma' (2011) 51 *British Journal of Criminology* 21, 21.

[75] A Barry, 'In the Middle of the Network' in Law and Mol (n 9).

[76] C Thompson, 'When Elephants Stand for Competing Philosophies of Nature: Amboseli National Park, Kenya' in Law and Mol (n 9).

surface regarding 'what the species is to be saved from, by whom it is to be saved, how and where it is to be saved, and how and by whom conservation gains and setbacks will subsequently assessed'.[77] What Thompson is indicating here is that normative impulses mask a range of uncertainties. In the case of mental health, when we decide that some personality trait or constellation of behaviours is a psychiatric disorder—let us call it ASPD—that needs to be treated, we must then ask: *how* should it be treated? *Who* should take responsibility for this and *where* should it be implemented? *How* should such treatments be funded? *Which* individuals are eligible for access—in other words, who has the right to be treated? Again, in forensic mental health these questions have important legal and ethical dimensions and are politically resonant.

This chapter has thus posed many questions, but has replied with few answers. Instead, these problems have been highlighted in order to give a sense of some of the complexities that are so characteristic of the multiple nexus points between law and regulation, biomedical innovation, and mental health. In aiming to articulate these problematics, I have necessarily engaged in my own form of 'pragmatic reductionism' in order to lend some kind of coherence to an essentially complicated situation.[78] As in science itself, such simplification of the relationship between the technoscientific and the socio-legal is necessary in order to render the world legible and comprehensible.[79] As we simplify the relationships constitutive of new health technologies in order better to grapple with the social, legal, and ethical problematics they present us with and regulate them accordingly, we must necessarily also reflexively engage one another with the ontological politics of such representations. In essence, what kinds of simplifications should we make? Which do we have the right to make? In so doing, what do we bring to the fore and relegate to the background, and what are the ethical implications of this ordering?[80] Representation and simplification have normative dimensions, shaping our intellectual and regulatory responses to the messages that are conveyed. As such, they demand our attention and reflection.

---

[77] Thompson (n 76).

[78] cf S Beck and J Niewöhner, 'Somatographic Investigations across Levels of Complexity' (2006) 1 *BioSocieties* 219, 223.

[79] See, eg SL Star, 'Simplification in Scientific Work: An Example from Neuroscience Research' (1983) 13 *Social Studies of Science* 205.

[80] Mol and Law (n 9).

16

Where the Wild Things Are: Xenotechnologies and European Hybrid Regulation

Siân M Beynon-Jones and Nik Brown *

A. Introduction

The 'transbiologies' of xenotechnologies,[1] chimerism, and hybrid embryology occupy remote wild territories at the margins of what it means to be human, animal,[2] and even a species. And yet, whilst trans-species biological innovation proceeds apace, the legal framing of what is to be regulated has been arguably less creative. Regulation has been criticized for an overwhelming tendency to downplay the novel hybridity of new biomedical technologies, preserving instead largely human-centred frameworks of interpretation and institutional regulation.[3] Transbiologies are problematic for the very reason that the regulatory institutions, agencies, and bodies that govern them have certain species-centric qualities, outlooks, and histories.[4] Regulatory bodies can be said to mirror institutional interpretations of naturalistic species bodies existing 'out there' in the world

* The authors would like to thank Erich Griessler for his help in locating vital documentary material for the analysis. The work presented here was supported by the project 'Impact of Citizen Participation on Decision-Making in a Knowledge Intensive Policy Field' (CIT-PART), Contract Number: SSH-CT-2008-225327, funded by the European Commission within the 7th Framework Programme for Research—Socioeconomic Sciences and Humanities. The authors would like to thank the Commission for its contribution. For more details see <www.cit-part.at>.

[1] Commenting on the constantly evolving regulatory (re)definition of the term 'xenotransplantation', Marie Fox has coined the term 'xeno technologies' out of dissatisfaction with the term 'xenotransplantation's' inability to convey a sense of the diverse interventions to which it potentially refers (M Fox, 'Reconfiguring the Animal/Human Boundary: The Impact of Xeno Technologies' (2005) 26 *Liverpool Law Review* 149). These include the therapeutic transplantation of animal tissues into humans, the *ex-vivo* perfusion of human blood through animal tissues, and the transplantation into humans of human cells which have been in *ex-vivo* contact with animal cells. We have likewise adopted this useful expression—where appropriate—in the analysis that follows.

[2] While we recognize the problems inherent in this approach, we use the term 'animal' as shorthand for 'non-human animal' throughout this chapter.

[3] D Haraway, *Modest_Witness@Second_Millennium.FemaleMan©_Meets_OncoMouse™: Feminism and Technoscience* (Routledge 1997); L Birke and M Michael, 'The Heart of the Matter: Animal Bodies, Ethics, and Species Boundaries' (1998) 6 *Society and Animals* 245; N Brown, 'Xenotransplantation: Normalizing Disgust' (1999) 8 *Science as Culture* 327; S Squier, 'Negotiating boundaries: From Assisted Reproduction to Assisted Replication' in E A Kaplan and S Squier (eds), *Playing Dolly: Technocultural Formations, Fantasies, & Fictions of Assisted Reproduction* (Rutgers UP 1999); Fox (n 1); S Parry, 'Interspecies Entities and the Politics of Nature' in S Parry and J Dupre (eds), *Nature After the Genome* (Blackwell/Sociological Review 2010).

[4] N Brown and M Michael, 'Risky Creatures: Institutional Species Boundary Change in Biotechnology Regulation' (2004) 6 *Health, Risk & Society* 207; G Haddow and others, 'Not "human" enough to be human but not "animal" enough to be animal—the case of the HFEA, cybrids and xenotransplantation' (2010) 29 *New Genetics and Society* 3.

or in the laboratory.[5] That is, regulation[6] is structured through species-oriented forms of technical specialization, terms of reference, and disciplinary competence. Attempts to accommodate the novel ontologies of hybrid species entities within the provinces of existing regulatory jurisdiction thus lead inevitably to the material reconfiguration of the 'nature' of transbiological hybridity. In this chapter we demonstrate the powerful consequences of this process by exploring how the hybridity of xenotechnologies becomes reconfigured through their incorporation into European-level regulation.

Following intense policy debate about xenotechnologies during the late 1990s, a collapse in expectations concerning the future of this innovation has led to its widespread characterization as a 'failed' technology. Currently, however, xenotechnological scientific research (particularly, the potential utilization of pig islet cells as a treatment for human diabetes) actually continues at a comparable level to that which existed during the height of policy concern with xenotechnologies during the late 1990s.[7] This has prompted social scientists from a number of disciplines to emphasize the need for ongoing regulatory vigilance with regard to developments in this field.[8] While previous work[9] has reviewed and considered the implications of the European-level regulation of xenotechnologies for (primarily) humans and (to a lesser extent) animals, no previous studies have explored how such regulation (re)configures the materiality of xenotechnologies in terms of the human-animal *relationships* which they embody. It is to this gap in the literature concerning the co-construction of regulation and human-animal relations that our analysis speaks.

In what follows, we draw upon hybrid theory and conceptualization in the work of prominent scholars, specifically, Derrida, Agamben, Santner, Latour, and Haraway, whose interest has centred on the historical, political, and legal interstices between the human and the animal. For Derrida, law itself is founded on the categorical binary that puts the realm of the beastly (*la bête*) beneath the law, whilst elevating the sovereign above it. In other words, and importantly for our discussion here, law's secret origins lie in the exception, the exclusion, the casting out into the 'wild' of the animal. This exclusion is incredibly fragile depending, as it does, upon the fact that the animal is always and remains inside the law of the human. It is the very category of the beastly that ultimately makes possible the legal constitutional standing of the human. As Derrida puts it, 'We must consider that there are "living creatures" whose plurality is not grouped under the single category of the animal kingdom in simple contrast to mankind.'[10]

Similarly, Agamben references the origins of law back to the separation of bare life (*zoe*) from legally qualified or protected life (*bios*).[11] The classical legal figure, *homo sacer*, is one who can be killed with impunity, one who is cast into the wild. This

    [5] Brown and Michael (n 4).

    [6] In what follows, we use the term regulation to encompass both 'hard' law and 'soft law', for example policy and guidance documents.

    [7] SM Beynon-Jones and N Brown, 'Time, Timing and Narrative at the Interface Between UK Technoscience and Policy' (2011) 38 *Science and Public Policy* 639.

    [8] S McLean and L Williamson, 'The Demise of UKXIRA and the Regulation of Solid-Organ Xenotransplantation in the UK' (2007) 33 *Journal of Medical Ethics* 373; L Williamson, M Fox and S McLean, 'The Regulation of Xenotransplantation in the United Kingdon after UKXIRA: Legal and Ethical Issues' (2007) 34 *Journal of Law and Society* 441; M Tallacchini and S Beloucif, 'Regulatory Issues in Xenotransplantation: Recent Developments' (2009) 14 *Current Opinion in Organ Transplantation* 180; Beynon-Jones and Brown (n 7).

    [9] Tallacchini and Beloucif (n 8); E Griessler and others, *The Challenge of Public Participation in a Multilevel System: EU Xenotransplantation Policies* (Institute for Advanced Studies <www.cit-part.at/CIT-PART_EU.pdf> accessed 18 June 2012).

    [10] J Derrida, 'The Animal That Therefore I Am (More to Follow)' (2003) 28 *Critical Inquiry* 415.

    [11] G Agamben, *Homo Sacer: Sovereign Power and Bare Life* (Stanford UP 1998); G Agamben, *The Open: Man and Animal* (Stanford UP 2004).

'casting out' and exclusion from within the threshold of politically protected life is the foundational substrate of law. The freedom to kill effectively allows all politically qualified life to act as sovereign, *homines sacri*. Such acts of exclusion are not the exception but the rule, the rule of law. Nevertheless, it is important not to overstate the similarities between Derrida and Agamben on their conceptions of the origins of law, the human, and sovereignty. Agamben draws something of a binary dichotomous distinction between bare and qualified life, an absolute plane or horizon between the two. His interest in the concentration camp as an illustration of the line between bare and political life is perhaps telling of his greater concern with humans than with animals, and tacit consent to their separability.

Derrida, however, is critical of any such absolutes, recognizing that the human and animal always presuppose each other, entailing both at once. The point for Derrida is to go further than Agamben by exploring the implications of biopolitics not just for the human but for the animal within the human and its impact on the lived lives of both humans *and* non-humans. This echoes themes central also to Santner's thinking on what he calls 'creaturely life', those forms of life 'abandoned' and 'discarded' to states of obscurity and invisibility.[12] He has argued, like others referred to here, for a more open acknowledgement of creaturely bodies as an important 'resource for new kinds of social links'.[13] These differing insights are relevant to our discussion, we would argue, because of the paradoxical regulatory tendency to 'play-down' the animals upon which xeno-technologies depend, and the hybrid natures they are intended to bring into being.

There are parallels here with Latour's point that modernity, not just the law, has relied upon a constitutional split between a science that speaks for non-human natures and a politics that represents human subjects.[14] Modernity is in question, he contends, because behind this artificial bifurcation lies an unacknowledged truth, a constant flux of hybridity generated through the mediated translation of humans and non-humans, politics and science, culture and nature. The modern constitution structurally denies hybridity (through 'purification') whilst in turn actually accelerating hybrid prolifer-ation ('translation'). This is important for our analysis, which illustrates how the denial of trans-species hybridity in European regulation, in turn serves to facilitate and expedite trans-species hybrid innovation in the form of xenotechnologies. Methodo-logically, we employ a detailed document-based historical comparison of the two principal legal orders through which 'Europe', as an increasingly supranational regula-tory 'space', has addressed xenotechnologies. Our analysis demonstrates that regulation by first, the Council of Europe and, subsequently, the European Union (EU) has progressively erased consideration of the technology's implications for the manage-ment, husbandry, welfare, and suffering of xenotechnologies' source animals.

Taken together, both of these regulatory developments illustrate our central argu-ment that the animal, or the creaturely in Santner's terms, has increasingly been effaced through processes of species (human-centric) purification. In line with the theorizations of hybridity described earlier, we highlight that this intensification in purification of the animal from the human makes the proliferation of xenotechnological hybrids all the more likely. At the same time, however, we identify relative *gradations* of purifying decontamination and associated hybrid proliferation throughout the history of the regulation of xenotechnologies in Europe. Specifically, initial regulation produced by

---

[12] EL Santner, *On Creaturely Life. Rilke, Benjamin, Sebald* (University of Chicago Press 2006).
[13] Santner (n 12) 30.
[14] B Latour, *We Have Never Been Modern* (Harvard UP 1993).

the Council of Europe[15] recognizes (albeit to a limited extent), the unprecedented way in which xenotechnologies mutually implicate humans and animals through their uniquely hybrid corporeality. However, formal recognition of this hybridity becomes completely depleted and concealed as we draw nearer to the present through consideration of the EU's subsequent incorporation of xenotechnologies into the regulatory regime of medicinal products legislation (and its associated policy guidance).[16] Our comparison of these two sites of regulation prompts us to look beyond the seemingly fixed binaries of much existing hybrid theory, which has tended to characterize the production and regulation of the human/animal interface in terms of dichotomous absolutes, in particular, inclusion/exclusion and translation/purification. Instead, we suggest, it is necessary to interrogate the subtleties, gradations, and nuances of purification, erasure, and abandonment. The denial (and consequent production) of hybrids is not absolute, we argue, but relative and variable with shifting thresholds and horizons according to different sites of regulation.

Our illustration of this phenomenon recalls Haraway's argument that the theorization of human/non-human hybridity is of limited significance if analysis stops short of critically interrogating the specificities of particular *kinds* of hybrid. Haraway draws upon the figure of 'OncoMouse^{TM}', a transgenic mouse engineered to develop human cancers (and patented by drug companies) and asks:

For whom does OncoMouse^{TM} live and die?...Who lives and dies...because OncoMouse^{TM} exists? What does OncoMouse^{TM} offer when...death rates in the United States for African American women from breast cancer increased 21 per cent, while death rates for white women remained the same...Is the suffering caused to research organisms balanced by the relief of human suffering?[17]

---

[15] Recommendation No. R (97) of the Committee of Ministers to the Member States on Xenotransplantation (1997 <www.coe.int/t/dg3/healthbioethic/texts_and_documents/Rec(97)15E.pdf> accessed 19 June 2012; Recommendation 1399 (1999) of the Parliamentary Assembly to the Committee of Ministers on Xenotransplantation <www.assembly.coe.int/Main.asp?link=/Documents/AdoptedText/ta99/EREC 1399.htm> accessed 21 June 2012; Xenotransplantation Recommendation 1399 (1999): Reply from the Committee of Ministers (1999) <www.assembly.coe.int/Mainf.asp?link=/Documents/WorkingDocs/Doc99/EDOC8363.htm> accessed 19 June 2012; 'Report on the State of the Art in the Field of Xenotransplantation' CDBI/CDSP-XENO (2003) 1 <www.coe.int/t/dg3/healthbioethic/Activities/06_Xenotransplantation_en/XENO(2003)1_SAR.pdf> accessed 19 June 2012; 'Explanatory Report to Recommendation Rec(2003) 10 of the Committee of Ministers to Member States on Xenotransplantation' CDBI/INF (2003) 12 <www.coe.int/t/dg3/healthbioethic/activities/06_xenotransplantation_en/INF_2003_12exenoER.pdf> accessed 19 June 2012; Recommendation Rec(2003)10 of the Committee of Ministers to member states on xenotransplantation <http://wcd.coe.int/ViewDoc.jsp?id = 45827> accessed 19 June 2012.

[16] In exploring this regulatory regime our analysis encompasses the following legislation and guidance: Directive 2001/20/EC of the European Parliament and of the Council of 4 April 2001 on the approximation of the laws, regulations and administrative provisions of the Member States relating to the implementation of good clinical practice in the conduct of clinical trials on medicinal products for human use [2001] OJ L121/34; Commission Directive 2003/63/EC of 25 June 2003 amending Directive 2001/83/EC of the European Parliament and of the Council on the Community code relating to medicinal products for human use [2003] OJ L159/46; Regulation (EC) No 1394/2007 of the European Parliament and of the Council of 13 November 2007 on advanced therapy medicinal products and amending Directive 2001/83/EC and Regulation (EC) No 726/2004 [2007] L324/121; Commission Directive 2009/120/EC of 14 September 2009 amending Directive 2001/83/EC of the European Parliament and of the Council on the Community code relating to medicinal products for human use as regards advanced therapy medicinal products [2009] L242/3; 'Guideline on Human Cell-Based Medicinal Products' (EMEA/CHMP/410869/2006) <www.emea.europa.eu/docs/en_GB/document_library/Scientific_guideline/2009/09/WC500003894.pdf.> accessed 18 June 2012; 'Guideline on Xenogeneic Cell-Based Medicinal Products' (EMEA/CHMP/CPWP/83508/2009) <www.ema.europa.eu/docs/en_GB/document_library/Scientific_guideline/2009/12/WC500016936.pdf> accessed 18 June 2012.

[17] Haraway (n 3) 113.

Taking our cue from Haraway, our analysis of the regulation of xenotechnologies in Europe centres explicitly upon the implications of this process for humans and other animals. Its findings offer important insights for legal scholars concerned with the future regulation of novel trans-species entities, both in Europe and beyond this context.

B. Gradations of Purification: Two Sites of European 'Hybrid' Regulation

1. Xenotechnologies Within the Council of Europe

The first attempt to develop a European-level response to the emergence of xeno-technologies within Europe came from the Council of Europe in the form of Recommendation No R 97 (15).[18] This raised questions about xenotechnologies' disruption of species boundaries, in particular, the possibility that they could allow new diseases to be transmitted between animals and humans. On this basis, it recommended that Member States should establish appropriate regulatory measures to deal with xenotechnologies. This was followed by Recommendation 1399 (1999)[19] through which the Parliamentary Assembly of the Council of Europe again drew attention to the possibility of trans-species disease and asked the Committee of Ministers to work towards the introduction of a legally binding moratorium on clinical (animal to human) xenotransplanation in all Member States. In highlighting the problems generated by xenotechnologies' hybrid nature, the Assembly explicitly acknowledged the intimate and mutual indivisibility of human and animal potential harms: 'There are considerable scientific, medical, ethical, social, and legal problems that should be answered before clinical xenotransplantations proceed. The ethical problems include the acceptability of xenotransplantations *as regards both humans and animals*.'[20]

Simultaneously, however, this acknowledgement implicitly frames the hybridity of the human-animal as, to some extent at least, a phenomenon which can be disaggregated, purified, and treated separately. As Latour puts it, this version of hybridity is in fact 'a mixture of two pure forms'[21] disentangled from one another (the Parliamentary Assembly highlights ethical problems 'as regards both humans *and* animals', rather than human-animal hybrids). As we elaborate later, this initial process of purification was rendered increasingly significant and explicit throughout the development of the Council of Europe's response to xenotechnologies.

Although it recommended that a moratorium be placed upon clinical xenotransplantation, the Parliamentary Assembly simultaneously asked the Council to formulate a working group to produce 'a strategy for balancing the ethical, medical, scientific, legal, social and public health aspects of xenotransplantation, before the scientific and medical establishment is permitted to proceed with clinical trials on humans'.[22] The implication here is that, following an initial period of caution, regulation should eventually be able to resolve the challenges posed by xenotechnologies' disruption of

---

[18] Recommendation No R (97) (n 15).
[19] Recommendation 1399 (1999) (n 15).
[20] Recommendation 1399 (1999) para 5 (emphasis added).
[21] Latour (n 14) 78.
[22] Recommendation 1399 (1999) (n 15) para 6iii.

species boundaries. As Felt and others[23] have illustrated, this approach is typical of broader regulatory approaches to innovation within Europe in recent decades, which have focused on the management of the downstream consequences of controversial technologies. This framing of the regulatory role implicitly positions all innovations as acceptable in principle and precludes deliberation concerning more 'upstream' questions (for example, the visions of society which are implicit in the decision to pursue particular forms of technology).[24] However, while the silencing of such 'upstream' deliberation was undoubtedly important in the regulation of xenotechnologies,[25] our interest here is with the implications of this framing of the regulatory role for xeno-technologies' species hybridity. Specifically, our concern is with the way that the positioning of regulatory hurdles as resolvable in principle opened the way for a further cleaving of the animal from the human. The interdisciplinary Working Party which the Committee of Ministers subsequently formulated was tasked with providing a report on xenotransplantation, as well as with developing draft guidelines. Its construction and work reflected the Parliamentary Assembly's prior framing of xenotechnologies as both 'hybrid' and 'purifiable'. This framing is visible in its terms of reference, which were to take into account: 'the various interests involved (in particular the fundamental rights of the patients, the public health goals, the priorities in health care, the *animal protection* and the interests of industry)'.[26] Simultaneously, human and animal interests are linked together through xenotechnologies and are hierarchically separated. Human recipients, in the form of patients, have 'fundamental rights', whereas source animals, whilst having relevant interests, require only 'protection'.

In keeping with this framing, the Working Party's Report[27] goes on to highlight and differentiate the threat that xenotechnologies' disruption of species boundaries poses both to humans and to animals. For humans, the Report draws attention to the risk that animal tissues will prove incompatible with the bodies of human patients into which they are incorporated (both physiologically and immunologically). These risks extend to the possibility that viruses carried by animals may prove *too* compatible with human patients, generating potentially pandemic threats to the health of the human population as a whole.[28] In the case of animals, the Report argues that, in addition to the obvious point that animal lives would have to be sacrificed to provide tissues for human use, the decision to pursue this clinical endeavour would represent a commitment to using thousands of animals during a vast pre-clinical experimental stage. Moreover, the Report also points out that, if clinical

---

[23] U Felt and others, *Expert group on science and governance. Taking European knowledge society seriously* (European Commission DG Research Science, Economy and Society 2007).

[24] A large body of literature has discussed this phenomenon. For examples, see B Wynne, 'Creating public alienation: Expert cultures of risk and ethics on GMOs' (2001) 10 *Science as Culture* 445; J Wilsdon and R Willis, *See-through Science: Why Public Engagement Needs to Move Upstream* (Demos 2004); A Irwin, 'The Politics of Talk: Coming to Terms with the "New" Scientific Governance' (2006) 36 *Social Studies of Science* 299.

[25] Felt and others (n 23); Beynon-Jones and Brown (n 7).

[26] Xenotransplantation Recommendation 1399 (1999): Reply from the Committee of Ministers (1999) (n 15) para 4b (emphasis added).

[27] 'Report on the State of the Art in the Field of Xenotransplantation' CDBI/CDSP-XENO (2003) 1 (n 15).

[28] For in-depth analyses of the ways in which these human/animal similarities and differences have been mobilized in public/regulatory discussion of xenotechnologies see Birke and Michael (n 3); N Brown, 'Debates in xenotransplantation: On the consequences of contradiction' (1999) 18 *New Genetics and Society* 181; Brown (n 3); N Brown and M Michael, 'Switching between Science and Culture in Transpecies Transplantation' (2001) 26 *Science, Technology, & Human Values* 3; Fox (n 1).

xenotransplantation did eventually become feasible, then source animals would have to be reared in extremely restrictive conditions in order to reduce the threat of trans-species disease transmission to humans. This latter point signals more than anything the uniquely problematic and novel features of xenotechnological hybridity:

physical health is only one component of overall welfare since the social and behavioural needs must also be satisfied. This is where there is a serious conflict of interests between the needs of the animals and the likely requirements of any xenotransplantation breeding and source animal programme. In order to maintain a disease free status, animals will need to be reared in a sterile environment in which it may be difficult, if not impossible, to provide for their behavioural needs.[29]

However, as noted earlier, while the Report contains multiple acknowledgements of the new connections which xenotechnologies forge between humans and animals, these connections are not taken to problematize underlying species hierarchical classifications. Instead, the Report re-inscribes conventional species hierarchies, thus purifying the troubling hybridity of xenotechnologies. A clear illustration of this process is provided by the Report's framing of the requirements that xenotechnologies ask of animals:

The first, and most significant, is whether as a matter of principle it is considered to be morally acceptable to use animals as a source of organs... If it is agreed that this is acceptable then there are questions to address regarding the limits that should be imposed on such use and the welfare of animals within any xenotransplantation programme... [I]t is important to consider whether high standards of humane care from birth to death of the animal can be ensured.[30]

By defining the central issue as a question of whether xenotechnologies represent an acceptable human 'use' of animals, this framing implicitly reinstates a hierarchical binary in which animals are positioned instrumentally as a potential resource for humans—as does the reference to the importance of acting 'humanely'[31] towards this resource. This dichotomy is then reinforced through the Report's discussion of the central questions concerning the permissible 'use' of animals:

A *logical* discussion of the use... needs to take into account the *existing relationship* between animals and humans and *what is currently considered acceptable* in this respect.... If some use is accepted, it is then necessary to determine what is, or is not, considered acceptable.... Animals are already widely used within human societies for a variety of purposes... food, clothing, companionship, for entertainment and as 'tools' for research in the biomedical sciences. Their tissues, for example pig heart valves and skin, are also used for medical purposes.[32]

Rehearsing and restating established social conventions, in which parallels are drawn between xenotransplantation and a wide range of superficially mundane uses to which animal bodies are put, clearly serves to purify the technology's potent and novel trans-species hybridity. Referring back to Latour's 'modern constitution', these dichotomizing distinctions firmly re-inscribe xenotechnologies within a long-standing and extensive system of hierarchical binaries. Humans are positioned as political cultural subjects or agents looming over their non-human natural objects. As both Derrida and Agamben

---

[29] 'Report on the State of the Art in the Field of Xenotransplantation' (n 15) 71.
[30] 'Report on the State of the Art in the Field of Xenotransplantation' (n 15) 69.
[31] R Twine, 'Searching for the "Win-Win"? Animals, Genomics and Welfare' (2007) 15 *International Journal of Sociology of Agriculture and Food* 8.
[32] 'Report on the State of the Art in the Field of Xenotransplantation' (n 15) 69–70 (emphasis added).

put it, the constitutionality of these rights over life elevates the human above the animal within the law, excluding the latter whilst raising the former to sovereign status. These techniques of mundane normalization were just as central to early UK policy work concerning xenotransplantation.[33] Indeed, the Report frequently cites this prior British analysis of the 'ethical issues' and restates its significance in framing the Working Party's deliberations.

In sum, the Parliamentary Assembly's founding assumption was that regulation could potentially render xenotransplantation's hybridity manageable. The Report consolidates and strengthens that position by articulating and rehearsing the parallels and similarities between this novel use of animals and more conventional ones. Subsequently, Rec(2003) 10,[34] the Recommendation provided to Member States by the Council on the basis of the Report, went on to purify the human/animal boundary in an even more explicitly hierarchical fashion by outlining 'stringent and demanding'[35] regulatory conditions through which to contain the dangers of xenotechnologies' troubling species boundary transgressions, whilst pursuing the use of (particular) animals for human therapies. In keeping with this privileging of human over animal well-being, Rec(2003) 10 also devotes far more space to reducing the risks posed by animals to humans, than it does to those threats posed by humans to animals. Member States' regulatory responsibilities in the latter case are limited to safeguarding the welfare of source and pre-clinical trial animals (for example, satisfying behavioural needs). However, in the context of EU legislation concerning xenotechnologies, to which we now turn, even these fairly minimal requirements become excluded from the focus of the developing regulatory gaze.

2. Xenotechnologies within EU Medicinal Products Legislation

In contrast to the Council of Europe's comparatively early intervention in 1997, the EU's first attempt to regulate xenotechnologies did not take place until the early 2000s. Within the EU, xenotechnologies are first referenced in an opinion paper produced by the European Commission's Scientific Committee on Medicinal Products and Medical Devices (SCMPMD).[36] Echoing the discussion within the Council of Europe, this paper focuses particularly on the possibility that xenotechnologies will generate trans-species disease and advises that, in view of the fact that such disease 'will not be limited by geographic boundaries',[37] it is important to generate binding supranational regulation of xenotechnologies. Significantly, the SCMPMD paper references the earlier work by the Council of Europe, which illustrates that concrete links existed between the Council of Europe and the EU as regards the regulation of xenotechnologies. However, as we will go on to illustrate, in spite of the EU's awareness of this prior regulatory work, the manner in which it went on to establish oversight of xenotechnologies produced a very different configuration of their species hybridity.[38] Specifically,

---

[33] Fox (n 1); Beynon-Jones and Brown (n 7).

[34] Recommendation Rec(2003) 10 of the Committee of Ministers to Member States on xeno-transplantation (n 15).

[35] 'Explanatory Report to Recommendation Rec(2003) 10 of the Committee of Ministers to Member States on Xenotransplantation' (n 15) 3.

[36] 'Opinion on the State of the Art Concerning Xenotransplantation' (SANCO/SCMPMD/2001/0002) <http://ec.europa.eu/food/fs/sc/scmp/out38_en.pdf> accessed 18 June 2012.

[37] 'Opinion on the State of the Art Concerning Xenotransplantation' (n 36) para 11.

[38] As Griessler and others (n 9) illustrate in their analysis of the production and aftermath of the SCMPMD paper, it is difficult to elucidate what, if any, impact this committee's opinion had on the subsequent regulation of xenotechnologies within the EU.

the EU has chosen to engage in the 'pharmaceuticalising'[39] of xenotechnologies by incorporating them into legislation applied to medicinal products for human use. By tracking xenotechnologies' inclusion within this regulatory regime, we demonstrate how this process has further erased the non-human, and in particular has reduced the scope of regulatory consideration of the technology's dependence on animals.

Abraham and Lewis[40] note in their history of EU medicinal products legislation, that this regulatory regime has been developed with explicit reference to two key (and potentially antagonistic) priorities. These are, first, the protection of EU (human) public health through the implementation of standards for the safety of medicinal products and, secondly, the promotion of the economic growth of the EU pharmaceutical industry through the harmonization of Member State regulations in order to create an internal market for medicinal products. In highlighting the resonance of the latter aim with pharmaceutical industry interests, Abraham and Lewis note the disproportionately greater influence of those working within this sector upon the dynamics of this regulatory regime. Faulkner and others have also illustrated the silences and gaps generated by the application of EU medicinal products legislation's narrowly restrictive 'organizing principles' to the novel field of human tissue engineering (TE).[41] They draw attention to the way the prioritization of safety and economic growth has excluded discussion of the relative therapeutic *efficacy* of TE products in comparison to existing treatments, allowing assessments of clinical benefit to escape critical interrogation.

Additional deliberative lacunas in relation to TE result from the way responsibility for different priorities (public safety and economic benefit) reflect an EU-level division of labour and contrasting institutional 'species identities'.[42] Legislation concerning the sourcing and procurement of human cells and tissues[43] was formulated by DG-SANCO responsible for public health. Commercialization of these materials was addressed by DG Enterprise and Industry—via a separate body of legislation concerning the manufacturing of medicinal products (discussed later). The Commission's insistence on the legislative separation of these two issues—procurement versus commercialization—has stifled attempts to discuss the relationship between the two processes, for example that the ends to which human tissue is put may be relevant to the bodies from whom it is sourced.[44]

[39] A Faulkner, *Medical Technology into Healthcare and Society: A Sociology of Devices, Innovation and Governance* (Palgrave Macmillan 2009) 176.

[40] J Abraham and G Lewis, *Regulating Medicines in Europe: Competition, Expertise and Public Health* (Routledge 2000).

[41] A Faulkner and others, 'Tissue-Engineered Technologies: Scientific Biomedicine, Frames of Risk and Regulatory Regime Building in Europe' (2008) 17 *Science as Culture* 195.

[42] A Faulkner and others, 'Purity and the Dangers of Regenerative Medicine: Regulatory Innovation of Human Tissue-Engineered Technology' (2006) 63 *Social Science & Medicine* 2277; J Kent and others, 'Towards Governance of Human Tissue-Engineered Technologies in Europe: Framing the Case for a New Regulatory Regime' (2006) 73 *Technological Forecasting and Social Change* 41; Faulkner and others (n 41); M Tallacchini, 'Governing by Values. EU Ethics: Soft Tool, Hard Effects' (2009) 47 *Minerva* 281.

[43] Directive 2004/23/EC of the European Parliament and of the Council of 31 March 2004 on setting standards of quality and safety for the donation, procurement, testing, processing, preservation, storage and distribution of human tissues and cells [2004] OJ L102/48. Hereafter, this legislation is referred to as the Human Tissues and Cells Directive.

[44] Faulkner and others (n 42); Kent and others (n 42).

In summary, existing social scientific analyses of the regulatory regime of EU medicinal products legislation have drawn attention to two key issues. First, the narrow set of problems given priority, namely, economic growth and [human] public health. Secondly, the ease with which the manufacture and commercialization of products based on living human cells/tissues has become separated from prior questions about the procurement of these materials from human bodies. Given these regulatory 'species characteristics', it may seem obvious that the incorporation of xenotechnologies into this regulatory regime would not be accompanied by any particular acknowledgement of the animal tissue source. Nonetheless, in what follows we demonstrate that a complete understanding of the way this effacement is sustained necessitates a more in-depth textual analysis of medicinal products legislation than has been provided by existing literature. In particular, we emphasize the manner through which the legislation's classificatory hierarchies (re)configure the hybridity of xenotechnologies as regulatory objects.

a. Flattening species' differences

In 2003, an important series of amendments to existing EU legislation concerning the marketing authorization of medicinal products for human use was introduced through Directive 2003/63/EC.[45] One of the key aims of this Directive was to regulate a set of therapeutic materials not yet accommodated within existing EU legislation, and to outline the marketing authorization requirements to be applied to them. The amended legislation introduces the term 'advanced therapy medicinal products' (ATMPs) to capture this novel group of therapies:

The treatment of... pathological dysfunctions in humans calls upon novel concept-based approaches based on the development of biotechnology techniques. The latter involve the *use of advanced therapy medicinal* products based on processes focused on various gene-transfer-produced bio-molecules (gene therapy medicinal products) and manipulated or processed cells (cell therapy medicinal products) as active substances. In so far as *they achieve their essential action through metabolic, physiological and immunological means to restore, correct or modify physiological functions in humans*, these novel complex therapeutic products representing [sic] a new category of biological medicinal products....[46]

A crucial feature of this definition is that it is grounded in the species specific classificatory hierarchy which has traditionally been central to EU medicinal products legislation.[47] That is, the legislation prioritizes the *mode-of-action* of a medicinal product and the way in which it achieves a particular function within human bodies. As becomes evident in the extracts that follow, this future-oriented focus on a product's therapeutic mode-of-action is also reflected in the way the Directive defines the two key ATMPs which are its objects of regulatory concern: gene therapy and somatic cell therapy. Together, these definitions mutually frame xenotechnologies in terms of their actions within human bodies by restoring a human body's ability to function. This, we argue, represents a key mechanism of purification erasing the wider and more tendrilous network of dependence between human biotechnological projects and animal lives and bodies. To make this point it is worth citing the Commission at length:

---

[45] Commission Directive 2003/63/EC (n 16).
[46] Recitals 9 and 10 (emphasis added).
[47] See eg Kent and others (n 42).

GENE THERAPY MEDICINAL PRODUCTS (HUMAN OR XENOGENEIC)... shall mean a product *obtained through a set of manufacturing processes aimed at the transfer, to be performed either in vivo or ex vivo, of a prophylactic, diagnostic or therapeutic gene* (i.e. a piece of nucleic acid), *to human/animal cells and its subsequent expression in vivo.* The gene transfer involves an expression system contained in a delivery system known as a vector ... The vector can also be included in a human or animal cell.[48]

SOMATIC CELL THERAPY MEDICINAL PRODUCTS (HUMAN AND XENO-GENEIC)... shall mean *the use in humans* of autologous (emanating from the patient himself), allogeneic (coming from another human being) or xenogeneic (coming from animals) somatic living cells, *the biological characteristics of which have been substantially altered as a result of their manipulation to obtain a therapeutic, diagnostic or preventive effect through metabolic, pharmacological and immunological means.* This manipulation includes the expansion or activation of autologous cell populations ex vivo (e.g., adoptive immuno-therapy), the use of allogeneic and xenogeneic cells associated with medical devices used ex vivo or in vivo (e.g., microcapsules, intrinsic matrix scaffolds, bio-degradable or not).[49]

An additional feature of these definitions is the clear significance which they attribute to the *processes* through which the functions of ATMPs are achieved; an emphasis which is also illustrated by a subsequent Commission statement concerning the distinctive nature of this group of products: 'They are based on complex, highly innovative manufacturing processes. The specificity of the product precisely lies *in* the process.'[50] This classificatory hierarchy (that is, the prioritization of the question of the *mode-of-action* of a medicinal product within human bodies, and the *process* through which this mode-of-action is produced) results in the species origins of ATMPs being positioned as a secondary (bracketed) concern. Through this deprioritization of species differences, human and animal tissues within the legislation become substitutable starting materials for particular kinds of manufacturing process/mode-of-action (gene therapy or somatic cell therapy). Framing the species involved in this way obscures the very asymmetrical legal protections accorded to human donors of tissues (for example, the consent requirements detailed in the Human Tissues and Cells Directive) versus animals reared and killed to provide tissues for xenogeneic therapies.

Directive 2003/63 has been updated by Regulation No 1394/2007 (hereafter, 'the Regulation on advanced therapies').[51] Its key aim was to address ongoing disparities between Member States' regulation of ATMPs by clarifying the definition of such products and making centralized European Medicines Agency (EMA) approval compulsory prior to their marketing within the EU. The major change which the Regulation on advanced therapies enacted was to extend the category of ATMPs contained within Directive 2003/63/EC. As outlined earlier, this added the third category of TE to those of 'gene therapy' and 'somatic cell therapy'. While many of the tensions involved in this process of classificatory extension have been explored by the existing literature,[52] the Regulation on advanced therapies' implications for the

---

[48] Commission Directive 2003/63/EC (n 16), Annex 1, Part IV, para 1 (emphasis added).
[49] Annex 1, Part IV, para 2 (emphasis added).
[50] Proposal for a Regulation of the European Parliament and of the Council on advanced therapy medicinal products and amending Directive 2001/83/EC and Regulation (EC) No 726/2004 2005/0227 (COD) <eur-lex.europa.eu/LexUriServ/LexUriServ.do?uri=COM:2005:0567:FIN:EN:PDF> accessed 21 June 2012 2 (emphasis in original).
[51] Regulation No 1394/2007 (n 16).
[52] N Brown and others, 'Regulating Hybrids: "Making a Mess" and "Cleaning Up" in Tissue Engineering and Transpecies Transplantation' (2006) 4 *Social Theory and Health* 1; Faulkner (n 39).

classification of human/animal boundaries have not previously been considered. This represents an important omission because, through its definition of TE, the Regulation clearly extends and perpetuates the flattening of species differences identified earlier. Echoing Directive 2003/63, it renders species origins secondary to the question of the mode-of-action of TE medicinal products and the processes through which they are produced. In doing so, it presents animal and human cells/tissues as effectively equivalent, interchangeable substances:

'Tissue engineered product' means a product that: contains or consists of engineered cells or tissues, and; is presented as having properties for, or is used in or administered to human beings with a view to regenerating, repairing or replacing a human tissue. A tissue-engineered product may contain cells or tissues of human or animal origin, or both.[53]

Furthermore, in the wake of the Regulation on advanced therapies, the Commission has moved to update its existing definitions of requirements concerning gene and somatic cell therapy through a new Directive.[54] This renders potential differences in the species origins of such products almost completely invisible. The new definitions of gene and somatic cell therapies which the new Directive contains focus *exclusively* on their mode-of-action within human bodies and the manufacturing process through which this mode-of-action is produced. Little, if any, reference is made to the species origins of the biological materials upon which such products are based. The only sites at which the species identity of these materials are (briefly) mentioned as a relevant consideration are in acknowledgement of the more stringent risk assessments necessitated by the utilization of cells derived from animals (a point to which we return later).

These observations concerning the 'pharmaceuticalising' of xenotechnologies resonate with previous work which has addressed recent revisions to UK legislation on the licensing of trans-species embryo research. Brown[55] shows how a pro-research lobby strategically emphasized the nuclear (human), rather than mitochondrial (animal), DNA as the key determinant of the species' identity of research embryos. This made it possible for regulation to designate so-called 'cybrid' embryos (created from the insertion of a human cell into an enucleated animal egg) as de facto 'human' entities. This privileging of the human was also reflected in the Department of Health's preference for the term 'human admixed embryos', downplaying animal or transspecies aspects of the proposed research. Similar rhetorical shifts were found in the discourse of scientists who increasingly spoke of 'despeciation' instead of the more conventional 'denucleation' when describing the standard practice of removing nuclear DNA from animal ova. Brown's central argument is that the UK's incorporation of trans-species embryos into a 'human' regulatory regime represents the successful outcome of the pro-research lobby's attempts firmly to re-inscribe speciesist hierarchies and obscure animal involvement in the production of these entities. As we have argued earlier, the flattening of species' differences within EU medicinal products legislation can likewise be understood as a hierarchical process of purification, through which animal suffering and sacrifice in the production of human therapies is successfully erased.

---

[53] Regulation No 1394/2007 (n 16) Art 2(1)(b).
[54] Directive 2009/120/EC (n 16).
[55] N Brown, 'Beasting the Embryo: The Metrics of Humanness in the Transpecies Embryo Debate' (2009) 4 *Biosocieties* 147.

b. Domesticating the wild: xenotechnologies as medicinal products

The EU's classification of xenotechnologies as medicinal products institutionalizes a process of purification by collapsing and de-emphasizing otherwise troubling species differences. As Santner might put it, this is a process of domestication and taming, an effacement of the specific creatureliness of the species bodies involved. However, the work involved in managing trans-species hybridity nonetheless continues to resurface throughout medicinal products legislation, as well as within the associated guidance produced by the EMA. The difficulties of amalgamating xenotechnologies into the EU's regulation of human medicinal products is perhaps most explicit in medicinal products legislation's invocation of the principle of 'ethical subsidiarity'.[56] Faulkner and others employ this term to capture EU regulators' tendency to negotiate intractable debates concerning the morality of utilizing specific kinds of biological material in research and therapies, in particular human embryonic stem cells. This is achieved by remaining silent on questions of 'ethics' and attempting to regulate only on 'technical' matters, in particular those of risks to human subjects.[57]

The employment of this strategy as a means of managing xenotechnologies' hybridity is visible from the first occasion on which xenotechnologies enter EU medicinal products legislation. Directive 2001/20/EC,[58] which concerns good clinical practice in the conduct of clinical trials of medicinal products for human use, makes it mandatory for those seeking to conduct clinical trials to obtain approval from the relevant Member State Ethics Committee and/or appropriate regulatory authority, placing a limit upon the length of time allowed for this process of authorization. However, it *extends* this time limit in the case of medicinal products for gene therapy, somatic cell therapy, and products based on genetic modification processes—removing it completely in the case of xenogeneic cell therapy medicinal products. As Griessler and others argue,[59] this regulation effectively devolves decision-making about the acceptability of xenotechnologies to Member States, because it allows them to impose a de facto moratorium on their clinical use in humans (via indefinite delay of Ethics Committee decisions). A related approach is clear within the more recent Regulation on advanced therapies statement that:

The regulation of advanced therapy medicinal products at Community level should not interfere with decisions made by Member States on whether to allow the use of any specific type of human cells, such as embryonic stem cells, or animal cells. It should also not affect the application of national legislation prohibiting or restricting the sale, supply or use of medicinal products containing, consisting of or derived from these cells.[60]

Decisions about the ontological status of human/animal cells/tissues are, on the surface, thus excised from EU regulation of medicinal products. However, as Faulkner and others point out,[61] important forms of ontological work are in fact still performed by those seemingly 'neutral' aspects of regulation which the EU *does* deem transnationally applicable, namely standards designed to minimize the risks involved in manufacturing

---

[56] Faulkner and others (n 42).
[57] See also Tallacchini (n 42).
[58] Directive 2001/20/EC (n 16).
[59] Griessler and others (n 9).
[60] Regulation No 1394/2007 (n 16) Recital 7.
[61] Faulkner and others (n 42).

medicinal products for human use. As noted previously, the attempt to manage innovatory 'risks' inevitably performs particular ontologies because it implies the in-principle acceptance and facilitation of a particular innovation trajectory.[62] In the case of xenotechnologies, while decisions about whether to 'allow' the use of animal cells/tissues are left to Member States, EU legislation nonetheless outlines a process of risk management through which xenotechnologies can safely enter the European market for human consumption. This situation might appropriately be expressed as one of national hybridization (translation) and transnational purification. The acknowledgement of animal bodies as the cell/tissue sources for xenotechnologies threatens to disrupt xenotechnologies' designation as a medicinal product for human use. However, through the invocation of the principle of 'ethical subsidiarity', such disruptions are confined to a 'national' level. Meanwhile, the transnationally applicable risk management standards of human medicinal products legislation serve to (re)purify xenotechnologies' hybridity, in a manner that facilitates their transnational production and use. In the remainder of this section we go on to illustrate this process of transnational purification by exploring some of these standards in further detail.

The first site at which this form of purification is attempted within EU regulation is within Directive 2003/63/EC, which concludes by making a 'specific statement on xenotransplantation medicinal products', that is, those products which incorporate:

any procedure that involves the transplantation, implantation, or infusion into a human recipient of either live tissues or organs retrieved from animals, or, human body fluids, cells, tissues or organs that have undergone ex vivo contact with live non-human animal cells, tissues or organs.[63]

This statement then goes on to list a set of issues to be considered in such cases, and in doing so, demarcates ATMPs involving live animal cells as a particularly risky and potentially disruptive set of products:

Specific emphasis shall be paid to the starting materials. In this respect, detailed information related to the following items shall be provided according to specific guidelines: Sourcing of the animals; Animal husbandry and care; Genetically modified animals (methods of creation, characterisation of transgenic cells, nature of the inserted or excised (knock out) gene); Measures to prevent and monitor infections in the source/donor animals; Testing for infectious agents; Facilities; Control of starting and raw materials; Traceability.[64]

While brief, this statement is significant for three reasons. First, it emphasizes that the riskiness of manufacturing and using xenotechnologies stems from their origins within animal bodies. Secondly, by framing animal bodies as 'starting materials' for the production of medicinal products for human use, it then automatically serves to purify xenotechnologies' hybridity by emphasizing the *temporal distance* between xenotransplantation medicinal products and the animal bodies from which they have been derived. Finally, this framing of animals as 'starting materials' configures them instrumentally as basic raw materials for subsequent human uses.

This dichotomous (subject/object, culture/nature) framing of the relationship between humans and animals emerges even more explicitly within the detailed guidance which the EMA has developed on the basis of EU legislation concerning ATMPs. Echoing the classificatory hierarchy evident in medicinal products legislation

---

[62] See eg Wynne (n 24); Felt and others (n 23).
[63] Directive 2003/63/EC (n 16) Annex 1, Part IV, para 4.
[64] Directive 2003/63/EC (n 16) Annex 1, Part IV, para 4.

(that is, the prioritization of mode-of-action in human bodies), the EMA's current Guideline on 'Xenogeneic Cell-Based Therapy' begins by defining xenogeneic cell based medicinal products in terms of the functions that they fulfil:

Xenogeneic cell-based therapy is the *use* of viable animal somatic cell preparations, suitably adapted for: (a) implantation/infusion into a human recipient or (b) extracorporeal treatment through bringing (non-human) animal cells into contact with human body fluids, tissues or organs. *The principal objective is reconstitution of cell/tissue/organ functions.*[65]

In keeping with the pattern identified earlier, the Guideline stresses that it is necessary to develop separate guidelines for therapies involving human cells and those involving animal cells, on the basis that the latter pose 'additional risks' to human bodies. Nonetheless, again, this brief acknowledgement of trans-species risk is not taken to threaten the overall logic of xenotechnologies. Rather, the EMA's guidance outlines the provisions necessary to *ensure* that the technology's animal origins do not obstruct their usefulness within human bodies: 'These general principles may apply to a range of products using animal tissues as the starting material, as the key objective is to ensure that the product to be administered is of acceptable quality and standard, and free from contamination.'[66]

The Guideline is able to portray this as an attainable goal through its invocation of the second aspect of the classificatory hierarchy central to medicinal products legislation described earlier, namely, the *process* through which a product's mode-of-action in humans is produced. Specifically, in addition to the suggestion of a void between the human and the animal implied by the term 'starting materials', this distancing is enlarged and expanded as the Guideline takes note of modern industrial manufacturing processes:

Three steps have been identified in the production of the xenogeneic cell-based product, which require specific consideration: source of animals; procurement (extraction of organs/tissues or cells); processing. Procurement and processing of the xenogeneic materials needs to be performed in facilities separated from the animal facilities. The manufacture of the active substance starts at the receipt of the animal starting materials in the GMP approved manufacturing facility.[67]

Regulation prescribes a series of temporal and spatial shifts through different institutional boundaries. Each cumulative stage in processing is intended to further purify, humanize, and tame animal-based therapies, rendering them free of risk for human treatment. And yet, it is this very purification, processing, and enhancement from which the human-animal xenogeneic hybrid emerges.

Another key dimension of descriptions of the xenogeneic manufacturing processes in the Guideline is its repeated insistence that all interventions in animal bodies be oriented with regards to the future safe functioning of animal tissues within human bodies. For example, 'Programmes for screening and detection of known infectious agents should be tailored to the source animal species and the manner in which the xenogeneic cell-based product will be used clinically.'[68] Indeed, this emphasis on the functioning of xenogeneic medicinal products within human bodies is so pronounced that the instant that the issue of animal health/welfare is explicitly mentioned (only once, during the introduction to the Guideline), this is immediately linked back to the broader goal of obtaining medicinal products for *human use*: 'Attention is also given to

---

65 'Guideline on Xenogeneic Cell-Based Medicinal Products' (n 16) 3 (emphasis added).
66 'Guideline on Xenogeneic Cell-Based Medicinal Products' (n 16) 3.
67 'Guideline on Xenogeneic Cell-Based Medicinal Products' (n 16) 4.
68 'Guideline on Xenogeneic Cell-Based Medicinal Products' (n 16) 7.

principles of animal health and welfare in the processes of sourcing of xenogeneic materials for the medicinal products intended for human use.'[69]

In keeping with this instrumental reduction of animal welfare to the management of risks to humans, the only context in which animal health/welfare is discussed in any detail within the Guideline is in relation to the process of ensuring the 'quality control' of the 'starting and raw materials' to be used. In other words, animal health is depicted as important only insofar as it is deemed vital that the source animals which provide the 'starting materials' for xenogeneic medicinal products are free of any diseases which could be transmitted to humans. Accordingly, the Guideline outlines the conditions under which source animals are to be reared in order to maintain their disease-free status:

The origin and derivation of source animals should be fully described considering possible infectious agents and diseases of the particular animal species. Founder and source animals should be healthy and should, at minimum, be Specific Pathogen Free (SPF) and raised in SPF conditions, including health monitoring and barrier systems.[70]

This depiction of animal health/welfare as a goal that can be addressed in a straightforward manner en route to the management of risks to human populations diverges sharply from the Council of Europe's acknowledgement of the complex problems which Specific Pathogen Free conditions pose for animal existences. In view of this, it seems fitting to conclude this section by returning to the latter's very different portrayal of the difficulties involved in attempts to accommodate animals within conditions which have been designed to protect the future health of human populations:

Restricted environments can lead to behavioural and physiological abnormalities. Adequate complexity is required . . . to allow the animal to carry out a range of normal behaviours. . . . In extensive systems, pigs spend many hours exploring their environment, using their highly sensitive snout to root; laboratory housed pigs have little opportunity to express this sort of behaviour. In the absence of suitable foraging substrate and when there is insufficient diet to maintain satiety, abnormal stereotypic behaviours, such as bar chewing, and increased aggression can develop.[71]

C. Concluding Discussion

This analysis highlights contrasting configurations of the human/animal boundary emerging from two very different sites of European transbiological regulation. We have argued that, although processes of purification and effacement can undoubtedly be discerned in the work undertaken by the Council of Europe, xenotechnologies emerge as vastly more 'hybrid' here than they do within the EU's medicinal products legislation. In the regulatory work conducted by the Council of Europe, humans and animals are recognized as entities with entwined interests that are placed at mutual risk through the hybrid corporeality facilitated by xenotechnological innovation. Although a degree of purification does take place, resulting in the Council's positioning of humans and animals as separate entities with unequal claims to the protection of the law, the implications of xenotechnologies for animal bodies and lives are fully acknowledged. In

---

[69] 'Guideline on Xenogeneic Cell-Based Medicinal Products' (n 16) 3.
[70] 'Guideline on Xenogeneic Cell-Based Medicinal Products' (n 16) 4–5.
[71] 'Explanatory Report to Recommendation' Rec(2003) 10 (n 15) 29.

particular, the risks of trans-species disease are seen as profound for humans, but also having a proportionately high impact on those source animals facing far greater biohazard restrictions (specific pathogen-free environments) than would customarily be the case in other areas of animal husbandry. In contrast, when xenotechnologies are incorporated into the very different regulatory space of EU medicinal products legislation, animals emerge as highly refined and processed technical objects—literally 'raw materials' for the development of commercially viable therapeutic applications for safe use within human bodies. Consideration of the potential or actual burdens placed on the sources of these assets in their raw state is entirely effaced.

In the variations on hybrid theory with which we began, such processes of purification, effacement, and silencing ('hybrid denial' in Latour's terms) actually make the proliferation of hybrids more possible. That is, the marginalization of the animals upon which xenotechnology depends necessarily allows it to develop in a way that it may conceivably otherwise not. At the same time, our reflections here suggest that these processes operate at differing levels whereby *gradations* of purification in European regulation can be discerned which facilitate the production of hybrids to *different extents*. In highlighting these nuances, our analysis points to the importance of moving beyond the dichotomous absolutes of much existing hybrid theory, specifically, its tendency to depict 'translation' and 'purification' (or 'inclusion' and 'exclusion') as binary ontological states.

Our analysis has illustrated that the Council of Europe's partial acknowledgement that xenotechnologies depend upon hybrid animal/human corporealities impedes the creation of hybrids in a way that EU medicinal products legislation's more thorough purification does not. The Recommendation to Member States which was ultimately produced by the Council of Europe[72] states that xenotransplantation requires humans to demonstrate that they have fulfilled a particular duty of husbandry and care towards source animals in terms of these animals' 'physiological, social and behavioural needs'.[73] In contrast, in the context of EU medicinal products legislation we find a more complete reinstatement of hierarchical human/animal, subject/object dichotomies. Here, the husbandry needs of animals are rendered entirely subordinate to the requirement that the manufacture of medicinal products for human use should utilize 'disease-free starting materials', allowing xenotechnological innovation to proceed unhindered (at least, with regards to this particular issue).

Throughout our analysis we have emphasized the significance of institutional 'species identity' in shaping processes of purification. In particular, we have highlighted the difference between: first, the novel (although still institutionally aligned) regulatory space which the Council of Europe constructed to address the specific question of xenotransplantation; and, secondly, the entrenched characteristics of the regulatory regime of medicinal products legislation into which the EU has incorporated xeno-technologies. In classifying its regulatory objects, EU medicinal products legislation has traditionally prioritized the processes through which the mode(s)-of-action of these objects are produced, as part of ensuring that these products are 'safe' for human consumers. We have suggested that the EU's decision to define xenotechnologies as medicinal products, and thus incorporate them into the classificatory framework imposed by this regulatory regime, leads automatically to the flattening of species' differences, with animal and human bodies being positioned as equivalent starting materials for a commercial manufacturing process. Whenever xenotechnological

---

[72] Recommendation Rec (2003) 10 (n 15).   [73] Art 23.

hybrids begin to threaten and disrupt their incorporation into the regulatory regime of EU medicinal products legislation, its classificatory hierarchy ensures that species dichotomies are firmly reinscribed. Decisions about the ontological significance of the bodies which contribute cells/tissues for xenotechnologies are delegated explicitly to Member States (national translation), while transnational manufacturing standards are constructed to enable the production of xenotechnologies which act safely within human bodies (transnational purification).

In reflecting upon the significance of institutional 'species identities' in producing particular gradations of purification, it is worth returning to Latour's proposal to ameliorate the harms caused by modernity's denial and dependence on the productiveness of hybrids. Specifically, he argues that practices of purification must cease, and that, as a consequence, 'we are going to have to slow down, reorient and regulate the proliferation of monsters by representing their existence officially',[74] in a democracy which extends to *non-humans* as well as humans.

However, there are several reasons to be sceptical about such a solution. First, 'Europe', as a supranational regulatory 'space', already generates peculiar difficulties with regards to the achievement of even conventional forms of human (let alone non-human) democratic representation.[75] Perhaps more crucially, however, regardless of the site (national, supranational, etc.) of regulation, there are always problems inherent in confidently asserting some kind of homologous parity between regulatory institutions and the bodies which they are supposed to 'represent'. One reason for this, demonstrated by this analysis and elsewhere,[76] is that regulatory bodies have particular 'species' identities which means that their attempts to represent subjects/objects will inevitably lead to the material (re)configuration *of* subjects/objects in species-specific terms. Another is highlighted by Haraway,[77] who, whilst echoing many hybrid theorists' insistence that humans too easily ignore the lively qualities of the non-human entities with whom they co-habit, is also equally concerned with the suggestion that humans might ever adequately 'represent' and 'include' the non-human world. As she points out, such claims risk reinstating speciesist hierarchies by positioning non-humans as representable objects ripe for human regulation/exploitation. On this basis, she argues that we must 'give up mastery but keep searching for fidelity, knowing all the while we will be hoodwinked . . . we are not in charge of the world.'[78]

Whilst emphasizing the non-human world's inevitable refusal to comply with human goals, Haraway nonetheless insists that it remains vital to interrogate *different* human representations/interventions and the varying harms that they imply for humans and non-humans.[79] Drawing on these insights, we would like to conclude by circumnavigating the dangers implicit within Latour's call for a 'Parliament of Things'. We would suggest that the critical challenge posed by our analysis is one of empirically characterizing the institutional forms of trans-species regulation which lead to greater, or less intense, purifications of species boundaries and which thus impede, or facilitate,

[74] Latour (n 14) 12.
[75] See eg Tallacchini (n 42).
[76] Brown and Michael (n 4).
[77] D Haraway, *Simians, Cyborgs, and Women: The Reinvention of Nature* (Free Association Books 1991); Haraway (n 3).
[78] Haraway (n 77) 199.
[79] Haraway (n 77) 199; Haraway (n 3).

attempts to articulate, and engage with, the interdependencies of the human and non-human. Such empirical work could form an important basis for future engagement between legal scholarship, European regulation, and new transbiologies. Specifically, it would generate important insights concerning the forms of purification performed through the 'species characteristics' of existing regulatory regimes, facilitating reflection upon the implications of applying particular regimes to novel hybrid forms of life.

17

When Sperm Cannot Travel:
Experiences of UK Fertility Patients
Seeking Treatment Abroad

Ilke Turkmendag*

A. Introduction

Assisted reproduction technology (ART) is a term referring to any technique or medical intervention that enables individuals to procreate, where such procreation would be unlikely to occur otherwise.[1] ART has become an object of legal intervention in many countries. National restrictions on the availability of ART, and the globalization of health care services, have expanded the growth of an international market for fertility services. The practice of travelling abroad to seek access to ART is often referred as 'reproductive tourism'. Seeking treatment across borders is a form of medical tourism that enables patients to take advantage of differences in reproductive consumer cultures reflected in variations in the cost and availability of treatments, success rates, and waiting lists. The label 'tourism', however, trivializes and obscures the serious issues that underlie cross-border travel in search of treatment. It may also be seen as a 'reproductive exile' where patients who are denied access to treatment at home try to find a legal regime under which the treatment they need will be available.[2] In the remainder of the chapter, a more neutral language will be used, and the phenomenon will be referred to as 'cross-border reproductive care' (CBRC) movement, a term suggested by Pennings.[3]

Although the United Kingdom has some of the most liberal ART regulations in Europe, increasing numbers of patients seek treatment using donor gametes across the borders of the European Union (EU). The main reason that drives UK patients abroad is the donor shortage. The most comprehensive study on CBRC to date was carried out by European Society of Human Reproduction and Embryology (ESHRE) Task Force on Cross-Border Reproductive Care, with data from forty-six clinics across Europe. Thirty-four per cent of UK resident patients—more than any other nationality within

* This work was supported by a Mildred Blaxter Post Doctoral Fellowship from the Foundation for the Sociology of Health and Illness. I am grateful to Thérèse Murphy for her thoughtful and detailed insights about the piece presented here. Many thanks to Mark Flear and to the anonymous referee for their constructive comments. Finally, I would like to acknowledge all those who gave up their precious time to be interviewed and to share their experiences with me, and my supervisors Robert Dingwall and Thérèse Murphy for their endless support during my doctoral work which led to the chapter presented here.

[1] ART is often used for infertility treatment. *In vitro* fertilization (IVF) is the most common ART treatment and it involves removal of sperm and eggs (gametes) from the couple to produce embryos in the laboratory. One or more embryos are then transferred to the female partner's uterus to achieve pregnancy.

[2] R Matorras, 'Reproductive Exile versus Reproductive Tourism' (2005) 20 *Human Reproduction* 3571.

[3] G Pennings, 'Reproductive Tourism as Moral Pluralism in Motion' (2002) 28 *Journal of Medical Ethics* 337.

Europe—cited 'difficulties accessing treatment' as their reason for travelling abroad.[4] Findings from a recent qualitative study of United Kingdom residents provide further insights about the access difficulties at home. Overall, 'a desire for timely and affordable treatment with donor gametes' was evident in 71 per cent of cases, making donor conception the most sought-after treatment amongst these CBRC travellers.[5] Most patients sought treatment within European borders, the most popular destinations being Spain and the Czech Republic.[6]

There is now growing concern in the United Kingdom about such CBRC movement, but as yet there seems to be little understanding of the extent to which the regulatory regime may be playing a contributory role. The study presented in this chapter draws on empirical evidence to encourage more engagement with that question. Drawing on semi-structured interviews with a group of patients who sought donor conception treatment across borders, the study discusses the reasons behind CBRC movement. The accounts of the patients presented here provide insights about rights and markets, in particular. The promotion and protection of children's right to know their genetic identity, a human rights assumption encouraged by the European Convention on Human Rights (ECHR)[7] and now embedded in the United Kingdom's regulation of donor conception, has aggravated the donor shortage. And, as we shall see, the implementation of the EU Tissues and Cells Directive's (EUTCD)[8] voluntary and unpaid donations policy for tissues and cells has made access to treatment even more difficult.

In what follows, I begin with a brief background to the donor conception regulations in the United Kingdom. I will then present the views of the UK patients who received fertility treatment abroad using donated gametes or embryos.

B. Donor Conception and the Law in the United Kingdom

Prior to the 1980s, donor conception was performed without central record-keeping or regulation.[9] In 1982, the UK Government commissioned the Committee of Inquiry into Human Fertilization and Embryology to report on the ethical and legal issues associated with assisted conception and related technologies, which led to the Human Fertilisation and Embryology Act 1990 (HFE Act). Section 31(3) of the HFE Act allowed children born following anonymous gamete donation to apply for information about the donor upon reaching the age of 18. The Act did not specify the content of the information but, in practice, donors were asked to provide some *non-identifying* information, which could be passed to potential recipients. The Code of Practice issued by the relevant regulatory body, the Human Fertilisation and Embryology Authority (HFEA), directed that 'the Act generally permits donors to preserve their anonymity'.[10]

---

[4] F Shenfield and others, 'Cross Border Reproductive Care in Six European Countries' (2010) 25 *Human Reproduction* 1361.

[5] L Culley and others, 'Crossing Borders for Fertility Treatment: Motivations, Destinations and Outcomes of UK Fertility Travellers' (2011) 26 *Human Reproduction* 2373.

[6] Culley (n 5).

[7] European Convention for the Protection of Human Rights and Fundamental Freedoms 1950, ETS 5. The ECHR was incorporated into domestic law in the United Kingdom via the Human Rights Act 1998.

[8] Directive 2004/23/EC of the European Parliament and of the Council of 31 March 2004 on setting standards of quality and safety for the donation, procurement, testing, processing, preservation, storage and distribution of human tissues and cells [2004] OJ L102/48.

[9] L Frith, 'Gamete Donation and Anonymity: The Ethical and Legal Debate' (2001) 16 *Human Reproduction* 818.

[10] Human Fertilisation and Embryology Authority Code of Practice (6th edn) part 5.7.v <www .hfea.gov.uk/docs/Code_of_Practice_Sixth_Edition.pdf> accessed 21 May 2012. The Code is now in its 8th edition.

Towards the end of the 1990s, there was an alarming decrease in the number of people coming forward as sperm donors in the United Kingdom. Interestingly, although donor shortage was therefore a growing concern, in 2001, the government chose to launch a consultation to review the legislation governing access to information for those conceived through gamete donation.

1. The Child's Right-to-Know Movement: *Rose and Another v Secretary of State for Health*[11]

The Children's Society (a national charity involved in campaigning and social policy work to support children) was the first organization that attempted to transform the anonymity of donors into a public concern.[12] In November 1998, the Society called for a change in the law so that people who were born by sperm or egg donation could access the same information about their donors that adopted children could access about their natural parents. The Society's call for legal change brought a response from government agencies: in 1999 the Department of Health confirmed that it was looking at the issue and would publish a consultation paper. And, although it took a further two years to start that consultation, the Children's Society had successfully initiated a controversy.

A few years later another intervention had an impact: this time it was an application for judicial review by two donor-conceived individuals, Rose and EM. Liberty, a human rights NGO, announced the case in a press release with the headline 'Donor insemination case: children can claim right to personal identity'.[13] Rose, an adult woman and EM, a six-year-old, had both been conceived using donor insemination.[14] They had sought access to information about their anonymous sperm donors and also the introduction of a contact register, but the Secretary of State for Health had rejected their requests on the ground that a consultation exercise on the issue of anonymity was already underway. They sought judicial review of this decision, relying on Articles 8 and 14 ECHR. Article 8 provides for a right to respect for private and family life, and the European Court of Human Rights has held that this right incorporates the concept of personal identity, including the right to obtain information about a biological parent.[15] The claimants also invoked Article 14 in conjunction with Article 8, arguing that there should not be discrimination between donor offspring and adoptees or between donor offspring (like Rose) born before the coming into force of the HFE Act and those (like EM) born thereafter.

The judge, Scott Baker J, said that he found it 'entirely understandable that A.I.D. children should wish to know about their origins'.[16] It was in his view quite clear that Article 8 ECHR and the existing jurisprudence of the European Court of Human Rights supported the idea that 'everyone should be able to establish details of his identity as a human being', and that this clearly included the 'right to obtain information about a biological parent who will inevitably have contributed to the identity of his child'.[17] Scott Baker J's judgment says nothing, however, about whether there

---

[11] *Rose and Another v Secretary of State for Health* [2002] EWHC 1593 (Admin).
[12] I Turkmendag, 'The Donor-conceived Child's "Right to Personal Identity": The Public Debate on Donor Anonymity in the United Kingdom' (2012) 39 *Journal of Law and Society* 58.
[13] Liberty, Press Release, 26 July 2002 <www.liberty-human-rights.org.uk/media/press/2002/donor-insemination-case-children-can-claim-right-to-personal-identity.php> accessed 21 May 2012.
[14] *Rose* (n 11).
[15] See eg *Mikulic v Croatia* [2002] 1 FCR 720; *Odièvre v France* [2003] 1 FCR 621.
[16] *Rose* (n 11) [18].
[17] *Rose* (n 11) [47]–[48].

had been a breach of Article 8 in this case: it focuses only on the fact that Article 8 is engaged. The reason for this is that, at a case management conference prior to the hearing, the judge had decided that the issue of breach should be 'stood over':

Once the consultation exercise was under way, and it was clear that the government was giving serious consideration to how to tackle this extremely difficult problem, it was obviously sensible that many of the issues in this litigation should be stood over pending ministerial decisions on what if any government action was appropriate.[18]

Ultimately, although Rose and EM's application for judicial review was successful at the first stage, the later hearing to determine whether there had in fact been a breach of Article 8 was delayed and then, in January 2004, the government announced that donor anonymity was to be lifted. With the implementation of the HFEA (Disclosure of Donor Information) Regulations 2004, from 1 April 2005, UK law was changed to allow children born through gamete donation to access *identifying* details of the donor.[19]

Baroness Andrews, speaking in the House of Lords, explained the reasons that made this change in the law seem so necessary.[20] She emphasized that the secrecy and even stigma surrounding assisted conception had faded; that public attitudes towards information and rights to information had changed dramatically (referring to the *Rose* case); and that such openness had worked successfully in recent years in relation to adoption. She argued:

Information now is much more readily accessible than it was in 1991 . . . In a century where access to information is regarded as a personal and political right, this [donor anonymity] does not seem any longer to be appropriate. It has already proved to be a bone of contention—the Government are very likely to be challenged about the provision of information to donor-conceived people, as the Department of Health has already been in an application brought by Liberty.[21]

Rose's case thus played a significant role in removal of donor anonymity. Although in English law, disputes about parenthood should be resolved according to the best interest or welfare principle stated in the Children Act 1989, the Human Rights Act 1998 which incorporated the ECHR into domestic law is also influential.[22] Under the terms of the Human Rights Act, section 3(1), judges must interpret domestic law in a way which is compatible with Convention rights. As we have seen, Scott Baker J said that respect for private and family life had been interpreted by the European Court of Human Rights to incorporate the concept of personal identity; that the concept of personal identity 'plainly includes the right to obtain information about a biological parent who will inevitably have contributed to the identity of his child'; and that in his judgment there was no great leap in construing Article 8 in this way.[23] Following *Rose*, then, rejecting right-to-know claims from children who had been born following gamete donation could have left the UK Government exposed to increasing numbers of similar cases, backed perhaps by human rights NGOs.

[18] *Rose* (n 11) [16].
[19] The Human Fertilisation and Embryology Authority (Disclosure of Donor Information) Regulations 2004, SI 2004/1511.
[20] HL Deb, 662 cols 344–8 (2003–4) col 344.
[21] HL Deb, 662 cols 344–8 (2003–4) col 344.
[22] E Steiner, 'The Tensions Between Legal, Biological and Social Conceptions of Parenthood in English Law' (2006) 10 *Electronic Journal of Comparative Law* 10.
[23] *Rose* (n 11) [48].

During the debate in Parliament, some peers stated their concerns about the potential shortage of eggs and sperm. In other jurisdictions, the removal of anonymity has generally had a negative impact on both the demand for, and the recruitment of, gamete donors.[24] However, Baroness Andrews said that the government was planning a campaign, costing up to £200,000, to reach out to donors. Moreover, the campaign would be conducted with the support of three organizations: the National Gamete Donation Trust, the British Fertility Society, and the Donor Conception Network.

2. Implementation of the EUTCD into UK Law

After the disclosure regulations passed, the Department of Health undertook a public consultation exercise over the summer and autumn of 2005 on possible changes to update the HFE Act. The exercise culminated in the Human Fertilisation and Embryology Act 2008, an amending statute. Prior to that, however, the HFE Act was amended with effect from 5 July 2007 in order to bring the EUTCD into UK law.[25]

Following the implementation of the EUTCD, the procurement, testing, processing, or distribution of any embryo or sperm and eggs intended for human use must be licensed by the HFEA or be subject to an agreement with a licensed service.[26] If patients are considering obtaining sperm, eggs, or embryos from within the EU, a licensed UK clinic can organize for a transfer to be made from that country. However, the sperm, eggs, or embryos transferred must meet UK requirements. All medical fertility and non-medical fertility services such as internet sperm providers have to abide by UK standards, which include all donors being identifiable. There are other requirements too: donors must have consented to the transfer of their gametes/embryos to the United Kingdom; they must be made aware of the legal position in the United Kingdom on identifying donors and the implications of this for donors; and they must have received no more than reasonable expenses or reimbursement of loss of earnings (that is, 'inconvenience' payments are not permitted).

One effect of the introduction of the EUTCD into UK law is that, although patients can exercise their rights to travel within the EU to receive gametes or embryos from a clinic that does not comply with UK standards, the position is different for *gametes and embryos*: they cannot travel if they do not meet UK requirements on screening.[27] In other words, UK patients cannot get anonymous gametes imported, even if the gametes were lawfully donated in another Member State of the EU.

Whilst the EU aims to promote a market model, the EUTCD seeks to promote an altruistic approach to gamete donation: as stated in Article 12, 'Member States shall endeavour to ensure that the procurement of tissues and cells as such is carried out on a non-profit basis.' Having endorsed this principle, and also lifted donor anonymity, UK

---

[24] I Turkmendag, R Dingwall, and T Murphy, 'The Removal Of Donor Anonymity in The UK: The Silencing of Claims by Would-Be Parents' (2008) 22 *International Journal of Law, Policy and the Family* 283.

[25] EUTCD (n 8). There are also two supplementary Technical Directives: 2006/17/EC; 2006/86/EC.

[26] HFEA, *FAQs about new EU Standards* (HFEA 2008) <www.hfea.gov.uk/fertility-clinic-questions-eu-standards.html> accessed 23 May 2012.

[27] Under the directly effective freedom to provide and *receive* services under Art 56 Treaty on the Functioning of the European Union: *R v Human Fertilisation and Embryology Authority, ex parte Blood* [1997] 2 All ER 687 (CA). See TK Hervey, 'Buy Baby: The European Union and Regulation of Human Reproduction' (1998) 18 *Oxford Journal Legal Studies* 207.

law now offers neither financial incentives nor anonymity to potential donors. And as we shall see later, this policy of non-anonymous and non-remunerated donation seems to be part of the reason that would-be parents are heading abroad.

3. The Impact on Access to Treatment

There was a gamete shortage in the United Kingdom prior to the removal of donor anonymity. Lifting anonymity appears, however, to have exacerbated that shortage. There were 417 sperm donors in 1996, whereas in 2004, the donor supply had fallen to 228 and it had only recovered slightly by 2008 when it was 284.[28] Around this time, acute donor shortages and long waiting lists for would-be parents were regularly reported in the media. According to a BBC investigation in 2006, fifty of the seventy-four clinics in the United Kingdom reported that they had insufficient sperm or none at all.[29] The British Fertility Society claimed that one effect of the change in legislation was that the cost of donor insemination (DI) had risen enormously in many centres, and the programme had effectively been removed from the National Health Service (NHS) as standard practice in most areas.[30]

Initially the HFEA showed no inclination to review the change in the law. Instead, in order to try to curb the numbers going abroad, it emphasized 'risk'. For example, in April 2006, the then chair of the HFEA, Suzi Leather issued a public statement warning people against the poorly regulated treatment in overseas clinics. In the statement Leather referred to those who travel abroad to get treatment as 'a relatively small number of people', and she associated CBRC movement with holiday packages:

We know that *a relatively small number* of people *choose to travel abroad to* undergo fertility treatment and that sometimes *the treatment is packaged as a 'holiday' where the patient can convalesce in the sun*. However, we are concerned about [sic] people who choose to have their treatment abroad should know about the *potential risks*. We have heard of some clinics which offer treatment to patients that is *so dangerous* that it has been banned in the UK. . . . It is very sad when we receive complaints from patients about their treatment abroad and we are not able to help or reassure them. *We would urge patients to think twice and consider the risks and implications before going abroad for treatment.*[31]

Many would-be parents shared their reactions to this statement on discussion forums for fertility patients on the internet. Would-be parents are generally well informed about the success rates, the treatment costs, the methods, and the consultation and follow-up processes provided by clinics in the United Kingdom and abroad. Not surprisingly, then, on the discussion forums of the Infertility Network UK there were patients who expressed the view that the HFEA's statement was infantilizing.

One year later the HFEA issued a further warning; this one cautioned patients against buying sperm online. In response to a news report about women purchasing sperm through the internet, the new chair of the HFEA, Professor Lisa Jardine, began

---

[28] S Norcross, 'HFEA Publishes New Sperm and Egg Donor Figures' (Bionews 519 2009) <www.bionews.org.uk/page_46313.asp> accessed 8 May 2012.

[29] BBC News, 'Figures from Scotland's IVF Clinics' (BBC News 2006) <http://news.bbc.co.uk/1/hi/scotland/5065050.stm> accessed 23 May 2012.

[30] British Fertility Society, *British Fertility Society Response to the White Paper on the Human Fertilisation and Embryology Act* (2007) <www.fertility.org.uk/news/documents/Final%20BFS%20response%20to%20White%20paper%2024.4.07.pdf> accessed 23 May 2012.

[31] S Leather, 'Press Release: Thinking of Going Abroad? Think Twice About Going Abroad for Fertility Treatment' (HFEA 2006) <www.hfea.gov.uk/632.html> accessed 23 May 2012. Emphasis added.

by emphasizing that it was a criminal offence to 'procure, test, process or distribute' any gametes (sperm and eggs) intended for human application without a licence from the Authority. She went on to say that would-be parents seeking donated gametes 'should only use licensed centres':

That way, they can be assured that the gametes have been subject to screening checks and that the centre complies with the standards set out in the HFEA code of practice. A further difficulty with using unlicensed centres is that the HFEA is unable to hold, in its statutory registers, information relating to donors or children conceived from gametes obtained from such centres.[32]

She then returned to the question of criminality:

Responsibility for prosecuting criminal offences rests with the police, and it is the practice of the HFEA to refer concerns about internet procurement to them. We strongly advise any person who becomes aware that a person or organization may be procuring, testing, processing or distributing gametes without a licence to contact the police. The women whose stories you tell are entitled to make such fundamental choices about their personal lives within a safe, clinically sound framework. It is the HFEA's responsibility to provide that framework, and to be vigilant for the safety of those who undergo fertility treatment. The internet sperm providers referred to in one of your examples are not licensed by the HFEA. The service they offer is unlawful and unsafe.

Two years later, in 2010, two men were convicted of running a fertility website, without a licence, selling sperm from anonymous donors to women trying to conceive. They each received a nine-month custodial sentence, suspended for two years, a £15,000 fine, and 200 hours of unpaid work, and were banned from future work in the industry. Nearly 800 women, however, had signed up to use the online service provided by the men's company, which had operated under various names including Sperm Direct Limited and First4Fertility.[33]

Fertility travel, internet sperm providers, and the grey market in gametes are phenomena addressed as 'unsafe', 'illegal', and 'unethical', respectively, by policy-makers. And, as we have seen, would-be parents have been warned against the consequences of considering any solution to their infertility, other than treatment in a licensed UK clinic. Far less, however, has been said about the reasons would-be parents seek out 'coping' or 'avoidance' strategies or how solutions might be found to the problems that lead such parents to use 'illegitimate' ways of obtaining gametes.

C. CBRC Movement From the Patients' Perspective

The interviews and the data analysis presented here draw on my PhD work which explored the reactions of patients to the removal of donor anonymity in the United Kingdom. The people whose views are presented are a sub-group of patients who received/or considered receiving fertility treatment abroad: for the most part I refer to them as 'would-be parents'. The data was collected by thirteen semi-structured qualitative interviews.[34] The interviews themselves assessed three areas of the donor-conception

---

[32] L Jardine, 'Internet Sperm Providers are Illegal' (*Guardian News and Media Limited* 2008) <www .guardian.co.uk/uk/2008/sep/23/ukcrime.law1> accessed 23 May 2012.

[33] The Independent, 'Two Spared Jail over Illegal Sperm Business' (*The Independent* 2010) <www .independent.co.uk/news/uk/crime/two-spared-jail-over-illegal-sperm-business-2104324.html> accessed 8 May 2012.

[34] Of the thirteen individuals interviewed, five were egg recipients, two were embryo recipients, one was a sperm recipient, one contracted a surrogate mother as well as donating eggs, one was an egg donor, and one was a sperm donor.

experience: first, the decision-making process; secondly, disclosure; and, thirdly, claims-making (both for and against policy change). Ethical concerns relating to informed consent, the right to privacy, and protection from harm were carefully considered both before and after the interviews.

In what follows, the themes that emerged from the interviews will be presented in five main sections: disclosure; donor shortage; rights; markets; and policymaking.

1. Disclosure: 'Being Forced to Tell'

During the donor anonymity debate in the public sphere, the view that donor-conceived children have a *right* to have access to identifiable information was legitimized by two principal claims. First, the position of donor-conceived people should be aligned more closely with that of adopted people, with access to identifying information about their donor.[35] Secondly, as studies on adopted children had shown, genealogical knowledge is necessary for the development of identity; by denying access to their donor's identity, the government infringes the human rights of donor-conceived children.[36] During the donor anonymity debate that led to the 2004 regulations, these claims were part of broader emphasis on openness and transparency—an emphasis that was not just strong but almost intimidating. For example, any inclination towards secrecy on the part of donor-conception families was portrayed as a potential threat to the resultant child's welfare; indeed, parents who intended not to disclose were accused of deception and violation of moral standards.[37] Similarly, the HFEA advised would-be parents that '[i]t is *certainly best* to be open with your child/children about the circumstances of their conception. *Secrecy* on this subject *isn't in their interests* and they will have a right to find out about their origins from our register when they reach 18.'[38] Such imposition of disclosure presupposes that there is one way of organizing family life and that transparency will and should work for every family.[39] In the next section, I use interview data to show the reactions of would-be parents to this disclosure discourse that asserts openness.

a. 'The information, once it is out, you can't get it back'

Parents who choose not to disclose may justify their non-disclosure on the ground that it protects the best interests of the child. In the first extract, Lindsay reflects on her views about the disclosure. Lindsay, who had a daughter, Sandy, as a result of embryo donation, told her 'you came in a different way, you are special'. Sandy is now four years old. Lindsay still struggles about how to manage the information about Sandy's origins:

I am struggling... that is, you know I have told people information that is basically Sandy's information and that is where I have the dilemma. Because she is not old enough to know who she would like to tell, and who she would not like to tell. And I am doing it on her behalf... And

---

[35] Turkmendag (n 12).
[36] Turkmendag (n 12).
[37] Turkmendag (n 12).
[38] HFEA, 'For Parents of Donor-Conceived Children' (HFEA 2008) <www.hfea.gov.uk/en/1185.html> accessed August 2008. Emphasis added. The content of the web page has been updated since.
[39] G Pennings, 'The "Double Track" Policy for Donor Anonymity' (1997) 12 *Human Reproduction* 2839.

the information, once it is out you can't get it back. That is the reason that I keep cautious, not anything to do with me but because she might not want anyone to know.

Alice has a similar dilemma about revealing the information about her twins' origins. Alice got pregnant using her late husband's frozen sperm and donor eggs. She notes that her twins might have trouble with the fact that their father passed away before they were born. Therefore, she wants to wait for the right time before telling the children about their means of origin. She expresses concern that if the egg donation is known, she cannot avoid her children being bullied at school by other kids. Hence, she has shared her treatment only with immediate family and close friends.

Lindsay and Alice regard the information about the donor-conceived child's origins as the child's own information. They are therefore reluctant to pass this information to other people on their child's behalf. They also express concern about a child's competence in managing the information. Young children may be eager to share the details of their origins at a young age. But once they start to realize the content of the information that they have been sharing with everyone, they might feel that they have made a mistake. These parents are concerned not to give the child greater autonomy 'at any cost'.

b. *'Being dictated what you have to tell the child, it doesn't seem right to me.'*

Some participants considered that the disclosure policy discriminates against donor-conception families by comparison with those with naturally conceived children who do not necessarily know their origins. People who conceive naturally (but, for example, as a result of an affair or a one-night stand) are not told what to tell to their children.

Fiona points out that the government does not intervene in other areas of family life and does not tell people how to bring up their children. She stresses that she is doubly discriminated against: nature has discriminated against her, and now it is the policy-makers who remind her that she is different.

The government don't intervene in other areas of family life. They don't tell people what they must tell their children or how they must bring them up. So when you are already had such a battle, by the time we get another donor now and if we go through a cycle of successful we will be been trying for a child for nine years. Now, that itself is hard enough and put an enormous strain on a relationship, as well. *Being dictated* what you have to tell the child, it doesn't seem right to me... Nature already discriminated against me and it feels like the law was written that way as well.[40]

Fiona and her husband have been foster parents to nine children; none of these children knew who their genetic father was. Thus, for Fiona, the disclosure policy is not only discriminatory against those who use donor conception, but also against the resultant children. Her foster children do not know who their fathers are, because their mothers were not encouraged to be open about their means of conception:

We had nine foster children and in every single case none of them have known their genetic father. They have all been a result of one-night stands or short relationships and the government isn't there, telling these mums that *they have to provide their* children with genetic background so... I can't help feeling a bit discriminated against. The young girls that we've got fostering at the moment they have no dads, there is six children in their family from the same mum with six different dad. Not one of them knows their dad and you know, their mum isn't forced to reveal anything to them, or even tell them the names of their dads or anything. And they know nothing

---

[40] Emphasis added.

about their background on their paternal side. So I do feel a bit sort of *preached* to be told that I have to tell any resultant children... At least *mine are wanted children* and they are gonna be *brought up in a stable mother and father relationship* unlike the foster children we have.[41]

In the following extract, Tina talks about family-building practices before the arrival of ARTs. She says that in the past, if one wanted a child, one could have an affair, and this would be unspoken. She points out that the removal of anonymity does not apply to people like her husband's ex-wife, who got pregnant as a result of an affair:

in 1960s or something... It was an unspoken thing, if you found out that the man had a problem, then the woman turned to see... She went off, had a little fling. Cause in those days you would expect a baby in a year. You would wonder how many women just go out... and men knew it... sort of... didn't say anything.

Some of participants suggested that the new disclosure policy may be increasing subterfuge rather than openness. For example, Fiona argued that the disclosure policy makes her 'rebellious' against openness. She would be more positive about disclosure if she were not 'forced'. Although under the current legislation she is not compelled to tell her donor-conceived child about its origins, Fiona feels that she is 'dictated', 'forced', and 'preached to' about disclosure:

I am not against it [disclosure]. I do think it is child's best interest to tell, I really do but that's an intellectual decision not an emotional decision as regards actually telling the child. If we are lucky enough to have one in the future, I hope I will, but I know that I would be really worried about telling, and I certainly don't like *being forced to tell*. I also think that we would come around to that conclusion a lot quicker if we weren't forced to tell. We would estimate that decision as good sensible parents. I think we would come to the right answer but *being forced to tell* sort of makes me back away, you know, makes me want to do the opposite, makes me feel a bit rebellious as well.[42]

Alice proposes that, instead of lifting anonymity, the HFEA could provide a detailed profile of the donor without giving identifying information. She claims that donor-conceived children will be satisfied with knowing about the characteristics of the donor; they do not necessarily need to know the identity of the donor:

Again going back to the whole child's right to know thing, I think there are ways of disclosing information without necessarily giving away the donors identity because I really wonder whether... it would make any difference to children who were born with donor egg or sperm to know who their donor is as oppose to the characteristics of about their donor.

The interview accounts show that these participants are not convinced that disclosing the means of conception is in the best interests of the child. These parents feel that maintaining secrecy, or limiting information, about the child's conception is the safest way to protect the child, themselves, and the extended family. The accounts also suggest that the disclosure policy in the United Kingdom creates a socio-legal environment that requires donor-conception families to display their differences from other families.

As Smart explains, however, nowadays there is an almost unquestionable presumption that it is best for children to know identifiable information about the gamete donor who played a role in their conception, and increasingly this welfare criterion is also linked to a rights-based argument.[43] For example, in *Re T (A Child) (DNA Tests:*

---

[41] Emphasis added.   [42] Emphasis added.
[43] C Smart, 'Law and the Regulation of Family Secrets' (2010) 24 *International Journal of Law, Policy and the Family* 397.

Paternity) the judge decided that the child in question had a right to respect for private life under Article 8 ECHR in the sense of having knowledge of his identity which also encompasses his true paternity. Smart is critical of the new enthusiasm about knowing the truth:

The tendency for public policy, with its enthusiasm for DNA testing, to assume that (genetic) truth is better than (relational) fiction means that the addition of more genetic kin through these means is inevitably seen as producing a positive outcome for children (and possibly for adults). Yet children live in webs of relationships that are delicately interconnected and adding more relatives may disrupt and even break some of these links.[44]

She also gives an example of a recent ruling where the disclosure of paternity meant that the child in question would have lost more kin (a putative paternal grandmother who was his significant carer, a putative half-sibling, and a cousin) than he would have gained (a genetic father who was a stranger to the child).[45] In this case, the child did *not* want to know the truth: not knowing would mean that he could keep his grandmother, his brother, and cousin, and remain living with them rather than living with his genetic father.

Smart's analysis of the case reminds us that not everyone in family relationships is necessarily going to see genetic truth as an unassailable guiding principle. The interview accounts presented in the following section echo this view.

2. Donor Shortage: 'Throwing Out the Baby with the Bath Water'

The would-be parents in my study were clear that the shortage of donors could be attributed to the new disclosure law. Rosie claimed that lifting anonymity has had a negative effect on donor recruitment in the United Kingdom. She compared the programme in the United Kingdom to that in Spain, arguing that the latter is successful because the donors are able to preserve their anonymity:

They say it [removal of donor anonymity] doesn't have any effect but I can't see how it doesn't. I mean I—I am sure it will. It is logical and I am sure the programme in Spain would not be so successful, let's say if the donors were not anonymous. I think that they want to be anonymous. I don't think they want to be known or want to be contacted.

Alice also took the view that the removal of donor anonymity had caused a reduction in donations. She claimed that the open donation system in the United Kingdom frightens donors, as the resultant child might contact them in the future:

how can you not equate the two? The removal donor anonymity will of course cause a huge deduction in donors who want to come forward, of course that will scare people and they are not going to want to donate. People who donate sperm have done it in past are frightened. People who egg share or donate sperm all have done so in the past are frightened, majority of them are. In 18 years past time this adult can come to the door step, say 'you are my genetic father and mother', that's why.

Alice had travelled to Spain and Poland, countries that allow the treatment she needed (to get pregnant using an embryo created by insemination of her late husband's frozen sperm using donor eggs). She could have received the treatment in the United Kingdom, but she did not want to wait for eggs. In Alice's view it is the removal of donor anonymity and the long waiting lists that drive people abroad:

---

[44] (n 43) 409.   [45] *Re D (paternity)* [2007] 2 FLR 26.

It is difficult because you know I can see what they are trying to doing but I just wonder, you know, whether, sorry to use this but throwing out the baby with the bath water really, because it is driving people abroad . . . People are not willing to wait and you know 30s, 40s . . . they are not going to wait a couple of years. They take the best option . . . going to Spain, Russia or Poland where there aren't any waiting lists, cost is not a problem.

For a majority of participants in my study, waiting was not an option. One participant, Tina, who received embryo donation, was in her early forties and had a chance of using her own eggs to conceive. However, after a few failed attempts with IVF, she did not want to try to conceive with her own eggs any longer. She feared that the procedure would be time-consuming, risking her chances of carrying a baby. Another participant, Rosie, felt a need to start her treatment immediately—her age gave her no other choice: 'I didn't want to wait any longer I wanted to get on with it.'

Infertility increases by age. The participants in this study who considered donor eggs were between 30 and 40 years old. Because age is a significant determinant of the effectiveness of treatment, they gave up using their own gametes after failed attempts in their early forties, yet they were then faced with long waiting lists in the United Kingdom. Crossing borders was, they believed, the only option available to them if they wanted to become parents.

The United Kingdom's donor shortage is also an obstacle for couples who want to receive donations from a donor with a physical resemblance to them. Clinics situated in countries where abundant supplies of gametes are available often promise to match the physical characteristics of the donors with those of the would-be parents. A brief review of the postings on message boards on the internet indicates that, by contrast, clinics in the United Kingdom avoid making such promises.[46] Accordingly, a would-be parent may need to travel abroad in order to find a donor with a reasonable match to their own physical characteristics, or those of their partner. One of the reasons that motivated Rosie and her partner to get treatment in Spain was the likelihood of finding a donor who resembled their physical appearance.

I am not actually English racially. I am actually Jewish, Polish Jewish and my partner is quite dark skinned . . . and we are not very tall . . . so we thought actually Spain is pretty good for us anyway in terms of matching. So I didn't look anywhere else.

Having a donor with physical similarities provides would-be parents with biological continuity.[47] There is a cultural expectation that children resemble their parents; thus, having a child that resembles oneself reduces the level of 'cognitive dissonance' that social parents experience.

3. Markets: The Commercial Side of the CBRC Movement

This section deals with payment to donors and helps us to understand how the participants in my study presented the commercial side of CBRC movement. Trade in gametes is driven by two imperatives: the need for infertility treatment, and the need for stem cell research.[48] Women are the primary providers of such reproductive material but, at least in the EU context, the economic value of their labour remains

---

[46] Turkmendag, Dingwall, and Murphy (n 24).

[47] G Becker, *The Elusive Embryo: How Women and Men Approach New Reproductive Technologies* (University of California Press 2000).

[48] C Waldby, 'Oocyte Markets: Women's Reproductive Work in Embryonic Stem Cell Research' (2008) 27 *New Genetics and Society* 19.

largely unacknowledged.[49] Reproductive tissue is constituted as a 'gift' from the 'donor' to the recipient. For example, Recital 18 of the EUTCD asserts: 'tissue and cell programmes should be founded on the philosophy of voluntary and unpaid donation, anonymity of both donor and recipient, altruism of the donor and solidarity between donor and recipient.'[50] According to Article 12(1) of the EUTCD on standards relating to the handling and use of human tissues and cells, '[d]onors may receive compensation, which is strictly limited to making good the expenses and inconveniences related to the donation.'

There are, as Waldby explains, both pros and cons of the gift system: whilst it prevents commodification of human bodily material, it often means that donors are simply treated as open sources of bodily material that can be profitably privatized by biotechnology companies. She argues that although it would contravene the prevailing European ethos opposing the commodification of the human body, it might be worth considering provision of reproductive tissues and cells as a form of labour.[51] As we shall see, the views expressed by the would-be parents in this study are similar; they consider donation (eggs in particular) as a form of labour that deserves incentives, a view that runs contrary to the EUTCD's non-profit donation system.

a. The United Kingdom's non-remunerative donation policy: 'I would get them paid'

There are wide discrepancies in how the gift system is interpreted across EU Member States. The UK policy makes sure that donors do not have financial gain from donating: donors are compensated for expenses and loss of earnings, but not for inconvenience. When the interviews were conducted, the amount an egg donor could claim for loss of earnings was up to a daily maximum of £63.12, with an overall limit of £250 per donation cycle. In many other EU countries there is a blanket fee for loss of earnings, expenses, and inconvenience. For example in Spain, egg donors are compensated by up to €900.[52] In the following extract, Rosie says that such payment is not 'huge' enough to encourage people to donate repeatedly:

I think it is good that they pay people [in Spain]. I mean they don't get a huge amount of money. It is only like seven or 800 Euros or something. Having been through IVF I mean, I don't think it is a lot of money because it is quite you know, quite a heavy process to go through. I know that they are ok, they get paid but it is not a big amount.

Rosie points out that she is comfortable with the idea of egg donors being paid, because then she can see the process as a 'business arrangement'. She thinks that for a student, for example, this is 'not a bad way of earning some money'. Rosie's account also indicates that the donors deserve to be paid for providing eggs which is a 'quite heavy process'. Similarly, Tina, too, draws attention to the difficulties of donating eggs. She thinks that egg donors should be paid, because unlike sperm donation, egg donation is not easy:

In Spain you pay woman 600 pounds. It is a cultural thing. It is not nice having been through it. You wouldn't keep doing it. For men it is easy.

Another participant, Alison, supports the open donation system, yet she expresses concern about the decreasing donor numbers and the long waiting lists. She says that

---

[49] ibid.   [50] EUTCD (n 8).   [51] Waldby (n 48).
[52] HFEA, 'HFEA FAQs for Donors' (HFEA 2012) <www.hfea.gov.uk/2627.html#2640> accessed 8 May 2012.

we expect too much of the donors: they are identifiable, and they only get their travel expenses paid. Like the other participants, Alison states that she would like egg donors to get paid.

I had mixed feelings because I would choose an identifiable donor but obviously it means that the supply is greatly reduced so it is tricky. If it was up to me, I would I'd leave the identified part, but I'd like them get paid.

Unlike sperm, eggs are not a self-renewing, copious, and accessible tissue, and they are never detached from the body in the normal course of events.[53] Donating eggs involves stimulating the ovaries and the multiple follicles, shutting down the donor's reproductive cycle, several hormone injections, and then a surgical procedure to retrieve the eggs. The participants had an understanding of all of this; they were familiar with the complexity of IVF procedures (and some had been involved in egg sharing). Many of them expressed the view that egg donation was not an easy process and that egg donors should be paid for their efforts. The participants did not think that payment would cause abuse; the amount paid would not be high enough, they said, to encourage people to go through this procedure repeatedly.

b. Standards of the clinics abroad: 'Why don't we go, it is in Barcelona, we like Barcelona, it is a nice place you know'

By making both international partnerships and patient bookings much easier, internet communication has facilitated the growth of CBRC.[54] All of the participants in my study had made use of the internet. For example, when Rosie needed egg donation, she started doing research about the procedure and found a website called IVF Connections. She read the postings on message boards and found out that success rates were high in Spain, especially in one clinic in Barcelona:

just reading the stuff from the board at that time. Everyone seemed to be successful, That was really incredible. It was just like very good feeling... so many people were getting pregnant and so basically I thought about it. If all these women try that, what's so special about me that I couldn't consider it? Why don't we go, it is in Barcelona, we like Barcelona, it is a nice place you know, go and have a consultation and I heard that they were very quick and the indication of the cost that was a concern but I was lucky. I had enough money to do it...

Alice is content with the treatment she received in Spain and Poland. She says that the consultation process is more open and advanced in comparison to the consultation provided in the United Kingdom. Moreover, the cost of the treatment is lower abroad:

What I experienced in Poland and Spain, compared to clinics here, they have more experience. The doctors are out there, [they] are willing to take time to talk to you. . . . In Poland you decide how many embryos can be implanted, they talk to you. This is our recommendation, you can have 2 or 3 . . . Even it is in different country you have their e-mails. I have the mobile number of the doctor . . . In cost of one treatment in this country I can have two treatments.

Some patients expressed ethical concerns around the services provided by *United Kingdom* clinics. Tina had embryo donation in Spain. She stressed that donor anonymity was the main reason that drove her abroad, but she also commented on her other motives. She started her treatment in the United Kingdom in a private clinic. When they found out that they could not conceive due to male factor infertility, Tina

---

[53] Waldby (n 48).   [54] Waldby (n 48).

and her husband decided to receive sperm donation. However, they were advised to get intra-cytoplasmic sperm injection (ICSI) instead, which would enable Tina to get pregnant using her husband's sperm. Given that ICSI is much more expensive than sperm donation, and more complicated, Tina did not take the clinicians' advice. When she heard from a friend that the success rate was only 5 per cent for her age group, she decided that the clinic was giving her false hope and her treatment was a waste of time. She thinks that private clinicians have business minds and, when money comes into the equation, their advice is not reliable:

In the beginning when we found out that it was him [my husband] we asked for DI. They said no, you must have ICSI. DI is for 500 pounds, ICSI is 5500. Lord Winston said when money comes to the equation, ethics go out the door. With donor sperm you have a straight insemination, 10% chance, it is not that great but it was... and they said no... your husband has some sperm and you must try to have your husband's child.

Tina and her husband finally decided to get treatment in Spain using anonymous frozen embryos. The clinic staff in the United Kingdom warned Tina against getting treatment abroad. They thought the clinic in Spain was not ethical:

My clinic here in England took an extremely poor view of me going to Spain... questioned the ethics and the professionalism of the clinic in Spain. They completely, you know, put a down view on the whole thing.

Despite the concerns raised by the clinicians, for Tina the advantages of undergoing treatment in Spain were obvious: the clinics were more advanced, there were donors available, anonymity was preserved, and there were no waiting lists.

In Spain, they are bigger. Their equipment is the latest thing. In England it is all rubbish, you wait for hours and you spend the same money, the same cost.... I would have done here, which you can't. There is no donor egg available.... And if you have one, you have to tell the child. Waiting lists are five years. At my age you couldn't wait. In Spain there is no waiting list.

The accounts quoted here indicate that the participants in the study consider the standards of infertility treatment in other EU countries to be as high, if not better, than those in the United Kingdom. Given that the cost of such services is approximately the same or less than the ones provided in the United Kingdom, and that by going abroad one can avoid the waiting lists at home, it should come as no surprise that growing numbers of patients seek treatment in other EU countries.

4. Policymaking: The HFEA and the Reproductive 'Tourism'

During the interviews some of the participants referred to the ways in which the HFEA had dealt with CBRC movement. Alice, for example, described the HFEA as being 'like an ostrich', burying its head in the ground. She did not think the Authority represented patients' opinions in its decisions. And she said that, in the absence of statistics revealing the number of people seeking treatment abroad, the HFEA will continue denying the facts.

There is so much opportunity going on at this moment. The way HFEA operates today, their statistics not include anyone who has gone abroad for treatment. So that's just completely not part of research to them, 'oh no one is going abroad for treatment, you know because we are not doing the research in that area anyway'.

Alice wondered how the HFEA would respond to statistics revealing a decrease in donor numbers following the removal of donor anonymity. Alice also expressed the view that the HFEA was responsible for the consequences of the donor anonymity policy, and the donor shortage, and that the Authority was not listening to the voices of would-be parents who were being driven abroad. Alice's account suggests that going abroad is not the patients' choice; but 'their [the HFEA's] making'. For Alice, CBRC movements are the end-result of policymaking that is not informed by the views of would-be parents:

And I see a couple of programmes where they have interviewed Suzi Leather. She's just said 'if people want to go abroad that's their issue, we don't look at clinics abroad we look at clinics from UK'. I am thinking yes, but it is actually your making that driving them abroad, you know and there is no recognition of that. No understanding. It is a bit like, the HFEA is like an ostrich, buried in the ground . . . Who represents the patients in these big decisions that they make? Is there anyone? Not that I know of . . . So I have mixed feelings about them.

The would-be parents also reacted to Leather's remark that fertility treatment was marketed as a holiday. Like many other would-be parents who sent their protests to online support groups, Tina stressed that infertility treatment is not a holiday.

You want a baby, the media made out this whole fertility tourism thing 'yeah, you go on holiday and have your treatment' and it is like 'yeah you get to go to a different place and some Spain or whatever'. But it is not a holiday, there are so much going on in your body in your mind, you know.

Alice stated that policymakers should have weighed the cost of lifting anonymity for would-be parents. Alice feels that having access to a donor's identity and being told about donor conception are different matters, and she is uncertain as to whether knowing the identity of the donor would make a big difference to the donor-conceived child. Disclosure policy, she thinks, is preventing couples from being parents:

Although I can understand, you know, for a child it is important to know what the background is, it is not possible in some families, even in natural families, and you have to weight out what the cost of removal of donor anonymity would be. It may make a difference, it may not. Look how many couples left in the situation, who want to be parents, left in the situation where they have to wait long periods. . . . I know we all want to our children best we can, but almost preventing couples to have the opportunity of becoming parents . . . It is a tricky one. For me personally, I am a bit biased, coming from the point that I have donor egg I would say the disclosure policy is not the best policy that HFEA came up with.

The would-be parents in this study saw the donor shortage as a direct consequence of the removal of donor anonymity, and they blamed the HFEA for the circumstances that 'oblige' them to seek treatment abroad. The fact that obtaining treatment abroad had been condemned by the HFEA was a cause of further frustration. The parents also expressed the view that their concerns were not taken into consideration by the HFEA. This suggests very strongly that further research examining the communication gap between such stakeholders and the HFEA would contribute to developing strategies that could, and should, inform policymaking.

On a positive note, the HFEA's approach does seem to be changing. In August 2010, in part because of concern regarding the numbers opting to go to countries such as Spain and Cyprus to receive gametes, the Authority launched a full public consultation into sperm and egg donation policies. In this consultation document, the HFEA noted that the landscape of donation had changed since the Authority looked at these rules in 2005, and it emphasized that it would like to make sure that the rules are up to date. It also expressed concern that some fertility centres overseas may offer substandard treatment, and that increasing numbers of people are purchasing unscreened sperm on the internet.[55] It asked if gamete supply could be improved by a change in policy, or withdrawal from commitments under the EUTCD.[56]

As a result of the consultation process, the HFEA decided to take a more proactive approach to donor recruitment, and increased the compensation amount that sperm and egg donors should be permitted.[57] Egg donors can now receive £750 per cycle of donation. Sperm donors can receive a £35 fee per individual visit. The donors remain non-anonymous, however.

D. Discussion

The removal of anonymity has had identifiable detrimental effects in the United Kingdom: donors are reluctant to donate; clinics cannot meet the demand for gametes; and there are long waiting lists for patients who wish to get treatment. Why then have would-be parents been reluctant to mobilize against it? It is argued here that this reluctance may reflect the variety of ways in which they can avoid the impact of the change in the law: CBRC, in particular, acts as a safety valve.

It has been argued that CBRC promotes moral pluralism; that it prevents the potential clash between minorities wishing to use ART, and majorities who place restrictions on these practices.[58] Others, however, see CBRC as a poor substitute for moral pluralism.[59] In fact, as Storrow argues, CBRC's function as a safety valve against organized resistance at home is precisely what enables national legislatures to introduce restrictive regulations limiting access to reproductive care: governments may feel justified in assuming a stricter position than they otherwise might, knowing that CBRC will temper resistance to the law.[60] Arguably, then, diversity between different EU Member States has enabled the United Kingdom to introduce restrictive laws with regard to donor recruitment and the procurement of gametes. However, crossing borders to seek treatment in other jurisdictions is hardly desirable for patients: indeed, the interview accounts presented here suggest that such 'reproductive exile' may add to the stigmatization of infertility.[61] In addition, as Robertson notes, CBRC as a solution 'is grossly unfair because it enables only those with funds to escape the law's strictures. Those who are able to travel to obtain services must also bear the additional burdens of being away from home for substantial periods, making the already psychologically fraught and stressful situation of infertility all the more difficult.'[62]

Irish abortion policy is another example of an approach to the regulation of reproduction 'where a government "chooses" to facilitate these services through "delegation and doubt"'.[63] In Ireland abortion is only permissible when there is a risk to the

---

[55] HFEA, *A Review of the HFEA's Sperm and Egg Donation Policies* (HFEA 2011) <www.hfea.gov.uk/docs/2011-01 13_Donation_review_background.pdf> accessed 23 May 2012.

[56] E Blyth, 'Gamete Donation Review: Not the HFEA's Finest Hour' (Bionews 605, 2011) <www.bionews.org.uk/page_94012.asp> accessed 23 May 2012.

[57] S Starr, 'HFEA Takes First Set of Decisions Following Donation Review' (BioNews 616, 2011) <www.bionews.org.uk/page_102199.asp> accessed 8 May 2012.

[58] Pennings (n 3).

[59] Pennings (n 3).

[60] RF Storrow, 'The Pluralism Problem in Cross-Border Reproductive Care' (2010) *Human Reproduction* 2939.

[61] JA Robertson, 'Protecting Embryos and Burdening Women: Assisted Reproduction in Italy' (2004) 19 *Human Reproduction* 1693.

[62] Robertson (n 61) 1696.

[63] See M Fox and T Murphy, 'Irish Abortion: Seeking Refuge in a Jurisprudence of Doubt and Delegation' (1992) 19 *Journal of Law and Society* 454.

pregnant woman's life. According to the Irish Family Planning Association, between January 1980 and December 2010, at least 147,912 women travelled from the Republic of Ireland for safe abortion services abroad.

Having been through reproductive 'exile' in order to terminate their pregnancies, in 2005, three Irish women challenged Ireland's abortion law at the European Court of Human Rights.[64] The applicants felt that their rights under Articles 2, 3, 8, and 14 of the ECHR had been breached.[65] The Court ruled that the Article 8 rights of all three applicants were engaged. However, it distinguished the situation of A and B (who sought abortion for health and/or well-being reasons) from C (who sought abortion as she felt that the pregnancy posed a risk to her life) and ruled that Ireland's abortion law violated applicant C's rights under Article 8 ECHR. The Court also decided that the Irish Government needed to implement an infrastructure to facilitate legal abortions within the jurisdiction, that is, where the woman's life is at risk.[66] Ultimately, however, the decision did not lead to any liberalization of Irish law on abortion: as McGuinness notes, the Court facilitated Ireland's restrictive abortion laws through its application of the 'margin of appreciation' doctrine. The Court considered, first, that abortion could not be disentangled from the question of when life begins; an issue on which there is no consensus in Europe.[67] Secondly, the judgment did not try to widen the category of cases when abortion would be legal in Ireland as it considered this to be a highly sensitive and controversial issue for the Irish public.[68]

The Court's decision also suggests that it does not see the risks created by the Irish abortion ban as a human rights issue. The ban risks women's health by causing abortions to be performed later than is necessary, and creates emotional upset for women at an already stressful time.[69] Moreover, as noted earlier, crossing borders to receive medical help is not an option for everyone. In Ireland, both illegal abortions, and the use of illegal abortion pills have become a necessity for women who cannot travel abroad to end their pregnancies. McGuinness argues: '[W]ould the Irish Government's "choice"' to deal with abortion through allowing the provision of information and travel when travel is not possible still fail to breach Article 8 rights?'[70]

The Court's reluctance to engage deeply with Irish abortion law suggests that European human rights law does not place limits on the power of strongly held moral views in Member States of the Council of Europe. This is problematic because, in a democratic society, because of the fundamental nature of the rights at stake in issues related to human reproduction, majoritarian sentiments should not override the interests of major stakeholders of the problem, even though they are in a minority.[71]

Besides, it is questionable whether the Irish abortion ban reflects the Irish public's view on the matter. According to McGuinness, in *A, B and C* the judgment was influenced by the Irish Government's insertion of 'anti-abortion' clauses in the Maastricht and Lisbon Treaties, which in fact, indicate a fear that 'Europeanization' could lead to abortion being forced on the Irish people, rather than reflecting a majoritarian attitude on abortion.[72] Similarly, the removal of donor anonymity had little to do with public attitudes on donor conception in the United Kingdom: prior to the removal of

---

[64] *A, B and C v Ireland* [2010] ECHR 2032.   [65] *A, B and C v Ireland* (n 64).

[66] S McGuinness, 'A, B, and C Leads To D (For Delegation!): *A, B and C v. Ireland* 25579/05 [2010] ECHR 2032' (2011) 19 *Medical Law Review* 476.

[67] McGuinness (n 66).

[68] McGuinness (n 66). On NHTs and the margin of appreciation, see also Chapters 3 and 13 in this collection.

[69] McGuinness (n 66).   [70] McGuinness (n 66) 491.

[71] Storrow (n 66).   [72] Storrow (n 66) 485.

donor anonymity, the Department of Health's own consultation indicated widespread agreement that more *'non-identifying'* information about donors should be made available to donor offspring.[73]

True, the promotion of the right to know may have shielded the UK Government from further cases akin to *Rose* but it has also exacerbated the donor shortage. The latter risk, moreover, was foreseen: the government knew the potential consequences of removing anonymity from donors, yet it decided that the child's right to know should be championed at any cost, rather than weighed against the competing interests of would-be parents and donors. Writing in a different context, Murphy and Whitty have argued that the assessment and management of risk has become a pre-eminent concern for governments and organizations alike, and that today managing risk involves managing the 'risk of rights'.[74] Moreover, as they also point out, 'risks exist in both engaging with, and rejecting, human rights'.[75] In the United Kingdom, promotion of children's right to know their gamete donor meant rejection of potential 'right to treatment' and perhaps 'right to respect for private and family life' claims that could be raised by would-be parents. For example, on what basis does the state strongly encourage disclosure? On what grounds does the HFEA advise that it is 'certainly best' to be open with children about the circumstances of their conception? Disclosure should be a matter for each family to decide for itself. But, due to the confidentiality concerns of those who were considering treatment, such claims were not raised: many would-be parents remained silent during the policy change. Their voices, therefore, went unheard by public bodies, like the HFEA, which can only deal with issues through formal and transparent modes of communication.[76] This silence gave the UK Government a great advantage in managing the 'conflicting' interests of would-be parents and donor offspring.

To date the United Kingdom's non-anonymous donor conception policy does not seem to have increased openness in families. In spite of the greater encouragement in recent years for parents to disclose their children's donor origins, a recent study shows that less than 8 per cent of egg-donation parents, and less than 5 per cent of those who used donor insemination, disclosed to their children.[77] In the near future, management of donor registers may become another problem. The Coalition Government is planning to abolish the HFEA and transfer its functions to the Care Quality Commission. There are concerns as to how effectively the Commission can maintain registers with donors' information.[78]

In conclusion, then, the current policy seems to undermine the sustainability of gamete donation while failing to promote communication within families. It is also questionable whether the new donor compensation policy will encourage more donors to come forward. The United Kingdom needs to work towards an inclusive, fully informed, debate on balancing the right to know one's genetic identity against a range of other rights and interests. Without such a debate, and a comprehensive policy review, more would-be parents will be obliged to seek treatment in jurisdictions where they forfeit any benefits or protections that the HFE Act would otherwise confer.

---

[73] Turkmendag, Dingwall, and Murphy (n 24).

[74] T Murphy and N Whitty, 'Is Human Rights Prepared? Risks, Rights and Public Health Emergencies' (2009) 17 *Medical Law Review* 219.

[75] Murphy and Whitty (n 74) 244.

[76] Turkmendag, Dingwall, and Murphy (n 24).

[77] S Golombok and others, 'Non-Genetic and Non-Gestational Parenthood: Consequences for Parent-child Relationships and the Psychological Well-being of Mothers, Fathers and Children at Age 3' (2006) 21 *Human Reproduction* 1918.

[78] T Hirsch, 'NHS Watchdog not Up to Taking on HFEA's Role' (Bionews 651, 2012) <www .bionews.org.uk/page_137301.asp> accessed 23 May 2012.

Being a Supranational Regulator in a Fast-Moving and Politically Sensitive Environment: The Case of the EU Ethics Review Procedure

Mihalis Kritikos

This perspective draws on the author's experience of working within the European Commission (Commission) and focuses on ethics review of research funding. This is the main mechanism for integrating ethics into research at European Union (EU) level. It provides for a case-by-case review of research proposals that are pre-selected for funding and raise sensitive ethical issues. The Commission's ad hoc ethics review panel procedure, which provides evaluations of sensitive ethical issues raised by selected proposals for EU research funding, highlights both the opportunities and the limitations of harmonization and standardization efforts with regard to EU-wide ethics oversight of research initiatives. What it also shows is that a completely harmonized approach in the field is neither feasible nor desirable. This perspective proceeds by first providing a brief overview of the management of ethical concerns in research at EU level. Thereafter, specific aspects of the ethics review procedure are examined, including institutional features, legal underpinnings, and organizational arrangements.

By the early 1990s, it was recognized that a more structured approach was needed at EU level with respect to dealing with ethical issues raised by the conduct of research. This was particularly so in politically sensitive areas of governance, such as those involving food products, where rapid changes had taken place in the wake of (bio) technological advances. This led to the opening up of ethics debate and review at EU level as a way of managing public concern over such changes, in addition to determining whether such developments were (ethically) desirable. Managing such concerns has been, and continues to be, a particularly important matter for the Commission. This is because the ethico-social implications of, as well as stakeholder concerns about, new (health) technologies need to be be addressed in order to ensure the EU, its market, and citizens benefit from them.

Although the EU is required to respect the ethical positions of its Member States (see Article 6(3) TEU), this does not mean that the incorporation of ethical norms has not taken place at EU level. In 1997, the European Group on Ethics in Science and New Technologies (EGE) was established to provide ethics advice to the Commission within its remit. Ethics-related norms are incorporated into EU law through secondary legislation, as well as soft law on clinical trials, good clinical practice, data protection, animal experimentation, genetically modified organisms, and the use of human biological tissues. Such norms are also to be found in EU research framework programmes, the opinions of the EGE, and the judgments of the Court of Justice of the European Union.

Notwithstanding the absence of a formal Treaty competence in relation to research ethics at EU level, the Commission's ethics review procedure does not take place in a legal void. Indeed, a series of EU legal instruments on research funding make explicit reference to, and highlight the importance of oversight and compliance with, ethical principles and standards. This has helped to define the institutional features and organizational mechanics of the ethics review procedure. Since 1994, all EU framework programme decisions on research have highlighted the importance of ethical conduct of research and the need for ethics review received legal recognition following the adoption of the Sixth Framework Programme (FP6).

All EU-funded research must comply with fundamental ethical principles, including those reflected in the EU Charter of Fundamental Rights and the opinions of the EGE. Moreover, the funding of certain fields of research is not permitted including those involving human cloning for reproductive purposes, modification of the genetic heritage of human beings which could make such changes heritable, and the creation of human embryos solely for the purpose of research or for the purpose of stem cell procurement. In relation to the funding of human stem cell research, there are also strict licensing and control procedures which must be adhered to in Member States where the research takes place. Those who receive EU funding for their research are also required to provide written confirmation to the Commission that they have local research ethics approval for their research; they have met all other necessary national and local regulatory requirements; and they will conduct their research in accordance with any additional requirements resulting from the EU ethics review procedure.

The organization of ethics review at EU level consists of three independent steps: ethics screening, ethics review, and ethics follow-up or audit. The management of this multilevel procedure is the responsibility of the Ethics Sector of the European Commission (DG Research and Innovation) which is located in the European Research Area Directorate. The Ethics Sector also acts as a liaison between those who receive framework programme funding, competent national authorities, and relevant ethics committees. It is also responsible for appointing members to ethics screening and review panels, as well as coordinating the entire evaluation process. Although ethics review of research proposals may take place before any selection decision by the Commission, such review is mandatory where research proposals involve some form of intervention with respect to human beings, research involving human embryonic stems cells, human embryos, and non-human primates.

Ethics review is carried out by independent experts. The panels reflect and comprise a variety of disciplines such as law, sociology, psychology, philosophy and ethics, medicine, molecular biology, chemistry, physics, engineering, and veterinary sciences. The panels are geographical and gender balanced. Their composition depends on the nature of the proposals under review. Each expert reads the proposals and then meets with other experts on the nominated panel to review ethical issues raised by such proposals. The aim is to reach a consensus on how best to deal with such issues and then to produce a report on how they should be managed. Typically, such reports include a list of identified ethical issues, details of the way in which they have been handled by the applicants, and any requirements and/or recommendations that the panel have for how such issues should now be dealt with by the applicants. These reports are then sent to applicants and the Commission takes the reports into account when decisions are made to fund projects. This is done by including the key findings from the report as requirements in grant agreements entered into by those applicants whose research projects are funded by the EU.

The Commission has also developed specific procedural rules regarding the formulation, designation, and working methods of ethics review panels. These include the appointment of members and chairs of panels, the duties and responsibilities of members, the allocation of reviewing tasks (for example, appointment of rapporteurs), the format for reports, the procedures to be adopted with regard to decision-making, the conditions for interaction with applicants for research funding, as well as local and/or national research ethics and other authorization bodies. A system for screening research proposals, remote and central ethics reviews, follow-up, and audit has also been developed. To assist panel members, guidance notes, background papers, assessment forms, templates, and checklists are also provided to assist with the review process. Guidance has also been prepared for research funding applicants/beneficiaries on matters that do not necessarily fall within the scope of EU law.

Notwithstanding the promotion of consistency in the EU ethics review procedure, there is a need to accept that there may be a degree of variation in approach adopted by the panels. This is due to their rotating composition, fluctuating group dynamics, and the fact that they review a diverse range of projects. This works in practice to limit the promotion of a standardized approach to examining ethical concerns that may be raised by projects under consideration. On occasion, where an individual research project raises a number of problematic ethical issues, it may be the case that the panel is unable to reach a consensus position. This may result in the panel offering a variety of views on particular issues, rather than attempting to reach a single consensus position.

A number of other concerns have been raised about the ethics review procedure which are worth noting here. First, it has been suggested that the procedure is promoting the Europeanization of research ethics which operates in a restrictive manner in practice. This is because it is limited to examining the ethical soundness of particular research protocols and to making recommendations regarding the conduct of ethical aspects of projects. The danger is that it may lead to a mechanistic approach to research ethics: namely, one that is limited to a set of pre-defined regulatory issues and organizational procedures. Secondly, the absence of a Treaty mandate in respect of research ethics that encompasses the composition, membership, and decision-making processes of ethics review panels has created legal and institutional ambiguity, particularly with regard to whether they should be subject to established methods of judicial or administrative review.

Notwithstanding such concerns, the informal and flexible approach adopted in relation to ethics review of research at EU level should be seen as one of its strengths. It has had a particularly positive influence at Member State level upon the design of research protocols and technological programmes, as well as in strengthening compliance with research ethics standards. It has been able to offer practical solutions to ethical conflict which may arise in relation to particular research projects. While such solutions may be offered, there is also a recognition that the views of ethics review panels cannot be substituted for that of Member State authorities with respect to the granting of approval for projects. In addition, the fact that ethics review is legally mandated in a variety of cases within the framework funding programmes means that it has become an authoritative point of reference for resolving ethical disputes that may arise in this regard with respect to the conduct and funding of research under such programmes. As a result of its normative influence, the ethics review procedure has evolved incrementally in both size and scope and there has been a significant increase in the number of research projects requiring ethics review and oversight in recent years.

The need to address problematic ethical issues raised by research projects means that the Commission has preferred to opt for a soft form of governance, as it permits flexibility in approach. In any case, an EU-wide harmonized framework for research ethics is unlikely to be legally feasible given that such a transfer of powers from Member State level would require unanimous political agreement in the Council of Ministers, as well as at an interinstitutional level. Legal feasibility concerns aside, an exhaustive harmonization of research ethics standards at EU level might not be desirable as ethical concerns regarding the conduct of research may be locally or nationally specific and linked to particular socio-cultural beliefs or historical narratives. A one-size-fits-all approach would not reflect such diversity and runs the risk of privileging particular views over others, with the potential to generate further conflict between Member States, as well as between Member States and EU institutions.

The Commission has been largely successful in promoting a workable, consistent, and centralized procedural approach to dealing with EU-wide ethics review of research funding, in the absence of a formalized Treaty mandate in the field. The emphasis has been on designing a procedural approach that respects ethical plurality while at the same time is sufficiently flexible to respond to the fast-moving nature of technological developments. It is an approach which provides an institutional space from which consensus may emerge and practical solutions can be found to promote important and ground-breaking research. It has proved to be particularly important in areas where non-scientific considerations regarding the funding of research are of particular concern. It has also provided a set of EU-wide procedural standards and mechanisms for the identification of what the ethical parameters should be in relation to research where such concerns have been raised.

More broadly, it has led over time to the development of a well-functioning organizational environment in relation to ethics governance of research at EU level. The ethics review panels have become more than advisory bodies that provide technical and ethical information at an institutional level. Situated at the intersection between law, ethics, and science, they have become important actors in their own right with respect to resolving, defining, and legitimating the boundaries of ethical acceptability regarding innovative research within EU's framework programmes on research. Their operation signifies a shift in the regulatory governance of research funding from a purely technocratic preserve to one where socio-cultural considerations are also seen as important.

What is emerging is a de facto Europeanization, as well as embedding, of an approach to research ethics. This should be seen as particularly important where Member States cannot agree *ex-ante* on the substantive content of aspects of research ethics and/or of the fundamental ethical principles. In such circumstances, the Commission's approach offers a wide range of potential solutions and non-binding viewpoints with respect to how problematic ethical issues should be interpreted and assessed in the context of an independent review procedure. This is assisted by the lack of a strict methodological protocol which allows panels to develop self-generated working practices and methods of evaluating specific types of research, including resort to a range of scientific, legal, and ethics sources and procedural options. The informal legal character of the panels, their rotating membership, the fact that they meet privately, and the diverse range of research protocols they are required to consider, are all factors that have contributed to the development of a distinctive EU approach to the assessment and management of research ethics. It is an approach which has become all the more necessary given the increased funding of research into new or emerging technologies where ethical plurality is much more likely to pose a problem. It has also helped to shape a 'responsible innovation' narrative in which ethics is to be seen as an inherent component in the design process of technologies, rather than as a constraint on advances in technology. In sum, it has been instrumental in promoting good governance in research within the EU.

PART V

BRINGING IT ALL TOGETHER

18

A European Law of New Health Technologies?

Mark L Flear, Anne-Maree Farrell, Tamara K Hervey,
*and Thérèse Murphy**

A. European Law and New Health Technologies

Setting out on this project, we asked ourselves: What—if any—are the defining features of European law approaches to new health technologies? What is the significance of European law to such technologies? To what extent and, if so, how is European law on new health technologies legitimated? What are—and what should be—the roles of markets, risk, rights, and ethics in that respect? Thus, our initial overarching research agenda concerned the relationships between European law *and* new health technologies.

In this chapter, we reflect on those relationships. In so doing, we ask a further question: To what extent does our investigation define a new field of scholarship—European law *of* new health technologies? To sharpen our focus, we begin by reflecting on our core concepts: first, 'new health technologies' and thereafter 'European law'.

1. New Health Technologies

What counts as a 'new health technology'? We do not offer a new singular definition—nor did we hope to do so. The concept seems to be insufficiently defined for both discursive practices (in varied contexts including academic, policymaking, and legislative) and effective regulation. This imprecision might well be quite deliberate and pragmatic: the risk of running behind the pace of scientific, and social, development gives both academics and policymakers good reason to eschew precise definitions.

But *novelty* is not necessarily a temporal phenomenon.[1] 'Old technology' can become 'new technology' where new applications or new linkages make its use more controversial.[2] Researchers and medical practitioners differ in what counts as a 'new' health technology.[3] Intellectual property also drives claims of newness.[4] Side effects, misconduct, and accidents also have profound effects on what is 'new'.[5] Novelty can thus be understood as almost entirely *context-specific*.

* Our thanks to David Fraser for an insightful peer review.

[1] eg some 'biotechnology medicines', such as recombinant insulin, have been on the market in the EU since the 1980s, see Chapter 2 in this collection.

[2] eg new applications of *in vitro* fertilization, see T Murphy, 'Repetition, Revolution, and Resonance' in T Murphy (ed), *New Technologies and Human Rights* (OUP 2009). See also Chapter 15 in this collection.

[3] Chapter 4 in this collection.

[4] Chapters 4 and 7 in this collection.

[5] See eg A Petryna, *Life Exposed: Biological Citizens after Chernobyl* (Princeton UP 2002).

What counts as 'new' may depend ultimately on human perceptions—what is seen or constructed as new, socially not just scientifically.[6] Thus, the visibility of technological developments may be more important than we imagine. Consumer, patient, or public attitudes to new health technologies, including whether they are desirable or undesirable, which feed into regulatory arrangements through democratic processes, depend more on perceived novelty than intrinsic qualities of a new (health) technology. Recognizing novelty as *constructed* explains why differences between perceived incremental change and perceived radical change also matter: the former is perceived as fundamentally less threatening, challenging, and risky than the latter.

Challenges of defining 'new health technology' also reflect the well-known difficulties in determining the meaning of '*health*'. Consider one of the widest definitions of health, that of the World Health Organization (WHO), and contrast this with the definitions found in the UN Millennium Declaration, or the Agreement on Trade-Related Aspects of Intellectual Property Rights (TRIPs). The former declares that 'the enjoyment of the highest attainable standard of health is one of the fundamental rights of every human bring without distinction of race, religion, political belief, or economic or social condition', and defines health as 'a state of complete, physical, mental and social well-being and not merely the absence of disease or infirmity'.[7] The latter, by contrast, focus upon those with the greatest health needs, for instance through the concept of 'essential medicines', or treating medically recognized disabilities or illnesses.[8]

Finally, what counts as a 'new health *technology*'? Going beyond medicines, medical devices, and surgical procedures, such technologies encompass organizational systems for health care provision, screening, technologies of health information, and 'eHealth'.[9] Even the simple technology of a book[10] challenges our notion of 'new health technology' and reminds us that novelty is not necessary instantiated in ways we might expect.

Our practical response to the definitional challenges was to leave the question of what counts as a 'new health technology' to our contributors: they represent a reasonably wide range of expertise. Reflecting on their approaches and choices, what can we learn? First, by and large, our contributors excluded 'green' technologies,[11] although of course these have important implications for (global) health. For example, the 'Green Revolution' of the 1960s and 70s was supposed to alleviate hunger in the global South;[12] relationships between genetically modified crops and allergies are

---

[6] Chapter 10 in this collection explores the concept of 'newness' in detail, drawing on the field of nanotechnology. On 'social not just scientific' see A Webster, *Health, Technology and Society: A Sociological Critique* (Palgrave Macmillan 2007) 171–5. See relatedly S Jasanoff, 'Experiments Without Borders: Biology in the Labs of Life', BIOS Annual Lecture, LSE 15 June 2006 <www.lse.ac.uk/bios> accessed 24 July 2012: 'I think that British politics of science and technology produces more dramatic pictures than America's, and more of British politics happens, a result, in the visual domain. . . . some of the best pictures that show what's going on in the public domain are produced [in the UK].'

[7] Constitution of the WHO, 22 July 1946, 14 UNTS 185 (1948), preamble.

[8] See further J Harrington and M Stuttaford (eds), *Global Health and Human Rights* (Routledge 2010); J Tobin, *The Right to Health in International Law* (OUP 2012); B Toebes (ed), *Health and Human Rights in Europe* (Intersentia 2012); B Toebes (ed), *Health and Human Rights in Europe* (Intersentia 2012).

[9] In the sense of technological support in health care practice, see the second Regulator's perspective in Part II of this collection.

[10] Chapter 15 in this collection.

[11] cf Chapter 10 in this collection.

[12] GS Khush, 'Green Revolution: Preparing for the 21st Century' (1999) 42 *Genome* 646; K Mechlem and T Raney, 'Agricultural Biotechnology and the Right to Food' in F Francioni (ed), *Biotechnologies and International Human Rights* (Hart 2007).

insufficiently understood;[13] bioremediation has important health implications.[14] The list could go on. Instead, the focus was primarily on 'red' technologies, which encompass the design and application of biomedicine. This focus is perhaps understandable given the use of such technologies to diagnose or alleviate (medically recognized) illness or disability. In any case, it represents an initial and important way forward towards considering the nature and scope of new health technologies, as well as offering an opportunity to expand the research agenda through the inclusion of, and/or comparison with, 'green' technologies in the future.

Secondly, the phrase 'new health technologies' resonates on at least three different levels.[15] It denotes a small number of generic groupings of types of technologies (for example, products, processes, or methods of using products). It can mean forms of technology organized by scientific or technical sphere. Or it can mean specific examples of these forms, with their applications. Our book offers a 'map' within which relationships between these different levels can be explored.[16]

Thirdly, *within* the field of 'new health technologies' we also find many definitional problems.[17] Law did not produce all of these problems; it does perpetuate them, however. For instance, European law distinguishes between pharmaceuticals/medicinal products, medical devices, treatment protocols/processes/therapies, surveillance, and diagnosis;[18] between curative, prophylactic, enhancing, and cosmetic technologies; between technologies for diagnosis, treatment, and monitoring; between pharmacological, immunological, or metabolic versus mechanical modes of action. Many of these distinctions are unconvincing in the context of new health technologies. New health technologies also overlap with categories generated by the interplay between science and regulation,[19] which have applications both within and outside health contexts. New health technologies thus fundamentally challenge the internal logics of Europe's regulatory regimes (particularly those of the European Union (EU)).[20] This challenge is one of the reasons for our frame of inquiry.

But what are the implications of the definitional conundrums that are highlighted here? First, regulatory authorities, forced to work within these definitional constraints, may struggle or fail to keep pace with technological developments, leading to a constant process of differentiation and adaptation through various mechanisms of governance to maintain (a degree of) connection.[21] Secondly, it can be unclear which regulatory regime

---

[13] The Royal Society, 'Genetic Modified Plants for Food Use and Human Health: An Update' (Royal Society, Policy Document 4/02, 2002) <http://royalsociety.org/uploadedFiles/Royal_Society_Content/policy/publications/2002/9960.pdf> accessed 18 July 2012.

[14] Bioremediation involves the use of micro-organisms to remove marine pollution, see Chapter 4 in this collection.

[15] As demonstrated by Chapter 4 in this collection in an analysis inspired by patent law.

[16] Chapter 4 in this collection. In similar vein, drawing out the concept of 'legal cartography', see B de S Santos, *Toward a New Legal Common Sense: Law, Globalization and Emancipation* (2nd edn, Butterworths 2002).

[17] Questions about definitions within the concept of 'new health technology' are picked up by several of the chapters in this collection, eg: Chapters 5, 7, 8, 12, and 15.

[18] Chapter 4, Section A and Table 4.1.

[19] Such as synthetic biology, nanotechnology, and biotechnology.

[20] See eg the following from this collection: Chapters 4, 9, 10, 12, and 16.

[21] See eg the following chapters in this collection: Chapters 9 and 12 and the first Regulator's Perspective in Part II and the Regulator's Perspective in Part III. On connection and new technologies, see more generally R Brownsword, *Rights, Regulation, and the Technological Revolution* (OUP 2008); R Brownsword and M Goodwin, *Law and the Technologies of the Twenty-First Century* (CUP 2012) 369–420.

applies, and due to the lack of clear legal definitions, undesirable regulatory gaps may appear.[22]

Thirdly, in the context of supranational/multilevel governance environments, technical or scientific developments which bring newness to health technologies are accompanied by complexity and even confusion arising from definitional imprecision. The problem of reaching consensus in European institutions (including science) makes governance of change a difficult task. It produces a resistance to unpicking what is agreed, contributing to the accumulation of a legal and regulatory heritage, and a potential misfit with new developments.[23] This highlights a paradox of technological novelty, yet often a response of governance continuity. There may be no easy solutions here except to allow for purposive disconnection between new health technologies and their governance, permitting the re-evaluation of definitional difficulties as and when they arise following implementation and practice,[24] and to adjust and reconnect accordingly.[25]

2. European Law

In our opening chapter, we defined '*European* law' as wider than the law of the EU, encompassing the law of the Council of Europe, as well as that of organizations such as the European Patent Office, the OECD, and WHO Europe. Moreover, because these overlapping legal orders reach into national legal orders in ways that belie hierarchical relations, we also conceptualize European law as both multilevel and pluralist.[26] Equally, we conceive '*law*' as a much wider category than 'legislation' and 'case law', with the legal institutions that develop it. 'Law' also includes within it ways in which these 'modes of governance' (if that is the 'meta-category') interact with regulatory strategies, including soft law such as technical guidelines, reporting obligations, and benchmarking and indicators.[27]

Arguably, our focus on *European law* was too narrow. If health technology is a global industry, why single out a *European* dimension? Perhaps our reference point should have been global law—for instance, including the law of the International Conference on Harmonisation of Technical Requirements for Registration of Pharmaceuticals for Human Use, the WHO UNESCO, and the World Trade Organization? Should we have discussed law from other jurisdictions, that is applied or avoided in European contexts? And why European *law*? Should we have had 'regulation', or even 'governance' as our central focus? However broadly one draws 'law', it is difficult to think of it as the 'meta-category', particularly once we depart from the nation-state as the geographical reference point or scale.

---

[22] As Chapter 12 in this collection notes for 'combined products'; similarly Chapter 8 in this collection points to the difficulties of defining drug delivery through nanotechnology, or innovative tissue engineering, in the terms of EU product liability law, which draws on the distinctions between 'medicinal products', 'medical devices', and 'blood, organs, human tissue and cells'.

[23] Chapters 10 and 12 in this collection.

[24] Chapter 5 in this collection.

[25] eg the decision of the Court of Justice of the European Union (CJEU) in Case C-316/09 *MSD Sharp & Dohme GmbH v Merckle GmbH* 5 May 2011 nyr prompted the EU Commission to propose amended legislation on information about prescription-only pharmaceuticals on the internet, see COM(2012) 48 final.

[26] Several of our contributors report on the implications of European law in various national contexts, see especially Chapters 5 and 8 in this collection.

[27] Such as found in the EU's 'new governance' approaches, see J Scott and DM Trubek, 'Mind the Gap: Law and New Approaches to Governance in the European Union' (2002) 8 *European Law Journal* 1; M Dawson, *New Governance and the Transformation of European Law* (CUP 2011).

But there are both practical and conceptual reasons for our focus. The practical reasons were discussed in the opening chapter of the book. If one sees European law as a multilevel pluralist legal system (and we do), the law of new health technologies in Europe *is* European law. In the policy and (some) legal discourse, and crucially in the discourses of the actors involved (regulators, industries, patients' groups, and the like), 'European' has a meaning—or, more precisely, a range of meanings. These encompass the different and arguably competing interests and aims of law and regulation—be they ethical, scientific, commercial/market, socio-cultural—concerning new health technologies and the multi-valuing of humans, their bodies, human cells, blood, tissue, and organs.[28] As outlined later, these are often presented as calibrated and 'in tune', but often essentially masking their (perhaps arguable) inherent incompatibility.

The conceptual reasons focus around heritage and, relatedly, imagined futures. Europe is home to many technological firsts, including both Louise Brown, the first 'test-tube' baby, and Dolly the sheep, the first successful attempt at cloning a mammal by means of nuclear transfer technology. It is the home, too, of legal experimentation. Consider the EU: it is neither state nor international, instead 'it stands between them, incorporates strains of each and interlocks with them both'.[29] The EU Charter of Fundamental Rights (EUCFR) is distinctive too. For instance, it establishes data protection as an autonomous fundamental right, a move that makes it stand out amongst human rights instruments which, by and large, hook data protection onto the right to privacy.[30] Or consider the European Court of Human Rights (ECtHR), praised as 'the crown jewel of the world's most advanced international system for protecting civil and political liberties'[31] and home to a body of case law that features strongly in the common law of human rights[32]—that is, in the migration of human rights ideas from one legal regime to another. And, just as interesting, in this common law realm, the ECtHR is both exporter *and* importer.[33]

Overall, these related institutional forms ensure that Europe's governance responses do not develop from a 'clean sheet', but are conditioned by what went before. Of course, this might generate both misfit between existing definitions or understandings and new developments, and regulatory gaps. It also means that 'European law' holds resources that can be refashioned and redeployed to 'keep up' and close any gaps, so as to govern in the face of the uncertainty, 'unknowing', 'cross-borderness',[34] and to shape technoscientific developments and futures.

---

[28] Chapter 9 in this collection, Sections C and D.

[29] N Walker, 'The Place of European Law' in J Weiler and G de Búrca (eds), *The Worlds of European Constitutionalism* (OUP 2011) 57.

[30] See European Union Agency for Fundamental Rights, *Data Protection in the European Union: The Role of National Data Protection Authorities* (Publications Office of the EU 2010) 6.

[31] L Helfer, 'Redesigning the ECHR: Embeddedness as a Deep Structural Principle of the European Human Rights Regime' (2008) 19 *European Journal of International Law* 125, 159.

[32] See C McCrudden, 'A Common Law of Human Rights' (2000) 20 *Oxford Journal of Legal Studies* 499; C McCrudden, 'Judicial Comparativism and Human Rights' in E Örücü and D Nelken (eds), *Comparative Law: A Handbook* (Hart 2007).

[33] See, respectively, *Opuz v Turkey*, App No 33401/02, Judgment of 9 June 2009 (wherein the ECtHR makes reference to communications of the UN Committee on the Elimination of All Forms of Discrimination against Women), and *Lawrence v Texas* 539 US 558 (2003) (wherein the US SCt makes reference to ECtHR case law).

[34] A term coined by Zhang, Marris, and Rose to describe a key but neglected regulatory challenge in the field of synthetic biology: JY Zhang, C Morris, and N Rose, 'The Transnational Governance of Synthetic Biology: Scientific Uncertainty, Cross-borderness and the "Art" of Governance' (2011) BIOS Working Paper No 4.

Indeed, Europe—encompassing European institutions, European governments, and European publics—is also the home of a range of imagined new-health-technology futures. These futures link in part to European pasts, actual (whether acknowledged or neglected) and possible.[35] They also link to the *non*-European: the EU, for instance, endorses a precautionary approach that has led to it being brought before a Panel of the WTO.[36] The influence of the non-European might also grow in the future in that the EU has been pitching itself as an actor in the international human rights field. This raises a host of interesting questions, including how going forward it can govern science and technology so as to avoid giving 'scientific' endorsement to ideas of racial superiority, and thereby give effect to the International Declaration on the Elimination of All Forms of Racial Discrimination: in its Preamble the latter emphasizes that 'any doctrine of racial differentiation or superiority is scientifically false, morally condemnable, socially unjust and dangerous, and that there is no justification for racial discrimination either in theory or in practice.'

Imagined futures, not surprisingly, draw heavily on markets. Individual European states see themselves in a race to techno-innovate; the EU is also in this race, having vowed to use scientific research to build the most competitive global-knowledge economy.[37] More speculatively, there may be distinctively European imaginaries around other ideas that organize much of the thinking, in Europe and elsewhere, on how new health technologies might be governed—ideas ranging from dignity to cross-borderness, to what can and cannot be patented, and who should have a say in such matters. Any such imaginaries will, of course, exert regulatory force, both in Europe and outside it, and both aspirationally and aversively (or, as some prefer to say, by means of 'policy learning').

In terms of why 'law' (rather than, say, governance), law remains an important part of the governance environment for new health technologies in Europe. Part of the reason is the way law engages with novelty. For instance, in the EU context, the European Medicines Agency's Road Map; or horizon scanning, through EuroScan on health technology assessment, stress the novelty of the science, rather than its continuity.[38] The ECtHR addresses the scientific and social novelty of new health technologies, which it represents as not only new,[39] but rapidly developing. This justifies the need to develop appropriate legal responses, which also includes anticipating developments in knowledge that could not be foreseen at the time of adjudication.[40] In both of these contexts there are some notable attempts to respond to novelty through new legal or regulatory ideas or institutions. Take, for instance, the rise of public bioethics: in the EU, through the European Group on Ethics in Science and New Technologies (EGE) and ethics committees; and in respect of the Council of Europe, the Oviedo

---

[35] See eg G de Búrca, 'The Road Not Taken: The EU as a Global Human Rights Actor' (2011) 105 *American Journal of International Law* 649; B Prainsack and R Gmeiner, 'Clean Soil and Common Ground: The Biopolitics of Human Embryonic Stem Cell Research in Austria' (2008) 17 *Science as Culture* 377, examining the impact of the past on Austria's stance on reproductive medicine.

[36] *EC-Measures Affecting the Approval and Marketing of Biotech Products*, Panel Reports WT/DS291/R, WT/DS292/R, WT/DS292/R, 29 September 2006.

[37] See eg Lisbon European Council Presidency Conclusions, 23–24 March 2000 <www.europarl.europa.eu/summits/lis1.en.htm#a> accessed 16 July 2012; European Commission, 'Europe 2020: A Strategy for Smart, Sustainable and Inclusive Growth' COM(2010) 2020 final.

[38] Chapter 4 in this collection.

[39] Of course, the technology at issue in *SH and Others* was not so new; as the applicants contended, it was 'common and readily available', and 'reliable'.

[40] Chapter 13 in this collection.

Convention[41] and the ECtHR's use of 'emerging consensus' in respect of new health technologies.[42]

Yet, in other examples, and arguably the dominant picture overall, existing legal ideas (rights, dignity, liabilities, authorization, etc.) and 'regulatory heritage'[43] (path dependency) are used to deal with what is at the same time presented as novel. For example, in the Council of Europe context, these might constitute 'fixed reference points'.[44] EU product liability law treats new health technologies in the same way as any other product. In fact, it strengthens the legal fiction that a comparative product is any other product in its 'development risks defence', which protects producers from liability for defects that could not be discovered at the time the product is put into circulation.[45] New health technologies, such as nanotechnology, are deemed insufficiently new to warrant new regulatory responses.[46] This reversion to pre-existing regulatory institutions, tools, and techniques, in an approach that can be described at best as 'incremental regulatory innovation'[47] is 'arguably the most pronounced feature of the EU's regulatory response to nanotechnology'.[48] So, in some important respects, European law of new health technologies not only is not so new itself, but also paradoxically quite often does not conceive of new health technologies as 'really new'. This dominance of legal continuity is therefore the reason for our focus on law.

Moreover, given the increasing attention paid to 'hybridity' and blurred boundaries between different forms of law,[49] between law and regulation, and in seeking optimal 'governance blends', we do of course need to think in terms of law's place—of how it does, and how it should, relate to other modes of governance.[50] But in so doing we must not lose sight of law. To guard against that risk, there needs to be attention to the *particular*—not just particular fields of law (intellectual property, crime, human rights) but also to particular legal and non-legal settings where the governance of new health technologies is determined or resisted. Our view is that law's part—including the part played by European law—in the governance of new health technologies is shaped by at least two forces. It is shaped, first, by the ways in which legal and non-legal forms of governance (ethics, for instance) are seen by legal actors and institutions. Secondly, it is shaped by the ways these different forms of governance are seen by non-legal and hybrid institutions and actors.[51]

There is one final, definitional point: Why European law and new health technologies?

---

[41] Chapter 3 in this collection.
[42] Chapter 13 in this collection.
[43] Chapter 10 in this collection.
[44] Chapter 3 in this collection.
[45] Chapter 8 in this collection.
[46] Chapter 10 and 12 in this collection.
[47] Chapter 12 in this collection, 272.
[48] Chapter 10 in this collection, 227.

[49] See eg Chapter 2 in this collection; F Cafaggi, 'New Foundations of Transnational Private Regulation' (2011) 38 *Journal of Law and Society* 20; G de Búrca and J Scott, 'Introduction: New Governance, Law and Constitutionalism' in G de Búrca and J Scott (eds), *Law and New Governance in the EU and US* (Hart 2006); G de Búrca, 'New Governance and Experimentalism: An Introduction' (2010) *Wisconsin Law Review* 227.

[50] The first Regulator's Perspective in Part II of this collection. See also SHE Harmon, G Laurie, and F Arzuaga, 'Foresighting Futures: Law, New Technologies, and the Challenges of Regulating for Uncertainty' (2012) 4 *Law, Innovation and Technology* 1.

[51] See further Chapter 13 in this collection; the various Regulators' Perspectives in this collection.

Why not, for example, European law and new technologies? Or European law and health? Or even European law and rights in health contexts? There are interesting questions here of classification and its consequences. There are also, we accept, existing strands of scholarship focused on each of these possible, alternative fields. This book, we think, contributes to those existing bodies of literature. But it also claims to do—or at least to attempt—more. It asks: Is there a distinctive 'European-ness' to the relationships between European law and new health technologies? And so we turn to our second main section of this chapter—to the defining features of European law approaches to new health technologies where we consider whether there is a European law *of* new health technologies.

B. Defining Features of European Law Approaches to New Health Technologies

Our inquiry began with the intuition that, if there is a European law of new health technologies, it is typified by a certain 'European-ness' in terms of four features: markets, risk, human rights, and ethics. The four frames are demonstrably overlapping and, in general, mutually supporting. This phenomenon presents us with some organizational difficulties in the text that follows. Rather than break up the flow of our discussion, or attempt to present an exhaustive coverage of all possible combinations of the four frames, we begin by considering each frame alone, before turning to examine some of the more pertinent combinations.

1. Four Frames

a. Markets

One (perhaps *the*) traditional economics view of the role of markets as a mode of governance is that markets promote free trade, which fosters efficiency. The role of law and other governance mechanisms is to 'hold the ring' for rational economic actors within a free market, and to correct for market asymmetries.[52] In other words, law or regulation is 'second best' to markets.[53] As examined in various chapters in this book, the relationship between markets, law, and regulation in the context of European law of new health technologies is more complex and nuanced than that account.

In the context of the EU, the market is the dominant frame for law on new health technologies.[54] Almost every area of the relevant EU law, especially its legislation, and the regulatory institutions and practices that surround it, refers to the market as its rationale. These references range from access of new products or services to the EU market; to regulation of research with a view to eventual marketing to protection of consumers (patients) once a new health technology is on the market. Even legislation that appears to have a stronger rationale than that of the market[55] is framed as being

---

[52] Such as informational asymmetries which might impede such rational behaviour.

[53] See T Prosser, *The Regulatory Enterprise* (OUP 2010) 2, drawing on one of the seminal works in the law and economics field of regulation: A Ogus, *Regulation: Legal Form and Economic Theory* (Hart 2004).

[54] Chapter 2 in this collection.

[55] eg the EU's Directive on Legal Protection of Biotechnological Inventions, which in many ways concerns the ethics of allowing patent protection on controversial inventions, eg those involving embryonic stem cells.

centrally concerned with the market.[56] The entire structure of EU regulation of new health technologies, the way the regulatory measures fit together, cross-refer to each other, and are justified, all concern the marketing of new health technologies. At a level of generality (though not at every aspect of the regulatory landscape), the EU's approach to risk, rights, and ethics is essentially all about the need to create, foster, and protect the EU's market.

Law and its supporting institutions are therefore used by the EU to facilitate market arrangements with respect to new health technologies. These legal concepts and institutions include (a) 'services' in health care; (b) the notion of 'product', especially 'safe product', for instance as applied to new health technologies that also involve parts of the human body; and (c) the institution of the 'competent authority', a trans-European requirement that presents itself as ensuring market parity for various actors within the context of development, production, and use of new health technologies.

Relevant EU regulation refers to the EU's 'internal market', and the perceived need for removal of barriers to trade within it, so as to optimize growth and economic opportunity for inventors, developers, producers, and distributors of new health technologies operating within the EU. Equally, patients have used the EU law focus on the internal market to escape perceived deficiencies in the regulatory environments in their home state. Likewise, Member States have used the 'safety valve' of availability of treatment abroad to sustain their regulatory choices in the face of local criticism.[57] In this assessment, the market rationale of EU law of new health technologies is legitimate. Pluralist arrangements whereby different countries may have different rules, but may not impede consumer (patient) access to markets in other countries, increase consumer (patient) choice and 'exit' from sub-optimal national regulatory arrangements.

By contrast, prizing a legally harmonized single EU market more highly than consumer rights has negative effects for consumers in countries where, for instance, prior to harmonization, product liability laws gave greater protection to consumers. The 'freezing' of EU law in time is also sub-optimal, as the law can fail to keep pace with technological developments.[58] The underlying rationale of EU legislation, to the effect that there is a single (albeit regulated) EU market in all products, is also flawed. The market for new health technologies is *not* a normal consumer-led market: the main 'consumers' are national health systems, and they do not behave like normal consumers—their decision-making is significantly more politically constrained. Similarly, 'slight deviations in domestic implementation' can be interpreted as leading to too much heterogeneity for optimal regulation, in terms of creating the space necessary for innovation to be translated into clinical or health care settings.[59]

Moreover, the binary division in European law between 'products' (which are the subject of 'ordinary' market trade, though may be regulated heavily if safety or quality is at issue) and 'the human body' (which is not, in European contexts, to be traded) is tested to destruction by the emergence of certain new health technologies.[60] The ways

---

[56] As strikingly seen in the *Brüstle* case in which the CJEU differed from the opinion of its AG to articulate a market-based rationale, rather than one based on dignity.

[57] eg Austria bars ova and sperm donation for IVF but recognizes the parental status of those who have gone abroad for treatment: see Chapter 13 in this collection. See also T Hervey, 'Buy Baby: The European Union and Regulation of Human Reproduction' (1998) 18 *Oxford Journal of Legal Studies* 207.

[58] Chapter 9, Sections C and D in this collection.

[59] Chapter 5 in this collection, 109. This argument is implicit in the chapter.

[60] Such as collagen scaffolds, for instance the decelluralized homograft valve being developed in Hannover's regenerative medicine research cluster: see Chapter 5 in this collection.

in which that binary division has infused the EU's legislative and regulatory structures for new health technologies (including the ways in which they are implemented in national contexts) not only provide opportunities for both a regulatory 'race to the top' as well as a 'race to the bottom', but can also be seen as nothing short of 'a manifestation of injustice'.[61] A comparison with the US approach highlights the deficiencies of the European law of this aspect of new health technologies. The implication is that, as a knowledge-based economy, the EU is not well served by the law. Of course, beyond the nation-state, law's reach is limited, as it represents the outcome of often intense political bargaining in a complex multilevel governance environment, with all of its messiness, deficiencies, and necessary silences or omissions designed to assuage political conflict.

EU law also refers to the place of the EU's new health technology industries within the *global* market, and the desirability of designing the EU's governance structures so as to optimize the ability of EU firms to compete there.[62] The ways in which individuals seek to escape or avoid governance arrangements within Europe that are perceived as sub-optimal are part of the way in which the global market frames European governance. A 'level playing field' is legitimated by pursuit of European industry's competitiveness in global markets. In addition, it could be argued that the EU uses its approach to governance in the field of health technologies as a way of positioning itself as a leading global actor in the field, by exporting its legal style to the global stage.[63]

Finally, in terms of the market frame, we note that new health technologies do not emerge fully formed *de novo* on the market, ready to be regulated, and only then become subject to law. Rather, law shapes the conditions for the emergence of new health technologies, their eventual constitution, and concrete manifestations and effects. As several of the chapters show, the market for new health technologies is *created*—through discourses of hope and expectation, promulgated by clinicians, patients, regulatory agencies, and health authorities.

b. Risk

The case studies of new health technologies in this book show that, in European contexts, it is not contested that a range of governance mechanisms is necessary to regulate risk. Furthermore, European law conceptualized as 'command and control' or as 'legislate and adjudicate' will capture only a small part of the story—hence our focus on law, whilst at the same time taking account of regulation and wider social norms.

The assessment and management of risk in the context of uncertainty and the legitimacy of risk-management institutions and regulatory structures resonates particularly in European contexts in relation to emerging new health technologies.[64] The *legitimacy* of EU governance of new health technologies may be assessed by reference to procedural or constitutional institutional standards; democratic standards;[65] functional or effectiveness standards; or value-based standards, depending on the objectives of the regulatory regime.[66] This latter conceptualization resonates strongly with risk-based standards of assessing the EU's regulatory regime for new health technologies, as the

---

[61] Chapter 5 in this collection, 113.

[62] Chapter 12, Section D3 in this collection.

[63] For an example of the EU's approach in this regard in the case of environmental policy, see RD Kelemen, 'Globalizing European Union Environmental Policy' (2010) 17 *Journal of European Public Policy* 335.

[64] Nanotechnology being the prime contemporary example here.

[65] Such as participation, transparency, deliberation, accountability.

[66] Chapter 9 in this collection.

expressed values of the EU's relevant legislation place 'consumer' or even 'patient' safety centre frame. In terms of effectiveness, the EU's regulatory strategies can be seen to be deficient, in that they tend to lock regulatory responses into established analytical frameworks, rather than being open to 'variation and evolution over time and between contexts',[67] lacking comprehensiveness and leaving regulatory gaps, and revealing deficiencies in regulatory capacity.[68] Effective EU governance of new health technologies needs to move beyond the 'risk as safety' frame, to conceptualize risk as a social and cultural construct, shaped by public perceptions and ethical concerns.[69]

In addition to the problems created by such a narrow construction of risk, the structures of EU law[70] also operate in practice to privilege relationships between regulators and the pharmaceutical industry, to the detriment of clinical investigators.[71] Implicit in this analysis is that EU law (as part of the global regulation of pharmaceuticals) is woefully inadequate to protect patients against risk. Moreover, the legal threat of enforcing contractual provisions with respect to confidentiality at least affects the timing of release of information about clinical trials to the scientific community and/or regulatory authorities, and may operate to intimidate some researchers into silence. Far from protecting patients against risk, in this account the 'dark side' of the law is instrumentalized to protect a powerful industry, which has integrated itself with both regulatory authorities and research institutions (universities) alike.[72]

As implied earlier, risk in EU law on new health technologies is normally conceptualized as patient, or even consumer, safety. However, this is not always the case. Risks faced by industries with respect to regulatory uncertainty and sub-optimality also feature fairly strongly in the relevant legal and policy instruments. The calculation of risk varies as between expert and non-expert views.[73] There is a tendency in the EU to focus almost exclusively on expert calculations of risk, and this is a key part of the 'regulatory heritage' of new health technologies in that context.[74] Equally, in EU law, the policy and regulatory debate is said to follow a peculiarly narrow trajectory focused around risk.[75] This 'European' approach to risk, which has been characterized as essentially protectionist, may be contrasted with the US approach, which is said to view risk as opportunity.[76]

The EU's reliance upon risk regulation of new health technologies as a means of *legitimation*[77] can be seen through considering three main factors:[78] the 'fit' of risk as

---

[67] Chapter 10 in this collection, 233.
[68] Chapter 12 in this collection.
[69] Chapter 9 in this collection.
[70] In particular, the narrow notion of *locus standi* in judicial review claims before the CJEU.
[71] Chapter 11 in this collection.
[72] Chapter 11 in this collection.
[73] Chapter 8 in this collection.
[74] Chapter 10 in this collection, using examples from nanotechnology.
[75] Chapter 10 in this collection.
[76] There is a diversity of views on point. Eg it has also been argued that the difference between the EU and the USA is one of process (EU) versus product (USA) in relation to risk assessment: see S Jasanoff, *Designs on Nature: Science and Democracy in the United States and Europe* (Princeton UP 2005) 83. See further JB Wiener, MD Rogers, JK Hammitt, and PH Sand, *The Reality of Precaution: Comparing Risk Regulation in the United States and Europe* (RFF Press 2011); D Vogel, *The Politics of Precaution: Regulating Health, Safety, and Environmental Risks in Europe and the United States* (Princeton UP 2012).
[77] See Chapter 10's analysis in this collection of European Parliamentary discourse around nanotechnology; Chapter 9's analysis in this collection of management of risks to public health from new health technologies.
[78] Chapter 9 in this collection.

defined by EU regulation with risk and ethics' concerns of relevant actors; the 'immanent critique' of whether regulation meets its stated aims; and the procedural arrangements for facilitating transparency and evaluation of the regulatory regime. The EU continues to make claims that its regulation of risk enhances public trust, even where assessing risk to consumers, patients, or the public within standard epistemologies is fundamentally challenged by the novelty of health technologies.[79] Moreover, far from opening up debate through legal requirements of transparency and accountability, in the context of a powerful global pharmaceutical industry, European law can be used to close down contestation, and to narrow the debate among medical experts and other relevant stakeholders.[80]

So far, we have considered, of course, only one element of European law of new health technologies: EU law. One inquiry suggested that the Council of Europe does not feature in the (standalone) market frame: however, as regards the risk frame, we would argue that it is present as 'rights as risk'.[81] By this we mean the potential for human rights to operate as a risk when failure to comply with rights or otherwise meet the requisite standards undermines institutional or organizational reputation and standing. Human rights, in other words, are an 'institutional risk' that must be managed. But the imbalance in coverage needs to be addressed further, and to do so we turn now to the third of our legitimating frames: human rights. The law of the Council of the Europe and the law of the EU are present here. We also find both domestic and international human rights law, as well as a range of rights- and anti-rights activism (some of which might link to what science and technology studies (STS) describes as 'biocitizenship').[82]

c. Human rights

Generally, human rights operate as a kind of bridge between theoretical and emotional grounds for action—and from there to the fundamentally practical. Put differently, there is a strong empowering and *instrumental* dimension to human rights; they provide a form of attention to the world that underpins action that might disrupt or shape trajectories in innovation, through concrete techniques and practices, especially law. Indeed, this might be part of the reason why some have asked if they will replace (bio) ethics in the governance of the life sciences and related technologies.[83]

Human rights, on the face of it, are an important dimension of European law of new health technologies. There is no shortage of legal rules (albeit some of them are on the 'softer' end of the rule-spectrum): most notably, there is the European Convention on Human Rights (ECHR), the European Charter of Fundamental Rights (EUCFR), and both the European Social Charter and the Oviedo Convention, as well as rights protections (including direct incorporation of the ECHR) in the legal frameworks of individual European states. More than this, rights-based approaches to the regulation of new health technologies have been recommended by advisory groups such as the EGE.[84] The EU, given both the commitment to seek accession to the ECHR and the status of

---

[79] Such as nanotechnology, see Chapter 10 in this collection.
[80] Chapter 11 in this collection.
[81] Chapter 17 in this collection. On 'rights as risk' and 'risk within rights', see more generally T Murphy, *Health and Human Rights* (Hart 2013 forthcoming) ch 4.
[82] Chapter 13 in this collection.
[83] Chapters 13 and 14 in this collection.
[84] See eg G Hermerén, 'Accountability, Democracy, and Ethics Committees' (2009) 2 *Law, Innovation and Technology* 153; House of Commons Committee on Science and Technology, 'Human Reproductive Technologies and the Law' HC 7, 2004–2005.

the EUCFR, also seems to be signalling its own human rights intentions, perhaps a more coherent human rights policy than previously.[85] And, the ECtHR, for its part, seems alert both to the need for substantive rights protections and to the ways that human rights encourage, or even mandate, certain principles of governance.[86] It is also alert to new technologies as a threat to human rights, and to the ways that new 'techno-enabled' rights could threaten the balancing of rights and interests mandated by, for instance, Article 8 ECHR.[87]

There is, however, a counter-story. As regards health, it could be said that EU law has been less about human rights and more about rights to information, to provide services, and to avail of such services.[88] More generally, the European Economic Community at its inception may well have been more human rights-robust than today's EU.[89] The lack of cases on new health technologies before the ECtHR is, of course, another reason to doubt the centrality of human rights law to European law of new health technologies. Relatedly, the ECtHR usually provides a wide 'margin of appreciation' to contracting states when it considers that there is no European consensus, 'either as to the relative importance of the interest at stake or as to the best means of protecting it, particularly where the case raises sensitive moral or ethical issues'.[90]

Still, there is a direction of movement in the jurisprudence of the ECtHR towards increasing scrutiny of national policies in contexts where health technologies are developing.[91] More importantly, in terms of European law of new health technologies—specifically, in terms of human rights having not just a role in the governance of new health technologies but a role that could be said to be distinctively European—the margin of appreciation doctrine[92] seems to be central. We say this for two reasons. First, this doctrine is an ongoing experiment in the negotiation of a core human rights question and, relatedly, of European identity: namely, how to achieve a balance between universalism and particularism? Secondly, the doctrine signals the productive nature of European law: the ECtHR does not simply reflect consensus, but can also be seen to play a significant role in *creating* the consensus.[93] In similar vein, as we discuss later, because the ECtHR sees human rights as having a procedural dimension, rights may also shape what is expected both when European law of new health technologies is 'in the making' and when that law aims to be 'future proof'.[94]

Attention to human rights also highlights how the European law of new health technologies is pluralist—but with a minimum core. This is apparent in, for example, the notion of margin of appreciation and in strong variations in terms of national interpretations of EU law at the stage of implementation of EU Directives.[95] New

---

[85] The call for greater coherence was made, eg, in 'Leading By Example: A Human Rights Agenda for the European Union for the Year 2000'.

[86] Chapter 3 in this collection.

[87] See respectively *S and Marper v United Kingdom* [GC] (2009) 48 EHRR 50 at para 71, 112; *Odièvre v France* [GC] (2003) 38 EHRR 871.

[88] Chapters 6 and 17 in this collection. See further TK Hervey and JV McHale, *European Union Health Law* (CUP 2014 forthcoming).

[89] As Gráinne de Búrca has argued (n 35).

[90] *Evans v United Kingdom* [GC] (2008) 46 EHRR 34, para 77.

[91] Examples include gender reassignment surgery, and the relatively strong steer given to contracting states, as well as strong dissenting opinions, in cases concerning ARTs. See Chapters 3 and 13 in this collection.

[92] Chapter 3, Section C and Chapter 13 in this collection.

[93] Chapter 3, Section C and Chapter 13 in this collection.

[94] See text at nn 105 and 159. See more generally Chapters 3 and 13 in this collection.

[95] Chapters 5, 8, 9, 10, 12, and 17 in this collection.

health technologies, as many have noted, raise issues of deep and reasonable disagreement: constitutional pluralism is how Europe manages these disagreements, and both constitutes itself as a distinct order in the global system and projects itself within it by offering examples of governance approaches to new health technologies.

Within the general framework of pluralism, we discern a 'minimum core' of non-negotiable *substantive* European law of new health technologies. Emanating from the Council of Europe, and implicit in the ECtHR's jurisprudence, this minimum core focuses around human rights (mainly 'civil and political' rights, but also to some extent economic and social rights)—in particular, rights related to autonomy or privacy,[96] as well as to some extent equality and the right to health.[97] In EU law, the non-negotiable focuses on the right to privacy and related rights. Thus, human rights in the European law of new health technologies are not infinitely malleable. This minimum core of European law of new health technologies may include implications such as obligations to ensure adequate information is given to users of new health technologies on the benefits and risks of their use; to help and protect people (the young, the very old, those who lack capacity) who are unable to make their own health care decisions; to ensure quality and safety of new health technologies for the public in general; and to ensure that new health technologies do not increase existing social inequalities. Such obligations flow from extant standards within the Council of Europe; most of them are also reflected in EU law.[98]

We also discern an increasingly accepted notion of a minimum core of *procedural and institutional* European law of new health technologies. European human rights law prescribes which interests have to be considered, promoted, and balanced in whatever regulatory framework is adopted (at national or transnational levels) and, to an increasing extent, the institutional arrangements through which these processes must take place. Although the substantive balance of these interests is contextually variable, the procedural requirement to consider relevant interests is non-negotiable. In the discourse,[99] this minimum core includes strong notions of transparency, thereby facilitating broad public debates which are said to legitimate law and regulation of new health technologies. So, for instance, the ECtHR accepts stronger differences in approach, through the legal doctrine of the margin of appreciation, where there is evidence of wide public deliberation on the new health technology at issue. Indeed, for the ECtHR, 'good' European law of new health technologies is regularly reviewed and revised, taking into account not only developments in science, but also those in society.[100] In the EU context, the notion of a 'competent authority', with obligations to report to the EU's institutions, used in the harmonization strategies of the EU in many of its legislative instruments, imposes a non-negotiable institutional obligation on Member States, even if the details of operation of national 'competent authorities' vary significantly.[101]

Finally, notions of the 'human' in human rights are likewise salient to European law of new health technologies. Generally, although not discussed directly in this collection

---

[96] The consent principle, respect for private and family life.

[97] The 'minimum core' identified in Chapter 3, Section F in this collection.

[98] With the possible exception of the last, although EU law does recognize the principle of inequality, and is committed to promoting 'health for all' in many of its policies, see European Commssion Communication on *Solidarity in Health: Reducing Health Inequalities in the EU*, COM (2009) 567 final.

[99] Though would be difficult to defend the idea that this has been realized in practice.

[100] Chapter 13, Section E3 in this collection.

[101] See Chapters 9 and 10 in this collection.

in, say, discussions touching on the embryo in European law[102] (or so-called 'post-humans'[103]), this salience is apparent in relation to, for instance, the question of the rights holder and who has rights protections in the field of xenotransplantation.[104] In the EU the human holds rights, and the non-human is subject to weak welfare considerations, but is largely effaced from law. This process of the sequestration of the 'creaturely' in EU governance of new health technologies is, perhaps unsurprisingly, related to its specific concerns, especially around safety, and by implication its focus on markets, that is, ensuring consumption of products. By contrast, however, the Council of Europe, recognizes the unprecedented transpecies-hybridity of xenotechnologies and the need for more robust protections for the non-human. Overall, however, the non-human is largely 'rubbed out' of European law. Nevertheless, in this way the meaning of 'human' in human rights is highlighted in European law of new health technologies, raising the question: Are human rights themselves future proof? Of course, European law of new health technologies relies not only on *human* rights, but also on other non-market frames, such as ethics, to which we now turn.

d. Ethics

What about ethics, the final frame in our quartet? One point stands out: ethics, for a range of reasons, is hard to pin down. This seems true as a general claim; it is also true in the context that concerns us—European law of new health technologies. Why is this so? First, ethics has not been a dominant feature of the European policy landscape.[105] True, ethics has been a strong frame in EU research funding regulation[106] and in the use of human biological materials[107] and the ECtHR does grant a wider margin of appreciation where there is no European consensus, 'particularly where the case raises sensitive moral and ethical issues'.[108] However, none of these developments places ethics as a central influence on policy or on law. There is also a tendency, prevalent across the European law and policy landscape, to make references to ELSI (ethical, legal, and social implications), to 'ethics and rights' or 'law and ethics', or to 'sensitive moral or ethical issues'. These relentless linkages do not help when the question is: What is the role of ethics in European law of new health technologies?

Secondly, if we accept that European law is, or could be, influenced by the emerging international governance framework on new health technologies,[109] we face a further problem: the 'bioethical triangle'.[110] Human rights are a point of departure in the international framework, but they do not stand alone—rather, they are one part of an ethical plurality, sharing the regulatory terrain with both a dignitarian ethic and a

---

[102] Itself implicated in several chapters, eg Chapters 2 and 13 in this collection.
[103] I Karpin, 'The Uncanny Embryos: Legal Limits to the Human and Reproduction Without Women' (2006) 28 *Sydney Law Review* 599.
[104] Chapter 16 in this collection.
[105] Chapters 2, 3, and 14 in this collection.
[106] See further the Regulator's Perspective in Part IV of this collection.
[107] See Chapters 5 and 9 in this collection.
[108] *Evans* (n 90).
[109] See in particular the UN Declaration on Human Cloning 2005 and UNESCO's clutch of international biotechnology instruments: the UDBHR 2005, the International Declaration on Human Genetic Data 2003, and the Universal Declaration on the Human Genome and Human Rights 1997.
[110] See eg R Brownsword, 'Human Dignity, Ethical Pluralism, and the Regulation of Modern Biotechnologies' in Murphy (n 2).

utilitarian one.[111] Occasionally, the plurality will converge around a consensus: more often, however, 'choices will have to be made'.[112]

So-called 'regulatory ethics' adds to the difficulty. Even if we look only at medical ethics and bioethics, casting these as two forms of ethics that exert regulatory influence in Europe, we are faced with a range that includes academic, clinical or professional, corporate, and public bioethics. Each of these contributes to the governance of new health technologies and to what is, and what is not, seen as within (European) law's reach. For instance, to avoid the legal risk of rights, and other legal and non-legal risks, science and technology companies may work on 'ethical prophylaxis';[113] in other words, on finding ways to protect their technologies by means of their own 'good practice'.

Academic bioethics, in the wake of the 2005 UNESCO Declaration on Bioethics and Human Rights, has spent time investigating not just the tensions within that Declaration but also two far broader questions: namely, could human rights subsume bioethics, and should it?[114] Human rights lawyers—in Europe and elsewhere—have shown no particular interest in those questions or in the analyses being offered by bioethicists. Dignity has drawn their attention,[115] and the Oviedo Convention has sparked interest too, but outside these developments there is little of note.[116] The ECtHR, for its part, has been less than encouraging: giving advice on Recommendation Rec(2003) 10 of the Committee of Ministers concerning xenotransplantation, representatives of the Court suggested that the ECHR 'should be understood as a legal instrument aimed at securing individual rights and as such it may be of limited relevance to policy issues in the field of bioethics'.[117] So is the ethics frame a sideshow or even an irrelevance in European law of new health technologies?

The answer is that ethics is neither a sideshow nor irrelevant: in what follows we explain why. Let's start with public bioethics—whether that be the EGE or an ethics advisory group in a particular European state.[118] For us, this is a particularly interesting regulatory force. Our decision to include a set of regulators' perspectives testifies to our interest: several of these regulators serve, or have served, on bodies that are engaged in

---

[111] See eg Universal Declaration on Bioethics and Human Rights (UDBHR), Art 2(d).

[112] H Somsen, 'Regulating Human Genetics in a Neo-Genetic Era' in Murphy (n 2); see the notion of 'ethical subsidiarity' in Chapter 16 in this collection.

[113] The phrase comes from S Franklin, 'Ethical Biocapital' in S Franklin and M Lock (eds), *Remaking Life & Death: Toward an Anthropology of the Biosciences* (SAR Press 2003). She notes that ethical concerns are increasingly being 'built into' new life forms, as eg, in the development of a stem cell extraction procedure which removes one cell from the blastocyst without impinging on its ability for further development.

[114] See eg Chapter 14 in this collection, and RE Ashcroft, 'The Troubled Relationship Between Human Rights and Bioethics' in MDA Freeman (ed), *Law and Bioethics: Current Legal Issues, vol 11* (OUP 2008).

[115] See eg C McCrudden, 'Human Dignity and Judicial Interpretation of Human Rights' (2008) 19 *European Journal of International Law* 655; T Murphy, 'Taking Revolutions Seriously: Rights, Risk and New Technologies' (2009) 16 *Maastricht Journal of European and Comparative Law* 15.

[116] Doing human rights 'ethically' is an emergent theme (see eg T Murphy, 'Public Health *Sans Frontières*: Human Rights NGOs and "Stewardship on a Global Scale"' (2011) 62 *Northern Ireland Legal Quarterly* 659) but this has not translated into increased interest in rights, ethics, and new health technologies.

[117] Draft Memorandum to Recommendation Rec(2003)10 of the Committee of Ministers to Member States on Xenotransplantation—Explanatory Memorandum. 5 June 2003, CM(2002) 132 Addendum, at Appendix <http://wcd.coe.int/ViewDoc.jsp?id=45827> accessed 18 July 2012. Cf 'Research Report: Bioethics and the Case-law of the Court' (Council of Europe/European Court of Human Rights, 2012) <www.echr.coe.int> (Case-law–Case-Law Analysis–Research Reports).

[118] The UK's Nuffield Council on Bioethics being one illustration.

public bioethics.[119] What we cannot do, however, is specify the nature or the extent of the regulatory force that is being exerted by this form of ethics. Equally, we cannot say whether it has a distinctive 'European-ness' to it. Hence, our proposal for work diagnosing why, policy-wise, bioethics has been the 'go to' discipline for contributory expertise (rather than say law or, within that, human rights law). We also called for work that examines how individual advisory groups treat legal knowledge and, indeed, legal experts where they form part of the membership.[120]

Work of this sort is important because it will bring to light whether and how public bioethics expresses and fosters European (and not just EU) citizenship or, what STS calls, 'biological citizenship' (and the related matter of who—or what—is excluded or largely effaced, that is, the non-human).[121] It will also help us to dissect claims that public bioethics plays another, rather different role—of providing a focus for expert-generated discourse, which produces and legitimates an expert-led EU regulatory environment that supports innovation.[122] Finally, it should help us to answer the interesting question of whether there is a European bioethics and allows us to discern the reach, content, and meaning of that bioethics.[123]

For now the answer we give to the question of whether there is a Europena bioethics is 'no' (or at least not yet). Any claim that the precautionary principle constitutes such a European bioethic can be dismissed because as yet, even in the apparently advanced engagement by the EU, this principle has neither an agreed meaning nor a commonly accepted normative force.[124] In similar vein, if we look at Council of European law, any claim focusing on dignity as the core European bioethics also needs to be dismissed or, at all events, put on hold.[125] Obviously, for some, the place of dignity in the EUCFR is grounds for optimism.[126] And, looking ahead to an EU that has acceded to the ECHR, we may imagine an enhanced role for the dignity, focused Oviedo Convention.[127]

However, in tension with this notion of a European law of new health technologies founded on a European bioethic of dignity, we see the EU as a framework within which ethical differences are managed, in the pursuit of the 'prize' of creating and sustaining the internal market, and a sufficiently globally competitive industry.[128] The ethics of actually providing patient *access* to new health technologies[129] are not the subject of European law.[130] Perhaps this should not surprise us: ethical questions are a 'national matter' in EU contexts, and the ECtHR sees the lack of a European consensus, 'particularly where the case raises sensitive moral or ethical issues', as one of the triggers

---

[119] See the Regulator's Perspectives in Parts I, II, III, and IV of this collection.

[120] For these proposals, see Chapter 13 in this collection.

[121] Chapter 16 in this collection.

[122] Chapters 2 and 16 in this collection.

[123] This question is posed in Chapter 14 in this collection.

[124] See the discussion in Chapter 14 in this collection. For a developing argument on the principle's role in a rights-based community, see Brownsword (n 21) and Brownsword and Goodwin (n 21).

[125] Chapter 3 in this collection.

[126] Chapter 9 in this collection.

[127] Chapter 14 in this collection.

[128] Chapters 2 and 6 in this collection; Syrett in this collection.

[129] Say, to members of vulnerable groups such as those suffering rare diseases.

[130] Save, perhaps, emergent Council of Europe law on the 'right to health' combined with the principle of equality; and, perhaps, the emergent governance processes in the EU's promotion of exchange of information between national health technology assessment agencies: see, respectively, Chapters 3 and 2 in this collection.

for a wide margin of appreciation.[131] In any event, if we are seeking a European bioethic, as a central frame or feature of today's European law of new health technologies, both precaution and dignity fall short of the mark.

Still, the EU's 'ethical market'—an idea developed in a number of chapters—seems an interesting offshoot of the question about a European bioethic. Might it be an entity that is at once distinctly European and distinctly ethical? And by drawing in the European Patent Convention, with its reference to morality,[132] could we broaden this ethical market beyond an EU-identity? Could we also draw in the Council of Europe and, in so doing, introduce the idea of a human rights-based market? The potential is there. On the other hand, there are grounds to be doubtful. The EU successfully navigated significant differences over the ethical dimensions involved in the donation of blood, human tissue and cells, and organs. To do so, the EU invoked the authority of the Council of Europe in matters concerning ethics and human rights. The reality of the market (particularly in blood) in Europe was almost entirely suppressed in the text of the relevant legislation.[133] We would do well to be sceptical over whether this market-suppressing approach contributes to the effective management of risk, especially in clinical settings. Likewise, EU law on gamete donation asserts that it is based on an ethic of altruism, ignoring the very real market in gametes (both for infertility treatment and for stem cell research) and the different positionings of women and men, and of different women, in this market.[134]

In summary, then, although we have shown that the place and roles of ethics in our new field of inquiry—European law of new health technologies—are important, for now we cannot do much more than raise some of the questions as to why this is so and point to importance of following up this frame.

2. Frames in Combination

a. Markets and...

In general,[135] EU law of new health technologies conceives the need to protect against risks as fundamentally linked to the market frame. The need to safeguard patients, consumers, or public health from undesirable outcomes, in the context of uncertainty, is justified by the need to create and sustain markets in those new health technologies. We see this in the range of EU law on new health technologies, including product safety and product liability legislation. This legitimation of European law of new health technologies is found strongly in EU law, but also seems to be associated with other legal orders, such as the World Health Organization (WHO),[136] although it is not represented in Council of Europe law.

Our case studies show that, in general, markets and risk reinforce one another in EU law in two closely related ways—either a risk narrative *supports* the market frame, or the risk narrative is *embedded within* the market frame. Areas such as EU law on research

---

[131] See, respectively, Chapters 2, 13, and 14 in this collection.
[132] Odell-West in this collection.
[133] Chapter 7 in this collection.
[134] Chapter 17 in this collection.
[135] Although we note here that we were unable to agree whether this holds true for EU law on the human body and new health technologies; further investigation would be necessary to resolve this difference of opinion.
[136] Chapter 2, n 102, in this collection.

funding, research processes, intellectual property, and product safety are all examples of these connections between markets and risk. The constant reference point in these areas of EU law is the aim of getting new products or services to market, in such a way that consumers will have confidence in their quality and safety.[137] The legitimacy of regulatory management of uncertainties and risks entailed in new health technologies is assessed by reference to the ways that it supports the EU's market in new health technologies.

Having said that, a more nuanced approach is required if we are to understand the interrelationship between risk and markets in the context of European law regarding the collection and supply of human biological materials, whether in their raw form or as part of tissue engineered products. Running strongly through European social thought is the need to avoid the instrumentalization or commodification of the human body. This has become embedded not only in key (bio)ethical texts and declarations, but also in rights-based legal instruments such as the EUCFR and the Council of Europe's Oviedo Convention. So how can this be squared with the commercial value that is now ascribed to such materials in the wake of scientific and technological advances?

Reliance has been placed on the ill-defined notion of human dignity to exclude the commodification of, as well as trade in, such materials.[138] This is at odds with the reality of a thriving and lucrative European and, indeed, global market in human biological materials, such as blood and various types of tissue. These high-level ('constitutional') legal instruments may be read as one way in which the EU seeks to reconcile the relationship between risk and markets in this context. At the level of legislation, however, the EU does not fully acknowledge the dimensions of the market in the context of the design of the EU-wide blood regulatory regime for blood, for example. This failure has adverse implications not only for facilitating effective risk governance in the context of market activity, but also for broader questions concerning regulatory legitimacy.[139]

In terms of legitimation, here we also see the idea that the EU's market itself embodies or embeds a particular approach to risk management, and that the EU's market is constructed as one which is safe for consumers/patients.[140] Risk and market are also deployed to construct the EU as a democratic order. Risk operates in support of the market, which is therefore kept working, but at the same time also provides a way of making the EU capable of being audited and inspected as it relates to its citizens and broader publics. The risk/market narrative thus plays a key role in legitimating EU regulation.

The Council of Europe's approach to both risk and markets is more difficult to unravel. The ECtHR's approach to the 'right to health' may be seen as incorporating a 'precautionary' approach to risk, especially in the context of environmental threats to health, but also carried over into contexts concerning the right to information about an individual's health (such as results of genetic testing).[141] In general, both markets and risk, and the market/risk nexus are much less visible in Council of Europe governance than in the EU context. Indeed, in *SH and Others v Austria* the Grand Chamber of the ECtHR, upholding Austria's ban on third party donation for IVF, mentions the

---

[137] eg products must be tested in ways that ensure minimization of risks to consumers when they reach markets.
[138] Chapter 3 in this collection.
[139] Chapter 9 in this collection.
[140] Chapters 2 and 9 in this collection.
[141] Chapter 3, Sections C1, D1, and D3 in this collection.

opportunity for Austrians to travel abroad for treatment and have their parental status recognized at home, yet it makes no mention of any of the risks that attach to cross-border reproductive care.[142] So, if we are serious about a *European* (and not simply a *European Union*) law of new health technologies, we probably cannot characterize that law as constructed entirely through market-based legitimation of risk regulation.

To summarize, European law of new health technologies works to articulate the notion that the European market in new health technologies is safer, more respectful of human rights, and more ethical, than other markets. European law of new health technologies is thus constructed as the polar opposite of a 'global Vegas', where more or less 'anything goes'. European institutions have to grapple with a balance between, on the one hand, a totalizing discourse which pushes 'European' standards towards higher standards (a position associated with the European North and West), so that no one can 'escape', and a notion of European diversity and pluralism, or even regulatory competition (a position associated with the European East and South), which enhances choice (for those who can move within Europe).[143] Choice itself, as a core manifestation of autonomy in the human rights and ethics frames discussed later, is thus a legitimating factor in European law of new health technologies.

The apparent primacy of the market in the European context might be disrupted, for example, by the EUCFR and its relation to the ECHR. If the EUCFR represents how the EU characterizes and formulates governance (with respect to new health technologies), by reference to human rights, in terms of its immanent, self-proclaimed values, this *if demonstrated* would represent a fundamental change to the EU's self-representation as understood here. The implications of that discourse include that the EU is not a market organization, or not just a market organization, with its regulatory activities legitimated by reference to the efficiency of markets. Rather, the EU would be laying claim to the legitimating elements of human rights, and resonating with the heritage of the Council of Europe, to justify its regulatory activities. But while this discourse is discernible at the level of abstract legal instruments (such as the EUCFR), it disappears almost entirely when the frame or scale of reference[144] changes to the detail of legislation or regulatory norms.

b. Human rights and ethics

Earlier we mentioned 'ELSI'—ethical, legal, and social implications of new health technologies. We were unable to tease out the relationships between the individual components; doing so is, we think, an important ongoing task—one that calls not for grand diagnoses but for close, careful studies of legal and non-legal sites where decisions are made about what is ethical, what is legal, the links between them,[145] and so on. Imagine, however, that it is not ELSI but rather 'ethics and human rights', a combination of two of our four frames, which needs to be dissected. Is this more straightforward? Maybe, but it is not by much.

One challenge is that human rights manifest as law and as discourse.[146] 'Ethics and human rights' will have different meanings depending on whether one reads

---

[142] Chapter 13 in this collection.
[143] Chapter 17 in this collection.
[144] Da Sousa Santos (n 16).
[145] R Brownsword, 'Bioethics: Bridging from Morality to Law' in Freeman (n 114).
[146] Chapters 2, 13, and 17 in this collection.

'human rights' to mean law, discourse, or both. And where the combination changes to 'ethics and *rights*', other possibilities—consumer rights, rights for non-humans[147]—will emerge.

Both the recent and the more distant past produce challenges too. Some may tell a story of the birth of human rights and bioethics in the Nuremberg Trials, and of overlapping or shared experiences subsequently (notably around the rise of informed consent), thus claiming a 'European-ness' to human rights and ethics as a feature of European law of new health technologies. Yet origin stories are always controversial and others will downplay, or even dismiss, these overlaps between human rights and bioethics.

The recent past, too, is unlikely to produce consensus on the relationship between ethics and rights. It has, to be sure, been a time of internationalization and institutionalization: there has been almost a 'race to the top' for ethics and human rights, both separately and in tandem. One instance of the latter is the 2005 UNESCO UDBHR.[148] Another is the rise of an 'almost unquestionable presumption' that it is best for children to know about the gamete donor(s) who played a role in their conception.[149] This presumption draws both from the ethical notion of 'best interests' and from the human rights commitment to respect for private life[150] (and, in places, from the impropriety of state-supported deception[151]). A third illustration is provided by EU orphan medicines legislation.[152] The aim of this legislation is to entitle patients suffering from rare conditions to the same quality of treatment as other patients, which we may see as 'equity' and 'non-abandonment' (a notion reflected in the very term 'orphan'), meaning a combination of an ethic of solidarity (which is embedded in European health care systems) and the right to equal treatment.

Turning to the EU's general approach to regulating new health technologies,[153] we may be more explicit again. In general, ethics and (human) rights in this context can be *melded*, as their roles in EU regulation of new health technologies are similar. We particularly note 'an ethics or (human) rights-based approach to markets' in three areas: first, research funding and intellectual property rights promoting research; secondly, safety in research processes and products; and, thirdly, consent in research processes. Of course, even if the overall conclusion is that rights and ethics are used 'more as a means of legitimating other framing choices than as a frame in themselves',[154] this too is a melding of rights and ethics.

But 'in tandem' is not the only, or even the dominant, mode for ethics and human rights. The UDBHR—a universal declaration on bioethics *and* human rights—has already attracted a wide range of criticism.[155] Meanwhile, as noted earlier, European law (both the law of the EU and that of the Council of Europe) has effaced the animal (and with it the ethic of animal welfare), placing humans (with their human rights) in the centre of its frame.[156] There has also been concern at the 'demoralisation of

---

[147] Chapter 16 in this collection.

[148] Chapter 14 in this collection.

[149] Chapter 17 in this collection.

[150] It is not clear if the ECtHR would back this 'right to know' to the exclusion of competing rights and interests: see eg *Odièvre v France* (n 87).

[151] Discussing the United Kingdom, see J McCandless, 'The Changing Form of Birth Registration?' in F Ebtehaj and others (eds), *Birth Rites and Rights* (Hart 2011).

[152] Chapter 6 in this collection.

[153] Chapter 2 in this collection.

[154] Chapter 2 in this collection, 30.

[155] Chapter 14 in this collection.

[156] Chapter 16 in this collection.

medicine'—a trend attributted in part to the manner in which rights-based systems can corrode trust in professionals and in professional ethics, and potentially pitch law against ethics in damaging ways.[157]

Imagined futures, too, offer different prognoses on the rights/ethics relationship in European law of new health technologies. For instance, does human rights, because of its capacity for empowerment, have an edge over bioethics?[158] Is it, in other words, seen as more 'future proof?' We could, of course, imagine a developing normative framework for European governance of biomedicine, and the institutionalization of a human rights approach, through a transposition of the Oviedo Convention from its rather minor role as a persuasive authority in the interpretation of the ECHR, to a rather more important role as a guiding set of principles for the governance of biomedicine within the EU.[159]

Yet inquiry not imagination is what is required. The best prescription, therefore, has to be close study of the relevenace of the interactions (or not) of ethics and human rights (as law and as discourse) in both legal and non-legal sites where the governance of new health technologies is determined or, indeed, resisted.[160] In this way we might begin to understand the relationships between these modes of governance and, of course, whether there is a certain European-ness to any of them, standing alone or in combination.

C. Agendas Going Forward

So, in light of our findings, we move now to reflect on agendas for future research. Much supranational governance has been focused on the promotion of trade and international markets. While this may not be a problem in some areas, it is in the case of technologies that have the potential to impact upon human health and well-being. Legal and regulatory responses to technologies beyond the nation-state at the supranational level present persistent problems for legitimacy and legitimation, and law's role in this regard is likely to be vital. The contributions to this book have made a start in addressing these problems, simply because health matters, it is political, and it affects citizens directly.

More specifically, in the foregoing discussion of the defining features of European law of new health technologies, credibility, trust, and accountability are raised, and the roles of markets, risk, human rights, and ethics in promoting those have been discussed. In this context of the four frames as legitimating devices, we might typify markets as preoccupied with efficiency; risk as preoccupied with safety; human rights as preoccupied with freedom and dignity; and ethics as preoccupied with freedom, dignity, justice, and 'fundamental morality'. Understood thus, these four legitimating frames claim (mostly) mutual separation. For instance, the regulatory legitimacy which follows from efficiency is mutually inconsistent with that which follows from safety, freedom and dignity, or justice, and so on. We might say, then, that European law of new health

---

[157] J Montgomery, 'Law and the Demoralisation of Medicine' (2006) 26 *Legal Studies* 185. He does accept, however, that rights—notably ECHR rights—have, within them, a capacity to 'remoralise' medicine.

[158] Ashcroft (n 114).

[159] Arguing against the 'cynical story' about bioethics, the international human rights movement, and the UDBHR, see TA Faunce and H Nasu, 'Normative Foundations of Technology Transfer and Transnational Benefit Principles in the UNESCO Universal Declaration on Bioethics and Human Rights (2009) 34(3) *Journal of Medicine and Philosophy* 296.

[160] Chapter 13 in this collection.

technologies has very disparate and even contradictory claims to legitimacy. This requires further study.

Further, several of the chapters consider the extent to which the aspects of European law upon which they focus are legitimate, defined in various ways, including by reference to effectiveness, to fairness or equality, to democracy or accountability. Their findings suggest, in general and overall, that both political and institutional legitimacy with respect to the use of (new) health technologies is a salient issue and at the same time is problematic for supranational polities, such as those occupying the European space. Traditional methods of achieving legitimacy may not be possible at supranational level, given the existence of non-majoritarian institutions and decision-making processes.[161] As such, techniques of legitimation become important. We have focused on the use of law (broadly defined) as a key legitimation technique in various guises. But further attention is required to tease these out, begging at least one question: In what areas are new legal techniques in need of development, what shape should they take, and what values should they seek to uphold?

Moreover, in asking what the roles of markets, risk, human rights, and ethics are in the legitimation of European law on new health technologies, we are also asking a question of a different order. We are interested not so much in the legitimacy of European law's approach in terms of its outcomes, but more in how these ideas are used as ways of legitimating regulatory purposes and practices—and, indeed, of legitimating ideas of 'Europe' itself. Overall, then, there is a need to examine both legitimacy and legitimation in greater depth.

Secondly, we need to explore further the promise and the pitfalls (for legal modes of governance, for legal method, and more broadly for the governance of new health technologies) of particular ways of seeing law. The ECtHR, as we have seen, has faith in law—technologies may be fast-moving, they may even be a threat to human rights but law can, does, and should, move in ways that are a match for this. For the ECtHR, then, law is not fundamentally unsuited for the challenges posed by new health technologies. Yet this notion of faith in law is strongly challenged in the 'empirical realist' account of two of the sociologists who contributed to this collection: for them the law, far from being benign or protective of dignity and freedom, is an instrument of already powerful actors, and thus perpetuates (undesirable) relationships that are fundamentally unequal.[162] The upshot is that both faith in law and no faith in law merit further study, as do the range of positions in-between.

As part of this might be asked: Is there something specific to *European* law that could justify faith in it—or a leap of faith? In particular, how does—or could—that law deal with the future, with degrees of uncertainty, and with the scope for unknowing (in a scientific sense) inherent to new health technologies in Europe's context of intense internal cross-borderness? How is this to be described? In the context of European law's ongoing experiment in melding universalism and particularism, via doctrines such as the margin of appreciation, the notion of 'European consensus', the doctrine of subsidiarity, or locally crafted compliance with generally framed obligations as in the case of EU Directives, does this amount to a new way of thinking about—and doing—law?

A third area for further exploration concerns relationships between law, new health technologies, and identity. In ongoing processes, European institutions essentially seek to construct an identity that is distinct as compared to other (global) regulators. For

---

[161] A notable exception being the European Parliament.
[162] Chapter 11 in this collection.

example, the EU's projection of its identity as a supranational order founded on the rule of law (as framed and legitimated around markets) is used to underpin a process of knowledge production leading to application in material objects, such as new health technologies. In addition, this collection offers a few glimpses into the complex, interacting, and mutually constitutive techniques, practices, and processes of the 'making up' of both individual and collective identity in relation to European law.

For instance, even as state practices often remain distinct,[163] European law and its constitutive features of markets, ethics, risk, and rights, work with technoscience, (biomedical) knowledge, and imagined futures to provide a basis for individual and collective identification, 'European-ness', or European biocitizenship. This can be seen in the ways that 'other' hospitals, research centres, products, and technoscientific processes are increasingly being used, consumed, and thought of as not so foreign. These offer multiple means of identification: European citizens, European consumers, and now European patients. The permutations of these, as well as who is included— Europeans *and* non-Europeans who are affected by European law?—and law's roles in fabricating identities, such as through instantiations of imagined technoscientific futures, are ripe for further exploration.

There is scope for consideration of whether and, if so, to what extent, and which, Europeans (and even non-Europeans) are enrolled in European law (or not). What are the rationales for their involvement? That is, to what extent is citizen or public participation truly an effort to mobilize and facilitate substantive involvement in European law, and to direct and shape the material outputs of new health technologies? Are such efforts, for instance in the field of synthetic biology, merely attempts at legitimating governance that regulate and seek to calm citizen discontent and contestation?[164] How are biocitizens making use of traditional legal sites and fora (such as courts) in order to demand and contest decision-making over new health technologies and life itself?[165] What newer or alternative legal sites and fora are being used—or might be needed—in order to facilitate involvement? Who is included and who is marginalized and silenced and even excluded in attempts to demand and contest decision-making?

Moreover, identities change: the WHO estimates that by 2020 depression will be the second largest cause of morbidity worldwide.[166] For this and other reasons, the neurosciences now command considerable attention—from states and from others too.[167] What new European biocitizens—and non-European biocitizens—might emerge from this increasing centrality of neurology and mental health care? Do ECtHR judgments on the rights of mental patients, and the associated rights-activist tradition within some European states, notably the United Kingdom, give Europe a degree of legal preparedness? Or are these 'old' rights ill-suited to emergent science, illness, and patient activism? And, more than this, are rights—or at least rights as law—entirely the wrong frame?[168]

---

[163] Chapter 17 in this collection.

[164] ML Flear, 'The EU's Biopolitical Governance of Advanced Therapy Medicinal Products' (2009) 16 *Maastricht Journal of European and Comparative Law* 113; ML Flear and MD Pickersgill, 'Regulatory or Regulating Publics? The European Union's Regulation of Emerging Health Technologies and Citizen Participation' (2013) *Medical Law Review* forthcoming.

[165] A potential and practice highlighted in at least a couple of contributions, eg NGO interveners at Strasbourg in Chapter 13 in this collection; identity issues identified by Chapter 17 in this collection.

[166] See <www.who.int/mental_health/management/depression/definition/en/>.

[167] See further J Abi-Rached and N Rose, *Neuro: The New Brain Sciences and the Management of the Mind* (Princeton UP 2013 forthcoming).

[168] For views, see N Rose, 'Unreasonable Rights: Mental Illness and the Limits of the Law' (1985) 12 *Journal of Law and Society* 199; LO Gostin, 'From a Civil Libertarian to a Sanitarian' (2007) 34 *Journal of Law and Society* 594. On ECtHR case law, see P Bartlett, O Lewis, and O Thorold, *Mental Disability and the European Convention on Human Rights* (Martinus Nijhoff 2006).

Fourthly, there is scope for more comparative scholarship. Ultimately, a claim to the effect that a 'European law of new health technologies' is distinctive would be more convincing in the context of comparison to other governance systems.[169] We would like to know, for instance, is there a 'law of the Americas of new health technologies', or an 'Asian law of new health technologies'? There is also scope for a more thorough comparison of European law of new health technologies with the emerging international framework.

A final question is that of the redistributive consequences of European law of new health technologies. The frame of law[170] which we have adopted in this book, and the focus on the European level, in themselves diverted us from a thorough consideration of the redistributive consequences of what we have explored here. Some of our contributors do consider questions of redistribution—who are the 'winners' and 'losers' in European law of new health technologies?[171] But there is much more work to be done here to unravel what it means for redistribution, which in the current pluralist European constitutional settlement is a matter for national or sub-national governments and governance processes—although the Eurozone bailout deals are already having a significant influence on European health systems.[172] It is unimaginable that the contexts within which that redistribution must take place remain unaffected by European law of new health technologies. But what are the implications?

Related questions are about regulation through control of resources[173] and, crucially, about relationships between redistribution, ethics, and human rights. If the EU wishes to be recognized as a global human rights actor,[174] and if the ECtHR wants to live up to the claim that it is 'the jewel in the crown of the world's most advanced international system for protecting civil and political liberties',[175] each needs to think carefully about the right to enjoy the benefits of scientific progress and its applications,[176] about the obligation of international cooperation and assistance, and relatedly, about how a human rights conception of intellectual property might differ from existing ways of promoting innovation and creativity. International human rights law and practice, as well as developing states and a range of NGOs and INGOs, are engaging with these questions.[177] Scholars, too, are interested.[178]

Yet the EU, like the USA, has been pursuing bilateral agreements, known as TRIPs-plus, seeking to avoid TRIPs flexibilities that allow states to use public health needs to invoke compulsory licensing. The ECtHR for its part has had little to say on crossing

---

[169] But note Theodore Marmor's warning against unthinking comparison of health systems, see T Marmor, RB Freeman, and K Okma, 'Comparative Perspectives and Policy Learning in the World of Health Care' (2005) 7 *Journal of Comparative Policy Analysis*, 331.

[170] Though in its broader governance contexts.

[171] Chapters 6, 11, 13, and 17 in this collection.

[172] N Fahy, 'Who is Shaping the Future of European Health Systems?' (2012) 344 *British Medical Journal* 1712.

[173] What Daintith calls 'government by dominium': see T Daintith, 'The Techniques of Government' in J Jowell and D Oliver (eds), *The Changing Constitution* (OUP 1994) 209.

[174] See eg G de Búrca, 'The EU in the Negotiation of the UN Disability Convention' (2010) 35 *European Law Review* 174.

[175] Helfer (n 31).

[176] See eg International Covenant on Economic, Social and Cultural Rights (adopted 16 December 1966, entered into force 3 January 1976) 993 UNTS 3 (ICESCR), Art 15(1)(b).

[177] See eg Venice Statement on the Right to Enjoy the Benefits of Scientific Progress and Its Applications 2009 <http://shr.aaas.org/article15/Reference.Materials/VeniceStatementJuly2009.pdf> accessed 16 July 2012; 'The Right to Enjoy the Benefits of Scientific Progress and Its Applications': Report of Farida Shaheed, Special Rapporteur on cultural rights, UN Doc A/HRC/20/26 (14 May 2012).

[178] See eg T Pogge and others (eds), *Incentives for Global Public Health: Patent Law and Access to Essential Medicines* (CUP 2010); M Sunder, *From Goods To A Good Life: Intellectual Property and Global Justice* (Yale UP 2012).

borders for health purposes—whether Europeans crossing borders to other European states or further afield, or seriously ill non-Europeans being returned to their countries of origin.[179] All of these phenomena have serious redistributional consequences. They also limit the prospects of European law of new health technologies as an experiment in ethical or human rights-based markets. That observation concludes our main candidates for future directions, and it brings us to our final question.

D. Conclusion

Where are we, at the end of our project? Our overall argument runs something like this. Together, the detailed analyses within this book demonstrate that, taking a broad-brush, high-level view, there is sufficient cohesion around the legitimating factors of markets, risk, human rights, and ethics, alone and in various combinations, to justify our claim to have created a new field of scholarship: European law of new health technologies. Our 'map' of that new legal field sets out its broad parameters, identifies its key features, and establishes an agenda for both research and reform into the future. We are not claiming that European law of new health technologies is a unitary or unified legal system—rather, it is a pluralist network of legal sites, focused around a legitimating process of determining 'European-ness'. This is not a surprise, as Europe's identity is (and probably always will be) a process, and the institutional and legal instantiations of 'Europe' (the Council of Europe, the EU, and so on) relate to and co-construct the very notion of what it is to be 'European'. One of the tantalizing features of that 'European-ness' is the promise of escape from the globalizing force of market power. For sure, markets are writ large in the legitimation of European law of new health technologies. But they do not tell the whole story. And that is why European law of new health technologies represents a perfect case study for reflecting on power, democracy, legitimacy, global justice, and redistribution: some of the most salient issues in our fast changing world.

---

[179] On the latter see the ECtHR judgments in *D v United Kingdom* and *N v United Kingdom*, discussed in Chapter 3 in this collection.

Select Bibliography

Abbing HDC, 'The Convention on Human Rights and Biomedicine: An Appraisal of the Council of Europe Convention' (1998) 5 *European Journal of Health Law* 377.

Abi-Rached J and Rose N, *Neuro* (Princeton UP 2012).

Abraham J, *Science, Politics and the Pharmaceutical Industry* (Routledge 1995).

—— 'Partial Progress: Governing the Pharmaceutical Industry and the NHS, 1948–2008' (2009) 34 *Journal of Health, Politics, Policy and Law* 943.

—— and Lewis G, *Regulating Medicines in Europe: Competition, Expertise and Public Health* (Routledge 2000).

Agamben G, *Homo Sacer: Sovereign Power and Bare Life* (Stanford UP 1998).

Alston P, with Bustelo M and Heenan J (eds), *The EU and Human Rights* (OUP 1999).

Altenstetter C, 'Medical Device Regulation and Nanotechnologies: Determining the Role of Patient Safety Concerns in Policymaking' (2011) 33 *Law and Policy* 227.

Andorno R, 'Global Bioethics at UNESCO: In Defence of the Universal Declaration on Bioethics and Human Rights' (2007) 33 *Journal of Medical Ethics* 150.

Annas GJ and Grodin MA (eds), *The Nazi Doctors and the Nuremberg Code: Human Rights in Human Experimentation* (OUP 1995).

Ashcroft RE, 'The Troubled Relationship between Bioethics and Human Rights' in MDA Freeman (ed), *Law and Bioethics: Current Legal Issues 11* (OUP 2007).

—— 'Could Human Rights Supersede Bioethics?' (2010) 10 *Human Rights Law Review* 639.

Ayres I and Braithwaite J, *Responsive Regulation* (OUP 2002).

Baldwin R and Black J, 'Really Responsive Regulation' (2008) 71 *Modern Law Review* 59.

—— Cave M, and Lodge M, 'Regulation, the Field and the Developing Agenda' in R Baldwin, M Cave, and M Lodge (eds), *The Oxford Handbook on Regulation* (OUP 2011).

Bartlett P, Lewis O, and Thorold O, *Mental Disability and the European Convention on Human Rights* (Martinus Nijhoff 2006).

Bartolini S, 'New Modes of European Governance: An Introduction' in A Héritier and M Rhodes (eds), *New Modes of Governance in Europe* (Palgrave Macmillan 2010).

Bates E, *The Evolution of the European Convention on Human Rights* (OUP 2010).

Baxi U, *Human Rights in a Posthuman World: Critical Essays* (OUP 2007).

Beetham D and Lord C, *Legitimacy and the EU* (Longman 1998).

Bernstein G, 'In the Shadow of Innovation' (2010) 31 *Cardozo Law Review* 2257.

Beyleveld D and Brownsword R, *Human Dignity in Bioethics and Biolaw* (OUP 2001).

Beynon-Jones SM and Brown N, 'Time, Timing and Narrative at the Interface Between Technoscience and Policy' (2011) 38 *Science and Public Policy* 639.

Bickerton C, 'Europe's Neo-Madisonians: Rethinking the Legitimacy of Limited Power in a Multi-Level Polity' (2011) 59 *Political Studies* 659.

Black J, 'What is Regulatory Innovation?' in J Black, M Lodge, and M Thatcher (eds), *Regulatory Innovation: A Comparative Analysis* (Edward Elgar 2005).

Borrás S and Ejrnæs A, 'The Legitimacy of New Modes of Governance in the EU: Studying National Stakeholders' Support' (2011) 12 *European Union Politics* 107.

Brownsword R, *Rights, Regulation, and the Technological Revolution* (OUP 2008).

—— and Goodwin M, *Law and Technologies of the Twenty-First Century* (CUP 2012).

—— and Somsen H, 'Law, Innovation and Technology: Before We Fast Forward—A Forum for Debate' (2009) 1 *Law, Innovation and Technology* 1.

—— and Yeung K (eds), *Regulating Technologies: Legal Futures, Regulatory Frames and Technological Fixes* (Hart 2008).

Busby H, Hervey TK, and Mohr A, 'Ethical EU Law: The Influence of the European Group on Ethics in Science and New Technologies' (2008) 33 *European Law Review* 803.

Butler J, *The Ethics of Health Care Rationing: Principles and Practices* (Sage 1999).

Callahan D, 'Why America Accepted Bioethics' (1993) 23 *Hastings Center Report* 8.

Cavaliere A, 'Product Liability in the European Union: Compensation and Deterrence Issues' (2004) 18 *European Journal of Law and Economics* 299.

Chalmers D and Nicol D, 'Commercialisation of Biotechnology: Public Trust and Research' (2004) 6 *International Journal of Biotechnology* 116.

Christoffersen J and Madsen RM (eds), *The European Convention on Human Rights* (OUP 2011).

Cloatre E and Pickersgill M (eds), *Knowledge, Technology and Law: Interrogating the Nexus* (Routledge 2013 forthcoming).

Cohen JC, Illingworth P, and Schuklenk U (eds), *The Power of Pills* (Pluto 2006).

Craig P, 'Constitutions, Constitutionalism and the European Union' (2001) 7 *European Law Journal* 125.

—— and de Búrca G, *EU Law: Text, Cases, and Materials* (5th edn, OUP 2011).

—— and de Búrca G, *The Evolution of EU Law* (2nd edn, OUP 2011).

Daintith T, 'The Techniques of Government' in J Jowell and D Oliver (eds), *The Changing Constitution* (3rd edn, OUP 1994).

Daniels N, *Just Health: Meeting Health Needs Fairly* (CUP 2008).

Dawson M, *New Governance and the Transformation of European Law: Coordinating EU Social Law and Policy* (CUP 2011).

De Búrca G, 'The Road Not Taken: The EU as a Global Human Rights Actor' (2011) 105 *American Journal of International Law* 649.

—— and Scott J (eds), *New Governance and Constitutionalism in the EU and the US* (Hart 2006).

De la Rosa S, 'The Directive on Crossborder Healthcare or the Art of Codifying Complex Case Law' (2012) 49 *Common Market Law Review* 15.

De Sousa Santos B, *Toward a New Legal Common Sense: Law, Globalization and Emancipation* (2nd edn, Butterworths 2002).

Dorbeck-Jung B and Chowdhury N, 'Is the European Medical Products Authorisation Regulation Equipped to Cope with the Challenges of Nanomedicines?' (2011) 33 *Law and Policy* 276.

Dratwa J, 'Representing Europe with the Precautionary Principle' in S Jasanoff (ed), *Reframing Rights: Bioconstitutionalism in the Genetic Age* (MIT Press 2011).

Ehlers D (ed), *European Fundamental Rights and Freedoms* (De Gruyter Recht 2007).

Everson M and Vos E (eds), *Uncertain Risks Regulated* (Routledge-Cavendish 2009).

Fairgrieve D and Howells G, 'Rethinking Product Liability: A Missing Element in the European Commission's Third Review of the European Product Liability Directive' (2007) 70 *Modern Law Review* 962.

Farmer P and Gastineau Campos N, 'New Malaise: Bioethics and Human Rights in the Global Era' (2004) 32 *Journal of Law Medicine and Ethics* 243.

Farrell A-M, *The Politics of Blood: Ethics, Innovation and the Regulation of Risk* (CUP 2012).

—— Price D, and Quigley M (eds), *Organ Shortage: Ethics, Law and Pragmatism* (CUP 2011).

Faulkner A, *Medical Technology into Healthcare and Society: A Sociology of Devices, Innovation and Governance* (Palgrave Macmillan 2009).

—— Lange B, and Lawless C (eds), 'Special Issue: Material Worlds— Intersections of Law, Science, Technology and Society' (2012) 39 *Journal of Law and Society* 1.

Faunce TA and Nasu H, 'Normative Foundations of Technology Transfer and Transnational Benefit Principles in the UNESCO Universal Declaration on Bioethics and Human Rights' (2009) 34 *Journal of Medicine and Philosophy* 296.

Felt U and others, *Expert Group on Science and Governance: Taking European Knowledge Society Seriously* (European Commission DG Research Science, Economy and Society 2007).

Fisher E, *Risk Regulation and Administrative Constitutionalism* (Hart 2007).

Fisher M, *Fundamentals of Patent Law* (Hart 2007).

Flear ML, 'The EU's Biopolitical Governance of Advanced Therapy Medicinal Products' (2009) 16 *Maastricht Journal of European and Comparative Law* 113.

—— 'The Open Method of Coordination on Health Care after the Lisbon Strategy II: Towards a Neoliberal Framing?' (2009) 13 *European Integration online Papers* (Article 12).

—— and Pickersgill MD, 'Regulatory or Regulating Publics? The European Union's Regulation of Emerging Health Technologies and Citizen Participation' (2013 forthcoming) *Medical Law Review*.

—— and Ramshaw S (eds), 'Symposium: New Technologies, European Law and Citizens' (2009) 16(1) *Maastricht Journal of European and Comparative Law*.

—— and Vakulenko A, 'A Human Rights Perspective on Citizen Participation in the EU's Governance of New Technologies' (2010) 10 *Human Rights Law Review* 661.

Foucault M, *The Birth of Biopolitics: Lectures at the Collège de France, 1978–1979* (Palgrave Macmillan 2008).

Fovargue S, *Xenotransplantation and Risk: Regulating a Developing Biotechnology* (CUP 2011).

Francioni F (ed), *Biotechnologies and International Human Rights* (Hart 2007).

Franklin S and Lock M (eds), *Remaking Life & Death: Toward an Anthropology of the Biosciences* (SAR Press 2003).

Freeman MDA (ed), *Law and Bioethics* (OUP 2008).

Garrido MV, Kristensen FB, Nielsen CP, and Busse R, 'Health Technology Assessment and Health Policy-Making in Europe' (World Health Organization 2008) <www.euro.who.int/__data/assets/pdf_file/0003/90426/E91922.pdf>.

Gevers JKM, Hondius E, and Hubben JH (eds), *Health Law, Human Rights and the Biomedicine Convention* (Martinus Nijhoff 2005).

Goodwin M, Koops BJ, and Leenes R (eds), *Dimensions of Technology Regulation* (Woolf 2010).

Haas E, *The Uniting of Europe: Political, Social and Economic Forces 1950–1957* (California UP 1968).

Hancher L, 'The EU Pharmaceuticals Market: Parameters and Pathways' in E Mossialos, G Permanand, R Baeten, and TK Hervey (eds), *Health Systems Governance in Europe: The Role of EU Law and Policy* (CUP 2010).

Haraway D, *Simians, Cyborgs, and Women: The Reinvention of Nature* (Free Association Books 1991).

—— *Modest_Witness@Second_Millennium.FemaleMan©_Meets_OncoMouseTM: Feminism and Technoscience* (Routledge 1997).

Harmon SHE, Laurie G, and Arzuaga F, 'Foresighting Futures: Law, New Technologies, and the Challenges of Regulating for Uncertainty' (2012) 4 *Law, Innovation and Technology* 1.

Harrington J and Stuttaford M (eds), *Global Health and Human Rights* (Routledge 2010).

Harris-Short S, 'A Feminist Judgment in *Evans v Amicus Healthcare Ltd and Others*' in R Hunter, McGlynn C, and E Rackley (eds), *Feminist Judgments: From Theory to Practice* (Hart 2010).

Hatzopoulos V, 'Why the Open Method of Coordination Is Bad for You: A Letter to the EU' (2007) 13 *European Law Journal* 309.

Hedgecoe A and Martin P, 'The Drugs Don't Work: Expectations and the Social Shaping of Pharmacogenetics' (2003) 33 *Social Studies of Science* 3.

Helfer LR, 'Redesigning the ECHR: Embeddedness as a Deep Structural Principle of the European Human Rights Regime' (2008) 19 *European Journal of International Law* 125.

—— and Austin G, *Human Rights and Intellectual Property: Mapping the Global Interface* (CUP 2011).

Héritier A and Rhodes M (eds), *New Modes of Governance in Europe* (Palgrave Macmillan 2011).

Hermerén G, 'Accountability, Democracy, and Ethics Committees' (2009) 2 *Law, Innovation and Technology* 153.

Hervey TK, 'Buy Baby: The European Union and Regulation of Human Reproduction' (1998) 18 *Oxford Journal of Legal Studies* 207.

—— 'The "Right to Health" in EU Law' in T Hervey and J Kenner (eds), *Economic and Social Rights under the EU Charter of Fundamental Rights: A Legal Perspective* (Hart 2003).

—— 'We Don't See a Connection: The "Right to Health" in the EU Charter and European Social Charter' in G de Búrca and B de Witte (eds), *Social Rights in Europe* (OUP 2005).

—— 'The European Union's Governance of Health Care and the Welfare Modernization Agenda' (2008) 2 *Regulation & Governance* 103.

—— and Black H, 'The European Union and the Governance of Stem Cell Research' (2005) 12 *Maastricht Journal of European and Comparative Law* 3.

—— and McHale JV, *Health Law and the European Union* (CUP 2004).

Hestermeyer H, *Human Rights and the WTO: The Case of Patents and Access to Medicines* (OUP 2007).

Hodge G, Bowman D, and Maynard A (eds), *International Handbook on Regulating Nanotechnologies* (Edward Elgar 2012).

Hodges C, *European Regulation of Consumer Product Safety* (OUP 2005).

Hood C, Scott C, and Baldwin R, *The Government of Risk: Understanding Risk Regulation Regimes* (OUP 2001).

Hooghe L and Marks G, *Multilevel Governance and European Integration* (Rowman & Littlefield 2001).

Hoppe N, *Bioequity: Property and the Human Body* (Ashgate, 2009).

Hottois G, 'A Philosophical and Critical Analysis of the European Convention of Bioethics' (2000) 25 *Journal of Medicine and Philosophy* 133.

Jackson E, *Law and the Regulation of Medicines* (Hart 2012).

Jasanoff S, *The Fifth Branch: Science Advisers as Policy-Makers* (Harvard UP 1990).

—— *Science at the Bar: Law, Science, and Technology in America* (Harvard UP 1997).

—— (ed), *States of Knowledge: The Co-Production of Science and Social Order* (Routledge 2004).

—— *Designs on Nature: Science and Democracy in Europe and the United States* (Princeton UP 2005).

—— (ed), *Reframing Rights: Bioconstitutionalism in the Genetic Age* (MIT Press 2011).

—— and Kim SH, 'Containing the Atom: Sociotechnical Imaginaries and Nuclear Power in the US and Korea' (2009) 47 *Minerva* 119.

Kent J, *Regenerating Bodies: Tissue and Cell Therapies in the Twenty-First Century* (Routledge 2012).

—— and others, 'Towards Governance of Human Tissue Engineered Technologies in Europe: Framing the Case for a New Regulatory Regime' (2006) 73 *Technological Forecasting and Social Change* 41.

Klein R, Day P, and Redmayne S, *Managing Scarcity* (Open UP 2006).

Kopelman LM, 'The Incompatibility of the United Nations' Goals and Conventionalist Ethical Relativism' (2005) 5 *Developing World Bioethics* 234.

Kritikos M, 'Traditional Risk Analysis and Releases of GMOs into the European Union: Space for Non-Scientific Factors?' (2009) 34 *European Law Review* 405.

Kuhn TS, *The Structure of Scientific Revolutions* (University of Chicago Press 1962).

Lakoff A, *Pharmaceutical Reason: Knowledge and Value in Global Psychiatry* (CUP 2005).

Latour B, *Science in Action: Following Scientists and Engineers through Society* (Harvard UP 1987).

—— *We Have Never Been Modern* (Harvard UP 1993).

—— *Pandora's Hope: Essays on the Reality of Science Studies* (Harvard UP 1999).

Lee M, *EU Regulation of GMOs: Law and Decision-Making for a New Technology* (Edward Elgar 2008).

—— 'Beyond Safety? The Broadening Scope of Risk Regulation' (2009) 62 *Current Legal Problems* 242.

—— 'Risk and Beyond: EU Regulation of Nanotechnology' (2010) 35 *European Law Review* 799.

Lenk C, Sandor J, and Gordijn B (eds), *Biobanks and Tissue Research: The Public, The Patient and the Regulation* (Springer 2011).

Lenoir N, 'Biotechnology, Bioethics and Law: Europe's 21st Century Challenge' (2006) 69 *Modern Law Review* 1.

Lessig L, *Code: And Other Laws of Cyberspace* (Basic Books 1999).

Letsas G, *A Theory of Interpretation of the European Convention on Human Rights* (OUP 2009).

McCrudden C, 'Human Dignity and Judicial Interpretation of Human Rights' (2008) 19 *European Journal of International Law* 655.

McGuinness S, 'A, B and C Leads to D (for Delegation!): A, B and C v Ireland 25579/05 [2010] ECHR 2032' (2011) 19 *Medical Law Review* 476.

Macklin R, 'Yet Another Guideline? The UNESCO Draft Declaration' (2005) 5 *Developing World Bioethics* 244.

Macpherson CC, 'Global Bioethics: Did the Universal Declaration on Bioethics and Human Rights Miss the Boat?' (2007) 33 *Journal of Medical Ethics* 588.

Maduro MP, *We the Court: The European Court of Justice and the European Economic Constitution* (Hart 1998).

Majone G, *Regulating Europe* (Routledge 1996).

Mayrhofer MT and Prainsack B, 'Being a Member of the Club: The Trans (Self-) Governance of Networks of Biobanks' (2009) 12 *International Journal of Risk Assessment and Management* 64.

Merton RK, 'The Normative Structure of Science' in NW Storer (ed), *The Sociology of Science* (University of Chicago Press 1942).

Montgomery J, 'Law and the Demoralisation of Medicine' (2006) 26 *Legal Studies* 185.

Moran M, 'Understanding the Regulatory State' (2002) 32 *British Journal of Political Science* 391.

Moses LB, 'Recurring Dilemmas: The Law's Race to Keep up with Technological Change' (2007) *Journal of Law, Technology and Policy* 239.

Mossialos E, Permanand G, Baeten R, and Hervey TK (eds), *Health Systems Governance in Europe* (CUP 2010).

Motoc IV, 'The International Law of Genetic Discrimination: The Power of "Never Again" in T Murphy (ed), *New Technologies and Human Rights* (OUP 2009).

Murphy T (ed), *New Technologies and Human Rights* (OUP 2009).

—— 'Taking Revolutions Seriously: Rights, Risk and New Technologies' (2009) 16 *Maastricht Journal of European and Comparative Law* 15.

—— 'Technology, Tools and Toxic Expectations' (2009) 2 *Law, Innovation and Technology* 181.

—— 'Public Health *sans Frontières*: Human Rights NGOs and "Stewardship on a Global Scale"' (2011) 62 *Northern Ireland Legal Quarterly* 659.

—— *Health and Human Rights* (Hart 2013).

—— and Ó Cuinn G, 'Works in Progress: New Technologies and the European Court of Human Rights' (2010) 10 *Human Rights Law Review* 601.

Navarro-Michel M, 'Institutional Organisation and Transplanting the "Spanish Model"' in A-M Farrell, D Price, and M Quigley (eds), *Organ Shortage: Ethics, Law and Pragmatism* (CUP 2011).

Newdick C, 'Citizenship, Free Movement and Health Care: Cementing Individual Rights by Corroding Social Solidarity' (2006) 43 *Common Market Law Review* 1645.

Ogus A, *Regulation: Legal Form and Economic Theory* (Hart 2004).

Parry S and Dupre J (eds), *Nature After the Genome* (Blackwell/Sociological Review 2010).

Petryna A, *Life Exposed: Biological Citizens after Chernobyl* (Princeton UP 2002).

Pickersgill M, 'Standardising Antisocial Personality Disorder: The Social Shaping of a Psychiatric Technology' (2012) 34(4) *Sociology of Health & Illness* 544.

Plomer A and Torremans P (eds), *Embryonic Stem Cell Patents: European Law and Ethics* (OUP 2009).

Pogge T and others (eds), *Incentives for Global Public Health: Patent Law and Access to Essential Medicines* (CUP 2010).

Pottage A, 'The Socio-Legal Implications of the New Biotechnologies' (2007) 3 *Annual Review of Law and Social Science* 321.

Power M, *Organized Uncertainty* (OUP 2007).

Prainsack B and Buyx A, 'Solidarity: Reflections on an Emerging Concept in Bioethics' (Nuffield Council on Bioethics 2011).

—— and Gmeiner R, 'Clean Soil and Common Ground: The Biopolitics of Human Embryonic Stem Cell Research in Austria' (2008) 17 *Science as Culture* 377.

Prosser T, *The Regulatory Enterprise* (OUP 2010).

Rabinow P, 'Afterword' in S Gibbon and C Novas (eds), *Biosocialities, Genetics and the Social Sciences* (Routledge 2007).

Rapp R, *Testing Women, Testing the Fetus: The Social Impact of Amniocentesis in America* (Routledge 2000).

Research Division of the European Court of Human Rights, 'Research Report: Bioethics and the Case-law of the Court' (Council of Europe/European Court of Human Rights 2012).

Rose N, *The Politics of Life Itself* (Princeton UP 2007).

—— and Novas C, 'Biological Citizenship' in A Ong and SJ Collier (eds), *Global Assemblages, Politics and Ethics as Anthropological Problems* (Blackwell 2005).

Royal Academy of Engineering, 'Synthetic Biology: Scope, Applications and Implications' (RAEng 2009).

Salter B, 'Bioethics, Politics and the Moral Economy of Human Embryonic Stem Cell Science: The Case of the European Union's Sixth Framework Programme' (2007) 26 *New Genetics and Society* 269.

Scharpf F, *Governing in Europe: Effective and Democratic?* (OUP 1999).

Scott C, 'Governing without Law or Governing without Government? New-ish Governance and the Legitimacy of the EU' (2009) 15 *European Law Journal* 160.

Scott J and Trubek DM, 'Mind the Gap: Law and New Approaches to Governance in the European Union' (2002) 8 *European Law Journal* 1.

Selgelid M, 'Universal Norms and Conflicting Values' (2005) 5 *Developing World Bioethics* 267.

Sen A, 'Elements of a Theory of Human Rights' (2004) 32 *Philosophy & Public Affairs* 315.

Sheldon S, 'Gender Equality and Reproductive Decision-Making' (2004) 12 *Feminist Legal Studies* 303.

Silbey SS and Ewick P, 'The Architecture of Authority: The Place of Law in the Space of Science' in A Sarat, L Douglas, and M Umphrey (eds), *The Place of Law* (University of Michigan Press 2003).

Simmons BA, *Mobilizing for Human Rights: International Law in Domestic Politics* (CUP 2009).

Slaughter A-M, Stone Sweet A, and Weiler JHH (eds), *The European Courts and National Courts—Doctrine and Jurisprudence: Legal Change in Social Context* (Hart 1998).

Smart C, 'Law and the Regulation of Family Secrets' (2010) 24 *International Journal of Law, Policy and the Family* 397.

Somsen H, 'Regulating Human Genetics in a Neo-Genetic Era' in T Murphy (ed), *New Technologies and Human Rights* (OUP 2009).

Stokes E, 'Nanotechnology and the Products of Inherited Regulation' (2012) 39 *Journal of Law and Society* 93.

—— 'Demand for Command: Responding to Technological Risks and Scientific Uncertainties' (2013 forthcoming) *Medical Law Review*.

Stone Sweet A, *Governing With Judges: Constitutional Politics in Europe* (OUP 2000).

Sunder M, *From Goods to a Good Life: Intellectual Property and Global Justice* (Yale UP 2012).

Tallacchini M, 'Governing by Values. EU Ethics: Soft Tool, Hard Effects' (2009) 47 *Minerva* 281.

Timmermans S and Berg M, *The Gold Standard: The Challenge of Evidence-Based Medicine and Standardization in Health Care* (Temple UP 2003).

Titmuss RM, *The Gift Relationship: From Human Blood to Social Policy* (George Allen & Unwin 1970).

Tobin J, *The Right to Health in International Law* (OUP 2012).

Toebes B, Hartley M, Hendriks A, and Rothmar Hermann J (eds), *Health and Human Rights in Europe* (Intersentia 2012).

Turkmendag I, Dingwall R, and Murphy T, 'The Removal of Donor Anonymity in the UK: The Silencing of Claims by Would-Be Parents' (2008) 22 *International Journal of Law, Policy and the Family* 283.

Valverde M, Levi R, and Moore D, 'Legal Knowledges of Risk' in Law Commission of Canada (ed), *Law and Risk* (UBC Press 2005).

Van Dam C, *European Tort Law* (OUP 2006).

Van de Gronden JW, Szyszczak E, Neergaard U, and Krajewski M (eds), *Health Care and EU Law* (Springer 2011).

Von Tigerstrom B, *Human Security and International Law: Prospects and Problems* (Hart 2007).

Vos E, 'EU Food Safety Regulation in the Aftermath of the BSE Crisis' (2000) 23 *Journal of Consumer Policy* 227.

Waldby C and Cooper M, 'From Reproductive Work to Regenerative Labour: The Female Body and the Stem Cell Industries' (2010) 11 *Feminist Theory* 3.

Warnock M, *A Question of Life: The Warnock Report on Human Fertilisation and Embryology* (Basil Blackwell 1985).

Webster A, 'Crossing Boundaries: Social Science in the Policy Room' (2007) 32 *Science, Technology & Human Values* 458.

—— *Health, Technology and Society: A Sociological Critique* (Palgrave Macmillan 2007).

Weiler JHH, *The Constitution of Europe* (CUP 1999).

—— and de Búrca G (eds), *The Worlds of European Constitutionalism* (OUP 2011).

Whittaker S, *Liability for Products: English Law, French Law, and European Harmonization* (OUP 2005).

—— (ed), *The Development of Product Liability* (CUP 2010).

Williams SJ, Martin P, and Gabe J, 'The Pharmaceuticalisation of Society? A Framework for Analysis' (2011) 33 *Sociology of Health & Illness* 710.

Wilsdon J and Willis R, 'See-Through Science: Why Public Engagement Needs to Move Upstream' (Demos 2004).

Winickoff D, Jasanoff S, Busch L, Grove-White R, and Wynne B, 'Adjudicating the GM Food Wards: Science, Risk, and Democracy in World Trade Law' (2005) 30 *Yale Journal of International Law* 81.

Yeung K and Dixon-Woods M, 'Design-Based Regulation and Patient Safety: A Regulatory Studies Perspective' (2010) 71 *Social Science and Medicine* 502.

Zhang JY, Marris C, and Rose N, 'The Transnational Governance of Synthetic Biology: Scientific Uncertainty, Cross-borderness and the "Art" of Governance' (2011) BIOS Working Paper No 4.

Index

Introductory Note

References such as '178–9' indicate (not necessarily continuous) discussion of a topic across a range of pages. Wherever possible in the case of topics with many references, these have been divided into subtopics and/or only the most significant discussions of the topic are listed. Because the entire volume is about 'new health technologies' and 'European law', the use of these terms (and certain others which occur throughout) as entry points has been minimized. Information will be found under the corresponding detailed topics.

Printed and bound by CPI Group (UK) Ltd, Croydon, CR0 4YY